European Commission

General Report
on the Activities of
the European Union

2002

Brussels • Luxembourg, 2003

The *General Report on the Activities of the European Union — 2002* was adopted by the European Commission on 24 January 2003 under reference number SEC(2002) 1000 final.

Europe Direct is a service to help you find answers to your questions about the European Union

New freephone number:
00 800 6 7 8 9 10 11

A great deal of additional information on the European Union is available on the Internet. It can be accessed through the Europa server (http://europa.eu.int).

Cataloguing data can be found at the end of this publication.

Luxembourg: Office for Official Publications of the European Communities, 2003

ISBN 92-894-4688-9

The President and the Members of the European Commission to the President of the European Parliament

Sir,

We have the honour to present the General Report on the Activities of the European Union for 2002, which the Commission is required to publish by Article 212 of the EC Treaty, Article 17 of the ECSC Treaty and Article 125 of the EAEC Treaty.

In accordance with the procedure described in the declaration on the system for fixing Community farm prices contained in the Accession Documents of 22 January 1972, the Commission will shortly be sending Parliament the 2002 Report on the Agricultural Situation in the European Union.

And, in accordance with an undertaking given to Parliament on 7 June 1971, the Commission is preparing its XXXIInd Annual Report on Competition Policy.

Yours faithfully,

Brussels, 11 February 2003

Romano PRODI President	**Günter VERHEUGEN**
Neil KINNOCK Vice-President	**Christopher PATTEN**
Loyola de PALACIO del VALLE-LERSUNDI Vice-President	**Pascal LAMY**
Mario MONTI	**David BYRNE**
Franz FISCHLER	**Michel BARNIER**
Erkki LIIKANEN	**Viviane REDING**
Frederik BOLKESTEIN	**Michaele SCHREYER**
Philippe BUSQUIN	**Margot WALLSTRÖM**
Pedro SOLBES MIRA	**António VITORINO**
Poul NIELSON	**Anna DIAMANTOPOULOU**

NOTE

Legislative instruments under the co-decision procedure are mentioned in the Report followed by '(Table I)'. Instruments under the consultation procedure are followed by '(Table II)'. International agreements are followed by '(Table III)'. No footnotes are given for these instruments, which are listed in three separate tables annexed to the Report. The relevant references (OJ, COM, Bull.) for all the stages of the legislative procedure concerning each instrument, together with the appropriate point numbers in the text, are given in the tables.

As a rule, no references are given in the text for intermediate stages of procedures which started before 1 January 2002 and were not completed at 31 December 2002. These references also appear in the tables.

Contents

The European Union in 2002 — Overview

The year began with the introduction of euro notes and coins in 12 Member States and ended with the decision of the Copenhagen European Council to admit 10 new Member States to the European Union. Between these two historic turning points, and in addition to continuing progress and achievements in many Community policies, the interplay of the past and future of the European Union was very much in evidence. It was a year of significant landmarks: much of the period was taken up by the work of the convention set up to consider the future of the European Union, while July saw the end of the 50-year existence of the first European Community — the ECSC.

*

* *

A powerful symbol of a new era of European integration, the euro became part of everyday life for ordinary people on 1 January 2002, with the introduction of the new notes and coins. The public's response to the new currency in the 12 Member States of the euro zone, with their total population of over 300 million, lived up to the expectations of all those at Community and national level who had worked so hard to prepare for the introduction of the single currency: by the beginning of February, payments in euro already accounted for 95 % of cash payments, and the withdrawal of the national currencies from circulation in the Member States concerned was completed at the end of that month. The process received an extra impetus on 1 July when the regulation on the simplification of cross-border payments came into force. This regulation, which aims to create a single payment area in the euro zone, should enable European citizens to take full advantage of the benefits of the single currency, by harmonising charges for national and cross-border transactions (cash withdrawals and payments by bank card or credit card). Given the success of the physical introduction of the euro, economic and monetary union undoubtedly qualifies as one of the significant landmarks in European integration, an example of the 'real solidarity' beloved of Jean Monnet, ranking alongside such earlier achievements as the customs union of 1968 and the single market of 1992.

Completing a process launched nine years earlier in the same city, the Copenhagen European Council on 12 and 13 December concluded the negotiations with

10 candidate countries (Cyprus, the Czech Republic, Estonia, Hungary, Latvia, Lithuania, Malta, Poland, Slovakia and Slovenia) paving the way for the single greatest enlargement in the history of the European Union.

The success in December was the culmination of intense negotiations, coupled with preparations for the accession of the candidate countries, which continued throughout the year and built on the efforts and achievements of previous years. A turning point came at the end of October following publication of the Commission's reports on the progress of each candidate country towards accession. These formed the basis for a decision by the Council and then the European Council, meeting in Brussels, to complete the negotiations with the 10 countries selected from the 13 applicants for EU membership to form the first wave. October also brought another positive signal for the European Union in the shape of the 'yes' vote in the Irish referendum. Reversing the vote in 2001, the new referendum removed the final obstacle to ratification of the Nice Treaty signed on 26 February 2001. Ratification was completed by five Member States in 2001 and by another nine in the course of 2002.

As well as endorsing the outcome of the negotiations, the Copenhagen European Council was able to reach agreement on the financial framework associated with enlargement for the period 2004–06. Following the first step taken at the European Council in Brussels and subsequent amendments arising from the negotiating package prepared by the Danish Presidency, consensus was finally reached on a budget of EUR 40.8 billion, very close to the figure recommended by the Commission itself in its communication in January.

The decisive step taken in Copenhagen having cleared the way for enlargement, the timetable now provides for the Accession Treaty to be signed in Athens on 16 April 2003 and enlargement to take effect on 1 May 2004 after completion of the necessary ratification procedure. This timetable should enable the new Member States to take part in the elections to the European Parliament in spring 2004 and in the next Intergovernmental Conference on the institutional reform of the European Union. It also provides for the appointment of a new Commission on 1 November 2004.

As far as the other applicant countries are concerned, the Copenhagen European Council confirmed the aim of admitting Bulgaria and Romania to the European Union in 2007, as suggested in October, provided the pace of progress in these two countries matches the roadmaps prepared by the Commission. In the case of Turkey, the European Council deferred a decision on opening negotiations until its meeting in December 2004, at which point it will consider the recommendations the Commission is to present and whether Turkey satisfies the political criteria for accession to the European Union laid down in Copenhagen in 1993.

The policies and activities relating to the many internal aspects of Community integration developed around four main axes in 2002.

Firstly, most areas of activity continued to feel the effect of the momentum generated by the pursuit of the objectives defined at the Lisbon European Council in March 2000, relating to the promotion of a knowledge-based economy, competitiveness and growth compatible with higher levels of employment and social cohesion. The impact in terms of methods was felt mostly in the area of policy coordination in the medium and long term. The Commission, for example, began a process of rationalising the annual cycles for coordinating economic policy and employment policy, in the interests of consistency and efficiency. Solid achievements were recorded in several areas, such as the Community health and safety at work strategy, the Commission's commitment to lifelong learning, the liberalisation of the markets in services and the energy market, and the reform of the regulatory framework for telecommunications. Legislation on integrating rail markets was also tabled.

In the second place, further initiatives were developed as part of the reform agenda for the regulatory framework. A first example of this was the Commission's desire to help simplify and improve the legislative process in general and the way it exercises its executive powers, building on the process launched in 2001 with the publication of its White Paper on European governance. It presented several communications on this subject, one of which was accompanied by an action plan. In a similar vein, moves were made during the year to create new authorities or agencies to improve safety in various areas. As a result, the European Parliament and the Council established the European Food Safety Authority in January, the European Maritime Safety Agency in June and the European Aviation Safety Agency in July.

In the third place, the impetus for reform also produced measures in specific areas of activity. In the field of competition, for example, a new regulation implementing the antitrust provisions of the Treaty made possible a recasting of the legislation that had applied since 1962, notably by opening the way to decentralised enforcement of these rules in cooperation with the authorities in the Member States. Similarly, the Commission proposed a review of the merger regulation and launched a reform aimed at simplifying the procedures for monitoring State aid. Measures were taken in the area of economic and social cohesion to allow better management of the Structural Funds, with an emphasis on simplification. The Commission also undertook a review of its approach to industrial policy, adopted in 1990, to take account of recent developments such as globalisation and EU enlargement. Indeed, whole areas of Community policy came under review in 2002, an example being the common fisheries policy, where work continued throughout the year on reforms aimed at ensuring the sustainable development of the sector both environmentally and economically.

In July, the Commission presented an important communication on the mid-term review of the common agricultural policy, where it outlined ideas for improving the common market organisations, introducing simpler and more sustainable direct support for producers and consolidating and strengthening the rural development aspect (the second pillar).

The fourth development in 2002 was the launch of a number of programmes or action plans covering all or part of the present decade, and even beyond. One example was the adoption of the sixth framework programme of research and technological development for the period 2002–06, aimed at providing a financial basis for the establishment of the European research area and promoting better organisation of European research and innovation activities. Following the call by the Barcelona European Council for the launch of the Galileo programme for satellite radio-navigation, the Council adopted a regulation setting up the Galileo joint undertaking. The Commission completed the implementation of the 'eEurope 2002' action plan and at the same time adopted a new 'eEurope 2005' action plan aimed at both developing private investment and modernising public services to meet the challenges of the information society. The sixth environmental action programme, which was also adopted this year, established a new framework for Community policy in this area for the years to come. Finally, the new action programme in the field of public health seeks to foster new forms of cooperation between Member States and promote a more integrated approach, coordinated with other Community programmes and schemes.

The massive enlargement of the European Union currently being prepared will dramatically alter the shape of its external frontiers, and the prospect is already having an impact on certain aspects of the EU's external policy. In recent years a desire to foster good relations with its neighbours has led to the revitalisation of the Euro-Mediterranean partnership. The year 2002 saw a number of new developments, such as the adoption in Valencia of an action plan at the end of a conference that brought together the foreign ministers of all the partners concerned. The new proximity will also affect future relations with eastern Europe. The new situation lends extra significance to the support for the stabilisation and association process under way in the western Balkans, which has been important not only in terms of the financial aid provided in 2002 but also, and more particularly, because of the Community contribution to the progressive alignment of the legal and economic systems of these countries with those of the European Union. The same is true of the increasing importance attached to questions such as respect for human rights and the promotion of democracy or the transition to a market economy in the political dialogue with countries like Russia and Ukraine. The progress made in 2002 towards solving the problems posed by the situation of the Russian enclave of Kaliningrad vis-à-vis future EU Member States should also be viewed in the light of this new relationship with its neighbours.

A number of initiatives outside the European continent reflect the role which the European Union sees for itself on the international scene — a role which the Commission would like to see evolve into the responsibility of a world power (as it argued in a contribution to the deliberations of the Convention on the Future of the European Union). The EU kept up its tradition of bilateral summits with major partners, which included, as well as Russia and Ukraine, the United States, Canada, Japan, China and India. Other examples, this time at bi-regional level, include the second EU–Latin America Summit in Madrid in May and the fourth Asia–Europe Summit in Copenhagen in September. The European Union also made important contributions to and was instrumental in the success of the two major international conferences that took place in 2002. The first was the meeting in Monterrey (Mexico) in March on financing for development, which called for a new partnership between rich and poor countries entailing more generous financial contributions from the former and greater structural reforms by the latter. The second was the World Summit on Sustainable Development in Johannesburg (South Africa) from 26 August to 4 September which, 10 years after the Rio Earth Summit, adopted a medium- and long-term action plan. Similarly, the European Union strove to implement the agenda agreed in Doha (Qatar) in 2001 for a new round of multilateral trade negotiations under the World Trade Organisation. The importance the European Union attaches to promoting better integration of developing countries in the world economy and international trade was also reflected in the launch of negotiations on regional economic partnership agreements with the African, Caribbean and Pacific countries. In third countries that receive substantial financial aid from the European Union the devolution of aid management to the Commission delegations, which began a year ago as part of the Commission reform, was considerably stepped up in 2002.

In the area of the common foreign and security policy, the European Union focused its attention on two areas, in addition to its busy programme of regular activities. On one hand, it became increasingly involved in crisis management and resolution, as demonstrated by its work on behalf of peace in the Middle East, its contribution to the political, institutional and economic reconstruction of Afghanistan, and the support it gave to Argentina as it faced serious social and economic problems. On the other hand, the European Union demonstrated its determination, confirmed by the Seville European Council in June, to step up its role in the fight against terrorism, for example through the European security and defence policy. Similar concerns led the EU authorities to develop proposals to ensure integrated management of Member States' external frontiers and a joint approach to matters such as asylum and immigration, as part of their efforts to create an area of freedom, security and justice.

At institutional level, 2002 was marked by two developments pulling in opposite directions. The first was the disappearance of the first foundations of the

Community structure — the ECSC. Far from being an act of destruction this was more like the removal of a mould after the model has been cast, in that the Treaty of Paris which established the European Coal and Steel Community was concluded for a period of 50 years. Having entered into force in 1952, it duly expired on 23 July. Various commemorative events were organised to mark the occasion, and practical measures were enacted in several areas to safeguard the financial, technical and legal legacy of this, the original European Community.

The second development, at the other end of the scale, was the launch of the Convention on the Future of the European Union, as planned by the Laeken European Council at the end of 2001. The convention, consisting of 105 members and chaired by Valéry Giscard d'Estaing, started work on 28 February and continued for the remaining 10 months of the year, in two stages. The first 'listening' phase was devoted to gathering existing information and views. This was followed by a 'deliberating' phase, from September to the end of the year, when the reports prepared by the convention's various working groups were presented. The 'synthesis' phase in 2003 will draw together the conclusions in preparation for the negotiations at the next Intergovernmental Conference in 2004, which will have the job of designing a new institutional architecture for what will by then be a 25-member European Union.

Three other aspects of the convention deserve special mention here:

• the first concerns its composition: the convention includes representatives of national executives and parliaments (including those of the countries applying for EU membership), the European Parliament and the Commission, together with observers representing other Community bodies and the social partners. The participants include many eminent figures holding senior positions;

• the second aspect concerns the importance of the written contributions presented to the convention by the various interested parties, including the European Parliament, the Committee of the Regions, the European Economic and Social Committee and the Commission. The Commission, for example, presented a communication to the convention on 4 December suggesting various changes to the EU's institutional system and a simplification of the decision-making process without upsetting the balance between the Parliament, the Council and the Commission. It also advocates reinforcing the common foreign and security policy by creating the post of Secretary of the European Union, to be held by a member of the Commission who would be accountable to the Council. It also proposes changes to the way the Council operates and suggests that the Commission, under the leadership of a president elected by the European Parliament, should in future be politically accountable to Parliament and the Council. Finally, the Commission wants *these proposals to be incorporated in a constitutional treaty that would also contain the charter of fundamental rights of the European Union proclaimed in December 2000;*

- *the third significant feature of the procedure adopted for debating the future of the European Union is the determination to involve civil society and the general public, as asserted in the declaration of the Laeken European Council. By setting up a forum on the future of the European Union, complete with its own Internet site, which has collected over 400 contributions, and by creating a special network of contacts with different sectors of civil society, it has been possible to extend the debate beyond the usual political and institutional circles. The quality of the latter's contribution remains extremely high. But the preparation of a new European Union, coming to terms with the changes wrought by an almost doubling of its membership, will be imbued with the 'added value' of the public's contribution, illustrating just how far we have come in the half century since Europe set in train the historic process founded on the mines and blast furnaces that were so essential to its reconstruction in those early days.*

Chapter I

Institutional questions and the future of the Union

Section 1

Treaty of Nice (¹)

1. *Ratification of the Treaty*. Signed in Nice on 26 February 2001 (²), the Treaty amending the Treaty on European Union and the Treaties establishing the European Communities must be ratified by the 15 Member States in accordance with their respective constitutional requirements. Table 1 shows the corresponding procedure for each Member State.

2. *Ireland*. Following the failure of the Treaty of Nice referendum held in Ireland in June 2001 (³), the European Council, first in Barcelona (⁴), then in Seville (⁵), expressed its support for the Irish Government's efforts to conclude the ratification process successfully. In a 'national declaration' annexed to the conclusions of the Seville European Council (⁶), of which the latter took cognisance (⁷), Ireland recalled its commitment to the common foreign and security policy as set out in the Treaty on European Union, while confirming that its participation in that policy did not prejudice its traditional military neutrality. The 2001 referendum sparked a national debate and a new referendum was organised on 19 October, resulting this time in a positive vote for Treaty of Nice approval (62.89 % 'yes' against 37.11 % 'no', with a participation rate of 49.47 %) (⁸).

(¹) OJ C 80, 10.3.2001. Further information is available on the Europa server (http://europa.eu.int/comm/nice_treaty/index_en.htm).
(²) 2001 General Report, point 1.
(³) 2001 General Report, point 5.
(⁴) Bull. 3-2002, point I.45.
(⁵) Bull. 6-2002, point I.5.
(⁶) Bull. 6-2002, point I.29.
(⁷) Bull. 6-2002, point I.30.
(⁸) Bull. 10-2002, point 1.1.2.

TABLE 1

Treaty of Nice ratification process

Country	Procedure	Instrument of ratification deposited	Bulletin reference
Belgium	Parliamentary (approval by the seven parliaments at the different levels of power)	26.8.2002	Bull. 7/8-2002, point 1.1.6
Denmark	Parliamentary (Folketing)	13.6.2001	Bull. 6-2001, point 1.1.2
Germany	Parliamentary (Bundestag and Bundesrat)	11.2.2002	Bull. 1/2-2002, point 1.1.5
Greece	Parliamentary	3.6.2002	Bull. 6-2002, point 1.1.4
Spain	Parliamentary (Congreso and Senado)	27.12.2001	Bull. 12-2001, point 1.1.2
France	Parliamentary (Assemblée nationale and Sénat)	19.10.2001	Bull. 10-2001, point 1.1.1
Ireland	Parliamentary (Seanad and Dail) and referendum	18.12.2002	Bull. 12-2002, point 1.1.3
Italy	Parliamentary (Camera and Senato)	9.7.2002	Bull. 7/8-2002, point 1.1.4
Luxembourg	Parliamentary (Chambre des députés)	24.9.2001	Bull. 9-2001, point 1.1.1
Netherlands	Parliamentary (Eerste Kamer, Tweede Kamer)	28.12.2001	Bull. 12-2001, point 1.1.3
Austria	Parliamentary (Nationalrat and Bundesrat)	8.1.2002	Bull. 1/2-2002, point 1.1.6
Portugal	Parliamentary (Assembleia da República)	18.1.2002	Bull. 1/2-2002, point 1.1.8
Finland	Parliamentary (Eduskunta)	29.1.2002	Bull. 1/2-2002, point 1.1.7
Sweden	Parliamentary (Riksdag)	25.1.2002	Bull. 1/2-2002, point 1.1.9
United Kingdom	Parliamentary (House of Commons and House of Lords)	25.7.2002	Bull. 7/8-2002, point 1.1.5

3.   *Entry into force of the Treaty*. Under the terms of the Treaty of Nice, it will enter into force on the first day of the second month following that in which the instrument of ratification is deposited with the Italian Government by the last Member State to fulfil that formality. Since Ireland completed this procedure on 18 December, the Treaty will enter into force on 1 February 2003.

Section 2

The future of the Union

Overview

4.   *Following on from the adoption by the Laeken European Council, on 15 December 2001, of a declaration on the future of the European Union* (¹) *and the decision to convene a convention for examining the key issues in respect of the Union's future development* (²), *the convention, bringing together the main parties involved in the debate on the future of the Union, started its work on 28 February. The discussions and analyses conducted over a 10-month period proved to be very worthwhile, encompassing plenary session debates, numerous written contributions presented by the convention members, the viewpoints of other institutions and bodies, and the preparation by working groups of reports on a number of specific subjects. Almost all the members of the convention were in favour of having a draft constitutional treaty drawn up, and the framework for this has already been prepared and presented by the Praesidium.*

Convention on the Future of the European Union (³)

General aspects

5.   *Composition of the convention.* The convention has 105 members: the Chairman, Mr Giscard d'Estaing; two Vice-Chairmen, Mr Amato and Mr Dehaene; 28 representatives of the Heads of State or Government of the 15 Member States and the 13 candidate countries; 56 members of national parliaments (two from each Member State and candidate country); 16 members of the European Parliament; and two Commission representatives, Mr Barnier and Mr Vitorino. The members of the convention may be replaced by alternates. The convention also has 13 observers: six representatives of the Committee of the Regions, three representatives of the European Economic and Social Committee, three social partner representatives and the European Ombudsman.

(¹) 2001 General Report, point 13.
(²) 2001 General Report, point 14.
(³) http://european-convention.eu.int.

There are 12 members of the Praesidium: the chairman and the two vice-chairmen, representatives of the governments of the three Member States holding the Council Presidency during the period of the convention, two national parliament representatives, two representatives of the European Parliament and two representatives of the Commission. In addition, one representative of the candidate countries is invited to attend the Praesidium's meetings.

6.   *Working groups.* The working groups initially set up in May were: Group I, focusing on compliance with the principle of subsidiarity; Group II, looking at the possible inclusion of the EU charter of fundamental rights ([1]) in the Treaty; Group III, studying the consequences of explicit recognition of the European Union's legal personality; Group IV, seeking to define the role of national parliaments in the current architecture of the Union; Group V, examining 'complementary' competencies; and Group VI, concerned with economic governance. These groups, which started work in June, presented their conclusions at the September and October sessions. Four new groups were set up at the plenary session on 12 September: Group VII, focusing on the Union's external action; Group VIII, dealing with the subject of defence; Group IX, considering the simplification of procedures and instruments; and Group X, covering the area of freedom, security and justice. These four groups presented their conclusions in the course of November and December. Lastly, Group XI was set up on 6 December to examine issues raised in the context of social Europe.

7.   *Financing.* On 21 February, with a view to organising the financing of the convention, the representatives of the Member States meeting within the Council adopted a decision ([2]) setting up a fund and laying down the financial rules for its management. The European Parliament and the Commission became involved on 28 February, when the presidents of the three institutions signed an interinstitutional agreement ([3]) on their respective contributions to the convention's first financial year. Accordingly, of the EUR 4 million in expenditure estimated for 2002, a million was to be financed by the European Parliament, 0.4 million by the Council and 2.6 million by the Commission. The budget for this fund was subsequently approved by Parliament on 10 April ([4]) and by the Member States on 18 April ([5]). On 20 December, the representatives of the Member States meeting within the Council extended the decision setting up the fund until the end of the convention's proceedings, or until 31 December 2003 at the latest ([6]). Also on 20 December, the budget of the fund for financing the convention for the financial year 2003, totalling EUR 950 000, was adopted ([7]).

([1]) 2000 General Report, points 15 to 21.
([2]) Decision 2002/176/EU (OJ L 60, 1.3.2002; Bull. 1/2-2002, point 1.1.1).
([3]) OJ C 54, 1.3.2002; Bull. 1/2-2002, point 1.1.2.
([4]) Bull. 4-2002, point 1.1.3.
([5]) OJ L 123, 9.5.2002; Bull. 4-2002, point 1.1.4.
([6]) Decision 2002/997/EU (OJ L 349, 24.12.2002; Bull. 12-2002, point 1.1.7).
([7]) Decision 2002/998/EU (OJ L 349, 24.12.2002; Bull. 12-2002, point 1.1.7).

Both these decisions followed the signing, on 12 December, of a new interinstitutional agreement extending the initial agreement of 28 February (¹).

Activities of the convention

8.   Three-phase division. Mr Giscard d'Estaing decided to divide the convention's proceedings into three phases: the first one, designated the listening phase, was designed for gathering information and taking advance positions; the second, deliberative phase, running from September until the end of the year, gave rise to reports drawn up by the different working groups of the convention; the third, summarising phase, will be conducted in 2003, during which conclusions will be drawn from the work carried out and the 'final document' will be drafted, to serve as a starting point for negotiations at the new Intergovernmental Conference.

9.   Listening phase. The convention opened in Brussels on 28 February (²). At the inaugural session, Mr Giscard d'Estaing outlined the matters to be discussed, the objectives and the organisation of the convention's work. The second meeting, held on 21 and 22 March (³), marked the start of the listening phase. Many of the convention's members called for 'more Europe', particularly with regard to the area of security and justice, and the Union's action on the international scene. The importance of certain principles was also discussed, such as equality between Member States and subsidiarity, and the need for the Union to have a treaty with constitutional status. The aim of the third meeting, held on 15 and 16 April (⁴), was to define the missions of the European Union. There was initial broad consensus on the view that the present remit should not be called into question, and also that the criteria of subsidiarity and proportionality should be used to determine the missions to be ascribed to the Union. The majority of participants wanted explicit reference to be made in the Treaties to the principle whereby non-EU missions continue to be the responsibility of the Member States. At the same time, they supported a flexible system for the delimitation of competence, together with some form of control mechanism. Continuing with this theme, the members of the convention met on 23 and 24 May (⁵) to consider ways of ensuring the effectiveness and legitimacy of the Union's missions. Particular emphasis was placed on the need to redefine and simplify the legislative instruments available to the Union, and on the need for parliaments (European and national) to be more involved in the decision-making process. The session of 6 and 7 June (⁶) involved mainly a discussion on the role of the

---

(¹) Bull. 12-2002, point 1.1.7.
(²) Bull. 1/2-2002, point 1.1.3.
(³) Bull. 3-2002, point 1.1.5.
(⁴) Bull. 4-2002, point 1.1.1.
(⁵) Bull. 5-2002, point 1.1.2.
(⁶) Bull. 6-2002, point 1.1.2.

Member States and the Union in establishing an area of freedom, security and justice, while giving further consideration to the role of national parliaments in the European architecture. The convention also approved the composition of the first six working groups *(→ points 5 and 6)*.

After hearing a progress report from the convention's chairman, the Seville European Council of 21 and 22 June held an exchange of views on the development of discussions and expressed its support for the general approach followed by the convention ([1]).

In connection with the consultation of civil society and following on from an information and dialogue meeting, held on 18 April ([2]), involving Mr Dehaene and 100 or so representatives of organisations, the sixth session on 24 and 25 June ([3]) was devoted to hearing the views of civil society. The representatives of the eight contact groups focusing on specific sectors *(→ point 16)* were each able to speak on the matters for which they were responsible. The seventh session took place on 11 and 12 July ([4]). It dealt with the programme and working method of the convention, and received the report drawn up by the 'European youth convention', which met in Brussels from 9 to 12 July *(→ point 16)*.

10.   *Deliberating phase.* The eighth session, on 12 and 13 September ([5]), was concerned mainly with the simplification of instruments and procedures. It also gave the go-ahead for four additional working groups to be set up *(→ point 6)*. The ninth session, on 3 and 4 October ([6]), saw the presentation of reports from the working groups concerned with the European Union's legal personality and compliance with the principle of subsidiarity. The highlight of the session held on 28 and 29 October ([7]) was the presentation, by Mr Giscard d'Estaing, of the preliminary draft Constitutional Treaty drawn up by the Praesidium. Also during this session, reports were presented by the working groups dealing with the charter of fundamental rights, economic governance, complementary competencies and the role of national parliaments. The 11th session, which took place on 7 and 8 November ([8]), was dominated by debates on the reports from the working groups on economic governance and complementary competencies, as well as on social Europe and the preliminary draft Constitutional Treaty, following on from the discussion initiated at the 10th meeting of the convention. At the plenary session of 5 and 6 December ([9]), the Commission President presented the communication which the Commission had adopted on the subject

---

([1]) Bull. 6-2002, point I.3.
([2]) Bull. 4-2002, point 1.1.2.
([3]) Bull. 6-2002, point 1.1.3.
([4]) Bull. 7/8-2002, point 1.1.3.
([5]) Bull. 9-2002, point 1.1.1.
([6]) Bull. 10-2002, point 1.1.3.
([7]) Bull. 10-2002, point 1.1.4.
([8]) Bull. 11-2002, point 1.1.3.
([9]) Bull. 12-2002, point 1.1.5.

of the Union's institutional architecture *(→ points 12 and 37)*. This session also gave rise to discussion of the reports from the working groups concerned with the simplification of instruments and procedures, and security and justice. Discussions at the 13th and final meeting of the year ([1]), on 20 December, focused on the reports from the working groups dealing with the Union's external action and defence.

Contributions to the work on the future of the European Union

11.   In 2002, the members of the convention presented more than 160 written contributions to the convention, with the working groups making additional contributions. Besides the part played by their representatives within the convention, the different Community bodies also made a specific contribution to the debate on the future of the Union.

12.   *Commission initiatives*. The Commission set out its 'Project for the European Union' in a communication adopted on 22 May ([2]). Seeking to respond to people's expectations, this project embraces the three fundamental tasks of the Union: consolidating its model of economic and social development; building up the area of freedom, security and justice; and exercising the responsibilities of a world power. To this end, the Commission proposes establishing a constitutional text, clarifying the way in which the Union exercises and implements its powers, and ensuring that the principles of subsidiarity and proportionality are adhered to.

On 4 December, the Commission supplemented this initiative with a communication entitled 'For the European Union — peace, freedom, solidarity' ([3]), outlining its vision of the institutional architecture designed to underpin the European project. With this contribution to the convention's proceedings, the Commission proposed various changes to the Union's institutional system and simplification of the decision-making process, with due regard for the balance between the European Parliament, the Council and the Commission. It envisaged a greater role for Parliament in the legislative and budgetary sphere, dispensing with voting patterns requiring unanimity and introducing the simple dual majority scheme for taking Council decisions deemed to be adopted if they have the support of a majority of the Member States representing a majority of the Union's population. The Commission believed also that it should retain its right of initiative, as the cornerstone of the Community method and a guarantee of defending the general European interest. It proposed also that the common foreign and security policy be strengthened, with the creation of the post of Sec-

---

([1]) Bull. 12-2002, point 1.1.6.
([2]) COM(2002) 247; Bull. 5-2002, point 1.1.1.
([3]) COM(2002) 728; Bull. 12-2002, point 1.1.4.

retary of the European Union, who would be a member of the Commission reporting also to the Council. With regard to the Presidency of the Council, the Commission recommended maintaining the six-monthly rotation for the European Council, the General Affairs Council and the Committee of Permanent Representatives; for the other Council formations, the members of the Council could elect a President for a period of one year, with such a system ensuring equality of access by all States to the Council Presidency. Finally, the Commission proposed that its own President be elected by the European Parliament and that the Commission itself should in the future be politically accountable to both Parliament and the Council. The Commission wanted all these proposals to be adopted in a Constitutional Treaty, which would also include the charter of fundamental rights, and the key principles and policies of the Union.

13.   *European Parliament initiatives.* In a resolution adopted on 7 February ([1]), Parliament called for both its own role and that of national parliaments to be enhanced, and for cooperation between them to be stepped up. It also stressed the importance of, and need for, the participation of MEPs and national parliament representatives in the Convention on the Future of the Union, and more generally in the reform of the Treaties. In a resolution adopted on 16 May ([2]), Parliament proposed that the exercise of competences be based on the principles of subsidiarity and proportionality, with a clear distinction drawn between the competences of the States, those of the Union and those which are shared, while making provision for a review clause in order to avoid establishing a rigid system of division. In this same resolution, referring to a viewpoint expressed on 14 March ([3]), Parliament argued that the European Union should be endowed with legal personality in order to clarify its status and improve both its capacity for action and its image. On 17 December ([4]), Parliament adopted a new resolution on the typology of acts and the hierarchy of legislation in the European Union. It recommended the introduction of a completely revamped typology of Union acts based on the principles of simplification, democratisation and specialisation, according to the rule of 'one act, one procedure, one name', entailing classification of acts on the basis of function. To this end, a distinction ought to be made between three blocs: the 'constitutional bloc', in terms of the provisions to be contained in a treaty; the 'legislative bloc', comprising the acts adopted under the co-decision procedure by Parliament and the Council, acting by a qualified majority on a proposal from the Commission; and the 'implementing bloc', ensuring that legislative acts are implemented by means of executive provisions and delegated regulations.

([1]) OJ C 284 E, 21.11.2002; Bull. 1/2-2002, point 1.1.4.
([2]) Bull. 5-2002, point 1.1.3.
([3]) Bull. 3-2002, point 1.1.4.
([4]) Bull. 12-2002, point 1.1.8.

14.   Committee of the Regions initiatives. In an opinion delivered on 13 March ([1]), the Committee of the Regions expressed the view that the division of powers between the Union and the Member States should be based on the principle of subsidiarity. A contribution to the convention ([2]) was, moreover, adopted by the committee on 4 July, stating its principal views on the future of the Union. The committee wanted to be recognised as having institutional status and to have the power to bring actions before the Court of Justice, at least in defence of its prerogatives and the subsidiarity principle, with its functions being strengthened. In an own-initiative opinion adopted on 10 October, entitled 'Towards a constitution for European citizens', the committee advocated a European constitutional framework and considered that the future Constitutional Treaty should be a basic treaty strengthening the institutions with a view to redressing the Union's present democratic deficit. Three further own-initiative opinions adopted by the committee, on 21 November, dealt respectively with the role of regional and local authorities in European integration ([3]), a better division and definition of powers in the Union ([4]), and the need for more democracy, transparency and efficiency in the Union ([5]).

15.   European Economic and Social Committee initiatives. On 19 September, the European Economic and Social Committee adopted a resolution addressed to the convention ([6]), announcing its intention of helping particularly to ensure that the debate on the future of the Union is opened up as widely as possible within organised civil society.

Debate on the future of the European Union

16.   With a view to broadening the debate on the future of the Union and involving all citizens, as provided for in the Laeken European Council's declaration ([7]), the convention organised various exchanges with civil society organisations and citizens in the context of the forum on the future of the Union. A forum web site was thus opened on the Internet ([8]), offering civil society organisations the opportunity to submit their contributions at any time, resulting in more than 400 contributions being presented to the members of the convention. Moreover, eight contact groups were brought together with specific sectors of civil society: social sector; environment; universities and think tanks; citizens and European institutions; regions and local authorities; human rights;

([1]) OJ C 192, 18.8.2002; Bull. 3-2002, point 1.1.3.
([2]) Bull. 7/8-2002, point 1.10.30.
([3]) Bull. 11-2002, point 1.1.4.
([4]) Bull. 11-2002, point 1.1.5.
([5]) Bull. 11-2002, point 1.1.6.
([6]) Bull. 9-2002, point 1.1.2.
([7]) 2001 General Report, point 13.
([8]) http://europa.eu.int/futurum/forum_convention/index_en.htm.

development; and culture. A plenary session of the convention, on 24 and 25 June, was devoted to presenting and discussing the contributions from these groups. In addition, the 'European youth convention', held from 9 to 12 July, resulted in the adoption of a final text on the future of the Union. During the listening phase of the convention's work *(→ point 9)*, various meetings were organised between the members of the convention and civil society, with the backing of the European Economic and Social Committee. The Commission meanwhile continued to make all the appropriate documents and links concerning the future of the Union available on the 'Futurum' Internet web site (¹), designed to accompany the debate and to facilitate citizens' involvement.

(¹) http://europa.eu.int/futurum/index_en.htm.

Section 3

Relations with civil society

17.   Standards for consultation. Having regard to the series of communications adopted by the Commission on 5 June for the purpose of simplifying and improving the regulatory environment *(→ point 25)*, relations with civil society are covered more specifically by the communication advocating a reinforced culture of consultation and dialogue. To tie in with this approach and the strategy on governance *(→ point 23)*, a database of consultative bodies has been set up and published on the Internet ([1]). On 11 December, the Commission adopted a communication on general principles and minimum standards for consultation of interested parties ([2]).

18.   Participation in the debate on the future of the European Union. In cooperation with the Convention on the Future of the European Union, the European Economic and Social Committee has organised regular information and dialogue meetings with civil society networks within the Union. It has also endeavoured to bring into the debate forthwith civil society organisations in the candidate countries. On 19 September, the Committee adopted a resolution addressed to the convention *(→ point 15)*, reaffirming, among other things, that the dialogue with civil society is a key factor in enhancing the Union's democratic legitimacy.

19.   Participation in development cooperation policy. On 7 November, the Commission adopted a communication on participation of non-governmental actors in this policy *(→ point 835)*.

([1]) http://europa.eu.int/comm/civil_society/coneccs/index_en.htm.
([2]) COM(2002) 704; Bull. 12-2002, point 1.1.10; Internet: http://europa.eu.int/comm/secretariat_general/sgc/consultation/index_en.htm.

Section 4

Transparency [1]

20.   *Commission initiatives.* In line with its policy in recent years of promoting transparency, the Commission published its work programme for 2002 [2] on its Europa Internet server, and adopted several Green Papers and White Papers for the purposes of consultation or public debate [3].

21.   *Public access to documents.* Pursuant to the new Regulation (EC) No 1049/2001 regarding public access to European Parliament, Council and Commission documents [4] in respect of which the three institutions adapted their rules of procedure [5], the interinstitutional committee provided for in that regulation was set up on 13 March. It met on 10 April and 9 July. Its role is to develop best administrative practice and ensure that the regulation is applied in a coherent way by the three institutions. In a resolution dated 14 March, Parliament welcomed the establishment of the committee but noted that discrepancies remained in the way the regulation was being applied [6]. It also called on the Commission and the agencies and similar bodies established by the institutions to take, as a matter of urgency, the measures required to bring agencies' access rules into line with the new regulation [7]. The proposed amendments to the instruments setting up Community bodies, which the Commission adopted on 17 July following the adoption of the new Financial Regulation *(→ point 1048)*, extends the scope of Regulation (EC) No 1049/2001 to include agencies and similar bodies. On 19 August, the Commission suggested amending Regulation (EEC, Euratom) No 354/83 concerning the opening to the public of the Historical Archives of the European Economic Community and the European Atomic Energy Community *(→ point 1168)*, so as to bring it into line with Regulation (EC) No 1049/2001. Also pursuant to Regulation (EC) No 1049/2001, Parliament and the Commission opened a public register of documents on 3 June. These registers and the one opened by the Council in 1999 [8] are accessible on the Internet [9]; they contain references, such as the title, date and author of the documents, but also enable direct access to the full text of some categories of

---

[1] Further information is available on the Europa server (http://europa.eu.int/scadplus/leg/en/lvb/a18000.htm).
[2] http://europa.eu.int/comm/off/work_programme/index_en.htm.
[3] http://europa.eu.int/comm/off/index_en.htm.
[4] OJ L 145, 31.5.2001; 2001 General Report, point 21.
[5] Parliament Decision of 13.11.2001 (OJ C 140, 13.6.2002); Council Decision 2001/840/EC (OJ L 313, 30.11.2001); Commission Decision 2001/937/EC (OJ L 345, 29.12.2001); 2001 General Report, point 21.
[6] Bull. 3-2002, point 1.1.8.
[7] 2001 General Report, point 21.
[8] Decision 2000/23/EC (OJ L 9, 13.1.2000); 1999 General Report, point 984.
[9] http://europa.eu.int/comm/secretariat_general/sgc/acc_doc/index_en.htm.

document. Lastly, the three institutions have produced an information brochure for the general public on rights of access to documents, published in all the official languages of the European Union ([1]).

22. *Legislative transparency.* Parliament, the Council and the Commission are endeavouring to make documents linked to the law-making process directly available, with the aid of registers where appropriate. The Commission also publishes its meeting agendas and ordinary minutes on the Internet ([2]). In a resolution dated 16 May on the Council reform ([3]), Parliament stated that the Council should open its meetings to the public and admit television cameras to film debates and voting.

([1]) Catalogue number: KA-41-01-187-EN-C.
([2]) http://europa.eu.int/comm/secretariat_general/meeting/index_en.htm.
([3]) Bull. 5-2002, point 1.1.4.

Section 5

Governance (¹)

23.   *White Paper on European governance.* Amongst the many positive reactions to this document, adopted by the Commission in July 2001 (²), the Committee of the Regions put its case, on 13 March (³), for both its own role and that of the regions being given greater prominence, whilst the European Economic and Social Committee emphasised, on 20 March (⁴), that it could play a key role in defining and structuring civil dialogue.

24.   *New Commission initiatives.* Following on from its White Paper, the Commission adopted, on 5 June, a series of communications concerned specifically with simplifying and improving the regulatory environment (→ *point 25*), setting out a plan of action, introducing a new method for assessing the impact of legislative proposals and paving the way for a reinforced culture of consultation and dialogue. On 11 December, the Commission presented a report on European governance (⁵), drawing lessons from the public consultation on the White Paper and taking stock of the progress made in the 16 months since the White Paper was published. On the same day, the Commission adopted a further series of communications linked to the theme of governance:

- the first communication takes a further step towards a reinforced culture of consultation and dialogue by laying down general principles and minimum standards for consultation of interested parties by the Commission (⁶): it advocates building a flexible framework in the interest of transparency, giving feedback to contributors and responding within a reasonable minimum period of eight weeks. From 2003 onwards, these principles and standards will apply at least to all major policy initiatives foreseen in the Commission's legislative and work programme (→ *point 1094*);

- the second communication deals with principles and guidelines for the collection and use of expertise (⁷). It seeks to boost public confidence by ensuring that the Commission mobilises and exploits the most appropriate expertise, while adhering to the core principles of quality, openness and

---

(¹) Further information is available on the Europa server (http://europa.eu.int/comm/governance/index_en.htm).
(²) COM(2001) 428; 2001 General Report, points 24 and 25; Internet (http://europa.eu.int/comm/governance/white_paper/index_en.htm).
(³) OJ C 192, 18.8.2002; Bull. 3-2002, point 1.1.6.
(⁴) OJ C 125, 27.5.2002; Bull. 3-2002, point 1.1.7.
(⁵) COM(2002) 705; Bull. 12-2002, point 1.1.9; Internet (http://europa.eu.int/comm/governance/index_en.htm).
(⁶) COM(2002) 704; Bull. 12-2002, point 1.1.10.
(⁷) COM(2002) 713; Bull. 12-2002, point 1.1.11.

effectiveness; the guidelines to be applied from 2003, will cover expertise in the wide sense, going beyond the purely scientific dimension;

- the third communication is concerned with the operating framework for the European regulatory agencies ([1]), in view of the growing role played by these entities. The framework thus established encompasses detailed criteria for creation of the agencies, their functioning (powers and responsibilities, management, boards of appeal, budgetary and administrative procedures) and control mechanisms (administrative, political, financial and judicial supervision). The aim of the initiative is to improve the implementation and application of Community rules, whilst safeguarding the unity and integrity of the executive function at Community level;

- the fourth communication clarifies the framework for target-based tripartite contracts and agreements ([2]) between the Community, the Member States and regional or local authorities for the implementation of Community policies. The Commission makes a distinction between target-based tripartite contracts concluded in direct application of binding secondary Community law and target-based tripartite agreements concluded outside a binding Community framework; the intention is to launch pilot target-based tripartite agreements and, after assessing these initial experiments, to introduce tripartite contracts.

Other governance-related initiatives have to do with the proposed revision of the 'committee procedure' system *(→ point 33)* and the application of Community law *(→ point 1064)*.

([1]) COM(2002) 718; Bull. 12-2002, point 1.1.15.
([2]) COM(2002) 709; Bull. 12-2002, point 1.1.12.

Section 6

Simplifying and improving the regulatory environment

25.   *General approach*. Following on from publication of its White Paper on European governance in July 2001 and the open consultations held on that occasion *(→ point 23)*, on 5 June the Commission adopted a series of communications on simplifying and improving the regulatory environment.

• The first communication, which makes a direct reference to European governance, presents as a whole the initiatives designed to improve European Union legislation. It also announces the adoption of a second package of measures (¹) *(→ point 24)*.

• The second communication, presented to the European Council following a long process of consultation, outlines an action plan introducing a strategy for further coordinated action to simplify and improve the regulatory environment (²). The action plan differentiates between the different tiers of authority in the Community legislative process. For its part, the Commission has promised to expand the explanatory memoranda of its proposals, to set up a network on better lawmaking and to define the circumstances in which it may withdraw its proposals. It also calls on Parliament and the Council to come to an agreement on the use of less detailed directives and the methods of co-regulation and self-regulation, and to institute a programme for simplifying and reducing the body of Community law. Finally, it proposes a number of measures which Member States could take to improve the transposal of Community legislation.

• The third communication concerns one of the action-plan measures that is specific to the Commission — a new integrated method of assessing the impact of proposals (³), which will be introduced gradually from 2003 to cover economic, social and environmental aspects, in line with the guidelines adopted at the Laeken European Council (⁴).

(¹) COM(2002) 275; Bull. 6-2002, point 1.1.6.
(²) COM(2002) 278; Bull. 6-2002, point 1.1.7.
(³) COM(2002) 276; Bull. 6-2002, point 1.1.8.
(⁴) Bull. 12-2001, point I. 27.

- The fourth communication describes the approach proposed by the Commission for promoting a culture of consultation and dialogue, in particular the adoption of minimum standards for consultation ([1]). The Commission adopted these standards in December (→ point 24), after conducting a public survey. It is also compiling a database of information on the various bodies consulted ([2]).

The Seville European Council welcomed these communications from the Commission on better lawmaking, and invited Parliament, the Council and the Commission to adopt an interinstitutional agreement, in order to improve the quality of Community legislation and the conditions for its transposal into national law ([3]).

On 17 July, the Commission presented a communication on applying the 'Simplifying and improving the regulatory environment' action plan to environmental agreements (→ point 554).

More generally, in parallel with the 'Better lawmaking' initiative (→ point 28), the Commission has developed, as part of its interactive policy-making (IPM) initiative ([4]), a series of Internet tools ([5]) (on-line consultation, business panel and feedback mechanism) designed to encourage stakeholders to play a more active part in the policy-making process. These tools will also enable the Commission to act on feedback more openly and effectively (→ points 21 and 22).

In an opinion adopted on 21 March ([6]), the European Economic and Social Committee welcomed the Commission's communication of December 2001 on simplification ([7]) and proposed that regulatory assessment offices be set up at European and national level. On 21 May, the Council also approved the approach presented by the Commission ([8]). In its conclusions of 3 September, the Council reaffirmed the high priority it attaches to simplifying the regulatory environment, to be achieved by appropriate action at all stages of the Community legislative process and at national level ([9]). In an own-initiative opinion adopted on 21 November ([10]), the Committee of the Regions stressed the need to assess the impact of Community legislation on local and regional authorities and the importance of the quality of legislation as a matter of principle; it also

[1] COM(2002) 277; Bull. 6-2002, point 1.1.9.
[2] http://europa.eu.int/comm/civil_society/coneccs/index_en.htm.
[3] Bull. 6-2002, point I.6.
[4] 2001 General Report, point 20.
[5] http://europa.eu.int/yourvoice/index_en.htm.
[6] OJ C 125, 27.5.2002; Bull. 3-2002, point 1.1.9.
[7] COM(2001) 726; 2001 General Report, point 26.
[8] Bull. 5-2002, point 1.1.6.
[9] Bull. 9-2002, point 1.1.3.
[10] Bull. 11-2002, point 1.1.8.

supported the holding of prior consultations and argued that instruments such as the open method of coordination, self-regulation and co-regulation should be enshrined in a future constitutional treaty.

26.   *Codification and recasting of Community legislation.* In 2002, the Commission adopted two codification proposals intended to replace five legislative instruments and one recasting proposal covering seven legislative instruments. In connection with its communication of November 2001 on the codification of the *acquis communautaire* (¹), it asked for the consolidation of 908 instruments and began codifying 211 instruments.

(¹) COM(2001) 645; 2001 General Report, point 28.

Section 7

Subsidiarity and proportionality

27.   The Commission's legislative activity throughout the year continued to be guided by the principles of subsidiarity and proportionality, as laid down in Article 5 of the EC Treaty and in the Amsterdam Treaty Protocol on the application of these principles. As in previous years, the Commission was ever mindful of the criteria determining the appropriateness of a Community initiative as opposed to action at national level, namely that it should be necessary and effective.

28.   The Commission presented to the December European Council its annual 'Better lawmaking' report ([1]) on the application of these principles. Adopted on 11 December, this 10th report is unique in two respects: firstly, in line with the commitments stemming from the White Paper on European governance ([2]), the report focuses on the objectives of European Union policies, and hence on the legislative proposals made by the Commission in this context (security of citizens and safety of transport, sustainable development and development cooperation); secondly, the 2002 report looks at the way in which Parliament and the Council have applied the principles of subsidiarity and proportionality. Following on from the other reports, the Commission has also included a section on improving the quality of legislation (consultation, impact assessment, consolidation, codification, recasting, accessibility and drafting quality) *(→ points 25 and 26)*.

([1]) COM(2002) 715; Bull. 12-2002, point 1.1.17.
([2]) COM(2001) 428; 2001 General Report, point 24.

Section 8

Co-decision (¹)

29.   General information. As a result of the Treaty of Amsterdam, the co-decision procedure applies to more than 50 % of legislative proposals under the first pillar, with the emphasis on transport, the environment, social affairs and employment, and certain aspects of development cooperation. Accordingly, in the course of 2002, the Commission drew up 74 proposals under this procedure. The European Parliament and the Council for their part signed, or reached a consensus prior to signing, 79 dossiers, most of which were in progress before 1 January 2002.

30.   Adoption at first reading. Agreement on 20 proposals was reached at first reading. Although the list of cases concluded without the need for a second reading consists largely of technical matters and consolidated texts, or has to do with relations with third countries, it includes other subjects such as quarterly non-financial accounts governing relations between the Member States' national administrations *(→ point 177)*. Other cases concluded at first reading, dealing for example with solvency margin requirements for life and non-life insurance undertakings *(→ point 166)*, are of some interest in the economic sphere or are politically sensitive, such as the directive on tobacco advertising and sponsorship *(→ point 178)*.

31.   Adoption in two readings. More than half of the legislative proposals (40 dossiers) were adopted in two readings. These include the significant (for the European scientific community) adoption of the sixth multiannual framework programme for research, technological development and demonstration activities (2002–06) *(→ points 288, 299 to 301)* and the dossier relating to postal services determining, in this sector, the timetable for liberalisation *(→ point 170)*. Topics of further interest include the agreement making it possible to register '.eu' top-level domain names on the Internet, and the processing of personal data and protection of privacy in the electronic communications sector *(→ point 343)*.

In 19 cases, the adoption process required the intervention of the Conciliation Committee. In nine of these cases, a joint text was approved by the committee without discussion ('A item'), particularly as a result of earlier interinstitutional negotiations in which the Commission played a mediating role as provided for

---

(¹) Further information is available on the Europa server (http://europa.eu.int/scadplus/leg/en/cig/g4000c.htm#c4).

in the Treaty. Most of the areas requiring deeper discussion had to do with environmental issues (sixth action programme for the environment, environmental noise) *(→ points 551 and 552)*, human health (public health programme; human blood) *(→ points 685 to 689)*, transport (civil aviation security) *(→ point 654)* and social affairs (employment incentive measures; implementation of the principle of equal treatment and protection of workers against noise and vibrations) *(→ point 132)*. The dossier concerning the directive on cosmetic products ran into further difficulties, but the negotiations were nevertheless concluded before expiry of the deadline *(→ point 280)*.

32. *Outlook*. On 4 and 5 November, an interinstitutional seminar on co-decision was held, focusing on transparency, the evolving roles of the three institutions and the future of the co-decision procedure within an enlarged Union. The seminar proved highly constructive, resulting in specific conclusions intended to contribute to the work of the Convention on the Future of the European Union *(→ points 11 to 15)*.

Section 9

Implementing powers conferred on the Commission

33. Most legislative instruments adopted in 2002 conferred implementing powers on the Commission in accordance with Article 202 of the EC Treaty. Under the committee procedure *(comitologie)* system established by Council Decision 1999/468/EC of 28 June 1999 (¹), the advisory procedure was selected in a dozen cases, the management procedure in more than 50 and the regulatory procedure also in more than 50. In some instances more than one procedure was used by a single committee because of the matters being dealt with.

34. Following the agreement reached between Parliament and the Commission in February 2000 on the procedures for implementing the abovementioned Decision 1999/468/EC (²), the Commission sent 2 251 documents to Parliament in 2002, 105 of them in accordance with its right of scrutiny of measures implementing instruments adopted by co-decision procedure on the basis of Article 251 of the EC Treaty.

35. In accordance with the abovementioned decision and its previous report for 2000 (³), on 13 December the Commission adopted a report on the workings of the committees during 2001 (⁴).

36. With a view to implementing the provisions of Council Decision 1999/468/EC and the attached statements, the legislative proposals transmitted by the Commission in December 2001 and which were designed to bring the existing rules into line with the new decision (⁵) were examined during the year by Parliament and Council bodies. The existing committees also continued adapting their rules of procedure on the basis of the standard rules of procedure adopted by the Commission on 31 January 2001 (⁶); by the end of 2002 almost half of the committees' rules of procedure had been duly amended.

37. Lastly, in its communication on the institutional architecture, submitted to the Convention on the Future of the Union in December *(→ point 12)*, the

---

(¹) OJ L 184, 17.7.1999; 1999 General Report, point 981.
(²) OJ L 256, 10.10.2000; Bull. 1/2-2000, point 1.9.3.
(³) OJ C 37, 9.2.2002, COM(2001) 783; 2001 General Report, point 36.
(⁴) COM(2002) 733; Bull. 12-2002, point 1.1.14.
(⁵) 2001 General Report, point 36.
(⁶) OJ C 38, 6.2.2001; 2001 General Report, point 36.

Commission proposed amending Article 202 of the EC Treaty in order to establish a new system for delegating powers which more closely reflects the legal and political realities of the situation and the operating requirements of an enlarged Union. Pending the entry into force of a new treaty, on 11 December the Commission adopted a proposal amending the abovementioned Decision 1999/468/EC (Table II); this initiative is designed to clarify the exercise of executive functions and to place Parliament and the Council on an equal footing as supervisors of the Commission's exercise of the implementing powers conferred on it as regards the areas covered by the co-decision procedure.

Section 10

Interinstitutional cooperation

38.   In the field of interinstitutional cooperation, the main occurrences in 2002 were:

- the signing, and subsequent extension, of an interinstitutional agreement between the European Parliament, the Council and the Commission on the financing of the Convention on the Future of the European Union *(→ point 7)*;

- the setting-up of an interinstitutional committee to implement the regulation of public access to documents of the institutions *(→ point 21)* and approval, by Parliament and the Council, of an agreement concerning access by Parliament to sensitive information of the Council in the field of security and defence;

- the signing of an interinstitutional agreement between the European Parliament, the Council and the Commission on the financing and operation of a European Union Solidarity Fund for providing assistance to disaster-stricken peoples and regions *(→ point 362)*;

- the establishment of a European Communities Personnel Selection Office, common to the European Parliament, the Council, the Commission, the Court of Justice, the Court of Auditors, the European Economic and Social Committee, the Committee of the Regions and the European Ombudsman *(→ point 1137)*.

Section 11

Expiry of the ECSC Treaty

39. The Treaty of Paris establishing the European Coal and Steel Community expired on 23 July as stipulated by the Amsterdam Treaty in 1997. At the formal session of the ECSC Consultative Committee *(→ point 1124)* held in Luxembourg on 27 June to mark this event, speeches were made by Ms Polfer, the Luxembourg Minister for Foreign Affairs and Trade, Mr Poos, MEP and European Parliament Quaestor, Ms Birulés i Bertrán, the Spanish Minister for Science and Technology, Ms Loyola de Palacio, Vice-President of the Commission, Mr Frerichs, President of the European Economic and Social Committee and Mr Gibellieri, President of the ECSC Consultative Committee. A series of events and seminars and a round table to mark the event took place in Luxembourg between 25 and 27 June. Several publications, including a commemorative volume containing contributions from 34 leading figures on the ECSC's achievements in the industrial field, social dialogue and competition, and on the lessons to be learnt from the 'institutional laboratory' which the ECSC represented, as well as documents from various Commission directorates-general were also produced ([1]). On 23 July, following a highly symbolic ceremony in front of the building in Brussels where the President of the Commission has his office, a symposium on the history and future of the European Union was held at the headquarters of the European Economic and Social Committee with speeches by Mr Prodi, President of the Commission, Ms Ana Palacio, the Spanish Minister for Foreign Affairs and acting President of the Council, Mr Frerichs, Mr Gibellieri and others.

40. At its final ordinary session, held on 26 June, the ECSC Consultative Committee *(→ point 1125)* adopted a resolution on the legacy of the ECSC ([2]) in which it expressed its satisfaction at the efforts made to preserve the Community's achievements after the Treaty expires, particularly as regards the continuation of coal and steel research, structured dialogue and monitoring of aid to the steel sector and the coal industry. The committee also called on the EU institutions to take a balanced view of the economic, environmental and social constraints facing firms in the two ECSC sectors concerned and drew their attention to the importance of international negotiations on world-level reductions in the steel industry's excess capacity and to particular aspects of these problems in the light of the impending enlargement of the European Union. The committee also expressed concern at the gradual termination of various ECSC social measures,

---

([1]) http://europa.eu.int/ecsc/index_en.htm.
([2]) OJ C 176, 24.7.2002; Bull. 6-2002, point 1.7.4.

the abandonment of the sectoral approach in the use of the Structural Funds and the failure to guarantee the future of the Paul Finet Foundation and reiterated the need to continue treating prevention in the mining industry as a special case. Lastly, the committee wished to express its gratitude to the workers and all other parties involved in the two industries.

41. Various decisions have been adopted to deal with the practical consequences of the expiry of the ECSC Treaty:

- in the financial field, pursuant to a protocol written into the EC Treaty by the Nice Treaty following the Nice European Council ([1]), the representatives of the governments of the Member States, meeting within the Council, adopted on 27 February a decision ([2]) on the transfer of the ECSC's funds to the European Community when the Treaty expired and on the creation of a common research fund for the coal and steel industries. The Commission will administer these funds in accordance with the special rules set out in the decision;

- in the competition field, on 21 June the Commission adopted a communication concerning certain aspects of the treatment of cases resulting from the transition from the ECSC to the EC regime *(→ point 205)*;

- with regard to the international agreements concluded by the ECSC with third countries, on 19 July the representatives of the governments of the Member States, meeting within the Council, adopted a decision ([3]) providing for the rights and obligations flowing from those agreements to be devolved to the European Community when the Treaty expired. On the same date ([4]) the Council instructed the Commission to inform the third countries concerned of these arrangements, to undertake all necessary technical amendments in order to make the agreements compatible with EC rules and, where appropriate, to negotiate amendments to the agreements.

([1]) 2000 General Report, point 76.
([2]) Decision 2002/234/ECSC (OJ L 79, 22.3.2002; Bull. 1/2-2002, point 1.7.11).
([3]) Decision 2002/595/EC (OJ L 194, 23.7.2002; Bull. 7/8-2002, point 1.7.12).
([4]) Decision 2002/596/EC (OJ L 194, 23.7.2002; Bull. 7/8-2002, point 1.7.13).

Chapter II

Human rights and fundamental freedoms

Section 1

Actions within the European Union

42. Charter of fundamental rights ([^1]). In a resolution adopted on 23 October ([^2]), Parliament asked the Convention on the Future of the European Union *(→ point 13)* to make the charter legally binding by incorporating it in the future Treaty, so that legal actions can be brought on the basis of the rights laid down therein.

43. Traffic in human beings ([^3]). During the year, various initiatives relating to trafficking in human beings and the exploitation of children were taken or proposed within the framework of the area of freedom, security and justice *(→ point 489)*.

44. Daphne programme. In its report of 8 April, the Commission described the progress made with the Daphne programme (2000–03) ([^4]) since its adoption in January 2000 ([^5]). The programme is designed to prevent violence towards children, adolescents and women. In a resolution passed on 4 September, Parliament expressed satisfaction with the implementation of the programme at the half-way stage and recommended that the budget allocation be extended for the coming financial years ([^6]).

45. Fight against intolerance. At its meeting on 25 and 26 April, the Council denounced the racist acts committed at various places in the European Union in

---

([^1]) OJ C 364, 18.12.2000; 2000 General Report, points 15 *et seq.*; Internet (http://europa.eu.int/comm/justice_home/unit/charte/index_en.html).
([^2]) Bull. 10-2002, point 1.2.2.
([^3]) http://europa.eu.int/comm/justice_home/project/stop_prov_en.htm.
([^4]) COM(2002) 169; Bull. 4-2002, point 1.2.2.
([^5]) Decision No 293/2000/EC (OJ L 34, 9.2.2000; 2000 General Report, point 22 and http://europa.eu.int/comm/justice_home/project/daphne/en/index.htm).
([^6]) Bull. 9-2002, point 1.2.1.

the recent past and expressed its determination to strengthen the prevention of, and fight against, racist violence, anti-Semitism and all forms of intolerance (¹).

46. *Women's rights*. On 13 March, stating its views on the situation of women confronted with fundamentalism, Parliament stressed in particular that within the European Union the defence of women's rights meant that it was impossible to apply rules or traditions that are incompatible with those rights (²). In a resolution passed on 3 July (³), it highlighted current inequalities within the European Union with regard to sexual and reproductive health and rights, covering family planning, contraception, sex education, abortion and pregnancy. Emphasising that it is the Member States which are competent in the field of reproductive health, it recommends that high-quality national programmes be drawn up.

47. *Sakharov Prize*. On 17 December, the President of the European Parliament awarded the Sakharov Prize for Freedom of Thought to Mr Payá Sardiñas, founder of the Christian Liberation Movement in Cuba (⁴) and promoter of non-violent democracy based on dialogue and reform.

48. *European Group on Ethics (EGE)* (⁵). On 7 May, at the Commission's request, the EGE published an opinion on *Ethical aspects of patenting inventions involving human stem cells*. It also launched a discussion on the ethical aspects of clinical research in developing countries, in conjunction with the activities of the sixth framework programme for research *(→ points 298 and 312)*. In the context of these deliberations, it held a round table in Brussels on 1 October, which was attended by representatives from the Commission's departments, Parliament, international organisations such as the World Health Organisation and the Council of Europe, national ethics bodies, academic and industrial circles, religious bodies, associations and the media. Under the Spanish Presidency, the EGE held a working meeting in Barcelona on 18 and 19 April and took part in the platform on European–African partnership on clinical trials programmes for poverty-related diseases. It also held a working meeting in Copenhagen and took part in the international conference on future food and bioethics, organised by the Danish Presidency from 23 to 25 October.

(¹) Bull. 4-2002, point 1.2.4.
(²) Bull. 3-2002, point 1.2.2.
(³) Bull. 7/8-2002, point 1.2.1.
(⁴) Bull. 12-2002, point 1.2.1.
(⁵) http://europa.eu.int/comm/european_group_ethics/index_en.htm.

Section 2

Actions outside the European Union

49. Overall approach. On 21 October, the Council adopted the fourth annual report of the European Union on human rights in the world (^{1}), which gives an overview of Community policy on human rights within and outside the Union.

50. Respect for human rights and promotion of democratisation in third countries. The European Union continued its policy of promoting and consolidating democracy and the rule of law and universal respect for human rights and fundamental freedoms. The Commission communication of May 2001 on the EU's role in promoting human rights and democratisation in third countries (^{2}) was endorsed by the European Parliament on 25 April (^{3}). Parliament, for its part, proposed an interinstitutional code of conduct.

A large number of the EU's common strategies, common positions and joint actions specifically concern human rights and democratisation or contain substantial elements relating to human rights *(→ point 753).* The EU continued to take action against all those countries still committing serious violations of democratic principles and human rights, either through private censure *(→ points 749 and 756)* or by public condemnation of such practices *(→ point 762).* On 30 December, the Commission proposed the adoption of a regulation aimed at regulating trade in certain equipment and products liable to be used for torture or to inflict capital punishment or other kinds of cruel, inhuman or degrading treatment (^{4}).

51. Monitoring of elections. This remained an important facet of the EU's policy to promote human rights and democracy in the world. Observer missions were dispatched to Cambodia, Republic of Congo (Brazzaville), East Timor, Ecuador, Kenya, Madagascar, Pakistan, Sierra Leone and Zimbabwe.

52. EU action in international bodies. The importance the EU attaches to respect for democratic principles and human rights was also reflected in its contribution to the work of international bodies such as the UN General Assembly and the UN Commission on Human Rights (^{5}), the Organisation for Security and Cooperation in Europe (OSCE) (^{6}) and the Council of Europe (^{7}).

(^{1}) Bull. 10-2002, point 1.2.1.
(^{2}) COM(2001) 252; 2001 General Report, point 45.
(^{3}) Bull. 4-2002, point 1.2.5.
(^{4}) COM(2002) 770; Bull. 12-2002, point 1.2.4.
(^{5}) http://www.un.org/rights/index.html.
(^{6}) http://www.osce.org/odihr/hdim2002/.
(^{7}) http://www.coe.int/portalT.asp.

53.   International Criminal Court (ICC) [1]. In its conclusions of 17 June [2], the Council welcomed the entry into force of the ICC Statute while regretting the decision of the United States not to become party to it. On 20 June [3], it amended its Common Position 2001/443/CFSP [4] in order to underscore the Union's support for the early establishment of the ICC, its effective functioning and the widest possible participation of the international community. In its conclusions of 30 September [5], the Council set out conditions and guiding principles for the Member States' response to US proposals for bilateral agreements on 'non-execution of a request for surrender' to the ICC. The entry into force of the ICC Statute also prompted a Presidency statement on behalf of the European Union *(→ point 762)*.

54.   Action by the European Parliament. As in previous years, Parliament adopted, on 25 April [6], a resolution on human rights in the world in 2001 and on EU human rights policy. It gave its opinion on human rights and respect for democratic principles in a number of countries, as set out in Table 2, and addressed important issues such as the entry into force of the Statute of the International Criminal Court [7] and the stance of the United States to the ICC [8], the Union's priorities in the UN Commission on Human Rights [9], child labour in the production of sports goods [10] and the abolition of the death penalty in Japan, South Korea and Taiwan [11].

55.   Technical and financial assistance. As set out in the Commission communication of 8 May 2001 on the EU's role in promoting human rights and democratisation in third countries [12], geographical and thematic priorities were identified for 2002–04. In accordance with the regulations adopted by the Council on 29 April 1999 [13], financial support will be provided for measures to promote and defend human rights and fundamental freedoms, support the process of democratisation and assist in conflict prevention (EUR 103.7 million).

---

[1] http://www.iccnow.org/.
[2] Bull. 6-2002, point 1.2.2.
[3] Common Position 2002/474/CFSP (OJ L 164, 22.6.2002; Bull. 6-2002, point 1.2.3).
[4] OJ L 155, 12.6.2001; 2001 General Report, point 815.
[5] Bull. 9-2002, point 1.2.3.
[6] Bull. 4-2002, point 1.2.6.
[7] OJ C 271 E, 7.11.2002; Bull. 1/2-2002, point 1.2.1.
[8] Bull. 10-2002, point 1.2.3.
[9] OJ C 271 E, 7.11.2002; Bull. 1/2-2002, point 1.2.2.
[10] Bull. 6-2002, point 1.2.1.
[11] Bull. 6-2002, point 1.2.9.
[12] COM(2001) 252; 2001 General Report, point 45.
[13] 1999 General Report, point 26.

TABLE 2

Parliament resolutions on human rights in certain countries

Country	Subject	Reference
Afghanistan	Human rights situation	Bull. 9-2002, point 1.2.5
Argentina	Economic crisis	Bull. 7/8-2002, point 1.2.3
Bangladesh	Human rights situation	Bull. 11-2002, point 1.2.1
Belarus	Obstacles to an OSCE mission	Bull. 6-2002, point 1.2.6
	Press freedom	Bull. 7/8-2002, point 1.2.4
Cambodia	Violence during elections	Bull. 1/2-2002, point 1.2.3
	Closure of refugee camps	Bull. 4-2002, point 1.2.7
China	Situation of Tibetans	Bull. 12-2002, point 1.2.7
Colombia	Renewed violence	Bull. 3-2002, point 1.2.4
Democratic Republic of Congo	Persistence of violence	Bull. 6-2002, point 1.2.12
Egypt	Violation of human rights	Bull. 7/8-2002, point 1.2.5
	Case of Saad Eddin Ibrahim	Bull. 9-2002, point 1.2.6
Eritrea	Violation of human rights	Bull. 1/2-2002, point 1.2.4
Equatorial Guinea	Violation of human rights	Bull. 6-2002, point 1.2.8
Guatemala	Human rights situation	Bull. 4-2002, point 1.2.8
Iran	Human rights situation	Bull. 10-2002, point 1.2.5
	Death sentence on Hashem Aghajari	Bull. 11-2002, point 1.2.2
Iraq	Human rights situation	Bull. 5-2002, point 1.2.2
Kyrgyzstan	Imprisonment of an MP	Bull. 3-2002, point 1.2.5
Madagascar	Presidential elections	Bull. 1/2-2002, point 1.2.6
Malaysia	Human rights situation	Bull. 6-2002, point 1.2.10
Moldova	Human rights situation	Bull. 3-2002, point 1.2.6
	Disappearance of an MP	Bull. 4-2002, point 1.2.9
Myanmar	Violation of human rights	Bull. 4-2002, point 1.2.10
Nepal	Flare-up of violence	Bull. 6-2002, point 1.2.11
	Internal conflict	Bull. 10-2002, point 1.2.6
Nigeria	Respect for women's rights	Bull. 4-2002, point 1.2.11
	Amina Lawal case	Bull. 9-2002, point 1.2.7
Russia	Violation of press freedom	Bull. 1/2-2002, point 1.2.7
		Bull. 7/8-2002, point 1.2.6
Sudan	Human rights situation	Bull. 11-2002, point 1.2.3
Sri Lanka	Ethnic conflict	Bull. 3-2002, point 1.2.7
Syria	Individual rights (Riad Turk case)	Bull. 6-2002, point 1.2.13
Tunisia	Judicial procedures	Bull. 3-2002, point 1.2.8
Turkey	Respect for minorities	Bull. 1/2-2002, point 1.2.8
United States	Detention conditions at Guantanamo Bay	Bull. 1/2-2002, point 1.2.5
Vietnam	Respect for minorities	Bull. 4-2002, point 1.2.12
Zimbabwe	Incidents during elections	Bull. 3-2002, point 1.2.9

Chapter III

The Community economic and social area

Section 1

Economic and monetary policy (¹)

Overview

56.   *The introduction of euro notes and coins at the beginning of the year marked a decisive step in the history of European integration. Thanks to meticulous preparation and to the enthusiastic welcome given by a large majority of the public, the changeover to euro notes and coins was an unprecedented success that marked the birth of a currency area comprising over 300 million people. Economic and monetary union rests on the undertaking to conduct sound macroeconomic policies, and these have contributed to the emergence of a new culture of economic stability in Europe. It is this stability that has enabled the Union to cope with the slowdown in the world economy. Faced with this slowdown, the monetary authorities have cut interest rates, and budgetary policy has operated through the automatic stabilisers, which help to smooth out fluctuations in the growth of production. However, in the light of recent developments and in the absence of the recovery forecast in the spring, budget deficits have increased. Under these circumstances, the Commission has proposed improved coordination of economic policy and, in particular, of the Stability and Growth Pact. In order to strengthen and facilitate the coordination process even further, it launched a new quarterly report on economic developments in the euro area. In the interests of consistency and efficiency, it also launched a process for streamlining the annual economic and employment policy coordination cycles. The Commission has thus reinforced the medium- and long-term perspective for coordination in line with the strategy embarked on at the Lisbon European Council and followed up at the Gothenburg European Council and has placed*

(¹) Additional information is available on the Europa server (http://europa.eu.int/comm/economy_finance/index_en.htm).

the emphasis on implementing the policy guidelines and achieving tangible results.

Economic situation

57.   A modest economic recovery was discernible at the start of the year, following the slight dip in gross domestic product (GDP) in the fourth quarter of 2001. In the ensuing months, however, it became clear that the recovery was running out of steam. Internal demand was still weak, as were private consumption and, especially, investment. Persistent underlying inflation eroded household purchasing power before falling back in the second quarter, thereby boosting purchasing power. Consumer confidence nevertheless remained close to its long-term average, with no signs of any pick-up. The uncertainties surrounding labour market developments and prices, particularly as a result of the changeover to the euro, probably had an adverse impact on private consumption, prompting consumers to defer their early-year purchases. There was also some deterioration in the budgetary situation in terms of the objectives spelt out in the stability and convergence programmes, with budget deficits widening to slightly above 2 % of GDP in the euro area. The economic situation alone did not account for this deterioration in public finances since spending overruns but also the effects of tax changes were significant factors in larger deficits.

After declining markedly from 10.7 % in 1998 to 8 % in mid-2001, unemployment started to climb again in the wake of the economic slowdown. This reflects the response of the labour market to the contraction in economic activity. Since fewer jobs are being created, unemployment will not fall in the short term. The timing and intensity of the recovery in growth in the European Union are still uncertain, with mounting tension in the Middle East and Iraq and the related movements in oil prices being the main sources of concern. Other risks stem from the impact on consumer and investor confidence of the recent correction in share prices, the volatility of financial markets and the possible effects of contagion from the economic crises affecting some countries in Latin America. In this context, the forecasts for growth in the European Union in 2002 have had to be revised downwards. The average growth rate for the euro area should be 0.8 %, according to the Commission's autumn 2002 forecasts, compared with the 1.4 % forecast earlier.

Economic policy coordination

58.   *Reinforcing economic policy coordination.* The Barcelona European Council identified a need for further progress towards economic policy coordi-

nation and called on the Commission to present proposals before the European Council scheduled to take place in the spring of 2003 ([1]). To that end, the Commission presented, on 27 November, a communication on strengthening the coordination of budgetary policies ([2]) with a view to improving the implementation of the Stability and Growth Pact and the way in which Member States' budgetary policies are conducted. In connection with this initiative, the Commission adopted on the same date two further communications aimed at upgrading the quality of economic and budgetary statistics for the European Union ([3]) and the euro zone *(→ point 100)*. In addition, the Barcelona European Council called on the Council and the Commission to streamline their coordination processes ([4]). On 3 September, the Commission advocated streamlining the annual economic and employment policy coordination cycles in order to enhance the efficiency of policy coordination and improve coherence and complementarity between the various processes and instruments ([5]). In particular, it suggested synchronising these processes, adopting more of a medium-term perspective in the policy guidelines and focusing on monitoring their implementation by Member States. On 5 December, Parliament welcomed this Commission communication ([6]). For its part, the Council adopted, on 3 December, its own report on this matter, in which it made several recommendations ([7]). Moreover, in a communication of 22 May addressed to the Convention ([8]), the Commission set out suggestions for strengthening economic policy coordination in a future treaty in order to assert the Community interest more effectively. The European Economic and Social Committee contributed to the debate in an exploratory opinion on the coordination of long-term economic policies adopted on 29 May ([9]) and in an own-initiative opinion of 12 December on economic governance in the Union ([10]). In these opinions, it stressed the Commission's role as the body representing the Community interest.

Broad economic policy guidelines

59. *Preparation of the 2002 guidelines.* As a precursor to the broad economic policy guidelines for 2002, the Commission presented the 'EU economy 2001 review' ([11]) with a view to launching a debate on questions of economic policy. As part of the multilateral surveillance procedure, it assessed the

---

([1]) Bull. 3-2002, point I.5.
([2]) COM(2002) 668; Bull. 11-2002, point 1.3.5.
([3]) COM(2002) 670; Bull. 11-2002, point 1.3.6.
([4]) Bull. 3-2002, point I.39.
([5]) COM(2002) 487; Bull. 9-2002, point 1.3.3.
([6]) Bull. 12-2002, point 1.3.7.
([7]) Bull. 12-2002, point 1.3.6.
([8]) COM(2002) 247; Bull. 5-2002, point 1.1.1.
([9]) OJ C 221, 17.9.2002; Bull. 5-2002, point 1.3.3.
([10]) Bull. 12-2002, point 1.3.2.
([11]) Published in *European Economy*, No 73, and on the Internet (http://europa.eu.int/comm/economy_finance/publications/european_economy/the_eu_economy_review2001_en.htm).

implementation of the 2001 broad economic policy guidelines [1] in a report dated 21 February [2]. It took the view that macroeconomic policies had been adapted in appropriate fashion to the economic slowdown in 2001 but that more still needed to be done on the structural policy front. On 14 March, Parliament adopted a resolution in preparation for the 2002 guidelines [3]. It advocated sound public finances, a counter-cyclical macroeconomic policy mix and further progress in structural reforms. The European Economic and Social Committee gave its views on these matters in an own-initiative opinion adopted on 20 March [4]. In another opinion adopted on 21 March, it examined the economic policies of the euro-zone countries [5].

60.   *Broad guidelines for 2002* [6]. The 2002 broad economic policy guidelines for the Member States and the Community were formally adopted on 21 June by the Council [7], which confirmed and broadened the policy strategy set out in the previous guidelines *(→ point 59)* in the light of the results of the Barcelona European Council [8]. It stated that, by way of growth- and stability-oriented macroeconomic policies and structural reforms, efforts should focus on:

- safeguarding and further strengthening the macroeconomic framework,

- raising the employment rate and combating unemployment,

- strengthening conditions for high productivity growth, and

- promoting sustainable development for present and future generations.

The Council reaffirmed among other things its attachment to the Stability and Growth Pact and the consolidation of Member States' public finances. In accordance with Article 99(2) of the EC Treaty, these guidelines had previously been the subject of a Commission recommendation dated 24 April [9]. Parliament welcomed the Commission recommendation on 16 May [10] but suggested some amendments concerning for the most part investment and labour market policy. On 20 June, the Council finalised a draft recommendation [11] that was approved by the Seville European Council [12].

---

[1] COM(2002) 93; Bull. 1/2-2002, point 1.3.3; Internet (http://europa.eu.int/comm/economy_finance/publications/european_economy/implement2001_en.htm).
[2] Council Recommendation 2001/483/EC (OJ L 179, 2.7.2001; 2001 General Report, point 56).
[3] Bull. 3-2002, point 1.3.6.
[4] OJ C 125, 27.5.2002; Bull. 3-2002, point 1.3.7.
[5] OJ C 125, 27.5.2002; Bull. 3-2002, point 1.3.5.
[6] Published in *European Economy*, No 4/2002, and on the Internet (http://europa.eu.int/comm/economy_finance/publications/european_economy/broadeconomypolicyguidelines2002_en.htm).
[7] Council Recommendation 2002/549/EC (OJ L 182, 11.7.2002; Bull. 6-2002, point 1.3.3).
[8] Bull. 3-2002, point I.4.
[9] COM(2002) 191; Bull. 4-2002, point 1.3.2.
[10] Bull. 5-2002, point 1.3.4.
[11] Bull. 6-2002, point 1.3.3.
[12] Bull. 6-2002, point I.16.

61.   *Preparation of the 2003 guidelines.* The Commission launched the preparations for 2003 by presenting on 11 December the 'EU economy 2002 review' ([1]), which examines various aspects of macroeconomic developments, structural changes and enlargement.

Stability and Growth Pact; public finances

62.   *Stability and Growth Pact.* On 12 July, the Council adopted conclusions ([2]) on the methods for assessing output gaps, which form part of the Stability and Growth Pact.

63.   *Stability programmes.* Acting on a recommendation from the Commission ([3]), the Council adopted on 22 January ([4]) and 12 February ([5]) opinions on the updated stability programmes for the euro-area countries. On 12 February, it also adopted two statements on the budgetary situation of Germany ([6]) and Portugal ([7]). In a resolution dated 15 May, Parliament expressed concern at the failure by those two Member States to apply the Stability and Growth Pact strictly as this could harm its credibility and result in its differential application ([8]). In this resolution, it also welcomed Ireland's determination to apply the Commission's 2001 recommendation ([9]). As regards surveillance of budgetary deficits, the Commission adopted, on 24 September, a report on the public finance situation in Portugal. This report, which is a first stage in the excessive deficit procedure, was drawn up following official confirmation that the general government deficit in 2001 was equivalent to 4.1 % of GDP, clearly exceeding the reference value of 3 %. On 19 November, the Commission adopted a further report on the general government deficit in Germany, noting that the reference value of 3 % of GDP had been exceeded in 2002. On the same date, it decided to initiate the early-warning procedure in respect of France with a view to preventing the emergence in the medium term of an excessive deficit. On 5 November, acting on a recommendation from the Commission, the Council acknowledged the existence of an excessive deficit in Portugal and decided to issue a recommendation to that Member State with a view to remedying the situation ([10]).

([1]) COM(2002) 712; Bull. 12-2002, point 1.3.5. Published in *European Economy,* No 6/2002 and on the
    Internet (http://europa.eu.int/comm/economy_finance/publications/european_economy/the_eu_economy_
    review2002_ en.htm).
([2]) Bull. 7/8-2002, point 1.3.4.
([3]) Bull. 1/2-2002, points 1.3.4, 1.3.5, 1.3.7 to 1.3.15 and 1.3.17.
([4]) OJ C 33, 6.2.2002; Bull. 1/2-2002, points 1.3.4 (Belgium), 1.3.12 (Luxembourg), 1.3.13 (Netherlands),
    1.3.14 (Austria) and 1.3.17 (Finland).
([5]) OJ C 51, 26.2.2002; Bull. 1/2-2002, points 1.3.5 (Germany), 1.3.7 (Greece), 1.3.8 (Spain), 1.3.9 (France),
    1.3.10 (Ireland), 1.3.11 (Italy) and 1.3.15 (Portugal).
([6]) Bull. 1/2-2002, point 1.3.6.
([7]) Bull. 1/2-2002, point 1.3.16.
([8]) Bull. 5-2002, point 1.3.5.
([9]) 2001 General Report, point 59.
([10]) Bull. 11-2002, point 1.3.7.

64. *Convergence programmes.* On 22 January ([1]), 12 February ([2]) and 5 March ([3]), the Council adopted three opinions on the updated convergence programmes of the Member States not participating in the euro. With specific regard to Sweden, a Commission report adopted on 22 May found that it did not fulfil the exchange rate criterion and that it was not, therefore, ready to adopt the single currency ([4]).

65. *Public finances.* In its third report on public finances adopted on 14 May, the Commission, after reviewing the Member States' budgetary performances in 2001 and their prospects for 2002, examined some of the questions relating to budgetary policy at EU level, including the operation of the budgetary surveillance framework, the quality of public spending, the role of discretionary fiscal policies and the key budgetary challenges facing the candidate countries ([5]).

Other coordination processes ([6])

66. *Follow-up to the Lisbon process.* On 16 January, the Commission reviewed progress in implementing the Lisbon strategy ([7]) in its annual spring report to the European Council. It recalled that, even though economic and monetary union had contributed to macroeconomic stability in the European Union, decisive structural reforms were still needed. The Barcelona European Council had welcomed the Commission communication on the follow-up to the Lisbon strategy ([8]). On 28 February, Parliament called for acceleration of the Lisbon process and for closer coordination of economic, structural and employment policies with a view to staving off the current downward economic trend ([9]). On 20 March, it welcomed the outcome of the Barcelona European Council and reiterated that the Lisbon policy mix should be maintained and taken further at each spring European Council ([10]). On 16 October, the Commission presented the new list of structural indicators ([11]) that it was intending to use in drawing up its next annual spring report to the European Council. The previous list ([12]) had been amended slightly in order to take account of the improved quality of data and the new political priorities while maintaining a

---

([1]) Sweden: OJ C 33, 6.2.2002; Bull. 1/2-2002, point 1.3.18.
([2]) United Kingdom: OJ C 51, 26.2.2002; Bull. 1/2-2002, point 1.3.19.
([3]) Denmark: OJ C 64, 13.3.2002; Bull. 3-2002, point 1.3.8.
([4]) COM(2002) 243; Bull. 5-2002, point 1.3.6.
([5]) COM(2002) 209; Bull. 5-2002, point 1.3.2.
([6]) 1997 General Report, point 1140 (Luxembourg); 1998 General Report, point 1081 (Cardiff); 1999 General Report, point 1025 (Cologne); 2000 General Report, point 1145 (Lisbon).
([7]) COM(2002) 14; Bull. 1/2-2002, point 1.3.2.
([8]) Bull. 3-2002, point I.3.
([9]) OJ C 293 E, 28.11.2002, Bull. 1/2-2002, point 1.3.35.
([10]) Bull. 3-2002, point 1.3.3.
([11]) COM(2002) 551; Bull. 10-2002, point 1.3.1.
([12]) COM(2001) 619; 2001 General Report, point 62.

degree of continuity. On 3 December, the Council approved the definitive list of structural indicators (¹).

67.   *Environmental matters.* Pursuing the Community strategy launched last year, the Council, in a report to the Barcelona European Council adopted on 5 March (²), welcomed the fact that environmental policy had been taken into account in the broad economic policy guidelines. On 18 September, the European Economic and Social Committee also welcomed the progress made in various areas of the Lisbon strategy and recalled the importance of integrating environmental policy and sustainable development into Community economic policy (³).

Monetary policy

68.   *Activities of the European Central Bank (ECB)* (⁴). The European Central Bank continued implementing a monetary policy geared towards maintaining price stability in the medium term, thus helping to promote growth and employment in the euro zone. On the basis of its ongoing evaluation of the risks threatening such stability, the ECB Governing Council took the measures necessary to meet what is its main objective. The ECB also continued to ensure the transparency of its monetary policy by making public the economic analyses underlying its decisions at regular press conferences, in its monthly bulletin, in various other publications and in the speeches given by members of its Governing Council. In addition to the statutory reporting obligations incumbent on the ECB under its Statute, its President spoke before Parliament's Economic and Monetary Committee and before Parliament itself in plenary session. Eager to increase the transparency of its decision-making process still further and to obtain information in return from credit institutions and the public, the ECB has started to organise public consultations, publishing documents on a range of issues on its web site and asking experts or members of the public to submit their comments.

In May, the ECB published its 'Convergence report 2002', in which it examined Sweden's degree of sustainable convergence and the compatibility of Swedish legislation with the Treaty establishing the European Community and the Statute of the ESCB (European System of Central Banks).

(¹) Bull. 12-2002, point 1.3.1.
(²) Bull. 3-2002, point 1.3.2.
(³) Bull. 9-2002, point 1.3.1.
(⁴) http://www.ecb.int.

Target (¹), one of the world's largest payment systems, has continued to contribute considerably to the integration of the euro money market and to play an important part in the smooth implementation of the single monetary policy. The Governing Council also took a strategic decision on the next generation of the Target system (Target2), which is expected to become operational in a few years' time. The main objective of the Eurosystem is to ensure that Target evolves towards a system that better meets customers' needs, ensures cost efficiency and can adapt swiftly to future developments (including enlargement). In July, the ECB approved the inclusion of the euro in the continuous linked settlement (CLS) system, which became operational in September 2001, settling foreign exchange deals in seven currencies. Within its basic task of promoting the smooth functioning of payment systems, the ECB is closely following the developments in cross-border retail payments and has worked on the definition of security objectives for e-money and oversight standards for retail payment systems. Work has continued between the ESCB and the CESR (Committee of European Securities Regulators) in preparing recommendations and/or standards for securities clearing and settlement systems and for central counterparts at the European level.

The ECB and the Eurosystem as a whole have continued to promote cooperation among the competent national authorities on prudential supervision and financial stability. The main focus has been on monitoring and analysing the main structural and cyclical developments in the banking and financial sector and on areas of cooperation between central banks and other supervisory authorities. Its output included several reports, some of which were published. Furthermore, the ECB has contributed actively to the debate on the EU architecture for financial regulation, supervision and stability.

The ECB has continued to publish statistical information collected and compiled by the ESCB, mainly on monetary and banking statistics, securities issues, interest rates and balance of payments.

At European level, the ECB has participated in meetings of the Ecofin Council, the Eurogroup, the Economic and Financial Committee and the Economic Policy Committee and in the macroeconomic dialogue. At international level, it has been involved in the activities of multilateral institutions and forums, either as a member (i.e. OECD, Bank for International Settlements, G7, G10 Governors and G20) or as an observer (i.e. IMF, G10 Ministers and Governors, and the Financial Stability Forum).

The ECB has intensified further its relations with the central banks of the candidate countries. The annual high-level policy seminar was held in Genval, Bel-

---

(¹) Trans-European automated real-time gross settlement express transfer system (2001 General Report, point 74).

gium, in December. The Eurosystem also provided extensive technical cooperation and published a number of reports, in particular in the fields of payment and securities settlement systems, legal issues and statistics. At the Commission's request, and within the framework of the enlargement negotiations, the ECB has assessed the payment and securities clearing and settlement infrastructure and related oversight functions in the candidate countries.

The activities of the ECB are described in greater detail in its annual report, which was published in April, and in other publications. The 2001 annual report was the subject of a Parliament resolution of 3 July welcoming the pragmatism shown by the ECB ([1]).

69. *Regulatory and statutory aspects.* The ECB has issued opinions on Community and Member States' draft legislation in its field of competence. Some of these opinions were made public at the ECB's own initiative. In December, the ECB Governing Council unanimously agreed on the content of a proposal for a recommendation to be submitted to the Council following the entry into force of the Nice Treaty, which would adapt its voting arrangements ahead of the possible extension of the euro zone in an enlarged Europe. The members of the ECB Governing Council agreed on a code of conduct reflecting their special responsibility for safeguarding the integrity and reputation of the Eurosystem and for maintaining the effectiveness of its operations ([2]). Acting on a recommendation from the ECB ([3]), the Council adopted, on 22 January, a regulation clarifying the powers of the ECB regarding minimum reserves (Table II). Information relating to the composition of the ECB is to be found in Section 1 ('Composition and functioning of the institutions and bodies') of Chapter IX *(→ point 1107).*

Practical aspects of the euro

70. *Physical introduction of the euro.* The euro was launched in the form of notes and coins on 1 January ([4]). The currency changeover had been the subject of systematic and meticulous preparation by all concerned following a Commission information campaign. It took only a few days for the national currencies to be replaced by the new euro notes and coins even though the end of dual circulation was scheduled for 28 February. By the end of the first week in January, for example, most payments were made in euro and at the beginning of February the euro was used in over 95 % of cash transactions. These points were highlighted by the Commission in a communication to the Barcelona European Council dated 6 March ([5]) that reviewed the physical changeover to euro notes

---

([1]) Bull. 7/8-2002, point 1.3.1.
([2]) OJ C 123, 24.4.2002.
([3]) OJ C 89, 20.3.2001.
([4]) Bull. 1/2-2002, point 1.3.20.
([5]) COM(2002) 124; Bull. 3-2002, point 1.3.4.

and coins and summarised the findings of the Eurobarometer surveys ([1]). This success can thus be traced both to the enthusiasm with which the general public in Europe welcomed the euro and to the meticulous preparations by all the parties involved in the changeover.

71.   *Review of the euro's existence.* The Commission reviewed the first three years of the euro in a communication of 19 June ([2]) designed to inform the public of the new economic and political environment created by the single currency. One year after the successful introduction of euro notes and coins, the Commission focused in its communication of 19 December on the initial practical experience with the use of the new currency ([3]). In its Recommendation 2002/664/EC of 19 August, it proposed precise definitions of the terms 'euro', 'euro symbol' and 'medals and tokens' similar to euro coins ([4]). On 5 November, the Council adopted conclusions on euro-denominated collector's coins ([5]).

72.   *Cross-border payments.* Regulation (EC) No 2560/2001 ([6]), which aims to create a single payment area in the euro zone, entered into force on 1 July. It provides for two major advances that will allow individuals in Europe to take full advantage of the single currency. Charges for cash withdrawals will now be the same, irrespective of whether the cash dispenser is located in the country where the user has his bank account or in another Member State. The same principle of uniform charges for domestic and cross-border euro transactions will be applied to payments by bank card and credit transfers (up to EUR 12 500).

International economic and financial matters

73.   *G8 'Finance'.* The G8 finance ministers met on 14 and 15 June in Halifax mainly in preparation for the meeting of Heads of State or Government in Kananaskis *(→ point 924)*.

74.   *International monetary and financial system.* In a communication dated 13 February, the Commission reviewed the international monetary and financial system in a globalised world and the issue of promoting and financing development ([7]) *(→ point 809)*. In this connection, it proposed a reform of the international financial and monetary architecture as a response to global financial crises. Information concerning the IMF and the World Bank is to be found in Section 2 ('International organisations and conferences') of Chapter VI *(→ point 765)*.

([1]) http://europa.eu.int/comm/public_opinion/.
([2]) COM(2002) 332; Bull. 6-2002, point 1.3.2.
([3]) COM(2002) 747; Bull. 12-2002, point 1.3.4.
([4]) OJ L 225, 22.8.2002; Bull. 7/8-2002, point 1.3.3.
([5]) Bull. 11-2002, point 1.3.3.
([6]) OJ L 344, 28.12.2001; 2001 General Report, point 197.
([7]) COM(2002) 81; Bull. 1/2-2002, point 1.3.22.

75.   *Candidate countries.* Economic dialogue with the candidate countries continued in 2002 within the framework of the Europe agreements. It was reinforced and expanded under the decisions taken by the Council in 2000 (¹) and implemented in 2001 (²). The accession negotiations in the field of economic and monetary union (EMU) and on the liberalisation of capital movements were provisionally concluded with all the countries involved *(→ points 711 and 713).* Pre-accession fiscal surveillance continued with all the candidate countries. It is designed to prepare their public finances for participation in EMU. It has two components: notification of the fiscal situation in the light of EU standards and presentation of pre-accession economic programmes. In 2002, for the second time, the 13 candidate countries notified their fiscal situation and their pre-accession economic programmes to the Commission. These documents and their assessment by the Commission served as a basis for a more intensive economic dialogue between the members of the Economic and Financial Committee and their counterparts in the candidate countries as well as at the level of the economic and finance ministers and their counterparts. Monitoring the challenge of establishing macroeconomic and financial stability in the candidate countries was stepped up and a detailed Commission report on the matter published in March. The Commission continued to produce and publish twice a year macroeconomic forecasts for the candidate countries.

76.   *International capital market.* In an own-initiative opinion dated 18 September, the European Economic and Social Committee, stressing the growing importance of the international capital market, advocated a new financial architecture involving reform of the international financial institutions (³).

Financial operations

77.   *Financial assistance for balances of payments.* On 18 February, the Council established a facility providing medium-term financial assistance for the balances of payments of existing and future Member States which have not adopted the euro (Table II).

Macrofinancial assistance

78.   *General aspects.* On 3 July, the Commission adopted its report on the implementation of macrofinancial assistance to third countries in 2001, in which it reviewed the operations carried out the previous year and proposed that the emphasis be placed on the economic and structural conditions attached

---

(¹) 2000 General Report, points 706 and 708.
(²) 2001 General Report, points 81 and 779.
(³) Bull. 9-2002, point 1.3.5.

to such aid ([1]). Commenting on the report on 8 October, the Council took the view that the principles, conditions and procedures for implementing the entire range of EU instruments of a macrofinancial nature needed to be rationalised, in particular by updating the criteria to be met by those instruments through enhanced complementarity with the international financial institutions ([2]).

79. *Assistance for the countries in the western Balkans.* On 5 November, the Council decided to grant additional financial assistance of EUR 130 million (including EUR 75 million in outright grants) to the Federal Republic of Yugoslavia (Table II) over and above the aid already granted by the Community in 2001 ([3]) (EUR 345 million, including EUR 120 million in grants). On the same date, it granted assistance of EUR 60 million (including EUR 40 million in grants) to Bosnia and Herzegovina (Table II)

80. *Assistance for Moldova.* On 19 December, the Council decided on additional macrofinancial assistance of EUR 15 million in the form of outright grants for Moldova (Table II). This decision replaces that taken in 2000 regarding assistance for the same amount ([4]).

81. *Assistance for Ukraine.* On 12 July, the Council adopted Decision 2002/639/EC, which replaces the 1998 decision ([5]) in the light of changes in the financial situation of Ukraine vis-à-vis its creditors and grants it macrofinancial assistance in the form of a loan not exceeding EUR 110 million with a maximum maturity of 15 years (Table II).

82. *Aid for Romania.* In its conclusions of 22 January ([6]), the Council welcomed Romania's progress in the field of macroeconomic stability and took note of the Commission's intention to grant it EUR 100 million, subject to satisfactory progress in the country's structural adjustment process.

Development of financing techniques

83. *Phare programme* ([7]). Within the context of the Commission communication on the impact of enlargement on regions bordering candidate countries ([8]), an initial amount of EUR 35 million from the Phare 2002 budget was earmarked for a new instrument developed by the EIB, the municipal infrastructure facility, which is designed to facilitate small investments (less than EUR 5 million) in

---

([1]) COM(2002) 352; Bull. 7/8-2002, point 1.3.7.
([2]) Bull. 10-2002, point 1.3.2.
([3]) 2001 General Report, point 978.
([4]) Council Decision 2000/452/EC (OJ L 181, 20.7.2000; 2000 General Report, point 69).
([5]) Council Decision 98/592/EC (OJ L 284, 22.10.1998; 1998 General Report, point 77).
([6]) Bull. 1/2-2002, point 1.5.7.
([7]) http://europa.eu.int/comm/enlargement/pas/phare/index.htm.
([8]) COM(2001) 437; 2001 General Report, point 776.

municipal infrastructures in seven candidate countries bordering the European Union. The EIB will commit at least EUR 175 million for the facility's initial tranche. An amount of EUR 44 million was also committed under the Phare 2002 budget for the establishment of a facility for encouraging banks to extend their municipal infrastructure financing operations. The municipal finance facility concerns the 10 candidate countries in central and eastern Europe and has been set up jointly by the Commission, on the one hand, and the EIB, the EBRD and the Council of the European Development Bank (CEB/KfW), on the other. These three 'sponsors' will provide a total of at least EUR 220 million.

84.   *SME finance facility programme.* The Commission continued to implement this programme, which is designed to encourage financial intermediaries in the candidate countries in central and eastern Europe to expand their SME financing operations. At the beginning of the year, the EBRD, the CEB/KfW and the EIB earmarked EUR 450 million, EUR 263 million and EUR 300 million respectively for the facility, alongside Phare resources totalling EUR 191 million. Cooperation with those institutions was stepped up, representing an additional Phare commitment of EUR 50 million overall. At the end of December, Phare resources totalling EUR 142 million had been allocated to the projects. The Commission extended the facility's mechanisms to Turkey by using EUR 4 million from the MEDA budget.

Financing ECSC and Euratom activities

85.   *ECSC financing.* The ECSC's financial report for 2001 was adopted by the Commission on 5 June. In view of the expiry of the ECSC Treaty on 23 July (→ *point 39)*, the ECSC concluded no further loans.

86.   *Euratom financing.* A second payment of EUR 40 million was made under the EUR 212.5 million loan granted in 2000 for the modernisation and improvement of safety at the nuclear power station at Kozloduy (Bulgaria), bringing the total amount granted to EUR 80 million.

European Investment Bank (EIB)[1]

87.   *Loans granted.* The EIB granted loans totalling EUR 39.6 billion (EUR 36.8 billion in 2001) in support of European Union objectives, of which EUR 33.4 billion in the Member States, EUR 3.6 billion in the candidate countries (Cyprus, Malta, central Europe) and EUR 2.5 billion in partner countries

---

[1] Copies of the EIB's annual report and of other publications relating to the Bank's work and its operations can be obtained from the main office (Information and Communications Department, 100 Boulevard Konrad Adenauer, L-2950 Luxembourg, fax (352) 43 79-3189) or from its external offices or can be consulted on the Internet (http://www.eib.org/).

(Table 3). The Commission's report of 3 December describes the use to which EIB loans were put in each geographical area (¹).

88.   *Within the European Union.* Loans granted in the European Union totalled EUR 33.4 billion, including EUR 21.2 billion in individual loans and EUR 12.2 billion in global loans concluded with around 100 partner banks and financial institutions with a view to financing small to medium-scale investment projects in industry, services, education and health, or small infrastructure projects for local authorities. Of individual loans, 59 % were granted for investment contributing to the development of the less-favoured regions. Contracts signed under the Innovation 2000 initiative totalled EUR 3.4 billion for 10 Member States and related to education, telecommunications, the audiovisual industry and research. Individual loans for environmental protection totalled EUR 9.3 billion, while those for the supply and efficient use of energy totalled EUR 2.7 billion and loans for European communications infrastructure amounted to EUR 7.5 billion. Assistance totalled EUR 3.5 billion in the industrial and service sectors and EUR 1.3 billion in education and health.

A budget of EUR 700 million was granted to the accelerated financing mechanism, making it possible to finance 75 % instead of 50 % of the cost of certain projects in the sectors worst affected by the economic slowdown in the European Union and the candidate countries.

89.   *Outside the European Union.* Altogether, operations outside the European Union amounted to EUR 6.2 billion (EUR 5.6 billion in 2001).

In the candidate countries, assistance totalled EUR 3.6 billion, of which EUR 3.1 billion under the pre-accession facility. It was allocated chiefly to communications infrastructures intended to strengthen links with the European Union. In addition, the value of contracts signed under the Innovation 2000 initiative was EUR 212 million in the education and telecommunications sectors, and an aid programme with a total budget of EUR 5 billion was established to finance the work of repairing the damage caused by the floods in central Europe. An amount of EUR 425 million was granted in the Balkans for investment projects associated with the rebuilding of the region's economic potential, priority being given to infrastructure projects and SMEs.

Following the decision by the Barcelona European Council, the Bank stepped up its activities in the Mediterranean by establishing a Euro-Mediterranean investment facility to support the development of the private sector and the emergence of regional projects under the 'South–South' cooperation programme. Financing in this region (apart from Cyprus and Malta) amounted to EUR 1.6 billion, of which EUR 37 million in risk capital. In the ACP countries

---

(¹) COM(2002) 685; Bull. 12-2002, point 1.3.8.

and OCTs, total financing was EUR 298 million, of which EUR 175 million in risk capital, while in South Africa it amounted to EUR 50 million. Lastly, the EIB continued its operations in the countries of Latin America (EUR 85 million) and Asia (EUR 90 million).

TABLE 3

Contracts signed in 2002 and from 1998 to 2002

(million ECU/EUR)

Country	2002		1998–2002	
	Amount	%	Amount	%
Belgium	479	1.2	2 430	1.4
Denmark	1 027	2.6	4 826	2.8
Germany	6 504	16.4	29 103	16.9
Greece	1 072	2.7	6 607	3.8
Spain	5 426	13.7	21 302	12.3
France	4 023	10.2	18 209	10.5
Ireland	400	1.0	1 647	1.0
Italy	6 041	15.2	25 451	14.8
Luxembourg	74	0.2	489	0.3
Netherlands	538	1.4	2 295	1.3
Austria	998	2.5	3 489	2.0
Portugal	1 770	4.5	8 515	4.9
Finland	744	1.9	3 011	1.7
Sweden	720	1.8	3 490	2.0
United Kingdom	3 328	8.4	15 175	8.8
Other (¹)	300	0.8	1 174	0.7
European Union — Total	33 442	84.4	147 213	85.2
Central and east European candidate countries	3 421	8.6	13 435	7.8
Cyprus and Malta	220	0.6	575	0.3
Candidate countries — Total	3 641	9.2	14 010	8.1
(including pre-accession facility)	3 141	7.9	9 895	5.7
Mediterranean countries (except Cyprus and Malta) (²)	1 588	4.0	5 890	3.4
ACP, OCTs and South Africa	348	0.9	2 772	1.6
Latin America and Asia	174	0.4	1 921	1.1
Balkans	425	1.1	1 050	0.6
Partner countries — Total (³)	2 534	6.4	11 633	6.7
Grand total	39 618	100.0	172 856	100.0

(¹) Projects of Community interest located outside the territory of the Member States, granted under Article 18 of the Statute of the EIB.

(²) Including Turkey, the Bank's operations in Turkey (561 million) are carried out under a number of mandates, with 281 million under the Euro-Mediterranean partnership.

(³) Includes risk capital and other loans from budgetary resources:
   — ACP–OCTs: 175 million in 2002 and 1.155 billion from 1998 to 2002;
   — Mediterranean: 37 million in 2002 and 206 million from 1998 to 2002.

In addition, the EIB participates in the Community 'northern dimension' initiative ([1]). In this context, it was authorised to participate in the financing of projects to promote investment in environmental protection in the north-east of Russia up to a total amount of EUR 100 million; its operations were conducted in close cooperation with other international financial institutions.

90.   *Activity on capital markets.* The EIB obtained the funds needed for its lending activities by borrowing a total of EUR 38 billion on capital markets, 51 % of which was raised, prior to conversion, in Community currencies and in euro.

91.   *EIB 2001 annual report.* In a resolution of 5 February on the EIB annual report ([2]), Parliament congratulated the EIB on its conduct of lending operations, and in particular the financial assistance offered to candidate countries. It also encouraged the EIB to contribute to the Lisbon process by offering more loans to small enterprises. Lastly, it wanted to see more information on transparency concerning the EIB's activities and stressed the need to take account of the environmental dimension when approving loans.

European Investment Fund (EIF) ([3])

92.   *EIF activities.* As a result of the reform introduced in 2000 ([4]), the EIF now manages all the Community's venture-capital instruments and the SME guarantee mechanism, whether funded from its own or EIB resources or from the Community budget. Under its new statutes, it acts in support of the Community's objectives.

93.   *Venture-capital investment.* The EIF continued its venture-capital investment operations, albeit at a lower level than in 2001 (EUR 471.5 million invested in 36 operations, compared with EUR 800 million in 57 funds in 2001) on account of the difficulties encountered on this market, which a number of investors shunned, and the difficulty for a large number of funds to finalise their financing plans. In this depressed climate, the EIF's investment effort, geared to seed and start-up capital, accounts for a large share (around 20 %) of the venture capital for the setting-up of high-technology firms in Europe. The EIF's investment activities continued to focus on support for leading-edge technology (including a project with the European Molecular Biology Laboratory in Heidelberg) so as to exploit research findings; it also continued its regional activities and the launching of operations in the candidate countries. Operations under the Fund's SME guarantee mechanism expanded to EUR 1.25 billion (EUR 958 mil-

---

([1]) 2000 General Report, point 953.
([2]) OJ C 284 E, 21.11.2002; Bull. 1/2-2002, point 1.3.27.
([3]) http://www.eif.org/.
([4]) 2000 General Report, point 83.

lion in 2001). They continued to be financed from the Fund's own resources (credit enhancement, securitisation) to the extent of EUR 523.7 million and from Community resources managed under mandate in the context of the SME guarantee mechanism facility.

94.   *Commission financial instruments.* The Commission financial instruments are managed by the EIF under the multiannual programme for enterprise covering the period 2001–05 (¹). The EIF invested EUR 24.7 million under the European technology facility (ETF) start-up scheme, which is geared to financing seed-capital and incubator funds, and it can also promote the recruitment of young managers of this type of capital by way of the seed-capital programme. The SME guarantee facility, which has been extended to include microcredit, SME investment in information and communication technologies, and equity holdings, still accounted for the bulk of the Fund's guarantee operations; microcredit operations (signed in Belgium, France, Germany and Spain) got off to a promising start.

95.   *New activities.* The EIF is planning to develop new consultancy activities, including technical support for regions receiving financial engineering loans from the Structural Funds and for research centres benefiting from Community aid under the sixth framework research programme *(→ point 295)*. These new activities are set to enhance the synergies with the Union's regional and research policies, in line with the EIF's objective.

European Bank for Reconstruction and Development (EBRD) (²)

96.   *EBRD general meeting.* The 11th general meeting (³) was held in Bucharest from 18 to 20 May in the presence of Mr Solbes Mira, Member of the Commission and EBRD Governor (⁴). The meeting provided an opportunity for him to hold bilateral discussions with the EBRD President, with the President and Prime Minister of Romania, with the finance ministers of Bulgaria, the Czech Republic, Poland, Slovakia and Ukraine, and with representatives of the Former Yugoslav Republic of Macedonia, Bosnia and Herzegovina, Croatia and the Federal Republic of Yugoslavia. The meeting underscored the shareholders' support for the EBRD's activities, the significant economic progress made in Romania and the positive relationship between EU enlargement and the economic transition of countries benefiting from EBRD action. It also emphasised the strides made with cooperation in promoting the environment and assisting SMEs.

(¹) Decision 2000/819/EC (OJ L 333, 29.12.2000; 2000 General Report, point 261).
(²) http://www.ebrd.org/index.htm.
(³) Previous meeting: 2001 General Report, point 99.
(⁴) Bull. 5-2002, point 1.6.34.

97.   *EBRD financing.* On the basis of an initial evaluation of the results for 2002, the EBRD committed a total of EUR 3 billion in new operations, of which 11 % as equity and 89 % in the form of loans. The Commission disbursed EUR 7.425 million following the European Community's decision to subscribe extra shares in the capital of the EBRD ([1]).

([1]) Decision 97/135/EC (OJ L 52, 22.2.1997).

Section 2

Statistical system (^{1})

Overview

98.   The activities of 2002 in the field of statistics were centred on completing the implementation of the 1998–2002 Community statistical programme (^{2}) and preparing the next programme, which is to provide an overview of the strategies and priorities for a high-quality statistical information service designed to support the decision-making process. The importance attached to statistics on the euro area for backing up economic policies already shows how the Commission has embarked on this course.

Policy aspects

99.   2003–07 Community statistical programme. On 16 December, the European Parliament and the Council adopted the 2003–07 Community statistical programme (Table I), which sets out the statistical requirements for each of the policy areas in the Treaty, having regard to the main priorities among Community policies, namely economic and monetary union, enlargement, competitiveness, sustainable development and the social agenda.

100.   Economic policy. In response to the request from the Barcelona European Council (^{3}), on 27 November the Commission presented a communication (^{4}) on improving and harmonising the methods used for drawing up euro-area statistics and indicators and backing up the European Union's economic policies. On the same day, it also adopted a communication on improving budget statistics (→ *point 58*).

101.   European system of accounts (ESA). On 12 February, the European Parliament and the Council adopted a regulation on the use of ESA 95 in the determination of Member States' payments to the VAT-based own resource (Table I). Similarly, on 10 June, the European Parliament and the Council

---

(^{1}) Further information is available on the Europa server (http://europa.eu.int/comm/eurostat/).
(^{2}) Decision 1999/126/EC on the Community statistical programme (OJ L 42, 16.2.1999; 1999 General Report, point 79).
(^{3}) Bull. 3-2002, point I.56.
(^{4}) COM(2002) 661; Bull. 11-2002, point 1.3.4.

adopted a new regulation defining the content of the quarterly non-financial accounts for general government and laying down the list of the ESA 95 categories to be transmitted by Member States (Table I). On 15 May, the Commission proposed amending Regulation (EC) No 2223/96 (¹) in order to shorten the time allowed for transmitting the main aggregates of quarterly national accounts, abolish the derogations granted to Member States, which prevent these aggregates and the annual aggregates from being compiled for the euro area, and bring in the transmission of employment data for national accounts in hours worked (Table I).

In its report of 21 June (²) on the implementation of Regulation (EC) No 448/98 (³) concerning the allocation of financial intermediation services indirectly measured (FISIM), the Commission also welcomed the results of the qualitative and quantitative analysis of the effects on national accounts of applying the experimental methods during the trial period (1995–2001). On 15 October, it proposed harmonising gross national income (GNI) at market prices. This proposal defines the methods of calculating GNI on the basis of ESA 95 and specifies the Member States' obligations to transmit data in order to reinforce the comparability, reliability and exhaustiveness of GNI data (Table II).

102.   *Social statistics*. On 8 October, the European Parliament and the Council adopted Regulation (EC) No 1991/2002, which institutes in all the Member States a continuous sample survey of the labour force (Table I).

103.   *Environment*. In response to the Council's request (⁴), on 20 September the Commission presented an analysis (⁵) of the 'open list' of 34 indicators in order to choose from them the key environmental indicators for sustainable development. This analysis led to a classification of the indicators into four groups, ranging from those that can be drawn up straight away to those that are never likely to be drawn up. On 25 November, the European Parliament and the Council adopted a regulation on waste statistics (Table I).

104.   *Enterprise*. On 5 November, the European Parliament and the Council adopted Regulation (EC) No 2056/2002, which serves mainly to add two new annexes to Regulation (EC, Euratom) No 58/97 (⁶), thus incorporating structural statistics on credit institutions and on pension funds (Table I).

(¹) OJ L 310, 30.11.1996; 1996 General Report, point 95.
(²) COM(2002) 333; Bull. 6-2002, point 1.3.11.
(³) OJ L 58, 27.2.1998; 1998 General Report, point 98.
(⁴) 2001 General Report, point 612.
(⁵) COM(2002) 524; Bull. 9-2002, point 1.3.7.
(⁶) OJ L 14, 17.1.1997; 1996 General Report, point 98.

105.   Industry. On 11 July, the Commission adopted a report ([1]) on the implementation of Decision 1999/297/EC ([2]) establishing a Community statistical information infrastructure relating to the industry and markets of the audiovisual and related sectors. This report summarises the action taken and recommends continuing the implementation of the decision.

106.   Transport. On 16 December, the European Parliament and the Council adopted a regulation organising the collection by the Member States of statistics on rail transport to provide information to underpin the drawing up of new common rules in this field (Table I).

107.   ECSC statistics. On 30 September, the European Parliament and the Council decided to maintain the present system of ECSC statistics after the expiry of the ECSC Treaty (Table I). On 25 October, the Commission proposed a regulation on the production of annual Community steel statistics for the period 2003–09 (Table I).

108.   Agriculture statistics. On 13 February, the Commission adopted its second progress report ([3]) on the implementation of Council Decision 96/411/EC ([4]) on the improvement of Community agricultural statistics. On 21 October, the European Parliament and the Council extended this decision until 2007 so that more account can be taken of foreseeable developments in the common agricultural policy, particularly with regard to enlargement (Table I).

Publications

*109.   Eurostat's main publications in 2002 were: the *Eurostat yearbook*, the *Yearbook of the Regions, European business — facts and figures, The life of women and men in Europe* and the *Economic portrait*. There were also various other publications in the series *Statistics in focus*, for example in the domains of the economy, social development, agriculture, transport, education and research and development. Some 150 press releases were issued, on the subject of Euro-indicators, publications and international events. A new home page for the web site was produced.

([1]) COM(2002) 384; Bull. 7/8-2002, point 1.3.10.
([2]) OJ L 117, 5.5.1999; 1999 General Report, point 82.
([3]) COM(2002) 79; Bull.1/2-2002, point 1.3.29.
([4]) OJ L 162, 1.7.1996; 1996 General Report, point 99.

Section 3

Employment and social policy (¹)

Overview

110.   *In line with both the Lisbon strategy and the social agenda launched at the Nice European Council, the Commission consolidated the progress made in the social sphere by presenting a series of proposals including the Community strategy for health and safety at work, a directive on the status of temporary workers and a communication on corporate social responsibility. It also embarked on consultation of the social partners on the social aspects of corporate restructuring. Besides adopting its proposed joint report on employment, the Commission confirmed the usefulness of the open method of coordination, with an evaluation of the European employment strategy being carried out and use of this method being extended to the pensions field.*

Social policy agenda follow-up

111.   *Scoreboard.* The second scoreboard on implementing the social policy agenda, adopted by the Commission on 19 February (²), showing the progress made so far, supplemented the summary report (³) submitted to the Barcelona European Council *(→ point 66).* Earlier, Parliament had adopted a resolution, on 7 February (⁴), calling on the Commission to respond to its 2000 resolution (⁵) and to make operational the policy initiatives announced in the social policy agenda. It subsequently adopted, on 4 September (⁶), a resolution calling on the Commission to speed up its work on implementing the social agenda. The European Economic and Social Committee and the Committee of the Regions also gave their opinion on the scoreboard communication, on 17 July (⁷) and 10 October (⁸) respectively.

(¹) Further information is available on the Europa server (http://europa.eu.int/comm/employment_social/index_en.htm).
(²) COM(2002) 89; Bull. 1/2-2002, point 1.3.39.
(³) COM(2002) 14; Bull. 1/2-2002, point 1.3.2.
(⁴) OJ C 284 E, 21.11.2002; Bull. 1/2-2002, point 1.3.38.
(⁵) OJ C 197, 12.7.2001; 2000 General Report, point 97.
(⁶) Bull. 9-2002, point 1.3.14.
(⁷) OJ C 241, 7.10.2002; Bull. 7/8-2002, point 1.3.15.
(⁸) Bull. 10-2002, point 1.3.14.

Employment

112. Implementation of the employment guidelines for 2002. On 18 February, following the Laeken European Council's endorsement [1], the Council adopted Decision 2002/177/EC on guidelines for Member States' employment policies for the year 2002 (Table II), together with a recommendation concerning implementation of the Member States' employment policies [2]. At the Barcelona European Council in March [3], it was made clear that the European employment strategy [4] had to be reinforced, with continuing emphasis on reform of employment and labour-market policies. Decision No 1145/2002/EC on incentive measures in the field of employment (Table I), adopted on 10 June, bolstered this Community strategy with activities geared to analysis, research and cooperation among the Member States. With regard to the Lisbon European Council's objective of boosting employment in terms of both quantity and quality [5], the Commission presented an action plan for skills and mobility *(→ point 123)*. The European Parliament meanwhile adopted a resolution on 28 February [6], in preparation for the Barcelona European Council, on the strategy for full employment and social inclusion *(→ point 66)*.

113. European employment strategy. On 17 July [7], the Commission took stock of the European employment strategy, reviewing the results and confirming the structural character of the improved performance of the European Union's labour market. It also noted that employment policies had converged towards the priorities set in the guidelines and that the method of coordination under the Luxembourg process [8] had proved effective. The European Parliament for its part noted, on 25 September [9], that the European employment strategy had been very successful but nevertheless called on the Commission to propose changes in the strategy so as to turn it into a process involving the various actors at national, regional and European levels.

114. 2002 joint employment report. On 13 November, the Commission adopted its draft joint employment report for 2002 [10], in which it noted that the European Union's employment performance had continued to improve in 2001 despite the economic slowdown; the Member States were accordingly asked to step up their efforts to reform labour markets.

---

[1] 2001 General Report, points 117 and 1208.
[2] OJ L 60, 1.3.2002; Bull. 1/2-2002, point 1.3.37.
[3] Bull. 3-2002, points I.26 to I.29.
[4] http://europa.eu.int/comm/employment_social/empl&esf/ees_en.htm.
[5] 2000 General Report, point 97.
[6] Bull. 1/2-2002, point 1.3.35.
[7] COM(2002) 416; Bull. 7/8-2002, point 1.3.13.
[8] 1997 General Report, point 1140.
[9] Bull. 9-2002, point 1.3.17.
[10] COM(2002) 621; Bull. 11-2002, point 1.3.18.

115.   Local action for employment ([1]). The Commission's strategy in this area ([2]) was endorsed by the Committee of the Regions on 13 March ([3]), although it was pointed out that local and regional authorities ought to be involved in local employment strategies. On 24 April ([4]), the European Economic and Social Committee also welcomed this strategy while stressing the importance of the social partners' role in implementing local policies. The European Parliament endorsed the strategy in a resolution adopted on 4 July ([5]), in which it advocated more effective coordination of employment action plans at national and regional level.

116.   Employment services. The Commission continued to support and promote the network of public employment services in the European Union and the European Economic Area, particularly through initiatives aimed at evaluating the European employment strategy, strengthening cooperation with other service providers, adopting an action plan on mobility *(→ point 123)* and preparing the candidate countries' public employment services for accession. The plan for EURES reform, adopted by the Commission on 23 December, is another element of this approach.

Social protection and social security ([6])

117.   Coordination of social security schemes. On 6 February, the Commission adopted a proposal for extending the provisions of Regulation (EEC) No 1408/71 to nationals of third countries not already covered by those provisions solely on the grounds of their nationality (Table II). This proposal followed the withdrawal, on the same day, of the Commission's 1997 proposal for a regulation ([7]). Acknowledging the work being done to modernise and reform Regulation (EEC) No 1408/71, the Council called, on 26 June ([8]), for better cross-border cooperation on access to high-quality health services in order to promote patient mobility throughout the Community.

118.   Pensions. On 11 April, Parliament welcomed the launch of an open coordination method on pensions ([9]), while pointing out that national strategies needed to be adopted swiftly with a view to guaranteeing safe and sustainable pensions. On 29 May, in connection with the open method of coordination, the

---

([1]) http://europa.eu.int/comm/employment_social/ld/index_en.htm.
([2]) 2000 General Report, point 103; 2001 General Report, point 121.
([3]) OJ C 192, 12.8.2002; Bull. 3-2002, point 1.3.18.
([4]) OJ C 149, 21.6.2002; Bull. 4-2002, point 1.3.11.
([5]) Bull. 7/8-2002, point 1.3.14.
([6]) http://europa.eu.int/comm/employment_social/soc-prot/index_en.htm.
([7]) Bull. 1/2-2002, point 1.3.40.
([8]) Bull. 6-2002, point 1.4.71.
([9]) Bull. 4-2002, point 1.3.13.

European Economic and Social Committee suggested various options for the reform of pension schemes ([1]). The Commission presented its analysis of the first national strategy reports on pensions, on 17 December ([2]). This communication doubled as a joint report from the Commission and the Council to the spring 2003 European Council.

119.   Ageing of the population. On 18 March, the Commission adopted a communication ([3]) as a contribution to the second World Assembly on Ageing ([4]), setting out Europe's response to world ageing. In a resolution adopted on 11 April ([5]), Parliament called on the Council and the Commission to incorporate the issue of ageing into all relevant policy areas and Community programmes, with particular regard to cooperation *(→ point 826).*

On 24 January, the Commission adopted a report to Parliament and the Council ([6]) looking at ways of increasing the employment rate and prolonging working life through a number of priority actions. On 5 March, the Council approved this report from the Commission ([7]), which was also the subject of a Committee of the Regions opinion ([8]) adopted on 3 July. On the basis of the Commission's December 2001 communication ([9]) on the future of 'healthcare and care for the elderly', the Council adopted, on 24 January, a report to the European Council defining the main parameters for future discussions of general policy on this subject and proposing various activities to be carried out in 2002.

Measures to promote social integration ([10])

120.   Social inclusion. On 12 January, a new Community action programme was launched with the aim of encouraging cooperation between the Member States to combat social exclusion. This programme, which will run until 2006, will help to improve the understanding of poverty and social exclusion, mainly by means of comparable indicators, and will be instrumental in facilitating policy exchanges in the context of national action plans and developing the capacity of those involved, particularly through networking at European level ([11]). On 14 March ([12]), the Committee of the Regions gave a favourable opinion on the

---

([1]) OJ C 221, 17.9.2002; Bull. 5-2002, point 1.3.14.
([2]) COM(2002) 737; Bull. 12-2002, point 1.3.18.
([3]) COM(2002) 143; Bull. 3-2002, point 1.3.16.
([4]) http://europa.eu.int/comm/employment_social/soc-prot/ageing/news/tokyo_en.htm.
([5]) Bull. 4-2002, point 1.3.9.
([6]) COM(2002) 9; Bull. 1/2-2002, point 1.3.32.
([7]) Bull. 3-2002, point 1.3.15.
([8]) OJ C 287, 22.11.2002; Bull. 7/8-2002, point 1.3.12.
([9]) COM(2001) 723; 2001 General Report, point 123.
([10]) http://europa.eu.int/comm/employment_social/soc-prot/index_en.htm.
([11]) Decision 2002/50/EC (OJ L 10, 12.1.2002; 2001 General Report, point 130).
([12]) OJ C 192, 12.8.2002; Bull. 3-2002, point 1.3.21.

joint Council and Commission report on social inclusion ([1]). The European Parliament for its part reaffirmed, on 11 June ([2]), that promoting a high level of employment and social protection, increasing living standards and quality of life, and economic and social cohesion, must be priorities for the European Union in order to contribute to reducing poverty and social exclusion. Parliament also adopted, on 7 February, a resolution on illiteracy and social exclusion ([3]). The Council meanwhile, in a resolution adopted on 2 December ([4]), invited the social partners to identify possible partnership mechanisms and approaches for specific activities aimed at increasing social inclusion.

121. *Integration of people with disabilities.* On 17 July, the European Economic and Social Committee stressed the need to adopt a specific action programme at European level with the aim of making allowance for people with disabilities in all Community policies ([5]).

122. *Social indicators.* In an opinion delivered on 29 May ([6]), the European Economic and Social Committee welcomed the Social Protection Committee's report on social indicators, which helped to improve the understanding and comparability of poverty and social exclusion in the Union.

Free movement of workers ([7])

123. *Mobility of workers.* On 13 February, the Commission adopted an action plan ([8]) designed to make European labour markets more open and accessible. It proposed taking specific measures to boost occupational mobility, mainly by removing the legal and administrative barriers to geographical mobility and encouraging the cross-border recognition of qualifications *(→ point 159)*. This action plan was endorsed by the Council on 3 June ([9]). The Council was also in favour of creating a one-stop Internet web site providing information on employment and vocational training opportunities, and of introducing a European health insurance card. It also stressed the importance of supporting the development of EU statistics to monitor geographical mobility and skills shortages. On 10 October ([10]), the European Parliament also welcomed this new action plan, which tied in with its recommendation on the broad economic policy guidelines *(→ points 59 and 60)*. It noted, however, that aware-

---

([1]) COM(2001) 565; 2001 General Report, point 128.
([2]) Bull. 6-2002, point 1.3.15.
([3]) OJ C 284 E, 21.11.2002; Bull. 1/2-2002, point 1.3.42.
([4]) Bull. 12-2002, point 1.3.20.
([5]) OJ C 241, 7.10.2002; Bull. 7/8-2002, point 1.3.17.
([6]) OJ C 221, 17.9.2002; Bull. 5-2002, point 1.3.13.
([7]) http://europa.eu.int/comm/employment_social/fundamri/movement/index_en.htm.
([8]) COM(2002) 72; Bull. 1/2-2002, point 1.3.33.
([9]) OJ C 162, 6.7.2002; Bull. 6-2002, point 1.3.14.
([10]) Bull. 10-2002, point 1.3.15.

ness of different cultures, acquisition of linguistic skills and the concept of citizenship also helped to boost mobility. On 21 November ([1]), the Committee of the Regions endorsed this action plan. Moreover, on 11 December ([2]), the Commission adopted a communication highlighting some of the problems encountered by migrant workers and their families, which prevented workers and employers from exploiting fully the benefits and potential of geographical mobility.

124. *Supplementary pensions.* On 3 June, in accordance with Article 138 of the EC Treaty, the Commission launched the first phase of consulting the European social partners on the acquisition of supplementary pension rights, their preservation and transferability.

Labour law and industrial relations

125. *Organisation of working time.* In a resolution adopted on 7 February ([3]), the European Parliament gave its opinion on the Commission's report ([4]) on the state of implementation of Council Directive 93/104/EC ([5]) concerning certain aspects of the organisation of working time. Parliament was disappointed to note that some Member States were reluctant to implement this directive fully. The Commission meanwhile proposed, on 24 June, that Directives 93/104/EC and 2000/34/EC, dealing with certain aspects of the organisation of working time, be consolidated into a single directive without making substantive changes (Table I). On 11 March, the European Parliament and the Council adopted Directive 2002/15/EC establishing minimum requirements for the organisation of working time aimed at improving the safety and health protection of persons performing road transport activities, and aligning conditions of competition (Table I).

126. *Employee information and consultation.* On 11 March, the European Parliament and the Council adopted Directive 2002/14/EC establishing a general framework for informing and consulting employees in undertakings or establishments operating within a Member State and employing at least 50 or 20 employees respectively, with the emphasis both on promoting the social dialogue and on ensuring that employees' representatives are properly informed and consulted (Table I).

127. *Employee financial participation.* In a communication adopted on 5 July ([6]), the Commission set out guidelines for the development and promo-

---

([1]) Bull. 11-2002, point 1.3.16.
([2]) COM(2002) 694; Bull. 12-2002, point 1.3.21.
([3]) OJ C 284 E, 21.11.2002; Bull. 1/2-2002, point 1.3.44.
([4]) COM(2000) 787; 2000 General Report, point 114.
([5]) OJ L 307, 13.12.1993; Twenty-seventh General Report, point 450.
([6]) COM(2002) 364; Bull. 7/8-2002, point 1.3.19.

tion of employee financial participation, mainly in the form of a framework for Community action over the period 2002–04.

128.   *Protection of employees.* Directive 80/987/EEC relating to insolvency of an employer was amended on 23 September by Directive 2002/74/EC, mainly to take account of insolvency situations with a cross-border dimension (Table I).

129.   *Corporate social responsibility.* The Commission's Green Paper 'Promoting a European framework for corporate social responsibility' (¹) elicited critical responses from the Committee of the Regions (²) and the European Economic and Social Committee (³), on 14 and 20 March respectively. The European Parliament for its part, in a resolution adopted on 30 May (⁴), called on the Commission to impose an obligation on certain types of companies to produce social and environmental reports; it also urged the Commission to ensure that the principle of corporate social responsibility is taken into account in all areas of Community competence, and called for this principle to be incorporated into the annual employment guidelines and the European employment strategy. Taking these comments on board, the Commission adopted, on 2 July, a communication (⁵) summarising the situation and outlining a European strategy to promote corporate social responsibility in the interest of sustainable development. The Council for its part, in a resolution adopted on 2 December (⁶), called upon the Commission to take account of the views of all concerned in developing a European strategy on corporate social responsibility. It also called upon the Member States and future Presidencies to continue to encourage debate on this subject.

130.   *Temporary workers.* On 20 March, the Commission adopted a proposal for a directive on working conditions for temporary workers (Table I).

Health and safety at work (⁷)

131.   *New Community strategy.* On 11 March, in response to the Lisbon European Council's objective (⁸) of providing more and better jobs, the Commission adopted a communication setting out the new Community strategy on health and safety at work (2002–06) (⁹). This strategy is based on a comprehen-

---

(¹) COM(2001) 366; 2001 General Report, point 137.
(²) OJ C 192, 18.8.2002; Bull. 3-2002, point 1.3.24.
(³) OJ C 125, 27.5.2002; Bull. 3-2002, point 1.3.24.
(⁴) Bull. 5-2002, point 1.3.16.
(⁵) COM(2002) 347; Bull. 7/8-2002, point 1.3.18.
(⁶) Bull. 12-2002, point 1.3.22.
(⁷) http://europa.eu.int/comm/employment_social/h&s/index_en.htm.
(⁸) 2000 General Report, point 1145.
(⁹) COM(2002) 118; Bull. 3-2002, point 1.3.26.

sive approach to well-being at work, mainly by consolidating a culture of risk prevention, including related physical, psychological and social risks. With a view to implementing this policy effectively, the Commission proposed to the Council, on 3 April, that a recommendation be made to the Member States to extend the relevant legislation to self-employed workers (Table II). As a further element of the strategy, it proposed, on 4 September ([1]), that the two advisory committees be merged in order to rationalise their work and operation, thereby creating a single advisory body. The Council meanwhile adopted, on 3 June, a resolution on the new 2002–06 strategy ([2]), in which it welcomed the Commission's communication and called on the Member States, the social partners and the Commission to play an active part in promoting health and safety at work. In a resolution of 23 October ([3]), the European Parliament also welcomed the Commission's initiative but asked for a detailed action plan to be drawn up, together with financial commitments and a timetable for every major proposal. The Committee of the Regions and the European Economic and Social Committee also gave their opinions on this new strategy, on 3 ([4]) and 17 July ([5]) respectively, but were disappointed by the lack of a plan of action.

132.   Health and safety risks. On 25 June, the European Parliament and the Council adopted a directive on the minimum health and safety requirements in terms of daily limit values for the exposure of workers to vibrations (Table I). In December, pursuant to Article 138(2) of the EC Treaty, the Commission launched the first phase of Community-level consultation of the social partners on 'stress and its effect on health and safety at work'.

Social dialogue

133.   Promotion of social dialogue. In a communication adopted on 26 June, entitled 'The European social dialogue, a force for innovation and change' ([6]), the Commission summarised the progress made with the social dialogue since the entry into force of the Amsterdam Treaty. It also gave pointers for reinforcing the social dialogue in an enlarged Europe, outlining various measures aimed at promoting and enhancing dialogue. On the same day, the Commission put forward a proposal for a decision establishing a tripartite social summit for growth and employment, designed to ensure that there is continuous concertation, in advance of the European Councils, between the Heads of State or Government, the Commission and the cross-industry social partners, so that the latter may make a full

---

([1]) COM(2002) 486; Bull. 9-2002, point 1.3.21.
([2]) OJ C 161, 5.7.2002; Bull. 6-2002, point 1.3.18.
([3]) Bull. 10-2002, point 1.3.16.
([4]) OJ C 287, 22.11.2002; Bull. 7/8-2002, point 1.3.21.
([5]) OJ C 241, 7.10.2002; Bull. 7/8-2002, point 1.3.21.
([6]) COM(2002) 341; Bull. 6-2002, point 1.3.19; Internet (http://europa.eu.int/comm/employment_social/news/2002/jul/socdial_en.html).

and meaningful contribution to the various components of the strategy launched in Lisbon: structural and economic reform, employment and social protection, and macroeconomic policies. A further aim of this proposal is to formalise the social summits like those held in Stockholm ([1]) and Barcelona ([2]) (Table II). The ninth Social Dialogue Summit was held in Genval (Belgium) on 28 November ([3]). It was chaired by Mr Prodi and Mrs Diamantopoulou, respectively President and Member of the Commission. The goal of the summit was that the social partners should present their joint multiannual work programme (2003–05) as announced in their joint declaration to the Laeken Summit in December 2001.

Structural operations

134.   European Social Fund (ESF). Information on the ESF is given in Section 10 ('Economic and social cohesion') of this chapter *(→ points 366 to 369).*

European Foundation for the Improvement of Living and Working Conditions ([4])

*135.   The first forum organised by the Foundation on 'the European social model' was held in Dublin on 29 and 30 August. Furthermore, the portal of the European Monitoring Centre on Change ([5]) was launched in November. Continuing with the 2001–04 programme to support socioeconomic progress ([6]), the Foundation provided results, advice and analysis based on comparative research conducted from a European point of view. Within its three main areas of activity (industrial relations, working conditions and living conditions), the Foundation concentrated on promoting better jobs and boosting gender equality.

European Agency for Safety and Health at Work ([7])

*136.   The Agency continued to provide the Commission with support, particularly in relation to two key aspects of the new Community strategy on health and safety at work. Under the Spanish Presidency, it organised a seminar to look at ways of incorporating health and safety issues more effectively into education ([8]) and training. Under the Danish Presidency, the Agency ran a major

---

([1]) 2001 General Report, point 1204.
([2]) Bull. 3-2002, points I.20 to I.29.
([3]) Bull. 11-2002, point 1.3.21.
([4]) http://www.eurofound.ie/.
([5]) http://www.eurofound.ie/index.htm.
([6]) 2001 General Report, point 150.
([7]) http://europe.osha.eu.int/.
([8]) http://europe.osha.eu.int/good_practice/sector/osheducation/.

awareness-raising campaign on the growing problem of stress at work and organised a conference on the subject in November.

International cooperation

137.   G8 *'Labour and employment'*. Ministers from the eight most industrialised countries *(→ point 925)* responsible for social policy, along with Mrs Diamantopoulou and Mr Lamy, Members of the Commission, met in Montreal from 24 to 28 April (¹). The meeting, chaired by Mrs Stewart, the Canadian Minister for Human Resource Development, focused on lifelong learning, with discussions also taking place on corporate social responsibility, promotion of minimum labour standards and integration of immigrants into the labour market.

138.   *Promoting core international labour standards.* On 4 July, the European Parliament adopted a resolution (²) approving the Commission's communication (³) aimed at promoting core labour standards and achieving a better balance in the overall system of social governance in the context of globalisation. Parliament also called on the Member States and the candidate countries to ratify the International Labour Organisation (ILO) conventions (⁴).

(¹) Bull. 4-2002, point 1.3.12.
(²) Bull. 7/8-2002, point 1.6.41.
(³) COM(2001) 416; 2001 General Report, point 153.
(⁴) http://www.oit.org/public/english/index.htm.

Section 4

Equal opportunities (¹)

139. Gender equality programme (2001–05) (²). In a resolution adopted on 4 July (³), the European Parliament called on the Commission to prepare a report evaluating the Member States' compliance with the existing legislation on gender equality, so that the urgent measures to be taken in implementing the programme could be properly targeted.

140. Gender mainstreaming in other policies. On 25 April, Parliament adopted a resolution (⁴) on the programme of action for the mainstreaming of gender equality in Community development cooperation *(→ point 829)*, referring to the operational arrangements needed to implement the 2001 work programme (⁵). In its 2001 annual report on equal opportunities (⁶), the Commission pointed out that improving the gender dimension in the Union's external policies and in the Structural Funds would continue to be a political priority in 2002.

The Council, in its conclusions of 27 May (⁷), encouraged the Member States to strengthen the participation of women in the new rural development processes and called for an improvement in systems producing gender-desegregated statistical information in order to provide an overview of the European rural context as a basis for drafting policies in this area. Moreover, on 2 December (⁸), it urged the Commission to devise a plan for integrating gender aspects into relevant policy initiatives, and requested future Presidencies to continue the practice of gender mainstreaming within all formations of the Council. On 20 December (⁹), the Commission adopted a communication providing an overview of the incorporation of gender mainstreaming in the Structural Funds programming 2000–06, taking stock of the progress made.

(¹) Further information is available on the Europa server (http://europa.eu.int/comm/employment_social/equ_opp/index_en.htm).
(²) http://europa.eu.int/comm/employment_social/equ_opp/strategy_en.html.
(³) Bull. 7/8-2002, point 1.3.22.
(⁴) Bull. 4-2002, point 1.3.17.
(⁵) COM(2001) 295; 2001 General Report, point 926; http://europa.eu.int/comm/employment_social/equ_opp/report_en.html#prg.
(⁶) http://europa.eu.int/comm/employment_social/equ_opp/report_en.html.
(⁷) Bull. 5-2002, point 1.3.20.
(⁸) Bull. 12-2002, point 1.3.27.
(⁹) COM(2002) 748; Bull. 12-2002, point 1.3.29.

141.   Equal opportunities report. On 25 April(¹), Parliament welcomed the Commission's 2000 annual report on equal opportunities for women and men in the European Union. On 28 May, the Commission adopted its sixth annual report (2001) (²) presenting an overview of the main developments and achievements at European and national levels in 2001, and looking ahead to 2002 with increasing focus on reconciliation of work and family life.

142.   Implementing the principle of equal treatment. On 23 September, the European Parliament and the Council amended Directive 76/207/EEC to update its provisions in the light of evolving case-law and to ensure consistency with the two directives (³) adopted on the basis of Article 13 of the EC Treaty (Table I).

143.   Associations and social partners. In a resolution adopted on 25 September (⁴), Parliament called on the Commission to make a start on the compilation of data and the establishment of a database relating to the representation of women among the social partners and to the outcome of collective bargaining in the context of equal opportunities.

(¹) Bull. 4-2002, point 1.3.18.
(²) COM(2002) 258; Bull. 5-2002, point 1.3.21.
(³) Council Directive 2000/43/EC (OJ L 180, 19.7.2000; 2000 General Report, point 111); Council Directive 2000/78/EC (OJ L 303, 2.12.2000; 2000 General Report, point 111).
(⁴) Bull. 9-2002, point 1.3.24.

Section 5

Internal market (¹)

Overview

144.   *In order to concentrate political attention on the most important areas of the internal market, the Commission, with the Council's support, updated its internal market strategy for the third time and reduced the number of target actions. The year 2002 saw important advances in the financial services field, particularly with the adoption of directives concerning undertakings for collective investment in transferable securities, financial collateral arrangements, insider dealing and market manipulation, solvency in insurance matters and intermediation in insurance and financial conglomerates. Progress was also made with applying the Council regulation on Community designs, with applying international accounting standards and with the simplification and modernisation of public procurement legislation. In the field of taxation, the 'Fiscalis 2007' programme adopted in December will allow further improvements to be made to the systems of indirect taxation in the internal market by means of more effective cooperation between the authorities concerned.*

General strategy (²)

145.   *Legislative implementation.* Considering that the proper functioning of the internal market was, with entrepreneurship, one of the keys to growth and job creation, the Barcelona European Council emphasised the importance to this end of fully implementing all the relevant legislation (³); in this context, it regretted that, in spite of the progress made, only seven Member States had achieved 98.5 % transposition, the interim objective set the previous year in Stockholm (⁴). This mediocre performance led the European Council to extend the deadline for achieving this objective to March 2003; in parallel, it set a new objective of total transposition (100 %) by the Member States of all the directives which should have been transposed more than two years previously (⁵). In

---

(¹) Further information is available on the Europa server (http://europa.eu.int/comm/internal_market/en/index.htm).
(²) http://europa.eu.int/comm/internal_market/en/update/strategy/index.htm.
(³) Bull. 3-2002, points I.13 and I.14.
(⁴) 2001 General Report, point 161.
(⁵) Internal market scoreboard: http://europa.eu.int/comm/internal_market/en/update/score/index.htm.

preparation for the Barcelona European Council, in conclusions adopted on 1 March ([1]) the Council advocated the elimination of the remaining technical obstacles to trade within the framework of the internal market to strengthen confidence in markets, goods and services, and the opening up to competition of utilities and network industries providing services of general interest. In a communication of 23 December ([2]), the Commission set out the conditions under which notification must be given of certain national measures that are incompatible with harmonisation measures and the principles it will apply in examining these measures, in accordance with Article 95 of the EC Treaty.

146. Internal market strategy. On 11 April, the Commission presented a communication ([3]) in which it updated for the third time ([4]) the target actions provided for under the strategy defined in 1999 ([5]). While there had been some notable achievements in 2001, overall progress had not been fast enough, and the 'delivery gap' had to be closed or the overall credibility of the Lisbon strategy would be called into question. While the three institutions shared responsibility for the unachieved objectives, the Commission, though recognising that it had itself not met certain deadlines (action plan for better regulation and services strategy), noted that most of the delays had arisen in the European Parliament and the Council (the Community patent, the legislative package on public procurement and the directive on takeover bids). It therefore recommended continuing to concentrate on the same broad objectives, but reducing the total number of target actions so as to ensure that the most important domains received political decision-makers' full attention. The Council endorsed this approach and, in conclusions adopted on 21 May ([6]), reaffirmed its commitment to seeking early agreement on those target actions which were of particular relevance to the internal market, such as public procurement *(→ point 202)* and the Community patent *(→ point 193)*. The European Economic and Social Committee also commented on the communication, in an opinion adopted on 18 July ([7]). On 23 December, the Commission presented its fifth report on the functioning of Community product and capital markets ([8]), which stresses in particular that the internal market has produced not inconsiderable advantages for the citizens of Europe, and not just in terms of reducing the prices of many consumer products; according to the Commission there is, however, still scope for major advances, particularly in financial services and public procurement.

([1]) Bull. 3-2002, points I.58 and 1.3.30.
([2]) COM(2002) 760; Bull. 12-2002, point 1.3.34.
([3]) COM(2002) 171; Bull. 4-2002, point 1.3.19.
([4]) Previous update: COM(2001) 198; 2001 General Report, point 161.
([5]) COM(1999) 624; 1999 General Report, point 127.
([6]) Bull. 5-2002, point 1.3.22.
([7]) OJ C 241, 7.10.2002; Bull. 7/8-2002, point 1.3.23.
([8]) COM(2002) 743; Bull. 12-2002, point 1.3.31. Previous report: 2001 General Report, point 204.

147.   Simpler legislation for the internal market (SLIM) (^{1}). On 16 January, the European Economic and Social Committee adopted a further additional opinion (^{2}) in connection with this objective. Following on from its initiatives in 2000 (^{3}) and 2001 (^{4}), this aims to update the information on the PRISM (Progress report on initiatives in the single market) exercise. Other information concerning the general approach to legislative simplification can be found in Section 6 ('Simplifying and improving the regulatory environment') of Chapter I *(→ point 25)*.

148.   Problem solving. As part of the 'Dialogue with business and citizens', a 'Citizens' signpost' service was launched on 1 July (^{5}). This provides information and practical advice on internal market rights and where necessary directs enquirers to the authorities or services which are in a position to resolve the problems raised. In conclusions adopted on 1 March (^{6}), the Council welcomed the Commission's communication on setting up the Solvit network (^{7}), conceived as an effective system for resolving problems resulting from misapplication of internal market rules by government departments, and endorsed the Commission's recommendation laying down the principles for using the network, which has been operational since 1 July.

149.   Principle of mutual recognition. On 23 July, the Commission presented a second biennial report (^{8}) on the application of this principle in the single market. It stressed that there remained difficulties with technically complex products and products which could pose safety or health problems.

150.   Product liability. In a resolution of 19 December (^{9}), the Council considered that an assessment should be made of Directive 85/374/EEC concerning liability for defective products (^{10}) in order to judge whether there should be a further amendment to allow national legislation on the liability of intermediaries to be based on the same system as that for producers.

(^{1}) http://europa.eu.int/comm/internal_market/en/update/slim/index.htm.
(^{2}) OJ C 80, 3.4.2002; Bull. 1/2-2002, point 1.3.48.
(^{3}) OJ C 14, 16.1.2001; 2000 General Report, point 138.
(^{4}) OJ C 48, 21.2.2002; 2001 General Report, point 162.
(^{5}) http://europa.eu.int/citizensrights/signpost/front_end/signpost_en.htm.
(^{6}) Bull. 3-2002, point 1.3.31.
(^{7}) OJ L 331, 15.12.2001; COM(2001) 702; 2001 General Report, point 165; http://europa.eu.int/comm/internal_market/solvit/index_en.htm.
(^{8}) COM(2002) 419; Bull. 7/8-2002, point 1.3.24. Previous report: SEC(1999) 1106; 1999 General Report, point 131.
(^{9}) Bull. 12-2002, point 1.3.32.
(^{10}) OJ L 210, 7.8.1985; Nineteenth General Report, point 250. Previous amendment: Directive 1999/34/EC (OJ L 141, 4.6.1999; 1999 General Report, point 129).

Free movement of goods (¹)

Implementation of Articles 28 to 30 of the EC Treaty

151.   Statistics. The Commission continued monitoring compliance with Articles 28, 29 and 30 of the EC Treaty concerning the elimination of quantitative import and export restrictions between Member States and measures with equivalent effect. As of 31 December, 360 cases were still under examination, while 173 new complaints were received in 2002.

Technical aspects

152.   Information on the harmonisation of certain technical legislation on specific products or equipment (chemical substances, pharmaceutical products, machinery, motor vehicles, etc.) is dealt with in the corresponding thematic sections, and in particular in Section 7 ('Enterprise policy') of this chapter *(→ point 255)* and in Section 6 ('Transport') of Chapter IV *(→ points 639 et seq.)*.

Veterinary and plant-health legislation

153.   Information on veterinary and plant-health legislation can be found in Section 7 ('Consumer health and protection') of Chapter IV *(→ points 674 to 680)*.

Special schemes

154.   Cultural goods. On 21 January (²) the Council formally adopted its resolution of 5 November 2001 (³) on the Commission report of May 2000 (⁴) on the implementation of Council Regulation (EEC) No 3911/92 on the export of cultural goods (⁵) and Council Directive 93/7/EEC on the return of cultural objects unlawfully removed from the territory of a Member State (⁶).

155.   Dual-use goods and technology. Under Regulation (EC) No 1334/2000 (⁷), there is an exception to the principle of free movement within the Community for certain dual-use items and technologies. In order to limit breaches of this

---

(¹) http://europa.eu.int/comm/internal_market/en/goods/index.htm.
(²) OJ C 32, 5.2.2002; Bull. 1/2-2002, point 1.3.59.
(³) 2001 General Report, point 178.
(⁴) COM(2000) 325; 2000 General Report, point 142.
(⁵) OJ L 395, 31.12.1992; Twenty-sixth General Report, point 161.
(⁶) OJ L 74, 27.3.1993; Twenty-seventh General Report, point 96.
(⁷) OJ L 159, 30.6.2000; 2000 General Report, point 825; last amended by Council Regulation (EC) No 2432/2001 (OJ L 338, 20.12.2001; 2001 General Report, point 897).

fundamental principle, however, the Council decided, by adopting Regulation (EC) No 880/2002 of 27 May (¹), to remove from the annex to this regulation certain items which are now considered less sensitive.

Customs

156.   Information on customs can be found in Section 3 ('Common commercial policy') of Chapter VI *(→ points 782 and 783).*

Free movement of persons (²)

Freedom of movement and right of residence

157.   Information on freedom of movement and right of residence can be found in Sections 1 ('Area of freedom, security and justice') and 2 ('Union citizenship') of Chapter IV *(→ points 454 et seq.).*

Free movement of workers

158.   Information on the free movement of workers can be found in Section 3 ('Employment and social policy') of this chapter *(→ points 116 and 123).*

Mutual recognition of qualifications

159.   Consolidation and rationalisation of the acquis. On 7 March, the Commission proposed incorporating the existing directives on the recognition of qualifications in the field of the regulated professions into a single consolidated directive (Table I). Intended to encourage clarity and speed, the proposal also aims to preserve the guarantees the system already provides and in particular to permit greater liberalisation of cross-border services and more flexibility in the procedures for updating the minimum training requirements for professions currently governed by the sectoral directives.

(¹) Regulation (EC) No 880/2002 (OJ L 139, 29.5.2002; Bull. 5-2002, point 1.6.36).
(²) http://europa.eu.int/comm/internal_market/en/people/index.htm.

Freedom to provide services (^{1})

160.   State of the internal market for services. In a report of 30 July (^{2}), presented as part of the first phase of the internal market strategy for services (^{3}),
the Commission drew up as comprehensive an inventory as possible of the continuing barriers in this market (restrictions on the freedom to provide services
and the freedom of establishment). It also analysed the common features of
these barriers, made a preliminary assessment of their economic impact and
concluded that, a decade after the planned completion of the internal market,
there is a still huge gap between the vision of an integrated EU economy and the
reality experienced by European citizens and service providers. In conclusions
adopted on 14 November (^{4}), the Council welcomed the Commission's report
and considered that it formed an excellent basis for the second phase of the
strategy.

Financial services (^{5})

161.   Referring to the interconnection of the European economies, the Barcelona European Council (^{6}) reaffirmed its commitment to implementing the
financial services action plan (^{7}) and achieving full integration of the securities
and risk capital markets by 2003 and of the financial services markets by 2005.
This determination to pursue the financial services action plan was reaffirmed
by the Seville European Council (^{8}). In conclusions adopted on 12 July (^{9}), the
Council called on its Economic and Financial Committee to prepare, with Commission support, a new approach to integration for all financial services based
on the system developed for securities (^{10}). In conclusions adopted on
3 December (^{11}), it called for the establishment of separate regulatory committees for the banking, insurance and securities sectors and for reinforced cooperation on financial supervision.

162.   Action plan for financial services. The Commission presented its
sixth (^{12}) and seventh (^{13}) progress reports on this initiative on 3 June and
29 November respectively. It concluded that tangible progress had been made

---

(^{1}) http://europa.eu.int/comm/internal_market/en/services/services/index.htm.
(^{2}) COM(2002) 441; Bull. 7/8-2002, point 1.3.27.
(^{3}) COM(2000) 888; 2000 General Report, point 156.
(^{4}) Bull. 11-2002, point 1.3.26.
(^{5}) http://europa.eu.int/comm/internal_market/en/finances/index.htm.
(^{6}) Bull. 3-2002, point I.30.
(^{7}) COM(1999) 232; 1999 General Report, point 148.
(^{8}) Bull. 6-2002, point I.17.
(^{9}) Bull. 7/8-2002, point 1.3.28.
(^{10}) 2001 General Report, point 189.
(^{11}) Bull. 12-2002, point 1.3.41.
(^{12}) COM(2002) 267; Bull. 6-2002, point 1.3.30.
(^{13}) SEC(2002) 1314.

in this area and that the pace had to be maintained to meet the 2005 deadline set by the Lisbon European Council (^{1}) for fully implementing the action plan. In a resolution of 5 February (^{2}), Parliament had stressed the need to accelerate legislative procedures in the field of financial services. In two resolutions of 21 November, the European Parliament, noting that the Council intended to extend the 'Lamfalussy process' in order to speed up and introduce more flexibility into the reform of the European framework for financial markets, considered this move to be premature with regard both to the financial services sector as a whole (^{3}) and, more particularly, to the regulation and supervision of the banking and insurance sectors (^{4}).

163. *Securities.* On 21 January, Parliament and the Council amended Directive 85/611/EEC of 20 December 1985 on the coordination of laws, regulations and administrative provisions relating to undertakings for collective investment in transferable securities (UCITS) by adopting two new directives (Table I). Directive 2001/107/EC, which essentially concerns UCITS management companies, covers rules on market access and the conditions for doing business, together with the prudential standards to be met by these companies, and introduces a simplified prospectus to provide better information for investors; Directive 2001/108/EC extends the range of the financial assets in which approved UCITS may invest. In a communication of 28 May (^{5}), the Commission called for the creation of an integrated clearing and settlement environment as an essential precondition for efficient post-trade processing of all securities transactions in the European Union. On 5 November, the Council reached agreement on the proposal for a directive on the prospectus to be published when securities are offered to the public or admitted to trading (Table I). After a second reading by the European Parliament on 24 October, the Council approved the directive on insider dealing and market manipulation (Table I), which aims to enhance investor confidence by ensuring conditions of equality for all economic operators in the Member States.

164. *Financial collateral arrangements.* On 6 June, Parliament and the Council adopted Directive 2002/47/EC establishing a clear and uniform Community framework for the provision of securities and cash as collateral (Table I). This aims to limit risk in transactions and to improve the operation and the stability of European financial markets.

165. *Investment services.* On 19 November, the Commission adopted a proposal for a directive on investment services and the securities markets, replacing Directive 93/22/EEC (^{6}), in order to respond to the changes affecting the profes-

(^{1}) Bull. 3-2000, point I.10; 2000 General Report, point 159.
(^{2}) OJ C 284 E, 21.11.2002; Bull. 1/2-2002, point 1.3.63.
(^{3}) Bull. 11-2002, point 1.3.31.
(^{4}) Bull. 11-2002, point 1.3.32.
(^{5}) COM(2002) 257; Bull. 5-2002, point 1.3.33.
(^{6}) OJ L 141, 11.6.1993; Twenty-seventh General Report, point 107.

sions concerned by these sectors of activity and to place on an equal footing sales of securities on the regulated markets (stock exchanges) and unregulated markets in the European Union (Table I).

166. *Insurance.* On 5 March, the European Parliament and the Council adopted Directives 2002/12/EC and 2002/13/EC, which update the solvency margin requirements that had applied to life assurance and non-life insurance undertakings for over 20 years (Table I). On 28 May, the Commission proposed amending the existing directives on the annual accounts and the consolidated accounts of certain categories of insurance undertakings *(→ point 187).* On 7 June, it proposed amending the existing directives on motor insurance, with the particular aim of plugging regulatory gaps and creating a more efficient internal market in motor insurance (Table I). On 5 November, the European Parliament and the Council adopted Directive 2002/83/EC on life assurance (Table I), which recasts in a single text and replaces all the directives in the life assurance field adopted since 1979. On 9 December, the European Parliament and the Council adopted Directive 2002/29/EC establishing the regulatory framework for completing the internal market for insurance intermediaries (Table I). This directive, which repeals Directive 77/92/EEC ([1]), aims to guarantee a high level of professionalism among insurance and reinsurance intermediaries and to protect consumers who deal with them. It thus requires mandatory registration of all insurance and reinsurance intermediaries in their Member States of origin and requires them to provide consumers with clear explanations of the reasons for their advice on the purchase of a given insurance product.

167. *Financial conglomerates.* The European Parliament and the Council approved the content of a directive (Table I) on the supplementary supervision of credit institutions, insurance undertakings and investment firms in a financial conglomerate and amending Council Directives 73/239/EEC, 79/267/EEC, 92/49/EEC, 92/96/EEC, 93/6/EEC and 93/22/EEC and Directives 98/78/EC and 2000/12/EC of the European Parliament and the Council. Since the heightened tempo of internationalisation and consolidation in the financial sector, together with the blurring of boundaries between financial subsectors, has led to the emergence of cross-sector financial groups, the directive introduces a complementary supervisory system for financial conglomerates that supplements the existing sectoral rules for the businesses concerned.

168. *Risk capital action plan (RCAP).* In a resolution of 11 April([2]), the European Parliament warmly welcomed the Commission's communication of October 2001 ([3]) on the considerable progress made in the risk capital field since the adoption of the RCAP([4]). On 16 October, the Commission presented a

([1]) OJ L 26, 31.1.1977.
([2]) Bull. 4-2002, point 1.3.26.
([3]) COM(2001) 605; 2001 General Report, point 195.
([4]) 1998 General Report, point 263.

synopsis of the progress made in the course of 2001 and, in certain respects, during the first half of 2002 ([1]). It considers that recent developments show that the accompanying measures to develop European risk capital have undergone profound and positive changes and concludes that efforts must be maintained in a long-term perspective.

169.   Cross-border credit transfers. In a report dated 29 November ([2]), the Commission presented the arrangements for implementing the directive on cross-border credit transfers ([3]), with regard both to its transposition into national law and to the practical application of the provisions by the banking sectors in the Member States.

Other services

170.   Postal services. On 10 June, the European Parliament and the Council adopted Directive 2002/39/EC (Table I), which fulfils the mandate laid down in 1997 under Directive 97/67/EC ([4]) for a gradual controlled extension of the liberalisation of postal services. Taking effect as of 31 December, the new directive also aims to resolve various ancillary issues relating to the smooth operation of the internal market in this field. On 25 November ([5]), the Commission presented a report on the application of Directive 97/67/EC.

171.   Services of general economic interest. Encouraged by the Council and the Barcelona European Council ([6]) with a view to the forthcoming Seville European Council, on 18 June the Commission adopted a communication defining a methodology for the horizontal evaluation of services of general economic interest ([7]). The aim is to improve the performance of these services throughout the Union by helping to identify the ways of providing them which guarantee consumers the best quality and the best prices. The Commission methodology develops the approach defined in October 2001 in its report on services of general economic interest ([8]). Thus it intends, from 2003 onwards for the current 15 Member States and from 2005 for the new Member States, to produce annual performance assessments of services of general economic interest, in principle in the following sectors: transport, electricity, gas, postal services and telecommunications. Particular attention will be paid to how consumers see the performance of these services and to the impact of the process of economic reform and opening up to competition that they are undergoing. In an opinion

---

([1]) COM(2002) 563; Bull. 10-2002, point 1.3.23.
([2]) Bull. 11-2002, point 1.3.33.
([3]) Directive 97/5/EC (OJ L 43, 14.2.1997; 1997 General Report, point 202).
([4]) OJ L 15, 21.1.1998; 1997 General Report, point 521.
([5]) COM(2002) 632; Bull. 11-2002, point 1.3.35.
([6]) Bull. 3-2002, points I.35 and I.58.
([7]) COM(2002) 331; Bull. 6-2002, point 1.3.36.
([8]) COM(2001) 598; 2001 General Report, point 164.

adopted on 17 July (¹), the European Economic and Social Committee made a series of suggestions for reinforcing the status of these services at Community level. On 4 December, the Commission adopted a communication on the progress made in examining a proposal for a framework directive on services of general interest (²).

Media (³)

172.   *Cable and satellite.* In a report of 26 July (⁴) on the application of Council Directive 93/83/EEC on the coordination of certain rules concerning copyright and rights related to copyright (⁵), the Commission presented its thoughts on citizens' difficulties in accessing satellite transmissions from outside the Member State in which they are resident. This report also indicated that, in the light of the development of the media in the information society, there was a need for close scrutiny of the principle of collective management of cable retransmission rights and the resolution of disputes arising from retransmission.

173.   *Media concentration.* In a resolution of 20 November (⁶), the European Parliament called on the Commission and the Member States to safeguard pluralism and to ensure that the media within the European Union are free and diversified and stressed the need to establish a European market in this sector.

Free movement of capital (⁷)

174.   Several points concerning the movement of capital appear in Section 1 ('Economic and monetary policy') of this chapter *(→ point 78)*, Section 1 ('Area of freedom, security and justice') of Chapter IV *(→ point 485)*, Section 3 ('Common commercial policy') of Chapter VI *(→ points 784 to 786)* and Section 2 ('Decisions by the Court of Justice and the Court of First Instance') of Chapter VIII *(→ point 1068)*.

(¹) OJ C 241, 7.10.2002; Bull. 7/8-2002, point 1.3.31.
(²) COM(2002) 689; Bull. 12-2002, point 1.3.44.
(³) http://europa.eu.int/comm/internal_market/en/media/index.htm.
(⁴) COM(2002) 430; Bull. 7/8-2002, point 1.3.38.
(⁵) OJ L 248, 6.10.1993; Twenty-seventh General Report, point 118.
(⁶) Bull. 11-2002, point 1.3.34.
(⁷) http://europa.eu.int/comm/economy_finance/about/activities_en.htm.

Taxation (¹)

175. General matters. On 14 March (²) the European Parliament welcomed the Commission's communication of May 2001 on EU tax policy and its priorities for the years ahead (³). It considered in particular that tax competition between the Member States could help to prevent tax pressure from reaching excessive levels. In an own-initiative opinion delivered on 25 April (⁴), the European Economic and Social Committee also emphasised the beneficial effects of such competition on companies' competitiveness. In its conclusions of 4 June on the 'tax package' (⁵), the Council noted the progress made by its 'Code of conduct' group on company taxation. In the same context, with regard to the taxation of savings it cited the negotiations begun in 2001 (⁶) with Andorra, the United States, Liechtenstein, Monaco, San Marino and Switzerland on those countries' adoption of equivalent measures to those contained in a proposal for a directive to ensure the effective taxation within the Community of savings income in the form of interest payments. These negotiations were the subject of a report from the Commission dated 27 November (⁷). The Seville European Council on 21 and 22 June noted with satisfaction the Council's progress report on the tax package (⁸).

In conclusions on administrative cooperation in tax matters adopted on 4 June (⁹), the Council stated its wish to step up appropriate action for strengthening cooperation between the Member States. It also invited the Commission, on completion of the preparatory studies being carried out, to submit a proposal for amending Directive 77/799/EEC on mutual assistance between the competent authorities of the Member States (¹⁰). The Seville European Council welcomed these conclusions (¹¹). In addition, legislative work continued in various fields relating to administrative cooperation in tax matters (Table I) and in the field of the computerisation of checks (Table I).

Direct taxation

176. Companies. On 11 March (¹²), the Council backed the establishment of an EU joint forum to examine the practical problems arising in the internal mar-

---

(¹) http://europa.eu.int/comm/taxation_customs/taxation/taxation.htm.
(²) Bull. 3-2002, point 1.3.43.
(³) OJ C 284, 10.10.2001, COM(2001) 260; 2001 General Report, point 206.
(⁴) OJ C 149, 21.6.2002; Bull. 4-2002, point 1.3.28.
(⁵) Bull. 6-2002, point 1.3.38.
(⁶) 2001 General Report, point 210.
(⁷) SEC(2002) 1287; Bull. 11-2002, point 1.3.39.
(⁸) Bull. 6-2002, point I.19.
(⁹) Bull. 6-2002, point 1.3.39.
(¹⁰) OJ L 336, 27.12.1977; Eleventh General Report, point 230.
(¹¹) Bull. 6-2002, point I.20.
(¹²) Bull. 3-2002, point 1.3.41.

ket from the application of the tax rules on transfer pricing. The forum met for the first time on 3 October. In an own-initiative opinion of 17 July ([1]), the European Economic and Social Committee expressed its support for the guidelines defined by the Commission with the aim of adopting a harmonised tax base for all companies in the European Union ([2]). These guidelines were also the subject of a general discussion in the Council on 1 July.

Indirect taxation

177. *'Fiscalis' programme* ([3]). On 17 January, the Commission presented a proposal for a decision, accompanied by a communication on the case for pursuing the initiative ([4]), with a view to adopting the 'Fiscalis 2007' programme for improving the operation of taxation systems in the internal market by more effective cooperation between the administrations concerned. Decision No 2235/2002/EC adopting this programme was signed by the European Parliament and the Council on 3 December (Table I).

178. *Tobacco.* On 12 February, the Council amended Directives 92/79/EEC, 92/80/EEC and 95/59/EC with the aim of helping to combat fraud and smuggling in the Community by closer harmonisation of the structure and rates of excise duty applied on manufactured tobacco in the Member States (Table II).

179. *Labour-intensive services.* On 3 December, the Council adopted Directive 2002/92/EC extending the possibility of authorising Member States to apply reduced rates of VAT for some of these services (Table II), in view of the time needed to make an in-depth assessment, in terms of the effectiveness of the measure for job creation, of the national reports drawn up by the Member States which had taken up this possibility. On the same day, the Commission also extended the period of application of Decision 2000/185/EC ([5]), which authorised nine Member States to apply such a scheme until 31 December 2002 ([6]).

180. *Travel agents.* On 8 February, the Commission proposed amending Directive 77/388/EEC on the common system of value added tax, with a view to simpler and uniform application of the special scheme applicable to travel agents (Table II).

181. *Radio and television broadcasting services and electronic commerce.* On 7 May, the Council amended, partly on a temporary basis, Directive

---

([1]) OJ C 241, 7.10.2002; Bull. 7/8-2002, point 1.3.32.
([2]) COM(2001) 582, 2001 General Report, point 211 and http://europa.eu.int/comm/taxation_customs/taxation/company_tax/index.htm.
([3]) http://europa.eu.int/comm/taxation_customs/taxation/fiscalis/index_en.htm.
([4]) COM(2002) 10; Bull. 1/2-2002, point 1.3.66.
([5]) OJ L 59, 4.3.2000; 2000 General Report, point 170.
([6]) Décision 2002/954/EC (OJ L 331, 7.12.2002).

77/388/ EEC with regard to the VAT scheme applicable to radio and television broadcasting services and to certain electronically supplied services (Table II) and, temporarily, Regulation (EEC) No 218/92 on administrative cooperation in the field of indirect taxation with regard to new measures relating to electronic commerce (Table I). These amendments update the existing rules on VAT to cover the latest developments in electronic commerce and offer all service providers, based in the European Union or otherwise, a clear and certain regulatory environment.

182.   *Place of supply of services.* On 28 October, the Commission presented a report ([1]) on the review of Article 9 of the sixth VAT directive ([2]), which determines the place of taxation for the supply of services. The Council took note of this report on 5 November. On 5 December, the Commission proposed amending this sixth directive with respect to the place of delivery of natural gas supplied by pipeline and of electricity (Table II).

183.   *Fuels.* On 24 July, the Commission proposed amending the existing directives to introduce special tax arrangements for diesel fuel used for commercial purposes and to align the excise duties on petrol and diesel fuel (Table II). Legislative work also continued on the taxation of biofuels (Table II), the final adoption of a directive on this being linked to the directive on promoting the use of biofuels in transport *(→ point 644).*

184.   *Taxation of passenger cars.* On 6 September, the Commission presented a communication on the taxation of passenger cars in the European Union ([3]) with a view to launching discussion of a series of measures aimed at providing final solutions for the problems faced by citizens and the car industry. These solutions would improve the operation of the internal market and contribute to achieving the Kyoto Protocol commitments on reducing greenhouse gases *(→ points 487 to 589).*

185.   *Outermost regions.* A series of provisions adopted during the year authorise or extend specific exemptions for local production from those regions of the European Union which face handicaps primarily linked to insularity and geographical isolation *(→ points 379 to 382).*

([1]) COM(2002) 587; Bull. 10-2002, point 1.3.27.
([2]) Council Directive 77/388/EEC (OJ L 145, 13.6.1977; Eleventh General Report, point 219).
([3]) COM(2002) 431; Bull. 9-2002, point 1.3.39.

Company law (¹)

186.   Disclosure requirements. On 3 June, the Commission proposed amending Council Directive 68/151/EEC as regards disclosure requirements for certain types of companies (Table I). It proposes to accelerate the filing and disclosure of company documents and particulars by the use of modern technology, and to improve cross-border access to company information by allowing voluntary registration of company documents and particulars in additional languages.

187.   International accounting standards (IAS). On 28 May, the Commission proposed amending the existing directives concerning the annual accounts and consolidated accounts of certain categories of companies and insurance undertakings (Table I), in order to take account of changes in accounting standards and to encourage the gradual adoption of international accounting standards by unlisted companies. On 19 July, the European Parliament and the Council adopted Regulation (EC) No 1606/2002 on the application of these standards, with the aim of ensuring the comparability and transparency of the financial information presented by companies (Table I), which will be obliged to prepare their consolidated accounts in conformity with international accounting standards from 2005 onwards.

188.   Auditing. On 16 May, the Commission adopted a recommendation on the independence of the statutory auditor (²). This recommendation lays down a set of fundamental principles that auditors must comply with in order to maintain their independence and also provides for a series of specific safeguard measures.

189.   Takeover bids. On 2 October, the Commission adopted a new proposal for a directive concerning takeover bids (Table I). This proposal aims to respond to Parliament's concerns over the previous proposal, which it rejected in July 2001 (³), without compromising the Commission's fundamental principles, which the Council and Parliament broadly approved.

190.   Company law action plan. In conclusions adopted on 30 September (⁴), the Council gave priority to the preparation of an action plan covering among other things 'corporate governance' in order to improve and modernise the regulatory framework of company law. It called on the Commission to take initiatives to this end in conjunction with the Member States and to pay special attention to aspects such as management remuneration and responsibility and audit practices.

(¹) http://europa.eu.int/comm/internal_market/en/company/index.htm.
(²) Recommendation 2002/590/EC (OJ L 191, 19.7.2002).
(³) 2001 General Report, point 218.
(⁴) Bull. 9-2002, point 1.3.43.

Intellectual property (¹)

191. *Biotechnologies.* A Commission report of 14 January (²) presented an assessment of the implications for basic genetic-engineering research of non-publication or late publication of papers on subjects which could be patentable. On 7 October, the Commission adopted a report on the development and implications of patent law in the field of biotechnology and genetic engineering (³).

192. *Computer-implemented inventions.* On 20 February, the Commission proposed harmonising national laws concerning the patentability of such inventions and making the conditions relating to this more transparent (Table I). In particular, it recommended that the concept of 'technical contribution' count as an essential patentability criterion in this field.

193. *Community patent.* The Council took note of the progress of work in this field in its conclusions of 21 May (⁴). To facilitate continuing discussions within the Council, on 30 August the Commission adopted a working document on the planned Community patent jurisdiction (⁵).

194. *Designs.* Following the adoption in December 2001 of Council Regulation (EC) No 6/2002 on Community designs (⁶), since 6 March it has been possible to protect unregistered Community designs. The Commission has prepared the legal instruments necessary to allow registered Community designs to be registered with the Office for Harmonisation in the Internal Market from 2003 onwards (⁷).

195. *Community trade mark.* On 27 December (⁸), the Commission proposed amending Regulation (EC) No 40/94 on the Community trade mark (⁹) in order to improve a number of provisions in the existing system. On the same day, it adopted a report on the operation of the system of searches for Community trade marks (¹⁰) and a report on the functioning of the system of professional representation before the Office for Harmonisation in the Internal Market (¹¹).

196. *Public lending right.* In a report of 12 September (¹²) on the application of the public lending right, harmonised by Council Directive 92/100/EEC on

---

(¹) http://europa.eu.int/comm/internal_market/en/intprop/index_all.htm.
(²) COM(2002) 2; Bull. 1/2-2002, point 1.3.70.
(³) COM(2002) 545; Bull. 10-2002, point 1.3.29.
(⁴) Bull. 5-2002, point 1.3.37.
(⁵) COM(2002) 480.
(⁶) OJ L 3, 5.1.2002; 2001 General Report, point 220.
(⁷) Regulations (EC) No 2245/2002 and (EC) No 2246/2002 (OJ L 341, 17.12.2002).
(⁸) COM(2002) 767; Bull. 12-2002, point 1.3.54.
(⁹) OJ L 11, 14.1.1994; Twenty-seventh General Report, point 117.
(¹⁰) COM(2002) 754; Bull. 12-2002, point 1.3.52.
(¹¹) COM(2002) 766; Bull. 12-2002, point 1.3.53.
(¹²) COM(2002) 502; Bull. 9-2002, point 1.3.44.

rental and lending rights (¹), the Commission recalled the purpose and content of this right and the limits on exceptions to it and assessed its transposition in the Member States.

197.   *Databases.* On 17 September, the Commission proposed concluding an agreement with the Isle of Man (²) for a mutual extension of the *sui generis* protection of databases pursuant to Council Directive 96/9/EC (³) on the legal protection of databases.

198.   *Ownership of rights to cinematographic and audiovisual works.* In a report of 6 December concerning the ownership of rights to cinematographic and audiovisual works (⁴), the Commission examined the effects on the exploitation of works of the provisions on the initial ownership of these rights and on their transfer.

Data protection (⁵)

199.   *European data protection controller.* On 1 July, the European Parliament, the Council and the Commission adopted Decision No 1247/2002/EC (⁶) on the regulations and general conditions governing the performance of this independent authority's duties.

200.   *'Echelon' system.* In a resolution of 7 November (⁷), the European Parliament deplored the fact that, more than a year after the conclusion of its enquiry into the worldwide interception system 'Echelon' (⁸), neither the Council nor the Commission had taken the appropriate steps to give effect to its recommendations.

201.   *Privacy protection.* Information on this point appears in Section 9 ('Information society') of this chapter *(→ point 343).*

Public procurement (⁹)

202.   *Simplification of legislation.* In connection with the 'legislative package' put forward by the Commission to simplify and modernise the public-

---

(¹) OJ L 346, 27.11.1992; Twenty-sixth General Report, point 143.
(²) COM(2002) 506; Bull. 9-2002, point 1.3.46.
(³) OJ L 77, 27.3.1996; 1996 General Report, point 142.
(⁴) COM(2002) 691; Bull. 12-2002, point 1.3.51.
(⁵) http://europa.eu.int/comm/internal_market/en/dataprot/index.htm.
(⁶) OJ L 183, 12.7.2002; Bull. 7/8-2002, point 1.3.39.
(⁷) Bull. 11-2002, point 1.3.41.
(⁸) OJ C 72 E, 21.3.2002; 2001 General Report, point 225.
(⁹) http://europa.eu.int/comm/internal_market/en/publproc/index.htm.

procurement directives, on 21 May and 30 September respectively, the Council reached agreement with a view to a common position on firstly the proposal on coordination of the procedures for the award of public works, supply and service contracts (Table I) and secondly that on the procurement procedures of entities operating in the water, energy, and transport sectors (Table I). On 5 November, the Council and the European Parliament adopted Regulation (EC) No 2195/2002 on the common procurement vocabulary (CPV) (Table I). The CPV aims to simplify the rules on the publication of contract notices by the use of a single system for classifying public procurement. Its use by all public authorities will make it easier to identify the subject of procurement notices, to have invitations to tender translated into all the official languages of the European Union and to reinforce the openness and transparency of public procurement to the benefit of suppliers seeking market opportunities within the Union.

203.   Use of standard forms for publishing public procurement notices. On 1 May, the use of standard forms became obligatory for public contract notices published in the *Official Journal of the European Communities* pursuant to Commission Directive 2001/78/EC ([1]).

([1]) OJ L 285, 29.10.2001; 2001 General Report, point 227.

Section 6

Competition policy (¹)

Overview

204.   In 2002, the Commission pressed ahead with its work on modernising the Community rules in all areas of competition policy. In antitrust, its proposal for recasting Regulation No 17 implementing Articles 81 and 82 of the EC Treaty was adopted by the Council on 16 December, clearing the way for decentralised application of the Community rules in this field by national competition authorities acting in close cooperation with the Commission, as well as direct application by national courts. In addition, a new block exemption regulation in the motor vehicle sector will boost competition considerably in this vital area of the economy, at the level of both sales and after-sales service, and will benefit consumers in terms of prices and opportunities for cross-border purchases. The Commission also continued to give high priority to detecting, prosecuting and punishing unlawful agreements, which were the subject of numerous decisions imposing fines. On the mergers front, the observations made by interested parties in response to the Commission's Green Paper on the review of the merger regulation enabled it to draw conclusions on a whole series of concepts and approaches designed to improve the existing legislation. On 11 December, it adopted a proposal for amending the merger regulation. In the State-aid field, the Barcelona European Council endorsed the Council's appeals for continued efforts to reduce the overall level of aid and redirect resources towards objectives of common interest and to modernise the Community competition rules. For its part, the Commission launched a reform designed to simplify procedures for cases which do not raise major legal concerns so as to free up resources to handle the more important cases, as well as the cases which will arise after enlargement of the EU, in a context of greater transparency and predictability. On 29 April, it adopted the XXXIst Report on Competition

---

(¹) Only the most significant cases are dealt with in this section. For further information, as well as for detailed statistics on the cases handled by the Commission and on the relevant case-law, see the *XXXIInd Report on Competition Policy*, to be published in conjunction with this General Report. In conjunction with the XXXIInd Report (Part I), a report on the application of the competition rules in the European Union in 2002 (Part II), prepared under the sole responsibility of the Directorate-General for Competition, will also be available. Part I will be published in mid-2003 and Part II at a later date. Both reports can be obtained from the Office for Official Publications of the European Communities or accessed on the Europa server (http://europa. eu.int/comm/competition/index_en.html). The server also contains additional information on the European Union's competition policy.

Policy (¹), *which takes stock of its activity in the field in 2001 and which was the subject of a resolution adopted by the European Parliament on 21 November* (²).

Competition rules applying to businesses

General rules (³)

205.   *Consequences of expiry of the ECSC Treaty.* Following the expiry of the Treaty establishing the European Coal and Steel Community on 23 July *(→ point 39)*, the sectors previously covered by that Treaty and the procedural rules and secondary legislation derived from it became subject to the EC Treaty, and on 21 June the Commission issued a communication (⁴) dealing with certain aspects of the treatment of competition cases resulting from the changeover.

206.   *Fines in cartel cases.* Under a notice (⁵) adopted on 13 February, based on experience gained since 1996 (⁶) and aimed at strengthening the capacity to detect and prosecute cartel cases while improving legal certainty, the Commission can grant 'conditional immunity from fines' to the first firm contributing decisively to the identification or banning of a cartel.

207.   *New regulation implementing Articles 81 and 82 of the EC Treaty.* On 16 December, following a political agreement reached at the end of November, the Council adopted Regulation (EC) No 1/2003 on the implementation of Articles 81 and 82 of the EC Treaty, which marks the most fundamental overhaul of the antitrust rules since Regulation No 17 (Table II). One of the key aspects of the reform is the elimination of the practice of notifying agreements to the Commission. This will make procedures less cumbersome and will reduce legal costs for companies. The adoption of the new regulation before the large-scale enlargement of the European Union will also tighten application of the antitrust rules, including by the national courts, and will allow tasks to be shared more effectively between the Commission and the national authorities. The regulation will moreover allow the Commission and the national authorities to concentrate their resources on the task of combating price-fixing agreements and other types of agreement that really harm the market.

(¹) SEC(2002) 462; Bull. 4-2002, point 1.3.32; Internet http://europa.eu.int/comm/competition/annual_reports/2001/.
(²) Bull. 11-2002, point 1.3.43.
(³) Detailed statistics on the application of Articles 81 and 82 of the EC Treaty will be provided in the Report on Competition Policy, to be published in 2003.
(⁴) OJ C 152, 26.6.2002; Bull. 6-2002, point 1.3.46.
(⁵) OJ C 45, 19.2.2002; SEC(2002) 150; Bull. 1/2-2002, point 1.3.87.
(⁶) OJ C 207, 18.7.1996; 1996 General Report, point 156.

Permissible forms of cooperation

Sectoral approach

208.   Motor vehicle distribution. On 31 July, the Commission adopted a regulation ([1]) amending, from October onwards, the previous arrangements ([2]) in order to put right the competition problems identified in its November 2000 evaluation report ([3]). The goal of the new regulation is to boost competition and bring tangible benefits to European consumers as regards vehicle sales and after-sales servicing thanks, in particular, to multi-brand dealerships and easier cross-border purchases of new vehicles. There is a one-year transition period to allow adaptation of existing contracts. At Parliament's request ([4]), a longer transition period until the end of September 2005 has been specifically allowed for the removal of location clauses. On 30 September, the Commission published an explanatory brochure on the new competition rules on motor car sales and servicing ([5]) designed to provide the general public with information on the new rights and obligations of vehicle manufacturers, dealers and repairers and the rights of consumers under the new rules.

209.   Insurance. Since Regulation (EEC) No 3932/92 exempting certain categories of agreements in the insurance sector ([6]) is due to expire on 31 March 2003, the Commission published a new draft regulation ([7]) on 9 July on which it invited interested parties to give their opinion. The draft innovates with regard to indicative risk premiums, standard insurance policy conditions, common coverage of certain categories of risk (pools) and security equipment.

210.   IATA (International Air Transport Association) passenger tariff conferences. On 25 June, following a wide-ranging consultation of interested parties, the Commission adopted a regulation renewing the block exemption for the IATA passenger tariff conferences until 30 June 2005 ([8]).

Individual cases

211.   FIFA. By decision of 15 April, the Commission formally rejected a complaint against the rules governing the activities of players' agents laid down by the International Football Federation (FIFA), thereby recognising that FIFA was

---

([1]) Regulation (EC) No 1400/2002 (OJ L 203, 1.8.2002; Bull. 7/8-2002, point 1.3.60).
([2]) Regulation (EC) No 1475/95 (OJ L 145, 29.6.1995; 1995 General Report, point 142).
([3]) 2000 General Report, point 193.
([4]) Bull. 5-2002, point 1.3.49.
([5]) http://europa.eu.int/comm/competition/car_sector/#020930.
([6]) OJ L 398, 31.12.1992; Twenty-sixth General Report, point 198.
([7]) OJ C 163, 9.7.2002; Bull. 5-2002, point 1.3.47.
([8]) Regulation (EC) No 1105/2002 (OJ L 167, 26.6.2002).

entitled to regulate the profession with a view to upholding ethical standards provided that access remained open and non-discriminatory. By decision of 30 May, it also rejected two complaints against the rules governing international transfers of football players laid down by FIFA, which had to do mainly with unilateral breaches of contract by players (¹).

212.   *UEFA.* On 25 June, the Commission formally rejected the complaint lodged in 2000 by ENIC against UEFA, the governing body of European football, concerning the rule whereby two or more clubs participating in a UEFA club competition may not be directly or indirectly controlled by the same entity or managed by the same person (²). The Commission concluded that, although the UEFA rule was a decision taken by an association of undertakings, it could be exempted from the ban in principle set out in Article 81(1) of the EC Treaty provided that it did not exceed what was necessary in order to achieve the legitimate objective of guaranteeing the integrity of competitions and that it was applied in a non-discriminatory manner.

213.   *Austrian Airlines/Lufthansa.* On 5 July, the Commission exempted a cooperation agreement between Austrian Airlines and Lufthansa (³) up to 31 December 2005, i.e. six years from the date of notification. The exemption was granted only after the parties had accepted major changes to the agreement: they are required among other things to allocate up to 40 % of the slots available to any new entrants and to apply the same fare reductions they offer on a route on which they face competition to three other routes between Austria and Germany on which there is no competition. The Commission established, on the basis of the obligations imposed, that several competitors were interested in entering the market.

214.   *Visa.* On 24 July, the Commission granted conditional exemption for certain multilateral interchange fees (MIF) for cross-border payments by Visa card (⁴). The exemption, valid until 31 December 2007, was granted only after major changes to the Visa system. The new MIF will be reduced in absolute terms, capped at the level of relevant costs and made transparent for retailers.

215.   *International Federation of the Phonographic Industry (IFPI).* By adopting an exemption decision subject to conditions and obligations on 8 October, the Commission authorised a 'one-stop shop' for issuing broadcasters with licences to broadcast music recordings on the Internet (⁵). This is the first Commission decision concerning the collective management and licensing of copyright for the purposes of commercial exploitation of musical works on the Inter-

---

(¹) Bull. 5-2002, point 1.3.50.
(²) Bull. 6-2002, point 1.3.56.
(³) Bull. 7/8-2002, point 1.3.61.
(⁴) Bull. 7/8-2002, point 1.3.62.
(⁵) Bull. 10-2002, point 1.3.37.

net. The Commission took the opportunity presented by the notification of an agreement in the field to set out a number of important principles which it will apply in future in order to take account of the global reach of the Internet.

216. *Transatlantic Conference (TACA)*. On 14 November, the Commission exempted the revised agreement of the TACA, a grouping of shipping companies which provide regular container transport for freight between ports in northern Europe and the United States [1]. The new agreement (the 'Revised TACA') brings the activities of the TACA into line with the main guidelines for conference behaviour laid down by the Commission in a previous decision adopted in 1998 [2]. The substantial increase in the extent and intensity of competition faced by the members of the conference was a crucial factor in the Commission's decision to grant exemption to the Revised TACA.

Prohibited restrictive agreements

217. *Austrian banks*. On 11 June, the Commission imposed fines totalling EUR 124.26 million on eight Austrian banks for their participation in a wide-ranging price cartel covering the entire territory of Austria [3]. In a highly institutionalised price-fixing scheme (the 'Lombard Club'), the CEOs of the banks met regularly with a view to fixing deposit, lending and other rates to the detriment of businesses and consumers.

218. *Methionine producers*. On 2 July, the Commission, finding that the agreement was a very serious infringement, imposed substantial fines totalling EUR 127.12 million on two producers of methionine, one of the main amino acids used in compound feeds for all animal species, for taking part in a cartel with the basic aim of fixing price targets on the market in methionine [4]. A third producer, to which the prohibition decision was also addressed, was granted full immunity from fines under the 1996 leniency notice *(→ point 206)*.

219. *GFU*. On 17 July, the Commission decided to close the GFU case relating to the joint sale of Norwegian natural gas [5] following the commitments offered by certain Norwegian gas producers — most prominently Statoil and Norsk Hydro. These two producers confirmed in particular that they would market their gas individually and undertook to offer 13 billion and 2.2 billion cubic metres respectively for sale to new customers over a period of approximately four years. These commitments will contribute to the creation of a single

---

[1] Bull. 11-2002, point 1.3.48.
[2] 1998 General Report, point 208.
[3] Bull. 6-2002, point 1.3.57.
[4] Bull. 7/8-2002, point 1.3.65.
[5] Bull. 7/8-2002, point 1.3.66.

gas market in Europe since European purchasers will have a wider choice from among the Norwegian suppliers.

220. *Dutch industrial gas cartel.* On 24 July, the Commission imposed fines totalling EUR 25.72 million on seven Dutch industrial and medical gas companies [1]. The companies concerned were involved in agreements or concerted practices with the aim of fixing price increases for industrial cylinder and bulk gases, agreeing on the implementation of these increases and fixing other trading conditions related to the delivery of the products.

221. *Nintendo.* On 30 October, the Commission imposed a fine totalling EUR 167.8 million on the Japanese video games maker Nintendo and seven of its official European distributors for colluding to prevent low-priced exports to high-priced countries [2]. The fine on Nintendo alone was calculated at EUR 149 million to reflect its size in the market concerned, the fact that it was the driving force behind the illicit behaviour and also because it continued with the infringement even after it had been informed that the investigation was going on. Although the leniency notice *(→ point 206)* does not apply to this kind of infringement, the decision stresses the importance that the Commission attaches to cooperation by companies which have infringed the Community competition rules, in that it takes account both of Nintendo's decision to offer significant financial compensation to third parties which suffered material harm and of the general cooperation afforded by the companies during the administrative procedure.

222. *Fine arts auction houses.* On 30 October, the Commission found against the world's two leading fine arts auction houses, Christie's and Sotheby's, for having fixed vendors' commissions and other trading terms between 1993 and early 2000 [3]. Christie's was exempted from a fine under the 1996 notice on the non-imposition or reduction of fines for companies which provide decisive information on the existence of a cartel *(→ point 206)*. Sotheby's, which was granted a 40 % reduction for its cooperation, was fined EUR 20.4 million. The case was investigated in close cooperation with the relevant US authorities, which looked at it from the point of view of its impact in the United States.

223. *Plasterboard.* On 27 November, the Commission imposed fines totalling EUR 478 million on Lafarge SA, BPB plc, Gebrüder Knauf Westdeutsche Gipswerke KG and Gyproc Benelux SA/NV [4]. These four firms were involved, between 1992 and 1998, in a secret agreement covering the four main EU markets (Benelux, France, Germany and the United Kingdom) in plasterboard, a product

[1] Bull. 7/8-2002, point 1.3.67.
[2] Bull. 10-2002, point 1.3.40.
[3] Bull. 10-2002, point 1.3.41.
[4] Bull. 11-2002, point 1.3.49.

widely used in the building industry. The market concerned is the largest in terms of value to have been covered by a Commission cartel decision in the last 10 years or so. In the case of Lafarge and BPB, the Commission viewed as an aggravating circumstance the fact that this was their second infringement of Article 81. Only BPB and Gyproc cooperated with the Commission.

224.   Methylglucamine. Also on 27 November, the Commission adopted a decision imposing a fine of EUR 2.85 million on two companies in the Aventis group, Aventis Pharma and Rhône-Poulenc Biochemie ([1]). The Commission considered the two firms to be jointly and severally liable. Merck KGaA, to which the decision was also addressed, received full immunity under the 1996 leniency notice *(→ point 206)*. The Commission found that between 1990 and 1999 these companies held annual meetings with a view to fixing prices and market shares for methylglucamine, a chemical substance used in X-ray analyses.

225.   Graphite. On 17 December, the Commission imposed fines totalling EUR 51.8 million on SGL Carbon, Carbone-Lorraine, Ibiden, Tokai Carbon, Toyo Tanso, NSCC Techno Carbon, Nippon Steel Chemical, Intech EDM BV and Intech EDM AG for taking part in a price-fixing cartel on the market in isostatic graphite products, a group of products used to make tools for the aerospace, electronics and other industries ([2]). SGL Carbon was also fined a further EUR 8.81 million for its involvement in another cartel on a parallel market. Graf Tech International (formerly UCAR), on the other hand, which was also involved in the two cartels, was granted full immunity under the 1996 leniency notice *(→ point 206)*.

226.   Reinforcing bars. Likewise, on 17 December, the Commission adopted a decision imposing fines totalling EUR 85 million on nine undertakings, corresponding to 11 firms (Alfa Acciai, Feralpi Siderurgica, Ferriere Nord, IRO Industrie Riunite Odolesi, Leali and Acciaierie e Ferriere Leali Luigi, Lucchini and Siderpotenza, Riva Acciaio, Valsabbia Investimenti and Ferriera Valsabbia) and one trade association (Federacciai) ([3]). They had taken part in a cartel to fix prices for 'size extras' and base prices, to fix payment times and to restrict or control production and/or sales on the market in reinforcing bars in Italy, in flagrant violation of Article 65(1) of the ECSC Treaty.

227.   Nucleotides. Also on 17 December, the Commission imposed fines totalling EUR 20.56 million on three nucleotide manufacturers, Ajinomoto (Japan), Daesang (South Korea) and Cheil Jedang (South Korea) for taking part in a cartel to set target prices and share out customers on the market in nucleotides (food flavour enhancers) ([4]). A fourth firm, Takeda Chemical Industries

---

([1]) Bull. 11-2002, point 1.3.50.
([2]) Bull. 12-2002, point 1.3.72.
([3]) Bull. 12-2002, point 1.3.74.
([4]) Bull. 12-2002, point 1.3.73.

(Japan), to which the decision was also addressed, was granted full immunity from fines under the 1996 leniency notice (→ *point 206*).

Dominant positions

228. Liberalisation of postal services. The gradual opening-up of the postal sector to competition was confirmed by the adoption of a Parliament and Council directive on 10 June (→ *point 170*).

229. Electronic communication networks and services. On 9 July, the Commission adopted guidelines on market analysis and the assessment of significant market power (SMP)([1]), as required by Directive 2002/21/EC on a new common regulatory framework for electronic communications services (→ *point 341*). As the directive gives a new definition of a company with SMP, based on the concept of 'dominant position' within the meaning of Article 82 of the EC Treaty, the guidelines set out the principles that national regulatory authorities will apply in defining the relevant markets and assessing the existence of a dominant position on those markets. On 16 September, the Commission adopted Directive 2002/77/EC ([2]) repealing Directive 90/388/EEC on competition in the markets for telecommunications services ([3]) and the five directives amending it. Under this new directive, which brings together in a single text the six earlier liberalisation directives, Member States may no longer grant or maintain in force exclusive or special rights for the establishment and/or operation of electronic communications networks, or for the provision of publicly available electronic communications services.

Mergers([4])

General approach ([5])

230. Legislative review. The Green Paper([6]) on the review of the merger regulation([7]), which the Commission adopted in December 2001, was the subject of a Parliament resolution([8]) adopted on 4 July and a European Economic and Social Committee opinion([9]) delivered on 17 July. On 11 December, the

---

([1]) OJ C 165, 11.7.2002; Bull. 7/8-2002, point 1.3.64.
([2]) OJ L 249, 17.9.2002; Bull. 9-2002, point 1.3.59.
([3]) OJ L 192, 24.7.1990; Twenty-fourth General Report, point 209.
([4]) http://europa.eu.int/comm/competition/mergers/legislation/simplified_procedure/.
([5]) Statistical data on merger control will be included in the Report on Competition Policy to be published in 2003.
([6]) COM(2001) 745; 2001 General Report, point 233.
([7]) OJ L 395, 30.12.1989; Twenty-third General Report, point 376; Regulation as last amended by Regulation (EC) No 1310/97 (OJ L 180, 9.7.1997; 1997 General Report, point 242).
([8]) Bull. 7/8-2002, point 1.3.40.
([9]) OJ C 241, 7.10.2002; Bull. 7/8-2002, point 1.3.40.

Commission proposed a recasting of Regulation (EC) No 4064/89 (Table II), which will be the most major reform of the Community merger control system since that regulation entered into force in 1990. The amendments proposed in the new regulation clarify its application in oligopoly situations, do away with the unnecessarily rigid rules on notifying mergers and simplify the rules for referring cases between the Commission and the national competition authorities. Provision is also made for introducing more flexibility into the time-frame for complex investigations in relation to assessing remedies and for strengthening the Commission's investigative powers. Also on 11 December, the Commission adopted a draft notice on the appraisal of mergers between competitors, for the information of firms and the legal community [1]. Internal organisational measures within the Commission are also planned to improve decision-making procedures in merger cases [2].

Individual cases

231.   SEB/Moulinex. On 8 January, the Commission adopted two decisions on SEB's acquisition of Moulinex [3]. Both companies are French manufacturers of small household electrical appliances. In the first decision, the Commission referred the matter of the impact of the acquisition on the French market to the French competition authorities; in the second one, it concluded that the part of the transaction not referred to the French authorities was compatible with the common market provided that the parties complied with the undertakings given and, in particular, that SEB granted third parties exclusive licences to use the Moulinex brand name for a period of five years in nine European countries. Third parties (Philips and Babylis) lodged an appeal against these decisions with the Court of First Instance.

232.   Tetra Laval/Sidel and Schneider Electric/Legrand. On 30 January, following the decisions it adopted in 2001 prohibiting these mergers [4], which had gone ahead, the Commission took two decisions requiring the companies to demerge. The first decision set out measures for the divestiture of the stake held by the Swiss-based Tetra Laval in the French company Sidel, while allowing Tetra flexibility in choosing an appropriate buyer or buyers and a suitable method of divestiture within a fixed time limit; the second one laid down the arrangements for demerging Schneider Electric and Legrand, two French electrical equipment manufacturers, while leaving Schneider free to choose the legal form that the demerger would take although requiring it to divest all its shares in Legrand in a single transaction and to reduce its stake in Legrand to less than 5 %. In both cases, the companies concerned appealed to the Court of First

[1] SEC(2002) 1337; Bull. 12-2002, point 1.3.56.
[2] http://europa.eu.int/comm/competition/index_en.html.
[3] Bull. 1/2-2002, point 1.3.74.
[4] 2001 General Report, points 265 and 267.

Instance against both the initial prohibition decisions and the decisions requiring the demergers. Using the accelerated procedure for the first time, the Court annulled all the decisions by judgments of 22 and 25 October (→ point 1068).

233. *Hidroeléctrica del Cantábrico.* On 19 March, the Commission authorised the acquisition of joint control of Spain's fourth-largest utility company Hidroeléctrica del Cantábrico by Energie Baden-Württemberg (EnBW), Electricidade de Portugal SA (EDP) and Caja de Ahorros de Asturias (Cajastur), subject to compliance with certain undertakings given by the parties (¹). As in the recent bid for the Spanish company by EnBW and Grupo Villar Mir, the transaction would have led to the strengthening of the existing collective dominant position on the Spanish wholesale market for electricity. To allay these competition concerns, Électricité de France (EDF), which jointly controls EnBW, and EDF–RTE, the operator of the French electricity grid, undertook to increase to around 4 000 MW the commercial capacity of the interconnector between France and Spain.

234. *Bayer/Aventis.* On 17 April, the Commission decided to clear Bayer's acquisition of Aventis Crop Science, subject to compliance with the undertakings by the parties (²). As initially notified, the transaction would have led to the creation or strengthening of dominant positions on some 130 markets for crop protection, professional pest control and animal health products. But Bayer offered a comprehensive set of commitments, including the sale, in one single package, of Aventis Crop Science's entire European seed treatment business, which included the best-selling insecticide.

235. *Sulzer/Promatech.* On 24 July, the Commission authorised the acquisition of Sulzer Textil, the textile machinery division of the Swiss company Sulzer Ltd, by the Italian company Promatech SpA, another maker of weaving machinery, subject to compliance with the undertakings given by the parties (³). The Commission's in-depth investigation having shown that the deal could lead to the creation of a dominant position on the west European market for rapier weaving machines, Promatech offered to divest some of Sulzer Textil's operations in Italy and Switzerland.

(¹) Bull. 3-2002, point 1.3.51.
(²) Bull. 4-2002, point 1.3.36.
(³) Bull. 7/8-2002, point 1.3.50.

State aid

General policy (¹)

236.   *Reduction and redirection of State aid.* On 16 October, the Commission presented a progress report concerning reduction and reorientation of State aid (²). This initiative responds to the calls made by the European Council at Stockholm (³) and Barcelona (⁴) for the overall level of State aid as a percentage of GDP to be reduced and for such aid to be redirected towards horizontal objectives of common interest.

237.   *Reactions to Commission reports.* In a resolution (⁵) adopted on 6 February, Parliament commented on the Commission's ninth survey on State aid in the European Union (⁶).

238.   *State aid scoreboard.* On 22 May (⁷) and 27 November (⁸), the Commission published updated versions of the scoreboard, which is intended to increase transparency in the monitoring of State aid. In a resolution (⁹) adopted on 21 November on the spring update, Parliament stressed its interest in the scoreboard, while calling for additional information that would allow it to carry out more effective comparative analysis of the impact of such aid.

Horizontal aid and sectoral and regional schemes

239.   *Multisectoral framework.* On 13 February, the Commission approved the recasting of the rules applicable to regional aid for large investment projects, including in the motor vehicle and synthetic fibres sectors (¹⁰). The new framework will make for greater transparency and reduce the overall level of aid granted in the European Union; it also includes the restrictions on State aid to the steel industry which continue to apply after expiry of the ECSC Treaty in July *(→ point 39).*

(¹) For general statistical data and a discussion of the most significant individual cases, see the *XXXIInd Report on Competition Policy*, which will be published in the course of 2003.
(²) COM(2002) 555; Bull. 10-2002, point 1.3.43.
(³) Bull. 3-2001, point I.12.
(⁴) Bull. 3-2002, point I.58.
(⁵) OJ C 284 E, 21.11.2002; Bull. 1/2-2002, point 1.3.89.
(⁶) COM(2001) 403; 2001 General Report, point 269.
(⁷) Bull. 5-2002, point 1.3.53; Internet http://europa.eu.int/comm/competition/state_aid/scoreboard/index_en.html.
(⁸) COM(2002) 638; Bull. 11/2002, point 1.3.54.
(⁹) Bull. 11-2002, point 1.3.52.
(¹⁰) Bull. 1/2-2002, point 1.3.90.

240. *Steel and coal industry.* On 18 March, the Commission presented its report ([1]) on the implementation in 2001 of the steel aid code ([2]). On 27 May, it adopted its 17th report on the monitoring of Article 95 ECSC steel aid cases ([3]).

On 10 April, the Commission adopted a report on the application of the Community rules for State aid to the coal industry ([4]), which focused on the results of restructuring, rationalisation and modernisation in the five Member States that still produce coal. Pointing out that enlargement will bring in two large producers, the Commission stressed the need to keep up these efforts. On 23 July, the Council adopted Regulation (EC) No 1407/2002 on State aid for modernising and restructuring the coal industry (Table II). The aim of the regulation is to ensure that some coal-producing capabilities are maintained, in particular following the expiry of the ECSC Treaty *(→ point 40)*. On 17 October, the Commission established a joint framework for communication of the information necessary for the application of the regulation ([5]).

241. *Agriculture and fisheries.* On 27 November, the Commission adopted guidelines clarifying the conditions in which State aid may be granted for tests for transmissible spongiform encephalopathies (TSE), fallen stock and slaughterhouse waste ([6]).

242. *Shipbuilding.* On 27 June, the Council adopted a regulation on a temporary defensive mechanism for the Community industry *(→ point 805)*.

243. *Employment.* On 12 December, the Commission adopted Regulation (EC) No 2204/2002 on the application of Articles 87 and 88 of the EC Treaty to State aid for employment ([7]). The regulation exempts from the notification obligation certain types of aid aimed for example at the reintegration of disadvantaged or disabled workers into the labour market. As part of the consultation process ([8]) prior to its adoption, the European Economic and Social Committee delivered an opinion ([9]) on 18 July and Parliament adopted a resolution ([10]) on 4 September.

([1]) COM(2002) 145; Bull. 3-2002, point 1.3.54.
([2]) Decision No 2496/96/ECSC (OJ L 338, 28.12.1996; 1996 General Report, point 178).
([3]) COM(2002) 248; Bull. 5-2002, point 1.3.54.
([4]) COM(2002) 176; Bull. 4-2002, point 1.4.58.
([5]) Decision 2002/871/EC (OJ L 300, 5.11.2002; Bull. 10-2002, point 1.3.42).
([6]) OJ C 324, 24.12.2002. For a discussion of the most significant individual cases concerning State aid to agriculture and fisheries, see the *XXXIInd Report on Competition Policy*, to be published in 2003.
([7]) OJ L 337, 13.12.2002; Bull. 12-2002, point 1.3.75; corrigendum: OJ L 349, 31.12.2002.
([8]) OJ C 88, 12.4.2002.
([9]) OJ C 241, 7.10.2002; Bull. 7/8-2002, point 1.3.68.
([10]) Bull. 9-2002, point 1.3.60.

244.   R & D. On 24 April, the Commission decided([1]) to extend unchanged until the end of 2005 the existing Community framework for State aid for research and development ([2]).

245.   Services of general interest. On 5 June, as part of the follow-up to its October 2001 report to the Laeken European Council on services of general interest ([3]), the Commission adopted a report ([4]) on the status of work on the guidelines for State aid linked to services of this type. It supplemented this document by a further report adopted on 27 November ([5]).

International cooperation

246.   Japan. On 8 May, the Commission proposed to establish a negotiated framework for cooperation with the Japanese competition authority (Table III) with a view to enabling the antitrust rules to be applied more effectively and reducing the number of cases in which the EU and Japanese competition authorities are liable to take conflicting or incompatible decisions.

247.   United States and Canada. On 29 January, the Commission presented a report on implementation of the agreements on the application of competition rules with both countries in 2000 ([6]) and, on 17 September, a report on 2001 ([7]). It noted that the agreements continued to provide a framework for constructive cooperation between the parties which benefited both the competition authorities and the companies involved in cases which they helped effectively to resolve. On 30 October, the Commission and the US authorities published a set of best practices concerning bilateral cooperation in merger cases with a view to minimising the risk of divergent outcomes on either side of the Atlantic and reducing induced costs for the parties.

248.   Enlargement. Under the pre-accession strategy, the Commission and the Lithuanian Competition Council jointly organised the eighth annual competition conference between the Commission and the competition authorities of the candidate countries in Vilnius on 18 and 19 June ([8]).

([1]) Bull. 4-2002, point 1.3.46.
([2]) OJ C 45, 17.2.1996; 1995 General Report, point 163.
([3]) COM(2001) 598; 2001 General Report, point 164.
([4]) COM(2002) 280; Bull. 6-2002, point 1.3.58.
([5]) COM(2002) 636; Bull. 11-2002, point 1.3.55.
([6]) COM(2002) 45; Bull. 1/2-2002, point 1.3.118.
([7]) COM(2002) 505; Bull. 9-2002, point 1.3.66.
([8]) Previous conference: 2001 General Report, point 280.

249. Promoting international cooperation. The Commission continues to act as one of the driving forces behind the international competition network (ICN), which since its inception in 2001 ([1]) has been joined by more than 70 competition authorities from all five continents. The first tangible results of ICN projects were presented at its inaugural conference, held in Naples from 27 to 29 September. The Commission also played an active part in the International Cartel Workshop which took place in Rio (Brazil) in September.

([1]) 2001 General Report, point 282.

Section 7

Enterprise policy (¹)

Overview

250. Developments in enterprise policy must be seen in the context of the objective laid down in Lisbon in 2000 of making the economy of the European Union the world's most competitive economy by 2010. Thus, the Barcelona European Council(²) called for a more favourable environment for entrepreneurship and competitiveness. It called on Member States to speed up the implementation of the European Charter for Small Enterprises and to learn from best practice. It also called on them to resolutely pursue their efforts to simplify and improve the regulatory environment. A debate was also opened at ministerial level on how to achieve the objective of realising Europe's full growth potential and relaunch the Lisbon process. In addition, the Commission's communication on industrial policy, adopted in December, was expected to provide a fresh impetus; this puts the emphasis on the challenges in this field arising from the enlargement of the EU, globalisation, the growth of the single market and the vital role of industrial competitiveness.

Competitiveness and enterprise policy (³)

General

251.   *Global approach.* In a resolution adopted on 13 June (⁴), the European Parliament gave its assessment of the Commission communication of November 2001 entitled 'Sustaining the commitments, increasing the pace' (⁵) and in particular reaffirmed its support for the objectives defined at the Lisbon European Council (⁶). In addition, on 25 April, the European Economic and Social Committee adopted an opinion on the impact of tax competition on companies' competitiveness *(→ point 176).*

(¹) Further information is available on the Europa server (http://europa.eu.int/comm/enterprise/index_en.htm).
(²) Bull. 3-2002, point I.13.
(³) http://europa.eu.int/comm/enterprise/enterprise_policy/index.htm.
(⁴) Bull. 6-2002, point 1.3.76.
(⁵) COM(2001) 641; 2001General Report, point 284.
(⁶) Bull. 3-2000, point I.8; 2000 General Report, point 247.

In a communication dated 21 May entitled 'Productivity: the key to competitiveness of European economies and enterprises' (¹), the Commission examined the growth in labour productivity in the EU in recent years. It pointed to the need for greater political resolve in this field if the objectives of the Lisbon strategy were to be met (²). The 2002 report on European competitiveness (³), adopted simultaneously, examined issues such as the role of human capital in economic growth, productivity in services, sustainable development in manufacturing industry and the links between industrial policy and competition policy. In turn, at its meeting of 6 and 7 June (⁴), the Council adopted conclusions which focused on the need to strengthen in particular the main factors influencing productivity, such as innovation, research and development, new technologies and investment in and dissemination of information and communications technologies. In an opinion dated 12 December (⁵), the European Economic and Social Committee called for a rapid improvement in competitiveness.

On 7 November, the Commission adopted a communication entitled 'A better environment for enterprises' (⁶) which proposes the voluntary adoption, applying the open coordination method, of national quantitative objectives in a number of important areas of enterprise policy. At its meeting on 26 November (⁷), the Council expressed its support for the continuation of this approach and invited the Member States and the Commission to discuss national enterprise policies with a view to learning from each other.

252.   *Industrial policy.* In a communication dated 11 December on industrial policy in an enlarged Europe (⁸), the Commission reassessed the approach it had set out for this policy in 1990 (⁹). Confirming that the horizontal approach drawn up at the time was sound, it discussed how to respond to new challenges such as globalisation or society's new demands while preserving and improving competitiveness.

External aspects of enterprise policy

253.   *Euro-Mediterranean partnership.* At the fourth Euro-Mediterranean conference of industry ministers held in Malaga in April (→ *point 881*), in connection with the establishment of a free-trade area by 2010, the participants stressed the need to harmonise the Mediterranean partners' technical rules,

---

(¹) COM(2002) 262; Bull. 5-2002, point 1.3.65.
(²) Bull. 3-2000, points I.5 and I.8; 2000 General Report, point 247.
(³) SEC(2002) 528; Internet http://europa.eu.int/comm/enterprise_policy/competitiveness/index.htm#doc.
(⁴) Bull. 6-2002, point 1.3.78.
(⁵) Bull. 12-2002, point 1.3.82.
(⁶) COM(2002) 610; Bull. 11-2002, point 1.3.63.
(⁷) Bull. 11-2002, point 1.3.62.
(⁸) COM(2002) 714; Bull. 12-2002, point 1.3.83.
(⁹) COM(1990) 556; Twenty-fourth General Report, point 212.

standards and conformity assessment procedures with the European Union approach and to make these countries familiar with the European approach to enterprise policy.

254.   Eastern Europe. As regards Russia, the fourth round table of industrialists was held in Turin, while efforts continued to promote regulatory convergence with the European Union, in particular in connection with Russia's joining the World Trade Organisation and initial work on the concept of a common economic area. Parallel efforts were made with Ukraine.

Operation of the internal market, regulatory policy, standardisation, impact assessment

255.   Operation of the internal market. In accordance with Directive 98/34/EC laying down a procedure for the provision of information in the field of technical standards and regulations and the rules governing information society services ([1]), in 2002 the Commission received 508 notifications of draft technical regulations, including 478 on the rules governing products and 30 on the rules governing information society services. The number of notifications received in connection with this instrument for the preventive monitoring of trade barriers thus went from 530 in 2001 to 508 in 2002, primarily as a result of a decrease in notifications in the construction sector. In 47 cases ([2]), the Commission sent detailed opinions regarding the infringements of Community law to which the draft regulations might give rise. The Member States did likewise in 76 cases ([2]). These detailed opinions show that the sector causing most problems is the agriculture and food products sector. The number of notifications under the procedure for the provision of information in the field of technical regulations provided for by the Agreement on the European Economic Area (EEA) went from 22 in 2001 to 49 in 2002. For its part, the Commission, on behalf of the Community, sent a total of 10 observations to the EFTA countries that are signatories to the EEA Agreement.

Other information on the operation of the internal market is dealt with in Section 5 ('Internal market') of this chapter *(→ point 152).*

256.   Regulatory policy. A certain amount of information on this topic is dealt with in Section 6 ('Simplifying and improving the regulatory environment') of Chapter I *(→ points 25 and 26)* and in Section 5 ('Internal market') of this chapter *(→ points 145 to 150).* In particular, the assessment of the regulatory burden of achieving conformity with European regulations continues to be very

---

([1]) 1998 General Report, point 158; Internet http://europa.eu.int/comm/enterprise/tris/index_en.htm.
([2]) Figure on 1 January 2003. The deadline for delivering detailed opinions in response to drafts notified in 2002 is 31 March 2003.

important in ensuring conditions favourable to entrepreneurship, competitiveness and sustainable economic development. In this connection, the conclusions and recommendations of a pilot study on the practices of the Commission and of the Member States with regard to business impact assessments have been published (¹) and have served to give substance to the approach developed by the Commission in this field in its June communications on simplifying and improving the regulatory environment *(→ point 25)*.

257.   *Standardisation.* In conclusions adopted on 1 March (²), the Council noted the progress made by the European standardisation bodies and urged them to continue to diversify their product range, while calling on the national bodies to support them. It also pointed to the progress made by the candidate countries and their national standards bodies in becoming fully-fledged members of the European standardisation system. In addition, the Council advocated progress on questions related to standardisation, such as the capacity to respond to market needs, the role of public authorities, greater efficiency and financial viability.

Multiannual programme for enterprise and entrepreneurship (2001–05) (³)

258.   In accordance with Council Decision 2000/819/EC (⁴), the activities pursued in 2002 under the multiannual programme fall under three headings: the financial instruments managed by the European Investment Fund (EIF), the support services provided to enterprises at European level through the network of Euro Info Centres and the development of policies, including the BEST procedure launched in response to the Lisbon European Council's call for the creation of an open method of coordination (⁵). This last heading covers a limited number of BEST projects reflecting policy priorities agreed with the Member States, together with certain studies and exercises to collect data and disseminate information on enterprise policy. The Commission, in close cooperation with the national governments and other interested players, has launched new BEST projects on the following themes: technology transfer institutions; restructuring, bankruptcy and a fresh start; environmental management systems in SMEs. The results of these projects were communicated to the Council as a contribution to the discussions on enterprise policy*(→ point 251)*. In connection with the activities to promote entrepreneurship, there were very broad consul-

---

(¹) http://europa.eu.int/comm/enterprise/library/enterprise-papers/paper9.htm.
(²) OJ C 66, 15.3.2002; Bull. 3-2002, point 1.3.64.
(³) http://europa.eu.int/comm/enterprise/enterprise_policy/mult_entr_programme/programme_2001_2005.htm.
(⁴) Decision 2000/819/EC of 20 December 2000 (OJ L 333, 29.12.2000).
(⁵) Bull. 3-2000, point I.8.

tations as part of the work to revise the existing definition of SMEs applicable in Community law (¹).

European Charter for Small Enterprises (²)

259.   On 6 February (³), the Commission presented its second annual report on implementation of the charter. It highlighted the progress made in this respect, particularly in fields such as registration procedures and improvements to legislation, and stressed that there is a need to boost the representation of the interests of small businesses and to step up the promotion of the spirit of enterprise in the education system. The report was at the centre of discussions at the conference of ministers responsible for SMEs, held in Aranjuez (Spain) on 23 February, and was presented to the Barcelona European Council of 15 and 16 March, which called on the Member States to speed up the process of implementing the charter (⁴), and the Commission published the relevant national reports (⁵). In Slovenia on 23 April, the candidate countries signed the 'Maribor declaration', in which they accept the charter's recommendations.

Business services

260.   *Studies.* A study was published entitled 'Business services in European industry: growth, employment and competitiveness', which analyses the current situation in that sector and provides statistics (⁶). The Commission also published the results of its work on publicly funded and/or initiated support services for small businesses (⁷). The survey, conducted among 1 200 small businesses, reveals a certain imbalance between the needs expressed by businesses and the existing range of services. The questions discussed in the study include the quality of services, the training of small-business consultants and the evaluation of these services.

Industry and sustainable development

261.   *Enterprise policy.* In conclusions adopted at its meeting on 6 and 7 June (⁸), the Council stressed the essential role of enterprise policy in guaran-

---

(¹) Commission Recommendation 96/280/EC (OJ L 107, 30.4.1996); 1996 General Report, point 216.
(²) 2000 General Report, point 258; Internet http://europa.eu.int/comm/enterprise/enterprise_policy/charter/index.htm.
(³) COM(2002) 68; Bull. 1/2-2002, point 1.3.120. Previous report: COM(2001) 122; 2001 General Report, point 305.
(⁴) Bull. 3-2002, point I.13.
(⁵) http://europa.eu.int/comm/enterprise/enterprise_policy/charter/charter2002.htm#national.
(⁶) http://europa.eu.int/comm/enterprise/services/business_services/index.htm.
(⁷) http://europa.eu.int/comm/enterprise/entrepreneurship/craft/craft-studies/craft-supportserv.htm.
(⁸) Bull. 6-2002, point 1.3.77.

teeing the integration of sustainable development and ensuring a balance between its economic, social and environmental dimensions. It invited the Member States and the Commission to pursue their work in the area, in particular in fields such as the sustainable use of natural resources and waste management, chemical products, innovation, standardisation, indicators, voluntary action and general policy initiatives.

Research, innovation and change (¹)

262.   *Innovation scoreboard*. On 9 December, in line with the conclusions of the Lisbon European Council (²), the Commission presented the 2002 edition of this scoreboard, which analyses performance in terms of innovation in the Member States, the associated countries and the candidate countries (³).

Innovation projects

263.   As regards the fifth framework programme, the third call for proposals for innovation projects closed on 15 March. Of the 158 proposals submitted, 31 were selected for Community assistance totalling EUR 28.5 million. These projects were negotiated and launched in the course of the year. Under the fourth framework programme, 18 technology validation and transfer projects were completed in 2002. Extraction and analysis of the lessons to be learnt and of good practice have been completed and the results disseminated, in particular through the CORDIS service *(→ point 267)*.

Innovation networks

264.   *Innovation relay centres (IRCs)*. This network is an important infrastructure intended to facilitate the transnational transfer of technologies in Europe. During the year, the 68 IRCs forming the network completed their first phase of activity under the fifth framework programme. Their contracts were extended for a further two years, thus ensuring the continuity of the service until 31 March 2004. In addition, operating agreements for closer collaboration between this network and Eureka and with the European Space Agency (ESA) were signed and put in place.

(¹) http://www.cordis.lu/innovation-smes/home.html.
(²) 2000 General Report, point 247.
(³) SEC(2002) 1349; Internet http://trendchart.cordis.lu/. Previous scoreboard: 2001 General Report, point 292.

265. *Innovating regions in Europe* ([1]). The network links more than 100 regions (including central and eastern Europe) and is intended to encourage and help local public authorities to devise regional strategies for innovation and to exchange their good practice. Thirty new projects were launched in the Member States and the candidate countries. The network held its third conference in Stratford (United Kingdom) in June.

266. *Intellectual property rights (IPR) help desk.* This new help desk, intended to provide general information on the importance of protecting intellectual property rights, commenced its activities on 1 January for a period of three years (2002–04).

Dissemination of information

267. *CORDIS service* ([2]), *publications and conferences.* A new CORDIS service, aimed at the participants or potential beneficiaries of the sixth framework research programme (2002–06) (→ *point 301)*, was launched in September, while the multilingual 'Technology market' site, which provides summaries of the latest research results ready for exploitation by interested third parties, was relaunched. Other new services were also set up under CORDIS: 'CORDIS Wire' (free dissemination of information on research and innovation) and 'CORDIS Express' (an electronic weekly bulletin on current European research and innovation). In addition, the invitation to tender for providing the CORDIS service (2003-07) was published in November ([3]). Lastly, more than 40 publications appeared, and several conferences were held on innovation policy, innovating regions and the sixth framework programme.

Promoting entrepreneurship ([4])

Support measures for entrepreneurship and businesses

268. *European company statute.* In an own-initiative opinion of 21 March ([5]), the European Economic and Social Committee considered that an analysis of requirements confirmed the need for a European company project for small and medium-sized businesses, alongside the European company

---

([1]) http://www.innovating-regions.org.
([2]) http://www.cordis.lu/en/home.html.
([3]) OJ S 225, 20.11.2002.
([4]) http://europa.eu.int/comm/enterprise/entrepreneurship/index.htm.
([5]) OJ C 125, 27.5.2002; Bull. 3-2002, point 1.3.65.

statute (¹). The Council also approved general guidelines in that respect for cooperatives (→ point 272).

Support for access to financing

269. *Implementation of the financial instruments.* On 1 July (²), in application of Council Decision 98/347/EC on measures of financial assistance for innovative and job-creating small and medium-sized enterprises (³), the Commission presented its annual report on the progress achieved under this heading by 31 December 2001 with regard to the start-up facility, the Joint European Venture and the SME guarantee mechanism. In addition to an analysis of each instrument, it evoked their further development under the multiannual programme for enterprise and entrepreneurship 2001–05 (⁴). The European Parliament gave its opinion on this report in a resolution of 10 October (⁵).

Business support networks

270. *Euro Info Centres* (⁶). During the year, the foundations were laid for all Commission policies and programmes to benefit from the added value of the Euro Info Centres. The first step was to put their feedback function under the interactive policy-making initiative on a systematic basis (→ point 25). To this end, the Euro Info Centres were given a privileged position for listening to small and medium-sized enterprises. This liaison function should allow them also to play a role in the impact assessment sphere (→ points 25 and 256). In addition, the process of rationalising the business support networks continued throughout the year through consultations between all the departments responsible for these networks. Those consultations led to the definition of a methodology for action based on bringing the networks closer together rather than merging them. The annual conference held in Oulu (Finland) was also an opportunity to establish closer ties between the different networks.

(¹) Council Regulation (EC) No 2157/2001 (OJ L 294, 10.11.2001; 2001 General Report, point 219).
(²) COM(2002) 345; Bull. 7/8-2002, point 1.3.81.
(³) OJ L 155, 29.5.1998; 1998 General Report, point 262.
(⁴) 2000 General Report, point 261; Internet http://europa.eu.int/comm/enterprise/enterprise_policy/best-directory/index.htm.
(⁵) Bull. 10-2002, point 1.3.54.
(⁶) http://europa.eu.int/comm/enterprise/networks/eic/eic.html.

Improving the business environment and promotion of the interests of SMEs in Community policies and programmes

271.   *Island regions.* In an own-initiative opinion of 25 April ([1]), the European Economic and Social Committee pleaded in favour of establishing an integrated policy comprising specific positive measures in favour of businesses in the islands and the outermost island regions *(→ points 379 to 382)*.

Craft industries, small businesses, cooperatives and mutual societies

272.   *Cooperatives.* On 3 June, the Council approved general guidelines for a regulation and a directive on the European cooperative society ([2]). It recommends that the text of the regulation should essentially be based on that of the regulation on the European company ([3]), while taking account of the specific characteristics of cooperatives, in order to make available to cooperatives appropriate legal instruments to facilitate their cross-border and transnational activities, as the statute for a European company will do for public limited companies. Similarly, the rules in the directive on the involvement of employees would essentially copy those in the corresponding directive for the European company ([4]).

Industries and services

Basic industries: chemicals, steel, wood

273.   *Chemical substances.* On 25 June and 19 July, the European Parliament and the Council again amended Directive 76/769/EEC relating to restrictions on the marketing and use of certain dangerous substances and preparations in respect of short-chain chlorinated paraffins (Table I) and azo dyes (Table I), and in December they approved another amendment with regard to penta- and octa-bromodiphenyl ether (Table I). On 12 February, the Commission proposed a further amendment of this directive for substances classified as carcinogenic, mutagenic or toxic for reproduction (c/m/r) (Table I). On 16 August, it took a similar step for nonylphenol, nonylphenol ethoxylate and cement (Table I). In the field of precursors, on 10 September, the Commission proposed replacing Directive 92/109/EEC by a new regulation to improve the monitoring and supervision of trade in these products and at the same time simplify the

---

([1]) OJ C 149, 21.6.2002; Bull. 4-2002, point 1.3.75.
([2]) Bull. 6-2002, point 1.9.2.
([3]) Council Regulation (EC) No 2157/2001 (OJ L 294, 10.11.2001; 2001 General Report, point 219).
([4]) Directive 2001/86/EC (OJ L 294, 10.11.2001; 2001 General Report, point 140).

legislation and make it more user-friendly (Table I). On 9 July, it adopted Directive 2002/62/EC, which introduces a ban on the marketing of organostannic compounds used as biocides on ships ([1]), as these substances are known to be harmful to aquatic life with possible implications for the human food chain. On 12 July, it proposed the adoption of a regulation of the European Parliament and of the Council to prohibit the use of these products on any ship entering Community waters (→ *point 651*). On 4 September, it proposed replacing five directives on detergents by a new regulation to modernise and simplify the legislation while making it more user-friendly (Table I). On 26 September, the Commission proposed a legislative consolidation of the two directives on the inspection and verification of good laboratory practice (GLP) (Table I) and the approximation of laws, regulations and administrative provisions relating to the application of GLP (Table I).

274. *Steel industry.* On 14 January, the Commission adopted its draft forward programme for steel for 2002 ([2]). While noting difficulties related to the economic cycle, it underlined more generally the positive aspects of 50 years of implementing the ECSC Treaty (→ *point 39*), which have enabled the Community steel industry to attain an excellent level of competitiveness.

275. *Forest-based and related industries.* In November, a new Internet site ([3]) on forest-based industries was created in order to raise the profile and improve the dissemination of information on the Commission's activities which have an impact on this sector. In addition, the results of a quality study on the public image of forest-based industries were published in December ([4]).

276. *Rubber.* On 22 July, the Council adopted Decision 2002/651/EC allowing the Community to join the International Rubber Study Group (IRSG) ([5]).

Capital goods: mechanical engineering, construction, aerospace

277. *Electromagnetic compatibility.* On 23 December, the Commission proposed a revision of Directive 89/336/EEC on the approximation of the laws of the Member States relating to electromagnetic compatibility (Table I), for the purpose of improving legal security by laying down a clearer and more precise text.

([1]) OJ L 183, 12.7.2002.
([2]) SEC(2002) 12; Bull. 1/2-2002, point 1.3.122.
([3]) http://europa.eu.int/comm/enterprise/forest_based/.
([4]) *Perception of wood-based industries: Qualitative study on the image of the wood-based industries among the public in the Member States of the European Union* (available from the Office for Official Publications of the European Communities).
([5]) OJ L 215, 10.8.2002; Bull. 7/8-2002, point 1.6.84.

278.   *Construction.* With regard to the competitiveness of this industry (¹), two new working groups were set up by the Commission to develop the subject of 'e-building' and to analyse the lifelong costs of the built environment in the context of sustainable construction. In this area the Council, in its conclusions of 6 and 7 June on the contribution of enterprise policy to sustainable development (→ *point 261)*, welcomed the work done with regard to construction and invited the Member States and the Commission to continue the work with their own experts and those from the construction industry.

Consumer goods: pharmaceuticals, cosmetics, textiles, motor vehicles

279.   *Pharmaceutical products.* On 17 January, the Commission proposed amending Directive 2001/83/EC on the Community code relating to medicinal products for human use by adding a specific procedure for the registration of traditional plant-based products (Table I).

280.   *Cosmetic products.* On 15 April, the Commission adopted a 26th directive (²) adapting to technical progress Annexes II, III and VII to Council Directive 76/768/EEC on the approximation of the laws of the Member States relating to cosmetic products (³). On 6 November, the Conciliation Committee between the European Parliament and the Council adopted a compromise on the seventh amendment to Directive 76/768/EEC (Table I).

281.   *Motor vehicles.* In a resolution of 13 June (⁴) on the Commission communication of July 2001 'Pedestrian protection: commitment by the European automobile industry' (⁵), the European Parliament asked the Commission to come forward with a framework directive incorporating a clear timetable in this field and to devise means of enabling the Member States to play an appropriate part in its implementation. Further information relating to motor vehicles and their equipment can be found in Section 6 ('Transport') of Chapter IV (→ *point 642)*.

Other industries

282.   *Biotechnology.* Information on biotechnology, particularly on the Commission's important communication 'Life sciences and biotechnology —

(¹) COM(97) 539; 1997 General Report, point 295; Internet http://europa.eu.int/comm/enterprise/ construction/index.htm.
(²) Directive 2002/34/EC (OJ L 102, 18.4.2002).
(³) OJ L 262, 27.9.1976; Tenth General Report, point 124.
(⁴) Bull. 6-2002, point 1.3.80.
(⁵) COM(2001) 389; 2001 General Report, points 176 and 313.

A strategy for Europe', can be found in Section 8 ('Research and technology') of this chapter *(→ point 290)*.

E-business

283. *Small and medium-sized enterprises (SMEs).* On 16 January[1], the European Economic and Social Committee gave its opinion on the communication entitled 'Helping SMEs to go digital (*eEurope Go Digital*)' that the Commission presented in March 2001[2].

284. *Impact on businesses.* In conclusions adopted at its meeting on 6 and 7 June[3], the Council stressed the important implications of e-business for businesses' competitiveness. It considered that the rapid development and efficient use of information and communications technologies was an important part of the strategic goal set by the Lisbon Summit for the European Union to become the world's most dynamic and competitive knowledge-based economy[4]. In this context it called on the Member States and the Commission to identify specific objectives, to share best practice and to incorporate the e-business dimension into all policies and legislation relevant to competitiveness. At its meeting on 5 and 6 December[5], the Council stressed the need to support efforts to bridge the skills gap with regard to information and communications technology and e-business in Europe.

Electronic interchange of data between administrations (IDA)[6]

285. On 21 October, the European Parliament and the Council adopted Decisions No 2046/2002/EC and No 2045/2002/EC, amending Decisions No 1719/1999/EC and No 1720/1999/EC respectively, on guidelines and measures for trans-European networks for the electronic interchange of data between administrations (Table I). These amendments take account of the evaluation of IDA II carried out by the Commission in September 2001[7], the experience gained in the first few years of this operation, the context determined by the *eEurope initiative (→ points 331 to 337)* and the enlargement of the European Union, and the recommendations of the ministerial conference of November 2001 on 'e-government' and of the conference held in Sandhamn (Sweden) in June 2001 on pan-European services in this field. The new arrangements also

---

[1] OJ C 80, 3.4.2002; Bull. 1/2-2002, point 1.3.119.
[2] COM(2001) 136; 2001 General Report, point 316; Internet http://europa.eu.int/comm/enterprise/ict/ policy/godigital.htm.
[3] Bull. 6-2002, point 1.3.81.
[4] Bull. 3-2000, point I.13; 2000 General Report, point 247.
[5] Bull. 12-2002, point 1.3.84.
[6] http://europa.eu.int/comm/enterprise/ida/index.htm.
[7] COM(2001) 507; 2001 General Report, point 423.

relate to IDA's contribution to defining and promoting a framework for inter-operability between European administrations and the possibility of including non-member countries in the process of data interchange.

Tourism, commerce

286. Tourism. The communication on 'Working together for the future of European tourism' that the Commission presented in November 2001 ([1]) was welcomed in principle by the European Parliament, which put forward at the same time a series of supplementary proposals ([2]). Similarly, the future of European tourism was the subject of a Council resolution of 21 May ([3]) which also supported the Commission's approach and in turn called on it to take a number of initiatives. The European Economic and Social Committee and the Committee of the Regions likewise welcomed the Commission's communication, in opinions dated 18 September ([4]) and 10 October ([5]) respectively. In addition, the introduction of special tax arrangements for travel agencies was the subject of a proposal for a directive *(→ point 180)*.

287. Commerce ([6]). The Commission published a report on an economic analysis of the distribution sector in Europe.

([1]) COM(2001) 665; 2001 General Report, point 315.
([2]) Bull. 5-2002, point 1.3.67.
([3]) OJ C 135, 6.6.2002; Bull. 5-2002, point 1.3.68.
([4]) Bull. 9-2002, point 1.3.69.
([5]) Bull. 10-2002, point 1.3.55.
([6]) http://europa.eu.int/comm/enterprise/services/commerce/index.htm.

Section 8

Research and technology ([1])

Overview

288.　The year 2002 was marked by two events which will profoundly alter research and innovation in Europe both qualitatively and quantitatively. The first was the launching of the sixth framework programme for research and technological development covering the period 2002–06. Equipped with new implementation instruments, this programme has been designed to make a reality of the European research area, of which it is the financial arm, and improve the organisation of European research and innovation activities. Quantitatively, the Heads of State or Government agreed at the Barcelona European Council to raise investment in research and development from 1.9 % of gross domestic product in 2000 to 3 % by 2010.

Community RTD policy

Coordination and general developments

289.　Space. In a resolution adopted on 17 January ([2]) the European Parliament, referring to the Commission communication of September 2000 ([3]), welcomed the formulation of a European space strategy and stressed the importance of close cooperation with the European Space Agency (ESA). In this connection, on 27 May the Council adopted negotiating directives with a view to a framework agreement between the Community and the ESA (Table III).

290.　Life sciences and biotechnology. Stressing the importance of the sector in terms of potential, and in line with the public consultation which it launched in September 2001 ([4]), in a communication adopted on 24 January ([5]), supplemented by an action plan, the Commission proposed the formulation of a European strategy on this subject based on lines of action such as: reinforcing the sci-

---

([1]) http://europa.eu.int/comm/research/index_en.html.
([2]) OJ C 271 E, 7.11.2002; Bull. 1/2-2002, point 1.3.124.
([3]) 'Europe and space: Turning to a new chapter', COM(2000) 597; 2000 General Report, point 285.
([4]) COM(2001) 454; 2001 General Report, point 323.
([5]) OJ C 55, 2.3.2002, COM(2002) 27; Bull. 1/2-2002, point 1.3.126.

entific resource base, increased mobility and networking of operators; responsible harvesting of the potential of biotechnology while respecting European values and principles; the international role of the EU in this sector, together with its responsibility towards the developing countries; coherence in the implementation of the strategy, involving a regular monitoring report and the organisation of a forum between the parties concerned. This approach was welcomed by the Barcelona European Council ([1]), and subsequently by the Council which, in conclusions adopted on 6 June ([2]), called upon the Commission to cooperate closely with it to establish an operational road map of practical measures based on the abovementioned communication. The objectives of this road map were specified by the Council in conclusions adopted on 26 November ([3]) which recognised the importance of regular dialogue within society and greater coherence between the actions of the Member States and the European institutions. In an opinion delivered on 21 February ([4]), the European Economic and Social Committee delivered an opinion in the context of the abovementioned consultation. In an opinion delivered on 18 September ([5]) concerning the Commission communication, it called for the stakeholders concerned to become more involved in terms of competitiveness, growth and job creation. In a resolution adopted on 21 November ([6]), the European Parliament emphasised the urgent need to establish a harmonised legal framework and called upon the Commission to launch a 'B-Europe' policy in the field of biotechnology.

291.   *Ecotechnology*. On 13 March, the Commission adopted a report on the impact of new innovative technologies on sustainable development (→ *point 560*).

European research area ([7])

292.   *General developments*. On 16 October, 30 months after the European research area initiative was launched by the Lisbon European Council ([8]), the Commission took stock of the activities undertaken and the developments which have occurred in this connection, and indicated what should be done to give new momentum to the initiative ([9]). It suggested, in particular, measures aimed at substantially increasing the Member States' involvement in research, boosting the impact of the activities initiated, and consolidating the conceptual

---

([1]) Bull. 3-2002, points I.37 and I.38.
([2]) Bull. 6-2002, point 1.3.82.
([3]) Bull. 11-2002, point 1.3.65.
([4]) OJ C 94, 18.4.2002; Bull. 1/2-2002, point 1.3.127.
([5]) Bull. 9-2002, point 1.3.71.
([6]) Bull. 11-2002, point 1.3.64.
([7]) http://europa.eu.int/comm/research/era/index_en.html.
([8]) 2000 General Report, point 283.
([9]) COM(2002) 565; Bull. 10-2002, point 1.3.56.

and policy framework in which the ERA initiative is being implemented. In conclusions adopted on 26 November (^{1}), welcoming the progress achieved in developing the ERA, the Council called for the coordination of the RTD activities of the Member States and the Community. In a resolution adopted on 17 December (^{2}), the European Parliament gave its views on the Commission's December 2001 report on the RTD activities of the European Union in 2001 (^{3}).

293.   *Methodological approach.* The first recommendations (^{4}) arising from the benchmarking of the national research policies (^{5}) were taken into account in the conclusions of the Barcelona European Council. The results of the first benchmarking exercise, which were made public in September (^{6}), were widely disseminated for study and discussion at workshops and conferences. In addition, a pilot project relating to scientific and technological mapping was carried out in the fields of life sciences, nanotechnologies and economics. In addition, the action taken by the Commission following the Council conclusions of 26 June 2001 on infrastructures in the ERA (^{5}) led in the spring to the creation of a European Strategy Forum on Research Infrastructures, aimed at facilitating the development of a European policy in this connection. Lastly, the Commission published the 2002 edition of the key figures concerning progress towards the ERA which, in the form of indicators, maps out the European science and technology profile (^{7}).

294.   *Investment in research.* At the Barcelona European Council of 15 and 16 March, the Heads of State or Government agreed that investment in research and development in the EU should be increased, with the aim of approaching 3 % of gross domestic product by 2010 compared with 1.9 % in 2000 (^{8}). In order to launch a debate on the ways and means of achieving this objective, on 11 September the Commission adopted a communication (^{9}) identifying a number of areas in which policies should be mobilised in a coherent manner and under conditions such as: highly qualified human resources, a strong public research base, an appropriate competitive environment and favourable fiscal conditions.

295.   *Regional dimension.* In an opinion delivered on 16 May (^{10}) on the Commission communication of October 2001 (^{11}), the Committee of the Regions

---

(^{1}) Bull. 11-2002, point 1.3.66.
(^{2}) Bull. 12-2002, point 1.3.85.
(^{3}) COM(2001) 756, 2001 General Report, point 324.
(^{4}) SEC(2002) 129, 24.1.2002
(^{5}) 2001 General Report, point 325.
(^{6}) http://www.cordis.lu/rtd2002/era-developments/benchmarking.htm.
(^{7}) http://www.cordis.lu/rtd2002/indicators/home.html.
(^{8}) Bull. 3-2002, point I.37.
(^{9}) COM(2002) 499; Bull. 9-2002, point 1.3.70.
(^{10}) OJ C 278, 14.11.2002; Bull. 5-2002, point 1.3.69.
(^{11}) COM(2001) 549; 2001 General Report, point 325.

stressed the importance of establishing specific regional objectives in order to make the European economy competitive in the face of the reduction in growth and employment. On the ground, in connection with the strategic analysis of specific policy issues under the fifth framework programme, a series of actions with a regional dimension were undertaken, such as the development of systematic exchanges of experience through the drafting of country-specific guides to regional foresight, the holding of a conference in October bringing together over 250 experts and regional officers of the Member States and the accession candidate countries, and the announced creation of a European association of regions carrying out foresight exercises

296.   *Energy*. In an own-initiative opinion delivered on 17 July (¹) stressing the importance of security of energy supply for the EU *(→ point 602)*, the European Economic and Social Committee called upon the Commission to lay the foundations for a European research programme in this sector.

297.   *Health*. On 28 August the Commission proposed that the Community should participate in a research and development programme aimed at promoting new clinical interventions to combat HIV/AIDS, malaria and tuberculosis (Table I). This programme, which has already been undertaken by several Member States and Norway, entails long-term partnership between Europe and the developing countries.

298.   *Science and society*. The Commission began implementing the action plan adopted in December 2001 (²), which provides for 38 actions to strengthen the links between citizens, scientists and decision-makers through more systematic consideration of scientific advice in policy-making, greater public awareness of scientific issues, appropriate treatment of ethical issues relating to scientific research, and the promotion of equality between women and men in science. The 'Structuring the European research area' component of the sixth framework programme *(→ point 299)* is the main instrument for implementing the action plan. On 11 December, the Commission adopted principles and guidelines concerning the collection of expertise by its departments *(→ point 24)*.

Framework programme 2002–06 (³)

299.   *General programme*. On 27 June the European Parliament and the Council adopted the sixth multiannual European Community framework programme for research, technological development and demonstration activities (Table I). With a budget of EUR 16.27 billion for the period 2002–06, the pro-

---

(¹) OJ C 241, 7.10.2002; Bull. 7/8-2002, point 1.3.83.
(²) COM(2001) 714; 2001 General Report, point 321.
(³) http://europa.eu.int/comm/research/fp6/index_en.html.

gramme is intended to make a reality of the European research area by strengthening its foundations, integrating research capacities in Europe more effectively, and structuring and simplifying their implementation. This objective is based on two main principles: firstly, introducing instruments with integrating effects, such as networks of excellence and EU participation in jointly-implemented national programmes, and with structuring effects, such as the development of infrastructures; and secondly, greater concentration on certain priority areas where Community action can bring about the greatest value added (in particular genomics, information-society technologies and food safety). In addition, the new framework programme fully integrates the accession candidate countries into all its activities and offers scope for significant international cooperation. In parallel, on 3 June the Council adopted the sixth Euratom research framework programme (Table II), with a budget of EUR 1.23 billion, also for the period 2002–06. This programme covers all activities relating to research, technological development, international cooperation, dissemination and utilisation of results, as well as training in the following areas: waste treatment and disposal, controlled thermonuclear fusion, the nuclear activities of the Joint Research Centre, and activities relating to nuclear safety and safeguards (radiation protection and new processes for harnessing nuclear energy).

The sixth framework programme 2002–06 became operational at the end of the year, with the publication of the first calls for proposals ([1]). From 11 to 13 November, in Brussels, the Commission held a major conference to launch it, which attracted 8 500 participants and constituted a real European research forum, fostering numerous contacts and cooperation projects.

300. Specific programmes. On 30 September the Council adopted five specific programmes 2002–06 to implement the sixth framework programme, with an overall budget of EUR 17.5 billion, subdivided as follows: EUR 12.905 billion for structuring the European research area (Table II); EUR 2.605 billion for integrating and strengthening the area (Table II); EUR 760 million for direct actions carried out by the Joint Research Centre (JRC) for the European Community (Table II); EUR 290 million for direct actions carried out by the JRC for Euratom (Table II); and EUR 940 million for research and training in the field of nuclear energy (Table II).

301. Participation of operators. On 16 December, the European Parliament and the Council adopted Regulation (EC) No 2321/2002 concerning the rules for the participation of undertakings, research centres and universities and for the dissemination of research results for the implementation of the European Community framework programme (Table I). The regulation is intended to adapt the rules to the spirit and features of the new framework programme and

---

([1]) OJ C 315, 17.12.2002.

simplify them compared with the existing provisions. On 5 November the Council adopted a similar regulation for the implementation of the sixth Euratom framework programme (Table II).

Implementation of the fifth framework programme 1998–2002 [1]

302. In the course of 2002, over 4 500 RTD contracts were signed, representing a Community financial contribution of nearly EUR 3.6 billion, or some 25 % of the total budget for the fifth framework programme. Participation in the fifth framework programme totalled some 22 000 entities, more or less evenly divided between research centres, higher education establishments and businesses.

Quality of life and living resources

303. In 2002, 263 additional research projects were selected for financing during the last year of the programme, in the framework of which 1 841 projects were financed. In addition, 74 fellows will receive financial support by way of Marie Curie fellowships. The proportion of proposals selected (24 %) increased compared with 2001 (17 %). The projects selected made it possible to enhance the coverage of Community RTD priorities in areas such as health-related functional genomics, man/animal links in the transmission of infectious diseases, the resistance mechanisms of *staphylococcus aureus* and the investigation of antiviral peptides as therapeutic tools.

User-friendly information society

304. During the last year of operations under the fifth framework programme, the information society technologies (IST) programme gave rise to over 650 proposals for shared-cost actions, concerted actions, accompanying measures, specific measures for SMEs and training fellowships. The corresponding actions were selected following the seventh [2] and eighth [3] calls for proposals under the IST programme and the calls concerning IMS (intelligent manufacturing systems) [4] and SMEs [5]. These operations enabled the programme to increase support for the development of key technologies for the competitiveness of European industry and enable citizens to benefit more from information society services, with a major impact in areas such as health, transport and edu-

[1] http://europa.eu.int/comm/research/fp5_en.html.
[2] OJ C 191, 7.7.2001.
[3] OJ C 321, 16.11.2001.
[4] OJ C 27, 27.1.2001.
[5] OJ C 92, 1.4.1999.

cation and training. The IST programme succeeded in targeting longer-term research (5–10 years), while maintaining a high level of participation of SMEs (25 %). The programme also continued to make a contribution to EU policies concerning the information society, in particular the *e*Europe initiative *(→ point 331)* and the creation of the European research area *(→ points 292 to 298)*. In order to prepare for the sixth framework programme and encourage the establishment of partnerships for the first calls for proposals in this connection, the Commission launched a call for expressions of interest [1], which attracted over 3 000 replies, mainly relating to the IST thematic priority; strategic objectives were identified on this basis and in consultation with the Member States, the associated countries and the research community in the field concerned, mainly addressing integrated projects, networks of excellence and more traditional projects.

Competitive and sustainable growth

305.   Processes and materials. Following the call for proposals for CRAFT cooperative research aimed at SMEs [2], 489 proposals were received and 121 selected for Community financing totalling EUR 67 million. Of these proposals, 68 concerned the design or improvement of manufacturing and production processes and 28 the development or improvement of materials. The research actions supported by the EU in the fields of nanotechnologies and clean technologies for competitive and sustainable production were presented to the press in the course of the second half of 2002.

306.   Measurements, tests and infrastructure. Following the fifth targeted call published in the fields covered by the generic activity 'Measurements and tests' and 'Support for research infrastructures' [3], 15 research proposals, one INCO fellowship and 11 networks were selected for Community financing, totalling EUR 27 million. In addition, in the field of measurements and tests, a conference entitled 'Towards an integrated infrastructure for measurements' held in Warsaw in June, provided a forum for discussing the opportunities available to the accession candidate countries, in particular with a view to developing a joint European research infrastructure.

307.   Transport. A conference on 'Surface transport technologies for sustainable development', held in June in Valencia (Spain) made it possible to take stock of the progress made over the last five years and establish a common vision for the future in the context of national and European industrial research policies.

---

[1] OJ C 71, 20.3.2002.
[2] OJ C 72, 16.3.1999.
[3] OJ C 290, 16.10.2001.

Energy, environment and sustainable development

308.   Non-nuclear energy. Fifty-four projects under the key action 'Cleaner energy, including renewable energy sources', 65 projects under the key action 'Economical and efficient energy for a competitive Europe' and eight generic measures, including accompanying measures for the dissemination of innovative energy technologies, seven Marie Curie fellowships and 12 SME projects were selected in 2002. The various projects concerned renewable energy sources and their industrial applications. They were selected following calls for proposals aimed at improving the participation of the newly associated countries, published in August ([1]) and September 2001 ([2]), and the open call published on 24 October 2000 ([3]). The activities carried out in 2002 also included studies concerning the impact of the results of projects completed under the fourth framework programme, indicators and scientific and technological references in the field of non-nuclear energy and the launching of initiatives concerning the links between science and society in the energy sector.

309.   Energy, environment and sustainable development. This component gave rise to 371 contracts, including 172 for research projects, the remaining contracts concerning accompanying measures, Marie Curie fellowships and CRAFT contracts for SMEs. Extensive efforts were made to communicate and make use of results through the publication of numerous scientific articles and journals and the holding of high-level international conferences such as the Science and Technology Forum in Johannesburg in connection with the World Summit on Sustainable Development *(→ points 556 to 558).* The programme has made it possible to establish the role of scientific and technical research in the definition of the Community's sustainable development strategy. Considerable attention was also paid to support for Community policies, notably the action programme for the environment and its components concerning climate change, water and biodiversity, together with marine sciences *(→ point 552).* Numerous scientific references were produced for the drafting of Community guidelines on these subjects; in addition, the programme developed quantitative tools for sustainable development impact assessments now required by the Commission for *ex ante* policy evaluation.

Confirming the international role of Community research

310.   European cooperation. The Commission continued to support European cooperation in the field of scientific and technical research (COST), which the former Yugoslav Republic of Macedonia joined, bringing the total member-

---

([1]) OJ C 240, 28.8.2001.
([2]) OJ C 264, 20.9.2001.
([3]) OJ C 303, 24.10.2000; amendment published in OJ C 344, 6.12.2001.

ship to 34. Just under 200 COST projects were in progress in 2002. COST is continuing to develop vast research networks in Europe involving 25 000 scientists. In addition, in the context of the Eureka intergovernmental technological innovation initiative, various activities were conducted in order to enhance coordination and synergy between the EU's research programmes and Eureka.

311. Nuclear energy. Formal negotiations for the joint implementation of an international thermonuclear experimental reactor (ITER) were conducted under the auspices of the International Atomic Energy Agency. On 27 May ([1]) the Council widened the negotiating mandate given to the Commission in 2000 ([2]) in order to include aspects concerning the site for ITER and cost-sharing arrangements. In addition, various types of scientific and technical work were carried out in the laboratories of the Euratom fusion associations and by the industry with a view to the construction and operation of ITER.

312. Emerging economies and developing countries. On 23 September the Council signed an agreement for scientific and technological cooperation with Chile (Table III). On 25 June it concluded a similar agreement with India (Table III). On 12 July it also adopted negotiating directives with a view to cooperation with Mexico (Table III). On 3 December a cooperation agreement with Brazil was initialled (Table III.). Bi-regional dialogues with the Mediterranean countries made it possible to define research priorities for the main call for proposals aimed at financing projects in fields such as managing regional water resources, preserving and using the cultural heritage and promoting healthy societies. In this connection, 120 proposals were received of which 17 were firmly selected for financing and five were provisionally selected. On 5 November the Council adopted negotiating directives for the renewal of the agreement for scientific and technical cooperation concluded in 1999 with Israel (Table III). The calls for proposals aimed at financing research projects in the field of international cooperation with the developing countries having taken place in earlier years, accompanying measures were the main instrument for this cooperation in 2002. In this connection, 68 proposals were received, notably in the fields of health, ecosystems preservation and agriculture. In addition, 16 proposals were selected for the award of fellowships in the context of the INCO-DEV initiative for researchers from developing countries.

313. Accession countries. On 27 May the Council concluded the additional protocol to the association agreement with Malta to associate it with the fifth framework programme for research, technological development and demonstration activities (Table III). The calls aimed at increasing the participation of the candidate countries in the activities under the specific programmes in the context of the fifth framework programme were closed in 2002. In this connec-

---

([1]) Bull. 5-2002, point 1.3.73.
([2]) 2000 General Report, point 312.

tion, 297 proposals out of the 457 proposals received were selected to enable participants from the candidate countries to be associated with projects financed under the thematic priorities (NAS 1). With regard to the initiative 'Support for the integration of the candidate countries into the European research area' (NAS 2) aimed at integrating the candidate countries' research centres into the Member States' excellence structures through the organisation of conferences, exchanges and training, etc., 353 proposals were received, of which 126 were selected for financing. The call 'Strategic action for training and excellence' ([1]) attracted 80 proposals, of which 11 were financed in the field of life sciences, physics and chemistry. In addition, in the context of the open call ([2]) for the financing of accompanying measures encouraging researchers from the candidate countries to attend events in Europe or providing financial support for the organisation of scientific meetings in the countries in the pre-accession phase, 70 proposals were received, of which 20 were selected for financing

314.   *Independent States of the former Soviet Union.* On 4 July the Council signed an agreement for scientific and technological cooperation with Ukraine (Table III). In addition, the Community continued to cooperate with scientists from the new independent States by initiating, via the INTAS Association, 208 new research projects, granting 243 scholarships and launching 100 accompanying measures, totalling some EUR 22 million. Also, the scientific dialogue with Russia and the new independent States was intensified by means of four strategic workshops.

Promotion of innovation and SME participation

315.   *Promotion of research, development and innovation.* In a report adopted on 22 January on policies in this area ([3]), the Council formulated recommendations to the EU and the Member States. It advocated amending the legislation concerning State aid so as to promote innovation and the role of SMEs on the market, in particular by providing better information and advice concerning intellectual property rights. The growing economic and social importance of innovation was reflected in a series of studies launched by the Commission in 2002 ([4]). In April the support for access to private innovation financing give rise to the 'Gate2Growth' initiative aimed at strengthening networks and spreading good practice between innovation professionals in Europe. This support has resulted, in particular, in the creation of a European database concerning the opportunities for investment in innovating companies and the support

---

([1]) OJ C 261, 18.9.2001.
([2]) OJ C 367, 21.12.2001.
([3]) Bull. 1/2-2002, point 1.3.133.
([4]) http://www.cordis.lu/innovation-policy/studies/home.html.

granted to the European Venture Capital and Private Equity Association to launch, on a European scale, an entrepreneurship education initiative for commercial schools and universities. The completion of 30 projects, networks and accompanying measures in the context of the PAXIS pilot action to promote the setting-up and development of innovative companies made it possible to draw conclusions aimed at contributing to the formulation of innovation policy. Fourteen new contracts were signed to place the action on a wider scale. The Third European Forum for Innovative Enterprises held by the Commission in Stockholm in April looked at the latest trends in the creation of innovative start-ups, and 'awards of excellence' were presented in this connection.

316. *SME participation.* In the context of the specific measures to promote SME participation in the Community research programmes — exploratory awards and cooperative research (CRAFT) — 1 004 proposals involving 5 344 SMEs were received in 2002 of which 34 % were favourably assessed. Also, 1 374 requests for information were sent to the single entry point for SMEs that is common to all the programmes. Under the 'Economic and technological intelligence' scheme designed to help SMEs, 53 projects are in progress to help SMEs identify relevant information and subsequently embark upon projects with other partners to take advantage of perceived trends. In 2002 these projects gave rise to numerous partnerships between SMEs and helped forge links between just under 500 partners working with or for SMEs (regional development agencies, national SME contact points, industrial associations, etc.). To prepare for the next framework programme, a pilot collective research action was set up, resulting in the financing of five projects. In September the fourth SME Technology Days Conference brought together policy-makers, intermediaries and representatives of local SMEs.

Improving human potential and the socioeconomic knowledge base

317. *Infrastructure.* Following the third and last call for proposals concerning 'Improving access to research infrastructures' under the programme 'Improving human potential', proposals concerning transnational access were selected for financing, totalling EUR 3.279 million.

318. *Training and mobility of researchers.* In conclusions adopted on 18 February ([1]) concerning Special Report No 9/2001 of the Court of Auditors on this subject ([2]), the Council welcomed the Commission's efforts concerning the procedures for the Marie Curie fellowships. Following the last calls for proposals under the fifth framework programme, a total of 337 individual Marie Curie fellowships were proposed for financing. Where research training net-

---

([1]) Bull. 1/2-2002, point 1.3.128.
([2]) OJ C 349, 10.12.2001; 2001 General Report, point 1219.

works are concerned, 167 initiatives were proposed for financing. In addition, 284 high-level conferences received Community support in order to increase the participation of young researchers.

319.   Awards. In the context of the Archimedes Prize ([1]) for the best science projects drawn up by European students, 10 projects were selected following a call for proposals ([2]) and prizes were awarded in Munich on 5 December. The Descartes Prize ([3]) for cooperation in Europe on high-level research was also awarded in Munich on 5 December from a shortlist of 10 projects selected following a call for proposals ([4]). Lastly, 85 young people from 34 countries took part in the EU Contest for Young Scientists ([5]) which rewards the scientific achievements of European secondary school students. Nine projects received awards, and others received special prizes allowing the recipients to take part in training courses at European research centres.

320.   Raising public awareness of science and technology. The call for applications launched on this subject ([6]), which focused on scientific culture, was very successful. Three sectors of activity were addressed: mechanisms for involving the public in dialogue; the role of the media and science communicators; and the European Science and Technology Week 2003 ([7]), consisting of seven projects covering a range of targeted demonstration and discussion exercises for the public and a growing number of associated activities.

321.   Socioeconomic research. Under the key action 'Improving the socio-economic knowledge base', a final call for applications was launched, with a budget of EUR 63 million with a view to facilitating the transition from the fifth framework programme to the sixth, and in particular helping researchers prepare for the European research area by contributing to the Lisbon strategy. This call led to the initiation of 90 new research projects, thematic networks and accompanying measures. In addition, the organisation of dialogue between researchers and policy-makers in the form of workshops continued into 2002. Likewise, a horizontal group of high-level experts was set up to provide the interface between the social and human science community and Community research and innovation policy. As regards support for science and technology policy-making, five projects were initiated in connection with the strategic analysis of specific policy issues (Strata) and three projects concerning the development of a common basis for science, technology and innovation indicators (CBSTII). A high-level group of experts also produced a foresight analysis of the

---

([1]) http:// www.cordis.lu/improving/awards/archimedes.htm.
([2]) OJ C 246, 4.9.2001.
([3]) http://www.cordis.lu/descartes/.
([4]) OJ C 358, 15.12.2001.
([5]) http://europa.eu.int/comm/research/youngscientists/indexflash.htm.
([6]) OJ C 11, 15.1.2002.
([7]) http://www.cordis.lu/scienceweek/.

relationship between higher education and research with a view to better defining the policies to be pursued to achieve the Lisbon objective. The database on
local initiatives to combat social exclusion in Europe (LOCIN) was updated and
linked with other databases on the same subject.

Direct actions carried out by the JRC for the European Community

322. *General approach.* Two topics continued to occupy an important place
in the activities of the JRC: on the one hand, sustainable development and, on
the other, exposure to health hazards in the context of food, chemicals, pollution, water supply and noise. JRC work evolved during 2002 by integrating
database management, parameter assessment and monitoring into a functional
process for the study of impacts of pollutants on human health. Tools to assess
the influence of landscape factors, such as land-use changes on flooding problems were initiated, together with simulation, forecasting, and impact assessment. The multidisciplinary approach included numerical modelling and interpretation of remote sensing images. The JRC further developed its extensive set
of networks with more than 1 000 partner organisations around the world associated with its work.

323. *Chemical substances.* The JRC was particularly active in this area, providing independent scientific and technical support to the establishment of the Community regulatory framework *(→ point 273).* Furthermore it supported the work of
the competent authorities in the Member States in implementing the current policies
and supporting the development of future policies on chemicals risk assessment.

324. *European Centre for the Validation of Alternative Methods (ECVAM).*
This body, a centre for the development, and scientific and regulatory acceptance
of alternative testing methods, e.g. *in vitro* studies using cell tissue cultures and
computer-based testing continued its activities with the aim of replacing, reducing
or refining the use of laboratory animals in several fields of biomedical science.

325. *Training activities.* Research training and access to JRC facilities continued, and JRC projects provided access to dedicated laboratories and scientific
expertise. The development of links with candidate countries continued.

Nuclear energy: fission

326. Twelve generic actions, 13 accompanying measures, four Marie Curie
and 10 projects concerning access to research infrastructures were selected in
2002 concerning nuclear fission and radiation protection ([1]) following calls for

---

([1]) http://europa.eu.int/comm/research/energy/fi/fi_en.html.

proposals published in October 2001 (^{1}) and April 2002 (^{2}). In addition, major results were achieved in the areas of processing and disposal of long-lived radioactive waste, understanding the effects of low doses of radioactivity on human beings and the environment, nuclear accidents which may arise in power plants, decommissioning of power plants and optimisation of the use of radiation in medical applications.

Direct actions carried out by the JRC for Euratom

327.   The JRC's activities in the nuclear field supported Community policies in various areas. In the area of safeguards, the JRC provided the secretariat for the European Safeguards Research and Development Association (Esarda), continued the operation of the on-site laboratories at La Hague (France) and Sellafield (United Kingdom) and cooperation in the safeguards area with Russia and the United States. The transfer of expertise in the form of training courses and the competencies of the JRC's Community reference laboratory for radionuclide metrology were further exploited. Nuclear forensic science was deepened and applied in support projects, mainly for candidate countries, in counteracting illicit trafficking of nuclear materials. As regards the environment, advanced particle measurement techniques were developed to monitor contamination and possible detection of clandestine nuclear activities. With respect to nuclear waste management, both options of direct interim or final storage and of advanced reprocessing and re-irradiation were under evaluation. In the basic research area, the Actinide User Laboratory was put into operation, providing access to both specialised facilities and knowhow.

Coal and steel technical research

328.   The Council decided on a new steel research programme (2002–07) on 27 February. This programme is a continuation of the ECSC steel programme which came to an end in 2002 with the expiry of the ECSC Treaty (→ points 39 to 41).

Joint Research Centre (JRC) (^{3})

329.   The JRC continued to provide scientific and technical support for the implementation of Community policies during the last year of the fifth frame-

---

(^{1}) OJ C 290, 16.10.2001.
(^{2}) OJ C 79, 3.4.2002.
(^{3}) http://www.jrc.cec.eu.int/.

work programme. Special attention was paid to the candidate countries to help them implement the Community *acquis*, through the training of scientists and the establishment of collaborative links with research centres in those countries. Pilot actions were launched in order to prepare the ground for consolidated action during the sixth framework programme. This was helped by the creation of specialised working groups in order to tackle important strategic issues, including networking, training and actions relating to the enlargement of the EU. On 26 June the Commission adopted its annual report on the JRC [1]. On 17 December [2], the European Parliament adopted a resolution on this report, stressing the significant role that the JRC will play in connection with the sixth framework programme and the creation of the European research area.

---

[1] COM(2002) 306; Bull. 6-2002, point 1.3.90.
[2] Bull. 12-2002, point 1.3.85.

Section 9

Information society (¹)

Overview

330.   Apart from completing the implementation of the eEurope 2002 action plan, in order to maximise the results of the plan and respond to new challenges, the Commission adopted a new eEurope 2005 action plan, which was approved by the Seville European Council, the objective of which is to create an environment favourable to private investment and job creation, modernise public services (eGovernment, eHealth, and eLearning) and give everybody the opportunity to participate in the global information society. An in-depth reform of the telecommunications regulatory framework also took place in the course of the year.

eEurope initiative (²)

331.   eEurope action plans. In a communication adopted on 5 February (³), the Commission took stock of the eEurope 2002 action plan, and concluded that the e-economy is emerging in Europe but that there are still major disparities. At its meeting of 5 and 6 December the Council adopted a resolution on the implementation of the eEurope action plan. On 28 May the Commission presented a new action plan (eEurope 2005) (⁴) the aim of which is to stimulate the development of secure services, applications and content. The plan focuses on a limited number of priority areas such as online public services, generalised high-speed Internet access and network security, where action by the public authorities is decisive. For the purposes of monitoring progress, the plan also contains a proposal for a benchmarking exercise based on a set of policy indicators. In this connection, on 21 November the Commission adopted a communication (⁵) in which it proposes a list of benchmarking indicators for eEurope 2005. On 26 July it adopted a proposal for a decision adopting a multiannual programme (2003–05) creating a legal basis for continuing the dissemination of best practice and management activities provided for in the eEurope

---

(¹) Further information is available on the Europa server (http://europa.eu.int/information_society/index_en.htm).
(²) http://europa.eu.int/information_society/eeurope/action_plan/index_en.htm.
(³) COM(2002) 62; Bull. 1/2-2002, point 1.3.134.
(⁴) COM(2002) 263; Bull. 5-2002, point 1.3.78.
(⁵) COM(2002) 655; Bull. 11-2002, point 1.3.72.

2005 action plan (Table II). It also provides for preparatory measures to pave the way for a European policy on network and information security.

332.   Accessibility of public web sites. The strategy concerning the accessibility of public web sites and their content set out in a Commission communication adopted in 2001 ([1]), was favourably received by the European Economic and Social Committee on 20 February ([2]), the Committee of the Regions on 15 May ([3]), and the European Parliament on 13 June ([4]). The latter called upon the Commission and the Member States to promote dialogue with the representatives of disabled and elderly people in order to ensure that they have access to new technologies and do not suffer any form of discrimination in this respect. On 25 March the Council stressed the need to step up the efforts in this connection and, in particular, encourage the Member States to speed up accessibility to web sites and their content by means of appropriate national measures ([5]). In a resolution adopted on 2 December on e-accessibility ([6]) the Council called upon the Member States and the Commission to improve the access to the information society of people with disabilities by removing technical, legal and other obstacles to their effective participation.

333.   Public-sector documents. On 5 June the Commission adopted a proposal for a directive (Table I) based to a large extent on the communication which it adopted in 2001 ([7]) concerning the creation of a Community framework for the commercial exploitation of public-sector documents. The purpose of this proposal is to achieve minimum harmonisation of the rules concerning the reuse and commercial exploitation of public-sector documents in order to improve the functioning of the internal market. It is intended to achieve an adequate degree of legal certainty, so as to enable the market players to establish new trans-frontier information services based on public-sector information.

334.   Action plan on promoting safer use of the Internet. On 22 March ([8]) the Commission proposed extending until 31 December 2004 the action plan on promoting safer use of the Internet by combating illegal and harmful content on global networks (Table I). The last series of shared-cost projects arising from the calls for proposals for projects to raise awareness about safer use of the Internet and to advise self-regulation bodies on the preparation of codes of conduct began in the autumn. The final evaluation of the action plan in January 2003

([1]) COM(2001) 529; 2001 General Report, point 367.
([2]) OJ C 94, 18.4.2002; Bull. 1/2-2002, point 1.3.136.
([3]) OJ C 287 E, 22.11.2002; Bull. 5-2002, point 1.3.77.
([4]) Bull. 6-2002, point 1.3.96.
([5]) OJ C 86, 10.4.2002; Bull. 3-2002, point 1.3.68.
([6]) Bull. 12-2002, point 1.3.92.
([7]) COM(2001) 607; 2001 General Report, point 376.
([8]) COM(2002) 152; Bull. 3-2002, point 1.3.67.

should make it possible to examine in detail the results and impact of each of the projects covered by the plan.

335.   Cybercrime. Information on action to combat cybercrime is provided in Section 1 ('Area of freedom, security and justice') of Chapter IV *(→ point 474).*

336.   eHealth. In a communication (¹) adopted on 29 November the Commission called upon the Member States and the national and regional health authorities to apply precise quality criteria to health-related web sites and encourage the exchange of information about how these criteria are implemented.

337.   eLearning. Information on the *e*Learning initiative is provided in Section 3 ('Education and culture') of Chapter IV *(→ point 520).*

Electronic communications

338.   Internet. On 22 April the European Parliament and the Council adopted Regulation (EC) No 733/2002 on the implementation of the Internet top-level domain '.eu' (Table I). The introduction of this new '.eu' domain will create a real European identity in cyberspace for Internet users.

339.   Telecommunications. In June the Commission launched a public consultation on a draft recommendation on relevant markets in this sector. On 11 July it published guidelines on market analysis and the assessment of significant market power (²). Lastly, on 3 December it adopted its eighth report on the implementation of the telecommunications regulatory package (³) in which it assesses the development of the telecommunications market since liberalisation (⁴) and indicates the challenges with which the Member States are confronted in the run-up to the application of the new framework. In conclusions (⁵) adopted at its meeting of 5 and 6 December the Council also took stock of the situation in the telecommunications sector.

340.   Network and information security. On 28 January, following up the initiative launched by the Commission in 2001 (⁶), the Council adopted a resolution on a common approach and specific actions in the area of network and information security (⁷) in which it called upon the Member States to introduce

---

(¹) COM(2002) 667 et Bull. 11-2002, point 1.3.75.
(²) OJ C 165, 11.7.2002.
(³) COM(2002) 695; Bull. 12-2002, point 1.3.95.
(⁴) 1998 General Report, point 467.
(⁵) Bull. 12-2002, point 1.3.96.
(⁶) COM(2001) 298; 2001 General Report, point 371.
(⁷) OJ C 43, 16.2.2002; Bull. 1/2-2002, point 1.3.138.

concrete measures to encourage the exchange of information between the national players concerned. In a resolution adopted on 22 October (¹) the European Parliament emphasised the need to ensure that all citizens, businesses and administrations have access to the public electronic services of all the EU institutions via a secure and personalised access system. At its meeting of 5 and 6 December (²), the Council called upon the Member States and the industry to promote network and information security by developing a security culture.

341. *Electronic communications networks and services.* On 7 March the European Parliament and the Council adopted four directives intended to bring about an in-depth reform of the telecommunications regulatory framework in Europe, in particular as regards electronic communications (Table I). Directive 2002/21/EC establishes a harmonised regulatory framework for all electronic communications networks and services in response to the phenomenon of the convergence of the sectors. Directive 2002/19/EC regulates access to and the interconnection of electronic communications networks and associated facilities in order to guarantee legal certainty for market players, by establishing clear criteria concerning their rights and obligations and for regulatory intervention. Directive 2002/20/EC provides for the simplification and harmonisation of the national systems for the authorisation of electronic communications networks and services by reducing the administrative barriers to market entry. Lastly, Directive 2002/22/EC seeks to ensure universal service provision for public telephony services in a competitive environment. It also defines the rights of users and consumers of communication networks and services, aims to guarantee the interoperability of consumer digital television equipment and regulates the imposition of 'must carry' obligations on network operators.

342. *Radio spectrum policy.* On 7 March the European Parliament and the Council adopted Decision No 676/2002/EC, the aim of which is to establish a policy and legal framework in the European Community so as to harmonise the conditions regarding the availability and efficient use of the radio spectrum necessary for the establishment and functioning of the internal market in telecommunications (Table I).

343. *Data protection.* Directive 2002/58//EC, which was adopted on 12 July by the European Parliament and the Council, seeks to guarantee that consumers and users of communication services enjoy the same level of protection of their personal data and privacy irrespective of the technology used to send their electronic communications (Table I). This directive is the fifth directive in the context of the new telecommunications regulatory framework *(→ point 341)* which will enter into force in July 2003. Further information on the protection of personal data is provided in Section 5 ('Internal market') of this chapter *(→ point 199)*.

(¹) Bull. 10-2002, point 1.3.61.
(²) Bull. 12-2002, point 1.3.97.

344. Trans-European telecommunications networks. Information on trans-European telecommunications networks is provided in Section 12 ('Trans-European networks') of this chapter *(→ points 383 et seq.).*

Information society technologies

345. Next generation Internet. On 21 February the Commission adopted a communication on priorities for action in migrating to the EU IPv6 Internet Protocol (¹) in which it recommended that the Member States undertake a series of complementary actions, in particular in the context of the sixth framework programme for research and development *(→ point 299).* In conclusions adopted on 18 June (²), the Council welcomed the communication and called upon the Commission to evaluate the social impact of the implementation of IPv6 on society, citizens and businesses and to investigate security issues related to IPv6.

346. Third-generation mobile communications systems. In a communication adopted on 12 June (³), the Commission, as requested by the Barcelona European Council, after giving an overview of the situation regarding third-generation (3G) licences, analysed the financial, technical and regulatory challenges associated with the full roll-out of third-generation mobile communications.

Digital content

347. eContent programme (⁴). In the context of the *e*Content programme, the Commission selected 29 additional projects in support of the objectives of the programme with regard to the exploitation of public-sector information, and the linguistic and cultural adaptation of services offered by global networks. On 19 December the Commission adopted the work programme for 2003 and 2004 and a new call for proposals.

348. Preserving digital content. On 23 May the Council approved a resolution in which it proposed several measures aimed at stimulating the development of policies for preserving digital culture and heritage, as well as their accessibility (⁵). It also suggested addressing issues related to the promotion of the preservation concept and appropriate investment. A resolution adopted on 25 June also stresses the need to continue to develop methods and guidelines

---

(¹) COM(2002) 96; Bull. 1/2-2002, point 1.3.135.
(²) Bull. 6-2002, point 1.3.97.
(³) COM(2002) 301; Bull. 6-2002, point 1.3.103.
(⁴) http://www.cordis.lu/econtent/.
(⁵) Bull. 5-2002, point 1.3.82.

and practical measures, common to all the Member States, to preserve Europe's heritage in digital form (^{1}) and support it by developing research programmes and experimental applications.

349. *Open platforms.* As requested by the Seville European Council, the Commission launched a public consultation on a report on the obstacles which still prevent generalised access to new information-society services and applications thanks to open platforms in third-generation mobile communications (3G). The European Parliament adopted a resolution on this subject on 26 September (^{2}).

Regional and international aspects

350. *eEurope + action plan* (^{3}). The Commission organised the second ministerial conference (^{4}) with the accession candidate countries in Ljubljana (Slovenia) on 3 and 4 June (^{5}). The first report (^{6}) drawn up in this connection confirmed the efforts undertaken by the candidate countries to speed up the process of reform and modernisation of their economies in order to adapt them to the information society in the context of the *e*Europe + action plan.

351. *Cooperation with Russia.* The northern e-dimension action plan' (^{7}) (NeDAP) based on the *e*Europe (^{8}) and *e*Europe + (^{9}) action plans and adopted by the Feira European Council in the context of the northern dimension action plan (^{10}), focuses on transfrontier cooperation and the implementation of practical networking and knowledge-sharing projects. The NeDAP is, in this respect, an instrument to speed up the transition to the information society in the northern regions and establish greater cooperation with Russia.

352. *Cooperation with Latin America and the Caribbean countries.* The @LIS (Alliance for the information society) (^{11}) programme for cooperation with Latin America was officially launched on 26 and 27 April in Seville at a meeting between ministers, regulators, representatives of the private sector and civil society of the EU, Latin America and the Caribbean countries. The aim of this programme is to establish a partnership on policy, regulatory and standardisation

---

(^{1}) Bull. 6-2002, point 1.3.102.
(^{2}) Bull. 9-2002, point 1.3.74.
(^{3}) http://europa.eu.int/information_society/topics/international/regulatory/eeuropeplus/index_en.htm.
(^{4}) Previous conference: 2000 General Report, point 338.
(^{5}) http://emcis.gov.si/.
(^{6}) http://europa.eu.int/information_society/topics/international/regulatory/eeuropeplus/doc/progress_report.pdf.
(^{7}) http://europa.eu.int/comm/external_relations/north_dim/index.htm#5.
(^{8}) 1999 General Report, point 424.
(^{9}) 2001 General Report, point 379.
(^{10}) 2000 General Report, point 953.
(^{11}) http://europa.eu.int/comm/europeaid/projects/alis/index_en.htm.

frameworks in key areas for the development of the information society, such as telecommunications, e-commerce and e-government and develop interconnections between the research networks and communities of the two regions. It also comprises projects to demonstrate the applications of the information society in four priority areas: government, education, health and social cohesion.

353.   *Development cooperation.* The Council adopted conclusions concerning information and communication technologies in the field of development cooperation (→ *point 816).*

354.   *Action within the international organisations.* In cooperation with the Member States, the Commission helped to prepare the World Summit on the Information Society scheduled to be held in Geneva in December 2003 (¹) and in 2005 in Tunis. In this connection, it participated in various preparatory meetings and supported the regional conferences for Africa in Bamako in April and for Europe in Bucharest in November. Similarly, it participated in the World Conference for the Development of Telecommunications in April in Istanbul, the Conference of Plenipotentiaries of the International Telecommunication Union (ITU) in Marrakech in September and October and the work of the United Nations Task Force on Information and Communications Technologies (ICT) at the Secretariat-General of the United Nations.

(¹) http://www.itu.int/wsis/index.html.

Section 10

Economic and social cohesion ([1])

Overview

355.   In 2002 work concentrated on improving the quality of the Structural Funds programmes for the period 2002–06 and the projects to be carried out; the implementation and closure of operations decided on before 2000 also made considerable progress. Steps were taken to improve the financial management of the Funds, principally through simplification. The forthcoming enlargement of the European Union and reflections on the future of its policy on economic and social cohesion were features of much work done and many initiatives taken. The Union reacted rapidly to the catastrophic flooding in central Europe by establishing a Solidarity Fund to help the regions affected.

General outline

356.   Monitoring the Commission's reports ([2]). On 30 January, as part of the discussions on the analyses and proposals in its second report on economic and social cohesion which it had adopted early in 2001 ([3]), the Commission presented a progress report ([4]) updating the data, summarising the discussion on the future of cohesion policy and giving details of the administrative preparations required for the future implementation of the structural instruments in the accession countries. In its resolution of 7 February on this same report for 2001 ([5]), the European Parliament, while welcoming the results achieved in recent years as regards economic and social cohesion, noted that regional disparities which it regarded as unacceptable still remained. It asked the Commission to present a more detailed analysis of the impact on this cohesion of the principal Community policies and to supply it with a list of the measures it intended to apply to ensure compliance with the principle of additionality, which the Member States sometimes infringed. The progress report adopted early in the year was the subject of an opinion by the Committee of the Regions

---

([1]) Further information is available on the Europa server (http://europa.eu.int/comm/regional_policy/index_en.htm).
([2]) http://europa.eu.int/comm/Regional_policy/sources/docoffic/official/repor_en.htm.
([3]) COM(2001) 24; 2001 General report, point 383.
([4]) COM(2002) 46; Bull. 1/2-2002, point 1.3.145.
([5]) OJ C 284 E, 21.11.2002; Bull. 1/2-2002, point 1.3.146.

on 10 October (^{1}) and a resolution of the European Parliament on 7 November (^{2}). Parliament insisted in particular on the need for a long-term reform of the Union's structural policy and encouragement for spatial cohesion in Europe and the coherence of those Union policies having an impact on economic and social cohesion.

In its resolution of 13 June (^{3}), Parliament gave its opinion on other Commission reports, those on the implementation of the Structural Funds (2000) (^{4}), the work of the Cohesion Fund in 2000 (^{5}) and the Instrument for structural policies for pre-accession (ISPA) in 2000 (^{6}).

357.   Local partnerships and society. In its own-initiative opinion of 14 March (^{7}), the Committee of the Regions drew attention to the significant contribution which partnerships between local and regional authorities and social economy organisations could make to social cohesion, integration, employment and the establishment of firms.

358.   Cross-border cooperation. The communication presented by the Commission in 2001 on the impact of enlargement on regions bordering candidate countries was welcomed by Parliament and the Committee of the Regions (→ point 715).

359.   Island regions. In its own-initiative opinion of 13 March on these regions and their prospects in the context of enlargement (^{8}), the Committee of the Regions advocated a number of innovations, including in regard to the Treaty on European Union, so that better account could be taken of the position of the regions suffering from long-term structural handicaps such as insularity.

360.   Future of the cohesion policy. In its own-initiative opinion adopted on 17 July (^{9}), the Economic and Social Committee advocated a thorough reform of this policy, including the establishment of a single Fund, in preparation for the enlargement of the European Union. In an opinion adopted on 18 July (^{10}), it identified a series of challenges facing the Union in the area of cohesion.

361.   International Fund for Ireland. Council Regulation (EC) No 214/2000 of 24 January 2000 concerning Community financial contributions to the Inter-

---

(^{1}) Bull. 10-2002, point 1.3.63.
(^{2}) Bull. 11-2002, point 1.3.78.
(^{3}) Bull. 6-2002, point 1.3.104.
(^{4}) COM(2001) 539; 2001 General Report, point 383.
(^{5}) COM(2001) 602; 2001 General Report, point 405.
(^{6}) COM(2001) 616; 2001 General Report, point 791.
(^{7}) OJ C 192, 12.8.2002; Bull. 3-2002, point 1.3.70.
(^{8}) OJ C 192, 12.8.2002; Bull. 3-2002, point 1.3.72.
(^{9}) OJ C 241, 7.10.2002; Bull. 7/8-2002, point 1.3.94.
(^{10}) OJ C 241, 7.10.2002; Bull. 7/8-2002, point 1.3.93.

national Fund for Ireland, as it is due to expire on 31 December, the Council adopted, on 10 December, Regulation (EC) No 2236/2002, allowing the continuation of these contributions for a further two years, up to the end of the 'Peace II' programme in 2004 (Table II).

362. *European Union Solidarity Fund.* As a result of the flooding which affected Germany, Austria and several candidate countries during the summer, on 28 August the Commission adopted a communication to establish emergency aid through a European disaster relief fund and the reallocation of existing resources ([1]). On 5 September ([2]) Parliament asked the Commission to implement a general programme of rapid assistance based on the principles of solidarity and the fair sharing of burdens. Against this background, on 7 November Parliament, the Council and the Commission signed an interinstitutional agreement on the financing of the Union's Solidarity Fund and the conditions governing access to it (Table II). On 11 November the Council adopted Regulation (EC) No 2012/2002, which is designed to provide financial assistance to the inhabitants of the regions most affected by major natural disasters, including those applying for accession (Table II). That regulation provided the Solidarity Fund with a budget of EUR 1 billion per year.

Structural measures

General

363. *Management of the Structural Funds* ([3]). In its resolution of 7 February ([4]), the European Parliament asked the Commission to table specific proposals to make management of the Funds more flexible and streamlined. It also considered that the rules governing the various Funds should be more standardised, and even that a single regional development fund might be achieved in 2007. It also sought greater compliance with the principle of additionality. In its communication of 20 September on the budgetary implementation of the Structural Funds ([5]), the Commission set out the situation as regards outstanding commitments expected in the remainder of the period 2000–06, a system expected to reach a steady level in 2004. On 30 October it adopted the 13th report on the Structural Funds ([6]). On 22 January ([7]) and then on 22 February ([8]), the Council gave its opinion on two special reports by the Court

---

([1]) COM(2002) 481; Bull. 7/8-2002, point 1.4.19.
([2]) Bull. 9-2002, point 1.4.29.
([3]) http://europa.eu.int/comm/regional_policy/funds/prord/prord2_en.htm.
([4]) OJ C 284 E, 21.11.2002; Bull. 1/2-2002, point 1.3.147.
([5]) COM(2002) 528; Bull. 9-2002, point 1.3.77.
([6]) COM(2002) 591; Bull. 10-2002, point 1.3.65.
([7]) Bull. 1/2-2002, point 1.3.148.
([8]) Bull. 1/2-2002, point 1.3.149.

of Auditors, one on certain structural measures for employment [1] and one on the financial control of the Structural Funds [2].

364.   Mountain areas. In an own-initiative opinion on the future of these areas issued on 18 September [3], the Economic and Social Committee advocated their inclusion in the future policy of the Structural Funds and identified a number of measures which could be implemented under Community law as it stood at present.

Community support frameworks (CSFs) and single programming documents (SPDs)

365.   Since all the programmes concerned had been approved before the end of 2001, no new CSFs or SPDs were adopted in 2002. Complements to assistance already programmed were, however, considered.

366.   The breakdown by Member State of the commitments made in 2002 under Objective 1 is shown in Table 4.

367.   The breakdown by Member State of the commitments made in 2002 under Objective 2 is shown in Table 5.

TABLE 4

Commitments in 2002 — Objective 1

(million EUR)

Member State	ERDF	ESF	EAGGF (Guidance Section)	PEACE	FIFG
Belgium	63.990	29.717	6.965		0.328
Germany	1 655.301	872.436	494.304		24.954
Greece	2 413.532	713.499	384.984		33.464
Spain	3 541.728	1 293.200	759.720		220.000
France	338.795	136.586	101.728		5.188
Ireland	318.583	157.807	26.810		11.400
Italy	2 374.933	587.861	419.065		39.586
Netherlands	12.400	6.600	1.400		0.600
Austria	25.655	8.120	6.103		0.122
Portugal	1 961.697	677.343	329.557		33.914
Finland	69.188	38.806	29.027		0.979
Sweden	67.903	23.131	16.467		1.731
United Kingdom	585.693	268.335	53.959		15.013
Other				106.000	
Total	13 429.398	4 780.441	2 630.089	106.000	387.279

[1] Special Report No 12/2001 (OJ C 334, 28.11.2001; 2001 General Report, point 1219).
[2] Special Report No 10/2001 (OJ C 314, 8.11.2001; 2001 General Report, point 1219).
[3] Bull. 9-2002, point 1.3.76.

368. The rural development measures financed by the EAGGF Guarantee Section forming part of the programming for Objective 2 are included in Table 11 in Chapter III (→ point 400).

TABLE 5

Commitments in 2002 — Objective 2

(million EUR)

Member State	ERDF	ESF
Belgium	80.255	9.094
Denmark	20.863	8.136
Germany	530.516	79.193
Spain	357.920	49.080
France	819.384	130.751
Italy	491.100	
Luxembourg	7.450	
Netherlands	149.070	
Austria	105.135	4.371
Finland	59.824	16.177
Sweden	57.706	7.294
United Kingdom	670.900	77.100
Total	3 350.122	381.198

369. The breakdown by Member State of the commitments made in 2002 under Objective 3 ('Adaptation and modernisation of policies and systems for education, training and employment') is shown in Table 6.

TABLE 6

Commitments in 2002 — Objective 3

(million EUR)

Member State	ESF (excluding Objective 1 areas)
Belgium	111.729
Denmark	55.334
Germany	694.484
Spain	324.426
France	688.269
Italy	567.594
Luxembourg	5.760
Netherlands	255.599
Austria	80.045
Finland	61.095
Sweden	109.152
United Kingdom	692.514
Total	3 646.001

370.   The breakdown by Member State of the commitments made in 2002 under the Financial Instrument for Fisheries Guidance (FIFG) outside the Objective 1 regions is shown in Table 7.

TABLE 7

Commitments in 2002 — FIFG

(million EUR)

Member State	FIFG (excluding areas under Objective 1)
Belgium	5.2
Denmark	29.9
Germany	16.3
Spain	30.4
France	34.2
Italy	14.6
Netherlands [1]	10.2
Austria	0.6
Finland	4.7
Sweden	9.1
United Kingdom	18.3
Total	173.5

[1] The programme for the Netherlands was not adjusted until 2002 and the commitment made concerns the instalments for 2001 and 2002.

Community initiatives

371.   URBAN *(Community initiative for urban areas).* On 14 June the Commission presented an initial assessment [1] of the URBAN initiative, in which it reviewed the key characteristics of the programmes for 2000–06 [2]. As regards method, these concerned mainly administrative simplification, an integrated approach bringing together a number of factors, the 'indirect' zoning method allowing targeting of the least-favoured areas and the stress on local partnerships, which means that the municipalities themselves manage two-thirds of the projects with, in more than 80 % of the cases, a substantial participation by the local authorities, in line with the recommendations on developing competencies and participation in civil society in the Commission's White Paper on governance *(→ point 23).* The Commission's conclusions were considered at a conference which it organised on 'Cities for cohesion', which was held in London on 8 and 9 July at the invitation of the Mayor of London. At the end of that conference, attended by Mr Barnier, Member of the Commission, 75 mayors representing 60 million people signed the 'London declaration' solemnly proclaiming

[1] COM(2002) 308; Bull. 6-2002, point 1.3.105.
[2] COM(1999) 477, 1999 General Report, points 321 and 343; Internet (http://europa.eu.int/comm/regional_ policy/urban2/index_en.htm).

the need for more resources to be devoted to urban measures in the European Union. The Urbact programme, a further initiative for urban development, was adopted on 20 December. It seeks to associate the Member States and the cities which make up their own network using assistance from the Commission, which will enable them to exchange a considerable amount of experience, best practice and evaluation indicators through systematic learning cycles.

372.   *Interreg.* In 2002 this programme gave priority to work preparing for the integration of the applicant countries into the programme, with special finance totalling EUR 30 million for the frontier regions of those countries and better coordination and coherence between the Phare and Tacis programmes. On 16 December the Commission approved the Interact trans-European programme. This programme, which will receive EUR 25 million up to 2006 from the Interreg III Community initiative and EUR 10 million from the Member States, is intended to increase the impact of Interreg on economic and social cohesion and the intensity of regional cooperation both within the European Union and with neighbouring countries.

373.   The breakdown by Member States of the commitments made in 2002 under the Community initiatives is shown in Table 8.

TABLE 8

Commitments in 2002 — Community initiatives

(million EUR)

Member State	Leader	Interreg	Equal	Urban
Belgium	5.300		13.756	3.900
Denmark	2.500		5.028	0.900
Germany	53.889		86.838	25.200
Greece	26.500		17.580	4.300
Spain	73.629		87.056	19.100
France	38.900		54.056	17.300
Ireland	6.900		5.736	0.900
Italy	68.039		66.608	19.400
Luxembourg	0.308		0.726	
Netherlands	12.000		35.160	5.000
Austria	10.900		17.226	1.400
Portugal	23.400		19.250	3.200
Finland	8.000		12.198	0.900
Sweden	5.900		14.576	0.900
United Kingdom	20.635		67.452	21.100
Other		963.683		2.800
Total	356.800	963.683	503.246	126.300

Innovative measures and other regional operations

374. On 18 February the Council amended Regulation (EEC) No 2019/93 of 19 July 1993 introducing specific measures for the smaller Aegean islands concerning certain agricultural products (Table II). On 7 October the Commission adopted a report on the progress achieved in implementing those measures in 1998 and 1999 ([1]).

375. Following the announcement in 2001 of innovative measures and the innovative system of direct contracts with the regional authorities, 103 of the 154 regions eligible applied so that in 2002 a total of EUR 206 million was granted to projects financed in 81 regions. During the year 58 other applications were made.

Cohesion Fund ([2])

376. On 15 October, the Commission adopted the annual report on the work of the Cohesion Fund in 2001 ([3]). The equal balance between commitments for transport and the environment was broadly respected (48.5 % and 51.5 % respectively). Finance went mainly on the one hand to rail and on the other to the supply of drinking water and the treatment of waste water and solid waste. In view of the long time elapsing between the commitment of expenditure and payment noted during implementation, in 2002 the Commission took steps to reduce these delays, including drawing up guidelines on the extension of time for payments and a plan to close projects financed in 1993–99. These measures will be monitored by a Cohesion Fund coordinating group.

377. In 2002, total commitments to finance Cohesion Fund projects amounted to EUR 2 791.47 million. The breakdown of these commitments by country and area is given in Table 9.

Pre-accession instruments

378. The work of the instrument for structural policies for pre-accession (ISPA) is dealt with in Section 4 ('Pre-accession strategies') of Chapter V (→ *point 729*).

([1]) COM(2002) 546; Bull. 10-2002, point 1.3.66.
([2]) http://europa.eu.int/comm/regional_policy/intro/regions1_en.htm.
([3]) COM(2002) 557; Bull. 10-2002, point 1.3.64. Previous report: 2001 General Report, point 405.

TABLE 9
Commitments in 2002 — Cohesion Fund

Member State	Environment		Transport		Total	Breakdown
	(million EUR)	%	(million EUR)	%	(million EUR)	(%)
Greece	220.580	11.1	114.578	7.9	335.158	12.0
Spain	930.467	81.7	1 046.237	74.3	1 976.704	70.8
Ireland	75.378	3.7	107.283	3.4	182.661	6.5
Portugal	60.319	3.5	236.462	14.4	296.781	10.6
Technical assistance					0.165	0.01
Grand total	1 286.745	100	1 504.559	100	2 791.469	100

Section 11

Measures for the outermost regions (¹)

379.   *General approach*. Measures for the outermost regions (the French over-seas departments, Canary Islands, Azores and Madeira) continued in accord-ance with the strategy for the sustainable development of these regions set out in the Commission report of 14 March 2000 (²) on the measures to implement Article 299(2) of the EC Treaty. These measures concerned the three aspects of the strategy: traditional production (agriculture and fisheries), diversification and modernisation, and regional cooperation and the international environ-ment. In an own-initiative opinion on 29 May (³), the European Economic and Social Committee asked for preferential treatment for access by these regions to Community programmes and projects. The Seville European Council on 21 and 22 June (⁴) asked the Council and the Commission to make proposals to take account of the specific needs of these regions through the various common pol-icies, particularly transport, and when certain policies, especially regional pol-icy, were revised. On 19 December, the Commission adopted a half-yearly report on the implementation of Article 299(2) EC (⁵).

380.   *Fisheries*. On 25 March, the Council extended for one year up to 31 December 2002 the scheme to compensate for the additional costs incurred in the marketing of certain fishery products from the Azores, Madeira, the Canary Islands and French departments of French Guyana and Réunion as a result of those regions' remoteness (Table II).

381.   *Taxation*. On 18 February the Council authorised France to extend to 31 December 2009 the application of a reduced rate of excise duty on 'tradi-tional' rum produced in its overseas departments (Table II). On the same day, it authorised Portugal to reduce the rate of excise duty on rum and liqueurs from Madeira and on liqueurs and *eaux-de-vie* from the Azores (Table II). On 20 June, it authorised Spain to lay down, in respect of certain products, total exemptions from or reductions of the tax known as the *arbitrio sobre las importaciones y entregas de mercancías en las Islas Canarias (AIEM)*, until 31 December 2011 as part of its promotion of local activities in the Canary Islands (Table II). On 10 December the Council extended until 31 December 2003

(¹) Further information is available on the Internet (http://www.erup.net).
(²) COM(2000) 147; 2000 General Report, point 368.
(³) OJ C 221, 17.9.2002; Bull. 5-2002, point 1.3.84.
(⁴) Bull. 6-2002, point I.26.
(⁵) COM(2002) 723; Bull. 12-2002, point 1.3.101.

the exemptions currently in force from the dock duties to support local production in the French overseas departments (Table II).

382.   Customs. On 25 March, in order to enable the industrial sector in the Canary Islands to improve its competitiveness, the Council adopted Regulation (EC) No 704/2002 temporarily suspending autonomous common customs tariff duties on imports of certain industrial products and opening tariff quotas for certain fisheries products (Table II).

Section 12

Trans-European networks (¹)

General approach

383.   Guidelines. The Barcelona European Council called for the adoption of revised guidelines for the trans-European energy (²) *(→ point 390)* and transport (³) *(→ point 387)* networks, including the priority projects identified by the Commission, and revised financial rules for these networks *(→ point 385)*. In an own-initiative opinion adopted on 25 April (⁴), the European Economic and Social Committee advocated linking the islands of Europe with the trans-European networks so as to reduce the gap in terms of their development.

384.   Annual report. On 1 July, the Commission adopted the report for 2000 (⁵). While painting a generally positive picture, the Commission nevertheless identifies a series of weaknesses and gaps which it wishes to tackle in the years ahead, particularly in the implementation of the trans-European transport network, e.g. through the development of the railways to rebalance the modal split.

385.   Financial assistance. The legislative work with a view to drawing up new general rules for the granting of Community financial assistance in the field of trans-European networks continued throughout the year (Table I).

Community funding for the trans-European networks (TENs) is shown in Table 10. The TEN Financial Assistance Committee met six times during the course of the year and endorsed the commitment of EUR 618.4 million, of which EUR 581.4 million for transport, including intelligent transport systems, EUR 22 million for telecommunications and telematics and EUR 15 million for energy.

(¹) Additional information is available on Europa (http://europa.eu.int/comm/energy_transport/en/tn_en.html).
(²) Bull. 3-2002, point I.32.
(³) Bull. 3-2002, point I.33.
(⁴) OJ C 149, 21.6.2002; Bull. 4-2002, point 1.3.82.
(⁵) COM(2002) 344; Bull. 7/8-2002, point 1.3.97.

TABLE 10
Community financing of TENs in 2002

(million ECU/EUR)

Sector	Type of aid	Instrument	1993-96	1997	1998	1999	2000	2001	2002
Transport	Loans	EIB	11 170	4 943	4 415	5 977	4 010	5 066	4 908
	Guarantees	EIF	464	55	71	256	80	—(¹)	—(¹)
	Subsidies	Structural Funds	3 638	527	n.a.	n.a.	n.a.	n.a.	n.a.
		Cohesion Fund	4 216	1 251	1 337	444	1 277	1 563	1 504
	Subsidies, interest rebates, loan guarantees and co-financing of studies	TENs budget heading B5-70	905	352	474	497	592	572	581
		(of which the 14 priority projects)	573	211	305	266	253	221	211
Energy	Loans	EIB	2 998	854	393	174	392	0	185
	Guarantees	EIF	490	4	5	0	15	—(¹)	—(¹)
	Co-financing of studies and subsidies	Structural Funds	2 029	277	n.a.	355	n.a.	n.a.	n.a.
		TENs budget heading B5-71	21	24	19	29	13	19	15
Telecommunications	Loans	EIB	5 921	1 880	3 434	2 126	2 211	994	180
	Guarantees	EIF	184	276	230	44	140	—(¹)	—(¹)
	Financial contributions	Structural Funds	468	n.a.	n.a.	387	n.a.	n.a.	n.a.
	Co-financing of feasibility and validation studies	TENs budget heading B5-720	61	27	28	21	35	33	22
Telematic networks	Subsidies	TENs budget heading B5-721	163	47	15	24	20	22	23

(¹) The EIF's guarantee activity was transferred to the EIB at the end of 2000.
NB: n.a. = not available.

Transport

386.   *Inland waterways.* In an own-initiative opinion adopted on 16 January on the future of the trans-European inland waterway network (¹), the European Economic and Social Committee recommended increasing the efforts to promote intermodal transport, of which inland waterways are one component.

387.   *Revision of the guidelines.* In parallel with the continuation of the legislative procedure with a view to revising the guidelines adopted in 1996 for the development of the trans-European transport network (Table I), after amending its proposal on this subject in September the Commission set up a high-level group of representatives of the Member States and observers from the accession candidate countries to assist it with the revision process.

Telematics and telecommunications

388.   *Revision of the guidelines.* On 12 July, the European Parliament and the Council amended Decision No 1336/97/EC on the guidelines (Table I). The new decision redefines in particular the 'projects of common interest'.

389.   Electronic interchange of data between administrations (IDA) is dealt with in Section 7 ('Enterprise') of this chapter *(→ point 285)*.

Energy

390.   *Revision of the guidelines.* The legislative procedure with a view to revising the guidelines adopted in 1996 continued throughout the year (Table I), the most recent stage being the political agreement reached by the Council on 25 November with a view to a common position, following the European Parliament opinion on first reading delivered on 24 October.

Environment

391.   *Revision of the guidelines.* The Commission continued its evaluation (²) of the environmental aspects of Decision No 1692/96/EC on the development of the trans-European transport network *(→ points 386 and 387)*, with a view to revising the guidelines in connection with these particular aspects.

(¹) OJ C 80, 3.4.2002; Bull. 1/2-2002, point 1.3.153.
(²) 2001 General Report, point 427.

Section 13

Agriculture and rural development (¹)

Overview

392. *As regards internal affairs, in accordance with Agenda 2000 adopted by the Berlin European Council in 1999, the Commission presented a major communication on the mid-term review of the common agricultural policy, recommending, among other things, a number of reforms relating to aid mechanisms and the promotion of rural development. As regards external affairs, in addition to the successful conclusion of the enlargement negotiations on the agriculture chapter, the focus was on monitoring the agricultural part of the agenda agreed at Doha in 2001 for a new round of multilateral trade negotiations.*

Content of the common agricultural policy (CAP) (²)

393. *Mid-term review of the CAP.* In a communication of 10 July (³), the Commission proposed a review in line with the objectives and general framework (Agenda 2000) laid down by the Berlin European Council in 1999 (⁴). The proposal is aimed at stabilising the markets and improving the common market organisations (the first pillar of the CAP), introducing simpler and more sustainable direct support, achieving a better balance of support for sustainable agriculture and rural development and consolidating and strengthening rural development (the second pillar). To achieve this, the Commission makes the following proposals: direct aid should be decoupled from production; direct payments should be conditional on compliance with environmental, food safety, animal welfare and occupational safety standards; EU support should be substantially increased by modulating direct payments; a new farm audit system should be introduced; new rural development measures should be introduced to improve production quality, food safety and animal welfare and cover the costs of the farm audit. Turning to market policy, the Commission is proposing to

---

(¹) For more details see *Agriculture in the European Union — Statistical and economic information 2001*, the Internet site (http://europa.eu.int/comm/agriculture/agrista/2001/table_en/index.htm) and the 2000 Report available from the Office for Official Publications of the European Communities and on the Europa server (http://europa.eu.int/comm/agriculture/publi/agrep2000/index_en.htm). Additional information is also available on Europa (http://europa.eu.int/comm/dgs/agriculture/index_en.htm).
(²) http://europa.eu.int/comm/agriculture/mtr/index_en.htm.
(³) COM(2002) 394; Bull. 7/8-2002, point 1.3.100.
(⁴) 1999 General Report, points 6 and 495 to 501.

improve the competitiveness of Community agriculture by completing the process of reform started in 1992 ([1]), in particular by means of reductions in a number of intervention measures. The Commission communication was dealt with in a Parliament resolution of 7 November ([2]), a Committee of the Regions opinion of 21 November ([3]) and a European Economic and Social Committee opinion of 11 December ([4]).

394.   Future of the CAP. In an own-initiative opinion adopted on 21 March ([5]) the European Economic and Social Committee evaluated the changes in the CAP over the past decade and looked at present and future demands on farming from the standpoint of 'multifunctional agriculture' to which the Community is committed. Among other things it recommended modulation of aid to promote environmental protection schemes.

395.   Enlargement. On 30 January, the Commission adopted an issues paper on integrating the new Member States into the CAP, on which Parliament adopted a resolution on 13 June *(→ point 708)*. The adaptation of certain agricultural concessions in the form of tariff quotas for agricultural products from the applicant countries is covered in Section 4 (Pre-accession strategy) of Chapter V *(→ points 718 and 719)*.

396.   Promotion of the cultivation of plant proteins. Referring to the options set out by the Commission in March 2001 to achieve this objective ([6]), in an own-initiative opinion of 16 January ([7]) the European Economic and Social Committee recommended a number of measures, such as the development of research and the provision of appropriate funding. In a resolution of 3 September ([8]) Parliament took the view that the European Union's virtually exclusive reliance on imports of such products placed it in a vulnerable position and recommended that EU plant protein production should be encouraged by means of measures such as research programmes and authorising the cultivation of these crops on set-aside land and traditional fallow land.

397.   Recognition of producer organisations. On 14 October the Council adopted Regulation (EC) No 1881/2002 rectifying an error relative to the starting date of the transitional period laid down in Regulation (EC) No 2200/96 ([9]), to enable producer organisations to adjust to the new conditions on the fruit and vegetable markets (Table II).

([1]) Twenty-sixth General Report, points 506 to 512.
([2]) Bull. 11-2002, point 1.3.81.
([3]) Bull. 11-2002, point 1.3.82.
([4]) Bull. 12-2002, point 1.3.106.
([5]) OJ C 125, 27.5.2002; Bull. 3-2002, point 1.3.78.
([6]) COM(2001) 148; 2001 General Report, point 432.
([7]) OJ C 80, 3.4.2002; Bull. 1/2-2002, point 1.3.156.
([8]) Bull. 9-2002, point 1.3.80.
([9]) OJ L 297, 21.11.1996.

Agriculture and the environment, forests [1]

398.   New measures were introduced and legislative initiatives proposed on the protection of forests in the Community against atmospheric pollution and fire (→ point 572).

Rural development [2]

399.   *Agenda 2000.* In a resolution of 30 May [3] assessing progress made with the rural development pillar of the CAP introduced with the Agenda 2000 reform [4], Parliament called for this pillar to be strengthened, especially in budgetary terms, also taking account of enlargement. On 26 February the Commission adopted new detailed rules [5] for the application of Council Regulation (EC) No 1257/1999 on support for rural development from the European Agricultural Guidance and Guarantee Fund (EAGGF) [6], replacing Regulation (EC) No 1750/1999 [7].

400.   *Statistical data.* A breakdown of EAGGF Guarantee Section aid for rural development by Member State is given in Table 11.

TABLE 11

EAGGF Guarantee Section rural development payments, by Member State

Payments from 16 October 2001 to 15 October 2002

(million EUR)

Member State	EAGGF Guarantee Section
Belgium	47.5
Denmark	49.8
Germany	730.7
Greece	160.3
Spain	450.0
France	678.5
Ireland	333.0
Italy	652.6
Luxembourg	12.8
Netherlands	50.6
Austria	440.4
Portugal	167.7
Finland	320.1
Sweden	163.1
United Kingdom	161.8
Total	4 418.9

[1] http://europa.eu.int/comm/agriculture/envir/index_en.htm.
[2] http://europa.eu.int/comm/agriculture/rur/index_en.htm.
[3] Bull. 5-2002, point 1.3.90.
[4] 1999 General Report, points 6 and 495 to 501.
[5] Regulation (EC) No 445/2002 (OJ L 74, 15.3.2002).
[6] OJ L 160, 26.6.1999; 1999 General Report, point 502.
[7] OJ L 214, 13.8.1999; 1999 General Report, point 502.

Veterinary and plant health legislation

401. This is covered in Section 7 (Health and consumer protection) of Chapter IV (→ *points 674* et seq.).

Quality of agricultural products [1]

402. Protection of geographical indications and designations of origin. On 15 March the Commission proposed an amendment of Regulation (EEC) No 2081/92 [2] governing protection for agricultural products (Table II) to take account of the rules set by the 1994 agreement on trade-related aspects of intellectual property rights and the technical rules resulting from Community legislation. On 14 June it adopted a proposal for a regulation to register 'Feta' as a protected designation of origin [3].

403. Specific standards. In a report of 19 July [4] the Commission reviewed the application of Council Regulation (EC) No 2991/94 [5] laying down standards for spreadable fats.

404. Organic farming. On 16 October [6] the Commission proposed amendments to Regulation (EEC) No 2092/91 [7] exceptionally authorising the use of certain synthetic vitamins as additives in ruminant feed for a transitional period. This initiative is a response to various difficulties encountered in organic livestock farming.

Management of the common agricultural policy

Common market organisations (COMs)

405. Reform of the COMs in the context of Agenda 2000. In a resolution of 30 May [8] on the mid-term review of the reform, Parliament took the view that Community action in the agricultural sector must be developed, taking account of the principle of multifunctionality, enlargement, sustainability, negotiations in the World Trade Organisation, and the new requirements of society. It also

---

[1] http://europa.eu.int/comm/agriculture/qual/en/prod_en.htm.
[2] OJ L 208, 24.7.1992.
[3] COM(2002) 314; Bull. 6-2002, point 1.3.114.
[4] COM(2002) 411; Bull. 7/8-2002, point 1.3.106.
[5] OJ L 316, 9.12.1994; 1994 General Report, point 622.
[6] COM(2002) 561; Bull. 10-2002, point 1.3.70.
[7] OJ L 198, 22.7.1991; Twenty-fifth General Report, point 546.
[8] Bull. 5-2002, point 1.3.91.

wanted to see greater account taken of the interests of the poorest countries, called for a policy of support for rural development, producer groups and young farmers, and hoped that future reforms of the COMs would take full account of social, environmental and territorial factors.

Crop products

406.   Alcohol. The agreements on trade in wine and spirit drinks between the Community and South Africa initialled at the end of 2001 were signed on 28 January (Table III). On 21 January the Council exchanged letters with South Africa to amend some of the annexes to the Trade, Development and Cooperation Agreement signed in 1999 to adjust the quantity covered by the tariff quota for South African wine imported in bottles (Table III).

407.   Bananas. On 25 February ([1]) the Commission amended the rules for the application ([2]) of Council Regulation (EEC) No 404/93 as regards the system for importing bananas into the Community ([3]) as part of the second stage of the arrangements for the management of tariff quotas for this product agreed with the United States and Ecuador in April 2001 ([4]).

408.   Cereals. To provide for the application of the agreements currently being concluded between the Community and Canada and the United States (Table III) respectively, on 11 December the Commission proposed an amendment of the import arrangements in Council Regulation (EEC) No 1766/92 on the common organisation of the market in this sector (Table II).

409.   Potato starch. In conclusions of 18 February ([5]) the Council made various recommendations as regards the Court of Auditors' Special Report No 8/2001 on refunds and production aid for this product ([6]). On 27 May it rolled over the quota regime for the eight Member States concerned for the 2002/03, 2003/04 and 2004/05 marketing years (Table II).

410.   Fruit and vegetables. In a resolution of 14 March ([7]) Parliament condemned the unilateral measures taken by the United States in 2001 excluding Community clementines from the US market. On 18 March the Council extended the funding of plans for improving the quality and marketing of certain nuts and locust beans and introduced special aid for producers of hazelnuts

---

([1]) Regulation (EC) No 349/2002 (OJ L 55, 26.2.2002; Bull. 1/2-2002, point 1.3.161).
([2]) Regulation (EC) No 896/2001 (OJ L 126, 8.5.2001; 2001 General Report, point 449), as last amended by Regulation (EC) No 2351/2001 (OJ L 315, 1.12.2001).
([3]) OJ L 47, 25.2.1993; Twenty-seventh General Report, point 529.
([4]) 2001 General Report, points 449 and 880.
([5]) Bull. 1/2-2002, point 1.3.163.
([6]) OJ C 294, 19.10.2001; 2001 General Report, point 1219.
([7]) Bull. 3-2002, point 1.3.81.

(Table II). In a report of 10 July (^{1}) the Commission presented an analysis of the economic, social and environmental aspects of nut production in the European Union.

411. Hops. On 28 November (^{2}) the Council extended the special temporary measures introduced in the sector in 1998 by one year to stabilise the market (^{3}).

412. Olive oil. To ensure budget predictability, on 14 October the Council adopted Regulation (EC) No 1873/2002 setting the limits to the Community financing of work programmes drawn up by operators' organisations in the olive sector (Table II). On 26 November (^{4}) it extended the 1986 international agreement on olive oil and table olives (^{5}) to 30 June 2003. The Commission adopted rules of application for the funding of the work programmes of operators' organisations in the olive sector (^{6}) and regulations on physical and chemical characteristics (^{7}) and marketing standards for olive oil (^{8}), thus completing the regulatory framework for application of the quality strategy for olive oil in the European Union in accordance with the Council's conclusions of July 2001 (^{9}).

413. Rice. In a report of 10 July (^{10}) the Commission presented an in-depth analysis of the market, which is marked by persistent imbalance, and the current market organisation and medium-term forecasts with a view to making appropriate proposals for new mechanisms under the reform of the COM for rice.

414. Seeds. On 21 January the Council rolled over the current amounts of aid granted in the sector for the 2002/03 and 2003/04 marketing years and provided for the introduction of a stabiliser mechanism (Table II).

415. Tobacco. On 25 March the Council adopted Regulation (EC) No 546/2002 fixing the premiums and guarantee thresholds by variety group and Member State for the 2002, 2003 and 2004 harvests (Table II).

(^{1}) SEC(2002) 797; Bull. 7/8-2002, point 1.3.104.
(^{2}) Regulation (EC) No 2151/2002 (OJ L 327, 4.12.2002; Bull. 11-2002, point 1.3.83).
(^{3}) Council Regulation (EC) No 1098/98 (OJ L 57, 30.5.1998; 1998 General Report, point 578).
(^{4}) Bull. 11-2002, point 1.3.84.
(^{5}) OJ L 214, 2.8.1987. Previous amendment: OJ L 298, 3.12.1993.
(^{6}) Regulation (EC) No 1334/2002 (OJ L 195, 24.7.2002).
(^{7}) Regulation (EC) No 796/2002 (OJ L 128, 15.5.2002).
(^{8}) Regulation (EC) No 1019/2002 (OJ L 155, 14.6.2002).
(^{9}) 2001 General Report, point 455.
(^{10}) SEC(2002) 788; Bull. 7/8-2002, point 1.3.107.

Livestock products

416. Milk. In conclusions of 18 February ([1]) the Council reacted to the Court of Auditors' Special Report No 6/2001 on milk quotas ([2]). It recommended that the report be used as a contribution to the Commission's mid-term review of the development of the milk quota system. In a report of 10 July ([3]) adopted at the same time as its proposal for the mid-term review of the common agricultural policy *(→ point 393)* the Commission assessed application of the regime so far and the prospects for the Community milk market. To avoid a situation in which the specific measure exempting milk producers in Madeira (under the Poseima regulation) from the quota system ([4]) could be detrimental to the milk quota system in Portugal, on 11 November the Council adopted Regulation (EC) No 2028/2002 amending Regulation (EEC) No 3950/92 establishing an additional levy in the milk and milk products sector (Table II).

417. Sheepmeat. In a report of 12 June ([5]), while regretting the lack of progress in the use of the Community classification grid for sheep carcases ([6]), the Commission proposed that, having proved useful in those cases in which it had been applied, the system should remain unchanged.

Other work

Food aid

418. On 24 September the Council agreed on an extension of the 1999 Food Aid Convention ([7]). In 2002 the Union spent EUR 200 million on a food aid programme for the needy. Food aid for developing countries is covered in Section 4 (Development cooperation) of Chapter VI *(→ points 837 and 839).*

State aid schemes

419. These are covered in Section 6 (Competition policy) of this chapter *(→ point 241).*

([1]) Bull. 1/2-2002, point 1.3.165.
([2]) OJ C 305, 30.10.2001; 2001 General Report, point 1219.
([3]) SEC(2002) 789; Bull. 7/8-2002, point 1.3.105.
([4]) Council Regulation (EC) No 1453/2001 (OJ L 198, 21.7.2001; 2001 General Report, point 409).
([5]) COM(2002) 295; Bull. 6-2002, point 1.3.118. Previous report: COM(97) 250; 1997 General Report, point 628.
([6]) Council Regulation (EEC) No 2137/92 (OJ L 214, 30.7.1992), as last amended by Council Regulation (EC) No 2536/97 (OJ L 347, 18.12.1997; 1997 General Report, point 628).
([7]) OJ L 163, 4.7.2000; 1999 General Report, point 735.

Farm accountancy data network (FADN) ([1])

420. In 2002 the FADN published macroeconomic agricultural statistics for the 15 Member States, notably on farm incomes and production costs. These data, representative of farm types and sizes at regional level, were used for analytical work both in and outside the Commission, much of it devoted to assessment of common market organisations such as olive oil and tobacco. They were also widely used for preparing the mid-term review of the common agricultural policy (→ *point 393).*

Advisory committees and relations with professional organisations

421. At the 82 meetings of advisory committees and working parties held in 2002 the Commission maintained a dialogue on CAP developments, including the mid-term review, with representatives of producers, processors, traders, consumers, workers, and environmental protection and rural development organisations.

Agricultural management and regulatory committees

422. The committees' activities are given in Table 12.

Financing the common agricultural policy: the EAGGF ([2])

423. *Appropriations in the 2002 budget for the EAGGF Guarantee Section* totalled EUR 44.255 billion, broken down as follows (million EUR):

• Crop products	27 349
• Livestock products	10 859.58
• Ancillary expenditure	1 951.50
• Clearance, reductions/suspensions, appropriations, provisions	− 500
Total (subheading 1a)	39 660.08
• Rural development	4 595
Total (subheading 1b)	4 595
Guarantee Section total	44 255.08

([1]) http://europa.eu.int/comm/agriculture/rica/index_en.cfm.
([2]) http://europa.eu.int/comm/agriculture/fin/index_en.htm.

TABLE 12

Activities of agricultural management and regulatory committees

Committee	1 January to 31 December 2002			
	Meetings (¹)	Opinions for	No opinion	Opinions against
Management Committee for Cereals	45	608	46	0
Management Committee for Pigmeat	14	18	5	0
Management Committee for Poultrymeat and Eggs	13	76	0	0
Management Committee for Fresh Fruit and Vegetables	14	43	9	0
Management Committee for Wine	27	35	4	0
Management Committee for Milk and Milk Products	24	135	14	0
Management Committee for Beef and Veal	22	71	2	0
Management Committee for Sheep and Goats	4	7	0	0
Management Committee for Oils and Fats	17	21	12	0
Management Committee for Sugar	47	175	0	0
Management Committee for Live Plants and Floriculture Products	2	1	1	0
Management Committee for Products Processed from Fruit and Vegetables	12	20	1	0
Management Committee for Tobacco	9	9	0	0
Management Committee for Hops	5	3	1	0
Management Committee for Natural Fibres	7	7	0	0
Management Committee for Seeds	3	1	0	0
Management Committee for Dried Fodder	1	1	0	0
Implementation Committee for Spirit Drinks	3	1	0	0
Implementation Committee for Aromatised Wine-based Drinks	1	1	0	0
Management Committee for Bananas	6	11	1	0
Joint meetings of management committees (¹)	30	23	0	0
EAGGF Committee	17	16	0	0
Committee on Agricultural Structures and Rural Development	12	60	0	0
Community Committee on the Farm Accountancy Data Network	3	2	0	0
Standing Committee on Agricultural Research	1	0	0	0
Standing Forestry Committee	6	4	0	0
Standing Committee on Organic Farming	7	6	1	0
Committee on Protected Geographical Indications and Designations of Origin (²)	3	0	1	0
Committee on Certificates of Specific Character (²)	1	0	0	0
Committee on the Conservation, Characterisation, Collection and Utilisation of Genetic Resources in agriculture	1	0	0	0
Joint meetings of regulatory committees	0	0	0	0

(¹) Including those devoted to trade mechanisms (11 meetings), promoting agricultural products (10 meetings) and agrimonetary matters (two meetings).

(²) For agricultural and food products.

424.   Appropriations in the 2003 budget. When the 2003 budget was adopted on 19 December *(→ point 1029)* the appropriations allocated to the EAGGF Guarantee Section were EUR 44 780.45 million. Table 13 shows, by chapter, expenditure from 1999 to 2001 and the initial allocations in the 2002 and 2003 budgets.

TABLE 13

EAGGF Guarantee Section expenditure, by sector ([1])

(million EUR)

Sector or type of measure	Expenditure 1999	Expenditure 2000 ([2])	Expenditure 2001	Appropriations 2002 ([2])	Appropriations 2003 ([3])
Arable crops ([4])	17 865.9	16 663.1	17 466.2	17 916.0	16 790.0
Sugar	2 112.8	1 910.2	1 497.1	1 401.0	1 482.0
Olive oil	2 091.8	2 210.1	2 523.8	2 366.0	2 341.0
Dried fodder and dried legumes	376.4	381.3	374.8	385.0	389.0
Fibre plants	1 027.1	991.4	826.3	956.0	908.0
Fruit and vegetables	1 454.1	1 551.3	1 558.0	1 650.0	1 609.0
Wine	614.6	765.5	1 196.7	1 392.0	1 381.0
Tobacco	911.1	987.1	973.4	983.0	973.0
Other crop sectors or products	285.3	350.0	297.4	300.0	303.0
Milk and milk products	2 510.1	2 544.3	1 906.6	1 912.0	2 672.0
Beef and veal	4 578.6	4 539.6	6 054.0	8 095.0	8 404.0
Sheepmeat and goatmeat	1 894.3	1 735.6	1 447.3	672.0	1 805.0
Pigmeat, eggs and poultry, other	449.2	446.9	137.1	163.5	203.5
Fishery products	7.8	9.4	13.4	17.08	14.45
Non-Annex I products	573.4	572.2	435.6	415.0	415.0
Food programmes	390.5	308.9	281.8	306.0	306.0
POSEI programmes	223.7	226.9	183.6	253.9	264.0
Veterinary and plant health measures	—	—	565.5	569.5	190.0
Monitoring and preventive measures	23.3	74.6	32.1	57.3	48.0
Clearance and reductions/suspensions (B1-10 to 39)	− 606.2	− 1 077.9	− 569.7	− 500.0	− 500.0
Promotion and information measures	68.5	48.7	48.9	78.8	66.5
Other measures ([5])	100.2	933.1	469.8	271.0	18.0
Subheading 1a: total	39 952.5	36 172.2	37 719.7	39 660.08	40 082.45
Subceiling 1a		37 352.0	40 035.0	41 992.0	42 680.0
Margin		1 179.8	2 315.3	2 331.92	2 597.55
Rural development and accompanying measures (subheading 1b)	2 588.2	4 176.4	4 363.8	4 595.0	4 698.0
Subceiling 1b		4 386.0	4 494.5	4 595.0	4 698.0
Margin		209.6	125.7	0	0
Total (1a + 1b)	39 540.7	40 348.6	42 088.5	44 255.08	44 780.45
Guideline	45 188.0	46 549.0	48 788.0	50 867.0	51 889.0
Margin	5 647.3	6 200.4	6 699.5	6 611.92	7 108.55

([1]) In accordance with the nomenclature in the 2002 draft budget.

([2]) Including the appropriations entered in Chapter B-40 (reserves and provisions). Not including the monetary reserve entered in Chapter B1-60.

([3]) Commitment appropriations entered in the draft 2003 budget.

([4]) Cereals, oilseeds, protein crops and set-aside.

([5]) From the 1996 budget this chapter mainly covers agrimonetary aid.

425.   Financial reports. On 4 November the Commission adopted its 31st financial report on the EAGGF Guarantee Section for the 2001 financial year ([1]). On 22 November, in accordance with Council Regulation (EC) No 2040/2000 on budgetary discipline ([2]), it submitted a report to the budget authority on the impact on EAGGF Guarantee Section expenditure between 1 August 2001 and 31 July 2002 of movements in the euro/dollar exchange rate ([3]).

426.   Clearance of Member States' accounts (EAGGF Guarantee Section expenditure). The Commission adopted several decisions: on 12 June ([4]) in respect of the 2001 financial year; on 26 June ([5]) and 28 June ([6]) excluding from Community financing certain expenditure incurred by Member States; and on 14 October ([7]) in respect of the 1995 financial year.

427.   Integrated administration and control system (IACS). In conclusions of 28 January ([8]) on the Court of Auditors' Special Report No 4/2001 on the audit of the EAGGF Guarantee Section ([9]) the Council noted that the absence of uniform interpretation of the IACS rules in the Member States could lead to unequal treatment between farmers in the European Union and recommended that the Commission clarify and simplify the IACS rules and conduct cost-benefit assessments of the system on the basis of sound financial information on sanctions.

428.   Protection of the Community's financial interests. On 11 June the Commission proposed an increase in the period beyond which the financing of expenditure may no longer be refused from 24 to 36 months (Table II). On 28 November the Council adopted Regulation (EC) No 2154/2002 on scrutiny by Member States of transactions forming part of the system of financing by the EAGGF Guarantee Section to simplify the mechanisms introduced by Regulation (EEC) No 4045/89 and make them more flexible (Table II).

Pre-accession instruments

*429.   These are covered in Section 4 (Pre-accession strategy) of Chapter V (→ points 727 to 729).

([1]) COM(2002) 594; Bull. 11-2002, point 1.3.86.
([2]) OJ L 244, 29.9.2000; 2000 General Report, point 1050.
([3]) COM(2002) 648; Bull. 11-2002, point 1.3.87.
([4]) Decision 2002/461/EC (OJ L 160, 18.6.2002).
([5]) Decision 2002/524/EC (OJ L 170, 29.6.2002).
([6]) Decision 2002/523/EC (OJ L 170, 29.6.2002).
([7]) Decision 2002/816/EC (OJ L 280, 18.10.2002).
([8]) Bull. 1/2-2002, point 1.3.169.
([9]) OJ C 214, 31.7.2001; 2001 General Report, point 1219.

International cooperation

430.   Multilateral negotiations. As part of the measures to implement the Doha agenda *(→ point 780)*, the Community drew up agricultural proposals as a contribution towards the creation of a more market-oriented trading system by means of a reform programme covering rules and specific undertakings for support and border protection, to rectify and prevent restrictions and distortions on world agricultural markets. The Community's proposals focus on non-trade aspects and special, differentiated treatment for the developing countries.

431.   Trade agreements. The main developments in this field in 2002 related to cereals *(→ point 408)* and olive oil and table olives *(→ point 412)*.

432.   EAGGF Guarantee Section payments database. In a report of 25 June ([1]) presenting the results of the feasibility studies carried out to determine whether it would be technically possible to set up such a database to provide a breakdown of aid paid out by category of recipient, the Commission recommended using the CATS (clearance audit trail system) database, which has been in use for auditing purposes since 2000, making improvements to it where necessary.

([1]) COM(2002) 339; Bull. 6-2002, point 1.3.119.

Section 14

Fisheries (¹)

Overview

433.   One of the highlights of 2002 was work on the reform of the common fisheries policy aimed at ensuring the sustainable development of the industry, both from the environmental and the economic and social point of view through action to secure the economic viability and competitiveness together with a fair standard of living for people dependent on fishing. The Commission therefore recommended arrangements making it possible to help ensure responsible fishing, improve marine ecosystems and establish the rules of good governance and a multisectoral approach consistent with the other Community policies, especially the environment and development policies. The Community also laid particular importance on the control of unlawful, unreported and unregulated fishing. It proposed a range of initiatives for implementing the international action plan ratified by the United Nations organisation.

General

434.   *Reform of the common fisheries policy (CFP)* (²). In a resolution adopted on 17 January (³), the European Parliament, considering that the measures proposed by the Commission in its March 2001 Green Paper on the future of the common fisheries policy (⁴) were not sufficiently innovative, recommended that flexible instruments be introduced for managing resources and organising fishing fleets. It was opposed to any reduction in structural assistance to the fisheries sector but recommended that aid be distributed more fairly and called for better Community legislation on working conditions for fishermen. Turning to international aspects, it felt that the common fisheries policy should be more consistent with the Community's cooperation and development policy and adopt an overall approach to trade negotiations. In a resolution adopted on 14 March (⁵),

---

(¹) Further information is available on the Europa server (http://europa.eu.int/comm/dgs/fisheries/index_en.htm).
(²) http://europa.eu.int/comm/fisheries/reform/index_en.htm.
(³) OJ C 271 E, 7.11.2002; Bull. 1/2-2002, point 1.3.176.
(⁴) COM(2001) 135; 2001 General Report, point 475; Internet (http://europa.eu.int/comm/fisheries/greenpaper/green1_en.htm).
(⁵) Bull. 3-2002, point 1.3.88.

Parliament called for greater account to be taken in the reform proposals of fish processing activities.

The Commission, in a communication of 28 May ([1]), presented its action programme to reform the common fisheries policy along with a timetable for its implementation. Stressing the need to ensure sustainable resources and apply the principle of good governance, the Commission proposed a new multiannual framework for the conservation of resources and the management of fisheries, the latter to incorporate environmental concerns; the strengthening of technical measures; new rules on fleet policy, to reduce overcapacity; a new regulatory framework for control and enforcement, including effective penalties; new strategies for aquaculture and remote fisheries; initiatives to counter the consequences of fisheries restructuring and to reinforce sectoral dialogue. These strategies recommended by the Commission received the support of Parliament in a resolution of 20 November ([2]), which nevertheless called on the Commission to avoid a legal vacuum if its reform proposal failed to enter into force on 1 January 2003 and to establish a specific allocation for the reform. The European Economic and Social Committee also supported the Commission approach in an opinion of 12 December ([3]).

Following on its communication of 28 May, the Commission presented a communication on 'A strategy for the sustainable development of European aquaculture' on 19 September ([4]) consisting of a series of actions aimed at creating long-term employment in the sector, assuring consumers of the availability of healthy, safe and good-quality products and ensuring an environmentally sound industry.

Regarding the external aspects of the reform of the common fisheries policy, the Commission, in a communication of 23 December ([5]), put forward a new strategy for improving fisheries agreements with third countries, in particular developing coastal states: it recommended that bilateral relations in this area move progressively from agreements giving access *(→ point 443)* to genuine partnership agreements; these would cover both the protection of the interests of the European Union high seas fleet and the tightening of conditions making it possible for sustainable fishing to be carried on in the waters of partner countries.

435.   Multiannual guidance programmes for fishing fleets (MAGPs). On 1 August, the Commission adopted its annual report on the results of the *MAGPs* at the end of 2001 ([6]). It noted that during the five years of the fourth

---

([1]) COM(2002) 181; Bull. 5-2002, point 1.3.95.
([2]) Bull. 11-2002, point 1.3.90.
([3]) Bull. 12-2002, point 1.3.116.
([4]) COM(2002) 511; Bull. 9-2002, point 1.3.88.
([5]) COM(2002) 637; Bull. 12-2002, point 1.3.122.
([6]) COM(2002) 446; Bull. 7/8-2002, point 1.3.109.

programme that had elapsed, Community fleet capacity was cut by approximately 1.9 % in terms of tonnage and by 5.9 % in terms of engine power. The majority of the Member States, however, failed to achieve all the goals set in the programmes. In a resolution of 25 April ([1]) on the Commission's annual report on the results of the *MAGPs* at the end of 2000 ([2]), Parliament had earlier expressed regret about this situation. It called on the Council and the Commission to identify the causes of the failure and, in the context of the reform of the common policy *(→ point 434)*, to amend the MAGPs and in particular to adopt measures to ensure a balance between capacity and fishing effort, on the one hand, and effective catch opportunities, on the other. As part of the abovementioned reform, the Commission proposed abandoning the MAGPs and replacing them with a more effective system for managing capacity. To take account of the Council Decision prolonging MAGP IV by a year, the Commission, on 29 July, approved the implementing decisions for each country ([3]). On 3 September, it adopted a report on the interim results of the MAGPs at 30 June 2002 ([4]).

436. *Control of illegal, unreported and unregulated fishing.* In a communication of 28 May ([5]), the Commission proposed a number of new measures and initiatives at the level of Community regulation and within regional and multilateral fisheries organisations to implement the international plan of action endorsed by the Council of the United Nations Food and Agriculture Organisation (FAO) on 23 June 2001. The Council supported this strategy in its conclusions of 11 June ([6]), as did Parliament in its resolution of 20 November ([7]).

Referring, on 4 July ([8]), to the communication of November 2001 ([9]) in which the Commission expressed disapproval of behaviour detected in 2000 that seriously infringed the rules of the common fisheries policy, Parliament, expressing regret about the shortcomings noted both in relation to information provided by the Member States and regarding penalties, underlined that breaches should be classified according to their seriousness and that a uniform system of minimum penalties should be introduced. It also expressed the wish that the arrangements for notifying breaches be examined again as part of the policy reform process. In a communication of 5 December ([10]), the Commission drew up a new table showing how Member States imposed penalties for the same types of behaviour in 2001. Observing that there had been an increase in the

---

([1]) Bull. 4-2002, point 1.3.90.
([2]) COM(2001) 541; 2001 General Report, point 478.
([3]) Decision 2002/652/EC (OJ L 215, 10.8.2002; Bull. 7/8-2002, point 1.3.110).
([4]) COM(2002) 483; Bull. 9-2002, point 1.3.87.
([5]) COM(2002) 180; Bull. 5-2002, point 1.3.96.
([6]) Bull. 6-2002, point 1.3.120.
([7]) Bull. 11-2002, point 1.3.91.
([8]) Bull. 7/8-2002, point 1.3.108.
([9]) COM(2001) 650; 2001 General Report, point 487.
([10]) COM(2002) 687; Bull. 12-2002, point 1.3.112.

number of breaches reported, it again called on the Member States to show greater haste and initiative pursuing breaches.

Resource conservation and management

Internal aspects

437. *Sustainable balance between resources and their exploitation.* On 28 January, the Council prolonged to 31 December 2002 its Decision 97/413/EC ([1]) concerning the objectives and detailed rules for restructuring the Community fisheries sector with a view to achieving such a balance (Table II). It accordingly reduced the fishing effort of the Community fleet during the year and introduced the possibility of derogating from these measures for vessels of under 12 metres other than trawlers.

438. *Conservation of stocks.* On 20 December, the Council adopted Regulation (EC) No 2371/2002 on the conservation and sustainable exploitation of fish stocks under the common fisheries policy (Table II). These new framework rules provided a basis for the implementation of consistent fisheries management measures based on the precautionary principle. They are based on a multi-annual strategy for managing fish stocks comprising restrictions on fishing effort along with limits on catches and the targeted application of technical measures. They also constitute a new legal framework for establishing a Community system to control and enforce the rules. They set up regional advisory councils to give those involved in the sector a greater role in strengthening management. On 16 December the Council adopted Regulation (EC) No 2347/2002 on the management of catches and fishing effort for species occurring in deep water areas, such as blue ling and red bream (Table II). On the same date the Council established the fishing possibilities for deep water fish stocks for 2003 and 2004 with an annual review clause ([2]). On 20 December, it established the fishing possibilities for 2003 and the relevant conditions for certain fish stocks ([3]).

As part of the reform of the common fisheries policy *(→ point 434)*, on 9 October the Commission adopted a communication on the future strategy to be adopted for the management of fisheries in the Mediterranean ([4]), which takes account of the specific features of the region. On 16 December the Council expressed its views on this strategy ([5]). On 26 November, presenting a Commu-

---

([1]) OJ L 175, 3.7.1997.
([2]) Regulation (EC) No 2340/2002 (OJ L 356, 31.12.2002; Bull. 12-2002, point 1.3.118).
([3]) Regulation (EC) No 2341/2002 (OJ L 356, 31.12.2002; Bull. 12-2002, point 1.3.115).
([4]) COM(2002) 535; Bull. 10-2002 point 1.3.76.
([5]) Bull. 12-2002, point 1.3.114.

nity action plan to reduce discards ([1]), the Commission advocated various initiatives, including the preparation of pilot projects, the improvement of technical measures involving fishing gear, and consideration of the possibility of introducing a ban on discards following a consultation process. Parliament, in a resolution of 5 December ([2]), expressed concern about the socio-economic implications of a recent scientific opinion recommending the temporary stopping of fishing for cod in the North Sea, the Irish Sea, off the west of Scotland and Skagerrak.

439.   Replacement of stocks. In a resolution of 17 January ([3]) on the Commission communication of June 2001 on rebuilding stocks of cod and hake in Community and adjacent waters ([4]), Parliament called for a reduction in the severity of some of the technical measures on increasing mesh sizes. It also invited the Commission to adopt a new approach in implementing its stock recovery plans. On 12 February, the Council adopted Regulation (EC) No 254/2002 introducing measures to protect certain spawning grounds during the 2002 season in order to replenish the cod stock in the Irish Sea (ICES division VII a) (Table II). The legislative process for adoption of the draft regulation on the introduction of measures to replenish cod and hake stocks continued throughout the year, resulting in the tabling of an amended proposal by the Commission on 23 December (Table II). On 3 December, the Commission also proposed including in a complete set of technical measures the recent amendments on the protection of juvenile sea organisms (Table II).

440.   Monitoring of fishing activities. The Commission continued to monitor compliance with total allowable catches (TACs), quotas and technical measures in Community waters and in certain international waters. Following the exhaustion of permitted fishing possibilities, 24 fisheries were closed. Infringement proceedings under way relating to overfishing in past years were pursued. The Commission also monitored compliance with conservation measures and fisheries agreements with northern and ACP countries, continued surveillance work in the North-West Atlantic Fisheries Organisation (NAFO) regulatory area and participated in the inspection scheme for the North-East Atlantic Fisheries Commission (NEAFC) regulatory area. It also granted fishing licences for third country vessels operating under fisheries agreements in Community waters. It arranged further meetings of the Member States' expert group to review progress on the introduction of the satellite system for vessel monitoring. Against the background of its communication of 28 May on the reform of the common fisheries policy *(→ point 434)* and its proposal forming the basis of new stock conservation rules *(→ point 438)*, the Commission recommended

[1] COM(2002) 656; Bull. 11-2002, point 1.3.98.
[2] Bull. 12-2002, point 1.3.121.
[3] OJ C 271 E, 7.11.2002; Bull. 1/2-2002, point 1.3.175.
[4] COM(2001) 326; 2001 General Report, point 481.

strengthening the system for monitoring fishing activities and the establishment of uniform penalties. On 13 December, it proposed a new fishing effort scheme for the Atlantic to ensure the stability of the effort recently deployed by Member State vessels (Table II).

In a resolution of 4 July (^{1}) on the Commission report of September 2001 on the monitoring of the implementation of the common fisheries policy in the period 1996–99 (^{2}), Parliament expressed its concern about the substantial disparities in the extent to which the Member States had fulfilled their obligation to notify catches to the Commission and called upon it to reinforce the system and draw up a list of effective deterrent penalties. On 24 September (^{3}) and 16 December (^{4}), the Council amended Regulation (EC) No 2555/2001 (^{5}) in order to adjust certain total allowable catches as a result of new scientific evaluations, certain international fisheries agreements, decisions adopted recently in international bodies and a judgment of the Court of Justice of 18 April (^{6}).

441. *National conservation measures.* The Commission was informed of 20 measures notified by the Member States in 2002.

External aspects

442. *Community participation in the work of international fisheries organisations.* The Community participated in the work of a number of organisations, including the North-West Atlantic Fisheries Organisation (NAFO) (^{7}), the North-East Atlantic Fisheries Commission (NEAFC) (^{8}), the North Atlantic Salmon Conservation Organisation (NASCO) (^{9}), the General Fisheries Commission for the Mediterranean (GFCM), the Indian Ocean Tuna Commission (IOTC) (^{10}), the International Commission for the Conservation of Atlantic Tunas (ICCAT) (^{11}), the International Baltic Sea Fishery Commission (IBSFC) (^{12}), the Commission for the Conservation of Antarctic Marine Living Resources (CCAMLR) (^{13}), the Fisheries Committee of the Organisation for Economic Cooperation and Development (OECD) and the Standing Committee of the European Convention for the Protection of Animals kept for Farming

---

(^{1}) Bull. 7/8-2002, point 1.3.111.
(^{2}) COM(2001) 526; 2001 General Report, point 486.
(^{3}) Regulation (EC) No 1811/2002 (OJ L 276, 12.10.2002; Bull. 9-2002, point 1.3.89).
(^{4}) Regulation (EC) No 2256/2002 (OJ L 343, 18.12.2002; Bull. 12-2002, point 1.3.116).
(^{5}) OJ L 347, 31.12.2001; 2001 General Report, point 479.
(^{6}) Case C-61/96 (OJ C 144, 15.6.2002).
(^{7}) http://www.meds-sdmm.dfo-mpo.gc.ca/meds/Prog_Int/NAFO/NAFO_e.htm.
(^{8}) http://www.neafc.org/.
(^{9}) http://www.nasco.int/.
(^{10}) http://www.iotc.org/English/
(^{11}) http://www.iccat.es/.
(^{12}) http://www.ibsfc.org/.
(^{13}) http://www.ccamlr.org/.

Purposes concluded under the auspices of the Council of Europe. It participated in the work of four of the consultative bodies established by the Food and Agriculture Organisation of the United Nations (FAO): the Fishery Committee for the Eastern Central Atlantic (CECAF), the Western Central Atlantic Fishery Commission (WECAFC), the Committee on Fisheries and the Committee on Aquaculture of the GFCM. It also took part as an observer in the preparatory work for the establishment of the new organisation for tuna stock management in the western central Pacific.

On 22 July, the Council concluded the Convention on the Conservation and Management of Fishery Resources in the South-East Atlantic Ocean (Table III). On 3 July, the Commission proposed updating the Community rules transposing the measures for the monitoring of fishing activities (Table II) and the technical measures applying to them (Table II) under the CCAMLR. On 24 July, it proposed amending the rules in force concerning the catch documentation scheme for *Dissostichus spp.* (Table II) under the CCAMLR recommendations and for certain stocks of highly migratory species under the technical recommendations adopted by ICCAT and the IOTC (Table II). On 5 August, it proposed adopting a similar strategy for the introduction, in the Community, of a scheme for the statistical recording of bluefin tuna, swordfish and bigeye tuna (Table II).

443. Fisheries agreements with third countries and the overseas countries and territories. The Council adopted regulations on the conclusion, renewal or provisional application of the protocols annexed to the fisheries agreements with Angola (Table III) Cape Verde (Table III), Gabon (Table III), Guinea (Table III), Guinea-Bissau (Table III), São Tomé and Príncipe (Table III), Senegal (Table III), and Seychelles (Table III). It also authorised Spain and Portugal to prolong their fisheries agreements with South Africa to March and April 2003 ([1]) respectively. In addition, a draft agreement, the first of its kind concluded in the Pacific region, was initialled with Kiribati to determine tuna fishing opportunities for Member States off the coast of that country (Table III). A draft agreement with Mozambique was also initialled on 23 October (Table III). On 3 December ([2]), the Commission adopted a communication on the mid-term review of the fourth protocol on fisheries between the European Union and Greenland ([3]).

444. Agreements on fishery products with applicant countries. In October and November, the Council concluded agreements on fishery products in the form of additional protocols to the respective association agreements with the Czech Republic (Table III) and Bulgaria (Table III).

([1]) Decisions 2002/332/EC and 2002/333/EC (OJ L 116, 3.5.2002; Bull. 4-2002, point 1.3.91).
([2]) COM(2002) 697; Bull. 12-2002, point 1.3.124.
([3]) OJ L 209, 2.8.2001; 2001 General Report, point 492.

Market organisation

445.   Guide prices. On 19 December, the Council set guide prices for fishery products for the 2003 fishing year ([^1]).

446.   Outermost regions. On 25 March, the Council prolonged the scheme to compensate for the additional costs incurred in disposing of certain fishery products as a result of the remoteness of those regions *(→ point 380)*. On the same date, it opened tariff quotas for various fishery products likely to be imported into the Canary Islands *(→ point 382)*.

Fisheries and the environment ([^2])

447.   Integration of environmental concerns into the common fisheries policy. In a resolution of 17 January ([^3]) on the Commission communication of March 2001 on this integration strategy ([^4]), Parliament, considering that it could not be achieved by imposing restrictions on fishing alone, called on the Commission to formulate alternatives in a much wider context embracing management of the marine environment as a whole. The Council, in its conclusions of 18 February ([^5]) reiterating a position that had been set out in April 2001 ([^6]), proposed that the components of the strategy should be included in the proposals on the reform of the common fisheries policy *(→ point 434)*. The Barcelona European Council ratified those conclusions and gave priority to the safeguarding of biodiversity ([^7]). In a communication of 28 May ([^8]), the Commission presented a Community action plan for the adoption of this integration strategy, in which it proposed defining guiding principles, such as the precautionary principle and the 'polluter pays' principle, and applying them in the form of a work programme of priority measures (e.g. with a view to a reduction in pressure on fishing grounds and the protection of biological diversity), and additional measures. It also proposed setting up a system to monitor the process of integration of environmental protection requirements based on indicators. As a follow-up to this strategy, on 5 August the Commission adopted a proposal for a regulation banning the removal of shark fins on board fishing vessels where this is practised as a means of alleviating the difficulty of preserving the meat (Table II).

In a resolution of 20 November ([^9]), Parliament made a number of requests for the environmental protection of fisheries, including improving the stock evaluation

[^1]: Regulation (EC) No 2346/2002 (OJ L 351, 28.12.2002; Bull. 12-2002, point 1.3.128).
[^2]: http://europa.eu.int/comm/fisheries/doc_et_publ/factsheets/facts/en/pcp8_1.htm.
[^3]: OJ C 271 E, 7.11.2002; Bull. 1/2-2002, point 1.3.188.
[^4]: COM(2001) 143; 2001 General Report, point 497.
[^5]: Bull. 1/2-2002, point 1.3.189.
[^6]: 2001 General Report, point 497.
[^7]: Bull. 3-2002, point I.59.
[^8]: COM(2002) 186; Bull. 5-2002, point 1.3.100.
[^9]: Bull. 11-2002, point 1.3.97.

arrangements, promoting fisheries research and adopting emergency measures for attaining a sustainable balance between exploitation and stocks, in line with the goals set in Johannesburg *(→ point 557)*. On 20 December, Council Regulation (EC) No 2372/2002 (Table II) introduced specific measures to compensate fishermen together with the Spanish shellfish and aquaculture sectors affected by the pollution caused by the sinking of the tanker 'Prestige' *(→ points 574 and 648)*.

Structural action

448.   General approach. On 28 January, the Council amended Regulation (EC) No 2792/1999 (¹) laying down the detailed rules and arrangements regarding Community structural assistance in the fisheries sector (Table II). The new regulation reinforces, for the period from 1 January to 30 June 2002, the withdrawal requirement linked to the entry of new capacity in segments where the annual targets have not yet been achieved. On 20 December, out of concern to ensure consistency with the most recent rules on fisheries, the Council again amended the regulation (Table II): the new Regulation (EC) No 2369/2002 mainly concerns the limiting of public aid, measures to assist small-scale inshore fishing and socio-economic measures to encourage fishermen to change their skills or retrain for occupations in areas other than sea fisheries.

449.   Socio-economic action plan. On 6 November, the Commission presented an action plan to counter the social, economic and regional consequences of the restructuring of the EU fishing industry (²). In addition to assessing the impact in terms of job losses, the plan contains a list of all the existing means of alleviating these consequences under Community aid schemes and an analysis of the short and long-term options.

450.   Breaking up of fishing vessels. On 20 December, in order to deal with the imbalance between the Community fleet and fish stocks, the Council adopted Regulation (EC) No 2370/2002 making it possible for Member States to offer vessel owners affected by the reductions in fishing effort additional funds for breaking up (Table II).

*451.   The other structural measures implemented in 2002 are covered in Section 10 ('Economic and social cohesion') of this chapter *(→ point 365 et seq.)*.

State aid schemes

*452.   These are covered in Section 6 ('Competition policy') of this chapter *(→ points 236 to 245)*.

(¹) OJ L 337, 30.12.1999; 1999 General Report, points 332 and 550.
(²) COM(2002) 600; Bull. 11-2002, point 1.3.99.

Chapter IV

Citizenship and quality of life

Section 1

Area of freedom, security and justice (¹)

Overview

453.   The momentum generated by the Laeken European Council in December 2001 continued to bear fruit throughout the year. Important decisions agreed in principle were confirmed, including the European arrest warrant and the framework decision on terrorism. In the field of judicial cooperation in civil matters, significant progress was made in applying the principle of mutual recognition. And approval by the Council in December of the directive laying down minimum standards on the reception of applicants for asylum in Member States should be seen as the cornerstone of the common European asylum system. But the delays in certain areas noted at Laeken were not caught up with despite the fact that all the necessary proposals had been presented to the Council. The European Council meeting in Seville attempted to provide new impetus by stressing its determination to speed up implementation of all aspects of the programme adopted in Tampere for the creation of an area of freedom, security and justice in the European Union. Combating illegal immigration and introducing coordinated and integrated management of external borders were moved back to the top of the agenda.

General

454.   *Implementation of the area of freedom, security and justice.* In a resolution adopted on 7 February (²), Parliament reviewed the progress made in this

---

(¹) Further information is available on the Europa web site (http://europa.eu.int/comm/dgs/justice_home/index_en.htm).
(²) OJ C 284 E, 21.11.2002; Bull. 1/2-2002, point 1.4.1.

area in 2001 in line with the objectives set by the Tampere European Council in 1999 ([1]). It welcomed the progress made with regard to respect for fundamental rights, a common asylum and immigration policy and the building of an area of justice and security, but deplored the delays and deadlocks resulting from the separation of these matters between the first and third pillars. On 30 May ([2]) and 16 December ([3]), the Commission presented two communications providing a six-monthly update and setting out the priorities for the following six months (Tampere scoreboard).

455.   *Schengen Agreement.* In a decision adopted on 28 February ([4]), the Council approved Ireland's participation in some of the provisions of the Schengen *acquis*, including those concerned with judicial cooperation in criminal matters, police cooperation, the fight against drugs, and the Schengen information system.

456.   *Enlargement.* On the margin of the Council meeting of 14 and 15 October, the Member States' justice and home affairs ministers met their counterparts from the candidate countries ([5]). Discussions covered Schengen, the mutual recognition of judicial decisions in criminal matters, and the need for joint action to protect professional drivers from violent attacks.

457.   *AGIS framework programme.* On 22 July, the Council adopted a framework programme on police and judicial cooperation in criminal matters (AGIS) (Table II). Established for the period 2003–07 and allocated a budget of EUR 65 million, this programme sets out to help achieve the general objective of providing Union citizens with a high level of safety within an area of freedom, security and justice. It will finance cooperation in the following areas falling within the scope of Title VI of the Treaty on European Union: judicial cooperation in general and criminal matters, including training; cooperation between law enforcement authorities; cooperation between law enforcement authorities or other public or private organisations in the Member States involved in preventing and fighting crime; cooperation between Member States to achieve effective protection of the interests of victims in criminal proceedings. The programme is targeted at police and criminal-justice practitioners and other players (including private and non-governmental organisations) directly involved in combating and preventing crime. The AGIS programme replaces Grotius II — Criminal, Oisin II, STOP II, Hippokrates and Falcone, which expired in 2002.

([1]) 1999 General Report, point 889.
([2]) COM(2002) 261; Bull. 5-2002, point 1.4.1.
([3]) COM(2002) 738; Bull. 12-2002, point 1.4.1.
([4]) Decision 2002/192/EC (OJ L 64, 7.3.2002; Bull. 1/2-2002, point 1.4.17).
([5]) Bull. 10-2002, point 1.4.4.

Internal borders, external borders and visa policy (¹)

458. *General aspects.* On 7 May, the Commission adopted a communication in line with the conclusions of the Laeken European Council (²) entitled 'Towards integrated management of the external borders of the Member States of the European Union' (³). After reviewing progress and examining persistent needs, the Commission sets out measures for establishing a common policy in this area incorporating five components: a common corpus of legislation; a common and operational coordination and cooperation mechanism; common integrated risk analysis; staff trained in the European dimension and inter-operational equipment; and burden-sharing between Member States in the run-up to establishing a European corps of border guards. For its part, the Council adopted a decision on 13 June concerning an action programme for the period 2002–06 for the development of administrative cooperation between national agencies in the fields of external borders, visas, asylum and immigration (ARGO) (Table II).

459. *Visas and residence permits.* On 18 February, the Council adopted two regulations to improve safeguards against counterfeiting and falsification: Regulation (EC) No 334/2002 amending Regulation (EC) No 1683/95 laying down a uniform model for visas (Table II), and Regulation (EC) No 333/2002 on a uniform format for forms for affixing the visa issued by Member States to persons holding travel documents not recognised by the Member State drawing up the form (Table II). On 13 June, it adopted Regulation (EC) No 1030/2002 establishing a uniform format for residence permits for third-country nationals (Table II). Spain also presented an initiative with a view to adopting a Council regulation on the issue of visas at the border, including the issue of such visas to seamen in transit (Table II). On 28 November, the Commission presented a proposal for a regulation amending Regulation (EC) No 539/2001 of 15 March 2001 listing the third countries whose nationals must be in possession of visas when crossing the external borders and those whose nationals are exempt from that requirement (Table II); the proposal makes provision for including Ecuador in the first list and for making other technical adaptations to reflect developments in international law. At its meeting on 28 and 29 November, the Council called for the stepping-up of consular cooperation in relation to the issuing of visas (⁴).

460. *Repatriation and readmission.* In its conclusions of 28 February (⁵), the Council supported an exchange of information with a view to drawing up a

---

(¹) http://europa.eu.int/comm/justice_home/unit/libre_circulation_fr.htm.
(²) Bull. 12-2001, point I.17.
(³) COM(2002) 233; Bull. 5-2002, point 1.4.7.
(⁴) Bull. 11-2002, point 1.4.12.
(⁵) Bull. 1/2-2002, point 1.4.8.

guide to good practice for obtaining travel documents for the repatriation of people who do not fulfil or no longer fulfil entry or residence conditions.

461. Channel Tunnel. In view of the growing problem of refugees and the obstruction of rail freight in the Channel Tunnel, Parliament adopted a resolution on 11 April in which it called on France and the United Kingdom to take urgent measures to restore normal conditions and compensate operators adversely affected by this situation ([1]).

Asylum and immigration ([2])

462. General approach. Determined to speed up the implementation of all aspects of the programme adopted in Tampere for the creation of an area of freedom, security and justice in the European Union ([3]), the Seville European Council stressed the need for a common policy in the European Union on the separate but closely linked issues of asylum and immigration ([4]). It further identified a series of specific measures to combat illegal immigration, to gradually introduce coordinated and integrated management of the external borders, to integrate immigration policy into the European Union's relations with third countries and to speed up the ongoing process of adopting legislation defining a common asylum and immigration policy. At its meeting on 14 and 15 October, the Council stressed that the integration of third-country nationals legally resident in the Member States was an important element in the establishment of a European asylum and immigration policy, which could include integration requirements ([5]). In conclusions adopted on 18 November, it called for intensified cooperation with third countries on the management of migration flows ([6]). At its meeting on 28 and 29 November, it adopted a return plan for Afghanistan ([7]) and stressed the need for the creation of a network of immigration liaison officers ([8]). On 3 December, the Commission adopted a communication on integrating migration issues in the European Union's relations with third countries ([9]), which includes a report on the effectiveness of financial resources available at Community level for repatriation of immigrants and rejected asylum seekers, for management of external borders and for asylum and migration projects in third countries.

([1]) Bull. 4-2002, point 1.4.9.
([2]) http://europa.eu.int/comm/justice_home/unit/immigration_en.htm.
([3]) Bull. 10-1999, points I.3 to I.7; 1999 General Report, points 889 and 896.
([4]) Bull. 6-2002, points I.9 to I.13.
([5]) Bull. 10-2002, point 1.4.19.
([6]) Bull. 11-2002, point 1.4.1.
([7]) Bull. 11-2002, point 1.6.73.
([8]) Bull. 11-2002, point 1.4.9.
([9]) COM(2002) 703; Bull. 12-2002, point 1.4.2.

463. Comprehensive plan to combat illegal immigration. Adopted on 28 February by the Council (^{1}) in response to the conclusions of the Tampere (^{2}) and Laeken (^{3}) European Councils, this plan aims to define a common and integrated approach to all questions relating to illegal immigration and trafficking in human beings. It mentions several priority areas, including visa policy, readmission and repatriation policies, the monitoring of borders, Europol and penalties. On 15 April, the Council also stressed the need for effective cooperation from the countries of origin and transit involved in illegal immigration and called for early implementation of the measures outlined in the comprehensive plan (^{4}). At its meeting on 25 and 26 April (^{5}), the Council also insisted on the need to strengthen sea border controls. On 13 June, it asked for the problems of illegal immigration and trafficking in human beings to be integrated to a greater extent into the Union's external relations (^{6}). At its meeting on 14 and 15 October, the Council welcomed the measures already taken in response to the conclusions of the Seville European Council *(→ point 462)* and asked the Commission to continue giving high priority to illegal immigration as part of an integrated, comprehensive and balanced approach (^{7}). On 28 November, it adopted Framework Decision 2002/946/JHA which aims to strengthen the penal system to hinder illegal entry, movement and residence (Table II), and Directive 2002/90/EC which defines this strengthening (Table II). At its meeting on 19 and 20 December, it commented further on external border checks and combating illegal immigration (^{8}). Moreover, in an opinion adopted on 25 April (^{9}) on the Commission communication of November 2001 on a common policy on illegal immigration (^{10}), the European Economic and Social Committee stressed the importance of such a policy.

464. Return of illegal residents. On 10 April, in line with the conclusions of the Laeken European Council and the comprehensive plan referred to above *(→ point 463)* the Commission adopted a Green Paper on a common policy in this area (^{11}). The Commission's intention with this Green Paper is to trigger consideration of the different aspects of the problem, to create common standards and to introduce common measures. It insists that a Community return policy must fit in with and complement existing Community policies on immigration and asylum. It also focuses on future cooperation between the Member States on the return of illegal residents and on the development of a readmission

---

(^{1}) Bull. 1/2-2002, point 1.4.5.
(^{2}) Bull. 10-1999, points I.4 to I.7; 1999 General Report, point 896.
(^{3}) Bull. 12-2001, point I.16; 2001 General Report, point 502.
(^{4}) Bull. 4-2002, point 1.4.4.
(^{5}) Bull. 4-2002, point 1.4.5.
(^{6}) Bull. 6-2002, point 1.4.2.
(^{7}) Bull. 10-2002, point 1.4.6.
(^{8}) Bull. 12-2002, point 1.4.6.
(^{9}) OJ C 149, 21.6.2002; Bull. 4-2002, point 1.4.6.
(^{10}) COM(2001) 672; 2001 General Report, point 516.
(^{11}) COM(2002) 175; Bull. 4-2002, point 1.4.3.

policy with third countries. Finally, it proposes a range of issues to fuel a debate on the Green Paper. The European Economic and Social Committee gave an opinion on the Green Paper on 18 September ([1]) and 11 December ([2]) and the Committee of the Regions on 20 November ([3]).

In a communication presented on 14 October, the Commission set out the components of an action programme concerning the return of illegal residents ([4]). It advocated that operational cooperation be enhanced, that an integrated programme be defined to serve as a common framework and that cooperation with third countries be stepped up. The programme was endorsed by the Council at its meeting on 28 and 29 November ([5]). On 27 November, the Council signed an agreement with the Government of the Special Administrative Region of Hong Kong on the readmission of illegal residents *(→ point 964)*. In June, it adopted negotiating directives for a similar agreement with Ukraine *(→ point 918)*. And in November, negotiating directives were adopted for readmission agreements with Albania *(→ point 863)*, Algeria *(→ point 885)*, China *(→ point 964)* and Turkey.

465. *Short-term residence permit for victims that cooperate with national authorities.* On 11 February, to meet the objective of tackling illegal immigration at its source set by the Tampere European Council in October 1999 ([6]), the Commission adopted a proposal for a directive under which a short-term residence permit could be issued to victims of action to facilitate illegal immigration or trafficking in human beings provided they cooperate with the competent authorities (Table II). This proposal defines the criteria for issuing this document, the conditions of residence and the grounds for withdrawal or non-renewal of the permit.

466. *Asylum and immigration policy.* In an own-initiative opinion adopted on 21 March ([7]), the European Economic and Social Committee stressed the need for the social integration of immigrants and refugees and the importance of the role of civil society in this process. On 16 May ([8]), the Committee of the Regions welcomed the Commission's commitment to developing a better overall understanding of migration patterns, to reinforcing border controls and to stepping up the penalties against those who seek to profit from illegal immigration. In an opinion adopted on 29 May ([9]), the European Economic and Social Committee also approved the open method of coordinating Community policy advo-

[1] Bull. 9-2002, point 1.4.1.
[2] Bull. 12-2002, point 1.4.4.
[3] Bull. 11-2002, point 1.4.2.
[4] COM(2002) 564; Bull. 10-2002, point 1.4.2.
[5] Bull. 11-2002, point 1.4.6.
[6] 1999 General Report, point 889.
[7] OJ C 125, 27.5.2002; Bull. 3-2002, point 1.4.2.
[8] OJ C 278, 14.11.2002; Bull. 5-2002, point 1.4.3.
[9] OJ C 221, 17.9.2002; Bull. 5-2002, point 1.4.6.

cated by the Commission in its communications of July 2001 on immigration ([1]) and November 2001 on asylum ([2]). On 28 February ([3]), the Council laid down certain rules to implement Regulation (EC) No 2725/2000 concerning the establishment of the Eurodac system for comparison of the fingerprints of asylum seekers and certain nationals of non-member countries ([4]).

On 2 May, responding to the request by the Laeken European Council in December 2001 ([5]) and its concern about the slow progress of deliberations within the Council, the Commission presented a new amended proposal on the right to family reunification (Table II). The Seville European Council of 21 and 22 June, expressed its desire that the relevant directive be adopted before June 2003 ([6]). It also expressed an identical expectation concerning the status of third-country nationals who are long-term residents (Table II) and refugee status (Table II). On 18 June, the Commission adopted an amended proposal on minimum standards on procedures in Member States for granting and withdrawing refugee status ([7]). These proposals were discussed by the Council on 15 October.

On 7 October, the Commission adopted a proposal for a directive on the conditions of entry and residence of third-country nationals for the purpose of studies, vocational training or voluntary service (Table II).

467.   *Enlargement.* In a formal declaration made in the margins of the Council meeting of 14 and 15 October ([8]), the justice and home affairs ministers indicated that they would consider the candidate countries with which an Accession Treaty was being negotiated *(→ point 705)* to be 'safe countries of origin' for all legal and practical purposes in relation to asylum matters as from the date of signature of the Accession Treaty. In a statement adopted on 28 November ([9]), the Council also confirmed that, for Member States applying the principle of 'safe third countries', the candidate States may be presumed to be safe third countries from the date of the signature of the Accession Treaties. The Council also agreed that the members of EFTA may also be presumed to be safe third countries.

([1]) COM(2001) 387; 2001 General Report, point 513.
([2]) COM(2001) 710; 2001 General Report, point 519.
([3]) Regulation (EC) No 407/2002 (OJ L 62, 5.3.2002; Bull. 1/2-2002, point 1.4.24).
([4]) OJ L 316, 15.12.2000; 2000 General Report, point 456.
([5]) Bull. 12-2001, point I.16.
([6]) Bull. 6-2002, point I.13.
([7]) Bull. 6-2002, point 1.4.4.
([8]) Bull. 10-2002, point 1.4.3.
([9]) Bull. 11-2002, point 1.4.8.

Judicial cooperation in civil and commercial matters [1]

468. General aspects. At its meeting on 25 and 26 April, the Council adopted (EC) Regulation No 743/2002 establishing a general Community framework of activities to facilitate the implementation of judicial cooperation in civil matters for the period 2002–06 (Table II) with the aim of *inter alia* encouraging cooperation in this field and improving mutual understanding of Member States' judicial systems and information to the public on access to justice.

469. Access to justice in cross-border disputes. In a proposal for a directive to improve such access adopted on 18 January, the Commission advocated the establishment of minimum common rules on legal aid and other financial aspects of civil proceedings (Table II). This proposal was agreed by the Council on 14 October.

470. Litigation and alternative methods of dispute resolution. On 19 April, responding to the request formulated by the Council in May 2000 [2] and by the Laeken European Council [3], the Commission adopted a Green Paper [4] to initiate a broad-based consultation on out-of-court dispute resolution in civil and commercial law, stressing that interest in such alternative methods was growing in the European Union. It examines how these systems operate in the Member States, but excludes arbitration, which is already highly regulated, and outlines the political and legal issues surrounding the initiatives which might be taken. The European Economic and Social Committee delivered its opinion on this approach on 11 December [5]. On 20 December, in line with the conclusions of the Tampere European Council [6], the Commission adopted a new Green Paper initiating consultation on measures to be taken at Community level to create a European order for payment procedure and to simplify and speed up small claims litigation [7].

471. Enforcement of judgments, court settlements and authentic instruments. On 18 April, the Commission adopted a proposal for a regulation to enable creditors who have obtained an enforcement order regarding a claim which has never been disputed by the debtor to enforce it directly in another Member State (Table II). On the matter of jurisdiction and the recognition and enforcement of judgments in matrimonial matters and in matters of parental responsibility, the Commission adopted a proposal for a regulation on 3 May with a view to creating a complete system of rules in this field, agreed by the Council on

---

[1] http://europa.eu.int/comm/justice_home/unit/civil_en.htm.
[2] 2000 General Report, point 462.
[3] Bull. 12-2001, point I.19.
[4] COM(2002) 196; Bull. 4-2002, point 1.4.18.
[5] Bull. 12-2002, point 1.4.16.
[6] Bull. 10-1999, point 1-10.
[7] COM(2002) 746; Bull. 12-2002, point 1.4.17.

28 November (Table II). On 6 June (^{1}), it withdrew its previous proposal for a regulation (^{2}), the provisions of which had been incorporated into the later proposal. On 2 October, it proposed the signing of the Council of Europe Convention on Contact concerning Children (Table III). On 19 December (^{3}), the Council authorised the Member States to sign the 1996 Hague Convention on Jurisdiction, Applicable Law, Recognition, Enforcement and Cooperation in respect of Parental Responsibility and Measures for the Protection of Children.

472. *International aspects*. At its meeting on 14 and 15 October, the Council adopted negotiating directives concerning a draft convention between the Community and Denmark, on one hand, and Iceland, Norway, Poland and Switzerland, on the other, on jurisdiction and the recognition and enforcement of judgments in civil and commercial matters (Table III).

Judicial cooperation in criminal matters (^{4})

473. *Eurojust* (^{5}). By decision of 28 February (Table II), the Council set up the Eurojust unit, the task of which is to reinforce the fight against serious crime, in particular, organised crime, as a result of better judicial cooperation between Member States. Each of the Member States will second a national member — a prosecutor, a judge or a police officer of equivalent status — to this new European Union body, which will have its own legal personality.

474. *Security of information systems*. In a proposal for a framework decision adopted on 19 April, the Commission advocated measures to prevent attacks against information systems based on an approximation of criminal law and a strengthening of judicial cooperation between Member States (Table II).

475. *Approximation of sanctions*. At its meeting on 25 and 26 April, the Council recommended a flexible approach to the approximation of criminal penalties (^{6}). It advocated the introduction of ranges of years of imprisonment corresponding to the different severity of crimes. Belgium presented an initiative on the setting-up of a European network of national contact points for restorative justice (Table II) to develop and promote the various aspects of restorative justice at Union level.

(^{1}) COM(2002) 297; Bull. 6-2002, point 1.4.14.
(^{2}) COM(2001) 505; 2001 General Report, point 525.
(^{3}) Bull. 12-2002, point 1.4.18.
(^{4}) http://europa.eu.int/comm/justice_home/unit/penal_en.htm.
(^{5}) http://europa.eu.int/comm/justice_home/news/laecken_council/en/eurojust_en.htm.
(^{6}) Bull. 4-2002, point 1.4.26.

476.   European arrest warrant (¹). On 13 June, in line with the priorities of the Spanish Presidency, the Council adopted a framework decision on the establishment of a European arrest warrant so that any person sought under a judgment given in a Member State can be arrested and surrendered by other Member States (Table II).

477.   Confiscation of crime-related items. Denmark presented an initiative for a framework decision on the confiscation of crime-related proceeds, instrumentalities and property (Table II). Its purpose is to approximate national legislation on confiscation by requiring Member States to include such a provision in their national law. The initiative follows on from the Council framework decision of 26 June 2001 on money-laundering, the identification, tracing, freezing, seizing and confiscation of instrumentalities and the proceeds of crime (²) and is aimed at a horizontal harmonisation of certain aspects of confiscation orders. Denmark also presented an initiative for a framework decision on the execution in the European Union of confiscation orders (Table III).

478.   Disqualifications. Denmark presented an initiative for a Council decision on increasing cooperation between EU Member States with regard to disqualifications imposed on natural persons as part of a judgment or as a corollary of a criminal conviction (Table II).

479.   Joint investigation teams. On 13 June, the Council adopted a framework decision on joint investigation teams (Table II), the purpose of which is to implement the relevant conclusions of the Tampere European Council of October 1999 (³) in anticipation of the application of Article 13 of the convention of 29 May 2000 on mutual assistance in criminal matters (⁴).

480.   Compensation to crime victims. On 20 March, the European Economic and Social Committee (⁵) broadly approved the action proposed by the Commission in its Green Paper of September 2001 (⁶). In a resolution passed on 24 September, Parliament (⁷), while welcoming the Commission initiative, asked the Commission to propose a mechanism for mutual assistance between Member States and recommended the adoption of European minimum standards. On 16 October, the Commission presented a proposal for a directive laying down such standards (Table II).

(¹) http://europa.eu.int/comm/justice_home/news/laecken_council/en/mandat_en.htm.
(²) Decision 2001/500 /JHA (OJ L 182, 5.7.2001; 2001 General Report, point 545).
(³) 1999 General Report, point 910.
(⁴) 2000 General Report, point 464.
(⁵) OJ C 125, 27.5.2002; Bull. 3-2002, point 1.4.7.
(⁶) COM(2001) 536; 2001 General Report, point 530.
(⁷) Bull. 9-2002, point 1.4.6.

481.   Fight against racism and xenophobia. In conclusions adopted on 25 April on combating racism, anti-Semitism and xenophobia *(→ point 45)*, the Council emphasised the importance of the draft framework decision on combating racism and xenophobia currently under discussion in the competent Council bodies.

482.   Further information concerning judicial cooperation in criminal matters is given under 'Prevention of and fight against crime' and 'Combating terrorism' in this section *(→ points 488 et seq.).*

Police and customs cooperation (¹)

483.   Europol (²). On 28 November, following an initiative presented by Belgium and Spain, the Council established a protocol amending the convention establishing the European Police Office and two protocols annexed to it (Table II). The aim of this amendment is to enable Europol to participate in the joint investigation teams and their operational activities *(→ point 479)* and to authorise the office to ask Member States to initiate inquiries in specific cases. Given the growing importance of the office's role, the Commission presented a communication on 26 February (³) calling for stronger democratic monitoring of its activities and operation by the national parliaments and the European Parliament. Parliament supported this in a recommendation of 30 May (⁴), though it regarded the initiative as inadequate and asked for the convention and its protocols to be recast as a Council decision. On 19 December, following an initiative presented by Belgium, Luxembourg and the Netherlands, the Council amended the Staff Regulations applicable to Europol employees with a view to regulating the position of members of the Europol Directorate, in particular, their selection and possible disciplinary procedures (Table II). The same day, the Council reached a general approach on a draft protocol presented by Denmark which would amend the Europol Convention with a view to strengthening cooperation in Europol's areas of responsibility (Table II). On 20 December, an agreement was concluded (⁵) supplementing the agreement between the United States and Europol on the exchange of strategic information of 6 December 2001 (⁶); this supplemental agreement will allow the exchange of personal data.

484.   European Institute of Police Studies. Spain presented an initiative for a decision establishing a European Institute of Police Studies (Table II), whose

---

(¹) http://europa.eu.int/comm/justice_home/unit/police_en.htm.
(²) http://www.europol.eu.int/index.asp.
(³) COM(2002) 95; Bull. 1/2-2002, point 1.4.19.
(⁴) Bull. 5-2002, point 1.4.14.
(⁵) Bull. 12-2002, point 1.4.25.
(⁶) 2001 General Report, point 554.

main task would be to give effect to crime-related programmes decided on by the Council.

485.　*Specific forms of cooperation between Member States.* In two initiatives for draft decisions, Spain proposed setting up a European network for the protection of public figures (Table II), and a network of contact points of national authorities responsible for private security (Table II). The first of the two initiatives was translated into Council Decision 2002/956/JHA, adopted on 28 November. On 25 April, the Council decided to enhance security at international football matches by establishing a national football information point in each Member State to gather and exchange relevant police information (Table II). On 13 June, it adopted a framework decision to establish joint investigation teams between the authorities of two or more Member States *(→ point 479).* The same day, it recommended the Member States to cooperate on private security ([1]). In conclusions adopted at its meeting on 14 and 15 October ([2]), it called for the adoption of a mandatory legal instrument concerning electronic data-interchange between Member States' enforcement services. On 25 June, the Commission presented a proposal for a regulation on the prevention of money-laundering through customs cooperation. On 28 November, the Council approved the Security Handbook for the use of police authorities and services at meetings of the European Council and other similar events. On 19 December, at the initiative of Denmark, it adopted a decision on the common use of liaison officers posted abroad by the law enforcement authorities of the Member States, the main purpose of which is to develop cooperation between such liaison officers outside the Union (Table II).

486.　*Eurodac.* On 28 February, the Council adopted a regulation laying down certain rules to implement the Eurodac system for comparison of the fingerprints of certain nationals of non-member countries *(→ point 466).*

487.　*International cooperation.* At its meeting on 25 and 26 April, the Council expressed support for stronger cooperation between the Frontiers and False Documents Working Party and Europol, Interpol, the United States and Canada ([3]). On 25 April, the ministers for justice and home affairs of the Fifteen met their Russian counterparts in Brussels *(→ point 917).*

([1]) Bull. 6-2002, point 1.4.19.
([2]) Bull. 10-2002, point 1.4.16.
([3]) Bull. 4-2002, point 1.4.27.

Prevention of and fight against crime [1]

488.   Cooperation between Member States. On 13 June, the Council, in response to a Dutch initiative, decided to set up a European network of contact points in respect of persons responsible for genocide, crimes against humanity and war crimes to facilitate cooperation between the relevant national authorities (Table II). Denmark presented an initiative for a Council decision on the investigation and prosecution of *inter alia* war crimes and crimes against humanity (Table II). The aim of this draft decision is to strengthen the possibilities afforded to Member States for acting against persons who have committed or participated in the commission of war crimes or similar serious offences and to secure the necessary cooperation and information exchanges. On 13 June, the Council welcomed the results of the first annual report of the European crime prevention network, stressing its importance and approving both the work already done and the programme of future work [2]. At its meeting on 19 and 20 December, the Council adopted conclusions on information technologies and the investigation and prosecution of organised crime [3].

489.   Trafficking in human beings. In a framework decision adopted on 19 July (Table II), the Council defines offences concerning trafficking in human beings for the purposes of labour exploitation or sexual exploitation and provides for penalties to be imposed on offenders.

490.   Corruption in the private sector. Denmark presented an initiative for a framework decision to combat corruption in the private sector supplementing the joint action adopted in 1998 [4]. The main aim of this initiative is to ensure that both active and passive corruption in the private sector is a criminal offence in all Member States, that legal persons may also be held responsible for such offences, and that the offences incur effective, proportionate and dissuasive penalties. The Council reached agreement on the framework decision on 19 December.

491. Information on environmental protection by criminal law is given in Section 4 ('Environment') of this chapter *(→ point 595).*

Combating terrorism [5]

492.   General aspects. On 28 January, the Council adopted a strategic document on terrorism in Europe [6] to improve the coordination and targeting of

---

[1] http://europa.eu.int/comm/justice_home/unit/crime_en.htm.
[2] Bull. 6-2002, point 1.4.13.
[3] Bull. 12-2002, point 1.4.14.
[4] Joint Action 98/742/JHA (OJ L 358, 31.12.1998; 1998 General Report, point 972).
[5] http://europa.eu.int/comm/justice_home/news/laecken_council/en/terrorism_en.htm.
[6] Bull. 1/2-2002, point 1.4.9.

activities and, in particular, to strengthen control and security measures relating to explosives; on 19 December, it approved a similar document on control and security measures relating to the transport of nuclear, biological, chemical and radioactive substances. On 13 June, the Council adopted a framework decision to approximate the provisions of the Member States on the definition of terrorist offences and to provide for adequate penalties (Table II). On 31 July, the Commission proposed establishing a legal basis for financing certain Europol activities in this area (Table II). On 28 November, the Council adopted a decision establishing a mechanism for the collective evaluation of national anti-terrorism provisions (Table II), followed on 19 December by a decision on the application of specific police and judicial cooperation measures to combat terrorism (Table II).

In a resolution adopted on 7 February ([1]), Parliament called on the Council to let it play a greater role in the adoption of third-pillar measures and, referring to Council Common Positions 2001/930/CFSP and 2001/931/CFSP ([2]), regretted, in particular, that it was not consulted on the list of terrorist organisations. The Council updated this list on 2 May ([3]) and 17 June ([4]), when it also updated ([5]) the list of persons, groups and entities concerned by the regulation on specific restrictive measures ([6]). On 28 October, the Council updated a number of specific points ([7]), chiefly regarding more extensive information exchanges between Member States, Europol and Eurojust. These were further updated on 12 December ([8]). At its meeting on 14 and 15 November ([9]), and as part of the follow-up to the conclusions of the special European Council held in Brussels on 21 September 2001 ([10]), the Council also recommended Member States to introduce a standard form for exchanging information on terrorists.

On 24 April ([11]), the European Economic and Social Committee endorsed the recommendations put forward in December 2001 by the Commission for coordinated Community action to fight terrorism ([12]). The Seville European Council adopted a declaration on the contribution of the CFSP, including defence policy, to combating terrorism (→ point 758), and the Council adopted conclusions on the same subject on 22 July ([13]).

([1]) OJ C 284 E, 21.11.2002; Bull. 1/2-2002, point 1.4.12.
([2]) OJ L 344, 28.12.2001; 2001 General Report, point 535.
([3]) Common Position 2002/340/CFSP (OJ L 116, 3.5.2002; Bull. 5-2002, point 1.4.9).
([4]) Common Position 2002/462/ CFSP (OJ L 160, 18.6.2002; Bull. 6-2002, point 1.4.10).
([5]) Decision 2002/460/EC (OJ L 160, 18.6.2002; Bull. 6-2002, point 1.4.11).
([6]) Regulation (EC) No 2580/2001 (OJ L 344, 28.12.2001; 2001 General Report, point 546).
([7]) Decision 2002/848/EC; Common Position 2002/847/CFSP (OJ L 295, 30.10.2002; Bull. 10-2002, points 1.4.11 and 1.4.10).
([8]) Decision 2002/974/EC; Common Position 2002/976/CFSP (OJ L 337, 13.12.2002; Bull. 12-2002, points 1.4.8 and 1.4.9).
([9]) Bull. 11-2002, point 1.4.15.
([10]) Bull. 9-2002, point 1.8.
([11]) OJ C 149, 21.6.2002; Bull. 4-2002, point 1.4.14.
([12]) COM(2001) 743; Bull. 12-2001, point 1.4.5.
([13]) Bull. 7/8-2002, point 1.6.3.

493.   Commemoration of the attacks of 11 September 2001. On 11 March, the Council published a European Union declaration (¹) commemorating these terrorist attacks and reaffirmed its solidarity with the United States. Another solemn declaration was published on the anniversary of the attacks (→ *point 928).*

494.   Cooperation between Member States. In a recommendation adopted at its meeting on 25 and 26 April (²), the Council supported the establishment of ad hoc multinational investigation teams to combat terrorism. In November, at the initiative of Denmark, the Council adopted a recommendation on the use of profiling techniques by the Member States in the fight against terrorism.

495.   Armaments. On 15 April, the Council responded to the recrudescence of the terrorist threat by calling for a reinforcement of the multilateral dimension of the European Union's non-proliferation, disarmament and arms control policy (³).

Drugs (⁴)

496.   Implementation of the European Union action plan for the fight against drugs (2000–04) (⁵). In its communication of 4 November (⁶), the Commission presented a mid-term evaluation of the action plan. It stressed the significance of the progress achieved in the first two years of the plan and noted that there were still efforts to be made in the area of synthetic drugs and that this was a top priority for the Union and Member States. The report advocates a number of measures to this end, notably the development of more effective and efficient coordination. The communication was sent to the European Council in Copenhagen.

497.   Improvement of investigation methods. At its meeting on 25 and 26 April (⁷), in accordance with the action plan on drugs referred to above and in order to combat this type of crime more efficiently, the Council called on the Member States to conduct simultaneous investigations into drug trafficking and the identification of the relevant organisations' financial and asset structures.

498.   Cooperation with the candidate countries. On 28 February, the Council and the candidate countries adopted a joint declaration (⁸) stressing, in particu-

---

(¹) Bull. 3-2002, point 1.4.5.
(²) Bull. 4-2002, point 1.4.15.
(³) Bull. 4-2002, point 1.4.13.
(⁴) http://europa.eu.int/comm/justice_home/unit/drogue_en.htm.
(⁵) 2000 General Report, point 479.
(⁶) COM(2002) 599; Bull. 11-2002, point 1.4.25.
(⁷) OJ C 114, 15.5.2002; Bull. 4-2002, point 1.4.31.
(⁸) Bull. 1/2-2002, point 1.4.25.

lar, that the candidate countries would abide by the action plan guidelines (→ *point 496*). In addition, on 16 December, an agreement was concluded with Turkey to control trade in certain substances used in the illicit manufacture of drugs (Table III).

499. *Control and prevention measures.* The Council decision of 28 February ([1]) defines new control measures and criminal penalties concerning paramethoxymethamphetamin (PMMA). At its meeting on 25 and 26 April, the Council stressed the need to boost cooperation and information exchanges between the Member States' operational units specialising in the fight against trafficking in precursors ([2]). At the same meeting, in accordance with the drugs action plan, the Council called on the Member States to adopt a series of measures to prevent the recreational use of drugs ([3]). A resolution of 13 June ([4]), recommended the establishment of health promotion and drug-addiction prevention programmes in schools. On 3 June, the Council amended Regulation (EEC) No 3677/90 ([5]) laying down measures to be taken to discourage the diversion of certain substances to the illicit manufacture of narcotic drugs and psychotropic substances in accordance with United Nations instruments ([6]). In a resolution adopted on 28 and 29 November ([7]), the Council welcomed the Commission's initiatives on the generic classification of specific groups of synthetic drugs and adopted an implementation plan outlining possible action against these substances. Work continued in various areas of customs cooperation.

With a view to simplifying the legislation, the Commission presented a proposal on 10 September to convert Directive 92/109/EEC on drug precursors into a Parliament and Council regulation laying down harmonised monitoring and surveillance measures for certain chemical substances frequently used in the manufacture of illicit drugs (→ *point 273*). It also proposed a recommendation on the prevention and reduction of risks associated with drug dependence (→ *point 690*). Legislative work continued with a view to the adoption of a framework decision on criminal acts and penalties in the field of illicit drug trafficking (Table II).

([1]) Decision 2002/188/JHA (OJ L 63, 6.3.2002; Bull. 1/2-2002, point 1.4.26).
([2]) OJ C 114, 15.5.2002; Bull. 4-2002, point 1.4.30.
([3]) Bull. 4-2002, point 1.4.32.
([4]) Bull. 6-2002, point 1.4.21.
([5]) OJ L 357, 20.12.1990; Twenty-fourth General Report, point 167.
([6]) Regulation (EC) No 988/2002 (OJ L 151, 11.6.2002; Bull. 6-2002, point 1.4.20).
([7]) Bull. 11-2002, point 1.4.26.

External relations (¹)

500.   *Candidate countries.* The Commission pursued the monitoring process agreed with the Member States for the 10 countries with which negotiations have been completed and continued to make progress in the negotiations with Bulgaria and Romania. It also continued to provide assistance to the Turkish authorities to help them attain the accession partnership objectives in the area of freedom, security and justice and launched the pre-negotiation legislative screening process.

501.   *Western Balkans.* The Commission worked with other relevant players to optimise the overall consistency of regional initiatives on the justice and home affairs front, and thereby provide support for implementation of the justice and home affairs chapter of the stabilisation and association process. In May and June, missions responsible for assessing the situation visited the five countries in the region with a view to providing guidance for future action in this area. As part of the programme of Community assistance for reconstruction, development and stabilisation (CARDS), justice and home affairs projects continue to contribute to the political and economic development of the western Balkans.

502.   *Eastern Europe.* Under the various partnership and cooperation agreements with Russia and Ukraine, justice and home affairs troïkas were organised with these countries. In addition, in its communication of 18 September, the Commission examined the issue of transit to and from Kaliningrad *(→ point 917).* It also contributed to the implementation of existing instruments such as the action plan to combat organised crime in Russia (²) and the European Union–Ukraine action plan in the field of justice and home affairs. The action plan for the northern dimension *(→ point 921),* which includes a chapter on justice and home affairs, was updated, and the Commission continued to play an active part in the action group combating organised crime in the Baltic region (Visby).

503.   *Mediterranean countries.* Activities focused primarily on promoting the consideration of justice and home affairs issues on a regional basis as part of the Barcelona process, particularly under the regional programme approved in Valencia in April *(→ point 880).* The development of relations with these countries on justice and home affairs is also being pursued on a bilateral basis within the framework of the association agreements.

504.   *United States.* The United States and the European Union have both focused on stepping up cooperation in the fight against terrorism, including police and judicial cooperation in criminal matters, and frontier security.

(¹) http://europa.eu.int/comm/justice_home/unit/relex_en.htm.
(²) 2000 General Report, point 943.

Cooperation between the United States and Europol was also intensified (→ *point 483*).

505. International organisations. The Commission continued cooperation with and through multilateral organisations, in particular, the United Nations, the Organisation for Security and Cooperation in Europe, the Financial Action Task Force on Money-Laundering, and the Council of Europe. Activities focused primarily on putting in place a regular dialogue on questions of common interest, such as terrorism and the financing of terrorism, and developing key instruments, such as the United Nations Convention against Transnational Organised Crime and a future United Nations Convention against Corruption.

Section 2

Union citizenship

506. On 5 September, the European Parliament adopted a resolution (^{1}) on the third report on citizenship of the Union, adopted by the Commission in September 2001 (^{2}). The Committee of the Regions gave its opinion on the report on 21 November (^{3}).

Freedom of movement and right of residence (^{4})

507. Work continued on legislation concerning the right of Union citizens and members of their family to move and reside freely within the territory of the Member States (Table I).

Right to vote and stand as a candidate (^{5})

508. Municipal elections. On 30 May, the Commission adopted a report (^{6}) on the application of Council Directive 94/80/EC laying down detailed arrangements for the exercise of the right to vote and stand as a candidate in municipal elections (^{7}). Although from a legal standpoint all the Member States have transposed the directive, the Commission notes that its application is still somewhat marginal in practice, since the proportion of non-national citizens entered on the electoral roll for municipal elections in their country of residence is generally rather low. The Committee of the Regions gave an opinion on the report on 21 November (^{8}).

509. Elections to the European Parliament. Also on 21 November, the Commission and electoral experts from the Member States held a meeting on the application of Directive 93/109/EC laying down detailed arrangements for the exercise of the right to vote and stand as a candidate in elections to the European Parliament for citizens of the Union residing in a Member State of which they

---

(^{1}) COM(2001) 506; 2001 General Report, point 556.
(^{2}) Bull. 9-2002, point 1.4.11.
(^{3}) Bull. 11-2002, point 1.4.27.
(^{4}) http://europa.eu.int/comm/justice_home/unit/libre_circulation_en.htm.
(^{5}) http://europa.eu.int/comm/justice_home/unit/elections/elections_menu_en.htm.
(^{6}) COM(2002) 260; Bull. 5-2002, point 1.4.19.
(^{7}) OJ L 368, 31.12.1994; 1994 General Report, point 4.
(^{8}) Bull. 11-2002, point 1.4.27.

are not nationals (^{1}). The purpose of the meeting, held with an eye to the forth-coming elections to Parliament in 2004, was to work out a system of exchanging information to prevent citizens voting more than once. Representatives of the 10 candidate countries with an interest in the 2004 elections also attended the meeting as observers. The Commission acknowledged that this restriction was still justified. In a resolution adopted on 5 December (^{2}), recalling its resolutions of December 1998 (^{3}) and May 1999 (^{4}), Parliament called for the procedure for adopting the draft statute for its Members to be speeded up and completed.

Right of petition and right of access to the Ombudsman (^{5})

510.   Right of petition. On 26 September, Parliament adopted a resolution on the deliberations of the committee on petitions during the 2001 parliamentary year (^{6}). The Commission had been consulted on virtually all the 500 petitions examined and had sent communications on the various cases. Measures to strengthen the right of petition were the subject of a contribution by Parliament to the Convention on the Future of the European Union *(→ point 13)*.

511.   Regulations governing the Ombudsman. Exercising its right of initiative in this field under Article 195 of the EC Treaty, and after obtaining the opinion of the Commission on 6 March (^{7}), Parliament amended on 14 March (^{8}) the reg-ulations and general conditions governing the performance of the Ombuds-man's duties (^{9}). The purpose of the new decision is to take account of the cre-ation of a specific section for the Ombudsman in the general budget of the European Union (^{10}).

512.   Activities of the Ombudsman. On 26 September, Parliament adopted a resolution (^{11}) on the annual report of the European Ombudsman for the year 2001 (^{12}). On 17 December, it stated its opinion on two special reports by the Ombudsman, one to the Council (^{13}) and one to the Commission (^{14}), following

---

(^{1}) OJ L 329, 30.12.1993; Twenty-seventh General Report, points 15 and 590.
(^{2}) Bull. 12-2002, point 1.1.18.
(^{3}) OJ C 398, 21.12.1998; Bull. 12-1998, point 1.8.4.
(^{4}) Bull. 5-1999, point 1.8.6.
(^{5}) http://www.euro-ombudsman.eu.int/home/en/default.htm.
(^{6}) Bull. 9-2002, point 1.4.13.
(^{7}) COM(2002) 133; Bull. 3-2002, point 1.4.9.
(^{8}) Decision 2002/262/ECSC, EC, Euratom of the European Parliament (OJ L 92, 9.4.2002; Bull. 3-2002, point 1.4.9).
(^{9}) Decision 94/262/ECSC, EC, Euratom of the European Parliament (OJ L 113, 4.5.1994; 1994 General Re-port, point 6).
(^{10}) Council Regulation (EC, ECSC, Euratom) No 2673/1999 (OJ L 326, 18.12.1999; 1999 General Report, point 952).
(^{11}) Bull. 9-2002, point 1.4.12.
(^{12}) http://www.euro-ombudsman.eu.int/report/en/default.htm.
(^{13}) Bull. 12-2002, point 1.4.28.
(^{14}) Bull. 12-2002, point 1.4.29.

recommendations relating to complaints. In connection with the work of the Convention on the Future of the European Union, the Ombudsman formulated proposals on the charter of fundamental rights, legal remedies and cooperation between European, national and regional ombudsmen.

Right to diplomatic and consular protection

513.   Following completion of the requisite legislative procedures by all the Member States, the decision of 19 December 1995, regarding protection for citizens of the European Union by diplomatic and consular representations of the Member States in non-member countries, entered into force on 3 May ([1]). As a result, all Union citizens are now entitled to receive such protection if, in the territory where they are located, their own Member State — or another State representing it on a permanent basis — has no accessible permanent representation or accessible honorary consul competent for such matters.

([1]) Decision 95/553/EC of the Representatives of the Governments of the Member States meeting within the Council (OJ L 314, 28.12.1995; 1995 General Report, point 6).

Section 3

Education and culture (¹)

Overview

514.   In 2002, the European Union broke new ground with the implementation of major projects launched at the Lisbon European Council in the sphere of education and culture. Education and training now form an integral part of the employment guidelines with new emphasis on quality in work. The Barcelona European Council welcomed the Commission's initiatives for lifelong learning and the definition of concrete future objectives for education and training systems. The new eLearning programme also demonstrated the Commission's commitment to lifelong learning through the Internet and the opportunities it affords, while the adoption of the action plan for skills and mobility underlined the importance of the recognition of qualifications in the interest of mobility. Besides the continuation of programmes and activities focusing on education, vocational training and youth (Socrates, Leonardo da Vinci, Youth, etc.), increasing attention was paid to international cooperation, particularly in higher education and the youth field, through extension of the Tempus programme to the Mediterranean countries, renewal of the EuroMed/EuroMed Youth programme, and the proposal to launch the Erasmus World programme. These initiatives form part of the strategy to boost cooperation with third countries in the higher education field. In the cultural and audiovisual sectors, the MEDIA programme was extended to the candidate countries and a new work plan for improving cultural cooperation was adopted by the Council. Additionally, 2004 has been designated 'European Year of Education through Sport'.

Education and training (²)

Priority objectives

515.   Concrete future objectives of education and training systems. The European Parliament (on 6 February (³)) and the Council (on 14 February (⁴)), gave

---

(¹) Further information is available on the Europa server (http://europa.eu.int/comm/dgs/education_culture/index_en.htm).
(²) http://europa.eu.int/comm/education/index_en.html.
(³) OJ C 284 E, 21.11.2002; Bull. 1/2-2002, point 1.4.27.
(⁴) Bull. 1/2-2002, point 1.4.28.

their reactions to the Commission's report (¹) drawn up for the European Council concerning the detailed work programme (²) for following up the report on the objectives of education and training systems (³) in Europe. The Barcelona European Council welcomed these initiatives (⁴). In the context of the detailed work programme, the Commission proposed, on 20 November (⁵), that European benchmarks be adopted for education and training systems in areas seen as vital for achieving the strategic goal set by the Lisbon European Council. The Council meanwhile reaffirmed, on 11 November (⁶), its commitment to enhanced cooperation in education and vocational training, and called on the Commission and the Member States, in a resolution adopted on 19 December, to take appropriate steps in this direction (⁷). A ministerial meeting on the subject of European cooperation in vocational training and education was held on 29 and 30 November, with key participants including Mrs Reding, Member of the Commission, the education ministers of the Member States and candidate countries, and the social partners, in the course of which the Copenhagen declaration (⁸) was adopted.

516.   Lifelong learning. The Barcelona European Council (⁹), the Committee of the Regions (on 15 May (¹⁰)) and the Council (on 27 June (¹¹)), welcomed the Commission's communication on lifelong learning (¹²). The Council, in particular, stressed the need to consolidate the principles set out in the communication, and called upon all the parties involved to cooperate more effectively with this in mind. On 5 September (¹³), the European Parliament called on the Commission and the Member States to develop a European framework of basic skills to be acquired by all pupils before they leave compulsory school education, and called on the Commission to give universities a more prominent place in its programmes and policies, and to draw up a Green Paper on a future European higher education area.

517.   Employment policies. In an opinion adopted on 14 February (¹⁴), the Council stressed the importance of education and training within the employment guidelines *(→ point 112)*. It welcomed, in particular, the new horizontal objective aimed at improving quality in work, encompassing both qualifications

---

(¹) COM(2001) 501; 2001 General Report, point 563.
(²) Bull. 1/2-2002, point 1.4.29.
(³) COM(2001) 59; 2001 General Report, point 563.
(⁴) Bull. 3-2002, point I.36.
(⁵) COM(2002) 629; Bull. 11-2002, point 1.4.28.
(⁶) Bull. 11-2002, point 1.4.30.
(⁷) Bull. 12-2002, point 1.4.39.
(⁸) Bull. 11-2002, point 1.4.31.
(⁹) Bull. 3-2002, point I.36.
(¹⁰) OJ C 278, 14.11.2002; Bull. 5-2002, point 1.4.20.
(¹¹) OJ C 163, 9.7.2002; Bull. 6-2002, point 1.4.24.
(¹²) COM(2001) 678; 2001 General Report, point 567.
(¹³) Bull. 9-2002, points 1.4.15 and 1.4.16.
(¹⁴) Bull. 1/2-2002, point 1.3.36.

and lifelong learning. The Commission meanwhile adopted, on 13 February, an action plan for skills and mobility *(→ point 123)*, including proposals for a more effective system for recognising qualifications and diplomas.

518. Twinning between secondary schools. As requested by the Barcelona European Council ([1]), the Commission adopted, on 4 June, a report on the feasibility of twinning between European secondary schools ([2]). The objective is that all pupils should, during their time at school, be involved in exchanges with pupils from another country of the European Union. Besides the creation of a general framework for such cooperation, the Commission advocated a teacher-training drive and the establishment of a suitable support service.

519. Cooperation with third countries. In a resolution adopted on 11 April ([3]), concerning a Commission communication on strengthening cooperation with third countries in the field of higher education ([4]), the European Parliament called for exchanges to be stepped up and for a European quality label to be introduced for certain teaching modules.

520. eLearning ([5]). Implementation of the *eLearning* action plan ([6]), adopted in 2001, was boosted by an increase in funding making it possible to launch pilot projects and strategic studies on *eLearning* in Europe. Given the encouraging results, the Commission put forward a proposal, on 19 December, for adopting the *eLearning* programme ([7]) targeting three priority areas: the digital divide, virtual universities and twinning of schools via the Internet.

Programmes and actions ([8])

521. Education. In a resolution adopted on 28 February ([9]), the European Parliament called on the Commission to improve the implementation of the Socrates programme ([10]), to draw up annual activity reports on this subject and to promote cooperation with other Community programmes. The Commission, for its part, put forward a proposal, on 29 April, for amendment of an annex to Decision No 253/2000/EC establishing the second phase of the Socrates programme, aimed at reducing the administrative burden on beneficiaries (Table I). On 15 October, the Council endorsed the Court of Auditors' Special Report

([1]) Bull. 3-2002, point I.36.
([2]) COM(2002) 283; Bull. 6-2002, point 1.4.22.
([3]) Bull. 4-2002, point 1.4.36.
([4]) COM(2001) 385; 2001 General Report, point 605.
([5]) http://europa.eu.int/comm/education/elearning/index.html.
([6]) COM(2001) 172; 2001 General Report, point 564.
([7]) COM(2002) 751; Bull. 12-2002, point 1.3.94.
([8]) http://europa.eu.int/comm/education/programmes_en.html.
([9]) OJ C 293 E, 28.11.2002; Bull. 1/2-2002, point 1.4.32.
([10]) Decision No 253/2000/EC of the European Parliament and of the Council (OJ L 28, 3.2.2000; 1999 General Report, point 278; Internet http://europa.eu.int/comm/education/socrates.html).

No 2/2002 *(→ point 1104)* on the Socrates and Youth for Europe programmes (¹), stressing the importance of such programmes for boosting cooperation between the different players in the education sector. On 17 December (²), Parliament drew attention to shortcomings in the management and implementation of these programmes.

In school education (Comenius strand of the Socrates programme), the 'school partnerships' action gave rise to agreements with the national agencies of 30 countries. More than 10 200 schools were involved in partnerships, with some 35 000 pupils and 33 000 teachers benefiting from mobility. In connection with the training of school education staff, more than 6 000 language teachers have been able to enhance their skills through Europe-wide mobility, with 40 new transnational cooperation projects being selected for Community funding. The Comenius networks action engendered five new projects eligible for Community funding. Lastly, within the framework of the Arion action, the Commission granted 1 762 mobility grants to education specialists and decision-makers from 30 countries, enabling them to participate in the 170 or so study visits connected with the development of education policies in the Member States and candidate countries, covering the 22 themes of the programme.

In the higher education field (Erasmus strand of the Socrates programme), financial assistance was granted, in 2002/03, to 1 845 higher education establishments (including 34 establishments in the 12 associated countries); according to the latest statistics, 111 084 students and 14 356 teachers spent a period of time abroad with a mobility grant in 2000/01. During the 2002/03 academic year, 696 institutions benefited from the European credit transfer system. In addition, funding was provided for 107 joint syllabus development projects (77 programmes and 30 European modules) and 232 intensive programmes. Twelve new thematic network projects (bringing together faculties, departments, associations and socioeconomic partners from all the participating countries) became eligible for financial support, while eight projects were renewed for a second year of activity and 15 thematic networks received funding to disseminate and exploit the key results obtained at the end of a three-year cycle of activity. Moreover, 14 existing Erasmus curricular projects received additional aid for disseminating the results obtained during their three years of activity. This year, the Commission celebrated the millionth Erasmus student and, during the Erasmus Week from 18 to 25 October, launched the Erasmus student charter setting out the entitlements and obligations of students participating in the programme.

In the sphere of adult education and other educational pathways (Grundtvig strand of the Socrates programme), decentralised activities became more wide-

---

(¹) Decision 88/348/EEC (OJ L 158, 25.6.1988; Twenty-second General Report, point 468).
(²) Bull. 12-2002, point 1.4.31.

spread in 2002. Over 50 new cooperation projects involving more than 350 organisations throughout Europe were financed under 'Grundtvig 1', together with eight large-scale European networks encompassing more than 130 participating organisations under 'Grundtvig 4'. Over 200 'Grundtvig 2' learning partnerships involving more than 900 organisations across 30 European countries were also set up. Moreover, several hundred members of adult education staff (both teaching and administrative) received 'Grundtvig 3' grants enabling them to undergo continuing training in other European countries. The effectiveness of Grundtvig as a vector for lifelong learning was reinforced by the Grundtvig Working Group (advisory body created by the Socrates Committee). At the operational level, the Grundtvig action continues to be supported by its network of national agencies.

Within the framework of the 2001–02 action plan for equal opportunities under the Socrates programme, the Commission presented, at a conference in Budapest on 29 and 30 November, an analysis of the projects carried out under the Socrates programme in the sphere of equal opportunities for women and men. It supported the activities geared to dissemination (Internet web site, database, Euronews), study (classroom practice in standard primary education, transition from school to the labour market for young people with special needs) and analysis (improving the selection of quality projects for the participation of people with special needs or disabilities, including proposed quality indicators), and the work of the European Development Agency for special needs education, as well as collaboration with the Eurydice network for the creation of special education indicators.

522. In the course of 2002, the Eurydice network carried out the annual update of Eurybase, its database on the 30 education systems covered by the network. In this connection, two reports on the teaching profession, a survey on the teaching of key skills in compulsory education, a series of national reports on the evaluation of schools, and the final version of a glossary of staff responsible for management, quality control and guidance in Europe were published. The network also produced, jointly with Eurostat, the 2002 edition of *Key data on education in Europe*.

523. *Vocational training.* In a report adopted on 2 May ([1]), the Commission presented a positive assessment of the two years of operation of the system for European pathways in work-linked training, including apprenticeship ([2]). With regard to the Leonardo da Vinci programme ([3]), the Commission adopted, on 14 June, a positive report ([4]) on the start of implementation of the programme

---

([1]) COM(2002) 214; Bull. 5-2002, point 1.4.23.
([2]) Council Decision 1999/51/EC (OJ L 17, 22.1.1999; 1998 General Report, point 336).
([3]) Council Decision 1999/382/EC (OJ L 146, 11.6.1999; 1999 General Report, point 283; http://europa.eu.int/comm/education/leonardo/leonardo2_en.html).
([4]) COM(2002) 315; Bull. 6-2002, point 1.4.23.

over the 2000–06 period. It looked, in particular, at the management of decentralisation of part of the programme to the Member States and the simplification of procedures. Under this programme, 279 projects from 30 countries were selected in 2002, attracting EU funding of EUR 89.7 million to co-finance their activities. The projects cover a wide range of topics relating to education and vocational training. While the proposals are extremely varied, a number of European trends are nevertheless discernible: quality in training, transparency, validation and recognition of training; integration in the labour market; and use of information and communication technologies.

524.   *Cooperation with third countries.* On 11 February, the Commission proposed that the geographical scope of the Tempus trans-European cooperation scheme for higher education (¹) should be extended to include Mediterranean non-member countries for the third phase (2000–06), thereby opening the programme up to the Euro-Mediterranean partnership and taking it through to 31 December 2006. The Council endorsed these proposals in a decision of 27 June (Table II), and the sum of EUR 106 million was earmarked accordingly. On 17 June, moreover, the Commission adopted an annual report on the application of the programme in 2000 (²). In the course of the year 2002, it committed EUR 29.4 million for the funding of 90 joint European projects and 122 mobility grants in the Balkans, central Europe and Central Asia, totalling EUR 720 084. It also financed 19 cooperation projects for higher education and training, amounting to EUR 2.28 million, with the United States and Canada (³). Finally, two pilot projects for cooperation with Japan and Australia in the field of higher education were launched and given funding of EUR 594 682. The Commission also pressed on with its reform, simplification and revamping of the Tempus programme management. Moreover, on 17 July, it proposed that a programme be established to enhance quality in higher education and promote intercultural understanding (Erasmus World) through cooperation with third countries over the period 2004–08 (Table I).

525.   *Jean Monnet project* (⁴). For the 2002 Jean Monnet project (European integration in university studies), the Commission selected 185 teaching projects in Community law, European economics, European political studies and the history of European integration, thereby bringing to 601 the number of Jean Monnet chairs worldwide. Providing support for the setting up of regional and transnational research groups organised by the academic world (ECSA national associations and Jean Monnet centres of excellence), the Commission adopted six projects. Networks of Jean Monnet professors continued to be organised, and a symposium on intercultural dialogue was held on 20 and 21 March 2002,

(¹) http://europa.eu.int/comm/education/tempus/index.html.
(²) COM(2002) 323; Bull. 6-2002, point 1.4.27.
(³) Decisions 2001/196/EC and 2001/197/EC (OJ L 71, 13.3.2001; 2001 General Report, point 604).
(⁴) http://europa.eu.int/comm/education/ajm/index_en.html.

attended by more than 400 participants from academic and political circles and the EU institutions.

526. Cooperation with networks on European integration. The Commission continued its policy of supporting the activities of the national ECSA (European Community Studies Association) networks, with the award of seven grants (two in Member States, two in candidate countries and three elsewhere in the world). Globally, the ECSA network is made up of 49 national associations of professors and researchers specialising in European integration. On 5 and 6 December 2002, the Commission organised the sixth ECSA–World symposium on the theme of 'Peace, security and stability: international dialogue and the role of the European Union', attended by more than 350 participants from the 49 national ECSA associations. Lastly, in support of initiatives from the academic world aimed at promoting discussion, reflection and knowledge about the process of European integration, the Commission selected 39 projects on the topics of enlargement, the future of the European Union, the euro, the European Union and other nations of the world, and sustainable development.

Youth

527. Follow-up to the White Paper on youth. On 14 February([1]) and 30 May([2]), the Council reacted favourably to the White Paper entitled 'A new impetus for European youth'. Adopting a resolution on 30 May, it emphasised its desire to promote European cooperation in the youth field both through the open method of coordination and by paying greater heed to the youth dimension in other policies. On 7 May([3]), the Council decided to start applying the open method of coordination to two of the White Paper's priorities of participation and information. As regards paying greater heed to the 'youth' dimension in different policies, the Council adopted two resolutions on 27 June, one concerned with lifelong learning and the other focusing on cooperation in the youth field. The European Economic and Social Committee, the European Parliament and the Committee of the Regions endorsed the Commission's proposals contained in the White Paper on 25 April([4]), 14 May([5]) and 3 July([6]) respectively. In addition to the adoption of specific measures, Parliament wanted young people and youth organisations to be involved in policy matters at both national and local levels.

([1]) OJ C 119, 22.5.2002; Bull. 1/2-2002, point 1.4.34.
([2]) OJ C 168, 13.7.2002; Bull. 5-2002, point 1.4.25.
([3]) OJ C 119, 22.5.2002; Bull. 5-2002, point 1.4.24.
([4]) OJ C 149, 21.6.2002; Bull. 4-2002, point 1.4.35.
([5]) Bull. 5-2002, point 1.4.24.
([6]) OJ C 287, 22.11.2002; Bull. 7/8-2002, point 1.4.8.

528.   *Youth programme* (¹). In a resolution adopted on 28 February (²), Parliament welcomed the large number of projects funded. It pointed to the significant role played by the Member States, associated countries and national agencies in implementing this programme, and called on the Commission to improve its reporting on this aspect. Some 11 500 projects involving organisations from 50 countries received funding under the Youth programme, enabling more than 120 000 young people to take part in intercultural learning and non-formal education activities, with particular emphasis on mobility through exchanges and European voluntary service. The Commission also supported 12 large-scale European projects in connection with young people's cooperation, information and training, and 15 projects forming part of joint actions on topics such as young people's active citizenship.

529.   *EuroMed Youth.* Cooperation between the European Union and the 12 Mediterranean partner countries in the social, cultural and human fields is one of the pillars of the Barcelona process (³), with the EuroMed Youth programme providing the framework for youth-oriented cooperation activities encompassing the Mediterranean region. At the start of the year, the Commission launched the second phase of this programme (2002–04), for which the budget was adopted in 2001.

530.   *Voluntary work for young people.* On 14 February, the Council formally adopted a resolution (⁴) on the added value of voluntary work for young people in the context of the development of Community action in the youth field (⁵).

Language learning (⁶)

531.   *Follow-up to the European Year of Languages 2001.* The Council formally adopted, on 14 February, a resolution (⁷) on this subject, aimed at promoting the learning of foreign languages in education, vocational training and lifelong learning systems. In its report adopted on 4 November (⁸), the Commission was pleased to note that the objectives set in 2000 (⁹) had been fulfilled.

(¹) http://europa.eu.int/comm/education/youth/youthprogram.html.
(²) OJ C 293 E, 28.11.2002; Bull. 1/2-2002, point 1.4.36.
(³) 1995 General Report, points 839 and 840.
(⁴) OJ C 50, 23.2.2002; Bull. 1/2-2002, point 1.4.35.
(⁵) 2001 General Report, point 582.
(⁶) http://europa.eu.int/comm/education/languages_en.html.
(⁷) OJ C 50, 23.2.2002; Bull. 1/2-2002, point 1.4.33.
(⁸) COM(2002) 597; Bull. 11-2002, point 1.4.32.
(⁹) 2000 General Report, point 508.

European bodies and centres

532. *European Centre for the Development of Vocational Training (Cedefop)* ([^1]). The centre continued its activities within the framework of medium-term guidelines (2000–03) focusing on the development of European cooperation in the vocational training field, in line with the priorities established by the Council on 11 November ([^2]). It worked together with the European Forum on the transparency of vocational qualifications ([^3]), particularly through the creation of a European curriculum vitae. In close collaboration with the European Training Foundation, it also brought the candidate countries into various projects stemming mainly from the Leonardo da Vinci programme *(→ point 523)*. The new medium-term priorities for the 2003–06 period were adopted on 15 November by the Cedefop Management Board.

533. *European Training Foundation (Turin)* ([^4]). On 8 January, the Commission adopted a report ([^5]) on the European Training Foundation which seeks to promote high-quality, responsive vocational training systems in the countries of central and eastern Europe, the new independent States and Mongolia, and the Mediterranean area. The Commission described the foundation's activities in 2000 in the regions covered, with particular reference to its participation in the Phare, Tempus and Delphi I programmes. On 24 July, the Commission adopted a report on the foundation's activities in 2001 ([^6]), welcoming the emphasis placed on vocational training in the context of lifelong learning and the development of training and skills at corporate level.

534. *European University Institute (Florence)* ([^7]). The Commission contributed a total of EUR 5.3 million towards the 2002 budget of the European University Institute, which was earmarked for certain scientific and research activities (more specifically those of the Robert Schuman Centre, the European Forum and the Academy of European Law); EUR 1.1 million was accounted for by the historical archives of the European Communities *(→ points 1168 and 1169)*, which are managed by the institute. The four departments (history, economics, law, political and social sciences) hold 50 chairs, eight of them jointly with the Schuman Centre. There are around 500 grant-aided researchers (some of them from third countries), and 93 doctorates were awarded in 2001/02. In addition, the institute granted its first three doctorates *honoris causa* to Professors Mayntz, Drèze and Hirschman.

[^1]: http://www.cedefop.eu.int/.
[^2]: Bull. 11-2002, point 1.4.30.
[^3]: http://www.cedefop.eu.int/transparency/default.asp.
[^4]: http://www.etf.eu.int/.
[^5]: COM(2001) 810; Bull. 1/2-2002, point 1.4.37.
[^6]: COM(2002) 440; Bull. 7/8-2002, point 1.4.10.
[^7]: http://www.iue.it.

In connection with the activities of the Schuman Centre, the annual meeting of the Mediterranean programme brought together 250 specialists in the largest meeting of researchers from the Mediterranean region ever organised by the centre since the first meeting in March 2000. The centre's summer school, focusing on migration, was extended by the preparation of a database on this topic. The European Forum looked at 'Europe in the world: the external dimension of Europeanisation', while the Academy of European Law considered aspects of human rights and EU law. The Academy of European History held its first session, on the theme of 'Images of Europe, from antiquity to today'.

Several prominent European figures visited the institute in 2002. In January, Mr Fischer, German Minister for Foreign Affairs, gave his views on enlargement and the reform of the European Union. In February, Mr Kwasniewski, President of Poland, delivered a speech also on the subject of EU enlargement. On 26 September, the institute was honoured by the joint visit of Mr Ciampi, President of Italy, and Mr Klestil, President of Austria. Lastly, Mr Sampaio, President of Portugal, set out his personal views in a lecture entitled 'European governance: great expectations, main concerns'.

Culture ([1])

535.   *General aspects.* In two resolutions adopted on 21 January ([2]), the Council drew attention to the role of culture in the development of the European Union and to the links between culture and the knowledge society ([3]). On 25 June, it adopted a new work plan ([4]) aimed at improving European cooperation in the field of culture, mainly by creating a structured framework for discussion of priority topics. Lastly, on 19 December ([5]), it called on the Commission and the Member States to take concrete measures to promote the mobility of persons and circulation of works in the cultural sector. The European Parliament, for its part, on 22 October ([6]), underlined the importance of theatre and the performing arts in an enlarged Europe, and called on the Commission and the Member States to give more support to this sector, particularly by encouraging both the mobility of performers and other workers and the dissemination of productions. Accordingly, on 11 November ([7]), the Council invited the Member States and the Commission, within their respective spheres of competence, to take concrete measures in this field. Moreover, in accordance with the Com-

---

([1]) http://europa.eu.int/comm/culture/index_en.htm.
([2]) JO C 32, 5.2.2002; Bull. 1/2-2002, points 1.4.39 and 1.4.40.
([3]) 2001 General Report, point 595.
([4]) Bull. 6-2002, point 1.4.28.
([5]) Bull. 12-2002, point 1.4.34.
([6]) Bull. 10-2002, point 1.4.24.
([7]) Bull. 11-2002, point 1.4.33.

mission's proposal of 5 March ([1]), the Council adopted a decision, on 7 May ([2]), designating the city of Cork (Ireland) as the European Capital of Culture 2005.

536. *Culture 2000 programme* ([3]). Throughout the year, within the framework of the Culture 2000 programme, support was given to more than 230 European cultural cooperation projects covering a wide range of activities. This programme was, moreover, extended to Slovenia ([4]). The year also saw the introduction of a European cultural heritage prize and selection of the 2002 and 2003 Capitals of Culture. In a resolution adopted on 28 February ([5]), Parliament stressed the political significance of this programme, making several recommendations on more efficient management, the type of projects to be supported and closer cooperation with other Community programmes.

537. *Interactive media*. In two resolutions adopted on 11 November ([6]) and 19 December ([7]), the Council asked the Member States and the Commission to analyse interactive media content in Europe and to consider the cultural, linguistic and economic implications.

538. *Book prices*. On 16 May, following a complaint from an Austrian company, Parliament called on the Commission to submit a proposal for a directive on the fixing of book prices ([8]).

Audiovisual sector ([9])

539. *General aspects*. On 21 January ([10]), the Council formally adopted a resolution on the development of the audiovisual sector ([11]), advocating stronger action by the Commission in this field. Moreover, in an opinion delivered on 13 March ([12]) concerning a Commission communication on certain legal aspects relating to cinematographic and other audiovisual works ([13]), the Committee of the Regions supported the adoption of measures aimed at preserving audiovisual works. The European Parliament also gave its opinion on this initiative in a resolution adopted on 2 July ([14]), backing various activities announced in the

---

([1]) Bull. 3-2002, point 1.4.11.
([2]) JO C 124, 25.5.2002; Bull. 5-2002, point 1.4.27.
([3]) http://europa.eu.int/comm/culture/eac/c2000-index_en.html.
([4]) OJ L 115, 1.5.2002.
([5]) JO C 293 E, 28.11.2002; Bull. 1/2-2002, point 1.4.42.
([6]) Bull. 11-2002, point 1.4.36.
([7]) Bull. 12-2002, point 1.4.35.
([8]) Bull. 5-2002, point 1.4.28.
([9]) http://europa.eu.int/comm/avpolicy/index_en.htm.
([10]) OJ C 32, 5.2.2002: Bull. 1/2-2002, point 1.4.43.
([11]) 2001 General Report, point 598.
([12]) OJ C 192, 18.8.2002; Bull. 3-2002, point 1.4.12.
([13]) OJ C 43, 16.2.2002; COM(2001) 534; 2001 General Report, point 598.
([14]) Bull. 7/8-2002, point 1.4.11.

communication, including the creation of expert groups. With regard to the protection of minors and human dignity ([1]), Parliament adopted, on 11 April ([2]), a resolution in response to the report drawn up by the Commission on this subject ([3]), recommending, in particular, that steps be taken to promote exchanges of experience and international cooperation, and the creation of content filter and classification systems for more effective parental control.

540.   *Television without frontiers.* The Commission adopted, on 8 November, a communication on the application, in 1999 and 2000 ([4]), of the provisions of Directive 89/552/EEC ([5]) concerning the promotion and distribution of television programmes. This communication, drawn up in accordance with Article 4(3) of the directive, takes account of the application reports notified by the Member States and reflects the Commission's view that there is a positive and dynamic trend in the broadcasting of European works, including those by independent producers, in the context of a general increase in the number of channels. The Council, for its part, adopted conclusions, on 11 November ([6]) and on 19 and 20 December ([7]), to the effect that the Commission should establish a work programme geared to the preparation of a proposal for revising the directive in the light of technological developments in the field of television broadcasting.

541.   *Statistical infrastructure.* On 11 July ([8]), the Commission adopted implementing measures for the 2002–04 period in respect of the activities undertaken by national authorities and Eurostat with a view to establishing the statistical infrastructure decided on by the Council ([9]). On the same day, the Commission also adopted a report ([10]) on the implementation of the Council decision during the period from 1999 to autumn 2001.

542.   *European Audiovisual Observatory.* On 11 November, the Commission adopted a report ([11]) on the implementation, from 1999 to 2000, of the Council decision ([12]) providing for Community participation in the observatory's activities, pursuant to a partial agreement of the Council of Europe.

([1]) http://europa.eu.int/comm/avpolicy/regul/new_srv/pmhd_en.htm.
([2]) Bull. 4-2002, point 1.4.38.
([3]) COM(2001) 106; 2001 General Report, point 597.
([4]) COM(2002) 612; Bull. 11-2002, point 1.4.34.
([5]) OJ L 298, 17.10.1989; Twenty-third General Report, point 227; last amended by Directive 97/36/EC (OJ L 202, 30.7.1997; 1997 General Report, point 705).
([6]) Bull. 11-2002, point 1.4.35.
([7]) Bull. 12-2002, point 1.4.36.
([8]) Decision 2002/591/EC (OJ L 192, 20.7.2002; Bull. 7/8-2002, point 1.3.10).
([9]) Decision 1999/297/EC (OJ L 117, 5.5.1999; 1999 General Report, point 82).
([10]) COM(2002) 384: Bull. 7/8-2002, point 1.3.10.
([11]) COM(2002) 619; Bull. 11-2002, point 1.4.37.
([12]) Decision 1999/784/EC (OJ L 307, 2.12.1999; 1999 General Report, point 308).

543.   MEDIA programme. In accordance with Decision 2000/821/EC (¹) and Decision No 163/2001/EC (²), the Commission set about implementing the MEDIA programme (2001–05) (³), drawing up guidelines and publishing calls for proposals in the different sectors of the programme: training of professionals, development of audiovisual works, distribution (cinema, sales agents, networking and television) and promotion (festivals and access to markets). On 17 May and 17 December, it adopted a series of decisions allowing eight candidate countries to participate in the programme (⁴). On 18 December, the Commission adopted a further decision on Slovenia's participation.

544.   Netd@ys. The Netd@ys Europe initiative (⁵) promoting the use of new technologies, especially the Internet, in education and culture, concentrated on 'image' in 2002, while a link was also established with the CinEd@ys initiative celebrating Europe's film heritage. The high level of participation in the sixth year of Netd@ys confirmed the success of the initiative. More than 400 projects (competitions, short films, educational tools, virtual museums, on-line interaction, etc.) on the theme of image from 30 or so countries received the Netd@ys label. The Valencia EuroMed Council called for Netd@ys and e-Schola to be opened up to the Mediterranean countries.

Sport (⁶)

545.   Combating doping (⁷). In a communication of 6 May (⁸), on the Commission's participation in the World Anti-Doping Agency (WADA) (⁹) and its funding, the Commission sought to inform the Council about how it had implemented the latter's conclusions of December 2000 (¹⁰). It also annulled the appointment of Mrs Reding as the Community's WADA representative. In addition, it followed up 22 projects, covered by a budget of EUR 5 million, which were selected in 2001 after a call for proposals on a pilot project for campaigns to combat doping in sport in Europe, or in the framework of cooperation with the WADA. Moreover, funding of EUR 1.25 million was provided for the Paralympic Games.

546.   European Year of Education through Sport. On 19 December, the European Parliament approved the Council common position of 14 October, in respect of the proposal for a decision establishing the European Year of Education through Sport 2004 (Table I).

(¹) OJ L 13, 17.1.2001; 2000 General Report, point 520.
(²) OJ L 26, 27.1.2001.
(³) http://europa.eu.int/comm/avpolicy/media/index_en.html.
(⁴) Bulgaria, Cyprus, Estonia, Latvia, Lithuania, Poland, Czech Republic, Slovakia.
(⁵) http://www.netdayseurope.org/.
(⁶) http://europa.eu.int/comm/sport/index_en.html.
(⁷) http://europa.eu.int/comm/sport/key_files/doping/a_dop_en.html.
(⁸) COM(2002) 220; Bull. 5-2002, point 1.4.30.
(⁹) http://www.wada-ama.org/asiakas/003/wada_english.nsf/Home?OpenPage.
(¹⁰) OJ C 356, 12.12.2000; 2000 General Report, point 527.

Relations, partnerships and communication with civil society ([1])

Dialogue with citizens

547.   Relations and partnerships with civil society. The Commission continued to give financial support to the debates and deliberations on the future of Europe *(→ point 16)* proposed by civil society organisations *(→ point 18)*, including trade unions, non-governmental organisations and European interest groups and federations.

548.   Town twinning ([2]). The Commission continued to support meetings between citizens of towns and municipalities in Europe in order to encourage active and participatory European citizenship, and to strengthen intercultural dialogue. In 2002, the available budget was EUR 12 million. More than 2 401 grant applications were submitted, 2 088 of them concerned with exchanges between citizens of twinned towns and 313 connected with theme-based events and training seminars. In all, 1 306 projects were accepted: 1 131 exchanges between citizens involving 2 824 towns and municipalities, 498 (17.6 %) of them situated in the candidate countries, and 175 conferences, 41 (23.4 %) of which were organised in the candidate countries.

Specific communication actions on education and culture

*549.   Communication actions in 2002 helped to raise the profile of the Commission's activities and programmes, particularly in the form of specific initiatives including the media prize, CinEd@ys, Netd@ys and the celebration of 1 million Erasmus students. In addition, 40 or so publications and videos were produced and the Commission took part in 37 fairs and exhibitions, while 1 000 or so individual requests for information are handled each month in tandem with an ongoing programme of group visits.

Libraries

*550.   The Commission's central library ([3]), serving officials from all the institutions and outside researchers upon request, continued with the computerisation of its periodical collections and launched a feasibility study for creating an interinstitutional library. Moreover, it moved to new premises in the course of the year.

([1]) http://europa.eu.int/infonet/en/index.htm.
([2]) http://europa.eu.int/comm/dgs/education_culture/towntwin/index_en.html.
([3]) http://europa.eu.int/eclas/.

Section 4

Environment ([1])

Overview

551.   In 2002, a series of key decisions gave fresh impetus to Community environment policy for the years ahead. The spring European Council in Barcelona issued a reminder of the progress yet to be made by the EU in the light of the sustainable development strategy formulated by the Commission in 2001. The sixth environment action programme, adopted this year, in turn put in place a new framework for developing environment policy for the next 10 years. The EU also played an active part in promoting the sustainable development principle on the international scene by making practical contributions to the results of the World Summit on Sustainable Development and of the sixth conference of the parties to the Convention on Biological Diversity. The adoption of the Kyoto Protocol to reduce emissions of greenhouse gases was a sign of the strong commitment on the part of the EU to combating climate change.

Sixth action programme ([2])

552.   Action programme. The sixth Community environment action programme was adopted by the European Parliament and the Council on 22 July (Table I). This 10-year programme is the central environmental component of the Community's sustainable development strategy *(→ points 559 and 560)*. It proposes a new strategic approach to meeting its environmental targets in the light of the experience built up from implementing the previous programme ([3]). It pursues the objectives of the previous programme, focusing on four priority areas: climate change, nature and biodiversity, environment and health, and natural resources and waste. This new programme sets out to ensure fuller, wider application of these environmental priorities.

([1]) Further information is available on the Europa server (http://europa.eu.int/comm/dgs/environment/index_en.htm and http://europa.eu.int/comm/environment/policy_en.htm).
([2]) http://europa.eu.int/comm/environment/newprg/index.htm.
([3]) COM(92) 23; Twenty-sixth General Report, point 589.

Taking the environment into account in other policies

553. General strategy. The Barcelona European Council of 15 and 16 March (^{1}) issued a reminder that the sustainable development strategy means that the various policies should be consistent with the EU's long-term objectives and that, in this context, economic, social and environmental considerations must receive equal attention in policy-making and decision-making processes. In its conclusions of 17 October (^{2}), the Council stressed the importance of taking the environment into account in other policies by calling on the European Council to reinforce the Cardiff (^{3}) process and develop strategies to promote sustainable development. It also invited the Commission to introduce an annual stocktaking of the Cardiff process. On 10 December (^{4}), the Council adopted a report on the integration of environmental protection and sustainable development into the internal market aspects of competitiveness policy. On 3 September (^{5}), the European Parliament in turn stated that reporting on transposition should be separated from reporting on the effect of Community law on the state of the environment and that a system should be introduced for fining Member States which submit their reports late.

554. Environmental agreements. On 17 July, the Commission adopted a communication (^{6}) explaining how the provisions in the action plan 'Simplifying and improving the regulatory environment' (^{7}) can be applied in the context of environmental agreements. This communication was welcomed by the European Economic and Social Committee on 18 September (^{8}).

555. Other Community policies. The Commission proposals on the reform of the common fisheries policy *(→ point 434)* and the mid-term review of the common agricultural policy *(→ point 393),* adopted in May and July respectively, were milestones in the process of integration of environmental protection into other Community policies set in train by the Cardiff European Council in 1998 (^{9}). Further information on taking the environment into account in other Community policies is given in the sections dealing with those policies, in particular, in Sections 1 ('Economic and monetary policy') *(→ point 67)* and 7 ('Enterprise policy') of Chapter III *(→ point 261),* Sections 5 ('Energy') *(→ point 613)* and 6 ('Transport') *(→ point 634)* of this chapter and Section 4 ('Development cooperation') of Chapter VI *(→ point 821).*

(^{1}) Bull. 3-2002, points I.7 to I.12 and I.59.
(^{2}) Bull. 10-2002, point 1.4.27.
(^{3}) 1998 General Report, point 1081.
(^{4}) Bull. 12-2002, point 1.4.41.
(^{5}) Bull. 9-2002, point 1.4.17.
(^{6}) COM(2002) 412; Bull. 7/8-2002, point 1.4.13.
(^{7}) COM(2001) 726; 2001 General Report, point 26.
(^{8}) Bull. 9-2002, point 1.4.19.
(^{9}) 1998 General Report, point 1081.

Sustainable development ([1])

World Summit on Sustainable Development (Johannesburg) ([2])

556.   *Preparations for the Johannesburg Summit.* In preparation for this summit following on from the Rio Summit ([3]) within the framework of the United Nations Conference on Environment and Development, and in line with the guidelines issued by the Göteborg European Council ([4]), on 13 February, the Commission adopted a communication ([5]) analysing Europe's contribution to global sustainable development. On 4 March, the Council adopted conclusions on the internal and external dimensions of the sustainable development strategy ([6]). The European Parliament, in turn, adopted two resolutions ([7]) on 16 May, in which it suggested promoting sustainable development by taking effective action in a number of fields, such as management of natural resources, globalisation, poverty eradication and governance. It proposed the adoption of specific measures to this end. The Committee of the Regions and the European Economic and Social Committee likewise gave their views on sustainable development, the former in a resolution on 16 May ([8]), the latter in an opinion on 30 May ([9]), in which they called on the EU to take an active part in the Johannesburg Summit. The Council conclusions of 30 May, 4 June, 17 June and 22 July ([10]), provided further confirmation that the EU intended to contribute towards reaching pragmatic conclusions at the summit and, in particular, putting the results into action. These contributions to the preparations for the summit were approved by the Seville European Council in order to establish the EU's overall position at the Johannesburg Summit ([11]). This position stressed the EU's willingness to play a leading role in the preparation of the summit, with a view to reaching overall agreement.

557.   *Outcome of the Johannesburg Summit.* The World Summit on Sustainable Development, from 26 August to 4 September, brought together over 200 countries represented by 110 Heads of State or Government. The EU, represented by Mr Rasmussen, President of the Council, Mr Prodi, President of the Commission, and Mrs Wallström and Mr Nielson, Members of the Commission, played a major role and contributed actively to the adoption of a political

---

([1]) http://europa.eu.int/comm/environment/eussd/index.htm.
([2]) http://europa.eu.int/comm/environment/agend21/index.htm and http://www.johannesburgsummit.org/.
([3]) Twenty-sixth General Report, point 596.
([4]) 2001 General Report, point 611.
([5]) COM(2002) 82; Bull. 1/2-2002, point 1.4.44.
([6]) Bull. 3-2002, points 1.4.16 and 1.4.17.
([7]) Bull. 5-2002, points 1.4.35 and 1.4.36.
([8]) OJ C 278, 14.11.2002; Bull. 5-2002, point 1.4.38.
([9]) OJ C 221, 17.9.2002; Bull. 5-2002, point 1.4.37.
([10]) Bull. 5-2002, point 1.4.39; Bull. 6-2002, points 1.4.32 and 1.4.33; Bull. 7/8-2002, point 1.4.14.
([11]) Bull. 6-2002, point I.14.

declaration and a plan of implementation. In addition, over 200 partnership initiatives were launched in the course of the summit.

The plan of implementation set new targets in several fields:

• to halve by 2015 the proportion of people lacking access to basic sanitation and drinking water;

• to reduce significantly biodiversity loss by 2010;

• to halt the decline of fish stocks and stabilise fish stocks at sustainable levels by 2005; and

• to minimise harmful effects on human health from the production and use of chemicals by 2020.

This plan confirmed the commitment by every country involved to put a sustainable development strategy into action by 2005. The agreement to establish a 10-year work programme on sustainable consumption and production, with industrialised countries taking the lead, marked another big step forward. The EU also started two strategic partnerships for sustainable management of water and energy. To back up the commitments given by all the parties to increase the share of their energy supplies accounting for renewable resources, the EU announced the formation of a 'coalition of the willing' determined to act together to increase the use of renewable energy sources, based on clear, ambitious time frames and targets. Consequently, this summit gave a fresh boost to multilateralism and demonstrated that the international community is both willing and able to find multilateral responses to global problems.

558.   Follow-up to the summit. On 26 September ([1]), the European Parliament welcomed the declaration adopted at the summit but stressed the need to put the principles into action. On 30 September ([2]) and 14 and 15 October ([3]), the Council, in turn, welcomed the consensus achieved among Heads of State or Government in Johannesburg on the political declaration and the plan of implementation. On 17 October ([4]), the Council stated that it was determined to put into action the declaration and the plan adopted at the summit. It called on the European Council to reinforce the environmental dimension of the Lisbon process *(→ point 67)*. In its conclusions of 5, 18 and 25 November ([5]), the Council committed itself to contributing to the follow-up to the summit, particularly on issues such as sustainable development in a globalising world, implementation

---

([1]) Bull. 9-2002, point 1.4.22.
([2]) Bull. 9-2002, point 1.4.23.
([3]) Bull. 10-2002, point 1.4.26.
([4]) Bull. 10-2002, point 1.4.27.
([5]) Bull. 11-2002, points 1.4.39 to 1.4.41.

of the Doha agenda, financing development, debt relief and development of an institutional framework for sustainable development.

Sustainable development strategy

559. Barcelona European Council. The Barcelona European Council on 15 and 16 March ([1]), advocated further action, notably on environmental technologies, impact assessment, energy and transport in order to promote the Lisbon strategy and take account of sustainable development in the implementation of the various Community policies. It also contributed to the preparations for the Johannesburg World Summit on Sustainable Development *(→ point 556).* Finally, it welcomed the progress in the discussions with a view to the adoption of the sixth environment action programme *(→ point 552)* which is a key instrument for progress towards sustainable development. The preparations for this European Council meeting were also the subject of opinions adopted by the ECSC Consultative Committee on 25 January ([2]) and by the European Economic and Social Committee on 21 February ([3]) and a resolution of the European Parliament of 28 February ([4]).

560. Environmental technology. On 13 March, the Commission adopted the report 'Environmental technology for sustainable development' ([5]) which stressed that new and innovative, environment-friendly technologies have the potential to contribute to growth, by reducing the costs of environmental protection and creating new outlets for technologies, and proposed the development of an action plan to allow easier access to such technologies. This report is an important bridge between the economic, social and environmental components of the Lisbon strategy.

Management of resources: consumption and waste

561. Integrated product policy. In a resolution ([6]) adopted on 17 January on the Green Paper on integrated product policy ([7]), the European Parliament called for clear objectives to be set, with timetables for implementing them and indicators for monitoring progress with this key instrument for sustainable development policy.

([1]) Bull. 3-2002, point I.59.
([2]) OJ C 54, 1.3.2002; Bull. 1/2-2002, point 1.4.45.
([3]) OJ C 94, 3.4.2002; Bull. 1/2-2002, point 1.4.47.
([4]) OJ C 293 E, 28.11.2002; Bull. 1/2-2002, point 1.4.48.
([5]) COM(2002) 122; Bull. 3-2002, point 1.4.18.
([6]) OJ C 271 E, 7.11.2002; Bull. 1/2-2002, point 1.4.49.
([7]) COM(2001) 68; 2001 General Report, point 613.

562.   *Waste management.* On 16 December, the Council supplemented Directive 1999/31/EC ([1]) by establishing more precise criteria for characterising waste, checking its compliance and accepting it at landfills ([2]). At the sixth conference of the parties to the Basle Convention ([3]), held in Geneva from 9 to 13 December, progress was made, in particular, on numerous aspects of application of the convention on which guidelines and decisions were adopted ([4]). On 27 December, the European Parliament and the Council adopted two directives to restrict the use of hazardous substances in electrical and electronic equipment and to avoid generation of waste from electrical and electronic equipment, particularly by allowing recycling (Table I).

Sustainable urban development and coastal zones

563.   *Coastal zones.* On 30 May, the European Parliament and the Council adopted a recommendation concerning the implementation of integrated coastal zone management in Europe (Table I). This aims to provide a common vision on the part of Member States for the future of their coastal zones, based on sustainable economic choices involving employment opportunities, ecosystem integrity and sustainable management of all resources. The same recommendation also calls on the Member States to develop national strategies by February 2006, to promote integrated management of their coasts.

Environmental quality and natural resources

Protection of water, soil conservation, agriculture

564.   *Water management.* In a resolution adopted on 14 March ([5]), the European Parliament called on the Member States to transpose in a non-restrictive manner Directive 91/271/EEC ([6]) on urban wastewater treatment. In another resolution adopted on 30 May, the Council welcomed the overall framework set out in the Commission communication for integrating sustainable water management in development strategies and processes (→ point 817).

565.   *Protection of water.* On 17 July, the Commission adopted its report on the implementation of Directive 91/676/EEC concerning the protection of waters against pollution caused by nitrates from agricultural sources ([7]) in which

---

([1]) OJ L 182, 16.7.1999; 1999 General Report, point 453.
([2]) Decision 2002/53/EC (OJ L 11, 16.1.2003; Bull. 12-2002, point 1.4.45).
([3]) 1999 General Report, point 454.
([4]) Bull. 12-2002, point 1.4.43.
([5]) Bull. 3-2002, point 1.4.21.
([6]) OJ L 135, 30.5.1991; Twenty-fifth General Report, point 649.
([7]) COM(2002) 407; Bull. 7/8-2002, point 1.4.15.

it noted the progress made since 1998 ([1]), but expressed regret that the action programmes introduced by the Member States were insufficient.

566.   *New bathing water policy.* To follow up its communication on developing a new bathing water policy ([2]), on 24 October, the Commission proposed a revision of Directive 76/160/EEC ([3]) concerning the quality of bathing water, in line with the sustainable development strategy *(→ point 559)*, the sixth environment action programme *(→ point 552)* and the Community legislation on water, particularly the framework directive ([4]), the objective being to lay down the rules necessary for monitoring and classifying bathing water quality and supplying the relevant information to the public (Table I).

567.   *Protection of the marine environment.* On 2 October, the Commission adopted a communication ([5]) on a strategy to protect and conserve the marine environment in which it proposed a series of ambitious objectives. To attain these objectives, it proposed multilateral initiatives involving international and non-governmental organisations concerned with conservation of the marine environment from the Baltic to the Black Sea.

568.   *Maritime pollution.* On 21 January, the Council adopted a decision authorising the signature of a new protocol to the Barcelona Convention (Table III). More precisely, the measure took the form of amendments to the protocol on combating pollution of the Mediterranean Sea by oil ([6]) to insert the provisions necessary for developing a regional strategy for preventing pollution of the marine environment of the Mediterranean by ships. The protocol was signed in Malta on 25 January.

569.   *Soil protection.* On 16 April, the Commission adopted a communication ([7]) outlining its plans to develop a thematic strategy for soil protection, which gave an overview of policies and legislation on the subject and announced a series of measures to prevent pollution of the soil. The Council welcomed this communication in conclusions adopted on 25 June ([8]), issuing a reminder of the need to protect soil, both as a natural resource at regional level and as a means of combating poverty worldwide. On 18 September ([9]), the European Economic and Social Committee in turn endorsed this communication.

([1]) Previous report: COM(1998) 16; 1998 General Report, point 497.
([2]) COM(2000) 860; 2000 General Report, point 547.
([3]) OJ L 31, 5.2.1976.
([4]) Directive 2000/60/EC (OJ L 327, 22.12.2000; 2000 General Report, point 548), as last amended by Decision No 2455/2001/EC (OJ L 331, 15.12.2001; 2001 General Report, point 617).
([5]) COM(2002) 539; Bull. 10-2002, point 1.4.30.
([6]) Decision 81/420/EEC (OJ L 162, 19.6.1981).
([7]) COM(2002) 179; Bull. 4-2002, point 1.4.42.
([8]) Bull. 6-2002, point 1.4.36.
([9]) Bull. 9-2002, point 1.4.27.

Protection of nature and biodiversity, forests

570. *Biological diversity*. The sixth conference of the parties to the Convention on Biological Diversity (¹) was held in The Hague from 7 to 19 April. It adopted a strategic plan for the implementation of the obligations imposed by the convention with the aim of significantly reducing the current rate of biodiversity loss by 2010, together with a work programme on forest biological diversity, guidelines on access to genetic resources, and guiding principles for invasive alien species. In preparation for this conference, on 4 March, the Council adopted conclusions (²) reiterating the central role which the Convention on Biological Diversity should play in order to ensure closer coordination between the various existing conventions on biological diversity. On 25 June, the Council welcomed the outcome of this conference (³). It also took stock of 10 years' work on the internal dimension of biodiversity protection, and stressed the importance of protecting our common natural heritage and biodiversity. The Commission communication on biodiversity action plans (⁴) had already been endorsed by the European Parliament on 14 March (⁵).

571. *Protection of endangered species*. The seventh conference of the parties to the Bonn Convention (⁶) on the Conservation of Migratory Species of Wild Animal was held in Bonn from 18 to 24 September. On the basis of the negotiating directives (⁷) adopted by the Council on 22 July, the Commission and the Danish Presidency played an important part in formulating common Community positions, particularly on the conservation of wild birds, fishing and the conservation of whales, three more species of which were granted special protection status. The 12th meeting (⁸) of the parties to the Convention on International Trade in Endangered Species of Wild Fauna and Flora (CITES) (⁹) was held in Santiago (Chile) from 3 to 15 November (¹⁰). On 24 October (¹¹), the European Parliament in turn called on the Member States to support the moves to provide better protection for a number of species, particularly elephants, whales and turtles. On the conservation of wild birds, on 25 March, in its three-yearly official report (¹²), the Commission evaluated the action taken or being taken by the Member States to implement Directive 79/409/EEC (¹³). The big-

---

(¹) Decision 93/626/EC (OJ L 309, 13.12.1993; Twenty-seventh General Report, point 487).
(²) Bull. 3-2002, point 1.4.22.
(³) Bull. 6-2002, point 1.4.37.
(⁴) COM(2001) 162; 2001 General Report, point 620.
(⁵) Bull. 3-2002, point 1.4.25.
(⁶) OJ L 210, 19.7.1982; Sixteenth General Report, point 382.
(⁷) Bull. 7/8-2002, point 1.4.17.
(⁸) Previous session: 2000 General Report, point 550.
(⁹) http://www.cites.org/index.html.
(¹⁰) Bull. 11-2002, point 1.4.43.
(¹¹) Bull. 10-2002, point 1.4.33.
(¹²) COM(2002) 146; Bull. 3-2002, point 1.4.23.
(¹³) OJ L 103, 25.4.1979.

gest black spot identified was the almost 25 % decline in wild species in Europe, despite the efforts made over the last 20 years.

572. Protection of forests. On 18 February, the Council adopted conclusions ([1]) on the second session of the United Nations Forum on Forests, which was held in New York from 4 to 15 March. On 24 April, the European Economic and Social Committee delivered its opinion on how to manage the increase in the size of the European forestry sector following enlargement ([2]). On 15 April, the European Parliament and the Council amended Regulations (EEC) No 3528/86 ([3]) and (EEC) No 2158/92 ([4]) on the protection of the Community's forests against atmospheric pollution and fire respectively (Table I) in order to improve the knowledge available on the state of health of forests and on forest fires. As these two regulations were due to expire at the end of the year, on 15 July, the Commission adopted a proposal for a regulation intended not only to continue combating pollution and fires but also to promote monitoring of biodiversity, soils and carbon sequestration and to raise public awareness on forestry, with the aid of the 'Forest focus' system (Table I).

Civil protection, environmental accidents

573. Civil protection. In line with its 1994 ([5]) and 2001 ([6]) resolutions expressing the desire to develop cooperation between training centres active in the field of civil protection, in a resolution ([7]) adopted on 28 January, the Council invited the Commission to support the creation of a network between such establishments. As part of the Community response to the terrorist attacks on 11 September 2001, to follow up its communication ([8]) of 28 November 2001 responding to the request from the Heads of State or Government to improve cooperation between the Member States in this field, on 11 June, the Commission adopted a new communication ([9]) reporting on the progress made since 28 November 2001, particularly on the implementation of Decision 2001/792/EC ([10]). In a resolution adopted on 19 December ([11]), the Council invited the Member States to study the question of civil protection in the outermost, isolated, insular, remote and sparsely populated regions so that they can enjoy a level of safety similar to that existing in other areas of the EU.

[1] Bull. 1/2-2002, point 1.4.54.
[2] OJ C 149, 21.6.2002; Bull. 4-2002, point 1.4.44.
[3] OJ L 326, 21.11.1986, as last amended by Regulation (EC) No 1484/2001 (OJ L 196, 20.7.2001).
[4] OJ L 217, 31.7.1992, as last amended by Regulation (EC) No 1485/2001 (OJ L 196, 20.7.2001).
[5] 1994 General Report, point 510.
[6] 2001 General Report, point 624.
[7] OJ C 43, 16.2.2002; Bull. 1/2-2002, point 1.4.55.
[8] COM(2001) 707; 2001 General Report, point 624.
[9] COM(2002) 302; Bull. 6-2002, point 1.4.38.
[10] OJ L 297, 15.11.2001; 2001 General Report, point 624.
[11] Bull. 12-2002, point 1.3.98.

574. *Environmental accidents.* In response to the sinking of the oil tanker, *Prestige*, off Galicia, which unleashed an environmental disaster causing serious damage to the Spanish coasts, the European Parliament, in a resolution([1]) adopted on 21 November, and the Council, on 9 December([2]), called on the Commission not only to examine the possibilities offered by the Solidarity Fund for immediate funding for the disaster-stricken areas but also to put in place measures to make it safer to transport heavy fuel oil by sea *(→ point 647).*

575. *Prevention and limitation of risks.* On 20 December, the Commission and the Council adopted a joint programme on the prevention and limitation of the chemical, bacteriological, radiological or nuclear risks posed by a terrorist threat([3]). The objective of this programme, which sets out the action already taken or yet to be taken in this field, is to encourage the Member States to take action to limit and prevent such risks to the public and the environment.

576. *Rain and floods.* In response to the torrential rain which affected Tenerife and eastern Spain, on 11 April, the European Parliament adopted a resolution([4]) expressing its concern about climate change. Information on the establishment of a Solidarity Fund is given in Section 10 ('Economic and social cohesion') of Chapter III *(→ point 362).*

Environment and health ([5])

Chemicals

577. *International trade.* On 19 December, the Council approved a regulation aimed at incorporating into Community law the rules laid down in the Rotterdam Convention([6]) covering international trade in hazardous chemicals (Table I) and adopted a decision aimed at approving those rules (Table II).

578. *Pesticides.* In a communication adopted on 1 July([7]), the Commission called on the Community institutions to discuss a new thematic strategy on the sustainable use of pesticides, drawing on the measures put into practice by the Member States. On 9 December([8]), the Council called on the Commission to submit proposals for specific action based on this strategy by the beginning of

([1]) Bull. 11-2002, point 1.4.47.
([2]) Bull. 12-2002, point 1.4.49.
([3]) Bull. 12-2002, point 1.4.48.
([4]) Bull. 4-2002, point 1.4.45.
([5]) http://europa.eu.int/comm/environment/wssd/health_en.html.
([6]) 1998 General Report, point 489.
([7]) COM(2002) 349; Bull. 7/8-2002, point 1.4.20.
([8]) Bull. 12-2002, point 1.4.50.

2004 plus guidance on the key measures to be included in the national plans which the Member States will have to put into place.

579. *Mercury.* On 6 September, the Commission adopted a report concerning mercury from the chlor-alkali industry (¹). The report analysed the environmental problems which residual mercury from this industry could cause in the event of the total replacement of the mercury-cell technology called for in the medium term to implement Directive 96/61/EC (²) concerning integrated pollution prevention and control. On 9 December (³), the Council welcomed this report and the results of the Johannesburg Summit and reaffirmed the need for the EU to implement a Community policy on chemicals.

Biotechnology

580. *Genetically modified organisms (GMOs).* On 18 February, the Commission submitted a proposal for a regulation to incorporate into Community legislation the provisions of the Cartagena Protocol (⁴). In line with the precautionary principle, the objective of the proposal is to ensure an adequate level of protection for the transfer, handling and use of GMOs by means of mandatory notification of exports of GMOs intended for release into the environment plus an obligation to supply information, at international level, on the decisions taken on GMOs and the relevant legislation (Table I). The Council, in turn, adopted a decision on 25 June on the conclusion of the protocol by the Community, following which the EU deposited the instrument of ratification with the United Nations Secretariat-General in New York on 27 August (⁵) (Table III). On 24 July, the Commission adopted a decision establishing guidance notes supplementing Annex II to Directive 2001/18/EC (⁶). On 3 October, the Council adopted three decisions (⁷) supplementing and implementing certain aspects of Directive 2001/18/EC on the deliberate release into the environment of GMOs. The objective of these decisions is to establish a summary notification format containing comprehensive, clear and detailed information accompanied by notes explaining the objectives and the basic principles of the monitoring plans.

(¹) COM(2002) 489; Bull. 9-2002, point 1.4.34.
(²) OJ L 257, 10.10.1996; 1996 General Report, point 453.
(³) Bull. 12-2002, point 1.4.51.
(⁴) 2000 General Report, point 551.
(⁵) Bull. 7/8-2002, point 1.4.24.
(⁶) Decision 2002/623/EC (OJ L 200, 30.7.2002).
(⁷) Decisions 2002/811/EC, 2002/812/EC and 2002/813/EC (OJ L 280, 18.10.2002; Bull. 10-2002, point 1.4.39).

Air and noise

581.   Air quality. The 'Clean air for Europe' (CAFE) programme ([1]) launched in 2001 was endorsed by the European Parliament on 13 March ([2]), following on from the other institutions and bodies. The European Parliament and the Council also adopted Directive 2002/3/EC relating to ozone in ambient air on 12 February (Table I). The Commission in turn adopted an encouraging report ([3]) on 7 November, on the implementation of Directives 80/779/EEC ([4]), 82/884/EEC ([5]) and 85/203/EEC ([6]) on air quality in the period between 1997 and 1999.

582.   Emissions of gaseous pollutants. The new directive to reduce emissions of gaseous pollutants, adopted by the European Parliament and the Council on 19 July 2002, sets stricter emission limits than Directive 97/24/EC for two- or three-wheel vehicles and will apply from 2003 for new types of vehicles (Table I). On 9 December, the European Parliament and the Council adopted the directive on the approximation of the laws of the Member States relating to measures against the emission of gaseous and particulate pollutants from internal combustion engines to be installed in non-road mobile machinery (Table I). On 21 November, the Commission presented a new strategy to reduce the effects of atmospheric emissions from seagoing ships on the environment and human health ([7]). On the same day, it also proposed reducing the sulphur content of marine fuels used in the EU (Table I). On 23 December, it proposed a ban on placing on the market decorative paints and varnishes and vehicle refinishing products in order to reduce emissions of volatile organic compounds (Table I). On 27 December, it proposed amendments to the legislation on the emission of gaseous and particulate pollutants from internal combustion engines (Table I) and harmonisation of such legislation at world level as part of its strategy to combat climate change *(→ point 587).*

583.   Fuel quality. Promotion of biofuels is dealt with in Section 5 ('Energy') of this chapter *(→ point 615).*

584.   Noise. On 25 June, the European Parliament and the Council adopted Directive 2002/49/EC with the objective of defining a common approach intended to avoid, prevent or reduce on a prioritised basis the harmful effects, including annoyance, due to exposure to environmental noise (Table I).

([1]) COM(2001) 245; 2001 General Report, point 633.
([2]) Bull. 3-2002, point 1.4.27.
([3]) COM(2002) 609; Bull. 11-2002, point 1.4.50.
([4]) OJ L 229, 30.8.1980.
([5]) OJ L 378, 31.12.1982.
([6]) OJ L 87, 27.3.1985.
([7]) COM(2002) 642; Bull. 11-2002, point 1.4.53.

Radiation protection

585. Site security. On 18 March, the Commission proposed closer control by national authorities and operators over all high-activity sealed radioactive sources (Table II). Under the Euratom Treaty, the Commission also continued to verify the application of the safety standards for the protection of the health of the public and workers. Pursuant to Article 33 of the Euratom Treaty and taking account of the entry into force of Directives 96/29/Euratom and 97/43/Euratom, on 13 May, the Commission examined a number of draft national measures, but saw no need to issue recommendations on them. In accordance with Article 37 of the Treaty, it also delivered 17 opinions on plans for the disposal of radioactive waste and, under Article 35, it carried out one visit to verify the operation and efficiency of the facilities for monitoring the level of radioactivity in the environment.

586. International cooperation. On 30 September, the Commission adopted a decision on the signing of an agreement between the European Atomic Energy Community (Euratom) and non-member States on their participation in arrangements for the European Community Urgent Radiological Information Exchange (Ecurie).

Climate change and international dimension [1]

Global environment, climate change, geosphere and biosphere

587. Greenhouse effect. The Kyoto Protocol [2] to the United Nations Framework Convention on Climate Change was approved by the Council on 25 April, marking the commitment by the Community and its Member States to the process of reducing greenhouse gas emissions (Table II). The Council conclusions of 4 March [3] regretted the USA's refusal to sign the protocol. On 25 June [4], the Council also expressed disappointment with the announcement by the prime minister of Australia relating to the non-ratification of the protocol but satisfaction with the conclusion of the internal ratification process, after the EU's 16 instruments of ratification had been deposited at United Nations headquarters. In addition, on 17 and 24 October [5], the Council and the European Parliament welcomed the announcements of ratification by a number of countries, including South Africa, Brazil, China, India and Japan, and the announcements

[1] http://europa.eu.int/comm/environment/climat/home_en.htm.
[2] 1997 General Report, point 552, and Internet (http://www.unfccc/resource/docs/convkp/kpeng.html).
[3] Bull. 3-2002, point 1.4.33.
[4] Bull. 6-2002, point 1.4.42.
[5] Bull. 10-2002, points 1.4.45 and 1.4.46.

of forthcoming ratification by Canada, Poland and Russia. The last of these ratifications will clear the way for the Kyoto Protocol to enter into force. In its resolution of 25 September (¹), on the implementation of the first phase of the European climate change programme, the European Parliament approved the measures proposed by the Commission to honour the commitments given by the EU under the Kyoto Protocol but called on the Commission to cover more actions in its proposals. In a report (²) adopted on 9 December, on the mechanism for monitoring greenhouse gas emissions, the Commission announced that the emissions observed in 2000 were 3.5 % lower than in 1990 but that considerable progress remained to be made. On the same day, it adopted its third annual report (³) on the effectiveness of the Community strategy to reduce carbon dioxide emissions from cars (⁴) in which it stated that it was, on the whole, satisfied with the progress made by the automobile industries.

588.   *United Nations Framework Convention on Climate Change (UNFCCC).* The eighth conference of the parties (⁵) to the United Nations Framework Convention on Climate Change (COP8) (⁶) was held in New Delhi (India) from 23 October to 1 November. The conference ended with the adoption of the Delhi declaration which called on every country to ratify the Kyoto Protocol. The Council and the European Parliament had prepared for this conference on 17 and 24 October (⁷) respectively.

589.   *Ozone layer.* The fourth amendment ('Beijing amendment') to the Montreal Protocol was approved by Council Decision 2002/215/EC on 4 March. In particular, this protocol requires stricter control over trade in ozone-depleting substances (Table II). On 21 November, the Commission proposed amending Regulation (EC) No 2037/2000 with the objective of helping to speed up the process of regeneration of the ozone layer and complying with the requirements of the Montreal Protocol (Table I).

International cooperation

590.   *G8/Environment.* On 13 and 14 April (⁸), the first meeting of the environment ministers of the eight most industrialised countries was held in Banff (Canada) to prepare for the Johannesburg Summit *(→ point 556).* Three topics,

---

(¹) Bull. 9-2002, point 1.4.38.
(²) COM(2002) 702; Bull. 12-2002, point 1.4.56. Previous report: COM(2001) 708; 2001 General Report, point 643.
(³) COM(2002) 693; Bull. 12-2002, point 1.4.55. Previous report: COM(2001) 643; 2001 General Report, point 635.
(⁴) COM(95) 689; 1995 General Report, point 482.
(⁵) Previous conferences: 2001 General Report, point 644.
(⁶) http://unfccc.int/cop8/.
(⁷) Bull. 10-2002, points 1.4.45 and 1.4.46.
(⁸) Bull. 4-2002, point 1.4.51.

in particular, were discussed: environment and development; national and international environmental governance; and environment and health.

591. *North Sea Conference.* On 20 and 21 March ([1]), the fifth North Sea Conference ([2]) was held in Bergen (Norway). The ministers for the environment from the countries bordering on the North Sea and representatives of the Commission, international organisations and non-governmental organisations discussed issues concerning fisheries, marine pollution and protection of species and ecosystems. A declaration setting new objectives on combating pollution was adopted.

592. *Euro-Mediterranean conference on the environment.* On 10 July, the second ([3]) Euro-Mediterranean conference of ministers for the environment and of the Mediterranean Commission on Sustainable Development was held in Athens. The declaration adopted at the conference laid the foundation for a strategy to take the environment into account in Euro-Mediterranean regional cooperation.

593. *Transboundary air pollution.* On 30 January, the Commission proposed accession by the Community to the protocol to the 1979 Convention on Long-range transboundary Air Pollution to abate Acidification, Eutrophication and Ground-level Ozone (Table II).

594. *Inland waterways.* In its conclusions of 13 May ([4]), the Council welcomed the satisfactory outcome of the environmental cooperation in the Danube region, particularly the progress made in implementing the Commission's project to clear the stretch of the Danube in Yugoslavia.

Governance, communication and civil society

595. *Environmental liability.* After a series of accidents which had polluted the environment, particularly in 2001 ([5]), to follow up its 2001 communication ([6]) on sustainable development, the Commission adopted a proposal for a directive on 23 January, to introduce a liability scheme which will include not only compensation for damage to the environment, in accordance with the polluter-pays principle, but also the prevention of such damage (Table I).

([1]) Bull. 3-2002, point 1.4.35.
([2]) Previous conference: 1995 General Report, point 495.
([3]) Previous conference: 1997 General Report, point 572.
([4]) Bull. 5-2002, point 1.4.47.
([5]) 2001 General Report, point 625.
([6]) COM(2001) 53; 2001 General Report, point 610.

596.   *Implementation of the Aarhus Convention*([1]). On 10 December, the Conciliation Committee reached agreement on a joint text for a proposal for a directive providing for public participation in respect of the drawing-up of certain plans and programmes relating to the environment and of proposals which may have a significant impact on the environment. This proposal will cover the 'public participation' side of the Aarhus Convention and, hence, provide for public participation in decision-making and access to justice in environmental matters (Table I). On 16 and 18 December respectively, the Council and the European Parliament adopted a directive on public access to environmental information (Table I).

597.   *Non-governmental organisations (NGOs).* Decision No 466/2002/EC laying down a Community action programme promoting NGOs primarily active in the field of environmental protection was formally adopted on 1 March (Table I). Based on a 2001 report ([2]), the purpose of this programme is to promote systematic participation by such NGOs in drafting and implementing Community legislation.

([1]) 1998 General Report, point 518 and Internet (http://europa.eu.int/comm/environment/aarhus/index.htm).
([2]) COM(2001) 337; 2001 General Report, point 649.

Section 5

Energy (¹)

Overview

598. In line with its November 2000 Green Paper on the security of energy supply, the Commission pursued a policy based on improving energy supply while helping to make the European industry more competitive and combat environmental damage, in particular, by reducing greenhouse gas emissions. The agreement reached within the Council on the complete opening-up of the internal market for gas and electricity, allowing consumers a free choice of the most competitive suppliers and facilitating trans-frontier electricity trade, should also be seen in the context of this policy. In addition, the Commission put forward new proposals to improve the management of the Community mechanisms to deal with crises affecting oil and gas stocks. A series of proposals were also submitted to maintain nuclear energy technologies as an option for future generations while seeking to improve safety in this area in an enlarged EU, controlling the disposal of nuclear waste and combating global warming. To reduce greenhouse gas emissions, action was also undertaken to improve energy efficiency and promote new and renewable energies. The proposed launching of an 'Intelligent energy for Europe' programme illustrates these efforts and emphasises the integration of renewable energy and energy efficiency, together with promotional activities and legislative and technological initiatives, while complying with the commitments entered into by the Community to meet the objectives of the Kyoto Protocol.

General strategy

599. 'Intelligent energy for Europe' programme (²). As the previous framework programme (³) came to an end in 2002, on 9 April, the Commission submitted a proposal for a new multiannual programme for action in the field of energy for the period 2003–06 (Table I). Taking over the objectives of the Commission's Green Paper on security of energy supply, the proposed programme is

---

(¹) Further information is available on the Europa server (http://europa.eu.int/comm/dgs/energy_transport/index_en.html).
(²) http://europa.eu.int/comm/energy/intelligent/index_en.html.
(³) Decision 1999/21/EC, Euratom (OJ L 7, 13.1.1999; 1998 General Report, point 397).

intended to be the main Community instrument for non-technological support in this field, building on the successes of the SAVE, Altener and Synergy programmes. Four specific areas are covered: rational use of energy and demand management; new and renewable energy sources; the energy aspects of transport; and international promotion in the field of renewable energy and energy efficiency. Various types of action are proposed for each area, e.g. implementation of strategies, creation of financial and market instruments, and the development of information and education structures. Following the European Parliament's first reading on 20 November, the Council reached political agreement on 25 November with a view to a common position on this proposal, and, in particular, on a budget of EUR 190 million for four years ([1]).

600. *European energy and transport forum.* The Commission organised the first meeting of the forum on 8 October in Brussels. This forum is a consultative committee set up by a Commission decision of 11 July 2001 ([2]) with 34 high-level members covering a broad spectrum of areas of activity and expertise in the energy and transport sectors ([3]). Its role is, in particular, to give opinions, to advise the Commission, and to act as a monitoring centre for European energy and transport policies.

601. *Energy charter.* The work under the energy charter process ([4]) continued, including further negotiations on a transit protocol. Other work under the charter process, notably in the respective groups on trade, investment and energy efficiency, as well as in the context of the twice-yearly charter conference, also continued, with the Commission and the Community playing a major part in all these activities.

Security of supply

602. *Debate on the Commission Green Paper.* In a final report adopted on 26 June ([5]) concerning the results of the debate launched on the basis of its November 2000 Green Paper on the security of the EU's energy supply ([6]), the Commission stressed that a consensus has emerged around some key issues: the need to considerably improve energy efficiency, step up the promotion of renewables, reduce environmental damage caused by energy use, improve the investment climate in supplier and transit countries, and develop the producer–consumer dialogue. It also found that crucial issues were raised during the

---

([1]) Bull. 11-2002, point 1.4.57.
([2]) Decision 2001/546//EC (OJ L 195, 19.7.2001).
([3]) OJ C 158, 3.7.2002.
([4]) 1997 General Report, point 438.
([5]) COM(2002) 321; Bull. 6-2002, point 1.4.44.
([6]) COM(2000) 769, 2000 General Report, point 585 and Internet (http://europa.eu.int/comm/energy_transport/en/lpi_lv_en1.html).

debate prompted by the Green Paper, such as the effectiveness of the EU's emergency mechanisms, and the safety of nuclear generation, particularly in the accession candidate countries. Moreover, in most Member States, the debate prompted renewed consideration of the national options with regard to energy.

International cooperation

603.   *G8/Energy.* On 2 and 3 May ([¹]), the energy ministers of the eight most industrialised countries and Mrs de Palacio, Vice-President of the Commission, met in Detroit. To reduce the risks to the security of supply, both supply-side and demand-side approaches were considered. With regard to the oil market, the participants stressed their concern for greater price stability and increased market transparency through a producer–consumer dialogue. The importance of the action to combat climate change was also stressed, as was the possible contribution of nuclear energy.

604.   *International energy forum.* The eighth forum took place in Osaka, Japan, from 21 to 23 September. In the framework of the global producer–consumer dialogue, the energy ministers of 67 countries and nine international organisations discussed energy policy issues which have an impact on the oil and gas market. The Commission delegation was headed by Vice-President Loyola de Palacio, and 14 EU Member States took part in the discussions. The EU, in particular, expressed its views about the fact that the current price of oil is not helping to bring about the economic recovery that is needed, the guarantee given by OPEC to maintain an appropriate level of supply in the event of interruption (the Iraq problem) and the need to make progress in the field of renewable energy sources and energy efficiency. In addition, Mrs de Palacio had bilateral meetings with the energy ministers of Algeria, China, France, India, Iran, the Netherlands, Norway, Saudi Arabia and the United States.

605.   *Euro-Mediterranean conference of energy ministers.* This conference was held in Tunis on 6 May on the subject of the security of energy supply in the Mediterranean region ([²]), and was attended by Commission Vice-President Loyola de Palacio who stressed the importance of the trans-European energy and transport networks and interconnections to enhance the security of supply and trans-frontier trade.

606.   *Dialogue with Russia.* The energy dialogue launched at the EU–Russia Summit in October 2000 ([³]) continued on the basis of the priorities adopted at the October 2001 summit ([⁴]). The Moscow Summit in May *(→ point 917),*

([¹]) Bull. 5-2002, point 1.4.54.
([²]) Bull. 5-2002, point 1.6.75.
([³]) 2000 General Report, points 589 and 944.
([⁴]) 2001 General Report, points 660 and 1022.

while noting the progress that has been made, identified three new areas for joint examination, namely the interconnection of electricity networks and electricity trade, the oil market and trade in nuclear material. The Brussels Summit in November *(→ point 917)*, welcomed the progress that has been made concerning the legislative framework for production-sharing contracts in Russia and took note of the non-existence of an alleged Community limit of 30 % for imports of fossil fuels from any country that is not a member of the EU. An EU–Russia energy technology centre opened in Moscow on 5 November.

607.   *Cooperation with Ukraine.* The agreements signed on 23 July 1999 (¹) with Ukraine on nuclear safety and controlled thermonuclear fusion were published in the *Official Journal of the European Communities* (²).

608.   *Cooperation with the developing countries.* On 17 July, the Commission adopted a communication on energy cooperation with the developing countries *(→ point 817)*. The initiatives launched at the Johannesburg Summit are dealt with in Section 4 ('Environment') of Chapter IV *(→ point 557)* and in Section 4 ('Development cooperation') of Chapter VI *(→ point 817)*.

Internal energy market

Natural gas and electricity

609.   *Complete opening-up of the market.* The Barcelona European Council of 15 and 16 March (³), urged the Council and the European Parliament to adopt, as early as possible, the pending proposals for the final phase of the opening-up of the internal market for gas and electricity. It also urged the Council to reach, as early as possible, an agreement for a tariff-setting system for cross-border electricity transactions, based on the principles of non-discrimination, transparency and simplicity. It also agreed to the target for Member States to achieve a level of electricity interconnections equivalent to at least 10 % of their installed production capacity by 2005. The Seville European Council of 21 and 22 June (⁴), addressed the progress of work concerning energy taxation. On 25 November, the Council reached political agreement with a view to common positions on the proposal for a directive aimed at amending the common rules concerning the internal market for electricity and natural gas (Table I) and the proposal for a regulation on conditions of access to the network for cross-border exchanges of electricity (Table I). The Council, in particular, confirmed

(¹) 1999 General Report, point 486.
(²) Decision 2002/924/Euratom (OJ L 322, 27.11.2002; Bull. 11-2002, point 1.4.64).
(³) Bull. 3-2002, point I.32.
(⁴) Bull. 6-2002, point I.18.

the two-stage approach proposed for the liberalisation of the markets concerned: opening-up by 1 July 2004 for non-household users, and 1 July 2007 for household users.

Infrastructures and cohesion

610. Cogeneration. In response to the need to curb energy demand, expressed in its Green Paper on the security of energy supply, and in the context of the rational use of energy *(→ points 616 and 617)*, on 22 July the Commission adopted a proposal aimed at promoting cogeneration (i.e. combined heat and power production) (Table I). The proposal for a directive in question provides for a methodological approach and the drawing-up of common rules for the Member States.

611. Oil and gas stocks. On 11 September, the Commission adopted a communication entitled 'The internal market in energy: coordinated measures on the security of energy supply' ([1]) accompanied by two proposals for directives aimed at improving the security of the EU's energy supply in the context of the internal market in energy, one concerning oil (Table I), the other concerning natural gas (Table I). Where oil is concerned, the Commission is proposing, in particular, the harmonisation of the Member States' security stocks systems and the establishment of a Community decision-making process concerning the use of the stocks in the event of a supply crisis; in the case of gas, the proposal provides, in particular, for the establishment of clear responsibilities for the market players and the definition of minimum standards concerning security of supply. In addition, on the same day, the Commission also submitted proposals aimed at repealing a series of directives concerning petroleum products (Table II).

Trans-European energy networks ([2])

612. Information on the trans-European energy networks is provided in Section 12 ('Trans-European networks') of Chapter III *(→ point 390)*.

Energy and environment

613. In 2002, the main activities to promote sustainability and a more environment-friendly energy policy concerned the following topics: single

[1] COM(2002) 488; Bull. 9-2002, point 1.4.43.
[2] http://europa.eu.int/comm/energy/ten-e/en/index.html.

energy market *(→ point 609)*, the energy framework programme and the preparation of the 'Intelligent energy for Europe' programme *(→ point 599)*, activities in the field of renewable energy *(→ point 614)*, biofuels in transport *(→ point 615)*, energy efficiency of buildings *(→ point 617)*, energy labelling of domestic appliances *(→ point 616)*, infrastructures for the trans-European energy networks *(→ point 390)* and nuclear safety *(→ point 627)*.

614.   *Energy framework programme.* As provided for in the Council decision adopting a multiannual framework programme for actions in the energy sector(¹), on 7 August, the Commission presented the conclusions of the mid-term assessment of the energy framework programme (1998–2002), together with its comments(²). The assessment, conducted by a panel of high-level independent experts, covers Community framework actions during the period 1998–2002.

New and renewable energy sources(³)

615.   *Biofuels.* In a resolution adopted on 22 October(⁴), the European Parliament welcomed the Commission's November 2001 communication on promoting the use of alternative fuels for road transportation(⁵) as a first step, and considered that increasing the market share of alternative fuels will have a positive impact on job-creation and the agricultural sector. On 18 November, the Council adopted a common position with a view to setting indicative targets for the use of biofuels in transport, in the framework of a future directive which is in the process of being adopted (Table I).

Energy efficiency and rational use of energy

616.   *Indication of consumption.* Pursuant to Council Directive 92/75/EEC, which provides for the labelling of the energy consumption of domestic appliances(⁶), on 22 March and 8 May respectively, the Commission adopted implementing directives concerning air conditioners(⁷) and electric ovens(⁸).

617.   *Energy performance of buildings.* Following the European Parliament's opinion on second reading on 10 October, on 25 November, the Council

---

(¹) Decision 1999/21//EC, Euratom (OJ L 7, 13.1.1999; 1998 General Report, point 397).
(²) COM(2002) 448.
(³) http://europa.eu.int/comm/energy/en/fa_3_en.html.
(⁴) Bull. 10-2002, point 1.4.49.
(⁵) COM(2001) 547; 2001 General Report, point 668.
(⁶) OJ L 297, 13.10.1992; Twenty-sixth General Report, point 690.
(⁷) Directive 2002/31//EC (OJ L 86, 3.4.2002).
(⁸) Directive 2002/40/EC (OJ L 128, 15.5.2002).

approved a directive aimed at improving energy performance in this sector which accounts for 40 % of total EU energy consumption (Table I).

Promotion of research and technological development

618. The implementation of the specific programme 'Energy, environment and sustainable development' of the fifth framework programme for research and technological development (1998–2002), and the launch of the sixth research framework programme are dealt with in Section 8 ('Research and technology') of Chapter III *(→ point 299).*

Individual sectors

619. Nuclear energy [1]. In a resolution adopted on 7 May [2], the Council urged the Member States to adopt the necessary measures to reduce as far as possible the radiological risks resulting from the presence of radioactive materials in metallic materials destined for recycling. On the same day [3], it extended until 2010 the joint undertaking status of Hochtemperatur-Kernkraftwerk GmbH (HKG), which is responsible for operating [4] and subsequently decommissioning [5] the Unna nuclear power plant in Germany. It also extended the related advantages [6] on account of the importance of the decommissioning and surveillance programmes for the future development of the nuclear industry in the Community.

620. Coal imports. In the context of the expiry of the ECSC Treaty *(→ points 39 to 41),* on 3 September the Commission proposed a new legal framework for requesting Member States to provide information about the price of imported coal [7], in particular, to monitor State aid to the coal industry *(→ point 241).*

[1] http://europa.eu.int/comm/energy/nuclear/index_en.html.
[2] OJ C 119, 22.5.2002; Bull. 5-2002, point 1.4.50.
[3] Decision 2002/355/Euratom (OJ L 123, 9.5.2002; Bull. 5-2002, point 1.4.51).
[4] Decision 74/295/Euratom (OJ L 165, 20.6.1974).
[5] Decision 92/547/Euratom (OJ L 352, 2.12.1992).
[6] Decision 2002/356/Euratom (OJ L 123, 9.5.2002; Bull. 5-2002, point 1.4.51).
[7] COM(2002) 482; Bull. 9-2002, point 1.4.45.

Euratom Supply Agency [1]

621.   *Uranium.* While the slight rise in natural uranium prices that began in 2001 continued in 2002, the agency continued to recommend covering users' needs by means of multiannual contracts with diversified producers and by establishing appropriate strategic stocks [2]. The pressure on the market as the result of surplus stocks in Russia eased, so the agency, in close collaboration with its consultative committee, was able to envisage a relaxation of its natural uranium policy along the lines of the lifting of restrictions that took place in 2001 with regard to Kazakhstan and Uzbekistan [3]. Where enriched uranium is concerned, the anti-dumping and anti-subsidy procedures launched by the US enricher USEC with the US authorities against its European competitors Eurodif and Urenco [4] continued to adversely affect trade in this product between the EU and the United States.

622.   *The agency's consultative committee.* In the context of the restructuring of the Commission departments responsible for nuclear energy, on 14 February the committee adopted a series of recommendations concerning its own role and the role of the agency. In addition, the committee helped prepare the EU–Russia Summit held on 29 May *(→ point 917)*, presenting on 30 April a working paper recalling the permanent need to ensure the security of energy supply *(→ point 602)* and the viability of the European industry. The agency's annual report for 2001 was published in May [5].

State aid to the coal industry

623.   State aid is dealt with in Section 6 ('Competition policy') of Chapter III *(→ point 240).*

Euratom safeguards

624.   *New regulatory basis.* Some 25 years after the entry into force of Commission Regulation (Euratom) No 3227/76 [6], on 22 March the Commission submitted to the Council, for approval, the text [7] of an updated regulatory

---

[1] http://europa.eu.int/comm/euratom/index_en.html.
[2] 2000 General Report, point 608.
[3] 2001 General Report, point 674.
[4] 2001 General Report, point 675.
[5] Available from the agency and on the Internet (http://europa.eu.int/comm/euratom/docum_en.html).
[6] OJ L 363, 31.12.1976; Tenth General Report, point 432; as last amended by Regulation (Euratom) No 2130/93 (OJ L 191, 31.7.1993; Twenty-seventh General Report, point 501).
[7] COM(2002) 99; Bull. 3-2002, point 1.4.40.

basis designed to meet new needs with regard to the reporting of nuclear material in accordance with the development of technology and the legal framework.

625. *Euratom Safeguards Office (ESO).* The Commission's July 2001 report [1] on the operation of the ESO (1999–2000) was favourably received by the European Parliament on 2 July [2]. Nevertheless, Parliament considered it necessary that certain aspects be improved, in particular, with the prospect of enlargement of the EU. It called for an increase in the ESO's budget and for the drawing-up of directives establishing a reference framework for activities relating to auditing. On 26 June, as part of the debate about the mission and operational objectives of the ESO, the Commission submitted a communication on this subject based on the work of a high-level expert group [3].

Nuclear safety

626. *Evaluation of nuclear plant safety in the candidate countries.* On the basis of the recommendations emerging from the evaluation carried out in 2001 by the Council [4], the implementation of recommendations by the countries concerned was monitored by the Council and the Commission in the first half of the year.

627. *Legislative initiatives.* In response to the request from the Laeken European Council for the regular presentation of reports on the state of nuclear safety in the EU [5], on 6 November the Commission adopted a communication summarising its proposals in this connection [6]. In this document it proposes the establishment of a new Community reference framework for nuclear safety standards, in particular, on the basis of a future directive setting out basic obligations and general principles concerning the safety of nuclear installations, and a directive concerning the management of irradiated nuclear fuel and radioactive waste.

---

[1] COM(2001) 436; 2001 General Report, point 678.
[2] Bull. 7/8-2002, point 1.4.35.
[3] SEC(2002) 658.
[4] 2001 General Report, point 681.
[5] Bull. 12-2001, point I.25.
[6] COM(2002) 605; Bull. 11-2002, point 1.4.62.

Section 6

Transport (¹)

Overview

628.   *The European Union has set about meeting the objectives the Commission set in its 2001 White Paper on transport policy. There were a number of major developments in 2002, above all in the field of security and safety and of improved quality and efficiency of transport modes, with particular emphasis on intermodal transport. In addition to establishing the Galileo joint undertaking, the Commission presented five legislative proposals aimed at promoting the integration of the rail sector in the internal market. The aviation sector was focused on managing the security consequences of the 2001 terrorist attacks, progress on passenger rights and the creation of the single European sky. Furthermore, a recent ruling by the Court of Justice confirming the Community's external competence opens up the way to consolidation of this sector. With regard to maritime transport, the Council adopted several important measures and the European Maritime Safety Agency was established. Following the sinking of the oil tanker, Prestige, the Commission announced a new package of measures in its communication on improving safety at sea. These proposals were endorsed by the Copenhagen European Council.*

General approach

629.   *Future of transport policy.* On 13 March (²), the Committee of the Regions endorsed the White Paper on European transport policy for 2010 (³), which the Commission presented in September 2001. The European Economic and Social Committee, which gave its opinion on 18 July (⁴), advocated a rebalancing of transport modes by measures that neither distort competition nor limit users' freedom of choice. In a resolution of 28 February (⁵), the European Parliament asked the Commission to take account of health considerations in its transport policy proposals.

(¹) Further information is available on the Europa server (http://europa.eu.int/comm/dgs/ energy_transport/ index_en.html).
(²) OJ C 192, 18.8.2002; Bull. 3-2002, point 1.4.42.
(³) COM(2001) 370; 2001 General Report, point 683.
(⁴) OJ C 241, 7.10.2002; Bull. 7/8-2002, point 1.4.38.
(⁵) OJ C 293 E, 28.11.2002; Bull. 1/2-2002, point 1.4.74.

630.   European energy and transport forum. The Commission organised the first meeting of this forum in Brussels on 8 October *(→ point 600).*

631.   Security of transport. On 24 October, the European Economic and Social Committee adopted an exploratory opinion recommending a number of measures to deal with the general climate of insecurity prevailing in the transport sector since the terrorist attacks of 11 September 2001 in the United States ([1]). The Committee, in particular, favoured introducing measures that went beyond mere policing. With regard to the transport of dangerous goods, the Commission proposed to the Council on 3 July under the comitology procedure *(→ point 33)* that the date from which pressure drums, cylinder racks and tanks for the transport of such goods by rail ([2]) and by road ([3]) have to comply with Directives 96/49/EC ([4]) and 94/55/EC ([5]) respectively, should be changed. As the Council had not commented within the time limit set by the procedure, the Commission adopted the two decisions on 7 November ([6]).

Galileo satellite radio-navigation programme ([7])

632.   Implementation. The Barcelona European Council of 15 and 16 March ([8]), welcoming the progress already made, called on the Council to take the necessary decisions to launch the programme. The Council took a step in this direction in its conclusions of 26 March ([9]), asking the Commission to release EUR 450 million for this purpose. On 21 May, it adopted Regulation (EC) No 876/2002 setting up the Galileo joint undertaking (Table II): the aim of the latter, based in Brussels and set up for four years, is to ensure uniform management and financial control over the project during its development phase. The Commission reported on progress with the programme in a communication of 24 September ([10]). At its meeting of 5 and 6 December, the Council adopted conclusions favourable to continuing with the development of the Galileo programme ([11]).

([1]) Bull. 10-2002, point 1.4.51.
([2]) COM(2002) 357; Bull. 7/8-2002, point 1.4.39.
([3]) COM(2002) 358; Bull. 7/8-2002, point 1.4.43.
([4]) OJ L 235, 17.9.1996; 1996 General Report, point 382.
([5]) OJ L 319, 12.12.1994; 1994 General Report, point 373.
([6]) Decision 2002/885/EC and Decision 2002/886/EC (OJ L 308, 9.11.2002).
([7]) http://europa.eu.int/comm/dgs/energy_transport/galileo/index_en.htm.
([8]) Bull. 3-2002, point I.33.
([9]) Bull. 3-2002, point 1.4.43.
([10]) COM(2002) 518; Bull. 9-2002, point 1.4.47.
([11]) Bull. 12-2002, point 1.4.69.

Transport and the environment

633.   Tokyo Conference. This ministerial conference on 15 and 16 January ([1]), was attended by representatives of the 15 countries of the European Union, the European Commission, a number of industrialised countries (Australia, Canada, South Korea, United States, Japan, Norway and Singapore), the Organisation for Economic Cooperation and Development and the International Maritime Organisation. An action plan for the prevention of marine pollution was drawn up at the conference, which also discussed urban transport and the issue of combating terrorism in the transport sector.

634.   Integrating environmental considerations in transport policy. In the conclusions adopted at its meeting of 5 and 6 December ([2]), the Council called on the Commission to attach an impact assessment of the economic, social and environmental aspects of sustainable development to all substantial regulatory proposals as of 2003. It also considers that further action is necessary on greenhouse gas emissions, noise and emissions of harmful substances from all transport modes.

635.   Environmental aspects of transport are also dealt with in the subsections on 'Inland transport' *(→ point 644),* 'Maritime transport' *(→ point 651)* and 'Air transport' *(→ point 659)* of this section.

Clean urban transport ([3])

636.   Pilot projects have been running since the beginning of the year in 19 European cities intent on adopting a package of innovative measures to improve urban transport. The Commission is giving financial support totalling EUR 50 million to these initiatives under the Civitas programme, for which a forum was launched in October in order to provide the cities concerned with a platform for the exchange of ideas and experience.

Trans-European transport networks ([4])

637.   The trans-European transport networks are dealt with in Section 12 ('Trans-European networks') of Chapter III *(→ points 386 and 387).*

([1]) Bull. 1/2-2002, point 1.4.76.
([2]) Bull. 12-2002, point 1.4.67.
([3]) http://europa.eu.int/comm/energy_transport/en/cut_en.html.
([4]) http://europa.eu.int/comm/transport/themes/network/english/hp_en/aatransen.htm.

Promotion of research and technological development

638. Research and technological development in the transport sector is dealt with in Section 8 ('Research and technology') of Chapter III *(→ point 307).*

Infrastructure

639. The Copenhagen European Council of 12 and 13 December lent its support to improving transport infrastructure in order to encourage the development of cross-border and regional cooperation with the European Union's neighbours (¹). On 30 December, the Commission, for its part, transmitted a proposal for a directive to the European Parliament and the Council setting out safety rules for road tunnels of more than 500 metres in length located on the trans-European network, with the aim of clarifying the respective roles and responsibilities of the various bodies in charge of safety (Table I). This proposal contains a comprehensive set of minimum technical requirements (technical equipment, traffic rules, training of operating staff, organisation of rescue services, information to users and means of communication in the event of accidents). It also includes a flexibility clause allowing Member States to apply less costly risk-prevention measures.

Inland transport (²)

Rail transport

640. *Railway package.* On 23 and 24 January, the Commission published five legislative proposals, together with an introductory communication, designed to promote the use of rail transport in the Community.

In addition to presenting the various parts of the package, the introductory communication entitled 'Towards an integrated European railway area' (³), contains analyses of the situation of rail freight and international passenger services. The Commission considers that they constitute an avenue for reflection on possible measures to improve both the quality of service and make rail transport in general more attractive, in keeping with the White Paper on European transport policy for 2010 *(→ point 629).* The legislative initiatives concern: a proposal for a directive on railway safety (Table I); a proposal for a directive

---

(¹) Bull. 12-2002, point I.7.
(²) http://europa.eu.int/comm/transport/themes/land/english/lt_en.html.
(³) COM(2002) 18; Bull. 1/2-2002, point 1.4.80.

amending the existing legislation on interoperability of the trans-European rail system (Table I); a proposal for a regulation establishing the European Railway Agency responsible for safety and interoperability (Table I); a recommendation for a decision authorising the Commission to negotiate the conditions for Community accession to the Convention concerning International Carriage by Rail (COTIF) (Table III); and a proposal for a directive designed to open up immediately the whole national and international freight market (Table I). This package was the subject of a policy debate at the Council meeting of 5 and 6 December.

641.   *High-speed trans-European rail system.* On 30 May, the Commission adopted a number of decisions ([1]) relating to the technical specifications of interoperability of six subsystems of this trans-European rail system, in application of Directive 96/48/EC ([2]).

Road transport

642.   *Vehicle characteristics and equipment.* On 18 February, the European Parliament and the Council amended the provisions of Directive 96/53/EC laying down the maximum authorised dimensions and weights for certain road vehicles, setting the maximum length of non-articulated coaches and buses at 15 metres (Table I).

On 5 November, the European Parliament and the Council adopted Directive 2002/85/EC amending Directive 92/6/EEC on speed limitation devices for certain categories of motor vehicles (Table I). This directive imposes a maximum speed limit, with the aid of a speed limitation device, of 90 km/h on all haulage vehicles of more than 3.5 tonnes and of 100 km/h on passenger transport vehicles carrying more than eight passengers.

On 16 January, the Commission initiated a new phase in the recasting of Directive 74/150/EEC on the type approval of agricultural or forestry tractors, aimed at extending its scope to cover more specific types of tractors, their trailers and interchangeable towed equipment (Table I).

On 13 June ([3]), the Commission again adapted to technical progress Council Regulation (EEC) No 3821/85 in respect of the recording equipment monitoring the working time of professional drivers (tachographs) ([4]), with which vehicles first registered after 5 August 2004 must be equipped.

[1] Decisions 2002/730/EC to 2002/735/EC (OJ L 245, 12.9.2002).
[2] OJ L 235, 17.9.1996; 1996 General Report, points 327 and 377.
[3] Regulation (EC) No 1360/2002 (OJ L 207, 5.8.2002).
[4] OJ L 370, 31.12.1985. Previously amended by: Council Regulation (EC) No 2135/98 (OJ L 274, 9.10.1998; 1998 General Report, point 442).

643.   *Drivers*. In order to permit efficient monitoring of the professional status of drivers of Community vehicles carrying out international transport under a Community licence, the European Parliament and the Council introduced a uniform document at European Union level (the 'driver attestation'), with effect from 1 March (Table I). On 11 March, they adopted a directive on the working time of professional drivers *(→ point 125)*. On 5 December, the Council adopted a common position on the proposal for a directive on the periodic training of drivers of certain road vehicles for the carriage of goods or passengers (Table I). On 25 March([1]), the Commission rectified the existing decision on equivalences between certain categories of driving licence([2]). On 28 March([3]), it adopted an interpretative communication clarifying certain aspects of Directive 91/439/EEC on driving licences([4]).

In a resolution of 7 February([5]), the European Parliament deplored the treatment of professional drivers from non-Community countries employed by an Austrian haulage company, who had been left stranded in Luxembourg. It called on Member States to end social exploitation in this sector.

644.   *Ecopoints*. On 24 July, the Commission approved the approach consisting in not submitting a legislative proposal to reduce the number of ecopoints for 2002 (108 % clause)([6]). The proposal for a regulation aimed at establishing an ecopoints system applicable to heavy goods vehicles transiting through Austria for 2004 (Table I) was discussed in the Council throughout the year but could not be adopted. The Copenhagen European Council therefore asked the Council to approve, by the end of the year, a regulation on an interim solution to the problem of the transit of heavy goods vehicles through Austria for the years 2004–06([7]). A Presidency compromise proposal was approved by the majority of the Member States at the Council meeting on transport on 31 December.

Inland waterway transport

645.   *Danube corridor*. In the context both of enlarging the European Union and bringing stability to the Balkans, the Commission adopted a decision on signature of a memorandum of understanding on the development of this inland waterway corridor on 25 January (Table III).

([1]) Decision 2002/256/EC (OJ L 87, 4.4.2002).
([2]) Decision 2002/275/EC (OJ L 91, 12.4.2002).
([3]) OJ C 77, 28.3.2002.
([4]) OJ L 237, 24.8.1991; Twenty-fifth General Report, point 221.
([5]) OJ C 284 E, 21.11.2002; Bull. 1/2-2002, point 1.4.91.
([6]) SEC(2002) 855.
([7]) Bull. 12-2002, point I.12.

646.   *Capacity of Community fleets.* In order to promote inland waterway transport, the Commission decided on 22 February (¹) to halve again the ratio (between old and new tonnage) introduced under the temporary 'old-for-new' scheme (according to which the owner of new tonnage to be brought into service must either scrap old tonnage or make a special contribution to the inland waterway fund) (²).

Maritime transport (³)

647.   *Maritime safety.* The European Parliament and the Council established the European Maritime Safety Agency by Regulation (EC) No 1406/2002 of 27 June (Table I). The aim of this independent body is to assist the Commission in preparing legislation in the field of maritime safety, to monitor implementation by the Member States, to assist the latter in implementing maritime safety measures, to coordinate investigations following accidents at sea and to provide assistance to the candidate countries. The European Parliament and the Council also adopted Directive 2002/59/EC on 27 June, which seeks to impose additional strict conditions on shipping in order to improve safety at sea and avoid shipping accidents of all kinds (Table I).

On 25 March, as part of the follow-up to its White Paper on the future of European transport policy *(→ point 629)*, the Commission adopted a communication on the safety of passenger ships (⁴). This sets out the Commission's opinion on how liability for damage caused to passengers in the event of accidents should be regulated. The communication is accompanied by two proposals for directives concerning respectively: the introduction of specific stability requirements for ro-ro passenger ships operating international services from or to Community ports (Table I); the introduction of new standards for high-speed craft and safety requirements relating to passengers with reduced mobility (Table I).

648.   *Effects of the sinking of the oil tanker,* Prestige. On 3 December, the Commission adopted a communication on improving safety at sea in response to the *Prestige* accident off the Spanish coast (⁵). In it, the Commission reiterates the need for earlier application, by the Member States, of the legislative measures adopted following the sinking of the *Erika* in December 1999 (⁶), for example concerning the recruitment of port State control inspectors. It also

---

(¹) Regulation (EC) No 336/2002 (OJ L 53, 23.2.2002; Bull. 1/2-2002, point 1.4.95).
(²) Council Regulation (EC) No 718/1999 (OJ L 90, 2.4.1999; 1999 General Report, point 410).
(³) http://europa.eu.int/comm/transport/themes/maritime/english/mt_en.html.
(⁴) COM(2002) 158; Bull. 3-2002, point 1.4.48.
(⁵) COM(2002) 681; Bull. 12-2002, point 1.4.72.
(⁶) 2000 General Report, point 645; 2001 General Report, point 711.

announced specific initiatives in the light of the *Prestige* accident. Accordingly, on 20 December, it adopted a proposal for a regulation aimed at speeding up the schedule for the withdrawal of single-hull tankers and prohibiting the transport of heavy fuel oil in single-hull tankers to or from EU ports (Table I). A proposal for a regulation on penal sanctions in the event of gross negligence which causes pollution is in preparation. At its meeting of 5 and 6 December ([1]), the Council, too, called on the Member States to implement speedily the measures adopted in the wake of the *Erika* accident and to support the establishment of a supplementary compensation fund under the auspices of the International Maritime Organisation to cover up to EUR 1 billion of the cost of the damage caused to the victims of oil spills. It also calls on Member States and the Commission to take measures to reinforce the mechanisms for controlling shipping off Europe's coasts. The Copenhagen European Council ([2]) welcomed the Community's efforts to improve safety at sea and the measures to prevent pollution, and the Community institutions' rapid response in dealing with such disasters and compensating the victims. The European Parliament also adopted a resolution on the consequences of this accident on 19 December ([3]), calling, in particular, for the establishment of a European coastguard service and a European civil protection force capable of intervening in the event of natural disasters or industrial accidents; Parliament also wants flags of convenience to be banned from the European Union's territorial waters and, while stressing the importance of proper ship maintenance, considers that Member States should be obliged to grant refuge to ships in distress.

649. Facilitation and monitoring of maritime traffic. On 18 February, the European Parliament and the Council adopted Directive 2002/6/EC designed to simplify the reporting formalities applicable to ships entering and leaving Member States' ports (Table I). On 5 November, the Council adopted a common position on the proposal for a directive on market access to port services (Table I).

650. Liberalisation of maritime cabotage. On 24 April ([4]), the Commission published its fourth report on the implementation of Regulation (EEC) No 3577/92 ([5]) applying the principle of freedom to provide services to maritime cabotage (1999–2000). This report was welcomed by the Council in its conclusions of 5 November ([6]).

651. Environmental protection. On 18 February, the European Parliament and the Council adopted Regulation (EC) No 417/2002 on the accelerated phasing-in of double-hull or equivalent design requirements for single-hull oil

([1]) Bull. 12-2002, point 1.4.73.
([2]) Bull. 12-2002, point I.11.
([3]) Bull. 12-2002, point 1.4.75.
([4]) COM(2002) 203; Bull. 4-2002, point 1.4.62.
([5]) OJ L 364, 12.12.1992; Twenty-sixth General Report, point 670.
([6]) Bull. 11-2002, point 1.4.71.

tankers (Table I). The objective of this regulation is to impose common rules to exclude single-hull oil tankers from European ports after a certain date. This process will begin in 2003 and is designed to eliminate a major source of pollution risk.

On 19 September, the Council authorised the Member States to sign or ratify the International Convention on Civil Liability for Bunker Oil Pollution Damage (Table III). On 18 November, Member States were also authorised to ratify the 1996 International Convention on Liability and Compensation for Damage in connection with the Carriage of Hazardous and Noxious Substances by Sea (Table III). On 5 November, the European Parliament and the Council adopted Regulation (EC) No 2099/2002 establishing a Committee on Safe Seas and the Prevention of Pollution from Ships (COSS) (Table I) and Directive 2002/84/EC concerning the conditions governing its activity (Table I).

On 12 July, the Commission proposed banning the application of organotin compounds in anti-fouling paints used on ships. On 5 December, endorsing the amendments adopted by the European Parliament on 20 November, the Council reached political agreement on a common position on this proposal (Table I).

652.   *Training and recruitment of seafarers*. The Commission's communication on this subject in April 2001 ([1]), was the subject of a European Economic and Social Committee opinion on 16 January ([2]), and a European Parliament resolution on 17 January ([3]).

Air transport ([4])

653.   *Aviation safety*. On 15 July, the European Parliament and the Council adopted Regulation (EC) No 1592/2002 (Table I), which has two objectives: firstly, to establish common rules in the field of civil aviation, in particular, for the certification and maintenance of aeronautical products; secondly, to establish a European Aviation Safety Agency which is independent with regard to technical matters and which has legal, administrative and financial autonomy. The purpose of the agency is to assist the Commission in preparing and implementing the necessary legislation, in particular, by issuing on its own account type-certificates for aeronautical products and by requiring the monitoring of national authorities charged with other certification tasks.

([1]) COM(2001) 188; 2001 General Report, point 709.
([2]) OJ C 80, 3.4.2002; Bull. 1/2-2002, point 1.4.96.
([3]) OJ C 271 E, 7.11.2002; Bull. 1/2-2002, point 1.4.97.
([4]) http://europa.eu.int/comm/transport/themes/air/english/at_en.html.

On 14 January, the Commission proposed a directive to formalise the assessment procedure for non-Community air carriers and require Member States to ground dangerous aircraft (Table I). In a resolution of 28 February ([1]), the European Parliament warned Member States and undertakings against any tendency to consider the terrorist attacks of 11 September 2001 in the United States as the sole cause of the cyclical downturn in the air transport sector.

654. *Common rules in the field of civil aviation security.* On 16 December, the European Parliament and the Council adopted Regulation (EC) No 2320/2002 establishing common rules intended to harmonise and reinforce security measures and procedures as a direct response to the terrorist attacks of 11 September 2001 in the United States (Table I); this regulation imposes certain obligations on Member States and introduces a system of inspections at Community level, to be conducted by the Commission.

655. *Incident monitoring and compensation.* The legislative work on the proposal for a directive on incident reporting in civil aviation (Table I) and the proposal for a regulation on establishing common rules on compensation and assistance to passengers in the event of denied boarding and of cancellation or long delay of flights (Table I) continued throughout the year.

656. *Liability in the event of accidents.* On 13 May, the European Parliament and the Council adopted Regulation (EC) No 889/2002 amending the existing provisions on air carrier liability in the event of accidents (Table I) in order to bring them into line with the Montreal Convention, to which the Community acceded in 2001 ([2]).

657. *Slot allocation in airports.* On 27 May, the European Parliament and the Council adopted Regulation (EC) No 894/2002 aimed at enabling airlines to adapt to the sharp fall in demand following the terrorist attacks of 11 September 2001 in the United States and to ensure the uniform application of the rules in question throughout the Community (Table I).

658. *Insurance in the aviation sector.* Following its October 2001 communication on the economic situation of the aviation sector following the events of 11 September 2001 ([3]), the Commission adopted a proposal for a regulation on 24 September on the insurance requirements applicable to air carriers and to aircraft operators (Table I). The proposal introduces minimum requirements in a neutral, non-discriminatory manner covering both Community carriers and operators and those of third countries. Soon after the events of 11 September 2001, the aviation industry also presented initiatives concerning the creation of

---

([1]) OJ C 293 E, 28.11.2002; Bull. 1/2-2002, point 1.4.103.
([2]) 2001 General Report, point 716.
([3]) COM(2001) 574; 2001 General Report, point 713.

two mutual funds to respond to the risks of war and terrorism at European level (Eurotime) and international level (Globaltime) respectively. In response to a Council request of 17 June ([1]), the Commission adopted a communication on insurance in the air transport sector on 2 July ([2]).

659. Noise emissions. On 26 March, the European Parliament and the Council adopted Directive 2002/30/EC with the aim of strictly regulating noise pollution by aircraft (Table I).

660. Unfair pricing practices. On 12 March, the Commission presented a proposal for a regulation concerning protection against subsidisation and unfair pricing practices in the supply of airline services by countries which are not members of the European Community (Table I). The aim of this initiative is to enable the Commission to take measures against unfair competition, which distorts trade on the routes destined to and originating in its territory, while the Community air transport sector is subject to strict rules on State aid.

661. Single European sky. As part of the global strategy to achieve the single European sky ([3]), a protocol of Community accession to the European Organisation for the Safety of Air Navigation (Eurocontrol) was signed on 8 October (Table III). The Commission also updated, on 4 June ([4]), Regulation (EC) No 2082/2000 adopting Eurocontrol standards relating to data exchange (OLDI, ADEXP) ([5]). On 5 December, the Council reached political agreement on a common position on various proposals relating to the single European sky concerning, respectively, the creation of a legal framework (Table I), the supply of air navigation services (Table I), the organisation and use of air space (Table I) and network interoperability (Table I).

662. Court of Justice ruling. On 19 November ([6]), the Commission adopted a communication on the consequences of the ruling by the Court of Justice against Germany, Austria, Belgium, Denmark, Finland, the United Kingdom and Sweden in respect of the 'Open skies' agreements they had concluded with the United States (→ *point 1070*), which infringe Community competence and distort competition within the European Union. The communication calls on the Member States concerned to denounce the agreements which the Court has declared illegal, and sets a number of objectives for the establishment of a Community policy on external relations in air transport.

---

[1] Bull. 6-2002, point 1.9.9.
[2] COM(2002) 320.
[3] COM(2001) 123; 2001 General Report, point 712.
[4] Regulation (EC) No 980/2002 (OJ L 150, 8.6.2002).
[5] OJ L 254, 9.10.2000.
[6] COM(2002) 649; Bull. 11-2002, point 1.4.78.

Intermodal transport [1]

663. *'Marco Polo' programme.* On 4 February, the Commission proposed the grant of financial aid under this programme in order to establish, for environmental reasons, an instrument that will help transfer a volume of goods corresponding to the planned growth in international road freight to other transport modes (Table I). At its meeting of 5 and 6 December, the Council reached political agreement on the allocation of a budget of EUR 75 million for this purpose for the period 2003–06 [2].

664. *Implementation of common rules.* In a report adopted on 2 May [3], the Commission presented a status report on the application from 1996 to 1999 of Directive 92/106/EEC [4] on the establishment of common rules for certain types of combined transport of goods between Member States.

State aid

665. State aid is discussed in Section 6 ('Competition policy') of Chapter III (→ *points 236 to 245).*

International cooperation

666. *International organisations.* In order to enable the European Union to play a role in the adoption of the international rules which govern transport to a very large extent, the Commission, on 9 April [5], recommended opening negotiations with the International Civil Aviation Organisation (ICAO) and the International Maritime Organisation (IMO) on the conditions for Community accession. As it is aware that accession to these organisations will take several years, it proposes a number of transitional measures. On 31 July, the Commission called on the Member States to support the ICAO's initiatives concerning new protection standards for cockpit doors [6].

667. *China.* On 6 December, the Council and China signed an agreement on maritime transport (Table III).

---

[1] http://europa.eu.int/comm/transport/themes/land/english/lt_28_en.html.
[2] Bull. 12-2002, point 1.4.82.
[3] COM(2002) 215; Bull. 5-2002, point 1.4.66.
[4] OJ L 368, 17.12.1992, Twenty-sixth General Report, point 652.
[5] Bull. 4-2002, point 1.4.60.
[6] COM(2002) 444; Bull. 7/8-2002, point 1.4.54.

668.   *Romania.* On 27 May, the European Parliament and the Council amended Regulation (EC) No 685/2001 concerning the distribution among Member States of the authorisations received pursuant to the agreement establishing certain conditions for the carriage of goods by road and the promotion of combined transport between the European Community and Romania (Table I).

669.   *Interbus Agreement.* On 3 October, the Council concluded an agreement designed to ensure a high degree of legislative harmonisation through the establishment of common rules of a social, fiscal and technical nature for occasional international passenger transport services by coach or bus (Table III). The contracting parties are, of the one part, the Community and, of the other, Bosnia and Herzegovina, Bulgaria, Croatia, Estonia, Hungary, Latvia, Lithuania, Moldova, the Czech Republic, Romania, Slovakia, Slovenia and Turkey.

Section 7

Health and consumer protection (¹)

Overview

670.   With the Food Safety Authority being established, the European Union will have at its disposal a wealth of independent scientific and technical advice enabling it to improve the quality of foodstuffs available to consumers. The adoption of the new programme of action in the field of public health will underpin the development of a Community health strategy promoting further cooperation between the Member States and an integrated, cross-sectoral approach in conjunction with other Community programmes and actions. Moreover, the new strategy for consumer policy is a key element in the establishment of clear guidelines for achieving a high level of protection for Europe's consumers and for taking their interests more fully into account in EU policy as a whole.

Food safety (²)

General aspects

671.   European Food Safety Authority (³). Regulation (EC) No 178/2002, establishing the European Food Safety Authority in accordance with the White Paper on food safety (⁴), was formally adopted by the European Parliament and the Council on 28 January (Table I). The authority's task is to provide the European Union with the independent scientific and technical advice needed for implementing policy and taking appropriate legislative measures. The regulation lays down the general principles and requirements of food law, and also extends the scope of the rapid alert system to cover animal feed and the rejection of consignments at the external borders of the European Union.

(¹) Further information is available on the Europa server (http://europa.eu.int/comm/dgs/health_consumer/index_en.htm).
(²) http://europa.eu.int/comm/food/index_en.html.
(³) http://www.efsa.eu.int.
(⁴) COM(1999) 719; 2000 General Report, point 660.

672.   *Food supplements*. The European Parliament and the Council adopted, on 10 June, Directive 2002/46/EC (Table I), aimed at reconciling a high level of public health protection with the principle of free movement of goods, ensuring that food supplements are safe to be marketed and are appropriately labelled. In the same vein, the Commission proposed, on 29 November, that Directive 95/2/EC be amended for the purpose of authorising a new food additive and allowing new applications for certain existing food additives (Table I).

673.   *Foodstuffs*. On 9 October, in its report on food irradiation ([1]), the Commission summarised the results of checks carried out between September 2000 and December 2001 by the Member States in irradiation facilities and at the product marketing stage, with a view to monitoring the quality of the treated products and ensuring that they are properly labelled. On 17 December ([2]), the European Parliament called on the Commission to establish a system for monitoring and controlling products liable to be illegally irradiated and unlabelled, so that they are not marketed in the territory of the Member States. Moreover, on 11 July, the Commission proposed the authorisation of two new sweeteners meeting the criteria laid down in Directive 89/107/EEC ([3]) (Table I). On 15 July, it advocated Community procedures for the safety assessment and authorisation of smoke flavourings intended for use in or on foods (Table I). Lastly, on 5 August, the Commission proposed that the authorisation to use the additive E 425 konjac in jelly mini-cups and jelly confectionery be withdrawn (Table I).

Veterinary and plant-health legislation

674.   *Products of animal origin*. In the light of new developments relating, in particular, to meat safety, the Commission presented, on 11 July, a proposal for a regulation laying down specific rules for the organisation of official controls on all types of products of animal origin intended for human consumption, with the aim of reducing the risk to human health (Table I). Moreover, on the basis of the results of an inspection by the European Food and Veterinary Office in November 2001, the Commission decided, on 30 January, to place an embargo on certain products of animal origin from China ([4]). As regards measures applicable to trade in live animals and animal products from New Zealand, the Commission put forward a proposal, on 13 September, for an agreement aimed at recognising the equivalence of certain products and of certification systems so that the EC–New Zealand veterinary agreement could enter into force (Table III). On 16 December, the Council adopted a regulation laying down animal-health rules

---

[1] COM(2002) 549; Bull. 10-2002, point 1.4.62.
[2] Bull. 12-2002, point 1.4.90.
[3] OJ L 40, 11.2.1989, as last amended by European Parliament and Council Directive 94/34/EC (OJ L 237, 10.9.1994; 1994 General Report, point 106).
[4] Decision 2002/69/EC (OJ L 30, 31.1.2002; Bull. 1/2-2002, point 1.4.111).

governing the placing on the market and importation of products with a view to preventing the spread of animal diseases (Table II).

675.   *Animal by-products.* The European Parliament and the Council adopted, on 3 and 21 October respectively, Regulation (EC) No 1774/2002 and Directive 2002/33/EC laying down new health rules governing the processing and disposal of animal waste, and the production, marketing, trade and import of animal by-products not intended for human consumption (Table I).

676.   *Animal diseases.* On 16 January, the European Parliament decided to set up a temporary committee to analyse EU policy on the overall management of the foot-and-mouth crisis ([1]). As the football World Cup competition coincided with the outbreak of foot-and-mouth disease in South Korea, Parliament also proposed, on 13 June, to tighten up control measures in respect of foodstuffs from that country ([2]). On 17 December, it adopted a resolution on measures to control foot-and-mouth disease in the European Union ([3]). The Commission meanwhile proposed, on 19 July, to reinforce the animal-health rules applicable to staging points, as a result of outbreaks of foot-and-mouth disease in 2001 linked to the commingling of animals at staging points (Table II). In the wake of the 2001 foot-and-mouth epidemic, the Commission proposed, on 12 September, aligning the animal-health requirements for intra-Community trade in sheep and goats with those approved for bovine animals and swine, in order to prevent the spread of major infectious diseases within the Community (Table II). It also proposed, on 13 December, introducing not only minimum measures to combat outbreaks of foot-and-mouth disease but also preventive measures (Table II). Furthermore, the Commission proposed, on the same day, that the provisions of Directive 92/102/EEC ([4]) (Table II) be reinforced so that sheep and goats may be traced rapidly in the event of a contagious disease. With regard to Teschen disease and African swine fever, the Council adopted, on 27 June ([5]), a directive designed to update Directive 92/119/EEC ([6]), mainly by including swine fever within its scope (Table II). Seeking to limit, as far as possible, the public-health consequences of the bovine spongiform encephalopathy (BSE) crisis, the European Parliament called on the Commission, in a resolution adopted on 6 February ([7]), to carry out a review of the relevant EU legislation. The Council, for its part, recommended, on 18 February ([8]), that the Commission should take steps to improve the legislation. It also urged the Member States not only to bring about improvement but also to speed up implementation. In this con-

[1] OJ C 271 E, 7.11.2002; Bull. 1/2-2002, point 1.4.110.
[2] Bull. 6-2002, point 1.4.75.
[3] Bull. 12-2002, point 1.4.95.
[4] OJ L 355, 5.12.1992; Twenty-sixth General Report, point 96.
[5] Directive 2002/60/EC (OJ L 192, 20.7.2002; Bull. 6-2002, point 1.4.66).
[6] OJ L 62, 15.3.1993.
[7] OJ C 284 E, 21.11.2002; Bull. 1/2-2002, point 1.4.113.
[8] Bull. 1/2-2002, point 1.4.115.

text, the Commission proposed, on 25 September, tightening up the animal-health requirements applicable to intra-Community trade in and imports of semen of animals of the bovine species (Table II).

677.   *Plants and plant products.* On 22 November, the Commission adopted a report on the results of the application of Article 13(9) and Articles 22, 23 and 24 of Directive 2000/29/EC (¹) on protective measures against the introduction into the Community of organisms harmful to plants or plant products and against their spread within the Community (²). On 28 November, the Council amended this directive in order to remove certain superfluous provisions, to take account of Decision 1999/468/EC (³) concerning the exercise of implementing powers conferred on the Commission, and to incorporate elements relating to the introduction of the principle of harmonised fees to be charged for plant-health import inspections and the establishment of customs clearance procedures, by the appropriate services of the Member States, in cooperation with the customs authorities (Table II). On 23 December (⁴), the Commission adopted a report on the results of application of Article 12 of Council Directive 98/56/EC (⁵) on the marketing of propagating material of ornamental plants.

678.   *Seeds and plants.* On 13 June, the Council adopted five directives in this sector, numbered 2002/53/EC (common catalogue of varieties of agricultural plant species), 2002/54/EC (marketing of beet seed), 2002/55/EC (marketing of vegetable seed), 2002/56/EC (marketing of seed potatoes) and 2002/57/EC (seed of oil and fibre plants), for the purpose of consolidating directives which had been adopted at the end of the 1960s and amended several times (Table II). The Council also amended, on 19 July, Directive 2002/57/EC, in order to bring seed of hybrid varieties of oil and fibre plants within the scope of certain definitions (Table II). On 14 February, the Council adopted Directive 2002/11/EC in order to harmonise legislation relating to the marketing of material for the vegetative propagation of the vine, in the interest of internal market consolidation (Table II). On 25 September, the Commission put forward a proposal for amending the Community legislation governing the marketing of seed and plant propagating material, making provision for the financial measures needed to maintain the post control system, which is recognised as a very important tool for harmonisation of marketing by the Member States (Table II).

On 18 June, by means of Decision 2002/580/EC (⁶), the Council extended until 30 June 2005 the period of validity of checks on practices for the maintenance of varieties for all the third countries listed in Decision 97/788/EC (⁷). More-

---

(¹) OJ L 169, 10.7.2000; 2000 General Report, point 674.
(²) COM(2002) 644; Bull. 11-2002, point 1.4.90.
(³) OJ L 184, 17.7.1999.
(⁴) COM(2002) 761; Bull. 12-2002, point 1.4.102.
(⁵) OJ L 226, 13.8.1998; 1998 General Report, point 569.
(⁶) OJ L 184, 13.7.2002; Bull. 6-2002, point 1.4.67.
(⁷) OJ L 322, 25.11.1997.

over, on 16 December (¹), it extended the period of validity for the equivalence of seed produced in third countries until 31 December 2007 for all the countries listed in Decision 95/514/EC (²) and for Estonia, Latvia and the Federal Republic of Yugoslavia.

679. *Plant protection products.* In a resolution adopted on 30 May (³), the European Parliament called for a revision of Directive 91/414/EEC (⁴), taking account of the shortcomings in the application of that directive from the point of view of risk assessment of the active ingredients in pesticides. In this context, on 16 December (⁵), the Commission proposed that authorisations for plant protection products containing aldicarb be withdrawn.

680. *International cooperation.* On 18 March, the Council stressed the importance of veterinary and plant-health agreements with third countries for ensuring a high level of human, animal and plant protection both in the European Union and worldwide (⁶). Following its decision of 27 May, the Council authorised the Community to sign the International Treaty on Plant Genetic Resources for Food and Agriculture (Table III). This treaty, adopted by the conference of the United Nations Food and Agriculture Organisation (FAO), provides a legally binding framework for the sustainable conservation of plant genetic resources for food and agriculture.

Animal nutrition

681. *Undesirable substances and products.* On 7 May, the European Parliament and the Council adopted Directive 2002/32/EC, extending the scope to cover additives, removing the possibility of dilution or derogation, and introducing action thresholds outside the maximum limits. These changes enhance the safety of animal feed (Table I).

682. *Compound feedingstuffs.* A new directive on the circulation of compound feedingstuffs was adopted by the European Parliament and the Council on 28 January, aimed at revising the rules on labelling in order to improve information for stock farmers (Table I).

683. *Additives.* On 22 March, the Commission adopted a proposal for a regulation on additives for use in animal nutrition, aimed mainly at ensuring that users and consumers are properly informed by means of detailed labelling

(¹) Decision 2003/17/EC (OJ L 8, 14.1.2003; Bull. 12-2002, point 1.4.101).
(²) OJ L 296, 9.12.1995.
(³) Bull. 5-2002, point 1.4.78.
(⁴) OJ L 230, 19.8.1991; Twenty-fifth General Report, point 619.
(⁵) COM(2002) 734; Bull. 12-2002, point 1.4.100.
(⁶) Bull. 3-2002, point 1.4.57.

(Table I). Moreover, on 23 September, the Council withdrew the authorisation to use the coccidiostat Nifursol as an additive in feedingstuffs, owing to its potential dangerousness for human health ([1]). On 16 October, the Commission proposed amending the regulation on organic production of animal feed (→ *point 404*).

Animal welfare

684.   On 18 November ([2]), the Commission presented an evaluation of animal welfare legislation in 73 countries engaged in trade in animals and animal products with the European Union. It noted that existing disparities between the measures in force could give rise to competitive disadvantages (which might or might not benefit EU producers) and advocated various courses of action to avoid such distortions. In its conclusions of 16 December ([3]), the Council welcomed the Commission's communication. On the same day, it asked the Commission to give thought to setting up a system for the exchange of information between Member States on aspects of animal welfare ([4]).

Public health ([5])

General aspects

685.   *Community action programme.* On 23 September, the European Parliament and the Council adopted a programme of Community action in the field of public health (Table I). The three basic objectives of this programme, covered by a budget of EUR 312 million over the 2003–08 period, are: to improve health-related information and knowledge; to boost the capacity to react swiftly and in a coordinated manner to threats to health; and to promote health and prevent diseases. The programme should thus help to remedy inequalities in this field and encourage cooperation between the Member States with a view to providing a high level of health protection. It should also foster the development of a cross-sectoral approach to health issues, particularly by integrating the health dimension more fully into other Community policies and activities. Furthermore, eight public health programmes, shown in Table 14, expired at the end of the year.

([1]) Regulation (EC) No 1756/2002 amending Directive 70/524/EEC (OJ L 265, 3.10.2002; Bull. 9-2002, point 1.4.71).
([2]) COM(2002) 626; Bull. 11-2002, point 1.4.92.
([3]) Bull. 12-2002, point 1.4.103.
([4]) Bull. 12-2002, point 1.4.104.
([5]) http://europa.eu.int/comm/health/index_en.html.

686. Medical devices. On 26 June, the Council adopted conclusions on medical devices ([1]), underlining the importance of administrative cooperation between the Member States, and between the Member States and the Commission, with a view to achieving a common understanding about the management of this sector.

687. Patient mobility and healthcare. In its conclusions of 26 June ([2]), the Council welcomed the Commission's intention of taking further appropriate action in its work programme *(→ point 1094)* tying in with the programme of Community action in the field of public health. It also stressed the importance of establishing, in close collaboration with health ministers and other key stakeholders, a high-level process of reflection geared to enhancing cross-border cooperation between the Member States as regards healthcare and patient mobility.

688. Palliative care. In an own-initiative opinion delivered on 20 March, the European Economic and Social Committee called for the networking of information on voluntary activities, with particular reference to hospice work ([3]).

689. Obesity. On 2 December, the Council underlined the need for a cross-sectoral approach in preventing and responding to problems associated with obesity.

Legislation

690. Drugs. On 8 May, within the framework of the anti-drugs strategy (2000–04) ([4]), the Commission proposed that the Council should recommend to the Member States that they make provision for a number of services and facilities for drug prevention and treatment (Table II). The Council meanwhile adopted a resolution on the incorporation of drug prevention in school curricula *(→ point 499)*.

691. Tobacco. On 2 December, the Commission supplemented the existing measures on the prevention of smoking, in accordance with Article 152 of the EC Treaty, mainly by further prohibiting sales to minors, stepping up preventive and information campaigns, and restricting tobacco advertising, particularly with young people in mind (Table II).

692. Substances of human origin. Noting a number of shortcomings and discrepancies in the rules on the therapeutic use of substances of human origin, the

([1]) Bull. 6-2002, point 1.4.72.
([2]) Bull. 6-2002, point 1.4.71.
([3]) OJ C 125, 27.5.2002; Bull. 3-2002, point 1.3.17.
([4]) COM(1999) 239; 2000 General Report, point 479.

Commission put forward, on 19 June, a proposal for a directive aimed at establishing a legislative basis to ensure a high level of quality and safety of tissues and cells of human origin for the protection of recipients of these substances (Table I). On 27 December, the European Parliament and the Council adopted a directive aimed at setting standards of quality and safety for the collection, testing, processing, storage and distribution of human blood and blood components (Table I).

Implementation of programmes

TABLE 14

Financing

Action programme	Number of projects financed in 2002	Total amount of financing (EUR million)	Adoption of interim report on implementation
Health promotion, information, education and training	18	6.7	
Health monitoring	8	3.1	21 October COM(2002) 547; Bull. 10-2002, point 1.4.69
Injury prevention	20	2.7	10 October COM(2002) 552; Bull. 10-2002, point 1.4.68
Combating cancer	8	12.7	
Preventing drug dependence	14	5.1	
Pollution-related diseases	4	0.9	
Rare diseases	7	1.3	
Preventing AIDS and certain other communicable diseases	30	9.4	
Total	109	41.9	

Consumer protection (¹)

General aspects

693. Consumer policy strategy. In a communication adopted on 7 May (²), the Commission set out its new strategy for consumer policy (2002–06). The three objectives of this strategy are: to ensure a high common level of consumer protection; to guarantee effective enforcement of consumer protection rules; and to involve consumer organisations in EU policies. These objectives will be pursued through a range of measures over the next five years. A short-term rolling programme, to be regularly reviewed, is envisaged. The stated objectives are intended to make it easier to integrate consumer concerns into all other EU policies, to maximise the benefits of the single market for consumers and to prepare for enlargement. In its resolution of 2 December (³), the Council welcomed this strategy and called upon the Commission to implement it.

694. Green Paper. On 20 March, giving its opinion on the Green Paper on consumer protection (⁴), the European Economic and Social Committee was in favour of establishing a general requirement for fair commercial practices and of having a 'grey' list of unfair practices drawn up (⁵). In its communication of 11 June (⁶), the Commission pointed out that the wide response to the Green Paper had revealed a broad consensus on the need to reform EU consumer protection legislation by means of a framework directive, and it intended to carry out further consultation on the detail. The Commission, accordingly, set out an action plan together with an outline of the scope of the framework directive.

Safety of products and services

695. Products. Throughout 2002 (⁷), the Commission continued to prolong the validity of Decision 1999/815/EC (⁸) on measures prohibiting the placing on the market of toys and childcare articles intended to be placed in the mouth by children under three years of age made of soft PVC containing certain phthalates.

(¹) http://europa.eu.int/comm/consumers/index_en.html.
(²) COM(2002) 208; Bull. 5-2002, point 1.4.82.
(³) Bull. 12-2002, point 1.4.112.
(⁴) COM(2001) 531; 2001 General Report, point 761.
(⁵) OJ C 125, 27.5.2002; Bull. 3-2002, point 1.4.65.
(⁶) COM(2002) 289; Bull. 6-2002, point 1.4.78.
(⁷) Decisions 2002/152/EC (OJ L 50, 21.2.2002), 2002/372/EC (OJ L 133, 18.5.2002), 2002/660/EC (OJ L 224, 21.8.2002) and 2002/910/EC (OJ L 315, 19.11.2002).
(⁸) OJ L 315, 9.12.1999; 1999 General Report, point 581.

696. *Services.* The Commission launched an open consultation on a draft Parliament and Council report on the safety of services.

Consumers' economic and legal interests

697. *Financial services.* On 23 September, the European Parliament and the Council adopted a directive laying down provisions on the distance marketing of consumer financial services, with the aim of introducing a legal framework to enhance the operation of the internal market and consumer protection (Table I).

698. *Immovable properties.* Pointing to the problems frequently experienced by consumers in relation to their right to use immovable properties on a time-share basis, Parliament called on the Commission, on 4 July ([1]), to propose new legislative measures aimed at introducing unified European rules guaranteeing effective consumer protection.

699. *Contract law.* On 17 July ([2]), the European Economic and Social Committee gave its backing to the creation of a uniform, general European contract law, by means of a regulation, as proposed by the Commission in its communication on this subject ([3]).

700. *Consumer credit.* On 11 September, the Commission put forward a proposal for a new Community framework for consumer credit designed to achieve full harmonisation of the rules in this area (Table I). It drew upon various reports ([4]) concerning the application of the 1987 directive ([5]), which revealed that the Member States' laws differed greatly, and referred also to an opinion of the European Economic and Social Committee of 24 April ([6]) on household over-indebtedness.

Consumer representation, information and education

701. *Tourism.* In a resolution adopted on 16 January ([7]), the European Parliament considered that Directive 90/314/EEC ([8]) on package travel, package holidays and package tours should be updated to take account of developments in case-law. It also recommended that the directive's scope be widened in order

([1]) Bull. 7/8-2002, point 1.4.69.
([2]) OJ C 241, 7.10.2002; Bull. 7/8-2002, point 1.4.70.
([3]) OJ C 255, 13.9.2001; COM(2001) 398; 2001 General Report, point 764.
([4]) COM(95) 117; 1995 General Report, point 652; COM(96) 79; COM(97) 465; COM(97) 309.
([5]) Directive 87/102/EEC (OJ L 42, 12.2.1987).
([6]) OJ C 149, 21.6.2002; Bull. 4-2002, point 1.3.7.
([7]) OJ C 271 E, 7.11.2002; Bull. 1/2-2002, point 1.4.121.
([8]) OJ L 158, 23.6.1990; Twenty-fourth General Report, point 553.

to provide consumers with access to information on their rights, thereby guaranteeing better legal protection.

702.   *Video games.* On 1 March, the Council adopted a resolution on the protection of consumers, with particular reference to young people, through the labelling of certain video games and computer games according to age group, stressing the need to provide clear information as regards assessment of the contents of such games and subsequent rating ([1]).

703.   *Foodstuffs.* Information on the traceability and labelling of products intended for human or animal nutrition is contained in the 'Food safety' part of this section *(→ point 673).*

([1]) OJ C 65, 14.3.2002; Bull. 3-2002, point 1.4.66.

Chapter V

Enlargement (¹)

Section 1

Overview

704.   *The year 2002 marked a historic turning point in the EU enlargement process. Over the last three months of the year decisive progress was made over several stages which followed in quick succession. On 9 October, the Commission adopted an 'enlargement package 2002' comprising a strategy paper and, for each candidate country, a regular report on progress towards accession. On 24 and 25 October, the Brussels European Council approved the conclusions and recommendations set out in this package. On 12 and 13 December, the Copenhagen European Council, taking its cue from these recommendations, concluded accession negotiations with Cyprus, the Czech Republic, Estonia, Hungary, Latvia, Lithuania, Malta, Poland, Slovakia and Slovenia. The accession of these 10 countries should take place in 2004. The same European Council approved the Commission's communication on the 'road maps' for Bulgaria and Romania, including proposals for substantially increased pre-accession aid to those countries, and confirmed the goal of accepting them as fully-fledged EU members in 2007 subject to their progress on the accession criteria. On Turkey, the European Council indicated that if at its meeting in December 2004, it decided, on the basis of a Commission report and recommendation, that Turkey fulfilled the political criteria defined at Copenhagen in 1993 for the accession of third countries to the EU, it would then open negotiations with that country without delay.*

(¹) Further information is available on the Europa server (http://europa.eu.int/comm/enlargement/index.htm).

Section 2

Regular reports

705. Under the title 'Towards the enlarged Union', the Commission adopted, on 9 October, a communication consisting of a strategy paper and a report on the progress towards accession by each of the candidate countries ([1]). The communication includes a 'regular report' on each of the 13 countries concerned ([2]).

In its conclusions, the Commission considers that the regular reports show that all candidate countries have made considerable progress in implementing the accession criteria. In the Commission's assessment, Cyprus, the Czech Republic, Estonia, Hungary, Latvia, Lithuania, Malta, Poland, Slovakia and Slovenia fulfil the political criteria. Bearing in mind the progress achieved by those countries and their track record in implementing their commitments and taking account of their preparatory work in progress, the Commission considers that these countries will have fulfilled the economic criteria and those relating to the Community *acquis* and will be ready for EU membership from the beginning of 2004. It recommends concluding the accession negotiations with those countries by the end of the year with the aim of signing the Accession Treaty in the spring of 2003.

With Bulgaria and Romania having set 2007 as their indicative date for accession, the Commission will strongly support the two countries in achieving that objective, which will continue to be guided by the principles of differentiation and own merits. On the basis of the analysis of the regular reports for 2002, the Commission will propose detailed road maps for those two countries with increased pre-accession aid. These road maps were the subject of a communication adopted on 13 November ([3]). As regards Turkey, it stressed the significant headway already made in three major areas, but considered that substantial efforts were still necessary; in this context, and with a view to the next stage of Turkey's candidacy, the Commission recommended that the EU enhance its support for the country's pre-accession preparations and make significant funds available for that purpose.

([1]) COM(2002) 700; Bull. 10-2002, point 1.5.2 and Internet (http://europa.eu.int/comm/enlargement/report 2002/index.htm).
([2]) SEC(2002) 1400 (Bulgaria); SEC(2002) 1401 (Cyprus); SEC(2002) 1402 (Czech Republic); SEC(2002) 1403 (Estonia); SEC(2002) 1404 (Hungary); SEC(2002) 1405 (Latvia); SEC(2002) 1406 (Lithuania); SEC(2002) 1407 (Malta); SEC(2002) 1408 (Poland); SEC(2002) 1409 (Romania); SEC(2002) 1410 (Slovakia); SEC(2002) 1411 (Slovenia); SEC(2002) 1412 (Turkey).
([3]) Bull. 11-2002, point 1.5.3.

Generally speaking, the Commission will continue to pursue, for each of the candidate countries until their actual accession, implementation of the required reforms and respect for all the undertakings made as regards the Community *acquis*. The Commission proposed including in the Accession Treaty, as a provisional measure in addition to a general economic safeguard clause, two specific clauses concerning the functioning of the internal market and justice and home affairs.

On 9 October, Mr Prodi and Mr Verheugen presented the 'enlargement package' to the Parliament. On 22 October, the Council gave its assent on the conclusions and recommendations formulated by the Commission and the Brussels European Council on 24 and 25 October endorsed them ([1]).

([1]) Bull. 10-2002, points I.4 and I.5.

Section 3

Accession negotiations (¹)

706. *Ministerial conferences.* Several series of ministerial conferences were held during the year. The conference on 28 June (²), organised under the Spanish Presidency, was attended by all candidate countries with the exception of Bulgaria. The conference on 1 October (³), under the Danish Presidency, enabled a significant number of negotiating chapters to be provisionally closed with the 10 countries included in the first wave of accessions in 2004 *(→ point 705)*. After intense preparatory work at the level of deputies in October and November, and after a final ministerial conference on 9 and 10 December (⁴), those chapters still open were closed at the Copenhagen European Council on 12 and 13 December (⁵) after an agreement had been reached on financial matters and on specific subjects still in abeyance. For Bulgaria and Romania, a ministerial conference was held on 18 November; a total of 23 and 15 chapters were closed with those two countries respectively at the end of the Danish presidency.

Table 15 summarises the state of the negotiations at the end of the year for all candidate countries.

707. *State of progress of the negotiations.* In its resolution of 13 June (⁶), the European Parliament examined the progress of the negotiations both overall and by country, and considered that no additional obstacles should be put in the way of enlargement and that the EU should not request more than was necessary from the candidate countries as regards implementation of the *acquis*. The Seville European Council on 21 and 22 June (⁷) welcomed the decisive breakthroughs made in the negotiations during the first half of the year and considered that the process was entering its final phase. The Brussels European Council on 24 and 25 October (⁸) took decisions enabling the EU to draw up negotiating positions on the issues still outstanding after the ministerial conferences on 1 October *(→ point 706)*. In Copenhagen on 28 October (⁹), the leaders of the candidate countries met Mr Anders Fogh Rasmussen, Danish Prime

---

(¹) Further information is available on the Europa server (http://europa.eu.int/comm/enlargement/negotiations/index.htm).
(²) Bull. 6-2002, point 1.5.8.
(³) Bull. 10-2002, point 1.5.3.
(⁴) Bull. 12-2002, point 1.5.1.
(⁵) Bull. 12-2002, point I.3 to I.8.
(⁶) Bull. 6-2002, point 1.5.7.
(⁷) Bull. 6-2002, point I.8.
(⁸) Bull. 10-2002, points I.3 and I.4.
(⁹) Bull. 10-2002, point 1.5.6.

Minister and President of the European Council, Mr Javier Solana, High Representative for the CFSP, Mr Romano Prodi, President of the Commission, and Mr Günter Verheugen, Member of the Commission. At the meeting, the EU representatives presented the details of the financial framework for accession (→ *point 711)* and the negotiating positions adopted at the Brussels European Council.

708. *Agriculture.* In line with the road map endorsed at the Laeken European Council (¹), all remaining negotiating issues (direct payments, production quotas, rural development, etc.) arising under this chapter were addressed by the EU during the first half of the year. To that end, the Commission adopted on 30 January an 'issues paper' (²) to offer the Member States a basis for the discussion of the issues concerned, with a view to formulating new common positions. Rejecting in particular the idea of a two-speed common agricultural policy in the long-term, the Commission underlined the need to restructure agriculture and the agri-food industries in the candidate countries, and to improve competitiveness in these areas. On 13 June (³), Parliament welcomed the Commission's document.

709. *Financial framework.* On 30 January, the Commission also presented a communication on the common financial framework 2004–06 for the accession negotiations (→ *point 711)*.

710. *Administrative and judicial capacity.* On 5 June (⁴), on the basis of its strategy paper 'Making a success of enlargement' (⁵) and in line with the Laeken European Council (⁶) conclusions, the Commission launched, for each of the countries participating in the negotiations, an action plan to strengthen their administrative and judicial capacities. This initiative was welcomed by the Brussels European Council (⁷). For its part, in an opinion of 20 November (⁸), the Committee of the Regions felt it was necessary to establish close relations between the different levels of power in those countries and to consolidate their administrative capacity. The EU justice and home affairs ministers met their counterparts from the candidate countries on the fringes of the Council meeting on 14 and 15 October.

(¹) 2001 General Report, point 768; Bull. 12-2001, point I.6.
(²) SEC(2002) 95; Bull. 1/2-2002, point 1.5.1.
(³) Bull. 6-2002, point 1.5.6.
(⁴) COM(2002) 256; Bull. 6-2002, point 1.5.5.
(⁵) COM(2001) 700; 2001 General Report, point 767.
(⁶) Bull. 12-2001, point I.6.
(⁷) Bull. 10-2002, point I.5.
(⁸) Bull. 11-2002, point 1.5.8.

TABLE 15

State of the accession negotiations (December 2002)

Chapter	Cyprus	Czech Republic	Estonia	Hungary	Poland	Slovenia	Bulgaria	Latvia	Lithuania	Malta	Romania	Slovakia
1. Free movement of goods	x	x	x	x	x	x	x	x	x	x	*** o	x
2. Free movement of persons	x	x	x	x	x	x	x	x	x	x	*** o	x
3. Free movement of services	x	x	x	x	x	x	x	x	x	x	—	x
4. Free movement of capital	x	x	x	x	x	x	x	x	x	x	* o	x
5. Company law	x	x	x	x	x	x	x	x	x	x	x	x
6. Competition	x	x	x	x	x	x	x	x	x	x	o	x
7. Agriculture	x	x	x	x	x	x	*** o	x	x	x	**** o	x
8. Fisheries	x	x	x	x	x	x	x	x	x	x	x	x
9. Transport	x	x	x	x	x	x	*** o	x	x	x	* o	x
10. Taxation	x	x	x	x	x	x	* o	x	x	* o	*** o	x
11. Economic and monetary union	x	x	x	x	x	x	x	x	x	x	x	x
12. Statistics	x	x	x	x	x	x	x	x	x	x	x	x
13. Social policy	x	x	x	x	x	x	x	x	x	x	x	x
14. Energy	x	x	x	x	x	x	x	x	x	x	*** o	x
15. Industrial policy	x	x	x	x	x	x	x	x	x	x	**** x	x
16. Small and medium-sized enterprises	x	x	x	x	x	x	x	x	x	x	x	x
17. Science and research	x	x	x	x	x	x	x	x	x	x	x	x
18. Education and training	x	x	x	x	x	x	x	x	x	x	x	x
19. Telecommunications and information technology	x	x	x	x	x	x	x	x	x	x	x	x
20. Culture and audiovisual policy	x	x	x	x	x	x	x	x	x	x	x	x
21. Regional policy	x	x	x	x	x	x	** o	x	x	x	o	x
22. Environment	x	x	x	x	x	x	** o	x	x	x	*** o	x
23. Consumer and health protection	x	x	x	x	x	x	x	x	x	x	*** x	x
24. Justice and home affairs	x	x	x	x	x	x	* o	x	x	x	**** o	x
25. Customs union	x	x	x	x	x	x	x	x	x	x	x	x
26. External relations	x	x	x	x	x	x	x	x	x	x	x	x
27. Common foreign and security policy	x	x	x	x	x	x	** o	x	x	x	x o	x
28. Financial control	x	x	x	x	x	x	x	x	x	x	**** o	x
29. Budget	x	x	x	x	x	x	—	x	x	x	—	x
30. Institutions	x	x	x	x	x	x	x	x	x	x	x	x
31. Other	x	x	x	x	x	x	x	x	x	x	x	x
Chapters opened	31	31	31	31	31	31	30	31	31	31	28	31
Chapters closed at 31 December 2002	31	31	31	31	31	31	23	31	31	31	15	31

NB: o   = chapter opened, being negotiated.
     x   = chapter provisionally closed.
     *   = chapter opened for negotiation under the Swedish Presidency.
     **   = chapter opened for negotiation under the Belgian Presidency.
     ***   = chapter opened for negotiation under the Spanish Presidency.
     **** = chapter opened for negotiation under the Danish Presidency.
     —   = chapter not yet open.

Section 4

Pre-accession strategy (¹)

Accession partnerships and general matters

711.   Financial framework for the accession negotiations. On 30 January, to enable the Council to assess within a common framework, from the start of the Spanish Presidency, financial issues connected with the negotiations in a number of sensitive areas, the Commission presented a communication on the expenditure linked with enlargement over the period 2004–06 (²). The financial framework envisaged, which reflects the adjustments to the scenario agreed at the Berlin European Council in 1999 under Agenda 2000 (³), provides for commitment appropriations totalling EUR 40.160 billion and payment appropriations totalling EUR 28.019 billion. The fields covered are agriculture, structural measures and the budget allocation for internal policies and funds specific to the settlement of the Cypriot question. A provisional compensation regime is also recommended so that no new Member State finds itself in a significantly less favourable budgetary situation than in the year preceding enlargement.

This approach by the Commission was endorsed by the Committee of the Regions in an own-initiative opinion of 16 May (⁴). Parliament also gave its opinion on this communication in a resolution of 13 June (⁵). The Brussels European Council on 24 and 25 October highlighted certain elements of this financial framework, namely direct payments, the overall level of allocations for structural measures, own resources and possible budget imbalances (⁶). It also stated that the Union's expenditure should continue to respect the imperatives of budgetary discipline and effectiveness and stressed that the enlarged Union should have sufficient resources to ensure smooth functioning of its policies to the benefit of all its citizens. Following the provisions thus agreed at the Brussels European Council and subsequent adjustments resulting from the negotiations, the EU Heads of State or Government formulated a final offer at the Copenhagen European Council on 12 and 13 December (⁷). This offer, amounting to

---

(¹) Further information is available on the Europa server (http://europa.eu.int/comm/enlargement/pas/index.htm).
(²) SEC(2002) 102; Bull. 1/2-2002, point 1.5.6.
(³) 1999 General Report, point 4; Bull. 3-1999, points I.5 to I.8.
(⁴) OJ C 287, 14.11.2002; Bull. 5-2002, point 1.5.6.
(⁵) Bull. 6-2002, point 1.5.13.
(⁶) Bull. 10-2002, points I.6 to I.9.
(⁷) Bull. 12-2002, point I.14.

EUR 40.8 billion, a figure very close to that proposed initially by the Commission, was accepted by the candidate countries.

712.   *Updating the accession partnerships*. Following the political agreement it reached in December 2001 (¹), the Council formally adopted, on 28 January, a series of decisions updating the principles, priorities, intermediate objectives and terms of the accession partnerships with all the candidate countries other than Turkey (²).

713.   *Macroeconomic and financial situation of the candidate countries*. In response to a request by the Council (³), the Commission tabled, on 12 March, a report (⁴) contributing to the dialogue with the candidate countries *(→ point 75)* by identifying the risks and sources of vulnerability for their economic integration and helping define strategies at macroeconomic level and for the stability of their financial sector. The report raises issues such as real convergence of the candidate countries with the current Member States, economic policy, budgetary policy, exchange rates, participation in economic and monetary union, restructuring and privatisation in the banking field and the business environment. In an opinion of 17 July on Romania's progress towards accession (⁵), the European Economic and Social Committee voiced its concern at the situation in that country while recognising the progress made towards macroeconomic stabilisation. In a similar opinion of 18 July on Slovenia (⁶), it welcomed that country's efforts to catch up with the European Union in all fields and the manner in which the transition process in the economic and social fields had unfolded; it considered, however, that linguistic minorities (Italian and Hungarian) could receive greater recognition, as could Slovenes in Austria and Italy. In an opinion of 18 September (⁷), it welcomed the swift progress made by Latvia and Lithuania on the road to accession; it stressed the need, however, for Latvia to improve the effectiveness and transparency of its public administration and adopt a rural development policy, and stressed that combating unemployment should be a priority, particularly in Lithuania. In opinions of 12 December, the European Economic and Social Committee gave its view on the economic and social consequences of enlargement in the candidate countries (⁸) and on its effects on the single market (⁹). On 5 November, the ministers for the economy and finance of the European Union and the candidate

---

(¹) 2001 General Report, point 778.
(²) Decisions 2002/83/EC (Bulgaria), 2002/84/EC (Cyprus), 2002/85/EC (Czech Republic), 2002/86/EC (Estonia), 2002/87/EC (Hungary), 2002/88/EC (Latvia), 2002/89/EC (Lithuania), 2002/90/EC (Malta), 2002/91/EC (Poland), 2002/92/EC (Romania), 2002/93/EC (Slovakia), 2002/94/EC (Slovenia) (OJ L 44, 14.2.2002; Bull. 1/2-2002, point 1.5.3).
(³) Bull. 11-2000, point 1.5.10.
(⁴) COM(2002) 135; Bull. 3-2002, point 1.5.1.
(⁵) OJ C 241, 7.10.2002; Bull. 7/8-2002, point 1.5.2.
(⁶) OJ C 241, 7.10.2002; Bull. 7/8-2002, point 1.5.3.
(⁷) Bull. 9-2002, point 1.5.7.
(⁸) Bull. 12-2002, point 1.5.3.
(⁹) Bull. 12-2002, point 1.5.4.

countries adopted joint conclusions recognising the progress made in 2002 by the candidate countries towards strengthening their capacity in view of participating in multilateral surveillance of the Union and coordination of their economic policies ([1]).

714. *Communication strategy* ([2]). In a report of 5 June entitled 'Explaining Europe's enlargement' ([3]), the Commission presented a panorama of the activities carried out under the strategy. It traced the broad lines for the future, notably in terms of concerted and decentralised cooperation in applying the strategy with the current and future Member States and the Community institutions. On 17 September and 12 November, the Commission held meetings with the national officials concerned to discuss coordination of communication strategy to be implemented over the period of Accession Treaty ratification.

715. *Frontier regions.* The Committee of the Regions, on 13 March ([4]), then Parliament, on 13 June ([5]), welcomed the Commission's communication of July 2001 on the impact of enlargement on regions bordering the candidate countries ([6]). Parliament supported the new guidelines for Community structural policy instruments for those regions and the transitional measures on free movement of workers and services. On 29 November, the Commission presented a progress report on the measures advocated in the above communication ([7]).

716. *Transport.* In an own-initiative opinion of 19 September on transport and enlargement ([8]), the European Economic and Social Committee, stressing the importance of the impact of integration of the Community *acquis* and the consequences of the accession of the candidate countries, said they had to be taken into account in the field of infrastructure and the environment.

Europe agreements and other agreements

717. *Industrial products.* The additional protocols to the Europe agreement concluded respectively with Latvia and Lithuania and concerning conformity assessment and acceptance of products were signed on 21 May and concluded on 25 June (Table III). A similar protocol with Slovenia was signed on 26 November (Table III), while those with Slovakia (Table III) and Estonia (Table III) were proposed for signing by the Commission. More generally, the

---

[1] Bull. 11-2002, point 1.5.5.
[2] http://europa.eu.int/comm/enlargement/communication/.
[3] COM(2002) 281; Bull. 6-2002, point 1.5.2.
[4] OJ C 192, 18.8.2002; Bull. 3-2002, point 1.3.71.
[5] Bull. 6-2002, point 1.5.4.
[6] COM(2001) 437; 2001 General Report, point 776.
[7] COM(2002) 660; Bull. 11-2002, point 1.5.2.
[8] Bull. 9-2002, point 1.5.1.

Council adopted, on 19 July, negotiating directives for draft agreements with the candidate countries on the conformity assessment of industrial products and on mutual recognition (Table III).

718. *Agricultural products*. As part of the negotiation process, the Commission presented, on 30 January, a discussion paper on the integration of the new Member States into the common agricultural policy *(→ point 708)*.

Pending the entry into force of a new additional protocol to the Europe agreement with Estonia, on 27 June the Council adopted, on an autonomous and transitional basis, a regulation ([1]) enabling swift implementation, from 1 July, of the results of the negotiations on agricultural tariff concessions agreed under the protocol, for which, on 21 October, the Commission proposed the conclusion (Table III). A similar approach was followed, on 22 July, for Latvia ([2]) and Lithuania ([3]), and, on 29 July, for Hungary ([4]). On 9 July, the Commission proposed concluding an additional protocol adapting trade aspects of the Europe agreement with Poland to take account of the outcome of the negotiations on new reciprocal agricultural concessions between the parties (Table III). The Commission proposed a similar formula for Slovenia on 6 November (Table III), Latvia on 22 November (Table III), the Czech Republic on 26 November (Table III), Lithuania on 6 December (Table III), Hungary (Table III) and Slovakia on 10 December (Table III) and Bulgaria on 29 December (Table III). At its meeting on 19 and 20 December, the Council decided to conclude a similar protocol with Romania with a view to adopting all the agricultural trade concessions agreed hitherto between the parties (Table III).

719. *Processed agricultural products*. In the framework of the negotiating round on improving trade arrangements for these products, which in 2001 already produced results for a number of candidate countries ([5]), a new liberalisation decision was taken in 2002 as regards Hungary ([6]). On 8 October, the Council authorised the Commission to negotiate new mutual concessions with each of the 10 associated countries of central and eastern Europe with a view to improving trade arrangements in the sector and furthering gradual economic convergence between the EU and the candidate countries ([7]). On 5 November, the Council adopted negotiating directives with a view to similar agreements with Cyprus and Malta (Table III). On 10 December, the Commission proposed a regulation aimed at applying autonomous measures for processed agricultural products originating in Poland ([8]).

([1]) Regulation (EC) No 1151/2002 (OJ L 170, 29.6.2002; Bull. 6-2002, point 1.5.9).
([2]) Regulation (EC) No 1362/2002 (OJ L 198, 27.7.2002; Bull. 7/8-2002, point 1.5.6).
([3]) Regulation (EC) No 1361/2002 (OJ L 198, 27.7.2002; Bull. 7/8-2002, point 1.5.6).
([4]) Regulation (EC) No 1408/2002 (OJ L 205, 2.8.2002; Bull. 7/8-2002, point 1.5.5).
([5]) 2001 General Report, point 780.
([6]) Decision No 2/2002 of the EU–Hungary Association Council (OJ L 172, 2.7.2002).
([7]) Bull. 10-2002, point 1.5.7.
([8]) COM(2002) 706 and Bull. 12-2002, point 1.5.12.

720. Fishery products. Additional protocols to the Europe agreements were concluded with certain candidate countries *(→ point 444).*

721. Information society. On 21 October, the Council authorised the Commission to negotiate with the countries of central and eastern Europe and with Cyprus and Malta agreements establishing an exchange of information on technical regulations applying to information society services (Table III). More generally, the candidate countries started, with the Commission's assistance, implementing the action plan '*eEurope +*', launched at the Göteborg European Council in June 2001 ([1]) and designed to speed up reform and modernisation of their economies, improve overall competitiveness and strengthen social cohesion *(→ point 350).*

722. Transport. The agreement concluded in 2001 with Romania on transport of goods by road and the promotion of combined transport was the subject of an implementing regulation *(→ point 668).*

723. Customs. On 17 October, the Commission proposed concluding an additional protocol to the association agreement with Malta on mutual administrative assistance in the customs field (Table III).

724. Candidate countries' participation in Community programmes. The association councils set up by the Europe agreements took new decisions relating to the participation of all the candidate countries in the multiannual programme for enterprise and entrepreneurship; on 27 May, the Council concluded an additional protocol to the association agreement with Malta aimed at involving it in the fifth Community framework programme in the field of research and technological development *(→ point 313).* On 29 October, memoranda of understanding were signed with a view to involving the countries of central and eastern Europe, Cyprus, Malta and Turkey in the sixth framework research programme (Table III). In a resolution of 20 November, Parliament welcomed the participation of the candidate countries in these research programmes ([2]). Also on 20 November, the Commission approved a protocol of agreement relating to the participation of Bulgaria, Cyprus, Czech Republic, Estonia, Latvia, Lithuania, Romania and Slovakia in the Community programme for the interchange of electronic data between administrations (IDA) ([3]) *(→ point 285).* More generally, in 2002, new legal frameworks establishing the general conditions and arrangements for participation of the candidate countries in Community programmes were put in place.

([1]) 2001 General Report, point 379.
([2]) Bull. 11-2002, point 1.5.9.
([3]) Bull. 11-2002, point 1.5.10.

725. *Joint bodies*. Meetings of the association councils, association committees and parliamentary committees also created by the Europe agreements are described in the subsection 'Bilateral issues' (→ *points 733 to 745*).

Financial and technical assistance

726. *Management of pre-accession aid*. The approach developed since 1999 ([1]) and designed to enable the candidate countries to manage themselves, as far as possible, the pre-accession aid without involving the Commission entered into its active phase as part of the system of extended decentralisation of management responsibilities (EDIS). To facilitate this decentralisation process, the Commission allocated an overall budget of EUR 6 million from the Phare appropriations and signed financing memoranda with each of the 10 countries concerned during the year. Cyprus and Malta also made considerable progress on greater autonomy of management of pre-accession aid. In an own-initiative opinion of 19 September ([2]), the European Economic and Social Committee called for greater transparency of financing and obligatory participation of the social partners and other elements of civil society in the beneficiary countries in the process of implementing the Phare (→ *point 727*), Sapard (→ *point 728*) and ISPA (→ *point 729*) programmes.

727. *Phare* ([3]). The programme's budget amounted to EUR 1.698 billion in 2002. The operations financed were:

- national programmes: EUR 1.168 billion, of which EUR 95 million for Bulgaria, EUR 30 million for Estonia, EUR 112 million for Hungary, EUR 32 million for Latvia, EUR 62 million for Lithuania, EUR 394 million for Poland, EUR 85 million for the Czech Republic, EUR 266 million for Romania, EUR 57 million for Slovakia and EUR 35 million for Slovenia;

- cross-border cooperation: EUR 163 million;

- phasing-out of nuclear plants: EUR 90 million (EUR 80 million for Lithuania and EUR 10 million for Slovakia);

- regional and horizontal programmes: EUR 277 million.

([1]) Council Regulation (EC) No 1266/1999 (OJ L 161, 26.6.1999; 1999 General Report, point 605) for the 10 Phare countries and Regulation (EC) No 555/2000 (OJ L 68, 16.3.2000; 2000 General Report, point 708) for Cyprus and Malta.
([2]) Bull. 9-2002, point 1.5.4.
([3]) http://europa.eu.int/comm/enlargement/pas/phare/index.htm.

In September, the Commission defined a strategy to enable the gradual phasing out of the Phare programme for countries actually joining the European Union and reviewed the rules applicable to the programme. In accordance with its strategy paper of November 2001, the Commission established with each of the countries concerned an action plan designed to strengthen their administrative and legal capacities *(→ point 710)*.

728. *Special accession programme for agriculture and rural development (Sapard)* (¹). On 30 July, the Commission adopted the report on the implementation of the programme in 2001 (²); for the first time, the report includes contributions from several beneficiary countries. In a resolution of 13 June (³) concerning the Commission report on the execution of the programme in 2000 (⁴), Parliament bemoaned the delay in setting up the programme. It called for greater support for the creation of alternative employment in the candidate countries' rural areas and a modification in the financial perspectives with a view to higher pre-accession aid for those areas.

In 2002, a budget of EUR 554.5 million was allocated to this instrument. Following the accreditation of their respective agencies and careful examination on the ground by Commission officials, the Czech Republic and Slovakia on 15 April, Poland on 2 July, Romania on 31 July, and Hungary on 26 November were given responsibility for managing programme funds. A seminar was organised in June with the participation of the 10 eligible countries on important aspects of the management (follow-up and assessment, financial management and control, and decentralisation). The monitoring committees set up in each country continued their tasks throughout the year with the participation of Commission representatives as advisers.

On 18 September, the Commission proposed adapting Regulation (EC) No 1268/1999 establishing Sapard to enable the Czech Republic and Slovakia, affected by the serious floods in August, to benefit from more favourable financing conditions (Table II). In an own-initiative opinion of 24 October (⁵), the European Economic and Social Committee welcomed this initiative while deploring the start-up problems and administrative weaknesses. On 22 October (⁶), the Commission proposed signing an annual financing agreement with each of the 10 countries eligible for the programme in 2002 in order to speed up the release of funds under the multiannual programming.

(¹) http://europa.eu.int/comm/enlargement/pas/sapard.htm.
(²) COM(2002) 434; Bull. 7/8-2002, point 1.5.9.
(³) Bull. 6-2002, point 1.5.14.
(⁴) COM(2001) 341; 2001 General Report, point 790.
(⁵) Bull. 10-2002, point 1.5.16.
(⁶) SEC(2002) 1115; Bull. 10-2002, point 1.5.15.

729. *Instrument for structural policies for pre-accession (ISPA)* (^{1}). On 30 October, the Commission adopted a first annual report on implementation of this instrument in 2001 (^{2}). In order to improve the implementation of the instrument, several seminars and training courses were organised for the recipient countries to enable their officials to take cognisance of correct award procedures and project preparation.

A breakdown by candidate country of commitments made in 2002 under the ISPA programme is given in Table 16.

TABLE 16

Commitments in 2002 — ISPA

(million EUR)

Candidate country	ISPA
Bulgaria	104.571
Czech Republic	80.534
Estonia	30.362
Latvia	46.549
Lithuania	61.180
Hungary	94.120
Poland	362.785
Romania	256.554
Slovenia	16.645
Slovakia	54.135
Other	1.608
Total	1 109.044

730. *Pre-accession aid to Turkey.* On 20 December, the Commission adopted guidelines for implementing Regulation (EC) No 2500/2001 concerning pre-accession financial assistance for Turkey (^{3}) and gave a legal basis to the first aid programme agreed under this heading. As for all the other accession candidates, financial aid is now targeted on priorities identified in the 'partnership for accession' (^{4}). Following the decision to establish a system of decentralised implementation of aid to Turkey, the Turkish Government started putting in place the relevant structures. In 2002, Turkey received assistance amounting to EUR 142 million. The inclusion of the Commission's representation in Ankara in the first wave of decentralisation of the management of Commission aid to its delegations *(→ point 1152)* enabled the programme to be implemented. In a strategy paper of 9 October *(→ point 705)*, the Commission advocated a doubling of the resources thus allocated up to 2006.

(^{1}) http://europa.eu.int/comm/regional_policy/funds/ispa/ispa_fr.htm.
(^{2}) COM(2002) 596; Bull. 10-2002, point 1.5.17.
(^{3}) OJ L 342, 27.12.2001; 2001 General Report, point 788.
(^{4}) Council Decision 2001/235/EC (OJ L 85, 24.3.2001; 2001 General Report, point 773).

731.   *Interventions of the European Investment Bank (EIB).* In 2002, the EIB granted loans to the candidate countries amounting to EUR 3.6 billion.

732.   *Macrofinancial assistance.* Information on this form of aid to certain candidate countries can be found in Section 1 ('Economic and monetary policy') of Chapter III *(→ points 78 to 82).*

Bilateral issues

733.   The Association Council and Association Committee with Bulgaria met respectively on 18 November in Brussels ([^1]) and 11 July in Sofia. The Joint Parliamentary Committee met in Brussels on 3 and 4 June and in Sofia on 29 and 30 October. On 11 and 12 April, Ms Loyola de Palacio, Commission Vice-President, went to Sofia where she had talks with President Georgi Parvanov, Mr Simeon Saxe-Coburg Gotha, Prime Minister, and several government ministers. On 6 September ([^2]), Ms Meglena Kuneva, Bulgarian Minister for European Integration, and Mr Nikolai Vasilev, Deputy Prime Minister and Minister for the Economy, met Mr Verheugen. On 2 October ([^3]), Mr Verheugen and Mr Prodi met President Parvanov. Ms Diamantopoulou went to Sofia on 29 October where she met Ms Lidiya Shuleva, Bulgarian Labour Minister ([^4]).

734.   The Association Council and Association Committee with Estonia met, respectively, on 19 February and 10 June in Brussels. The Joint Parliamentary Committee met in Tallinn on 27 May and in Brussels on 9 December. On 9 January, Mr Toomas Hendrik Ilves, Estonian Foreign Minister, met Mr Verheugen and Mr Patten and, on 10 January, Mr Hendrik Hololei, the Economy Minister, saw Ms de Palacio and Mr Bolkestein. On 6 and 7 March, Mr Siim Kallas, Prime Minister, met Mr Verheugen and Mr Prodi. On 18 September, Mr Fischler went to Estonia where he had talks with Agriculture Minister Jaanus Marrandi ([^5]). On 19 September, Mr Liikanen also paid a visit to Estonia. On 23 October, Ms Kristiina Ojuland, Foreign Minister, saw Mr Verheugen. On 28 November, President Arnold Rüütel was received by Mr Prodi and by Mr Verheugen.

735.   The Association Council and the Association Committee with Hungary met on 18 November ([^6]) and 24 May in Brussels. The Joint Parliamentary Committee met on 25 and 26 February in Budapest and on 7 and 8 November in

[^1]: Bull. 11-2002, point 1.5.18.
[^2]: Bull. 9-2002, point 1.5.5.
[^3]: Bull. 10-2002, point 1.5.18.
[^4]: Bull. 10-2002, point 1.5.19.
[^5]: Bull. 9-2002, point 1.5.6.
[^6]: Bull. 11-2002, point 1.5.19.

Brussels. Mr Prodi met the Hungarian Prime Minister, Mr Victor Orban, on 20 February, and his successor, Mr Peter Medgyessy, on 16 September, and met President Ferenc Madl in Strasbourg on 22 October. Mr Verheugen and Ms Wallström went to Budapest on 15 and 16 July and from 2 to 4 October respectively.

736. The Association Council and the Association Committee with Latvia met on 19 February and 12 June in Brussels. The Joint Parliamentary Committee met on 17 and 18 February in Riga. On 14 and 15 June, Mr Verheugen went to Riga, where he met Prime Minister Andris Berzins and other members of the government. On 17 September, Mr Fischler visited Latvia where he saw the President, Ms Vaira Vike-Freiberga, and Prime Minister Berzins (¹). On 3 October, President Vike-Freiberga met Mr Prodi and Mr Verheugen. Mr Verheugen also met Ms Sandra Kalniete, Foreign Minister, in Brussels, on 2 December.

737. The Association Council and the Association Committee with Lithuania met on 19 February and 14 June in Brussels. The Joint Parliamentary Committee met on 27 and 28 May in Vilnius and Kaunas and on 11 and 12 November in Brussels. The Joint Consultative Committee, newly created at the level of representatives of socioeconomic groups, went to Vilnius in December. Mr Cox, President of Parliament, visited Lithuania on 2 and 3 May. Mr Monti and Mr Verheugen visited the country from 15 to 18 June, and on 4 and 5 July. Mr Verheugen met Mr Valdas Adamkus, the President of Lithuania, and Mr Algirdas Brazauskas, Prime Minister, and Mr Antanas Valionis, Foreign Minister. Mr Brazauskas and Mr Verheugen met again in Brussels on 24 October.

738. The Association Council and the Association Committee with Poland met on 18 November (²) and 29 May in Brussels. The Joint Parliamentary Committee met on 18 April in Warsaw and on 4 November in Brussels. On 12 and 13 September, Mr Fischler visited Poland where he met President Aleksander Kwasniewski, Mr Jaroslaw Kalinowski, Deputy Prime Minister and Minister of Agriculture and Rural Development, Ms Danuta Hübner, Secretary of State for Foreign Affairs, and members of the Parliament and agricultural and food industry representatives (³). Many other visits to both sides took place throughout the year, notably a visit to Poland by Mr Kinnock, and a meeting in Brussels between Mr Prodi and Mr Leszek Miller, Polish Prime Minister.

739. The Association Council and the Association Committee with the Czech Republic met on 18 November in Brussels (⁴) and on 19 April in Prague. The Joint Parliamentary Committee met on 22 April in Prague and on 26 November

(¹) Bull. 9-2002, point 1.5.6.
(²) Bull. 11-2002, point 1.5.20.
(³) Bull. 9-2002, point 1.5.8.
(⁴) Bull. 11-2002, point 1.5.21.

in Strasbourg. On 23 and 24 May, Mr Milos Zeman, Prime Minister, visited Brussels, where he saw Mr Prodi and Mr Verheugen and Mr Solana, High Representative for the CFSP([1]). Mr Prodi and Ms Wallström went to the Czech Republic on 16 August during the floods which seriously affected the country. On 28 and 29 August, Mr Verheugen visited Prague, where he met President Vaclav Havel and Mr Vladimir Spidla, Prime Minister. Mr Spidla was received in turn on 25 November in Brussels, where he met Mr Prodi and Mr Verheugen.

740.   The Association Council and the Association Committee with Romania met on 12 March and on 3 December in Brussels. The Joint Parliamentary Committee met on 15 and 16 April in Brussels and on 4 and 5 November in Bucharest. Mr Solbes Mira, Mr Barnier and Ms Diamantopoulou went to Romania from 18 to 20 May, on 10 and 11 October, and on 28 October, respectively. The Romanian Prime Minister, Mr Adrian Nastase, saw Mr Verheugen on 16 April, and Mr Prodi, together with Mr Verheugen, on 26 September in Brussels.

741.   The Association Council and the Association Committee with Slovakia met on 26 June in Luxembourg and on 18 December in Bratislava. The Joint Parliamentary Committee met on 5 and 6 March in Brussels and on 15 and 16 October in Kosice. From 21 to 23 February, Mr Verheugen visited Slovakia, where he met Mr Mikulas Dzurinda, Prime Minister.

742.   The Association Council and the Association Committee with Slovenia met on 26 June in Luxembourg and on 15 February in Brussels. The Joint Parliamentary Committee met on 20 June in Brussels and on 3 December in Ljubljana. On 10 and 11 June, Mr Barnier visited Slovenia, where he met Mr Janez Drnovsek, Prime Minister, and Mr Janez Potocnik, Mr Dimitrij Rupel and Ms Tea Petrin, European Affairs, Foreign Affairs and Economy Ministers respectively. On 15 April, Ms Diamantopoulou went to Slovenia for talks with Mr Milan Kucan, President, Mr Borut Pahor, Speaker of the Slovenian Parliament, and Mr Vlado Dimovski, Minister for Labour, the Family and Social Affairs. On 22 and 23 April, Mr Busquin was received by Mr Rupel, Foreign Minister, and by Ms Lucija Cok, Education, Science and Sports Minister. Mr Liikanen took part, in June, in the 'eEurope 2005' conference and met Slovenian European Affairs Minister, Mr Potocnik, and Information Society Minister, Mr Pavel Gantar.

743.   The Association Council with Cyprus met on 22 and 23 May in Cyprus and on 4 and 5 November in Brussels. On 27 and 28 June, Ms Wallström went to Cyprus, where she was received by President Glafkos Clerides, Mr Costas Themistocleous, Cypriot Agriculture Minister, and Mr George Vassiliou, chief

---

([1]) Bull. 5-2002, point 1.5.7.

negotiator for the accession of Cyprus to the EU ([1]). From 16 to 18 November, Ms de Palacio also visited Cyprus, where she met Mr Clerides, and Mr Averof Neophytou, Communications Minister, and Mr Nicos Rolandis, Minister of Trade, Industry and Tourism.

744.   The Association Committee with Malta met on 29 November in Brussels. The Joint Parliamentary Committee met on 29 and 30 April in Valletta and on 28 and 29 November in Brussels. Mr Verheugen went to Malta on 17 October, where he met the Prime Minister, Mr Edward Fenech Adami.

745.   The Association Council with Turkey met on 15 April in Luxembourg. The Joint Parliamentary Committee met on 18 June in Brussels. On 19 February, Mr Verheugen saw Mr Nihat Akyol, head of the Turkish mission to the European Union ([2]). On 5 September, he met Mr Sükrü Sina Gürel, Turkish Foreign Minister. On 12 September, Mr Mesut Yilmaz, Deputy Prime Minister, came to Brussels, where he saw Mr Prodi and Mr Verheugen ([3]).

([1]) Bull. 6-2002, point 1.5.15.
([2]) Bull.1/2-2002, point 1.5.9.
([3]) Bull. 1/2-2002, point 1.5.10.

Section 5

Regional cooperation

746.   The Commission attended the 11th ministerial meeting of the Council of the Baltic Sea States (CBSS) in Svetlogorsk (Russia) and the fourth summit of the Baltic Sea States in St Petersburg. It also took part in the third ministerial meeting of the Arctic Council, which met in Inari (Finland). Commission representatives were also in regular attendance at meetings of the CBSS Committee of Senior Officials, the Barents Euro-Arctic Council [1] and the Arctic Council. Two conferences on the northern dimension were organised by the Danish Presidency of the EU. The first was held in Ilulissat (Greenland) in August and provided a first opportunity to discuss the second action plan 2004–06 for this geopolitical dimension. The second, held in Luxembourg in October, saw the adoption of the guidelines for the action plan drawn up jointly by the Danish Presidency and the Commission, on the basis of the Ilulissat conclusions. The Commission also attended the annual ministerial meeting of the Adriatic and Ionian Council in Athens, during which an agreement was reached to rationalise and improve the division of work between the various regional initiatives on south-east Europe.

[1] Denmark, Finland, Iceland, Norway, Russia, Sweden.

Chapter VI

Role of the Union in the world

Section 1

Common foreign and security policy (CFSP) (¹)

Overview

747. *The CFSP underwent further development in the light of decisions taken by the various bodies of the EU institutions concerned. In the external relations field, the Barcelona European Council underlined its determination to develop the Euro-Mediterranean partnership, particularly on the financial front, and called repeatedly on the Israelis and Palestinians to take immediate and effective steps to put an end to the violence. Committed to stepping up the EU's role in combating terrorism and recognising the important contribution of the CFSP, including the European security and defence policy (ESDP), the Seville European Council called for greater account to be taken of the capabilities required to combat terrorism. It also reaffirmed that the European Union was now in a position to take charge of crisis management operations, as its decision to conduct the police mission in Bosnia and Herzegovina in particular demonstrated. It pointed out that ESDP structures and decision-making procedures had been successfully tested during the first crisis management exercise conducted by the Union. In its contribution to the work of the Convention on the Future of the European Union, the Commission put forward its idea of a project based on a number of core tasks, including enabling the Union to exercise the responsibilities of a world power, and advocated reforms to that effect. The Union continued to develop and intensify political dialogue with certain countries and country groupings with a view to extending its action in the areas of human rights and fundamental freedoms and encouraging as many States as possible to ratify the Rome Statute on setting up the International Criminal Court. The EU also continued its policy of promoting peace by offering to mediate, contributing to the resumption of dialogue between warring parties and providing humanitarian aid to civilian populations.*

(¹) Further information can be found on the Internet (http://ue.eu.int/Pesc/default.asp?lang=en).

General issues

748. Annual report on the CFSP. During its meeting of 25 and 26 April, by way of complement to the chapter on external relations of the annual report of the European Council on the progress of the European Union in 2001, the Council presented a report to the European Parliament concerning the main aspects and basic choices of the CFSP ([1]). In a resolution on 26 September on the progress achieved in the implementation of the CFSP ([2]), Parliament proposed a comprehensive notion of security for the EU, which would involve instruments as diverse as aid, trade and diplomacy and make conflict prevention a guiding principle of EU foreign policy action. It noted that the events of 11 September 2001 in the United States had speeded up further development of the CFSP and ESDP and their implementation in the context of multilateral crisis management. Parliament also reviewed the main foreign policy issues.

749. Conflict prevention. As part of the implementation of the EU programme for the prevention of violent conflicts endorsed by the European Council in Göteborg in June 2001 ([3]), the Council adopted conclusions on 28 January ([4]) in which it reviewed potential conflicts in order to set clear political priorities for preventive actions; on 17 June, it approved a Presidency report on implementation of the programme ([5]) which was subsequently presented to the European Council in Seville; in its conclusions of 22 July ([6]), it identified specific regional and cross-cutting issues requiring close attention. Further information on conflict prevention can be found below in the section on European security and defence policy *(→ point 755)*.

750. CFSP management. In its conclusions of 5 March ([7]) on Court of Auditors' Special Report No 13/2001 on the CFSP ([8]), the Council admitted that there were still some shortcomings in the management of the policy and noted that additional efforts would have to be made, particularly to ensure sufficient flexibility in the CFSP budget.

751. Future of the CFSP. In its communication of 22 May entitled 'A project for the European Union', a contribution to the work of the Convention on the Future of the European Union *(→ point 12)*, the Commission noted that exercising the responsibilities of a world power was one of the EU's three core tasks. To realise that objective, the Commission recommended the following reforms

---

([1]) Bull. 4-2002, point 1.6.1.
([2]) Bull. 9-2002, point 1.6.2.
([3]) Bull. 6-2001, points I.29 and I.30.
([4]) Bull. 1/2-2002, point 1.6.5.
([5]) Bull. 6-2002, point 1.9.8.
([6]) Bull. 7/8-2002, point 1.6.3.
([7]) Bull. 3-2002, point 1.6.4.
([8]) OJ C 338, 30.11.2001; 2001 General Report, point 1219.

and innovations to be undertaken in accordance with arrangements and a time-table to be determined: conferring upon the High Representative for the CFSP a capacity for ensuring overall consistency of political initiative and a leading role in crisis management; merging the functions of High Representative and Commissioner for External Relations within the Commission; giving foreign policy the necessary resources; ruling out the use of unanimity and making majority decisions possible without prejudice to specific provisions which might apply for security and defence; ensuring coherent single representation of collective interests by the High Representative/Commissioner for External Relations.

752. *Special European Union representatives.* In its conclusions of 13 May (¹), recalling the essential role of the European Union special representatives (EUSRs) in the implementation of EU policy on the ground, the Council agreed on the principle of the extension of the functions of the EUSRs for the Former Yugoslav Republic of Macedonia *(→ point 868)* and Afghanistan *(→ point 948)*.

Common foreign policy

753.   *Common positions and joint actions* (²). In 2002, the Council:

- adopted eight joint actions concerning the western Balkans, including Joint Action 2002/210/CFSP concerning the European Union Police Mission (EUPM) in Bosnia and Herzegovina and Joint Action 2002/211/CFSP concerning the appointment of the European Union special representative to that country *(→ point 875)*;

- defined Common Position 2002/400/CFSP concerning the temporary reception by Member States of the European Union of certain Palestinians *(→ point 895)* and Common Position 2002/599/CFSP concerning the derogations from the embargo with regard to Iraq *(→ point 899)* and adopted Joint Action 2002/965/CFSP extending the mandate of the EU special representative for the Middle East peace process *(→ point 889)*;

- adopted Joint Action 2002/373/CFSP regarding an OSCE observer mission on the border between Georgia and Russia *(→ point 917)*;

(¹) Bull. 5-2002, point 1.6.1.
(²) Joint actions and common positions concerning a specific geographical area are covered more fully in the chapter section on the geographical area in question; this section simply lists them and gives references to the appropriate sections.

- defined four common positions and adopted three joint actions concerning Asia, including Common Position 2002/831/CFSP on Burma/Myanmar (→ *point 958*);

- defined 11 common positions and adopted one joint action concerning Africa, including Common Position 2002/495/CFSP on Angola (→ *point 1008*); Common Position 2002/457/CFSP concerning Liberia (→ *point 1005*); Common Position 2002/22/CFSP concerning Sierra Leone (→ *point 1005*); Common Position 2002/145/CFSP concerning Zimbabwe (→ *point 1008*); Common Position 2002/830/CFSP concerning Rwanda (→ *point 1007*); Common Position 2002/829/CFSP concerning the Democratic Republic of the Congo (→ *point 1007*); Joint Action 2002/962/CFSP extending the mandate of the EU special representative for the Great Lakes region (→ *point 1007*);

- defined five common positions and adopted two joint actions on general issues, including Common Positions 2002/340/CFSP, 2002/462/CFSP, 2002/847/CFSP and 2002/976/CFSP on combating terrorism (→ *point 492*); Common Position 2002/474/CFSP on the International Criminal Court (→ *point 53*); Joint Action 2002/406/CFSP on ballistic missile proliferation (→ *point 759*); Joint Action 2002/589/CFSP concerning small arms and light weapons (→ *point 759*).

The Council also adopted several decisions and joint actions implementing, extending or repealing joint actions and common positions ([1]).

754.   Other forms of action. Throughout the year, the EU made numerous representations to governments regarding human rights, in support of humanitarian action or in the field of non-proliferation and the prevention of armed conflict. The Union's external relations policy also entailed continuing political dialogue with associated countries, non-Member States and various international organisations.

European security and defence policy (ESDP)

755.   Crisis management. In a resolution on 10 April ([2]), Parliament welcomed the progress made towards the establishment of crisis management structures and procedures at EU level, as well as the commitments by Member States on military and civilian capabilities ([3]). In another resolution adopted the same

---

([1]) These decisions and joint actions are covered in the section in this chapter on the relevant geographical area.
([2]) Bull. 4-2002, point 1.6.3.
([3]) 2001 General Report, point 826.

day (^{1}), it stressed that a strong European armaments industry was vital to the development of the ESDP. Following on from the conclusions of the Nice European Council (^{2}), on 13 May (^{3}) the Council adopted a series of decisions concerning arrangements for consultation and cooperation on crisis management between the EU and Canada, the Russian Federation and Ukraine. The European Council in Seville on 21 and 22 June affirmed that the European Union was now in a position to take charge of crisis management operations (^{4}), as demonstrated by the decision on the European Union Police Mission (EUPM) in Bosnia and Herzegovina *(→ point 875)*. On 19 November (^{5}), the Council underlined the importance of ensuring coordination of the EU's civilian and military crisis management instruments in order to be able to respond effectively to a crisis. The Commission continued to ensure that the various instruments under its responsibility could respond to the requirements of crisis management, for instance developing the use of the rapid reaction mechanism (RRM) as a policy support tool for crisis resolution. It also reinforced its crisis centre and played a major role in the implementation of the emergency aid programme for the reconstruction of Afghanistan *(→ points 757 and 948)*.

756. *Conflict prevention.* The Commission continued to implement its new conflict prevention strategy as presented in its communication of April 2001 (^{6}). A special effort was made to incorporate a conflict prevention element in the documents programming Community external aid to different countries and regions of the world, particularly the developing countries, and to go beyond a solely CFSP-based approach. Meanwhile the Commission continued to develop its internal expertise in the field of conflict and strategies for its prevention. It also contributed to the Council's work on setting up early warning systems and developed its contacts with NGOs and international organisations active in the conflict prevention field.

757. *Rapid reaction mechanism.* The Commission used the rapid reaction mechanism set up in 2001 (^{7}) to intervene in various crisis situations in an attempt to mitigate them or prevent conflict. It approved funding from the RRM for a second programme of emergency reconstruction aid to Afghanistan, various peace initiatives in Somalia, Ethiopia/Eritrea and Sudan, emergency aid for the rehabilitation of the Palestinian Authority's administrative infrastructure and programmes to support conflict resolution in Nepal and the peace process in Sri Lanka. The RRM also provided invaluable technical back-up to the political discussions in a dispute over the sharing of water resources between

(^{1}) Bull. 4-2002, point 1.6.4.
(^{2}) Bull. 12-2000, point I.6; 2000 General Report, point 752.
(^{3}) Bull. 5-2002, point 1.6.11.
(^{4}) Bull. 6-2002, point I.7.
(^{5}) Bull. 11-2002, point 1.6.5.
(^{6}) COM(2001) 211; 2001 General Report, point 812.
(^{7}) Regulation (EC) No 381/2001 (OJ L 57, 27.2.2001; 2001 General Report, point 811).

Lebanon and Israel. Implementation of RRM projects continued in tandem with the Commission's conventional aid programmes. The total financial package allocated for the RRM in 2002 amounted to EUR 25 million.

758. *Combating terrorism.* In its conclusions of 15 April ([1]) on the implications of the terrorist threat on the non-proliferation, disarmament and arms control policy of the European Union, the Council recommended a list of practical measures with a view to the establishment of multilateral instruments, limits on arms exports, international cooperation and political dialogue on this subject. The Seville European Council issued a special declaration on the role of the CFSP in combating terrorism ([2]). Stressing that the fight against terrorism would continue to be a priority objective of the European Union, which would continue to maintain close coordination with the United States and other partners, it believed that the CFSP, including the ESDP, could play an important role in countering this threat to security and in promoting peace and stability. As part of a global approach, the European Council advocated a series of priority objectives, including deepening political dialogue with third countries, strengthening arrangements for sharing intelligence and using military or civilian capabilities to protect civilian populations against the effects of terrorist attacks. The Council reaffirmed this position in its conclusions on 22 July ([3]). On 24 October ([4]), Parliament welcomed the global anti-terrorism strategy laid down by the extraordinary Brussels European Council ([5]) through the adoption of the European action plan to combat terrorism, which was updated at the Laeken ([6]) and Seville ([7]) European Councils. Other aspects of the fight against terrorism are covered in Section 1 ('Area of freedom, security and justice') of Chapter IV *(→ point 492).*

759. *Arms proliferation.* On 27 May, the Council decided to provide EUR 55 000 in financial support to the international negotiating process for the adoption of an international code of conduct against the proliferation of ballistic missiles ([8]), a commitment which it reiterated in its conclusions of 30 September ([9]). On 12 July, it once again demonstrated the EU's commitment to combating the destabilising accumulation and spread of small arms and light weapons by adopting a new joint action ([10]) repealing Joint Action 1999/34/CFSP ([11]). On 21 October, the Council contributed EUR 200 000 on behalf of the European

---

([1]) Bull. 4-2002, point 1.4.13.
([2]) Bull. 6-2002, point I.31.
([3]) Bull. 7/8-2002, point 1.6.3.
([4]) Bull. 10-2002, point 1.6.8.
([5]) 2001 General Report, point 1206.
([6]) 2001 General Report, point 1210.
([7]) Bull. 6-2002, point I.31.
([8]) Joint Action 2002/406/CFSP (OJ L 140, 30.5.2002; Bull. 5-2002, point 1.6.2).
([9]) Bull. 9-2002, point 1.6.6.
([10]) Joint Action 2002/589/CFSP (OJ L 191, 19.7.2002; Bull. 7/8-2002, point 1.6.1).
([11]) OJ L 9, 15.1.1999; 1998 General Report, point 673.

Union to the South-East Europe Regional Clearinghouse for Small Arms Reduction ([1]). The second report on the implementation of Joint Action 2002/589/CFSP was published on 31 December ([2]). In a resolution on 26 September ([3]) on the Council's third annual report on the European Union code of conduct on arms exports ([4]), Parliament welcomed the progress achieved and expressed its view that the code should become legally binding and that the candidate countries should be involved in it.

760. *Military capabilities.* In its conclusions of 13 May ([5]), the Council reviewed the progress achieved towards the development of EU military capabilities in the light of the guidelines laid down at the Laeken European Council ([6]).

761. *Relations with NATO.* During the Brussels European Council of 24 and 25 October ([7]), the modalities were agreed for the implementation of the Nice provisions on the involvement of the non-EU European members of NATO in peacetime ESDP consultations. Attention was drawn to the obligation to respect the Treaty on European Union, particularly the objectives and principles of the CFSP set out in Article 11 of the Treaty. The Copenhagen European Council of 12 and 13 December ([8]) congratulated the Presidency and the CFSP High Representative, Javier Solana, for their efforts, which had enabled a comprehensive agreement to be reached with NATO on all outstanding permanent arrangements between the EU and NATO. It also confirmed the Union's readiness to take over the military operation in the FYROM as soon as possible in consultation with NATO.

Presidency and EU statements

762. Table 17 lists, in summary form and by geographical region, the positions set out in Presidency statements on behalf of the European Union and statements by the European Union on international political issues ([9]).

([1]) Decision 2002/842/CFSP (OJ L 289, 26.10.2002; Bull. 10-2002, point 1.6.76).
([2]) OJ C 330, 31.12.2002.
([3]) Bull. 9-2002, point 1.6.5.
([4]) OJ C 351, 11.12.2001.
([5]) Bull. 5-2002, point 1.6.10.
([6]) Bull. 12-2001, point 1.5; 2001 General Report, point 826.
([7]) Bull. 10-2002, point I.1; Annex II to the Presidency conclusions.
([8]) Bull. 12-2002, point I.9.
([9]) The full text of the statements listed can be found in the *Bulletin of the European Union* for the month in which they were adopted. The central and east European countries associated with the European Union, the associated countries Cyprus, Malta and Turkey, and the EFTA countries members of the European Economic Area aligned themselves with many of the Union's declarations in the CFSP framework and with a number of the common positions adopted by the Union.

TABLE 17

Presidency and EU statements under the CFSP

Region/country/entity	Subject	Date	Bulletin reference
Candidate countries			
Slovakia	Positive outcome of the elections	8.10.2002	Bull. 10-2002, point 1.6.26
Turkey	Reform measures	6.8.2002	Bull. 7/8-2002, point 1.6.36
Western Balkans			
Albania	Establishment of the new government	25.2.2002	Bull. 1/2-2002, point 1.6.6
	Election of the president of the republic	27.6.2002	Bull. 6-2002, point 1.6.8
Bosnia and Herzegovina	Constitutional reform	12.3.2002	Bull. 3-2002, point 1.6.5
	Constitutional reform	23.4.2002	Bull. 4-2002, point 1.6.7
	Accession to the Council of Europe	24.4.2002	Bull. 4-2002, point 1.6.8
	Launch of the EU Police Mission	31.12.2002	Bull. 12-2002, point 1.6.18
Croatia	Draft constitutional law on the rights of national minorities	6.12.2002	Bull. 12-2002, point 1.6.21
Former Yugoslav Republic of Macedonia	Successful conduct of elections	17.9.2002	Bull. 9-2002, point 1.6.7
Federal Republic of Yugoslavia	Election of the president and establishment of the government	6.3.2002	Bull. 3-2002, point 1.6.19
	Transfer to UNMIK of Kosovo Albanian detainees	27.3.2002	Bull. 3-2002, point 1.6.20
	Media and electoral legislation in Montenegro	27.7.2002	Bull. 7/8-2002, point 1.6.26
	Municipal elections in southern Serbia	30.7.2002	Bull. 7/8-2002, point 1.6.27
	Recent arrests in Kosovo	20.8.2002	Bull. 7/8-2002, point 1.6.28
	UN Secretary General special representative's plan for Mitrovica	4.10.2002	Bull. 10-2002, point 1.6.24
	Second round of the Serbian presidential elections	10.10.2002	Bull. 10-2002, point 1.6.25
Maghreb, Mashreq and the Middle East			
Egypt	Trial of civil society representatives	31.7.2002	Bull. 7/8-2002, point 1.6.12
Middle East	Attack in Netanya	28.3.2002	Bull. 3-2002, point 1.6.15
	Situation of the Palestinian people	20.4.2002	Bull. 4-2002, point 1.6.15
	Middle East peace process	20.9.2002	Bull. 9-2002, point 1.6.17

Region/country/entity	Subject	Date	Bulletin reference
Iraq	Diplomatic solution to the question of disarmament	20.5.2002	Bull. 5-2002, point 1.6.20
	Adoption of Security Council Resolution 1441 (Iraq)	14.11.2002	Bull. 11-2002, point 1.6.12
Syria	Human rights situation	8.8.2002	Bull. 7/8-2002, point 1.6.35
	Release of Riad Al Turk following a presidential amnesty	21.11.2002	Bull. 11-2002, point 1.6.16
Independent States of the former Soviet Union			
Azerbaijan	Illegitimacy of the presidential election in Nagorno Karabakh	2.8.2002	Bull. 7/8-2002, point 1.6.5
Belarus	Relations with OSCE	8.5.2002	Bull. 5-2002, point 1.6.12
	Relations with OSCE	4.6.2002	Bull. 6-2002, point 1.6.9
	Situation of human rights and democracy	26.8.2002	Bull. 7/8-2002, point 1.6.6
	Relations with OSCE	17.9.2002	Bull. 9-2002, point 1.6.9
	Free media and freedom of expression	16.10.2002	Bull. 10-2002, point 1.6.9
Georgia	Illegitimacy of parliamentary elections in Abkhazia	12.3.2002	Bull. 3-2002, point 1.6.9
	Attack and incidents targeting non-governmental and religious organisations	22.7.2002	Bull. 7/8-2002, point 1.6.13
	Violation of Georgian airspace	12.8.2002	Bull. 7/8-2002, point 1.6.14
	Violation of Georgian airspace	28.8.2002	Bull. 7/8-2002, point 1.6.15
Kazakhstan	Zhakiyanov case	31.3.2002	Bull. 3-2002, point 1.6.12
	Zhakiyanov case	12.8.2002	Bull. 7/8-2002, point 1.6.20
	Attacks on the independent media	29.5.2002	Bull. 5-2002, point 1.6.21
Kyrgyzstan	Confrontations in Jalal-Abad province	28.3.2002	Bull. 3-2002, point 1.6.13
Moldova	Transnistria conflict	4.12.2002	Bull. 12-2002, point 1.6.25
Russia	Situation of the media	29.1.2002	Bull. 1/2-2002, point 1.6.24
	Abduction of relief workers in the northern Caucasus	26.8.2002	Bull. 7/8-2002, point 1.6.29
	Release of the two kidnapped humanitarian aid workers	20.11.2002	Bull. 11-2002, point 1.6.14
Turkmenistan	Situation following the attempted assassination of President Niyazov	10.12.2002	Bull. 12-2002, point 1.6.32
Ukraine	Parliamentary elections	31.3.2002	Bull. 4-2002, point 1.6.17
Asia			
Afghanistan	Death of the Afghan vice-president	9.7.2002	Bull. 7/8-2002, point 1.6.4
	Kabul declaration of good neighbourly relations	22.12.2002	Bull. 12-2002, point 1.6.16
Bahrain	Smooth conduct of the Parliamentary elections	5.11.2002	Bull. 11-2002, point 1.6.6

TABLE 17 (*continued*)

Region/country/entity	Subject	Date	Bulletin reference
Cambodia	Withdrawal from negotiations with the UN	20.2.2002	Bull. 1/2-2002, point 1.6.9
China	Municipal elections	1.3.2002	Bull. 3-2002, point 1.6.6
North Korea	Visit by representatives of the Dalai Lama	12.9.2002	Bull. 9-2002, point 1.6.11
	Visit of the Japanese prime minister to Pyongyang	2.9.2002	Bull. 9-2002, point 1.6.18
	Visit of the Japanese prime minister to Pyongyang	19.9.2002	Bull. 9-2002, point 1.6.19
	Clandestine nuclear weapon programme	18.10.2002	Bull. 10-2002, point 1.6.13
India	Ballistic missile test	28.1.2002	Bull. 1/2-2002, point 1.6.16
	Killing of Mushtaq Ahmed Lone	18.9.2002	Bull. 9-2002, point 1.6.15
	Violence in Gujarat	26.9.2002	Bull. 9-2002, point 1.6.16
	Successful conduct of elections in Jammu and Kashmir	11.10.2002	Bull. 10-2002, point 1.6.15
India/Pakistan	Terrorist attacks in Jammu and Kashmir	26.11.2002	Bull. 11-2002, point 1.6.11
	Deteriorating relations between the two countries	22.5.2002	Bull. 5-2002, point 1.6.18
	Violence in Kashmir and Pakistan	7.8.2002	Bull. 7/8-2002, point 1.6.17
	Positive outcome of the situation	18.10.2002	Bull. 10-2002, point 1.6.16
Indonesia	Flooding in Jakarta, Tangerang and Bekasi	8.2.2002	Bull. 1/2-2002, point 1.6.17
	Peace agreement on the Moluccas	11.3.2002	Bull. 3-2002, point 1.6.11
	Autonomy for Aceh	17.5.2002	Bull. 5-2002, point 1.6.19
	Deliberations of the People's Consultative Assembly concerning the amendment of the constitution	16.8.2002	Bull. 7/8-2002, point 1.6.18
	Agreement between the Indonesian Government and GAM	4.11.2002	Bull. 11-2002, point 1.6.11
	Signature of the agreement on cessation of hostilities in Aceh	9.12.2002	Bull. 12-2002, point 1.6.23
Malaysia	Proceedings against the former deputy prime minister	19.7.2002	Bull. 7/8-2002, point 1.6.23
Burma (Myanmar)	Release of Aung San Suu Kyi	8.5.2002	Bull. 5-2002, point 1.6.25
	Recent politically motivated arrests	11.10.2002	Bull. 10-2002, point 1.6.18
Nepal	Worsening crisis situation	8.5.2002	Bull. 5-2002, point 1.6.26
	Favourable development of the situation	11.10.2002	Bull. 10-2002, point 1.6.20
	Human rights situation	18.12.2002	Bull. 12-2002, point 1.6.26
Pakistan	Attack in Karachi	26.9.2002	Bull. 9-2002, point 1.6.21
	Successful conduct of the general elections	15.10.2002	Bull. 10-2002, point 1.6.21
	Election of the prime minister	22.11.2002	Bull. 11-2002, point 1.6.13

Region/country/entity	Subject	Date	Bulletin reference
Sri Lanka	Ceasefire in the internal armed conflict	27.2.2002	Bull. 1/2-2002, point 1.6.28
	Peace process	26.6.2002	Bull. 6-2002, point 1.6.16
	Peace process	20.8.2002	Bull. 7/8-2002, point 1.6.34
East Timor	Ad hoc human rights tribunal on East Timor	21.8.2002	Bull. 7/8-2002, point 1.6.19
Latin America and the Caribbean			
Argentina	Crisis situation	3.1.2002	Bull. 1/2-2002, point 1.6.8
Belize and Guatemala	Rapprochement over the territorial differendum	3.10.2002	Bull. 10-2002, point 1.6.10
Bolivia	Presidential and legislative elections	5.7.2002	Bull. 7/8-2002, point 1.6.7
	Inauguration of President Gonzalo Sánchez de Lozada	7.8.2002	Bull. 7/8-2002, point 1.6.8
Brazil	Election of the new president	29.10.2002	Bull. 10-2002, point 1.6.11
Colombia	Resumption of dialogue and condemnation of violence	17.1.2002	Bull. 1/2-2002, point 1.6.10
	Agreement between the government and the FARC-EP	24.1.2002	Bull. 1/2-2002, point 1.6.11
	Breakdown of the peace process	22.2.2002	Bull. 1/2-2002, point 1.6.12
	Presidential election	29.5.2002	Bull. 5-2002, point 1.6.14
	Inauguration of President Alvaro Uribe	8.8.2002	Bull. 7/8-2002, point 1.6.11
Costa Rica	Agreement concerning the San Juan river	10.10.2002	Bull. 10-2002, point 1.6.14
Cuba	Accession to the Treaty on the Non-proliferation of Nuclear Weapons	27.9.2002	Bull. 9-2002, point 1.6.13
Ecuador	Smooth conduct of the presidential and legislative elections	26.11.2002	Bull. 11-2002, point 1.6.9
Guatemala	Fourth anniversary of the assassination of Bishop Gerardi	24.4.2002	Bull. 4-2002, point 1.6.10
Haiti	Continuing political crisis	24.1.2002	Bull. 1/2-2002, point 1.6.15
	Report of the inquiry into the events of 17 December 2001	19.7.2002	Bull. 7/8-2002, point 1.6.16
Jamaica	Elections of 16 October	14.10.2002	Bull. 10-2002, point 1.6.17
Mexico	Fight against corruption	27.9.2002	Bull. 9-2002, point 1.6.20
Nicaragua	Political situation	28.6.2002	Bull. 6-2002, point 1.6.13
	Agreement concerning the San Juan river	10.10.2002	Bull. 10-2002, point 1.6.14
Venezuela	Political and social developments	21.5.2002	Bull. 5-2002, point 1.6.28
	Political crisis	9.10.2002	Bull. 10-2002, point 1.6.31
	Deterioration of the internal situation	23.12.2002	Bull. 12-2002, point 1.6.33

TABLE 17 (continued)

Region/country/entity	Subject	Date	Bulletin reference
Africa			
African Union	First summit in Durban	9.7.2002	Bull. 7/8-2002, point 1.6.37
West Africa			
Cameroon	Legislative and municipal elections	7.8.2002	Bull. 7/8-2002, point 1.6.10
Cameroon/Nigeria	Ruling of the International Court of Justice on the common land and maritime boundaries	29.11.2002	Bull. 11-2002, point 1.6.7
Côte d'Ivoire	Internal violence	25.9.2002	Bull. 9-2002, point 1.6.12
	Urging parties to sign a protocol of agreement following the ceasefire	15.11.2002	Bull. 11-2002, point 1.6.8
	Condemnation of acts of violence	18.12.2002	Bull. 12-2002, point 1.6.20
Equatorial Guinea	Deterioration of the political situation	10.6.2002	Bull. 6-2002, point 1.6.10
	Democratisation process and elections	18.12.2002	Bull. 12-2002, point 1.6.22
Guinea/Liberia/			
Sierra Leone	Mano River Union Summit	26.2.2002	Bull. 1/2-2002, point 1.6.14
	Mano River Union Summit	12.3.2002	Bull. 3-2002, point 1.6.9
Liberia	Abuse of human rights	30.4.2002	Bull. 4-2002, point 1.6.11
	Escalation of fighting	24.5.2002	Bull. 5-2002, point 1.6.23
	Human rights situation	30.7.2002	Bull. 7/8-2002, point 1.6.21
Malawi	Amendment of the constitution	17.6.2002	Bull. 6-2002, point 1.6.11
Mali	Presidential election	7.6.2002	Bull. 6-2002, point 1.6.12
Nigeria	Catastrophic explosions in Lagos State	4.2.2002	Bull. 1/2-2002, point 1.6.22
	Acquittal of Safiya Hussaini	22.3.2002	Bull. 3-2002, point 1.6.16
	Sentence on Amina Lawal	21.8.2002	Bull. 7/8-2002, point 1.6.24
São Tomé and Príncipe	Successful conduct of elections	26.3.2002	Bull. 3-2002, point 1.6.21
Sierra Leone	Inauguration of President Kabbah	12.7.2002	Bull. 7/8-2002, point 1.6.30
Togo	Political situation	7.2.2002	Bull. 1/2-2002, point 1.6.29
	Legislative elections (mixed outcome)	5.11.2002	Bull. 11-2002, point 1.6.17
East Africa			
Ethiopia/Eritrea	Boundary Commission decision	15.4.2002	Bull. 4-2002, point 1.6.9

Region/country/entity	Subject	Date	Bulletin reference
Somalia	Resolution adopted by the ninth IGAD summit	1.2.2002	Bull. 1/2-2002, point 1.6.25
	Peace and reconciliation process	4.10.2002	Bull. 10-2002, point 1.6.27
	Cessation of hostilities	30.10.2002	Bull. 10-2002, point 1.6.28
	Situation in Somalia	6.12.2002	Bull. 12-2002, point 1.6.31
Sudan	Nuba mountains ceasefire agreement	1.2.2002	Bull. 1/2-2002, point 1.6.26
	Bombing of civilian targets	28.2.2002	Bull. 1/2-2002, point 1.6.27
	Humanitarian situation	25.6.2002	Bull. 6-2002, point 1.6.15
	Machakos agreement	23.7.2002	Bull. 7/8-2002, point 1.6.31
	Access for humanitarian aid	14.8.2002	Bull. 7/8-2002, point 1.6.32
	Death sentences	30.8.2002	Bull. 7/8-2002, point 1.6.33
	Suspension of peace negotiations	5.9.2002	Bull. 9-2002, point 1.6.23
	Humanitarian situation	4.10.2002	Bull. 10-2002, point 1.6.29
	Resumption of peace negotiations	14.10.2002	Bull. 10-2002, point 1.6.30
	Unimpeded humanitarian access	6.11.2002	Bull. 11-2002, point 1.6.15
Central Africa			
Burundi	Continuing violence	3.5.2002	Bull. 5-2002, point 1.6.13
	Upsurge in violence	5.8.2002	Bull. 7/8-2002, point 1.6.9
	Escalation of violence	26.9.2002	Bull. 9-2002, point 1.6.10
	Outcome of regional summit on Burundi (Dar-es-Salaam)	10.10.2002	Bull. 10-2002, point 1.6.12
	Signature of a ceasefire	4.12.2002	Bull. 12-2002, point 1.6.19
Central African Republic	Attempted *coup d'État*	31.10.2002	Bull. 10-2002, point 1.6.22
	State of insecurity	10.12.2002	Bull. 12-2002, point 1.6.27
Republic of the Congo (Brazzaville)	Presidential election	26.3.2002	Bull. 3-2002, point 1.6.18
	Confrontations in the Pool region	16.12.2002	Bull. 12-2002, point 1.6.30
Democratic Republic of the Congo	Inter-Congolese dialogue and meeting at Sun City	22.2.2002	Bull. 1/2-2002, point 1.6.23
	Suspension of inter-Congolese dialogue	22.3.2002	Bull. 3-2002, point 1.6.17
	Positive outcome of Sun City meeting	30.4.2002	Bull. 4-2002, point 1.6.16
	Upsurge in violence	23.5.2002	Bull. 5-2002, point 1.6.27
	Fighting in the east and north-east	22.10.2002	Bull. 10-2002, point 1.6.23
	Humanitarian situation in Ituri and serious violations of human rights	11.12.2002	Bull. 12-2002, point 1.6.28
	Conclusion of the inter-Congolese negotiations in Pretoria	17.12.2002	Bull. 12-2002, point 1.6.29

TABLE 17 (continued)

Region/country/entity	Subject	Date	Bulletin reference
Democratic Republic of the Congo and Uganda	Signing of the Luanda agreement	12.9.2002	Bull. 9-2002, point 1.6.22
Democratic Republic of the Congo and Rwanda	Signing of a peace agreement	30.7.2002	Bull. 7/8-2002, point 1.6.25
Southern Africa Angola	Call for an end to the internal conflict	28.2.2002	Bull. 1/2-2002, point 1.6.7
	Signature by the government and UNITA of a memorandum of understanding	17.4.2002	Bull. 4-2002, point 1.6.6
	Peace process	6.9.2002	Bull. 9-2002, point 1.6.8
	Satisfaction with the peace process	2.12.2002	Bull. 12-2002, point 1.6.17
Lesotho	General elections	29.5.2002	Bull. 5-2002, point 1.6.22
Zimbabwe	Restrictive measures	18.3.2002	Bull. 3-2002, point 1.6.22
	Arrest of trade union leaders	20.12.2002	Bull. 12-2002, point 1.6.34
Indian Ocean Comoros	Continuation of national reconciliation process	18.3.2002	Bull. 3-2002, point 1.6.7
Madagascar	Political crisis following on from elections	22.2.2002	Bull. 1/2-2002, point 1.6.20
	Call for a resumption of internal dialogue	28.2.2002	Bull. 1/2-2002, point 1.6.21
	Condemnation of outbreaks of violence linked to the deteriorating situation	17.4.2002	Bull. 4-2002, point 1.6.12
	Signature of an agreement between the parties to the internal conflict	22.4.2002	Bull. 4-2002, point 1.6.13
	Call for continued dialogue between the parties	8.5.2002	Bull. 5-2002, point 1.6.24
	Reconciliation process	11.7.2002	Bull. 7/8-2002, point 1.6.22
	Successful conduct of the parliamentary elections	23.12.2002	Bull. 12-2002, point 1.6.24
General issues International Criminal Court	Entry into force of the Rome Statute setting up the Court	11.4.2002	Bull. 4-2002, point 1.6.18
	Attitude of the United States	14.5.2002	Bull. 5-2002, point 1.6.16
	Entry into force of the Rome Statute	1.7.2002	Bull. 7/8-2002, point 1.6.38

Region/country/entity	Subject	Date	Bulletin reference
Reduction of strategic nuclear arsenals	New treaty between the United States and Russia	24.5.2002	Bull. 5-2002, point 1.6.17
International Day in Support of Victims of Torture	EU support	25.6.2002	Bull. 6-2002, point 1.6.18
Prevention and eradication of torture	Implementation of the EU guidelines	11.12.2002	Bull. 12-2002, point 1.6.36
	Adoption of the optional protocol to the International Convention against Torture	19.12.2002	Bull. 12-2002, point 1.6.37
Combating terrorism	Application of specific measures to combat terrorism	11.11.2002	Bull. 11-2002, point 1.6.18

Section 2

International organisations and conferences

United Nations and specialised agencies (¹)

763. *UN General Assembly.* The 57th session of the UN General Assembly opened in New York on 10 September, with the general debate taking place between 12 and 20 September (²). On 12 September, Mr Anders Fogh Rasmussen, Danish Prime Minister and President of the Council, made a statement on behalf of the European Union. Issued just after the ceremonies marking the anniversary of the attacks of 11 September 2001, the statement stressed the key role played by the United Nations in the fight against international terrorism and reiterated the EU's support for effective UN action in fields such as conflict prevention, human rights and sustainable development and the importance the EU attached to setting up the International Criminal Court, a historic landmark in the strengthening of respect for international humanitarian law and human rights. As in previous years, a number of ministerial meetings were held on the fringes of the General Assembly between the EU, represented by its troika, and other countries or regional groups and with UN Secretary-General, Kofi Annan.

764. *UN Security Council.* Following the first report it presented on 24 December 2001, the EU presented a second report on 9 August to the Security Council's Counter-Terrorism Committee on measures adopted in the framework of the EU Treaty and the EC Treaty to implement Security Council Resolution 1373 (2001). The report sets out a series of obligations which all Member States must fulfil to prevent and suppress terrorism.

765. *International Monetary Fund (IMF)* (³) *and World Bank* (⁴). On 20 April, the European Union, represented by Mr Rodrigo Rato, President of the Council, and Mr Solbes Mira, for the Commission, took part in Washington in the spring meetings of the IMF's International Monetary and Financial Committee (IMFC). The IMFC applauded the measures adopted by the international community following the events of 11 September 2001 to maintain financial stability, restore the momentum of world economic growth and reinvigorate the fight against poverty. It decided to continue its global action to combat money-

---

(¹) http://www.un.org/english/index.shtml.
(²) Bull. 9-2002, point 1.6.24 and Internet (http://www.un.org/ga/57/index.html).
(³) http://www.imf.org/external/index.htm.
(⁴) http://www.worldbank.org/.

laundering and the financing of terrorism. It reiterated the importance it attached to a collaborative approach by the IMF and its member countries to promote sustained, broad-based growth, by creating opportunities for productive employment, reducing vulnerabilities and opening up economies to trade and providing resources for a durable reduction of poverty.

The autumn meetings of the IMFC and the Development Committee took place in Washington on 28 September, with Mr Thor Pedersen, President of the Council, representing the EU. Mr Solbes Mira attended as an observer. The main topic on the IMFC agenda was the feeble growth of the world economy. The IMFC encouraged the advanced countries to continue policies to boost consumer and investor confidence. It reviewed progress made in collaboration with the financial action task force (FATF) in combating money-laundering and the financing of terrorist networks. The IMFC welcomed recent progress in resolving financial crises, in particular the willingness of some countries to include clauses in their bond contracts facilitating sovereign debt restructuring. It also invited the IMF to table for the next spring meeting a proposal to set up a sovereign debt restructuring mechanism (SDRM). The IMFC drew member countries' attention to the need to help finance the initiative for the highly indebted poor countries (HIPCs).

766.   *World Trade Organisation (WTO).* The activities of this organisation are covered in Section 3 ('Common commercial policy') of this chapter *(→ points 780 and 781).*

767.   *World Intellectual Property Organisation (WIPO)* ([1]). The Community, represented by the Commission and the Member States, continued to play an active role in the work of the WIPO, notably on protection of broadcasting organisations, protection of databases, protection of intellectual property rights, the Substantive Patent Law Treaty (SPLT), reform of the Patent Cooperation Treaty (PTC), access to genetic resources and the protection of traditional knowledge and expressions of folklore.

768.   *United Nations Economic Commission for Europe (UNECE)* ([2]). The 57th annual meeting of the United Nations Economic Commission for Europe took place in Geneva from 7 to 10 May. The main topics on the agenda were: economic aspects of security in Europe, the UN Secretary-General's initiative to strengthen the United Nations, the UNECE spring seminar on the challenges of the labour market in the UNECE region, regional preparations for the World Sustainable Development Summit, the World Summit on the Information Society, the World Assembly on Ageing *(→ point 770)* and the UNECE work programme and the possibility of providing technical assistance. On 30 and

[1] http://www.wipo.org/index.html.
[2] http://www.unece.org/.

31 October, Ms Brigita Schmögnerová, the UNECE's new executive secretary, met Mr Patten and Mr Verheugen to examine the consequences of enlargement for the EU's new neighbours and for Europe as a whole. Her visit to Brussels included meetings with senior officials on the follow-up to the Johannesburg World Sustainable Development Summit (→ point 558) and the World Summit on the Information Society (→ point 354).

769. United Nations Population Fund (UNFPA) (¹). On 30 May, the Council underscored the importance of the UNFPA's work and urged the main donor countries to continue their financial support so as to help resolve problems linked to population and health in developing countries (²). It also endorsed the Commission's intention to step up its cooperation with the UNFPA.

770. World Assembly on Ageing. This second world assembly was held in Madrid from 8 to 12 April. The Spanish Minister of Labour and Social Affairs, Mr Juan Carlos Aparicio Pérez, spoke on behalf of the European Union. Ms Anna Diamantopoulou, Member of the Commission, highlighted the work under way in the European Community on issues of ageing and stressed the gender dimension in the ageing process.

771. World Summit on Sustainable Development. Information on the Johannesburg Summit can be found in Section 4 ('Environment') of Chapter IV (→ points 556 to 558).

772. Development cooperation. The activities of international development cooperation bodies are described in Section 4 ('Development cooperation') of this chapter (→ points 831 to 833).

Organisation for Security and Cooperation in Europe (OSCE) (³)

773. Ministerial Council. The main OSCE meeting of the year was the Ministerial Council meeting on 6 and 7 December (⁴), which brought together in Oporto the foreign ministers of the 55 participating States. Representatives of the European Union (notably the Danish Presidency, represented by Danish State Secretary for European Affairs, Mr Carsten Søndergaard), the OSCE's Mediterranean partners (Algeria, Egypt, Israel, Jordan, Morocco and Tunisia), the partners for cooperation (Japan, South Korea and Thailand), UN agencies and other international organisations and regional groupings also attended the summit. The meeting ended by adopting a Charter on Preventing and Combat-

---

(¹) http://www.unfpa.org/.
(²) Bull. 5-2002, point 1.6.32.
(³) http://www.osce.org.
(⁴) Bull. 12-2002, point 1.6.38. Previous meeting: 2001 General Report, point 869.

ing Terrorism and agreeing guidelines for a strategy to address new threats to security and stability in the 21st century.

774. *Economic forum.* The 10th meeting of the OSCE economic forum took place in Prague from 28 to 31 May and was given over to cooperation within the OSCE to ensure the quality and sustainability of water. Preparatory seminars were organised in Zamora (Spain) on 11 and 12 February and in Baku (Azerbaijan) on 15 and 16 April.

775. *Human dimension.* The seventh OSCE human dimension implementation meeting was held in Warsaw from 9 to 19 September. The main topics discussed were trafficking in human beings, electoral standards and the prevention of torture.

Council of Europe ([1])

776. *Activities.* The Community, represented by the Commission, took part in the 110th and 111th sessions of the Council of Europe Committee of Ministers in Vilnius on 2 and 3 May and in Strasbourg on 6 and 7 November, the latter session devoted in particular to international action to combat terrorism. Mr Anders Fogh Rasmussen, President of the Council, and Mr Patten, for the Commission, took part in the quadripartite meeting held in Strasbourg on 25 September. On 9 March, Mr Prodi participated in the 50th plenary meeting of the European Commission for Democracy through Law (Venice Commission). On 1 October, Ms Reding took part in a conference in Mondorf-les-Bains (Luxembourg) on freedom of expression and information at pan-European level, bringing together the Council of Europe, the EU and the OSCE.

Traditional cooperation continued, notably through the Commission's participation in the deliberations of the committees of experts on legal issues, culture, youth, human rights and audiovisual policy. The Council of Europe took part in meetings and conferences organised by the Commission. Cooperation also continued through various projects and joint initiatives ([2]).

The Council of Europe's Committee of Ministers adopted a convention on contact concerning children. This agreement, open to participation by the Community, will enable the latter to become party to the convention at the end of the signing and ratification procedures. The European Community, which is already a contracting party to eight Council of Europe conventions or agreements, signed the European convention relating to questions on copyright law

([1]) http://www.coe.int/portalT.asp.
([2]) http://jp.coe.int.

and neighbouring rights in the framework of trans-frontier broadcasting by satellite, adopted in 1994.

Organisation for Economic Cooperation and Development (OECD) [1]

777.   *Annual Ministerial Council meeting*. This meeting was held in Paris on 15 and 16 May [2] and brought together ministers of OECD member countries, Mr Lamy and Mr Solbes Mira for the Commission, and ministers of certain non-member countries [3]. Aside from discussing the economic outlook and monetary and budgetary policy objectives and structural reform with a view to enhanced economic efficiency, job creation and raising living standards, OECD members addressed the issue of the integrity and transparency of the international economy. Member countries also condemned the use of protectionism, citing the recent example of the United States, as it was an obstacle to the development of the poorest countries. Reaffirming their commitment to multilateral rules, they called on the WTO and its members to incorporate in their negotiations the concerns of the developing countries and to meet their expectations, including those on market access. Stressing the priorities of poverty reduction and sustainable development, OECD members called on all countries to work towards making the Johannesburg Summit on Sustainable Development a success *(→ point 556)* and proposed framing a common OECD programme for development, the objectives of which would be to encourage consistent policies, support good governance and the developing countries' policy-framing capacity, make aid more effective and ensure an adequate volume of aid. OECD ministers met ministers from Algeria, Egypt, Nigeria, Senegal and South Africa in the framework of the New Partnership for Africa's Development (NEPAD) and agreed that the OECD should play a role in helping Africa by means of an overall and integrated approach to development in the context of NEPAD *(→ point 1000)*.

European Bank for Reconstruction and Development (EBRD)

778.   The activities of the EBRD are dealt with in Section 1 ('Economic and monetary policy') of Chapter III *(→ points 96 and 97)*.

---

[1] http://www.oecd.org.
[2] Bull. 5-2002, point 1.6.33. Previous meeting: 2001 General Report, point 873.
[3] Argentina, Brazil, China, India, Russia and South Africa.

Section 3

Common commercial policy (¹)

Overview

779.   The Community's top priority this year was the new round of multilateral trade negotiations. It was actively involved in all fields of the negotiations in the quest for an ambitious and durable outcome that would redound to the benefit of all members of the WTO. The Community not only worked towards integrating the developing countries into the multilateral trading system but also towards making the system compatible with the demands of sustainable development. At the Johannesburg and Monterrey Summits, the Community continued to defend this policy, combining promotion of trade interests and support for development. The Commission's own work also showed the need to help the developing countries benefit from world trade. As part of the implementation of the new strategy for customs union adopted in 2001, the Commission took several initiatives to extend and enlarge the scope of the 'Customs 2002' programme to simplify customs legislation and fight against money-laundering.

World Trade Organisation (WTO) (²)

780.   Follow-up to the Doha round. After the successful launch at the end of 2001 of a new round of trade negotiations (Doha agenda) (³), the European Union during 2002 spearheaded initiatives to obtain an ambitious and balanced outcome as regards continued liberalisation of market access, strengthening of WTO rules and promotion of sustainable development, framing proposals in almost all fields of negotiation. The EU also encouraged the strengthening of the WTO's transparency and effectiveness, greater coherence between the WTO and other inter-governmental organisations. It was behind initiatives to finance and support trade-related technical assistance, the aim of which is to help developing countries implement WTO rules — both existing and future — and participate more actively in the multilateral trading system. Against that background, the Commission presented in September a communication entitled 'Trade and development — assisting developing countries to benefit from

---

(¹) Further information is available on the Internet (http://trade-info.cec.eu.int/europa/index_en.php).
(²) http://www.wto.org/index.htm.
(³) 2001 General Report, points 876 to 878.

trade' (^{1}) (→ *point 819)*, in which it sets out its opinion on the link between trade and development and proposes measures to improve, through trade, the scope for fostering development and reducing poverty. It also continued to work constructively to facilitate the accession of new members to the WTO (^{2}). Chinese Taipei (Taiwan) joined the WTO in January. The WTO General Council approved the accession of the Former Yugoslav Republic of Macedonia in October and of Armenia in December. They will become WTO members after ratification by their parliaments. The European Community played a very active role in negotiations on the memorandum of understanding on dispute settlement. The Doha Development Agenda charged WTO members with clarifying and improving the memorandum by May 2003. The European Community was very active in that connection, tabling several innovative proposals (in particular, setting up a special panel and strengthening transparency and openness in dispute settlement procedures). It continued to take part in the work on harmonising non-preferential rules of origin at global level. Having received a report from the Rules of Origin Committee on this subject, the WTO General Council is now in charge of the dossier.

781. *Implementation of dispute settlement system.* The European Community also continued to promote its trade interests in disputes with its partners and had recourse on several occasions to the WTO dispute settlement system. As a plaintiff, it initiated a dispute settlement procedure (sometimes together with other WTO members) in several important cases, notably the steel safeguard measures (DS248 United States: definitive safeguard measures on imports of certain steel products), and in another case concerning trade defence instruments in the steel sector (DS262 United States: sunset reviews of anti-dumping and countervailing duties on certain steel products from France and Germany).

Cases were brought against the Community by other WTO members who contested certain aspects of the generalised system of preferences (DS242: case brought by Thailand and DS246: case brought by India), presumed export subsidies on sugar (DS266: case brought by Brazil and DS265: case brought by Australia) and certain aspects of Community arrangements affecting wine (DS263: case brought by Argentina).

The European Community obtained a favourable decision from panels in key disputes brought before the WTO in previous years (sometimes jointly with other WTO members), for instance the dispute over the Byrd amendment to US legislation (currently the subject of an appeal).

In another anti-dumping case involving the European Community against India, the WTO published, on 29 November, a report by the panel set up at

(^{1}) COM(2002) 513; Bull. 9-2002, point 1.6.47.
(^{2}) Bull. 10-2002, point 1.6.34.

India's request (DS141/RW). The report rejected India's arguments and confirmed that the EC had correctly implemented DSB decisions and recommendations designed to bring their anti-dumping duties on imports of cotton bedlinen from India into line with the rules.

The only case brought before the Appellate Body in which the European Community was not successful was the case brought by Peru (trade description of sardines). In two other cases concerning the United States' abusive use of countervailing duties (*de minimis* case and privatisation case), the Appellate Body agreed with the Community that the US measures were incompatible with WTO rules.

In the FSC case (United States: Tax treatment for 'foreign sales corporations'/tax relief on exports), the EC was permitted to take against the United States retaliatory measures amounting to USD 4 billion if the United States did not comply with the DSB's decisions and recommendations. For the first time in the history of WTO dispute settlement, the DSB fully endorsed a request in adopting the thrust of the EU's arguments.

Operation of the customs union, customs cooperation and mutual assistance

782.   Strategy for the customs union. As part of the strategy for the customs union adopted in 2001 (¹), the Council approved, on 16 December, the decision to extend and enlarge the scope of the 'Customs 2002' programme (²) to 2007 (Table I). This new decision includes the following improvements: intensification of preparations for enlargement and fight against fraud; new information technology initiatives to standardise specifications; correct treatment of data exchanged between economic operators and Member States; better structured objectives and working tools. On 25 June, the Commission adopted a report to the Council (³) on controls on cross-border cash movements and proposed a regulation on the prevention of money-laundering by means of customs cooperation (Table I). On 14 November, the Commission proposed amending the International Convention on the Simplification and Harmonisation of Customs Procedures with a view to meeting the requirements of international commerce more effectively (Table III).

783.   Preferential origin rules. On 12 July, the Commission proposed a consolidation of the rules applicable in the 14 agreements with the EFTA part-

---

(¹) COM(2001) 51 and 2001 General Report, point 884.
(²) http://europa.eu.int/comm/taxation_customs/customs/information_notes/c2002/c2002.htm.
(³) COM(2002) 328; Bull. 6-2002, point 1.3.7.

ner countries and the countries of central and eastern Europe (¹). On 28 October, the ACP–EC Customs Cooperation Committee granted the ACP countries a derogation from the rules of origin for tuna (²). The Commission also granted a derogation on 29 July for certain fishery products from the Falkland Islands (³).

Commercial policy instruments (⁴)

784. General. On 4 September, the Commission adopted its 20th annual report to Parliament on the Community's anti-dumping and anti-subsidy activities (2001) (⁵). In order to clarify the legal situation of anti-dumping and anti-subsidy measures, complaints or investigations under way after the expiry of the ECSC Treaty *(→ point 41)*, the Council adopted, on 3 June, Regulation (EC) No 963/2002 (⁶) which states explicitly that after 23 July these will be governed by the provisions of the basic anti-dumping and anti-subsidy regulations (⁷) adopted in accordance with Article 133 of the EC Treaty. On 22 October (⁸), Parliament welcomed the Commission's 19th report on the Community's anti-dumping and anti-subsidy activities (⁹) as an instrument for assessing the Union's anti-dumping policy in the context of the Doha undertakings and the promotion of fair trade. It also called on the Union to adapt the current Community methodology to make it more effective and enhance the transparency of the decision-making process. With China's accession to the WTO, the Commission put forward a proposal, on 25 June (¹⁰), to amend Regulation (EC) No 519/94 (¹¹) in order to review the existing safeguard mechanism, progressively eliminate non-textile quotas and abolish the surveillance measures currently applicable to certain products originating in China.

785. Anti-dumping proceedings (¹²). On 5 November (¹³), the Council amended Regulation (EC) No 384/96 (¹⁴) in order to incorporate into it what has been learnt so far from anti-dumping practice and to grant Russia the status of genuine market economy. The Council imposed definitive duties in 25 new

---

(¹) COM(2002) 370, 378 to 383, 385, 386, 388 to 392.
(²) Decision No 2/2002 (OJ L 311, 14.11.2002).
(³) Decision No 2002/644/EC (OJ L 211, 7.8.2002).
(⁴) http://europa.eu.int/comm/trade/policy/index_en.htm.
(⁵) COM(2002) 484; Bull. 9-2002, point 1.6.28.
(⁶) OJ L 149, 7.6.2002; Bull. 6-2002, point 1.6.21.
(⁷) Regulation (EC) No 384/96 (OJ L 56, 6.3.1996; 1996 General Report, point 711) and Regulation (EC) No 2026/97 (OJ L 288, 21.10.1997; 1997 General Report, point 772).
(⁸) Bull. 10-2002, point 1.6.37.
(⁹) COM(2001) 571; 2001 General Report, point 891.
(¹⁰) OJ L 227 E, 24.9.2002; COM(2002) 342; Bull. 6-2002, point 1.6.22.
(¹¹) OJ L 67, 10.3.1994; 1994 General Report, point 1016.
(¹²) http://europa.eu.int/comm/trade/policy/dumping/antidumping.htm.
(¹³) Regulation (EC) No 1972/2002 (OJ L 305, 7.11.2002 and Bull. 11-2002, point 1.6.22).
(¹⁴) OJ L 56, 6.3.1996; 1996 General Report, point 772.

cases ([1]). The measures concerned imports of urea originating in Belarus, Bulgaria, Croatia, Estonia, Libya, Lithuania, Romania and Ukraine ([2]), ferromolybdenum originating in the People's Republic of China ([3]), certain zinc oxides originating in the People's Republic of China ([4]), certain ring-binder mechanisms originating in Indonesia ([5]), recordable compact discs originating in Taiwan, sulphanilic acid originating in the People's Republic of China and India ([6]), certain tube and pipe fittings, of iron or steel, originating in the Czech Republic, South Korea, Malaysia, Russia, and Slovakia ([7]), certain welded tubes and pipes, of iron or non-alloy steel originating in the Czech Republic, Poland, Thailand, Turkey and Ukraine ([8]) and polyester filament yarn originating in India ([9]). The Council also closed an investigation without taking measures (ring-binder mechanisms originating in India ([10])). Following a review, it confirmed or amended definitive duties in 32 proceedings and closed 17 proceedings without renewing the measures.

The Commission published notices of initiation concerning 20 new investigations and 52 reviews. It also adopted 15 provisional measures and closed one investigation without taking measures. Following reviews, it confirmed or amended definitive duties in three proceedings and closed one investigation without renewing the measures. The Commission also published 14 notices of expiry for anti-dumping measures which had been in force for five years.

786.   *Anti-subsidy measures*. On 5 November ([11]), the Council amended the provisions in Regulation (EC) No 2026/97 ([12]) concerning the method for determining the amount of subsidies and the use of available data. The Council imposed definitive duties in three new cases. These measures concerned imports of certain ring-binder mechanisms originating in Indonesia ([13]) and imports of sulphanilic acid ([14]) and textured polyester filament yarn ([15]) originating in India. It also closed two investigations without taking measures. Following reviews, it confirmed or amended definitive duties in three proceedings.

([1]) For further information on specific cases, see the twenty-first annual report to Parliament of the Community's anti-dumping and anti-subsidy activities (2002). The *Bulletin of the European Union* sets out, without commentary, the various stages (opinions, undertakings, duties) in all the proceedings under way.
([2]) OJ L 17, 19.1.2002; Bull. 1/2-2002, point 1.6.33.
([3]) OJ L 35, 6.2.2002; Bull. 1/2-2002, point 1.6.34.
([4]) OJ L 62, 5.3.2002; Bull. 1/2-2002, point 1.6.37.
([5]) OJ L 150, 8.6.2002; Bull. 6-2002, point 1.6.47.
([6]) OJ L 196, 25.7.2002; Bull. 7/8-2002, point 1.6.46.
([7]) OJ L 228, 24.8.2002; Bull. 7/8-2002, point 1.6.51.
([8]) OJ L 259, 27.9.2002; Bull. 9-2002, point 1.6.29.
([9]) OJ L 323, 28.11.2002; Bull. 11-2002, point 1.6.25.
([10]) OJ L 150, 8.6.2002; Bull. 6-2002, point 1.6.24.
([11]) Regulation (EC) No 1973/2002 (OJ L 305, 7.11.2002; Bull. 11-2002, point 1.6.23).
([12]) OJ L 288, 21.10.1997 and 1997 General Report, point 772.
([13]) OJ L 150, 8.6.2002; Bull. 6-2002, point 1.6.47.
([14]) OJ L 196, 25.7.2002; Bull. 7/8-2002, point 1.6.47.
([15]) OJ L 323, 28.11.2002; Bull. 11-2002, point 1.6.32.

The Commission published notices of initiation concerning three new investigations. It also adopted two provisional measures and closed one investigation without taking measures. Four reviews were opened and three procedures were closed. In two cases, it confirmed or amended definitive duties.

787. *Safeguard measures.* On 27 March, the Commission adopted Regulation (EC) No 560/2002 imposing provisional safeguard measures ([1]) which it then amended on 3 June ([2]). It also initiated a safeguard investigation on 28 March ([3]). On 11 December ([4]), it extended the deadline for closing the safeguard investigation into certain products until 27 February 2003. On 27 September, it adopted Regulation (EC) No 1694/2002, imposing definitive safeguard measures ([5]).

788. *Trade-barriers regulation.* Under the regulation ([6]), the Commission opened two examination procedures concerning trade practices maintained by Canada for imports of certain wines ([7]) and South Korean trade practices impeding trade in commercial ships ([8]). It closed the proceedings relating to commercial practices maintained by Brazil on imports of sorbitol ([9]) and a proceeding on commercial practices maintained by the United States on imports of mustard ([10]).

789. *Technical barriers to trade.* Pursuant to the agreement on technical barriers to trade ([11]), the Commission notified the relevant WTO panel of Community draft legislation containing technical rules in a number of fields such as wine products and cosmetic products. It also examined the legislative drafts of other countries in order to prevent the appearance of barriers to trade for Community firms. It encouraged Member States to participate actively in the procedure, notably to give the firms the opportunity to reap the benefits of this international trade instrument. On 20 November, the Commission adopted its 18th annual report on barriers to trade and investment in the United States, in which it stressed the impact of internal protectionist forces on the US Administration's ability to honour its international obligations, including those concerning agriculture and steel. It also declared that the European Union was prepared to use WTO procedures to defend the rights of EU businesses in the face of the various obstacles which were restricting their access to the market.

([1]) OJ L 85, 28.3.2002; Bull. 3-2002, point 1.6.40.
([2]) Commission Regulation (EC) No 950/2002 (OJ L 145, 4.6.2002; Bull. 6-2002, point 1.6.50).
([3]) OJ C 77, 28.3.2002; Bull. 3-2002, point 1.6.41.
([4]) OJ C 308, 11.12.2002; Bull. 12-2002, point 1.6.66.
([5]) OJ L 261, 28.9.2002; Bull. 9-2002, point 1.6.41.
([6]) Regulation (EC) No 3286/94 (OJ L 349, 31.12.1994), as last amended by Regulation (EC) No 356/95 (OJ L 41, 23.2.1995; 1995 General Report, point 745).
([7]) OJ C 124, 25.5.2002; Bull. 5-2002, point 1.6.57.
([8]) Decision No 2002/818/EC (OJ L 281, 19.10.2002; Bull. 10-2002, point 1.6.60).
([9]) OJ L 151, 11.6.2002; Bull. 5-2002, point 1.6.58.
([10]) OJ L 195, 24.7.2002.
([11]) OJ L 336, 23.12.1994.

790.   *Dual-use items and technology.* On 27 May (^{1}), the Council amended Regulation (EC) No 1334/2000 on exports of dual-use items and technology *(→ point 155).* On 13 December (^{2}), the Commission put forward a proposal to amend and update the regulation.

Treaties, trade agreements and mutual recognition agreements

791.   *Industrialised third countries.* On 8 October, the Council harmonised the various procedures established in the mutual recognition agreements concluded with Australia, Canada, Japan, New Zealand and the United States and distributed the management tasks between the Council and the Commission (Table III). As the United States had refused to recognise the competence of the national designating authorities and apply the procedure for designating Community conformity assessment bodies pursuant to the sectoral annex on electrical safety (^{3}), thus effectively excluding Community products from US markets, the Commission proposed, on 2 October (^{4}), to remedy this situation by suspending the Community's own obligations.

792.   *Candidate countries.* The additional protocols attached to the Europe agreements with certain candidate countries concerning the assessment and acceptance of industrial products are dealt with in Section 4 ('Pre-accession strategy') of Chapter V *(→ point 717).*

793.   *San Marino.* Signed in 1991, the cooperation and customs union agreement between the European Economic Community and the Republic of San Marino (^{5}), now ratified by all Member States, entered into force on 1 April (Table III).

794.   *Mediterranean third countries.* Information on the Euro-Mediterranean association agreements can be found in Section 8 ('Relations with the southern Mediterranean and the Middle East') of this chapter *(→ points 885 et seq.)*

795.   *Latin America.* Information on the association agreements between Latin America and the European Union can be found in Section 12 ('Relations with Latin America') of this chapter *(→ point 970).*

(^{1}) Regulation (EC) No 880/2002 (OJ L 139, 29.5.2002; Bull. 5-2002, point 1.6.36).
(^{2}) COM(2002) 730; Bull. 12-2002, point 1.6.41.
(^{3}) Agreement on mutual recognition between the Community and the United States of America (OJ L 31, 4.2.1999; 1998 General Report, point 729).
(^{4}) COM(2002) 537; Bull. 10-2002, point 1.6.62.
(^{5}) OJ L 359, 9.12.1992; Bull. 7/8-1992, point 1.4.31.

796.   *Economic partnership agreements.* Information on the economic partnership agreements is to be found in Section 13 ('ACP countries and OCTs') of
this chapter *(→ point 992).*

Export credits

797.   *Export credit insurance.* On 29 April, the Commission adopted a report
concerning the experience gained and the convergence achieved in applying the
provisions laid down in Directive 98/29/EC (¹) on medium- and long-term
export credit insurance (²). This report underlines the need for further harmonisation of credit insurance in order not to distort competition between Community firms.

798.   *Ships.* On 22 July, the Council amended Decision 2001/76/EC (³) in
respect of export credits for ships (⁴) in application of the OECD arrangement
on guidelines for officially supported export credits.

Market access

799.   The market access strategy adopted in 1996 (⁵) is largely based on the
availability to the public and to companies of an interactive database on barriers
to trade (⁶). The Commission has considerably developed the information contained in this database, providing users with better targeted information while
adopting a more operational and systematic approach to eliminating trade barriers. An information campaign directed notably at small and medium-sized
enterprises was also conducted in order to boost the use of the database and the
Commission's information on barriers that companies come up against.

Trade and sustainable development (⁷)

800.   Placing globalisation and trade in a perspective of sustainability remains
a major political objective of the European Union. At the World Summit on Sustainable Development in Johannesburg *(→ point 557),* the EU played a key role
in efforts to reach an agreement on a number of positive support measures

(¹) OJ L 148, 19.5.1998; 1998 General Report, point 729.
(²) COM(2002) 212; Bull. 4-2002, point 1.6.31.
(³) OJ L 32, 2.2.2001.
(⁴) Decision 2002/634/EC (OJ L 206, 3.8.2002; Bull. 7/8-2002, point 1.6.77).
(⁵) COM(96) 53; 1996 General Report, point 721.
(⁶) http://mkaccdb.eu.int/.
(⁷) http://europa.eu.int/comm/trade/csc/intro.htm.

affecting trade and investment. These measures are designed to contribute to sustainable development on the fringes of the Doha Development Agenda and the International Conference on Financing for Development, staged in Monterrey, Mexico, by the UN *(→ point 610)*. The Commission adopted a communication on this subject on 18 September *(→ point 819)*. It continued to take an active part in the work of the WTO Committee on Trade and Environment, at both regular and extraordinary meetings, in particular in the framework of the Doha Development Agenda and also in other international forums *(→ points 663 et seq.)*. The Council, in its conclusions of 19 November ([1]), discussed the interaction between trade and sustainable development. It wanted to see the developing countries formulate poverty-reduction policies based on a respect for sustainable development that would boost trade. It also recommended that trade be incorporated into development strategies.

Individual sectors

Steel

801.   *United States.* The Commission took a series of measures following the US decision to impose extraordinary duties of up to 30 % on steel imports. On 7 March, it initiated a proceeding before the WTO's dispute settlement body. It also initiated safeguard measures *(→ point 787)*. On 13 June, the Council adopted a regulation establishing additional customs duties on imports of certain products originating in the United States ([2]). Parliament condemned this flagrant violation of WTO rules by the United States ([3]). The ECSC Consultative Committee, in a resolution of 10 April ([4]), also criticised the US measures which it deemed inappropriate as they seriously undermined the global economic situation and multilateral trade agreements.

On 17 July, the Commission presented a report to the Council on steel rebalancing action ([5]). It noted that many countries around the world had reacted to the US decision by adopting safeguard measures and lodging a complaint with the WTO. In its conclusions of 22 July ([6]) and 30 September ([7]), the Council stressed the Union's determination to obtain an early decision by the DSB on the illegality of the US safeguard measures for steel. This would entail rebalancing measures under Regulation (EC) No 1031/2002 ([8]) if the United States

---

([1]) Bull. 11-2002, point 1.6.20.
([2]) Regulation (EC) No 1031/2002 (OJ L 157, 15.6.2002; Bull. 6-2002, point 1.6.51).
([3]) Bull. 3-2002, point 1.6.39.
([4]) OJ C 128, 30.5.2002; Bull. 4-2002, point 1.6.32.
([5]) COM(2002) 428; Bull. 7/8-2002, point 1.6.79.
([6]) Bull. 7/8-2002, point 1.6.80.
([7]) Bull. 9-2002, point 1.6.42.
([8]) OJ L 157, 15.6.2002; Bull. 6-2002, point 1.6.51.

did not immediately lift its measures after being condemned by the WTO. The Commission presented a new report to the Council on 24 September (¹) recommending that it should not at this stage apply any re-balancing measures. The Council followed that recommendation in its conclusions of 30 September (²).

802.   Monitoring of imports. On 17 January, the Commission adopted Regulation (EC) No 76/2002 (³) introducing prior Community surveillance of imports of certain iron and steel products. On 18 February, the Council extended the double-checking system without quantitative limit on imports of certain steel products (⁴) for the Czech Republic, Poland and Slovakia (⁵). On 29 November (⁶) and 2 December (⁷), the Commission proposed that the system be extended until those countries joined. The system was also extended with the Former Yugoslav Republic of Macedonia and Romania, by regulations of 21 January and 20 June respectively (⁸). On 2 December, the Commission proposed that the double-checking system for Romania (⁹) be extended until accession. As regards Russia, Kazakhstan and Ukraine, the agreements were not signed despite the fact that, on 28 February, the Council adopted decisions relating to the conclusion of these agreements extending the double-checking systems.

803.   Trade agreements. On 9 July and 22 July, two new agreements were concluded between the ECSC and Russia and Kazakhstan (Table III). These agreements, which extend similar agreements which elapsed on 31 December 2001, set quantitative limits for certain iron and steel products and will apply until 31 December 2004. Each contains a review clause in the event of those countries' accession to the WTO and enlargement of the Community after expiry of these agreements. A similar agreement with Ukraine could not be signed before the expiry of the ECSC Treaty *(→ point 39)* despite the assent given by the Council on 17 June to the draft Commission decision on the conclusion of the agreement (¹⁰). However, the same day, representatives of the governments of the Member States decided that exports of certain products originating in Ukraine should remain subject to quantitative limits for 2002 (¹¹). On

---

(¹) COM(2002) 532; Bull. 9-2002, point 1.6.40.
(²) Bull. 9-2002, point 1.6.42.
(³) OJ L 16, 18.1.2002, as last amended by Regulation (EC) No 1337/2002 (OJ L 195, 24.7.2002).
(⁴) 1995 General Report, point 762.
(⁵) Poland: Regulation (EC) No 570/2002 (OJ L 87, 4.4.2002; Bull. 1/2-2002, point 1.6.69); Slovakia: Regulation (EC) No 1093/2002 (OJ L 166, 25.6.2002; Bull. 1/2-2002, point 1.6.69); Czech Republic: Regulation (EC) No 844/2002 (OJ L 135, 23.5.2002; Bull. 1/2-2002, point 1.6.69).
(⁶) COM(2002) 665, COM(2002) 666; Bull. 11-2002, points 1.6.34 and 1.6.35.
(⁷) COM(2002) 669, COM(2002) 674; Bull. 12-2002, point 1.6.63 (Poland); COM(2002) 675, COM(2002) 676; Bull. 12-2002, point 1.6.64 (Czech Republic).
(⁸) Regulation (EC) No 152/2002 (OJ L 25, 29.1.2002; Bull. 1/2-2002, point 1.6.68) and Regulation (EC) No 1499/2002 (OJ L 227, 23.8.2002; Bull. 6-2002, point 1.6.56).
(⁹) COM(2002) 677, COM(2002) 678; Bull. 12-2002, point 1.6.65.
(¹⁰) Assent No 6 (Bull. 6-2002, point 1.6.55).
(¹¹) Decision 2002/476/ECSC (OJ L 164, 22.6.2002; Bull. 6-2002, point 1.6.53) amending Decision 2001/933/ECSC (OJ L 345, 29.12.2001; Bull. 12-2001, point 1.6.10).

19 December (^{1}), the Council decided that quantitative limits should also apply to these products in 2003.

Textiles

804.   Trade agreements. On 12 July (^{2}), the Council amended Regulation (EC) No 517/94 (^{3}) on common rules for imports of textile products from certain third countries not covered by bilateral agreements, protocols or other arrangements, or by other specific Community import rules. On 19 August (^{4}), the Commission put forward a proposal to amend Regulation (EEC) No 3030/93 (^{5}) on common rules for imports of certain textile products from third countries. The Council approved the following bilateral agreements and authorised their provisional application: on 5 November, an agreement in the form of a protocol of agreement between the European Community and Brazil, on arrangements in the field of access to the textile and clothing market (Table III); on 16 December, renewal of an agreement on trade in textile products between the European Community and Nepal (Table III); on 16 December, renewal of an agreement on trade in textile products between the European Community and Cambodia (Table III).

Shipbuilding

805.   On 30 April, the Commission adopted its fifth report on the situation in world shipbuilding (^{6}). This report confirms the observation made previously on the dominant position in a number of segments and the dumping practices of Korean naval shipyards. The Commission was supported by Parliament, which, in a resolution of 30 May (^{7}), recommended implementation of the Commission's strategy of launching a WTO procedure against South Korea and establishing a temporary defence mechanism to protect European shipbuilding against unfair Korean practices. On 13 November, the Commission adopted its sixth report (^{8}) in which it reported further on the global crisis affecting the shipbuilding industry everywhere except Asia and noted the main causes. On 27 June, the Council adopted a regulation concerning a temporary defensive mechanism to shipbuilding (^{9}) and agreed to the initiation of a procedure against the Korean practices at the WTO. The Commission sought a negotiated solution

---

(^{1}) Decision 2002/1001/EC (OJ L 349, 24.12.2002; Bull. 12-2002, point 1.6.67).
(^{2}) Regulation (EC) No 1309/2002 (OJ L 192, 20.7.2002; Bull. 7/8-2002, point 1.6.82).
(^{3}) OJ L 67, 10.3.1994; 1994 General Report, point 1035.
(^{4}) COM(2002) 465; Bull. 7/8, point 1.6.83.
(^{5}) OJ L 275, 8.11.1993; Twenty-seventh General Report, point 885.
(^{6}) COM(2002) 205; Bull. 4-2002, point 1.6.36. Previous report: COM(2001) 219 and 2001 General Report, point 909.
(^{7}) Bull. 5-2002, point 1.6.60.
(^{8}) COM(2002) 622; Bull. 11-2002, point 1.6.41.
(^{9}) Regulation (EC) No 1177/2002 (OJ L 172, 2.7.2002; Bull. 6-2002, point 1.6.57).

with South Korea by 30 September. After two fruitless bilateral consultation sessions, the Commission decided on 8 October (^{1}) to bring the case before the WTO. On 21 October (^{2}), the Commission launched the dispute settlement procedure for South Korea, asking for consultations. The regulation setting up a temporary defence mechanism was implemented. It allows for direct national aid to be given for a limited period and for certain types of ships. This aid, for contracts, is limited to 6 %. Moreover, an agreement was reached at the OECD at a ministerial meeting in May to start multilateral negotiations for the conclusion of an agreement on fair competition in the sector. The work of the special negotiating group started at the end of 2002 and should be completed in 2005.

Other products

806.   *Civil aircraft.* On 5 March, the Commission proposed approving the protocol of 2001 modifying the annex to the Agreement on Trade in Civil Aircraft (Table III).

Services

807.   Within the framework established by the Doha agenda, the Commission continued to play a key role in the negotiations on services (^{3}) as the process entered into the market access phase with the presentation by the Community in July of more than 100 initial requests for improved access to third country markets. In return, the Commission started receiving from third countries initial requests for opening up the Community services market. The Commission also met a large number of trading partners in July, October and December, to examine those initial requests. The focus will now be on preparing initial offers to other WTO members which must be submitted by 30 March 2003. Meanwhile, it participated actively in the work of WTO working groups on issues such as national rules, GATS rules (safeguard measures, subsidies and government procurement), specific commitments and the work programme on e-commerce, review of the most-favoured-nation clause and the annex on air transport.

Generalised system of preferences

808.   On 1 January, the new regulation applying the scheme of generalised tariff preferences for the period 2002–04 (^{4}) entered into force. On 29 July, the

---

(^{1}) Decision 2002/818/EC (OJ L 281, 19.10.2002; Bull. 10-2002, point 1.6.60).
(^{2}) Bull. 10-2002, point 1.6.61.
(^{3}) 2000 General Report, point 809.
(^{4}) Regulation (EC) No 2501/2001 (OJ L 346, 31.12.2001).

Commission adopted Regulation (EC) No 1381/2002 ([1]) laying down detailed rules for opening and administration of the tariff quotas for raw cane sugar for refining, originating in the least developed countries, for the marketing years 2002/03 to 2005/06.

On 31 July, the Commission adopted Regulation (EC) No 1401/2002 ([2]) laying down detailed rules for the opening and administration of the tariff quotas for rice, originating in the least developed countries, for the marketing years 2002/03 to 2008/09.

([1]) OJ L 200, 30.7.2002.
([2]) OJ L 203, 1.8.2002.

Section 4

Development cooperation (¹)

Overview

809.   The European Union assumed new commitments to the developing countries and played an active role in the preparations for and activities of the International Conference on Financing for Development, in Monterrey (Mexico), the World Food Summit on Sustainable Development, in Johannesburg, and the World Food Summit, in Rome. Poverty reduction was confirmed as the central objective in the Community's development cooperation policy and new initiatives were taken on health, education, environment, trade and specific subjects such as water and energy. One year after the setting up of the EuropeAid Cooperation Office, reform of the management of external assistance continued, notably by speeding up devolution of management to Commission delegations in the developing countries.

General policy

810.   Financing of development. An International Conference on Financing for Development was held in Monterrey from 18 to 22 March (²) and was attended by around 60 Heads of State or Government and representatives of international organisations. The EU Presidency was represented by Spanish Head of Government José María Aznar and Spanish Foreign Minister Josep Piqué i Camps, President of the European Council and President of the Council of the European Union respectively, while the European Commission was represented by Mr Prodi and Mr Nielson. The conference adopted the 'Monterrey Consensus', a catalogue of measures to be taken at national and international levels in order to achieve more acceptable living conditions for people in the world's poor countries. Calling for a new partnership between rich and poor countries, the conference urged rich countries to provide more funds for the development of poor countries. The latter were exhorted to take structural reform measures. At EC level, the conference was prepared by a Parliament resolution of 7 February (³), a Commission communication of 13 February (⁴) and a

---

(¹) Further information is available on the Europa server (http://europa.eu.int/comm/development/index_en.htm).
(²) Bull. 3-2002, point 1.6.48 and http://europa.eu.int/comm/development/events_en.htm#monterey.
(³) OJ C 284 E, 21.11.2002; Bull. 1/2-2002, point 1.6.73.
(⁴) COM(2002) 87; Bull. 1/2-2002, point 1.6.74.

Council statement of 5 March ([1]). The Barcelona European Council ([2]) welcomed the commitments made or confirmed by the Member States to increase their budget allocation for official development aid, the aim being to achieve collectively an EU average of 0.39 % of gross national income by 2006. The results of this conference were the subject, on 25 April ([3]), of a Parliament resolution, which welcomed the fact that the Union had set official development aid at 0.33 % of GNP while regretting that the Monterrey consensus contained no binding obligations or time-frame. The Union's commitment was also welcomed by the Seville European Council ([4]).

811. Implementation of external assistance. In a report adopted on 12 September ([5]), the Commission presented a summary of the first year of implementation of external assistance by the EuropeAid Cooperation Office set up in January 2001 ([6]). It sets out the commitments (EUR 9.7 billion) and payments (EUR 7.7 billion) made in 2001 and gives an overview of the geographical and horizontal programmes. The Commission's report also describes progress made in the main areas of external assistance management reform *(→ point 1152)* and stresses the importance of coherence, coordination and complementarity across EC policies to promote development, poverty reduction and integration of partner countries into the world economy. It covers general priorities such as food security and presents regional aid programmes and the activities of ECHO, the European Community Humanitarian Office *(→ points 841 to 853)* and the European Investment Bank *(→ point 89)* in the field of external assistance. The Council welcomed this report in its conclusions of 18 November ([7]).

812. Untying of aid. In its communication of 18 November ([8]), the Commission presented its approach to the untying of aid, which should no longer be subject to the purchase of goods and services obtained from the donor country using that aid. It examined in particular the current situation as regards the untying of Community aid and the untying of bilateral aid from Member States and formulated recommendations designed to make aid more effective.

813. Emergency aid, rehabilitation and development. On 5 February ([9]), Parliament welcomed the Commission communication of April 2001 on the links

---

([1]) Bull. 3-2002, point 1.6.45.
([2]) Bull. 3-2002, point I.11.
([3]) Bull. 4-2002, point 1.6.37.
([4]) Bull. 6-2002, point I.14.
([5]) COM(2002) 490; Bull. 9-2002, point 1.6.46.
([6]) 2001 General Report, point 1263 and http://europa.eu.int/comm/europeaid/index_en.htm.
([7]) Bull. 11-2002, point 1.6.45.
([8]) COM(2002) 639; Bull. 11-2002, point 1.6.44.
([9]) OJ C 284 E, 21.11.2002; Bull. 1/2-2002, point 1.6.72.

between emergency aid, rehabilitation and development (¹), while highlighting its concerns about the persistence of certain grey areas.

814.   Globalisation. On 13 February, the Commission presented a communication entitled 'Responses to the challenges of globalisation: a study on the international monetary and financial system and on financing for development' (²). This document covers topics such as crisis prevention and management, reducing abuses of the international financial system, debt relief for the developing countries, promotion of foreign direct investment and alternative financial instruments. In a statement of 5 March (³), the Council welcomed the communication which it saw as a significant contribution to the debate on globalisation *(→ point 800)* and on the financing of development *(→ point 810).* It urged industrialised countries that had not yet done so to take measures similar to those already taken by the EU such as the 'Everything but arms' initiative (⁴).

815.   Good governance. In conclusions of 30 May (⁵), the Council stressed that support for capacity building and non-State actors was a key area of development cooperation. On 11 June (⁶), the Commission presented a report in which it examined the progress of cooperation with indigenous peoples in the light of the guidelines it had set out in a working document of May 1998 (⁷). The Council welcomed this report in its conclusions of 18 November (⁸).

816.   Information and communication technologies. In its conclusions of 30 May (⁹), the Council considered that information and communication technologies could contribute significantly to reducing poverty and achieving the objectives of development. It recommended a number of principles and priority measures, notably in the field of institutional capacity building.

817.   Water and energy. In a communication of 12 March (¹⁰) stressing the need to consider water management as a problem to be integrated into poverty reduction policies, the Commission proposed a comprehensive and integrated approach valid for all aspects of water resource management and all users. On 17 July, it adopted a communication on energy cooperation with the developing countries (¹¹). This document highlights the importance of access to energy serv-

---

(¹) COM(2001) 153; 2001 General Report, point 920.
(²) COM(2002) 81; Bull. 1/2-2002, point 1.3.22.
(³) Bull. 3-2002, point 1.6.44.
(⁴) 2001 General Report, point 916.
(⁵) Bull. 5-2002, point 1.6.63.
(⁶) COM(2002) 291; Bull. 6-2002, point 1.6.60.
(⁷) 1998 General Report, point 751.
(⁸) Bull. 11-2002, point 1.6.46.
(⁹) Bull. 5-2002, point 1.6.64.
(¹⁰) COM(2002) 132; Bull. 3-2002, point 1.6.47.
(¹¹) COM(2002) 408; Bull. 7/8-2002, point 1.6.85.

ices in the context of poverty eradication and sustainable development. The Commission proposed a framework for EU external action in this field and presented the key aspects of the Union's future activities such as reform of the energy sector, technology transfer, improved efficiency and diversification.

On the occasion of the Johannesburg World Summit on Sustainable Development (→ *point 557)*, two initiatives on water and energy were launched at the EU's instigation with particular stress on partnership between governments, business and civil society as a key element of the implementation of the undertakings made in Johannesburg. On the fringes of the summit and in the framework of the partnership on water, the Union signed two policy statements, one with the African countries and the other with 12 countries in eastern Europe, the Caucasus and Central Asia.

818.   Rural development. In a communication of 25 July (¹), the Commission presented the Community's policy and approach on rural development in the developing countries. This involved integrating the objectives of poverty reduction, food security and sustainable management of natural resources into a coherent framework. Breaking with the past, it recommends incorporating those objectives within the existing framework of policies, institutions and programmes together with a number of fields of action such as more equitable access to productive assets, markets and services, investment in human capital and risk management. On 24 October, Parliament adopted a resolution on sustainable agricultural policy, agrarian reform and rural development for self-reliance in the developing countries (²); it stated in particular that action to open up market access to agricultural products from those countries should be combined with financial and technical assistance to foster sustainable development and greater food security.

819.   Trade and development. In a resolution of 3 September (³), Parliament welcomed the new regulation on generalised preferences (⁴) *(→ point 808)*, while regretting the restrictive nature of certain provisions. It considered capacity building and technical assistance to be essential elements of all future economic development cooperation and called on multinational companies to promote standards of ethics and transparency in their investment activities. It also considered that Community policies should be reviewed, notably as regards trade liberalisation, agriculture, fisheries, the environment and public health. In a communication of 18 September dealing with the link between trade and sustainable development (⁵), the Commission stressed the need to translate the

---

(¹) COM(2002) 429; Bull. 7/8-2002, point 1.6.86.
(²) Bull. 10-2002, point 1.6.66.
(³) Bull. 9-2002, point 1.6.45.
(⁴) Regulation (EC) No 416/2001 (OJ L 60, 1.3.2001); Council Regulation (EC) No 2501/2001 (OJ L 346, 31.12.2001); 2001 General Report, point 916.
(⁵) COM(2002) 513; Bull. 9-2002, point 1.6.47.

undertakings made at the Doha ([1]), Monterrey *(→ point 610)* and Johannesburg *(→ point 557)* Summits into concrete action to strengthen the dialogue between the EU and its partners, make its technical assistance more effective and help strengthen international action.

Development, environment and tropical forests

820. Information on the World Summit on Sustainable Development at Johannesburg can be found in Section 4 ('Environment') of Chapter IV *(→ points 556 to 558).*

821. Financing. In 2002, the Community committed EUR 49 million in the field of the environment and tropical forests as part of development cooperation. The Commission approved strategic guidelines and priorities for interventions in 2002 and 2003 under Regulation (EC) No 2493/2000 and Regulation (EC) No 2494/2000 ([2]) to promote the environment and the conservation and sustainable management of tropical and other forests in developing countries. These priorities include the links between poverty and the environment, implementation of multilateral environmental agreements and inclusion of environmental issues in development policy. The Commission also collaborated with the United Nations, the World Bank and the United Kingdom to draw up a document on the links between poverty and the environment.

Generalised preferences

822. Issues relating to generalised preferences are covered in Section 3 ('Common commercial policy') of this chapter *(→ point 808).*

Commodities and world agreements

823. Jute. At its meeting of 15 and 16 March, the Council decided to conclude the agreement mandating the International Jute Study Group 2001 (Table III).

824. Rubber. On 22 July, the Council adopted Decision 2002/651/EC on the participation of the Community in the International Rubber Study Group (IRSG) *(→ point 276).*

([1]) 2001 General Report, point 876.
([2]) OJ L 288, 15.11.2000; 2000 General Report, point 848.

825.   *Cocoa.* On 18 November, the Council signed and concluded the International Cocoa Agreement approved in 2001 in the framework of the United Nations Conference on Trade and Development (Table III).

North–south cooperation in the fight against drugs

826.   In 2002, the EU's most significant contribution to the fight against drugs was through the financial support given to Afghanistan to help with rebuilding the country; EUR 40 million was assigned to reconverting poppy-growing areas. A regional project aimed at supporting the prevention of diversion of drug precursors in the Andes was also financed to the tune of EUR 1.6 million. The Union took part in the annual meeting of the Commission on Narcotics in Vienna in March and in the two annual sessions of the Dublin Group in Brussels. The EU–Latin America–Caribbean coordination and cooperation mechanism to fight against drugs held its annual meeting in Madrid in March, while the annual high-level meeting between the EU and the Andean region took place in Brussels in June. In October, the anti-drugs action plan between the Union and Central Asia was approved by all the countries of this region with the exception of Turkmenistan at a ceremony in Brussels and the EC–ASEAN subcommittee on narcotics met for the first time in Kuala Lumpur.

North–south cooperation on health

827.   *Fight against poverty diseases (HIV/AIDS, malaria and tuberculosis).* In line with the policies and principles on health and poverty it defined in 2001 in the context of development cooperation ([1]), the Commission proposed on 4 March replacing Regulation (EC) No 550/97 on HIV/AIDS-related operations ([2]) with a new legal instrument making it possible to extend this new approach (Table I) to the main communicable diseases in the developing countries. It recommended a financial allocation much higher than that in the previous regulation and proposed an initiative in the field of cooperation on research (→ *point 297).* In a communication of 22 March entitled 'Health and poverty reduction in developing countries' ([3]), the Commission establishes for the first time a single Community policy framework to guide investment in health, AIDS and population within the context of overall EU assistance to developing countries. This initiative was welcomed by the Council in a resolution of 30 May ([4]). On 30 October, the Commission proposed the adoption of a regulation aimed

([1]) 2001 General Report, point 938.
([2]) OJ L 85, 27.3.1997; 1997 General Report, point 816.
([3]) COM(2002) 129; Bull. 3-2002, point 1.6.50.
([4]) Bull. 5-2002, point 1.6.62.

at preventing pharmaceutical products used in the fight against HIV/AIDS, malaria and tuberculosis and exported to developing countries at tiered prices from finding their way back onto the European market (Table II).

828. *Population.* On 7 March, the Commission proposed replacing Regulation (EC) No 1484/97 (¹) on aid for population policies and programmes in the developing countries with a new regulation designed to give couples and individuals the right to full protection of their reproductive and sexual health (Table I).

North–south cooperation on education

829. *Education and poverty reduction.* In a communication of 6 March (²), the Commission presented an overall framework for the Community's objectives, priorities and methods in education and training in the developing countries. The role of education in reducing poverty is highlighted, in particular as far as basic education, vocational training and cross-cutting issues such as equality of the sexes and the fight against AIDS are concerned. Among the recommendations, the Commission stresses the importance of taking account of the needs and the involvement of the poorest sections of the population and of support in institutional development and capacity building. With regard to this approach, the Council defined on 30 May (³), two fundamental principles: free primary education for all and closure of the gender gap. It recommended establishing a 'development compact' whereby developing countries would implement credible education policies and reforms and developed countries would increase the volume and quality of their aid in support of such strategies.

Cooperation in the campaign against anti-personnel landmines (⁴)

830. On 3 December, the Commission adopted the EU strategy to combat mines for the period 2002–04 and a multiannual indicative programme which, as part of the various Community instruments (geographical budget headings, European Humanitarian Aid Office, anti-personnel landmines regulation, rapid reaction mechanism), will mobilise around EUR 105 million for that period. With those instruments, which will be used in an integrated way, the Community will provide support for activities to combat mines (studies, mine clearance

(¹) OJ L 202, 30.7.1997; 1997 General Report, point 805.
(²) COM(2002) 116; Bull. 3-2002, point 1.6.46.
(³) Bull. 5-2002, point 1.6.61.
(⁴) http://eu-mine-actions.jrc.cec.eu.int/demining.asp.

and assistance for victims) and for the economic and social rehabilitation of the regions concerned and resettled populations.

Action in international forums

831.   Cooperation with the United Nations. Referring to the Commission communication of May 2001, which stressed the need to strengthen cooperation with the UN in the fields of development and humanitarian affairs ([1]), the European Parliament, in a resolution of 16 May ([2]), advocated various measures with a view to drawing up policies and programmes, stepping up cooperation on the ground and establishing a financial framework.

832.   World Summit on Sustainable Development. Information can be found in Section 4 ('Environment') of Chapter IV *(→ points 556 to 558).*

833.   Information on the International Conference on Financing for Development, in Monterrey, and on the World Food Summit can be found under other headings of this section *(→ points 810 and 837).*

EC Investment Partners (ECIP)

834.   In accordance with Regulation (EC) No 772/2001 ([3]), the Commission wound up this programme.

Cooperation via non-governmental organisations and decentralised cooperation

835.   Decentralised cooperation. On 13 May, the European Parliament and the Council extended to 31 December 2003 Regulation (EC) No 1659/98 ([4]) on decentralised cooperation and set the budget at EUR 24 million for the period 1999–2003 (Table I). As part of the World Summit on Sustainable Development in Johannesburg *(→ point 557),* the Community made a significant contribution to the participation of representatives of African civil society. On 7 November, the Commission adopted a communication on the participation of non-State actors in EC development policy ([5]) in which it provides an overview of

---

([1]) COM(2001) 231; 2001 General Report, point 940.
([2]) Bull. 5-2002, point 1.6.65.
([3]) OJ L 112, 21.4.2001; 2001 General Report, point 943.
([4]) OJ L 213, 30.7.1998; 1998 General Report, point 770.
([5]) COM(2002) 598; Bull. 11-2002, point 1.6.43.

current practices by instrument and by region and stresses the need to strengthen those organisations in the developing countries.

Rehabilitation aid

836. In 2002, the Commission committed EUR 99 million, including EUR 67 million for the reconstruction and rehabilitation programme for Central America, EUR 28 million for East Timor and EUR 4 million for Sri Lanka.

Food aid and food security

837. *World Food Summit* ([1]). Ahead of the summit, held in Rome from 10 to 13 June, the European Parliament, on 16 May ([2]), then the Council, on 30 May ([3]), set out an approach to addressing the problem of food security on a broad front; account should be taken of the availability of foodstuffs and households' access to them and the root political, economic and social causes of hunger and poverty should be pinpointed.

838. The food crisis in southern Africa was the subject of solemn appeals by the Council *(→ point 1008).*

839. Aid granted in 2002 under the heading of food security and food aid is set out in Table 18.

Aid for refugees

840. In 2002, EUR 48.5 million was committed for refugees, notably for the Afghan people.

([1]) http://www.fao.org/worldfoodsummit/english/index.html.
([2]) Bull. 5-2002, point 1.6.67.
([3]) Bull. 5-2002, point 1.6.68.

TABLE 18

Food security and food aid programme, 2002

Region/organisation	Cereals (tonnes)	Oil (tonnes)	Sugar, milk and pulses (tonnes)	Other products (million EUR)	Cost of all products (incl. transport) (million EUR)	Inputs and tools (million EUR)	Support + storage + information systems (million EUR)	Foreign exchange facilities (million EUR)	Monitoring and technical assistance (million EUR)
Direct aid									
Europe	246 250				71			9.5	0.9
Africa							5.05	36.8	6.35
Latin America and Caribbean							6.35		1.14
Asia						11	4		
Mediterranean and Middle East							3.6	38	1.4
Caucasus								19	2.6
Central Asia									1
Total direct aid	246 250				71	11	19	103.3	13.39
Indirect aid									
Various NGOs	80 000						35		
NGO — Euronaid	261 939	2 000	4 500		50.5	10			
WFP	30 000	4 300	1 900	7	132				
ICRC					8				
CGIAR							17.56		
FAO						6			
UNRWA		2 075	5 251		5.1		9.8		0.1
Total indirect aid	371 939	8 375	11 651	7	195.6	16	62.36		0.1
Monitoring and technical assistance									12.25
Grand total	618 189	8 375	11 651	7	266.6	27	81.36	103.3	25.74

Section 5

Humanitarian aid

General strategy

841. During 2002, the EC Humanitarian Office (ECHO)(¹) continued to work with its operational partners to bring relief to the world's main crisis areas. ECHO, which is one of the biggest providers of humanitarian aid in the world, came to the active assistance of the most vulnerable people. The main theatres of humanitarian operations were in Afghanistan, Chechnya, the Middle East, southern Africa, Sudan, the Democratic Republic of the Congo, North Korea and Colombia.

842. Intervention strategy. ECHO continued to develop its programming cycle in line with activity-based management principles and defined its operational priorities for 2003 following a comprehensive process of identification and analysis of all humanitarian situations in the world. This exercise culminated in a framework strategy paper entitled 'ECHO Aid Strategy 2002'. It was the subject of consultations with the Member States and strategic programming dialogues with ECHO's partners (the UN, the Red Cross, NGOs). On the basis of this paper, ECHO then drew up its 2003 management plan, which sets out the objectives and indicators designed to measure progress in the implementation of its strategy in 2003.

843. Emergency response. ECHO also continued to consolidate its emergency management procedures, enabling it to respond to new crisis situations, to manage them and mobilise humanitarian relief in extremely short deadlines (decision, signing of financing contracts and transfer of funding to partners within less than five days).

844. Framework of relations with partners. During 2002, ECHO continued consultations with the signatory organisations to the framework partnership contract(²). The aim of this consultation exercise is a thorough revision and consolidation of the contract, which is due to enter into force in the second half of 2003. There has been a shift in emphasis so that greater priority is attached to the planning of objectives, indicators and results. This revision is the second

(¹) http://europa.eu.int/comm/echo/index_en.htm.
(²) 1999 General Report, point 740; Internet (http://europa.eu.int/comm/echo/partners/agreement_en.htm).

stage in bringing the framework contract into line with the objectives set by the Commission in its communication 'Assessment and future of Community humanitarian activities' (¹). In view of the importance attached to the quality of humanitarian aid, the annual meeting with ECHO's partners held in Brussels on 14 and 15 October covered the following topics: an analysis of quality management tools in the humanitarian aid sector and their application by non-governmental organisations (NGOs); an analysis of human resources management systems applicable to NGOs in humanitarian aid; an evaluation of humanitarian platforms as regards information technology and the possibility of using them as coordination instruments.

845.   Training, studies, communication and evaluation. In 2002, the grant facility for training, studies and communication amounted to EUR 2.8 million. In the training section (EUR 1.4 million) the priority was the application of financial tools by those involved in the supply of humanitarian aid. In the study section (EUR 400 000), the priority was management of the security of international humanitarian activities and guidelines on support for refugees and displaced persons. In the communication section (EUR 1 million), it was 'forgotten crises' (²) and also information campaigns targeted at children and teenagers in the European Union.

In response to the expectations of European citizens, ECHO has adapted its information and communication instruments and activities in order to describe more fully the practical activities and results of its humanitarian operations and also to make more use of the media. There have been more audiovisual productions, with the result that advertising spots and documentaries have been shown on several national channels. In order to improve its visibility, ECHO has been given a new visual identity tailored to all its activities. Its Internet site has been completely restructured and re-designed.

Evaluation (³). By focusing on *ex ante* evaluation of requirements while maintaining the traditional *ex post* element, evaluation has continued to play an important role in guiding current humanitarian operations and planning future operations. An operation to evaluate cooperation with the United Nations High Commissioner for Refugees (UNHCR) was completed in 2002, leading to constructive discussions with the UNHCR. A similar evaluation concerning the World Food Programme has begun and also a thematic evaluation of the humanitarian response to droughts.

(¹) COM(1999) 468; 1999 General Report, point 738.
(²) http://www.forgottencrises.dk/.
(³) http://europa.eu.int/comm/echo/evaluation/index_en.htm.

Humanitarian aid operations [1]

846. In 2002, the Commission, through ECHO, allocated EUR 537.845 million to humanitarian aid operations.

847. Balkans. Humanitarian aid amounted to EUR 43 million. Owing to the return to normality in the region and the decline in humanitarian needs, the allocation was half that of 2001. Most of the humanitarian aid for the region went to Serbia (EUR 37.5 million), where there are still large numbers of refugees and displaced persons. This was used to cover the humanitarian needs of the most vulnerable people (food aid, hygiene products, wood and other heating fuels); to build on previous health and psychosocial activities; to seek permanent solutions for refugees, both in the form of housing programmes in Serbia and help for refugees from Bosnia and Croatia to return home. The next largest beneficiary of humanitarian aid in the region was the Former Yugoslav Republic of Macedonia (EUR 3 million), where ECHO continued to build on its water supply and social sector projects. Refugees from Kosovo and those affected by the consequences of the conflict in 2001 continued to be assisted by the UNHCR. ECHO focused its efforts in this area on three priorities: emergency rehabilitation; food aid for displaced persons staying with host families; agricultural assistance (seeds and animal fodder) for displaced persons and residents of the areas affected by the conflict. In Kosovo, despite ECHO's withdrawal at the end of 2001, a last allocation of EUR 2 million was made to the UNHCR in support of its activities to protect minorities. In Albania and Montenegro, the activities financed in 2001 were completed in preparation for ECHO's withdrawal. Throughout the region, ECHO paid close attention to the link between relief and development [2].

848. Southern Mediterranean. ECHO continued its major aid programme for Sahrawi refugees in Algeria, with a global plan worth EUR 14.34 million to cover food requirements, supplementing the World Food Programme (WFP) and the most urgent non-food requirements. In the Middle East, the humanitarian situation worsened, especially in the Palestinian territories, as a result of incursions and partial reoccupation by the Israeli armed forces, together with large-scale destruction and bans on the movement of persons and goods. ECHO therefore had to become more involved, providing aid of EUR 35 million covering both needs in the Palestinian territories and the refugee camps in Lebanon, Jordan and Syria. In the Palestinian territories, this funding (EUR 27 million) is mainly used to cover drinking water access and supply, food aid, provision of basic health services, preventing cases of malnutrition from getting worse, organising psychosocial activities for traumatised children and adolescents and protection of the civilian population by the International Committee of the Red

[1] http://europa.eu.int/comm/echo/operations/index_en.htm.
[2] 2001 General Report, points 920 and 951.

Cross (ICRC). In Lebanon, EUR 6.3 million was earmarked for access to drinking water, repair of drainage systems, improving health services and aid for the disabled. ECHO allocated EUR 600 000 each to Jordan and Syria for temporary housing needs. It also granted EUR 1.59 million to the most vulnerable members of the rural population in Yemen, victims of tribal tensions and natural disasters.

849.   *Independent States of the former Soviet Union.* Humanitarian aid amounted to EUR 40.50 million. ECHO completed its withdrawal from Belarus, Moldova and Ukraine as part of a progressive shift to other more appropriate aid instruments. In Central Asia, ECHO continued its support (EUR 10 million) for Tajikistan, directing it more towards vulnerable groups now hit by the combined effects of drought, civil war and the socioeconomic crisis. In the southern Caucasus, despite a scaling-back of aid the previous year, ECHO had to come to the aid of those once more affected by drought (EUR 700 000 in Georgia and EUR 500 000 in Armenia), and then resume its assistance to the most vulnerable people in Georgia, especially around Abkhazia (EUR 1.3 million). In the northern Caucasus, ECHO continued to provide aid for victims of the conflict in Chechnya. Despite the persistent difficulties with access and increasingly precarious security conditions, EUR 28 million was allocated in 2002 to help the most vulnerable displaced persons in Chechnya, Ingushetia and Dagestan.

850.   *Asia.* ECHO provided: in East Timor, EUR 650 000 in order to prepare the link between emergency, rehabilitation and development aid and its withdrawal from the country following the establishment of the new independent government; in Indonesia, EUR 2 million to cover the needs of those affected by the clashes in the Moluccas, Sulawesi and central Kalimantan; in Myanmar (Burma), EUR 4 million for ethnic minorities and internally displaced persons and EUR 3.4 million for Myanmar refugees in camps on the border between Myanmar and Thailand; in Sri Lanka, EUR 8.3 million for displaced persons and victims of the internal conflict; in India, EUR 2 million for victims of community riots in Gujarat, people affected by the conflict in Jammu and Kashmir and Sri Lankan refugees from Tamil Nadu; in Nepal, EUR 3 million for Bhutanese refugees and for victims of the internal conflict; in Cambodia, EUR 5.5 million mainly for the poorest regions and for returning refugees; in Afghanistan, Pakistan and Iran, EUR 70 million for Afghan and Pakistani victims of the drought and aid for the permanent return of refugees from Iran or Pakistan and victims of the earthquakes in Iran and Afghanistan. ECHO was also active in Iraq (global plan totalling EUR 13 million) complementing the UN oil-for-food programme in the health, water and sanitation sector; in North Korea it provided EUR 19.5 million for the most vulnerable people, especially children and the sick, and the victims of the floods; and in China it provided EUR 4.4 million primarily for victims of the snowstorms and floods.

851.   Latin America. ECHO continued its operation in Colombia to help the victims of the internal conflict (EUR 9.2 million). It was also active elsewhere in South America, providing EUR 350 000 for the victims of the floods and landslides in Brazil, for the victims of the floods (EUR 800 000) and a volcanic eruption (EUR 400 000) in Ecuador and also for the victims of the snowstorms and low temperatures in Bolivia and Peru (EUR 1.3 million). In Central America (Guatemala, Honduras and Nicaragua), ECHO focused its response (EUR 4.5 million) on nutritional problems caused by irregular rainfall cycles. In El Salvador, EUR 528 000 was used to finance a training project to teach people how to build low-cost traditional housing with earthquake-resistant features in the wake of the earthquakes in 2001. In Mexico, ECHO allocated EUR 1 million to help settle indigenous peoples in Chiapas and in Cuba it provided EUR 600 000 to assist the victims of hurricanes Isidore and Lili.

852.   African, Caribbean and Pacific. A total of EUR 200.15 million was granted to ACP countries in humanitarian aid. The bulk of the aid went to the Great Lakes region in Africa (EUR 81.5 million for Burundi, the Democratic Republic of the Congo and Tanzania), with EUR 37 million for the Democratic Republic of the Congo alone to cover general humanitarian needs and the eruption of the Goma volcano. In the wake of the devastating effects of the drought in southern Africa, ECHO provided the region with aid totalling EUR 48.5 million, including EUR 12 million to cover the main humanitarian needs in Angola after the end of the civil war and EUR 30 million principally for the victims of the drought in the region. Humanitarian aid in the Horn of Africa amounted to EUR 31.6 million. Apart from Sudan (EUR 19 million), which continued to be the biggest recipient of humanitarian aid, ECHO's activities in the second half of the year centred on the drought in Ethiopia and Eritrea. ECHO's air service 'ECHO-Flight' continued to operate in the region (EUR 8.4 million) and extended its area of operation to the Democratic Republic of the Congo. In west Africa, the crisis involving Sierra Leone, Liberia and Guinea remained the focus of ECHO's activities (EUR 17 million to meet the needs of refugees and internally displaced persons in these three countries). ECHO also supported the campaign against the epidemic of yellow fever in Senegal (EUR 750 000) and of meningitis in Burkina Faso (EUR 175 000) and provided assistance for the victims of the fighting in Côte d'Ivoire. ECHO was also active in the Caribbean and the Pacific, helping the victims of natural disasters (EUR 1.675 million).

853.   Regional operations. ECHO adopted two action plans under the natural disaster preparedness and prevention programme (Dipecho). One was for South-East Asia and the other for Central America, each totalling EUR 3.2 million. These action plans are designed to continue the work undertaken since 1998 in these two regions, namely to strengthen the capacities of local communities and institutions to respond effectively to recurrent natural disasters each year. The Dipecho programme also sets out to pass on the lessons learnt from implementing activities at local level to national and regional level. ECHO also decided to grant additional funding of EUR 1.64 million to the second action plan for the Andean Community adopted in December 2001 (¹) for groups at risk from flooding and earthquakes. In preparation for a regional Dipecho action plan for Central Asia in 2003, an evaluation was carried out and a call for expression of interest was issued.

(¹) 2001 General Report, point 962.

Section 6

European Economic Area, relations with EFTA countries

European Economic Area (EEA) (¹)

854. The EEA Council met in Luxembourg on 22 October (²). Discussions focused in particular on the overall functioning of the EEA agreement and on the effects of the future enlargement of the European Union on the EEA. Political dialogue issues discussed included the Middle East, Iraq, Sri Lanka and the International Criminal Court. The EEA Joint Committee met on nine occasions. The Joint Parliamentary Committee met in Reykjavik on 27 and 28 May, and in Brussels on 26 November.

Relations with EFTA countries (³)

Switzerland

855. *Sectoral agreements.* On 28 February, the Council formally adopted the decision on the conclusion of the seven agreements with Switzerland signed in 1999 (Table III). These agreements are interlinked by a clause providing for their simultaneous entry into force and cover the following areas: free movement of persons, air transport, carriage of goods and passengers by rail and road, trade in agricultural products, mutual recognition in relation to conformity assessment, certain aspects of government procurement and scientific and technological cooperation. On 17 June, the Council authorised the opening of negotiations with Switzerland in four new areas (Table III): implementation of the Schengen *acquis*, the Dublin Convention determining the State responsible for examining applications for asylum, free trade in services and the audiovisual sector. On the occasion of the adoption of these negotiating directives, the Council, which had already expressed expectations in this respect (⁴), called on the EU Presidency and the Commission to establish early contact with the Swiss

(¹) http://europarl.eu.int/factsheets/6_3_2_en.htm.
(²) Bull. 10-2002, point 1.6.70.
(³) http://www.efta.int/.
(⁴) Bull. 4-2002, point 1.6.42.

authorities in order to make progress in the current negotiations on the fight against fraud, and to start negotiations on the taxation of savings ([1]). In its conclusions of 30 September ([2]), the Council stressed that the outcome of negotiations with Switzerland in other areas could hinge on obtaining a satisfactory result on this latter point.

EEA countries

856.   *Liechtenstein.* On 25 June ([3]), the Council called on the Commission to table a recommendation as quickly as possible on the negotiation with Liechtenstein of an agreement to associate that country, at the same time as Switzerland *(→ point 855)*, with the implementation of the Schengen *acquis* and the legislation on asylum. The Council also recommended associating Liechtenstein in the Eurodac system for the comparison of the fingerprints of asylum applicants ([4]). Negotiations were also conducted on the taxation of savings.

857.   *Norway.* The agreement between the European Community and Norway on certain processed agricultural products covered by protocol No 2 to the bilateral free trade agreement ([5]) was signed in Brussels on 27 November and entered into force the same day (Table III).

Other west European countries

858.   *Taxation of savings.* Negotiations were conducted with Andorra, Monaco and San Marino *(→ point 175)*.

([1]) Bull. 6-2002, point 1.6.64.
([2]) Bull. 9-2002, point 1.6.51.
([3]) Bull. 6-2002, point 1.6.62.
([4]) Council Regulation (EC) No 2725/2000 (OJ L 316, 15.12.2000; 2000 General Report, point 456).
([5]) OJ L 171, 27.6.1973.

Section 7

Relations with the western Balkans (¹)

Overview

859.   The stabilisation and association process still constitutes the European Union's key policy framework in its relations with the western Balkans. Furthermore it has proved to be a major driving force behind the political, institutional and economic reforms carried out by countries in that region. Through the three instruments relating to the process (stabilisation and association agreements, trade preferences, and technical and financial assistance), the Union is not just making a lasting contribution to stability and prosperity in the region but is also helping countries gradually to bring their judicial and economic systems into line with its own systems. Under the CARDS programme (Community assistance for reconstruction, development and stabilisation) (²), the primary aim of which is to provide financial support to help recipient countries take part in the stabilisation and association process, commitments totalling EUR 665 million were made in 2002. Furthermore, the setting up of a European Union Police Mission to take over from the United Nations forces in Bosnia and Herzegovina demonstrates how seriously the EU takes the role it intends to take on both in the field and as major player on the international scene.

General

860.   Overall assessment. On 3 April, the Commission presented its first annual report on the stabilisation and association process for south-eastern Europe (³). The report describes the progress made and the lessons to be learnt and concludes that the process is beginning to have the desired effect on stability and political and economic reforms in the run-up to accession to the European Union, though there are still some stubborn problems such as the weakness of the rule of law, administrative capacity, civil society and the media. The Council welcomed the report in its conclusions of 13 May (⁴), and once again stressed that stronger ties and cooperation at regional level were inextricably linked to

(¹) Additional information is available on Europa (http://europa.eu.int/comm/external_relations/see/intro/index.htm).
(²) http://europa.eu.int/comm/europeaid/projects/cards/index_en.htm.
(³) COM(2002) 163; Bull. 4-2002, point 1.6.44.
(⁴) Bull. 5-2002, point 1.6.72.

the process of moving closer to the EU. It also welcomed the country assessments attached to the Commission's report and endorsed the recommendations on the measures to be taken over the next 12 months. In its resolution of 7 November (¹), Parliament also welcomed the Commission's first report and signalled its agreement with the Council conclusions. Furthermore, the Council's conclusions of 22 July (²), 21 October (³), 19 November (⁴) and 10 December (⁵) signalled its interest in the situation in the western Balkans, particularly the plight of displaced persons, the fight against organised crime, arms sales, cooperation with the International Criminal Tribunal for the former Yugoslavia and the electoral process in various countries in that region.

861.   *European Union Monitoring Mission.* On 25 November, the Council extended the mandate of the EU's Monitoring Mission to the western Balkans, with the task of monitoring and analysing the political situation in the region, until 31 December 2003 (⁶). It also set the financial reference amount for implementation of the joint action in 2003 at EUR 5.18 million. On the same day, the Council also extended the mandate of Antóin Mac Unfraidh as Head of Mission, for the same length of time (⁷).

862.   *Coordination of the Stability and Growth Pact for South-Eastern Europe.* On 10 December, the Council extended the mandate of Erhard Busek, as Special Representative of the European Union, to act as a special coordinator of the pact until 30 June 2003 (⁸).

Stabilisation and association agreements (⁹)

863.   *Albania.* The European Parliament had no doubt that a stabilisation and association agreement would strengthen democracy in Albania and it took note in its resolution of 16 May (¹⁰) of the Albanian authorities' efforts in that direction. However, it felt that negotiations could not start until certain conditions had been met, particularly with regard to presidential elections and electoral reform. When the presidential elections in June went smoothly, Parliament reviewed its position and came out in support of opening negotiations at an inter-parliamentary meeting held on 9 and 10 September. On 21 October, the

---

(¹) Bull. 11-2002, point 1.6.51.
(²) Bull. 7/8-2002, point 1.6.92.
(³) Bull. 10/2002, point 1.6.73.
(⁴) Bull. 11/2002, point 1.6.49.
(⁵) Bull. 12/2002, point 1.6.81.
(⁶) Joint Action 2002/921/CFSP (OJ L 321, 26.11.2002; Bull. 11-2002, point 1.6.50).
(⁷) Decision 2002/922/CSFP (OJ L 321, 26.11.2002; Bull. 11-2002, point 1.6.50).
(⁸) Joint Action 2002/964/CFSP (OJ L 334, 11.12.2002; Bull. 12-2002, point 1.6.82).
(⁹) http://europa.eu.int/comm/external_relations/see/actions/index.htm.
(¹⁰) Bull. 5-2002, point 1.6.73.

Council adopted a brief for negotiations on a stabilisation and association agreement between the European Union and Albania (Table III).

864. *Former Yugoslav Republic of Macedonia.* On 21 January, the Council adopted a regulation (¹) laying down arrangements for the implementation of provisions on a number of issues including agriculture and fisheries, the stabilisation and association agreement and the interim agreement concluded with FYROM in 2001 (²). On 19 December, the Council amended and added to the regulation by another regulation enabling the Community to use swift, effective procedures to deal with situations that require a rapid response such as safeguard or anti-fraud measures (³).

865. *Croatia.* On 28 January, the Council concluded an interim agreement on trade with Croatia (Table III), linked to the stabilisation and association agreement that was signed in 2001 (⁴). The interim agreement entered into force on 1 March and the Interim Committee held its first meeting on 19 April. On 19 December (⁵), the Council amended and added to Regulation (EC) No 2248/2001 on certain procedures for applying the stabilisation and association agreement and the interim agreement (⁶) with aims similar to those behind the new regulation concerning the Former Yugoslav Republic of Macedonia (→ point 864).

866. Other information on the countries covered by the stabilisation and association process can be found in this section under 'Regional cooperation and bilateral relations' (→ point 872 et seq.).

Technical and financial assistance

867. *European Agency for Reconstruction* (⁷). At its meeting on 18 and 19 February (⁸), the Council referred to the Court of Auditors' report concerning the Agency's accounts for 2000 (⁹). Highlighting the efficiency with which it managed its budget, the Council concluded that the Agency was serving the purpose for which it was created and welcomed the measures the Agency and the Commission had taken so far to implement certain recommendations of the

---

(¹) Regulation (EC) No 153/2002 (OJ L 25, 29.1.2002; Bull. 1/2-2001, point 1.6.79).
(²) 2001 General Report, point 974.
(³) Regulation (EC) No 3/2003 (OJ L 1, 4.1.2003; Bull. 12-2002, point 1.6.83).
(⁴) OJ C 320, 15.11.2001; 2001 General Report, point 975.
(⁵) Regulation (EC) No 2/2003 (OJ L 1, 4.1.2003; Bull. 12-2002, point 1.6.83).
(⁶) OJ L 304, 21.11.2001; 2001 General Report, point 975.
(⁷) http://www.ear.eu.int/.
(⁸) Bull. 1/2-2002, point 1.6.81.
(⁹) OJ C 355, 13.12.2001; 2001 General Report, point 1220.

Court of Auditors. On 10 June, the Commission adopted its second annual report on the Agency's activities ([1]), relating to 2001. It noted that the programmes funded by the Community and administered by the Agency continued to focus on three main areas: material and economic reconstruction, development of a market economy and support for private enterprise, and establishment of democracy, human rights and the rule of law. In its resolution of 5 September ([2]) on the Commission's first annual report on the Agency's activities ([3]), Parliament congratulated the Agency on its efficiency in 2000. However, it asked for clarification concerning the respective remits of the Agency and the Commission delegations. In 2002, the Agency, originally set up to implement aid programmes in Kosovo, had its remit explicitly extended to include the Former Yugoslav Republic of Macedonia, in line with Council Regulation (EC) No 2415/2001 ([4]).

868.   *Former Yugoslav Republic of Macedonia.* At a conference organised by the Commission and the World Bank in Brussels on 12 March ([5]), 38 donor countries and 19 donor international organisations decided to grant EUR 308.83 million for reconstruction and EUR 273.94 million to assist economic development in 2002. Of these totals EUR 104 million and EUR 24.5 million respectively would come from the Community budget.

869.   *Macro-financial assistance.* Information on macrofinancial assistance can be found in Chapter III, Section 1 under 'Economic and monetary policy' *(→ points 78 to 82).*

870.   *Aid management.* At operational level, the Commission continued the work it had started in 2000 on reforming the way it manages external aid; it pushed ahead with the devolution of activities from Brussels to the Commission delegations *(→ point 1152)* in those countries in the region where there had not yet been devolution or where the aid is not administered by the European Agency for Reconstruction *(→ point 867).*

871.   *Statistics.* Table 19 gives a breakdown of assistance for the Balkans in 2002 by instrument and by recipient country/region.

---

[1] COM(2002) 288; Bull. 6-2002, point 1.6.67.
[2] Bull. 9-2002, point 1.6.53.
[3] COM(2001) 446 and 2001 General Report, point 981.
[4] OJ L 327, 12.12.2001; 2001 General Report, point 981.
[5] Bull. 3-2002, point 1.6.57.

TABLE 19

Aid for the Balkans (not including humanitarian aid or macrofinancial assistance)

(EUR million)

	CARDS (¹)	Other programmes	Total
Albania	44.9		44.9
Former Yugoslav Republic of Macedonia	41.5		41.5
Bosnia and Herzegovina	71.9	13.3	85.2
Croatia	59.0		59.0
Federal Republic of Yugoslavia	351.6		351.6
of which:			
— Expenditure by the European Agency for Reconstruction	21 (²)		21
— Integrated management of borders (CARDS) regional programme	9.7		9.7
— Kosovo	137.9		137.9
— Montenegro	13.0		13.0
— Serbia	170		170
Regional cooperation	43.5		43.5
Administrative expenditure	19.6		19.6
Civil administrations	33 (³)		33

(¹) Community assistance for reconstruction, development and stabilisation.
(²) Met from budget headings for Serbia/Montenegro and Kosovo.
(³) Transitional civil administrations.

Regional cooperation and bilateral relations

872.   The statements made by the Presidency on behalf of the European Union concerning the countries in the western Balkans are shown in Table 17 (→ point 762).

873.   *Regional cooperation.* The stabilisation and association process, which essentially grew out of the old regional approach and the Stability Pact for South-Eastern Europe, launched in 1999 (¹), remains an essential catalyst for regional cooperation in that part of the world. Following the 2001 memorandum looking forward to the conclusion of bilateral free-trade agreements (²), a number of agreements of this type have now been signed with countries in the region and a start has been made on implementation. Furthermore, on 15 November in Athens, Albania, Bosnia and Herzegovina, Bulgaria, Greece, the Former Yugoslav Republic of Macedonia, Romania, Turkey, the Federal Republic of Yugoslavia and the UN Secretary-General's special representative for Kosovo signed a memorandum dealing specifically with the regional electric-

(¹) Common Position 1999/345/CFSP (OJ L 133, 28.5.1999; 1999 General Report, point 758).
(²) 2001 General Report, point 969.

ity market in south-eastern Europe and paving the way for it to be integrated into the EU internal market.

874.   *Albania*. On 13 May, the Council adopted negotiating briefs for an agreement on the activities of the European Union Monitoring Mission (EUMM) which has been set up in Albania (Table III) and which has had its mandate extended to 31 December 2002 ([1]). On 5 December, Mr Patten visited Albania. The EU–Albania consultative task force met in Tirana in March, June and November.

875.   *Bosnia and Herzegovina*. During a visit on 19 and 20 September, Mr Patten told his hosts that, in the Commission's view, Bosnia and Herzegovina had essentially adhered to the 'road map' that constituted the first stage of the stabilisation and association process and that, consequently, the Commission would press for a feasibility report on negotiations as soon as a new government was in place. The Council endorsed this view in its conclusions of 30 September ([2]). In the conclusions adopted at its meetings on 28 January ([3]) and 18 and 19 February ([4]), the Council announced that the European Union was ready to take over from the UN International Police Task Force (IPTF) from 1 January 2003. On 11 March, it adopted a joint action setting up an EU Police Mission (EUPM) ([5]) and appointing Mr Sven Frederiksen as Head of Mission/ Police Commissioner of the EUPM from 1 January 2003 to 31 December 2005 ([6]). The same day, it appointed Lord Ashdown as EU Special Representative in Bosnia and Herzegovina from 3 June ([7]). Lord Ashdown is also High Representative of the international community. The European Council, meeting in Seville on 21 and 22 June, stressed the importance of the EUPM ([8]). On 30 September, the Council and the authorities in Bosnia and Herzegovina concluded an agreement concerning the status of the EUPM (Table III). In its conclusions of 10 December ([9]), the Council welcomed the progress made by the EUPM's planning team in Sarajevo with a view to ensuring that the mission would be fully operational throughout the country from 1 January 2003 onwards, and the close cooperation between the team and the international organisations with a presence in the country. On the same day, it allocated EUR 38 million to the EUPM for 2003, including EUR 20 million from the European Union's general budget ([10]). Also on 10 December, the Council concluded agreements with Bulgaria, Cyprus, the Czech Republic, Hungary, Iceland, Latvia, Lithuania, Nor-

---

([1]) Joint Action 2001/845/CFSP (OJ L 315, 1.12.2001; 2001 General Report, point 969).
([2]) Bull. 9-2002, point 1.6.52.
([3]) Bull. 1/2-2002, point 1.6.85.
([4]) Bull. 1/2-2002, point 1.6.86.
([5]) Joint Action 2002/210/CFSP (OJ L 70, 13.3.2002; Bull. 3-2002, point 1.6.59).
([6]) Decision 2002/212/EC (OJ L 70, 13.3.2002; Bull. 3-2002, point 1.6.59).
([7]) Joint Action 2002/211/CFSP (OJ L 70, 13.3.2002; Bull. 3-2002, point 1.6.60).
([8]) Bull. 6-2002, point I.7.
([9]) Bull. 12-2002, point 1.6.86.
([10]) Decision 2002/968/CFSP (OJ L 335, 12.12.2002; Bull. 12-2002, point 1.6.87).

way, Poland, Romania, Slovakia, Slovenia, Switzerland, Turkey and Ukraine with a view to their involvement in the EUPM ([1]).

876.   Croatia. In its conclusions of 30 September, 21 October and 19 November referred to above *(→ point 860),* the Council, with reference to Croatia, pointed out that all States and other entities in the region had to cooperate with the International Criminal Tribunal for the former Yugoslavia, irrespective of national law in order not to jeopardise their rapprochement with the European Union, if for no other reason.

877.   Federal Republic of Yugoslavia. The European Council meeting in Barcelona welcomed the agreement reached in Belgrade on 14 March on the principle of a single constitutional arrangement for Serbia and Montenegro ([2]), expressed its appreciation for the work done by Mr Javier Solana, CFSP High Representative, and stressed the importance of the agreement for stability in the region. The initiative was also among those encouraged then welcomed by the Council in its conclusions of 28 January ([3]), 18 February ([4]), 11 March ([5]), 15 April ([6]) and 17 June ([7]). In its conclusions of 30 September ([8]), the Council stressed the importance of adopting the new constitutional charter and the action plan on the internal market, trade and customs. It also called on the authorities in Belgrade to cooperate fully with the International Criminal Tribunal for the Former Yugoslavia. It reminded all countries concerned of this obligation in its conclusions of 21 October ([9]). Furthermore, in its conclusions of 19 November ([10]), the Council welcomed the agreement reached on 5 November between political leaders in Serbia and also the fairness of the municipal elections organised recently in Kosovo. In its conclusions of 10 December ([11]), it welcomed the progress made towards the establishment of a new constitutional charter but expressed its concern at the result of the presidential elections on 8 December in Serbia.

Ms Schreyer and Mr Patten visited Belgrade on 31 May and 2 July respectively and Kosovo on 29 to 30 May and 18 September. The EU–Federal Republic of Yugoslavia Consultative Task Force held three meetings in Belgrade in February, May and July and made joint recommendations concerning sectoral reforms. A

---

[1] Bull. 12-2002, point 1.6.88.
[2] Bull. 3-2002, point I.48.
[3] Bull. 1/2-2002, point 1.6.78.
[4] Bull. 1/2-2002, point 1.6.87.
[5] Bull. 3-2002, point 1.6.55.
[6] Bull. 4-2002, point 1.6.43.
[7] Bull. 6-2002, point 1.6.66.
[8] Bull. 9-2002, point 1.6.52.
[9] Bull. 10-2002, point 1.6.73
[10] Bull. 11-2002, point 1.6.49
[11] Bull. 12-2002, point 1.6.81.

meeting of donors for Kosovo was also held in Brussels on 5 November to assess progress made and coordinate international assistance in the future.

878.   Former Yugoslav Republic of Macedonia. Council extended Mr Alain Le Roy's mandate as Special Representative of the European Union until 30 June in the first place (¹) and then until 31 December 2002 (²). On 30 September (³), the Council endorsed the appointment of Mr Alexis Brouhns as the new EU special representative in Skopje. The appointment was endorsed on 21 October by the Council (⁴), which then extended his mandate to 30 June 2003 (⁵). On 21 and 22 June, the European Council, meeting in Seville, expressed the EU's willingness to take over from NATO in the Former Yugoslav Republic of Macedonia (⁶). It reaffirmed this at its meeting in Brussels on 24 and 25 October (⁷).

On 21 January, the Council set up a double-checking system for steel imports from the Former Yugoslav Republic of Macedonia *(→ point 802)*. On 21 October, it signed an agreement on the ecopoints system for heavy goods vehicles registered in the Former Yugoslav Republic of Macedonia and transiting through Austria *(→ point 644)*.

(¹) Joint Action 2002/129/CFSP (OJ L 47, 19.2.2002; Bull. 1/2-2002, point 1.6.84).
(²) Joint Action 2002/497/CFSP (OJ L 167, 26.6.2002; Bull. 6-2002, point 1.6.69).
(³) Bull. 9-2002, point 1.6.54.
(⁴) Joint Action 2002/832/CFSP (OJ L 285, 23.10.2002; Bull. 10-2002, point 1.6.79).
(⁵) Joint Action 2002/963/CFSP (OJ L 334, 11.12.2002; Bull. 12-2002, point 1.6.84).
(⁶) Bull. 6-2002, point I.7.
(⁷) Bull. 10-2002, point I.12.

Section 8

Relations with the southern Mediterranean and the Middle East (¹)

Overview

879. *Against a background of extreme tension in the Middle East, a series of initiatives were adopted in the framework of the Barcelona process started in 1995, while the strategic measures agreed subsequently were intensified. The Euro-Mediterranean Conference of Foreign Ministers in Valencia in April was a key event in this context with all participants stressing the importance of revitalising the Euro-Mediterranean partnership at political level through enhanced dialogue. Similar meetings took place for ministers with various sectoral responsibilities. The action plan adopted at the end of the Valencia conference reflected the desire to intensify the Euro-Mediterranean partnership in the political, economic, social and cultural spheres and in the human dimension, including cooperation in the area of counter-terrorism. At bilateral level, association agreements were signed with Algeria and Lebanon, while negotiations with Syria advanced. Financial and technical cooperation under the MEDA II programme continued with each of the beneficiary countries and bodies and at regional level.*

Overall strategy

880. *Euro-Mediterranean Ministerial Conference in Valencia* (²). The sixth Euro-Mediterranean conference on 22 and 23 April (³) brought together foreign ministers from the 15 EU Member States and Algeria, Cyprus, Egypt, Israel, Jordan, Malta, Morocco, the Palestinian Authority, Tunisia and Turkey. Lebanon and Syria declined to attend. Also present were Mr Javier Solana, High Representative for the CFSP, Mr Patten for the Commission and, as special guests, representatives of Libya, the Arab League, Mauritania and the Arab Maghreb Union.

(¹) Further information is available on the Europa server (http://europa.eu.int/comm/external_relations/med_mideast/intro/index.htm).
(²) http://europa.eu.int/comm/external_relations/euromed/conf/val/index.htm.
(³) Bull. 4-2002, point 1.6.50. Previous conference: 2001 General Report, point 994.

The participants stressed the importance of an enhanced dialogue and the relaunching of the principles and aims of the Barcelona Declaration of 1995 ([1]) aimed at making the Mediterranean region an area of peace and stability, development and shared prosperity, and of cooperation and understanding between cultures and civilisations. The ministers said that a solution to the Israeli-Palestinian conflict could not be a military one and that the parties should immediately halt recourse to arms and apply UN Security Council resolutions. They also adopted an action plan whose objectives covered the different fields of the Euro-Mediterranean partnership ([2]): strengthening political dialogue and a multilateral approach to the fight against terrorism; promoting the trade dimension of the partnership and financial cooperation and improved management of the MEDA programme, speeding up the creation of the Euro-Mediterranean free trade area, enhancing sustainable development and tourism; adoption of a framework document on the implementation of a regional justice and home affairs programme and launching a ministerial conference on migration; creation of a Euro-Mediterranean Foundation in the cultural field and of a Euro-Mediterranean parliamentary assembly at institutional level.

At Community level, the preparation of the Valencia conference was the subject of a Commission communication on 13 February ([3]), a Parliament resolution of 11 April ([4]) and Council conclusions on 15 April ([5]). In a resolution of 15 May ([6]), Parliament welcomed the outcome of the conference.

881.   Euro-Mediterranean sectoral ministerial conferences ([7]). A series of Euro-Mediterranean conferences on specific sectors also took place at ministerial level, including:

- the second conference of trade ministers in Toledo on 19 March ([8]), attended by Mr Lamy: talks centred on origin rules, regional integration (adoption of an action plan to facilitate trade and investment) and development and liberalisation of the services sector;

- the fourth conference of ministers for industry in Malaga on 9 and 10 April ([9]): in addition to the Middle East peace dimension, the parties noted the importance of Euromed industrial cooperation in the context of the establishment of a free trade area in the Mediterranean region by 2010 and set a number of priorities including harmonisation of the regulatory

---

([1]) 1995 General Report, point 839; Internet (http://www.euromed.net/key-docs/barcelona.htm).
([2]) http://europa.eu.int/comm/external_relations/euromed/conf/val/concl.htm.
([3]) SEC(2002) 159; Bull. 1/2-2002, point 1.6.91.
([4]) Bull. 4-2002, point 1.6.47.
([5]) Bull. 4-2002, point 1.6.48.
([6]) Bull. 5-2002, point 1.6.76.
([7]) http://europa.eu.int/comm/external_relations/euromed/conf/index.htm.
([8]) Bull. 3-2002, point 1.6.64.
([9]) Bull. 4-2002, point 1.6.49.

framework, improving the conditions for attracting investment, SME development and reinforcing the role of the private sector;

- a conference of energy ministers in Tunis on 6 May *(→ point 605)*;

- a meeting of environment ministers in Athens on 10 July to prepare the World Summit on Sustainable Development *(→ point 590)*.

882. *Euro-Mediterranean summit of economic and social councils.* This meeting, held in Athens on 6 and 7 March ([1]), was attended by representatives of economic and social councils and similar institutions in the Euro-Mediterranean countries. Participants voiced a common determination to combat all forms of intolerance and called for a lasting peace in the Middle East, a strengthening of the social, cultural and human dimension of the Euro-Mediterranean partnership and more intensive action to promote civil society.

883. *Women's rights.* Considering that thus far women had played only a marginal role in Euro-Mediterranean cooperation, Parliament called in a resolution of 7 February ([2]) for the gender dimension to be incorporated into the different facets of the Euro-Mediterranean partnership and for the principle of political, social and economic equality between the sexes to be respected.

884. Statements by the Presidency on behalf of the EU concerning the southern Mediterranean and the Middle East can be found in Table 17 *(→ point 762)*. Parliament resolutions concerning human rights in the southern Mediterranean and the Middle East can be found in Table 2 *(→ point 54)*.

Maghreb

885. *Algeria.* On 22 April, the Community and its Member States signed a Euro-Mediterranean association agreement ([3]) with Algeria for an indefinite period, replacing the cooperation agreement and the agreement on ECSC products signed in 1976 (Table III). The new agreement covers the following main areas: regular political dialogue; gradual establishment of a free trade area; provisions on service liberalisation, capital movements, competition rules, intellectual property and government procurement; closer economic and financial cooperation and cooperation in the area of justice and home affairs. On 10 October ([4]), Parliament called on the Algerian authorities to step up their efforts to ensure respect for fundamental rights.

([1]) Bull. 3-2002, point 1.6.65.
([2]) OJ C 284 E, 21.11.2002; Bull. 1/2-2002, point 1.6.90.
([3]) http://europa.eu.int/comm/external_relations/algeria/intro/ip02_597.htm.
([4]) Bull. 10-2002, point 1.6.82.

886.   Morocco. The Association Committee held its second meeting in Rabat on 13 March. The parties continued dialogue on political and regional issues of mutual concern, reviewed the progress of the various working parties and evaluated the measures taken towards the establishment of a free trade area between Morocco and the Community. On 27 June, Prime Minister Abderrahmane Youssoufi visited Brussels for talks with Mr Pat Cox, President of the European Parliament, Mr Javier Solana, High Representative for the CFSP and Messrs Prodi, Patten and Vitorino of the Commission. Mr Mohamed Benaissa, the Foreign Minister, also met with Messrs Cox, Solana, Prodi and Patten on 14 November ([1]).

887.   Tunisia. The third meeting of the EU–Tunisia Association Council took place in Brussels on 29 January ([2]). The parties concluded that cooperation was working well and focused their discussions on the trade and financial components of the agreement. They also called for greater focus on the social field and on services. Political aspects addressed included the subject of pluralist democracy and the situation in the Middle East.

888.   Arab Maghreb Union. Referring to the special nature of the EU–Maghreb partnership in a resolution of 11 June ([3]), Parliament called for compliance with the association agreements with the Maghreb countries, notably in relation to human rights, democracy and the rule of law. It highlighted the Union's role in settling conflicts and in fostering stability in the region and advocated greater EU openness to those countries' exports and a review of EU immigration policy.

Mashreq, Palestinian territories, Israel ([4])

889.   Situation in the Middle East. The Barcelona European Council of 15 and 16 March ([5]) adopted a declaration recognising that there was no military solution to the Israeli-Palestinian conflict and calling on both parties to stop the bloodshed. Welcoming the adoption of UN Security Council Resolution 1397, it called for urgent implementation thereof, and welcomed also the peace initiative by the Crown Prince of Saudi Arabia; condemning indiscriminate terrorist attacks, the European Council considered that Israel should immediately withdraw its military forces from areas placed under the control of the Palestinian Authority and demanded the removal of all restrictions on the freedom of movement of its President, Mr Yasser Arafat. Lastly, it pointed out that the European Union would make a substantial economic contribution to peace-building in the

---

([1]) Bull. 11-2002, point 1.6.53.
([2]) Bull. 1/2-2002, point 1.6.93; Internet (http://europa.eu.int/comm/external_relations/tunisia/intro/index.htm).
([3]) Bull. 6-2002, point 1.6.72.
([4]) http://europa.eu.int/comm/external_relations/mepp/index.htm.
([5]) Bull. 3-2002, point I.55.

region. In a further declaration adopted by the Seville European Council of 21 and 22 June (¹), the EU Heads of State or Government supported the convening of an international conference to address political and economic aspects as well as matters relating to security. Noting that a settlement could be achieved only through negotiation, the European Council considered that the end result should be two States living side by side within secure and recognised borders. It reaffirmed its willingness to continue to assist in the reforms to the Palestinian Authority. It also stated the Union's readiness to work with the parties and with its partners in the international community, especially in the framework of the quartet (United Nations, European Union, United States and Russia). The members of the quartet met in New York on 17 September (²), with Mr Patten and Mr Javier Solana, the CFSP High Representative, also participating. The meeting resulted in a three-stage plan based largely on the Union's proposals and including provision for free elections for the Palestinian people, the creation of a Palestinian State and negotiations between Israel and Palestine aiming at a final settlement by 2005.

The situation in the Middle East was also the subject of Council conclusions on 28 January (³), 13 May (⁴), 22 July (⁵) and 30 September (⁶), Common Position 2002/400/CFSP (⁷) and resolutions by Parliament on 7 February (⁸) and 10 April (⁹).

On 10 December (¹⁰), the Council extended the mandate of Mr Miguel Angel Moratinos as EU special representative for the Middle East peace process until 30 June 2003.

890.   *Egypt.* The Egyptian Prime Minister, Mr Atef Ebeid, visited Brussels on 30 October (¹¹) accompanied by Mr Youssef Boutros-Ghali and Mr Ahmed Nazif, the Minister for Foreign Trade and Minister for Communications and Information Technology, respectively.

891.   *Israel.* The second and third meetings of the Association Council, set up under the EU–Israel association agreement (¹²), were held in Jerusalem and Luxembourg on 8 and 21 October, respectively (¹³). Talks at the two meetings were mainly devoted to political dialogue, scientific cooperation, origin rules, agricul-

---

(¹) Bull. 6-2002, point I.32.
(²) Bull. 9-2002, point 1.6.56.
(³) Bull. 1/2-2002, point 1.6.96.
(⁴) Bull. 5-2002, point 1.6.78.
(⁵) Bull. 7/8-2002, point 1.6.99.
(⁶) Bull. 9-2002, point 1.6.59.
(⁷) OJ L 138, 28.5.2002; Bull. 5-2002, point 1.6.80.
(⁸) OJ C 284 E, 21.11.2002; Bull. 1/2-2002, point 1.6.98.
(⁹) Bull. 4-2002, point 1.6.52.
(¹⁰) Joint Action 2002/965/CFSP (OJ L 334, 11.12.2002; Bull. 12-2002, point 1.6.94).
(¹¹) Bull. 10-2002, point 1.6.85.
(¹²) OJ L 147, 21.6.2000; 2000 General Report, point 923.
(¹³) Bull. 10-2002, point 1.6.83.

tural negotiations and cultural cooperation. At the meeting in Luxembourg the Israeli Foreign Minister, Mr Shimon Peres, met Mr Patten and Mr Pat Cox, President of the European Parliament. In a resolution of 19 December ([1]), Parliament urged the Government of Israel to stop the plan to demolish parts of Hebron's Old City, an action which undermined the cultural heritage of Palestine.

892.   *Jordan.* On 25 March, the Council concluded a Euro-Mediterranean association agreement with Jordan (Table III). This agreement, which replaces the cooperation agreement and the agreement concerning ECSC products signed in 1977, entered into force on 1 May for an unlimited duration and contains a clause concerning respect for democratic principles and human rights. It provides for regular political dialogue, the gradual establishment of a free trade area over a maximum period of 12 years and the strengthening of cooperation between the two parties. It also includes a special clause whereby the parties undertake to examine the situation of trade in agricultural products in order to be able to decide on new mutual concessions as soon as possible after the agreement's entry into force. The EU–Jordan Association Council set up in the framework of the new agreement held its first meeting in Luxembourg on 10 June ([2]). The meeting provided the occasion for taking the necessary first steps for implementing the association agreement. The EU stressed its commitment to respect for human rights and democratic principles in Jordan and both parties also addressed the situation in the Middle East. On 12 June ([3]), King Abdullah visited Strasbourg where he addressed a plenary session of the European Parliament and met Mr Pat Cox, the President, and Mr Prodi.

893.   *Lebanon.* On 17 June, the Community signed a Euro-Mediterranean association agreement with Lebanon for an indefinite duration (Table III). The agreement covers the following main aspects: respect for democratic principles and human rights; regular political dialogue; establishment of a free trade area over a transitional period not exceeding 12 years; trade in services; economic issues, e.g. capital movements, competition and economic cooperation; dialogue and cooperation on social and cultural issues, and on immigration; financial cooperation to help Lebanon undertake economic reforms. An interim agreement covering trade and trade-related aspects of the association agreement (Table III) and an agreement in the form of an exchange of letters on cooperation on combating terrorism *(→ point 492)* were also signed.

894.   *Syria.* On 21 January, the Council updated the negotiating directives issued in 1997 to include the area of justice and home affairs in the future EU–Syria Euro-Mediterranean association agreement (Table III). Talks were held on this subject at meetings in June and November.

([1]) Bull. 12-2002, point 1.6.93.
([2]) Bull. 6-2002, point 1.6.73.
([3]) Bull. 6-2002, point 1.6.74.

895. *Palestinian refugees.* In a common position of 21 May (^{1}), the Council set out the conditions for certain Member States to take in 12 Palestinians evacuated from the Church of the Nativity in Bethlehem. On 23 September, the Community concluded a convention with the United Nations Relief and Works Agency for Palestine Refugees in the Near East (UNRWA) (^{2}) on the continued provision of financial assistance to refugees over the period 2002 to 2005 (Table III).

896. *Multilateral visits.* During a visit between 6 and 9 January (^{3}), Mr Javier Solana, the CFSP High Representative, accompanied by EU Special Representative Mr Miguel Ángel Moratinos, was received in Israel by Mr Ariel Sharon, Prime Minister, Mr Shimon Peres and Mr Binyamin Ben Eliezer, Foreign and Defence Ministers respectively; in the Palestinian territories by Mr Yasser Arafat, President of the Palestinian Authority; in Jordan by Mr Abdul Illah al-Khatib, Foreign Minister; and in Egypt by President Hosni Mubarak, Foreign Minister Ahmed Maher, and Mr Amre Moussa, Secretary-General of the Arab League. On 27 March (^{4}), Mr Solana attended the Arab League summit in Beirut. On a visit between 6 and 10 February (^{5}), Mr Lamy was received in Syria by President Bashar Al-Assad and Prime Minister Muhammed Miro, in Lebanon by President Emile Lahoud and Prime Minister Rafiq Hariri, and in Jordan by King Abdullah II and Prime Minister Ali Abu Ragheb. Mr Patten made a visit to Egypt and Jordan from 13 to 15 October (^{6}). In Egypt he met President Mubarak, Mr Maher and Mr Moussa, as well as Mr Atef Ebeid, the Prime Minister, Mr Ahmed Fathi Srour, Speaker of the People's Assembly, Mrs Fayza Aboulnaga, Minister of State, and Mr Mostafa Kamal Helmy, Speaker of the Shura Council. In Jordan he was received by King Abdullah II, Prime Minister Ragheb, Mr Marwan Muashar, the Foreign Minister, Mr Zaid Al Rifai, President of the Senate, and Mr Michel Marto, Finance Minister.

Middle East

897. *Gulf Cooperation Council (GCC)* (^{7}). At its 12th meeting in Granada on 27 and 28 February (^{8}), the Joint Cooperation Council between the European Union and the GCC (^{9}) took stock of the various joint measures undertaken or planned. The parties confirmed their desire to continue negotiations for the conclusion of a free trade agreement and raised a number of international and regional issues of mutual interest. Subsequent negotiations in the GCC in

---

(^{1}) Common Position 2002/400/CFSP (OJ L 138, 28.5.2002; Bull. 5-2002, point 1.6.80).
(^{2}) http://www.un.org/unrwa/index.html.
(^{3}) Bull. 1/2-2002, point 1.6.94.
(^{4}) Bull. 3-2002, point 1.6.72.
(^{5}) Bull. 1/2-2002, point 1.6.99.
(^{6}) Bull. 10-2002, point 1.6.84.
(^{7}) http://europa.eu.int/comm/external_relations/gulf_cooperation/intro/index.htm.
(^{8}) Bull. 1/2-2002, point 1.6.101.
(^{9}) Bahrain, Kuwait, Oman, Qatar, Saudi Arabia, United Arab Emirates.

March, May, July, October and December resulted in the adoption of a decision on the establishment of a customs union, an essential condition for the conclusion of the free trade agreement between the EU and GCC.

898.   Iran. In its conclusions of 17 June ([1]), the Council underscored the importance of relations with Iran and expressed its support for the country's reform process. On 12 July, it adopted negotiating directives for a trade and cooperation agreement between the European Community and Iran (Table III), while negotiations were opened in Brussels on 12 December concerning political dialogue and combating terrorism. The Iranian Foreign Minister, Mr Kamal Kharazzi, met Messrs Solana, Prodi and Patten on 18 and 19 November ([2]).

899.   Iraq. On 22 July, the Council updated Common Position 96/741/CFSP concerning derogations to the embargo on Iraq ([3]) with a new common position ([4]) which took account of the conditions set out in UN Security Council Resolution 1409(2002) on 14 May. In order to implement this initiative, an amendment was made on 25 July ([5]) to Regulation (EC) No 2465/96 concerning the interruption of economic and financial relations between the European Community and Iraq ([3]). On 19 November ([6]), the European Council welcomed the adoption of Security Council Resolution 1441(2002) which paved the way for weapons inspectors to return to Iraq.

Financial and technical cooperation

900.   General aspects. Under the new MEDA II regulation ([7]), the Commission committed, in 2002, around EUR 585 million under the national financing plans for all the Euro-Mediterranean partnership countries and EUR 16 million under the regional financing plan. A further EUR 2.5 million was committed to strengthening the programme of activities of the Middle East peace process. The West Bank and Gaza Strip, which are subject to separate commitments in view of the ongoing state of crisis, received a total of around EUR 220 million from the Commission under various programmes, mainly in the form of support for the peace process and aid to Palestinian refugees via UNRWA.

In the operational field, the reform of the management of external aid adopted by the Commission in 2000 saw the process of devolution from headquarters to the Commission's delegations accelerate over the year *(→ point 1152).*

([1]) Bull. 6-2002, point 1.6.78.
([2]) Bull. 11-2002, point 1.6.57.
([3]) OJ L 337, 27.12.1996; 1996 General Report, point 844.
([4]) Common Position 2002/599/CFSP (OJ L 194, 23.7.2002; Bull. 7/8-2002, point 1.6.103).
([5]) Council Regulation (EC) No 1346/2002 (OJ L 197, 26.7.2002; Bull. 7/8-2002, point 1.6.104).
([6]) Bull. 11-2002, point 1.6.59.
([7]) Regulation (EC) No 2698/2000 (OJ L 311, 12.12.2000; 2000 General Report, point 928).

901.   *Regional cooperation.* With the adoption of the 2002 regional financing plan, a major EUR 6 million programme of regional cooperation was launched in the areas of justice, action to combat drug-trafficking and organised crime, and counter-terrorism. The programme also contained a section dealing with immigration, social integration and mobility of persons. An additional EUR 4 million was committed to regional cooperation under the 'Euromed information and communication' programme.

902.   *Euro-Mediterranean Investment Facility.* In a report on 27 February ([1]), responding to the invitation made at the Laeken European Council ([2]) to examine the setting-up of a Euro-Mediterranean development bank, the Commission envisaged several options for creating a 'facility' or a fund on setting up the bank. It recommended the solution of a bank institution which would be a subsidiary of the European Investment Bank (EIB) and have as its main task the promotion of private sector development and contributing to infrastructure financing. In its conclusions on 14 March ([3]), the Council indicated its preference for the establishment, initially, of a reinforced Euro-Mediterranean Investment Facility in the EIB, complemented by the Euro-Mediterranean partnership arrangement and an EIB representative office in the area; the creation of a subsidiary would be considered and a decision taken, if necessary, one year after the launching of the facility. The Barcelona European Council endorsed this approach ([4]). On 4 June ([5]), the Council stressed the importance of implementing the new facility as soon as possible. In September, the Euro-Mediterranean investment facility was set up in the EIB. The new facility will be managed by the EIB and have a supervisory board consisting not only of the Member States and the Commission, but also the partner States and international financial institutions active in the Mediterranean region. The EIB will also manage technical assistance and venture capital projects financed from the Community budget to which the Commission has committed EUR 255 million for the period 2003–06.

903.   *Transport.* At its meeting of 25 and 26 March ([6]), the Council welcomed the achievements made in the field of Euro-Mediterranean cooperation on transport, particularly the adoption, with an allocation of EUR 20 million under the MEDA annual financing plan, of the Euromed transport project. It called for the development of other regional projects in the transport sector, particularly maritime security/safety and satellite navigation projects.

([1]) SEC(2002) 218; Bull. 1/2-2002, point 1.6.92.
([2]) Bull. 12-2001, point I.24.
([3]) Bull. 3-2002, point 1.6.66.
([4]) Bull. 3-2002, point I.42.
([5]) Bull. 6-2002, point 1.6.71.
([6]) Bull. 3-2002, point 1.6.67.

Section 9

Relations with the independent States of the former Soviet Union and with Mongolia (¹)

Overview

904.   *Regular political dialogue with these countries continued throughout 2002 via the joint cooperation bodies set up under the partnership agreements and other agreements concluded with each country and in summits with Russia and Ukraine. These various meetings focused on respect for human rights, promotion of democracy and the transition to a market economy while the issue of the future Russian enclave of Kaliningrad was also raised on several occasions with the prospect of EU enlargement.*

Partnership and other agreements

905.   *Southern Caucasus.* The fourth meeting of the Joint Cooperation Councils with Armenia and Azerbaijan was held in Brussels on 1 October (²). At the end of these meetings the parties recognised the importance of continued development of democracy and human rights as a factor for stability in the southern Caucasus region. They also confirmed their commitment to press freedom and the importance they attached to the holding of successful national elections in 2003. An improvement in the economic climate for investors remained a priority. The fourth meeting of the Joint Cooperation Council with Georgia was also held in Brussels on 1 October (²). The deterioration of the security situation in that country, and in particular the cases of abduction of European citizens was at the centre of the EU's concerns. The Union concluded that the amount and arrangements for future aid to Georgia and the decisions on implementation of assistance already under way would depend strongly on the EU's assessment of the domestic security situation in the country. The EU also reiterated its support for Georgia's territorial integrity.

(¹) Further information is available on the Europa server (http://europa.eu.int/comm/external_relations/ceeca/index.htm).
(²) Bull. 10-2002, point 1.6.88.

906.   *Central Asia.* The fourth meeting of the Joint Cooperation Council with Kazakhstan was held in Brussels on 23 July (¹). The importance for Kazakhstan of guaranteeing freedom of the press and freedom of expression and ensuring transparency in the judicial system was recognised as an essential condition for cooperation. In addition to human rights issues, the discussions focused on areas of the partnership such as justice and home affairs, energy, transport, investment, Kazakhstan's accession to the WTO and protection of intellectual, industrial and commercial property rights. The EU–Kyrgyzstan Cooperation Council held its fourth meeting in Brussels on 23 July (²). Stressing the fact that respect for democracy, the principles of international law and human rights was an essential condition for their cooperation, the parties recognised the importance for Kyrgyzstan of guaranteeing freedom of the press and freedom of expression and ensuring the transparency of the judicial and regulatory systems. Regional cooperation, the fight against terrorism, justice and home affairs and trade and investment were also discussed. The third meeting of the joint EU–Uzbekistan cooperation council was held in Brussels on 29 January (³). The parties confirmed their desire to step up their political dialogue and cooperation on issues such as trade and investment, democracy, the rule of law and respect for human rights. Prospects for cooperation on the fight against terrorism and illegal activities were also explored.

907.   *Moldova.* In the framework of the partnership and cooperation agreement with that country, the fourth cooperation council was held in Luxembourg on 16 April (⁴). Discussions focused on the four priority areas of cooperation: approximation of legislation and effective application of the law; trade and transfrontier cooperation; justice and home affairs; the prospects for a free trade agreement. The partners also discussed the political situation in Moldova and the conflict in Transnistria.

908.   *Mongolia.* The sixth joint EU–Mongolia Cooperation Council meeting was held in Brussels on 20 November. In the interests of efficiency Mongolia agreed in future to take part in the Community programme of assistance to the countries of Asia and Latin America *(→ points 967 and 985)* rather than the Tacis programme specific to the independent States of the former Soviet Union and to Mongolia.

909.   *Russia.* The EU–Russia cooperation council held its fifth meeting in Luxembourg on 16 April (⁵). It encouraged a high-level group recently created by the parties to continue its work on drawing up a concept for a common European economic area. It also welcomed the intensification of negotiations ahead of

(¹) Bull. 7/8-2002, point 1.6.111.
(²) Bull. 7/8-2002, point 1.6.113.
(³) Bull. 1/2-2002, point 1.6.105.
(⁴) Bull. 4-2002, point 1.6.56.
(⁵) Bull. 4-2002, point 1.6.57.

Russia's membership of the WTO. Other subjects broached were the launching of a structured energy dialogue, cooperation on nuclear safety, the fight against organised crime and terrorism, crisis management and conflict prevention.

910.   Ukraine. The fifth Joint Cooperation Council meeting was held in Brussels on 11 March (¹). The European Union stressed the need for continued economic and political reform in Ukraine. The partnership and cooperation agreement (²) was considered an important instrument in this field, notably in the areas of energy, trade, justice and home affairs, the environment and transport.

Financial assistance

911.   Statistics. In 2002, EUR 440 million was allocated for assistance to Armenia, Azerbaijan, Georgia, Mongolia, Russia, Ukraine and the countries of central Asia. This assistance covered six fields of cooperation: the need for institutional, judicial and administrative reform; support for the private sector and aid for economic development; aid to cushion the social consequences of transition to a market economy; development of infrastructure networks; strengthening of protection of the environment and management of natural resources; development of the rural economy. Each country had to confine itself to three sectors at most. All chose the first two listed above. Around EUR 100 million was put at the disposal of the countries concerned for various activities in the field of nuclear safety *(→ point 627).*

At the operational level, implementation of the Commission's reform of management of external assistance adopted in 2000 continued with accelerated devolution from EC headquarters to the delegations *(→ point 1152).*

912.   Regional cooperation. At a pledging conference on 9 July a support fund was created to support the environmental partnership for the northern dimension (NDEP) (³) with a view to financing projects in the field of the environment and nuclear safety, principally in north-west Russia.

*913.   Further information on macrofinancial assistance can be found in Section 1 ('Economic and monetary policy') of Chapter III *(→ points 78 to 82).* Information on the EU's contribution to nuclear safety can be found in Section 5 ('Energy') of Chapter IV *(→ points 626 and 627).*

(¹) Bull. 3-2002, point 1.6.80.
(²) OJ L 49, 19.2.1998; 1998 General Report, point 858.
(³) http://europa.eu.int/comm/external_relations/north_dim/ndep/index.htm.

Bilateral relations

914. Statements by the Presidency on behalf of the EU concerning the independent States of the former Soviet Union and Mongolia can be found in Table 17 *(→ point 762).* Parliament resolutions concerning human rights in these countries can be found in Table 2 *(→ point 54).*

915. *Belarus.* In a declaration on 21 October on Belarus and its relations with the Organisation for Security and Cooperation in Europe (OSCE) (¹), the Council emphasised the vital role played by the OSCE Advisory and Monitoring Group (AMG) in assisting the Government of Belarus and civil society in promoting democratic institutions; it could not therefore accept the Belarusian position that the AMG should be formally closed before negotiations on a new OSCE presence could begin.

916. *Kazakhstan.* Mr Nursultan Nazarbayev, the President of Kazakhstan, met Mr Prodi for talks in Brussels on 29 November (²). During his visit an agreement on nuclear fusion was signed.

917. *Russia* (³). In 2002, two EU–Russia summits were held, the first in Moscow on 29 May (⁴), the second in Brussels on 11 November (⁵).

In Moscow, Russia and the EU reaffirmed their commitment to democratic principles and human rights and their determination to work harder still to deal with the challenges facing them both, such as international terrorism, drug trafficking and illegal immigration. The Union announced its intention to grant Russia the status of a market economy, with the trade advantages attached to that, and reaffirmed its support for the creation of a common economic space and Russia's rapid accession to the WTO. The parties adopted joint declarations on the energy dialogue and on strengthening their political dialogue and cooperation on crisis management and security. They also examined the special situation of Kaliningrad which will become a Russian enclave within the EU after the enlargement. The parties broached issues of international politics, notably the situation in Afghanistan, the conflict in the Middle East and the deterioration in relations between India and Pakistan. Ahead of the summit, the European Parliament adopted on 15 May (⁶) a resolution in which it announced its support for the creation of a common European economic area and the intensification of cooperation between the parties on energy and science and technology. It also reiterated its support for media plurality and the develop-

---

(¹) Bull. 10-2002, point 1.6.91.
(²) Bull. 11-2002, point 1.6.62.
(³) http://europa.eu.int/comm/external_relations/russia/intro/index.htm.
(⁴) Bull. 5-2002, point 1.6.90. Previous summits: 2001 General Report, point 1022.
(⁵) Bull. 11-2002, point 1.6.63.
(⁶) Bull. 5-2002, point 1.6.89.

ment of the rule of law in Russia and stressed the need to find an immediate political solution to the conflict in Chechnya, a subject it specifically raised in a resolution of 10 April (¹).

The summit in Brussels saw considerable progress achieved towards a solution of the problem of the enclave of Kaliningrad: the parties adopted a joint declaration in which they agreed to make a special effort to respond to the interests of both parties, as regards Lithuania, and to promote the economic and social development of the region; they also reached agreement on a system of documents for Russian citizens wanting to travel between the enclave and other parts of Russia. The parties also formulated a declaration on the situation in the Middle East and discussed progress on the definition of a common European economic space and on the dialogue on energy issues. As part of the preparations for the Brussels summit, the EU troika visited Moscow on 17 October (²). In a resolution on 21 November following the summit (³), Parliament urged the Commission to monitor closely the mechanisms for implementation of the agreement on Kaliningrad. Reiterating its conviction that the war in Chechnya could not only be considered as part of the fight against terrorism, Parliament also advocated the adoption of a political solution based on dialogue. In its conclusions of 25 November (⁴), the Council stressed the importance of the ongoing dialogue on energy with Russia as a cornerstone of a coherent approach to this sensitive issue.

On 25 April, in Brussels, the Union's justice and home affairs ministers met their Russian counterparts (⁵). The participants at the meeting adopted a joint declaration on the designation of central contact points to exchange information on organised crime.

In an own-initiative opinion of 20 March (⁶), the European Economic and Social Committee recommended involving civil society more closely in the partnership with Russia. For its part, in a resolution of 15 May (⁷), Parliament formulated recommendations on the communication presented by the Commission in January 2001 (⁸) on the Kaliningrad enclave. The Council also gave its opinion on this subject on 17 June (⁹), as did the Seville European Council (¹⁰). Responding to an invitation from the European Council, the Commission presented, on 18 September, a study on the scope for resolving the issue of persons in transit

---

(¹) Bull. 4-2002, point 1.6.59.
(²) Bull. 10-2002, point 1.6.93.
(³) Bull. 11-2002, point 1.6.94.
(⁴) Bull. 11-2002, point 1.6.65.
(⁵) Bull. 4-2002, point 1.6.60.
(⁶) OJ C 125, 27.5.2002; Bull. 3-2002, point 1.6.79.
(⁷) Bull. 5-2002, point 1.6.88.
(⁸) COM(2001) 26 and 2001 General Report, point 1023.
(⁹) Bull. 6-2002, point 1.6.84.
(¹⁰) Bull. 6-2002, point I.23.

to and from Kaliningrad while respecting the Community *acquis* and in agreement with the two candidate countries concerned (¹). The Council welcomed this communication in its conclusions of 30 September (²), returning to the issue again in its conclusions of 22 October shortly before the summit in Brussels (³).

On 21 May, the Council adopted a joint action (⁴) with the aim of strengthening the capacity of the Georgian authorities to support and protect an OSCE observer mission at the frontier between Georgia and Russia. The same day, it adopted a decision (⁵) on an additional financial contribution for the experts coordinating the EU programme for non-proliferation and disarmament in the Russian Federation (⁶). In a report of 20 June to the European Council (⁷), the Council took stock of the implementation of the EU common strategy on Russia (⁸). The Brussels European Council of 24 and 25 October condemned the hostage situation taking place in a Moscow theatre (⁹).

918.   Ukraine. The EU–Ukraine summit was held in Copenhagen on 4 July (¹⁰). The Union was represented by Mr Anders Fogh Rasmussen, Danish Prime Minister and President of the European Council and by Mr Javier Solana, High Representative for the CFSP, and Mr Prodi, President of the Commission; Mr Leonid Kuchma, President of Ukraine, led his country's delegation. Recognising the progress made by its partner on political and economic reform, the Union stressed that strengthening the country's democratic institutions, the rule of law and the market economy was essential for Ukraine's development and stepping up mutual relations. On the continuation of their strategic partnership, the parties agreed to step up cooperation with a view to aligning Ukraine's legislation on EU norms and standards. They also reaffirmed their desire to develop their regional and trans-border cooperation and cooperation in the field of justice and home affairs, energy, transport and the environment, and on crisis management. The Union renewed its support for Ukraine's aim to acquire the status of a market economy and join the WTO. The parties discussed in detail international issues such as the conflict in the Middle East and the situation in Belarus. Finally, they signed an agreement for scientific and technological cooperation *(→ point 314)*.

(¹) COM(2002) 510; Bull. 9-2002, point 1.6.62.
(²) Bull. 9-2002, point 1.6.62.
(³) Bull. 10-2002, point 1.6.94.
(⁴) Joint Action 2002/373/CFSP (OJ L 134, 22.5.2002; Bull. 5-2002, point 1.6.86).
(⁵) Decision 2002/381/CFSP (OJ L 136, 24.5.2002; Bull. 5-2002, point 1.6.91). Previous decision: Decision 2001/493/CFSP (OJ L 180, 3.7.2001 and 2001 General Report, point 1021).
(⁶) Joint Action 1999/878/CFSP (OJ L 331, 23.12.1999 and 1999 General Report, point 798).
(⁷) Bull. 6-2002, point 1.6.85. Previous report: 2001 General Report, point 1021.
(⁸) Common Strategy 1999/414/CFSP (OJ L 157, 24.6.1999 and 1999 General Report, point 797).
(⁹) Bull. 10-2002, point I.16.
(¹⁰) Bull. 7/8-2002, point 1.6.116. Previous summit: 2001 General Report, point 1026.

On 13 June, the Council adopted negotiating directives with a view to concluding with Ukraine a readmission agreement for persons residing without authorisation (Table III).

919.   From 24 to 26 October Mr Lamy visited Russia where he met the Prime Minister, Mr Mikhail Kasyanov, the Deputy Prime Minister, Mr Aleksey Kudrin and the Trade Minister, Mr German Gref for talks focusing mainly on the ongoing negotiations concerning Russian membership of the World Trade Organisation ([1]).

On 10 January ([2]), Mr Anatoliy Zlenko, Ukraine's Foreign Minister, went to Madrid, where he met Mr Josep Piqué i Camps, President of the Council and Spanish Foreign Minister, and Mr Javier Solana, High Representative for the CFSP, Mr Patten, Member of the Commission, and Carsten Søndergaard, Danish State Secretary for European Affairs.

Regional cooperation

920.   *Cross-border cooperation.* In conclusions of 22 January ([3]) on the Special Report No 11/2001 of the Court of Auditors ([4]) concerning the Tacis cross-border cooperation programme, the Council, stressing the importance of such cooperation ahead of EU enlargement, felt it was necessary to speed up implementation of the programme, in particular by establishing frontier crossing points and management of frontiers. It also called for greater interoperability between that programme and the Phare *(→ point 727)* and Interreg programmes *(→ point 372)*. Significant coordination between the various programmes took place at the level of financing in 2002.

921.   *Meetings on specific regions.* Mentioning the Commission's 1999 communication on relations between the EU and the southern Caucasus ([5]), Parliament, in a resolution of 28 February ([6]), called on the Council swiftly to define an overall long-term common strategy which would aim to prevent violent conflicts and establish a framework for fostering security and cooperation in the region, based on the stability pact for the Balkans ([7]). On 30 October, the Commission adopted a regional strategy document setting out the objectives of cooperation with the central Asian region, including sustainable economic development and poverty reduction and providing for the doubling of financial

---

([1]) Bull. 10-2002, point 1.6.95.
([2]) Bull. 1/2-2002, point 1.6.107.
([3]) Bull. 1/2-2002, point 1.6.108.
([4]) OJ C 329, 23.11.2001 and 2001 General Report, point 1219.
([5]) COM(1999) 272; 1999 General Report, point 790.
([6]) OJ C 293 E, 28.11.2002; Bull. 1/2-2002, point 1.6.104.
([7]) 1999 General Report, point 758.

assistance under the Tacis programme from EUR 25 to 50 million per year by 2006. The third session of the ministerial conference on the northern dimension took place in Luxembourg on 21 October ([1]). With a view to the new three year (2004–06) action plan, the conference adopted guidelines which emphasised the need for action in areas such as the economy, education, research, the environment, nuclear safety and justice and home affairs and also addressed issues such as Kaliningrad and the Arctic region.

922.   *New neighbours initiative.* In its conclusions of 18 November ([2]), the Council announced that the forthcoming enlargement of the Union would allow it to enhance its relations with a number of new neighbours, including Belarus, Moldova and Ukraine. In view of this, it believed that the EU should take an initiative based on an integrated and differentiated approach with the objective of promoting democratic and economic reforms, sustainable development and trade, as well as cooperation across borders, between regions and with the relevant international organisations. This approach was welcomed at the Copenhagen European Council ([3]).

([1]) Bull. 10-2002, point 1.6.96.
([2]) Bull. 11-2002, point 1.6.68.
([3]) Bull. 12-2002, point I.7.

Section 10

Relations with the United States, Japan and other industrialised countries

Overview

923.   The events of 11 September 2001 gave rise to the need to deepen cooperation not only with the United States but also with all the EU's industrialised partners in order to provide a comprehensive response to the terrorist threat. The agendas of the main bilateral summits attended by the EU were dominated by issues of security and the fight against international terrorism. During the last quarter of 2002, attention focused on the situation in North Korea.

Group of Eight (G8)

924.   Annual summit. The summit was held in Kananaskis (Canada) on 26 and 27 June (¹). It brought together the Heads of State or Government of Canada, France, Germany, Italy, Japan, Russia, the United Kingdom and the United States. The EU was represented by Mr José María Aznar, Spanish Prime Minister and President of the Council and Mr Romano Prodi, President of the Commission. At the close of the summit, the parties adopted a series of statements relating mainly to the fight against terrorism, transport safety, the non-proliferation of arms and an action plan for a New Partnership for Africa's Development (NEPAD).

925.   Ministerial meetings. The members of the G8 met at ministerial level in the areas of foreign affairs (²), the environment *(→ point 590),* work and employment *(→ point 137),* energy *(→ point 603),* finance *(→ point 73).*

(¹) Bull. 6-2002, point 1.6.88 and Internet (http://www.g8.gc.ca/). Previous summit: 2001 General Report, point 1033.
(²) Bull. 6-2002, point 1.6.87.

United States

926. Annual summit. The meeting took place in Washington on 2 May (¹). The European Union was represented by Mr José María Aznar, President of the European Council, Mr Romano Prodi, President of the Commission, Mr Javier Solana, High Representative for the CFSP, Mr Pascal Lamy and Mr Christopher Patten, Members of the Commission, and Mr Josep Piqué i Camps, Spanish Foreign Minister; the United States was represented by President George W. Bush, Vice-President Dick Cheney and Ms Condoleezza Rice, National Security Adviser. The parties agreed to launch the Positive Economic Agenda, a programme that will deepen cooperation in fields such as financial markets, sanitary and phytosanitary standards, organic farming and the computerisation of customs procedures. Mr Bush undertook to reform US tax legislation to conform with WTO rulings on the exemption arrangements enjoyed by US exporters. Other issues addressed were the fight against terrorism and the Middle East.

927. Transatlantic partnership. In a resolution of 15 May (²), Parliament recalled the historic contribution of the partnership to the democratic values and stability of the EU. Deploring America's tendency towards unilateralism, it called for a strengthening of the partnership on an equal footing and in close cooperation. It called on the EU and the United States to coordinate their economic and trade policies, especially vis-à-vis developing countries, and formulated proposals for a transatlantic partnership for the third millennium. It condemned the recent decision of the US authorities to approve a huge increase in farm subsidies to US producers, as well as the decision not to ratify the treaty establishing the International Criminal Court (ICC). Parliament again criticised the United States' stance on the ICC in a resolution of 4 July (³) on the draft US American Servicemembers' Protection Act (ASPA), which aims, *inter alia*, at exempting US personnel from the ICC's jurisdiction.

928. First anniversary of the terrorist attacks against the United States. On 11 September, EU Heads of State or Government, the President of the European Parliament, the President of the Commission and the High Representative for the CFSP adopted a joint statement (⁴) reaffirming the EU's solidarity with the American people and its determination to continue contributing to the international fight against terrorism. The statement also stressed the importance of inter-cultural dialogue and the construction of a just international order capable of promoting peace and prosperity for all.

(¹) Bull. 5-2002, point 1.6.94 and Internet (http://europa.eu.int/comm/external_relations/us/sum04_02/pc.htm). Previous summit: 2001 General Report, point 1034.
(²) Bull. 5-2002, point 1.6.96.
(³) Bull. 7/8-2002, point 1.6.117.
(⁴) Bull. 9-2002, point 1.6.14.

929.   *Specific areas of cooperation.* Information on police cooperation with the United States is to be found in Section 1 ('Area of freedom, security and justice') of Chapter IV *(→ point 487).* Other information concerning mutual recognition agreements appears in Section 3 ('Common commercial policy') of this Chapter *(→ point 791).* Information on cooperation with the United States on competition matters appears in Section 6 (Competition policy) of Chapter III *(→ point 247).*

930.   *US restrictions on imports.* This subject, together with the retaliatory measures envisaged by the EU, is dealt with in Section 3 ('Common commercial policy') of this chapter *(→ points 781 and 801).* Other restrictive measures applied to imports from the EU are mentioned in Section 13 ('Agriculture and rural development') of Chapter III *(→ points 407, 408 and 410).*

Japan

931.   *Annual summit.* The 11th EU–Japan Summit was held in Tokyo on 8 July (¹). It was attended by Mr Junichiro Koizumi, Japanese Prime Minister, Mr Anders Fogh Rasmussen, Danish Prime Minister and President of the Council, and Mr Romano Prodi, President of the Commission. Commissioners Liikanen and Lamy accompanied Mr Prodi. The parties congratulated themselves on their enhanced dialogue, due in particular to the implementation of the global action plan for Euro-Japanese cooperation adopted at the previous summit. They also noted the progress made in their cooperation in combating terrorism, also launched at the December 2001 summit. They expressed a desire to deepen the partnership in a number of priority international areas, such as support for developing countries, in particular Africa, sustainable development, peace in the Middle East, the fight against drugs and the tensions between India and Pakistan. The parties underlined their common understanding following the protectionist measures taken by the United States in the steel sector. They also expressed a desire to conclude an agreement on science and technology in the future.

932.   *Visits.* In April, Mr Prodi made an official visit to Japan, where he had an audience with Emperor Akihito and a series of meetings with political and business leaders. He was also the first Commission President to deliver a speech to the Japanese Diet. At the end of January and beginning of February, Mr Patten also went to Tokyo, on the fringes of the conference for Afghanistan donor countries *(→ point 948),* where he met Foreign Minister Makiko Tanaka and Finance Minister Masajuro Shiokawa, as well as political and business leaders.

(¹) Bull. 7/8-2002, point 1.6.121 and Internet (http://europa.eu.int/comm/external_relations/japan/sum07_02/state.htm). Previous summit: 2001 General Report, point 1048.

933. *Specific areas of cooperation.* Continuing their dialogue on regulatory reform, EU and Japanese representatives held high-level meetings in Brussels in March ([1]), and in Tokyo in November. Information on cooperation with Japan in the field of competition can be found in Section 6 ('Competition policy') of Chapter III *(→ point 246).* Other information on mutual recognition agreements is given in Section 3 ('Common commercial policy') of this chapter *(→ point 791).*

Canada

934. *EU–Canada summits.* Two summits were held in 2002, the first on 8 May in Toledo ([2]) and the second on 19 December in Ottawa ([3]). At the Toledo summit, Mr José María Aznar, President of the Council, and Mr Prodi, President of the Commission, met Mr Jean Chrétien, Canadian Prime Minister. The parties were in favour of strengthening judicial and police cooperation to deal with terrorism and organised crime. As regards foreign, security and defence policy, the EU undertook to put in place arrangements with Canada to enable the latter to take part in EU crisis management operations. The parties also wished to intensify cooperation in research, science and technology. They also decided to work closely together within the World Trade Organisation, in particular for the benefit of developing countries. They resolved to bilaterally strengthen their mutual trade relations and noted the progress made under the joint trade initiative launched in 1998 ([4]) to reduce barriers to trade and investment. They also undertook to continue cooperation in the fields of the environment and sustainable development. At the Ottawa summit, which brought together Mr Jean Chrétien, Mr Anders Fogh Rasmussen, Danish Prime Minister and President of the Council, Mr Romano Prodi, Mr Javier Solana, High Representative for the CFSP, and Mr Pascal Lamy, Member of the Commission, the EU and Canada focused on international and bilateral events, and on ways of strengthening the transatlantic link which unites them politically and economically. The parties discussed issues such as pursuing prosperity in both countries, and promoting peace, security and sustainable development through the recognition of agreements entered into and of the decisions of international bodies, and the resolution of their economic differences. The leaders agreed to strengthen and deepen cooperation especially in the northern regions, focusing in particular on environmental issues, to encourage partnerships between people, mainly through enhanced cooperation in education and training, and to fight against terrorism and crime.

---

[1] Previous meeting: 2001 General Report, point 1049.
[2] Bull. 5-2002, point 1.6.100 and Internet (http://europa.eu.int/comm/external_relations/canada/sum05_02/index.htm).
[3] Bull. 12-2002, point 1.6.98 and Internet (http://europa.eu.int/comm/external_relations/canada/intro/index.htm).
[4] 1998 General Report, point 890.

935. *Specific areas of cooperation.* Information on police cooperation with Canada is to be found in Section 1 ('Area of freedom, security and justice') of Chapter IV *(→ point 487)*. Other information on mutual recognition agreements features in Section 3 ('Common commercial policy') of this chapter *(→ point 791)*. Information on cooperation with Canada on competition matters appears in Section 6 ('Competition policy') of Chapter III *(→ point 247)*.

Australia

936. *Annual ministerial meeting.* The 18th meeting took place in Brussels on 18 April (¹). The EU was represented by Commissioners Fischler, Lamy, Patten and Vitorino, and Australia by Mr John Anderson, Deputy Prime Minister, Mr Alexander Downer, Foreign Minister, and Mr Philip Ruddock, Minister for Immigration and Multicultural Affairs. The parties agreed to strengthen bilateral cooperation, including in development aid and civil aviation. Discussions centred on the Asia-Pacific region, multilateral trade issues, agricultural and veterinary policy and global challenges such as sustainable development, climate change and the fight against illegal immigration and trafficking in human beings.

937. *Visits.* On 10 July, Mr John Howard, Australian Prime Minister, visited the Commission, meeting Mr Prodi and Commissioners Bolkestein, Byrne, Lamy, Nielson, Patten, Solbes Mira, Vitorino and Fischler. Mr Lamy and Mr Nielson went to Australia in July and October respectively.

938. *Specific areas of cooperation.* Information on mutual recognition agreements can be found in Section 3 ('Common commercial policy') of this chapter *(→ point 791)*.

New Zealand

939. *Visits.* In Copenhagen in September, a ministerial troika headed by Mr Per Stig Møller, Danish Foreign Minister, met a New Zealand delegation led by Mr Phil Goff, Foreign Minister. Mr Lamy and Mr Nielson went to New Zealand in July and October respectively.

940. *Specific areas of cooperation.* Information on mutual recognition agreements can be found in Section 3 ('Common commercial policy') of this chapter *(→ point 791)*. Other information on public health measures appear in Section 7 ('Health and consumer protection') of Chapter IV *(→ point 674)*.

(¹) Bull. 4-2002, point 1.6.68. Previous meeting: 2001 General Report, point 1052.

Republic of Korea

941. First EU–Korea Summit. The summit was held in Copenhagen on 24 September ([1]) on the fringes of the ASEM summit *(→ point 945)*. Among those attending were Mr Anders Fogh Rasmussen, Danish Prime Minister and President of the Council, Mr Romano Prodi, President of the Commission, and Mr Kim Dae Jung, President of South Korea. The parties underlined the significant breakthroughs in their bilateral relations, based on the Framework Agreement for Trade and Cooperation of March 2001 ([2]). They resolved to implement the Doha agenda *(→ point 780)* and to continue the trend towards a reduction in customs barriers. They also welcomed the adoption, at the ASEM conference, of a political statement for peace in the Korean peninsula. The Korean President also underlined the efforts made by the EU to encourage reform in North Korea through political dialogue and technical and humanitarian assistance. The EU welcomed the recent headway made in inter-Korean cooperation and reconciliation. The two parties also had in-depth discussions on aid to shipbuilding and agreed to organise a meeting of their respective experts in the near future to reach a rapid solution on the issue. A first ministerial meeting took place on 4 June, at which Mr Lamy and Mr Patten met Mr Choi Sung-Hong, Korean Foreign Minister.

942. Korean Peninsula. In a resolution of 7 November ([3]), the European Parliament called on North Korea to dismantle its uranium enrichment programme and to halt production of other weapons of mass destruction. Concerning the placing in reserve of the KEDO budget heading (Korean Peninsula Energy Development Organisation), Parliament stressed that a possible release of the funds would depend on how the situation evolved. For its part, on 19 November ([4]), the Council reiterated its concerns about the existence of such a programme which was a violation of the obligations incumbent on North Korea, in particular under the Non-Proliferation Treaty, and which was posing a serious threat to the process of reconciliation in the Korean Peninsula.

943. Presidency statements on behalf of the European Union on the Korean Peninsula are contained in Table 17 *(→ point 762)*.

([1]) Bull. 9-2002, point 1.6.65 and Internet (http://europa.eu.int/comm/external_relations/south_korea/intro/index.htm).
([2]) OJ L 90, 30.3.2001; 2001 General Report, point 1054.
([3]) Bull. 11-2002, point 1.6.69.
([4]) Bull. 11-2002, point 1.6.70.

Section 11

Relations with Asia (¹)

Overview

944.   This year saw the holding of the fourth ASEM summit (Asia–Europe Meeting) and summits with China and India which bore witness to the European Union's desire to continue its policy of engagement and dialogue with its Asian partners. The Union's relations with Asia unfolded against the background of major political and economic developments in the region. At the political level, the Union was actively involved, together with the Member States and more widely with the international community, in the process of political, institutional and economic reconstruction of Afghanistan, provided support for containing the rising tension between Pakistan and India, and continued to keep a close eye on political developments in Myanmar. At the same time, the EU contributed to putting in place an anti-terrorist campaign both bilaterally and multilaterally with ASEM and the ARF (ASEAN Regional Forum) and took appropriate measures within its powers. At the economic level, it conducted multilateral trade negotiations within the Doha round with its Asian partners, both bilaterally and within ASEM, and provided technical assistance to Asian developing countries to help integrate them more closely into the multilateral trading system. The Union actively strove to bring European civil society and Asian civil society closer together and to step up the dialogue between cultures and civilisations bilaterally and at ASEM level.

Asia–Europe Meetings (ASEM) (²) and relations with regional bodies

945.   Asia–Europe summit (ASEM). The fourth Asia–Europe summit (³) was held in Copenhagen from 22 to 24 September (⁴). Chaired by Mr Anders Fogh Rasmussen, Danish Prime Minister and President of the Council, the summit brought together Asian and European Heads of State or Government, with Mr Prodi in attendance for the Commission.

(¹) Further information is available on the Europa server (http://europa.eu.int/comm/external_relations/asia/index.htm).
(²) http://europa.eu.int/comm/external_relations/asem/intro/index.htm.
(³) Previous Summit: 2000 General Report, point 980.
(⁴) Bull. 9-2002, point 1.6.68.

Political dialogue focused on the consequences of the attacks of 11 September for international security and on major regional issues, notably the situation in the Korean peninsula, but also the situation in the Middle East and in Iraq. This dialogue led to the adoption of two statements, one on cooperation in the fight against international terrorism, accompanied by an action plan, and the other on the situation in the Korean peninsula, thus reaffirming the ASEM partners' support for the process of reconciliation and stabilisation in that area.

Economic issues and the international economic situation were also broached, notably the importance of continuing the WTO negotiating round started at Doha (→ point 780) and the need to strengthen economic ties by creating a task force covering three areas, namely trade, investment and financial matters.

For the first time, an informal session ('retreat') was held on the dialogue between cultures and civilisations, bringing together Heads of State or Government and enabling the participants to re-examine current international tensions from the point of view of cultural diversity and mutual knowledge and the need to ensure equal recognition of cultures. At the retreat, it was decided that a conference on the subject would be held at political level in 2003.

Other decisions were also adopted in the fields of development of human resources, social cohesion and the environment. The partners stressed the importance of educational exchanges and decided to strengthen the ASEM–DUO programme ([1]). They further highlighted the need to promote economic development that respected social balance (→ point 800). Implementation of the decisions on sustainable development taken at Johannesburg (→ point 557) and action on climate change were among the priorities in the field of environment.

This summit was prepared by a series of sectoral ministerial meetings bringing together the European ministers concerned, a member of the Commission and ministers of the different participating Asian countries ([2]). Environment ministers met in January ([3]), ministers responsible for migration in April ([4]), foreign ministers in June ([5]), finance ministers in July and economy ministers in September ([6]), just ahead of the summit. On 5 September ([7]), Parliament also presented its views on enhancing relations in the Asia–Europe partnership, notably within ASEM.

---

[1] http://www.asemduo.org/jsp/main.jsp.
[2] Brunei, China, Indonesia, Japan, Malaysia, Philippines, Singapore, South Korea, Thailand and Vietnam.
[3] Bull. 1/2-2002, point 1.6.112.
[4] Bull. 4-2002, point 1.6.69.
[5] Bull. 6-2002, point 1.6.100.
[6] Bull. 9-2002, point 1.6.67.
[7] Bull. 9-2002, point 1.6.66.

946.   ASEAN Regional Forum (ARF) (¹). The ninth ministerial meeting of the ASEAN regional forum was held in Brunei on 30 and 31 July with a European delegation headed by Mr Javier Solana, High Representative for the CFSP and Secretary-General of the Council, in attendance. Discussions focused on the political situation and respect for human rights in India, Pakistan and the Korean peninsula and on the international fight against terrorism and gave rise to the adoption of a statement on the financing of terrorism. On 1 August, the EU troika also took part in several ministerial meetings organised following the ARF, in the context of the ASEAN post-ministerial conference.

Bilateral relations (²)

947.   Presidency statements on Asia are to be found in Table 17 *(→ point 762)* and Parliament resolutions on human rights in the Asian countries can be found in Table 2 *(→ point 54).*

South Asia

948.   Aid for the reconstruction of Afghanistan. On 21 and 22 January, a second ministerial pledging conference for Afghanistan was held in Tokyo (³), the prime aim being to assemble the financial pledges of the international community to launch the country's reconstruction. At the conference, the Commission said it intended financing development aid to the tune of EUR 1 billion for the period 2002-06, in addition to humanitarian aid. As a guide to the achievement of these pledges, out of a total commitment of more than EUR 830 million for 2002, the Union had spent EUR 755 million by the beginning of December. The Commission, spent just over EUR 230 million on Afghanistan in 2002 (including emergency humanitarian aid). The Council stressed on 15 April (⁴) and on 22 July (⁵) that the EU's aid and policy for Afghanistan should conform to the political objectives of the Bonn process and provide political support for the reconstruction and modernisation of the country by the Afghan Interim Authority (AIA) while respecting the country's sovereignty and integrity. The second pledging conference for Afghanistan took place in Bonn on 2 December (⁶). On 10 December (⁷), the Council welcomed the decree adopted by the AIA during the conference and announced that it would support the authority in its action. Mr Patten went to Afghanistan from 20 to 22 May (⁸) to assess the political

(¹) http://europa.eu.int/comm/external_relations/asean/intro/arf.htm.
(²) http://europa.eu.int/comm/external_relations/asia/country.htm.
(³) Bull. 1/2-2002, point 1.6.113.
(⁴) Bull. 4-2002, point 1.6.71.
(⁵) Bull. 7/8-2002, point 1.6.122.
(⁶) Bull. 12-2002, point 1.6.102. Previous meeting: Bull. 12-2001, point 1.6.102.
(⁷) Bull. 12-2002, point 1.6.103.
(⁸) Bull. 5-2002, point 1.6.103.

changes made in the country and examine cooperation arrangements. For the period from 1 July to 31 December, the Council appointed Mr Francesc Vendrell, on 25 June, as special EU representative in Afghanistan ([1]) to replace Mr Klaus-Peter Klaiber whose mandate had been extended to 30 June on 27 May ([2]). The Council extended Mr Vendrell's mandate on 10 December ([3]) up to 30 June 2003.

949. Action against the Taliban. In January and February ([4]), the Commission updated Regulation (EC) No 467/2001 ([5]) and repealed Regulation (EC) No 337/2000 ([6]) to take account of developments in Afghanistan. In order to comply with UN Security Council Resolution 1390 (2002) of 16 January concerning a new government with no links to Usama bin Laden, the al-Qaida network and the Taliban, the Council decided on 27 May to adjust the scope of the financial measures and the various bans and to repeal the remaining sanctions put in place by Regulation (EC) No 467/2001 (Table II). Developments in the situation in Afghanistan also enabled the Council to repeal, on 21 January ([7]), Common Position 2001/56/CFSP ([8]) and, on 27 May ([9]), Common Positions 96/746/CFSP, 1999/727/CFSP, 2001/154/CFSP and 2001/771/CFSP ([10]). Other more general measures were adopted in order to combat international terrorism more effectively *(→ points 492 to 495).* On 5 September, the European Parliament, reaffirming its support for the international community's fight against terrorist networks, called on the UN to assess the situation and ensure that international law and conventions were fully respected ([11]).

950. India. Mr Nielson went to India from 28 January to 2 February ([12]) to take stock of the humanitarian aid measures put in place since the 2001 earthquake. On 14 February, a ministerial meeting took place between the EU and India ([13]), which was represented by Mr Jaswant Singh, external affairs minister. Discussions focused on the mounting tension between India and Pakistan. Mr Patten went to India on 24 May ([14]) and Mr Javier Solana, Secretary-General of the Council and High Representative for the CFSP, on 26 July. On 10 July,

---

([1]) Council Joint Action 2002/875/CFSP (OJ L 167, 26.6.2002; Bull. 6-2002, point 1.6.101).
([2]) Council Joint Action 2002/403/CFSP (OJ L 139, 29.5.2002; Bull. 5-2002, point 1.6.104).
([3]) Joint Action 2002/961/CFSP (OJ L 334, 11.12.2002; Bull. 12-2002, point 1.6.104).
([4]) Regulations (EC) No 65/2002 (OJ L 11, 15.1.2002), (EC) No 105/2002 (OJ L 17, 19.1.2002) and (EC) No 362/2002 (OJ L 58, 28.2.2002); Bull. 1/2-2002, point 1.6.115.
([5]) OJ L 67, 9.3.2001 and 2001 General Report, point 1065.
([6]) OJ L 43, 16.2.2000; 2000 General Report, point 986.
([7]) Common Position 2002/42/CFSP (OJ L 20, 23.1.2002; Bull. 1/2-2001, point 1.6.114.
([8]) OJ L 21, 23.1.2001; 2001 General Report, point 1065.
([9]) Common Position 2002/402/CFSP (OJ L 139, 29.5.2002; Bull. 5-2002, point 1.6.105).
([10]) OJ L 342, 31.12.1996 and 1996 General Report, point 904; OJ L 294, 16.11.1999 and 1999 General Report, point 835; OJ L 57, 27.2.2001 and 2001 General Report, point 1065; OJ L 289, 6.11.2001 and 2001 General Report, point 1066.
([11]) Bull. 9-2002, point 1.6.69.
([12]) Bull. 1/2-2002, point 1.6.120.
([13]) Bull. 1/2-2002, point 1.6.122.
([14]) Bull. 5-2002, point 1.6.109.

the Joint Committee met in Brussels. On 7 February, Parliament had already condemned the terrorist attacks against the Indian Parliament and called on India and Pakistan to resume their political dialogue ([1]). It reiterated its position in a resolution of 16 May ([2]).

On 10 October, the third EU–India summit took place in Copenhagen ([3]). It was attended by Mr Atal Bihari Vajpayee, India's Prime Minister, accompanied by Mr Yashwant Sinha, External Affairs Minister, and Mr Arun Shourie, Minister for Disinvestment, and their EU counterparts, Mr Anders Fogh Rasmussen, Prime Minister of Denmark and President of the Council, Mr Prodi and Mr Patten for the Commission, Mr Per Stig Møller, Danish Foreign Minister and Mr Solana. Discussions focused on progress made in relations with India since the second summit and notably on economic and trade relations. The latest developments in South Asia, notably the Kashmir issue, were also discussed. The political summit was preceded by a business summit on 8 and 9 October, attended by the Heads of State, at which recommendations on reform measures to foster investment and trade in key sectors were adopted.

951.   *Nepal*. On 27 and 28 August ([4]), Mr Sher Bahadur Deuba, Nepal's Prime Minister, met Mr Prodi, Mr Patten and Mr Lamy who confirmed the EC's support for the consolidation of democracy and development of Nepal. On 24 October ([5]), Parliament called for the end of the conflict, the opening of negotiations with the Maoist rebels and the calling of new legislative and local elections. In a statement on behalf of the Member States on 18 December, the Presidency expressed the EU's concern at the human rights situation in Nepal (→ *point 762*).

952.   *Pakistan*. Visiting Brussels on 4 February ([6]), Mr Abdul Sattar, Foreign Minister, met Mr Javier Solana, Secretary-General of the Council and High Representative for the CFSP, and Mr Patten. Mr Patten went to Pakistan on 23 May ([7]). The European Union sent an observer mission to the Pakistan national and provincial assembly elections held on 10 October. The mission criticised certain restrictions on participation in the elections. In a statement on behalf of the EU, the Presidency, while expressing its concern about reports of rigging, acknowledged that the elections represented a step forward in the gradual transition towards a consolidated democratic process in Pakistan (→ *point 762*). On 21 November ([8]), the European Parliament called on the Pakistan Government to ensure implementation of the recommendations of the

[1] OJ C 284 E, 21.11.2002; Bull. 1/2-2002, point 1.6.121.
[2] Bull. 5-2002, point 1.6.107.
[3] Bull. 10-2002, point 1.6.98. Previous summit: 2001 General Report, point 1061.
[4] Bull. 7/8-2002, point 1.6.130.
[5] Bull. 10-2002, point 1.2.6.
[6] Bull. 1/2-2002, point 1.6.125.
[7] Bull. 5-2002, point 1.6.115.
[8] Bull. 11-2002, point 1.6.79.

EU observer mission, following the mission's criticisms of the democratic legitimacy of those elections.

953. *Sri Lanka*. Visiting Brussels from 27 to 31 May ([1]), Mr Ranil Wickremesinghe, Prime Minister of Sri Lanka and Mr Tyrone Fernando, Foreign Minister, met Mr Prodi, Mr Lamy, Mr Patten and Mr Nielson. On 18 November ([2]), the Council confirmed its support for the peace process between the government and the Liberation Tigers of Tamil Eelam (LTTE) and welcomed the parties' determination to consolidate the ceasefire. It called on the European Union to strengthen its commitment to this process.

South-East Asia

954. *Trade promotion*. From 15 to 19 February ([3]), Mr Lamy visited Singapore, Indonesia and Cambodia to promote trade between the European Union and South-East Asia at regional and multilateral level.

955. *Cambodia*. Ahead of the municipal elections on 3 February, the European Union sent an observer mission to Cambodia. On 11 November, the Council extended Decision 1999/730/CFSP to 15 November 2003 by amending the EU's contribution to combating the accumulation and spread of small arms and light weapons in Cambodia ([4]).

956. *Indonesia*. On 16 May, Parliament expressed its concern at the violence in the Moluccas and the continuing conflicts in Aceh and Papua ([5]). It urged the Indonesian Government to combat terrorism in those provinces. On 21 October, the Council condemned the attacks in Bali on 12 October and proposed cooperating closely with Indonesia in the fight against terrorism. On the fringes of the ASEM summit, the EU and Indonesian delegations had an exchange of views on the political and economic situation in Indonesia and East Timor. The EU troika, visiting Indonesia on 7 and 8 November, was also received by President Megawati Sukarnoputri and several Indonesian ministers. The two parties discussed intensification of the political dialogue as part of the fight against terrorism.

957. *Malaysia*. On the fringes of the ASEM summit, Mr Prodi met Dr Mahathir bin Mohamad, Malaysian Prime Minister, with a view notably to the upcoming opening of a Commission delegation in Malaysia.

([1]) Bull. 5-2002, point 1.6.116.
([2]) Bull. 11-2002, point 1.6.81.
([3]) Bull. 1/2-2002, point 1.6.127.
([4]) Bull. 11-2002, point 1.6.75.
([5]) Bull. 5-2002, point 1.6.112.

958.   Myanmar. On 22 April ([1]), the Council extended for six months Common Position 96/635/CFSP ([2]) as it deemed progress on human rights and democratisation to be insufficient. On 21 October ([3]), it again extended this common position for a further six months and amended the list of persons affected by the freeze on funds and visa restrictions. The same day ([4]), the Council, welcoming the release of Aung San Suu Kyi, called on Myanmar to engage immediately in a thorough dialogue with the opposition leading to a peaceful political transition and national reconciliation. An EU troika mission went to Myanmar from 13 to 15 March and 9 to 10 September.

959.   Philippines. On 18 October, Mr Patten received the Philippine Foreign Minister, Mr Blas Ople. Discussions focused on deepening EU–Philippines relations as part of the cooperation programme between the Community and the Philippines on trade and the fight against international terrorism.

960.   Singapore. On 5 April, Mr Patten met Prime Minister Goh Chok Tong, Foreign Minister Shunmagar Jayakumar and Senior Minister Lee Kwan Yew in Singapore ([5]). The two parties reaffirmed their shared view of free trade at global and regional level and regional integration. Mr Patten also confirmed plans to open a new EC delegation office in Singapore. Mr Prodi, visiting Singapore on 6 July, met President Sellapan Rama Nathan, Mr Goh Chok Tong and Mr Lee Kwan Yew. Their discussions focused on EU–Singapore relations and Singapore's role on the regional and international stage.

961.   Thailand. On 11 February, Thai commerce minister Adisai Bodharamik met Mr Lamy in Brussels ([6]). On 13 June, Mr Prodi and Mr Lamy received Mr Thaksin Shinawatra, Thai Prime Minister, and other members of the Thai Government. The two parties decided to strengthen their relations and raised the possibility of a cooperation agreement.

962.   Vietnam. Mr Prodi, Mr Lamy, Mr Nielson and Mr Patten received the Vietnamese Prime Minister, Mr Phan Van Khai, and other members of his government. Discussions focused on all aspects of relations with Vietnam, notably intensification of economic relations between the two sides. Mr Prodi expressed his support for Vietnam in the process of internal reform and the country's accession to the WTO.

([1]) Common Position 2002/310/CFSP (OJ L 107, 24.4.2002; Bull. 4-2002, point 1.6.78).
([2]) OJ L 287, 8.11.1996 and 1996 General Report, point 903; last amended by Common Position 2001/757/CFSP (OJ L 286, 30.10.2001; 2001 General Report, point 1069).
([3]) Common Position 2002/831/CFSP (OJ L 205, 23.10.2002; Bull. 10-2002, point 1.6.103.
([4]) Bull. 10-2002, point 1.6.104.
([5]) Bull. 4-2002, point 1.6.80.
([6]) Bull. 1/2-2002, point 1.6.129.

Far East

963.   *China*. The Commission adopted on 1 March the strategic document on priorities for cooperation between the EU and China (¹) for the period 2002–06. The Union's strategy towards China, developed since 1998 (²), was also the subject of a Parliament resolution on 11 April (³). Parliament supported enhanced cooperation between the two parties based on a political and cultural dialogue which took account of economic interests and the promotion of human rights. On a visit to China from 27 March to 4 April (⁴), Mr Patten met President Jiang Zemin, deputy Prime Minister Qian Qichen and Foreign Minister Tang Jiaxuan. Mr Liikanen also visited China from 13 to 19 April (⁵), where he met deputy Prime Minister, Mr Li Lanqing, deputy economics and trade minister, Mr Jiang Quingui, industry and information minister, Mr Wu Jichuan and science and technology minister, Mr Xu Guanghua. On 17 and 18 October, Mr Lamy was received by Chinese foreign trade minister, Shi Guangsheng.

On 24 September, the fifth summit meeting (⁶) between the European Union and China took place in Copenhagen, attended by Mr Zhu Rongji, Prime Minister, Mr Anders Fogh Rasmussen, Danish Prime Minister and President of the Council, and Mr Prodi, President of the Commission. At the summit, the two parties expressed their mutual desire for an ever closer partnership. Discussions focused on trade relations and on human rights in Taiwan. The summit closed with the adoption of a joint statement taking stock of EU–China relations and setting out the subjects of future cooperation: clandestine immigration and tourism.

964.   *Special Administrative Regions (China)*. On 27 November, the Commission signed an agreement with the government of the Special Administrative Region of Hong Kong concerning the readmission of persons residing without authorisation (Table III). On 31 July the Commission adopted its second annual report on the Special Administrative Region of Macao (⁷) and, on 5 August, its fourth annual report on the SAR of Hong Kong (⁸). In a resolution of 19 December (⁹), Parliament expressed its concern at the anti-subversion bill of the government of the SAR of Hong Kong.

(¹) http://europa.eu.int/comm/external_relations/china/csp/index.htm.
(²) COM(1998) 181 and 1998 General Report, point 907; COM(2001) 265 and 2001 General Report, point 1075.
(³) Bull. 4-2002, point 1.6.74.
(⁴) Bull. 4-2002, point 1.6.73.
(⁵) Bull. 4-2002, point 1.6.75.
(⁶) Bull. 9-2002, point 1.6.72. Previous meeting: 2001 General Report, point 1073.
(⁷) COM(2002) 445, Bull. 7/8-2002, point 1.6.124 and Internet (http://europa.eu.int/comm/external_relations/macau/intro/index.htm). Previous report: COM(2001) 432 and 2001 General Report, point 1077.
(⁸) COM(2002) 450, Bull. 7/8-2002, point 1.6.125 and Internet (http://europa.eu.int/comm/external_relations/hong_kong/intro/index.htm). Previous report: COM(2001) 431 and 2001 General Report, point 1077.
(⁹) Bull. 12-2002, point 1.6.106.

965.   *Taiwan.* In a resolution of 14 March (¹), Parliament, considering that Taiwan's experience on health issues could be beneficial at world level, proposed that Taiwan be invited as an observer to the upcoming meeting of the World Health Assembly. In a resolution of 13 June (²), Parliament also called for the abolition of capital punishment.

Cooperation measures (³)

966.   *Financing of cooperation measures.* Under financial and technical cooperation with Asia (⁴), EUR 374 million was committed (of which EUR 127.5 million for Afghanistan). EUR 99 million was committed for political, economic and cultural cooperation.

967.   *Management of external assistance.* Implementation of the reform of the management of the Community's external assistance (⁵) continued with the speeding up of devolution from headquarters to the Commission delegations *(→ point 1152).* The Commission proposed a new framework for cooperation between the EC and the countries of Latin America and Asia *(→ point 985).*

(¹) Bull. 3-2002, point 1.4.63.
(²) Bull. 6-2002, point 1.2.9.
(³) Cooperation with Asian countries takes place chiefly under Regulation (EEC) No 443/92 (OJ L 52, 27.2.1992 and Twenty-sixth General Report, point 893).
(⁴) Details of measures financed by the EC can be found in the *Bulletin of the European Union.*
(⁵) 2000 General Report, point 1207.

Section 12

Relations with Latin America ([1])

Overview

968.   *Relations between the European Union and Latin America were characterised by the second bi-regional European Union–Latin America/Caribbean summit, which was held in Madrid. The strengthening of the strategic partnership confirms both regions' interest in cooperating on the defence of human rights and democracy, sustainable economic development and the quest for social equity. Relations between the two regions were also marked by the recession in Argentina, which began in December 2001 and has now spread to the social and political spheres and has jeopardised the economy and finances of several other Latin American countries. The European Union supported Argentina by temporarily increasing its imports of quality meat and by seeking a viable solution to Argentina's social and economic problems in international organisations. A series of bilateral ministerial meetings were held on 14 September in New York on the fringes of the UN General Assembly between the European Union troika and the Rio Group ([2]), the Andean Community, the San José Group and Mercosur.*

Relations with regional groupings

969.   *European Union–Latin America/Caribbean summit.* This second summit of Heads of State or Government of the 17 Latin American countries, 16 Caribbean countries and 15 EU Member States was held in Madrid on 17 and 18 May ([3]). Discussions focused on a more detailed approach to the strategic partnership launched in Rio in 1999 ([4]), and covered the political, economic, social and cultural fields. The summit concluded with the adoption of a political declaration containing clear commitments to a strategic partnership between the two regions and a document on the common values and positions on which the partnership will be built. An assessment report of the strategic

---

([1]) Further information is available on the Europa server (http://europa.eu.int/comm/external_relations/la/index.htm).
([2]) Argentina, Bolivia, Brazil, Chile, Colombia, Costa Rica, El Salvador, Ecuador, Guatemala, Honduras, Mexico, Nicaragua, Panama, Paraguay, Peru, Dominican Republic, Uruguay, Venezuela.
([3]) Bull. 5-2002, point 1.6.118; http://europa.eu.int/comm/world/lac/conc_en/index.htm.
([4]) 1999 General Report, point 848.

partnership's implementation since its introduction in 1999 was also adopted. Bilateral meetings were held on the fringes of the summit with Chile, Mexico, the Andean Community, Central America and Mercosur. On 30 May, Parliament endorsed the objective of a bi-regional strategic partnership adopted at the summit, and especially the desire to strengthen the multilateral system and promote free trade and the commitment to combat terrorism and organised crime ([1]). In preparation for this summit, Parliament adopted a resolution on 15 May ([2]) setting out the primary objectives of the new initiative for the strategic global partnership. On 21 February, the European Economic and Social Committee adopted an own-initiative opinion ([3]) urging the Latin American and Caribbean countries to choose an integration process based on the North American model (NAFTA ([4])) founded on free trade, or a more solidarity-oriented model such as the European one.

970.   *Mercosur* ([5]). In conclusions adopted on 28 January ([6]), the Council welcomed the Mercosur countries' ([7]) desire to strengthen their integration process and underlined the importance it attached to the establishment of an association agreement between the EU and Mercosur. Mr Lamy, on a visit to Brazil, Argentina and Chile from 26 February to 4 March ([8]), also stressed the importance of regional integration for the region's development and its integration into the global economy. The ministerial meeting with Mercosur on the fringes of the EU–Latin America/Caribbean summit gave political impetus to the trade negotiations between the two regions. The meeting between Mr Lamy and Mr Patten and Mercosur's Economy and Foreign Ministers in July ([9]) provided an opportunity to relaunch economic and trade negotiations by establishing the negotiating timetable and procedures for a future agreement. In a resolution of 26 September ([10]), Parliament deeply regretted the current situation of generalised crisis in the Mercosur countries and urged the relevant authorities in the Mercosur countries and also the EU Member States to commit themselves to carrying out economic programmes in conjunction with the international financial organisations. The eighth EU–Mercosur negotiating meeting was held in Brasilia from 11 to 14 November.

971.   *Andean Community* ([11]) *and Central America.* On 15 April, the Council adopted conclusions ([12]) on relations between the European Union and the Cen-

---

([1]) Bull. 5-2002, point 1.6.119.
([2]) Bull. 5-2002, point 1.6.117.
([3]) OJ C 94, 18.4.2002; Bull. 1/2-2002, point 1.6.131.
([4]) North American Free Trade Agreement.
([5]) http://europa.eu.int/comm/external_relations/mercosur/intro/index.htm.
([6]) Bull. 1/2-2002, point 1.6.130.
([7]) Argentina, Brazil, Paraguay and Uruguay.
([8]) Bull. 3-2002, point 1.6.91.
([9]) Bull. 7/8-2002, point 1.6.133.
([10]) Bull. 9-2002, point 1.6.80.
([11]) Bolivia, Colombia, Ecuador, Peru and Venezuela (http://europa.eu.int/comm/external_relations/andean/intro/index.htm).
([12]) Bull. 4-2002, point 1.6.82.

tral American and Andean Community countries. It underlined the importance of stepping up political dialogue and cooperation with each of the two regions, notably by negotiating an agreement on the basis of three objectives: establishment of political and social stability through democracy, human rights and good governance; completion of the process of regional integration at political and economic level and with a view to contributing to the environmental and social dimensions of poverty reduction. At the EU–Central America Joint Committee meeting, held in Brussels on 24 October, the parties took stock of Central America's regional economic integration process, particularly in the light of the adoption of an action plan for regional economic integration.

On the fringes of the second European Union–Latin America/Caribbean Summit (→ point 969), it was agreed that negotiations would begin on two political dialogue and cooperation agreements, one between the EU and the Andean Community and the other between the EU and Central America. The attainment of the objectives of these two agreements and closer cooperation would provide a basis, in the light of the results of the work programme adopted at Doha, for the negotiation of two practicable and mutually beneficial association agreements, mainly concerning the creation of a free trade area between the European Union and these two regions.

972. *San José dialogue.* The 18th ministerial meeting [1] of the San José dialogue [2] was held in Madrid on 18 May between the European Union, Colombia, Mexico, Venezuela and the San José Group countries [3]. The objective of the conference was to develop partnership ties with the Central American countries on the basis of fundamental principles and common values (democracy, promotion of development, eradication of poverty, peaceful settlement of disputes and respect for the environment). The participants adopted a renewed agenda for dialogue between the two regions and confirmed that the cooperation and political dialogue agreement would be launched to pave the way for a free trade agreement.

Bilateral relations

973. Presidency statements on behalf of the European Union on Latin America are shown in Table 17 (→ point 762). Parliament resolutions on human rights in Latin America are shown in Table 2 (→ point 54).

974. *Bilateral meetings.* The EU–Mexico Joint Council met in Brussels on 13 May [4]. Discussions at the EC Mexico Joint Committee, which was held in

---

[1] Bull. 5-2002, point 1.6.120.
[2] http://europa.eu.int/comm/external_relations/ca/index.htm.
[3] Costa Rica, El Salvador, Guatemala, Honduras, Nicaragua and Panama.
[4] Bull. 5-2002, point 1.6.123.

Puebla on 3 October, focused on consolidating bilateral relations on the basis of the economic partnership, political coordination and cooperation agreement (¹). The EC–Brazil Joint Committee met in Brasilia on 27 and 28 May. On 18 November the EU–Uruguay Joint Committee was held in Montevideo. Discussions covered management of the economic crisis in Uruguay, bilateral trade relations, the resumption of sanitary and phytosanitary negotiations, and the adoption of cooperation programmes scheduled for 2003. On 20 November the EU–Paraguay Joint Committee was held in Asunción. Talks covered the EU's support for strengthening Paraguay's democratic institutions, the opening of the EU delegation in Paraguay, the granting of a meat export quota, the timetable for the sanitary and phytosanitary negotiations as agreed on 5 November in Brussels and other outstanding bilateral issues. The meeting of the EU–Central America Joint Committee, held in Brussels on 24 October, provided an opportunity to assess the process of regional economic integration in Central America.

975. *Argentina.* On 22 January, the Council adopted a statement on behalf of the European Union, supporting the ongoing cooperation between the Argentine Government and the International Monetary Fund (²). It also underlined the EU's willingness to offer technical cooperation to the Argentine Government for the design and implementation of monetary and financial policies. On 4 March, Mr Fischler met Mr Miguel Ángel Paulón, Argentina's Agriculture Minister (³). At the meeting, Mr Fischler undertook to propose the opening of an extra autonomous import quota of meat because of the crisis in Argentina. On 27 June, the Council adopted Regulation (EC) No 1150/2002 (⁴) opening an additional autonomous quota of 10 000 tonnes for imports of high-quality beef from Argentina for one year.

976. *Brazil.* On 19 November, the European Community and Brazil signed a memorandum of agreement on market access for textiles *(→ point 804)* and a memorandum of agreement on cooperation for 2001 to 2006 (Table III). An agreement for scientific and technological cooperation was also initialled *(→ point 312).*

977. *Chile.* On 28 January, the Council endorsed the continuation of work to conclude a free trade agreement (⁵). The agreement, signed on 18 November, consists of three sections (political dialogue, cooperation and trade) and is designed to achieve trade liberalisation within seven years for industrial products and 10 years for agricultural products (Table III). The European Commu-

---

(¹) 2000 General Report, point 1012.
(²) Bull. 1/2-2002, point 1.6.133.
(³) Bull. 3-2002, point 1.6.92.
(⁴) OJ L 170, 29.6.2002.
(⁵) Bull. 1/2-2002, point 1.6.134.

nity and Chile also signed an agreement for scientific and technological cooperation (→ point 312).

978. *Colombia.* On 12 September, Mr Patten met the Colombian President, Mr Alvaro Uribe, in New York for talks on human rights, combating terrorism and bilateral cooperation. Foreign Minister Carolina Barco's visit to Brussels on 19 November provided an opportunity to discuss these issues in greater detail. In its conclusions of 10 December ([1]), the Council welcomed the Colombian President's efforts to develop a democratic State but called on the government to step up its efforts in this field.

979. *Costa Rica.* On 7 October, Mr Lamy received Mr Alberto Trejos, Costa Rica's Foreign Trade Minister. Talks focused on bilateral trade issues and multilateral aspects connected with the Doha agenda for development ([2]).

980. *Cuba.* In the context of the 11th assessment of the EU's Common Position 96/697/CFSP ([3]) on Cuba ([4]), the Council noted on 17 June that as the objectives of democratisation and economic recovery set out in the common position had still not been achieved, despite some progress, it would remain the basis of the EU's policy on Cuba. In its 12th assessment, it was decided to extend this common position. On 20 September, Mr Ricardo Cabrisas, Government Minister, was received by Mr Javier Solana, Secretary-General of the Council and CFSP High Representative, and Mr Nielson and Mr Lamy ([5]).

981. *Mexico.* On 8 March, Mr Byrne met the Mexican Agriculture Minister, Mr Javier Usabiaga ([6]). On 29 and 30 April, Mr Lamy visited Mexico ([7]). He met President Vicente Fox and the Economy Minister, Mr Luis Ernesto Derbez, to review preparations for the next WTO ministerial meeting scheduled for 2003 in Mexico.

982. *Peru.* On 5 December, Mr Prodi received President Alejandro Toledo of Peru, to discuss bilateral relations. On an official visit to Peru from 22 to 30 March, Ms Reding met the Foreign Minister, Mr Diego García-Sayan, and other representatives of the Peruvian Government.

([1]) Bull. 12-2002, point 1.6.112.
([2]) 2001 General Report, point 876.
([3]) OJ L 322, 12.12.1996; 1996 General Report, point 918.
([4]) Bull. 6-2002, point 1.6.110. Last assessment: 2001 General Report, point 1090.
([5]) Bull. 9-2002, point 1.6.81.
([6]) Bull. 3-2002, point 1.6.95.
([7]) Bull. 4-2002, point 1.6.85.

Cooperation measures

983.   *The information society*. The @LIS (¹) cooperation agreement was officially launched in Seville on 26 and 27 April *(→ point 352)*.

984.   *Education*. The Alßan cooperation programme was officially launched on 16 May at the EU–Latin America/Caribbean cultural forum. This programme of high-level scholarships will enable Latin American students and professionals to take advantage of the quality of European higher education. This year the programme has a budget of EUR 45 million.

985.   *Cooperation with ALA developing countries* (²). On 2 July, the Commission proposed setting up a new framework for cooperation between the Community and the Latin American and Asian countries (Table I). This framework sets out new arrangements for financing cooperation projects and programmes, in line with the requirements of the reform of the management of EC external assistance (³) *(→ point 1150)*.

986.   *Financing of cooperation*. In 2002, EUR 123 million was committed to financial and technical cooperation with Latin America. The projects financed chiefly concerned the environment and rural development, institutional support and the rule of law, regional integration and sectors that play a key role in increasing economic development and strengthening intra-regional trade. On economic cooperation, EUR 126 million was committed for projects of mutual interest essentially for regional measures in fields such as cooperation between European and Latin American SMEs (AL-Invest III programme (⁴) for a total amount of EUR 46 million), regional integration and higher education (Alßan programme (⁵) for a total amount of EUR 88.5 million, including EUR 45 million committed in 2002, and reinforcement of the Alfa programme (⁶) for an amount of EUR 17 million).

(¹) http://europa.eu.int/comm/europeaid/projects/alis/index_en.htm.
(²) Developing countries in Asia and Latin America.
(³) 2000 General Report, point 1207.
(⁴) http://europa.eu.int/comm/europeaid/projects/al-invest/index_en.htm.
(⁵) http://europa.eu.int/comm/europeaid/projects/alban/index_en.htm.
(⁶) http://europa.eu.int/comm/europeaid/projects/alfa/index_en.htm.

Section 13

ACP countries and OCTs

Overview

987.   Since not all EU Member States have ratified the Cotonou Agreement signed in June 2000, it has not entered into force. However, thanks to the measures giving effect to some of its provisions in advance, it was possible to push ahead, as in 2001, with programming the ninth European Development Fund (EDF), particularly, this year, with regional groupings of ACP countries, and to continue to apply the article enabling cooperation to be suspended in case of serious infringement of what are seen as the basic principles of ACP–EC cooperation (i.e. human rights, democratic principles and the rule of law). Negotiations on economic partnership agreements opened. They aim to integrate the ACP countries more fully into the global economy.

Relations with ACP countries (¹)

Institutions

988.   Joint Parliamentary Assembly ACP–EC (²). The fourth plenary session of the Joint Parliamentary Assembly was held in Cape Town from 18 to 21 March (³). During the discussions, the slow pace of ratification of the Cotonou Agreement signed in June 2000 *(→ point 990)* was criticised. Discussions also covered the European Development Fund, the economic partnership agreements *(→ point 992)*, the new initiative for Africa (NEPAD), *(→ points 924 and 1000)*, gender and health issues, sustainable development and the 10th anniversary of the Rio Conference on the Environment *(→ point 557)*, sensitive products (bananas, rice, sugar) and the situation in certain ACP countries and regions. The Assembly also adopted a declaration on trade. In a resolution of 14 March (⁴) on the work of the Assembly in 2001, Parliament was pleased to see that the political dimension had been put at the heart of the partnership and stressed that the central role conferred on the Parliamentary Assembly in imple-

(¹) http://www.acpsec.org/.
(²) http://www.acpsec.org/gb/jointass/default.htm.
(³) Bull. 3-2002, point 1.6.97. Previous sessions: 2001 General Report, point 1101.
(⁴) Bull. 3-2002, point 1.6.98.

menting this new approach, including the promotion of the democratic process, required a thorough review of its operating methods and its very nature. It also urged the Member States that had not yet ratified the Cotonou Agreement do so as soon as possible.

989.   ACP–EC Council([1]). The Council of Ministers met at Punta Cana (Dominican Republic) on 28 June ([2]). Discussions focused on the delays in ratification and implementation of the Cotonou Agreement *(→ point 990)* and on preparations for the World Summit for Sustainable Development *(→ point 556)*. The parties were unable to agree to draft guidelines on political dialogue or to ratify the draft document setting out the eligibility criteria with which civil society and the private sector must comply for access to EDF resources.

Implementation of the Lomé Conventions and the Cotonou Partnership Agreement([3])

990.   Cotonou Agreement: General aspects. On 17 January, Parliament gave its assent to the conclusion of the agreement (Table III). Given that not all Member States have yet ratified the agreement and the transitional measures agreed on in July 2000 ([4]) have been extended, the representatives of the Member States' Governments decided, on 25 June ([5]), that certain provisions of the draft internal agreement relating to the ninth European Development Fund would continue to be applied on a provisional basis until they entered into force. In an own-initiative opinion of 24 April ([6]), the European Economic and Social Committee welcomed the official recognition that the Cotonou Agreement accorded it by entrusting it with the organisation of meetings with ACP–EC economic and social operators. It nonetheless considered worrying the lack of instruments to bind non-State actors to the partnership.

991.   Conflict prevention and management. In its conclusions of 30 May on countries in conflict ([7]), the Council defined priorities that must be applied if the provisions and innovations of the Cotonou Agreement are to become operational for the ACP countries affected by conflict or crisis. In its conclusions of 22 October, it expressed its support for the international community's efforts, particularly the 'Kimberley process', an initiative from countries in southern Africa aimed at breaking the link between the diamond trade and the funding of armed conflict ([8]). This support was demonstrated by the adoption on

([1]) http://www.acpsec.org/gb/coumin_e.html.
([2]) Bull. 6-2002, point 1.6.113. Previous meeting: 2001 General Report, point 1102.
([3]) http://www.acpsec.org/fr/cotonou/accord1.htm.
([4]) 2000 General Report, point 1023.
([5]) OJ L 184, 13.7.2002.
([6]) OJ C 149, 21.6.2002; Bull. 4-2002, point 1.6.88.
([7]) Bull. 5-2002, point 1.6.126.
([8]) Bull. 10-2002, point 1.6.117.

20 December of a regulation implementing the Kimberley process certification scheme ([1]).

992.   *Economic partnership agreements (EPAs).* After welcoming the Commission's recommendations on 13 May ([2]), the Council adopted a mandate on 17 June to negotiate EPAs (Table III) and recalled that the objectives of these arrangements under the Cotonou Agreement were the smooth and gradual integration of the ACP States into the world economy, greater regional integration and the eradication of poverty. In a resolution of 26 September ([3]), Parliament put forward as negotiating priorities the contribution to sustainable development and the eradication of poverty, or the protection of the ACP economies against certain effects of globalisation. The ministerial negotiating committee held its first meeting in Brussels on 27 September after the ceremony officially opening the negotiations. It decided that the negotiations would be split into two stages: the first, general, stage would involve discussions with all ACP countries on common negotiating procedures with the regions; the second stage, consisting of region-by-region discussions, would begin in September 2003. The Commission's mandate allows considerable flexibility in both the negotiations and implementation of EPAs to take account of the different economic, social and environmental conditions in each ACP country.

993.   *Trade.* On 10 December, the Council adopted the new provisions concerning agricultural products and goods resulting from the processing of agricultural products originating in the ACP States ([4]) in accordance with the new system under the Cotonou Agreement. These provisions replace the previous regulation ([5]). On the same day, the Council replaced the procedure for implementing the safeguard measures provided for in the fourth Lomé Convention ([6]) with a new regulation taking account of the relevant provisions in the Cotonou Agreement ([7]).

994.   *Investment facility.* On 7 November ([8]), the Commission adopted a proposal for a decision concerning the coverage of costs incurred by the European Investment Bank for the management of the EUR 2.2 billion investment facility provided for by the first financial protocol (2000–05) to the Cotonou Agreement. The facility is intended to encourage private-sector development in the ACP countries.

([1]) Council Regulation (EC) No 2368/2002 (JO L 358, 31.12.2002; Bull. 12-2002, point 1.6.120).
([2]) Bull. 5-2002, point 1.6.124.
([3]) Bull. 9-2002, point 1.6.84.
([4]) Council Regulation (EC) No 2286/2002 (OJ L 348, 21.12.2002; Bull. 12-2002, point 1.6.119).
([5]) Council Regulation (EC) No 1706/98 (OJ L 215, 1.8.1998; 1998 General Report, point 936).
([6]) Council Regulation (EEC) No 3705/90 (OJ L 358, 21.12.1990; Twenty-fourth General Report, point 771).
([7]) Regulation (EC) No 2285/2002 (OJ L 348, 21.12.2002; Bull. 12-2002, point 1.6.118).
([8]) COM(2002) 603; Bull. 11-2002, point 1.6.87.

Stabex and Sysmin

995. *Sysmin.* Pursuant to the transitional measures on the use of Sysmin unexpended balances under the eighth EDF (¹), credits were allocated in 2002 for programmes to support the mining sector in Botswana (EUR 30 million), Ghana (EUR 40 million) and Papua New Guinea (EUR 50 million).

Debt and structural adjustment support

996. *Debt.* In a resolution of 25 April (²), referring to the initiatives taken to reduce the balance of all the special loans granted by the Community to ACP highly indebted poor least developed countries (³), Parliament called for the debt relief process to be speeded up. It asked the Commission and the Member States to provide technical assistance to ACP countries to devise debt management schemes. In addition to the initiative launched in 1999 by the International Monetary Fund and the World Bank for highly indebted poor countries (HIPCs) (⁴), the Community decided to provide funding worth EUR 60 million to cancel all the special loans the least development countries had taken out.

997. *Structural adjustment support.* Decisions were taken in 2002 to finance structural adjustment in 12 ACP countries, for a total of EUR 559.31 million. On 11 June (⁵), the Council welcomed Special Report No 5/2001 of the Court of Auditors (⁶) on counterpart funds from structural adjustment support earmarked for budget aid. It called on the Commission to monitor more closely the quality of public finance management in beneficiary countries and to step up coordination and cooperation with all the donors.

Support for ACP banana producers

998. The Community continued its support for the 12 traditional ACP suppliers of bananas under the special framework of assistance set up for them in 1999 (⁷). In June, the Commission approved individual allocations totalling EUR 44 million. All countries concerned applied. Implementation of previously funded projects continued in the form of support for improving competitiveness and encouragement for diversification in countries where banana production is no longer considered profitable. In accordance with the regulation setting up the

---

(¹) 2001 General Report, point 1105.
(²) Bull. 4-2002, point 1.6.86.
(³) COM(2001) 210; 2001 General Report, point 941; Decision No 2/2001 of the ACP–EC Council of Ministers (OJ L 56, 27.2.2002).
(⁴) 1999 General Report, points 713 and 810.
(⁵) Bull. 6-2002, point 1.6.125.
(⁶) OJ C 257, 14.9.2001; 2001 General Report, points 1108 and 1219.
(⁷) Regulation (EC) No 856/1999 (OJ L 108, 27.4.1999; 1999 General Report, point 870).

special framework of assistance, the Commission presented an implementation report for 2001–02 on 23 December (¹).

Protocols

999.   *Sugar.* On 22 April, the Council authorised the Commission to negotiate guaranteed prices for the 2001/02 to 2005/06 delivery periods for cane sugar originating in the ACP countries and India (Table III).

Relations with regional groupings

1000.   *Pan-African initiatives.* In the follow-up to the Europe–Africa ministerial conference in Brussels in October 2001 (²), the Community continued to step up its contacts with the New Partnership for Africa's Development (NEPAD) in both the framework of bilateral relations and the work of the G8. The Commission played an active role in drafting the Action Plan for Africa adopted in June by the G8 Summit in Canada in the presence of the African Heads of State who initiated the NEPAD *(→ point 924).*

Institutional and political contacts were also stepped up with the African Union, which was officially launched in July at the Durban pan-African Summit. In May, Mr Said Djinnit, Deputy Secretary-General of the Organisation of African Unity (OAU) was invited to report to the Council on the progress made in the transition from the OAU to the African Union and on the link between the latter and NEPAD. At the Durban summit, in a message to President Thabo Mbeki of South Africa, Mr Prodi welcomed the creation of the African Union and offered the EU's support for setting up new pan-African institutions, particularly in the peace and security field. The Commission's support took practical form in September with the announcement by Mr Nielson of a substantial contribution by the European Development Fund to the African Union's conflict settlement mechanism. At the World Summit on Sustainable Development in Johannesburg *(→ point 557),* Mr Prodi also met Mr Amara Essy, Secretary-General of the African Union.

Preparations for the second Europe-Africa Summit, which will be held in April 2003 in Lisbon, were stepped up in the second half of the year. The second Europe-Africa ministerial conference, held in Ouagadougou (Burkina Faso), on 27 and 28 November, issued a declaration on priority themes, adopted a joint statement on the fight against terrorism and agreed to draw up an action plan

---

(¹) COM(2002) 763.
(²) 2001 General Report, point 1115.

on trafficking in human beings. The conference also launched a discussion on how to continue the dialogue after the Lisbon summit.

1001. Subregional groupings. In most of the regions concerned, programming of the ninth European Development Fund was brought to a successful conclusion following extensive consultations with national governments, the private sector, civil society, the EU Member States, and also the other donors.

As regards west Africa, ninth EDF programming was finalised with the two mandated regional organisations (Ecowas and WAEMU). The regional strategy paper, approved by the Commission on 15 November, amounts to EUR 235 million and covers economic integration and trade, transport, and conflict management and prevention. In November, Mr Nielson went to Ouagadougou in the context of the political dialogue with Ecowas. On 10 December, the Council expressed its concern at the continuing instability in the Mano River Union region, containing Guinea, Liberia and Sierra Leone ([1]).

The ninth EDF regional strategy for central Africa was drawn up in conjunction with the mandated regional organisations (CEMAC and ECCAS). The regional strategy paper, approved by the Commission on 8 November, amounts to EUR 55 million and covers regional economic integration and trade, transport, sustainable management of natural resources and support for regional systems for conflict prevention.

The ninth EDF regional programme for the Caribbean was prepared over the course of the year in a broad dialogue with the Cariforum authorities. The regional strategy paper, submitted to the Commission, amounts to EUR 57 million and focuses on regional economic integration, international trade negotiations, the development of potential such as human resources, the private sector, information and communication technologies or transport, and on major factors of vulnerability such as anti-drugs monitoring and disaster management.

Regional indicative programmes were also signed on 5 October with the Pacific region and on 7 November with the Southern African Development Community (SADC) and with organisations mandated by the eastern and southern Africa region (Common Market of Eastern and Southern Africa, East African Community, Indian Ocean Commission and the Intergovernmental Authority on Development).

1002. Visits. In February, Mr Nielson attended the work of the Council of Ministers of the Indian Ocean Commission in Mauritius. In September he met Mr Erastus Mwencha, Secretary-General of Comesa, and Mr Albert Muchanga, Deputy Secretary-General of the Southern Africa Development Community

---

([1]) Bull. 12-2002, point 1.6.123.

(SADC). In October, he met the leaders of the Pacific Islands Forum in Fiji. On 7 and 8 November, he attended the ministerial conference help in Maputo (Mozambique) as part of the dialogue between the European Union and the SADC. At the end of November, Mr Lamy attended the meeting of Comesa trade ministers.

Bilateral relations

1003. The statements made by the Presidency on behalf of the European Union concerning the ACP countries is given in Table 17 *(→ point 762)*. Parliament's resolutions on human rights in the ACP countries are listed in Table 2 *(→ point 54)*.

1004. Suspension of the application of the Cotonou Agreement. Article 96 of the agreement providing for this possibility in the event of violation of one of its essential elements (respect for human rights, democratic principles and the rule of law) by one of the parties, was applied in 2002 against a few ACP countries. The Council accordingly decided on 21 January[1] to carry over until 31 December the measures taken in 2001 concerning Haiti[2]. On 11 December, the Commission proposed to review the measures[3] while maintaining the objectives adopted in earlier decisions. On 18 February[4], the Council terminated the consultations begun with Zimbabwe on 11 January and decided to apply appropriate measures, including the suspension of financing of all projects other than those of direct benefit to the people, especially in the social field, until the situation in Zimbabwe was once more such as to guarantee the said essential elements. By contrast, on 19 February[5] the Council decided to resume full cooperation with Côte d'Ivoire, which had been reduced after the coup of December 1999[6]. On 27 March[7], consultations with Liberia were concluded. Cooperation with Fiji was partially resumed in February but Article 96 still applies to it. Cooperation was also resumed with the Comoros, under the gradual, conditional approach to the resumption of these ties adopted in February 2000[8].

1005. West Africa. In addition to the procedure adopted under Article 96 of the Cotonou Agreement *(→ point 1004)*, on 13 June[9] the Council extended Common Position 2001/357/CFSP concerning restrictive measures against

[1] Decision 2002/131/EC (OJ L 47, 19.2.2002; Bull. 1/2-2002, point 1.6.141).
[2] Council Decision 2001/131/EC (OJ L 48, 17.2.2001; 2001 General Report, point 1116).
[3] COM(2002) 716; Bull. 12-2002, point 1.6.132.
[4] Decision 2002/148/EC (OJ L 50, 21.2.2002; Bull. 1/2-2002, point 1.6.156).
[5] Bull. 1/2-2002, point 1.6.140.
[6] 2000 General Report, point 1035; 2001 General Report, point 1116.
[7] Decision 2002/274/EC (OJ L 96, 13.4.2002).
[8] 2000 General Report, point 1035.
[9] Common Position 2002/457/CFSP (OJ L 155, 14.6.2002; Bull. 6-2002, point 1.6.117).

Liberia (^{1}) and on 22 July (^{2}), prohibited any provision of technical training or assistance connected with military activities and also imports of rough diamonds from Liberia. Bans on imports of rough diamonds from Sierra Leone were also imposed on 11 January (^{3}) and on 18 February (^{4}) and 19 December (^{5}).

As regards Nigeria, the Barcelona European Council (^{6}) urged the authorities to respect human rights and human dignity, with particular reference to women. On 27 May (^{7}), the Council repealed Common Position 2001/373/CFSP (^{8}) in order to implement an even more positive and constructive approach towards Nigeria in its efforts to consolidate democracy and advance its socio-economic development.

The worsening situation in Côte d'Ivoire from September onwards, prompted the Presidency to issue statements on behalf of the European Union *(→ point 762)*, and Parliament and the Council to state their positions on 10 October (^{9}) and 21 October (^{10}) respectively.

1006.   East Africa. In its conclusions of 17 June (^{11}), the Council welcomed the EU–Sudan political dialogue and defined several priorities in its relations with Sudan, namely promoting initiatives for a peace settlement, respect for human rights, the rule of law and democracy. Parliament adopted a resolution on the situation in Somalia on 4 July (^{12}), calling on the EU to assist the transitional government in re-establishing its authority, while urging strict application of the UN arms embargo against Somalia. In its conclusions of 22 July (^{13}), the Council also confirmed its support for the reconciliation process under way at regional level and endorsed a more proactive approach to support for good governance. On 10 December, it prohibited the supply of arms and related material from the European Union to Somalia (^{14}). On 19 December, the Commission adopted a proposal for a regulation defining the scope of the ban (^{15}).

In February, Mr Lamy visited Kenya for a meeting of the Joint Ministerial Trade Committee with that country.

(^{1}) OJ L 126, 8.5.2001; 2001 General Report, point 1126.
(^{2}) Regulation (EC) No 1318/2002 (OJ L 194, 23.7.2002; Bull. 7/8-2002, point 1.6.148).
(^{3}) Common Position 2002/22/CFSP (OJ L 10, 12.1.2002; Bull. 1/2-2001, point 1.6.148).
(^{4}) Council Regulation (EC) No 303/2002 (OJ L 47, 19.2.2002; Bull. 1/2-2002, point 1.6.149).
(^{5}) Common Position 2002/992/CFSP and Council Regulation (EC) No 2290/2002 (OJ L 348, 21.12.2002; Bull. 12-2002, point 1.6.139).
(^{6}) Bull. 3-2002, point I.54.
(^{7}) Common Position 2002/401/CFSP (OJ L 139, 29.5.2002; Bull. 5-2002, point 1.6.133).
(^{8}) OJ L 132, 15.5.2001; 2001 General Report, point 1123.
(^{9}) Bull. 10-2002, point 1.6.121.
(^{10}) Bull. 10-2002, point 1.6.122.
(^{11}) Bull. 6-2002, point 1.6.123.
(^{12}) Bull. 7/8-2002, point 1.6.152.
(^{13}) Bull. 7/8-2002, point 1.6.153.
(^{14}) Common position 2002/960/CFSP (OJ L 334, 11.12.2002; Bull. 12-2002, point 1.6.141).
(^{15}) COM(2002) 745; Bull. 12-2002, point 1.6.142.

1007.   Central Africa. On 11 March (¹), the Council referred to recent efforts to promote peace in the Great Lakes region. On the same day, replacing Common Position 2001/83/CFSP (²), it adopted a new common position (³) on EU support for the implementation of the Lusaka ceasefire agreement and peace process in the Democratic Republic of Congo. However, the Barcelona European Council expressed its concern at signs of a worsening in the situation there (⁴). On 21 October, the Council amended the embargo on arms supplies to this country to allow certain exemptions with a view to implementing the ceasefire agreement and the peace process (⁵). On the same day, the Council adopted Common Position 2002/830/CFSP (⁶) repealing Common Position 2001/799/CFSP (⁷), to take account of developments in the situation in Rwanda and support the process of national reconciliation, human rights, development and the transition to democracy. On 10 December (⁸), the Council extended Mr Aldo Ajello's mandate as the European Union Special Representative for the African Great Lakes region.

1008.   Southern Africa. In a statement of 30 May (⁹), the Council urged all donors and NGOs to take appropriate urgent action in response to the food crisis in southern Africa. It repeated its concerns in its conclusions of 22 July (¹⁰). For its part, the Commission allocated EUR 42 million to help combat the crisis affecting the region.

The third cooperation meeting provided for by the Trade, Cooperation and Development Agreement between the European Union and South Africa (¹¹) was held in Brussels on 7 June.

As regards Angola, the Barcelona European Council (¹²) encouraged the parties to implement fully the provisions of the Lusaka Protocol and asked the Angolan authorities to facilitate humanitarian activities. This progress towards peace was also supported in a Parliament resolution of 11 April (¹³) and by the Council conclusions of 13 May (¹⁴). On 25 June (¹⁵) the Council repealed Common Position 2000/391/CFSP (¹⁶) in order to redefine its support for the process of

---

(¹) Bull. 3-2002, point 1.6.102.
(²) OJ L 29, 31.1.2001; 2001 General Report, point 1121.
(³) Common Position 2002/203/CFSP (OJ L 68, 12.3.2002; Bull. 3-2002, point 1.6.104).
(⁴) Bull. 3-2002, point I.53.
(⁵) Common Position 2002/829/CFSP (OJ L 285, 23.10.2002; Bull. 10-2002, point 1.6.127).
(⁶) OJ L 285, 23.10.2002; Bull. 10-2002, point 1.6.125.
(⁷) OJ L 303, 20.11.2001; 2001 General Report, point 1122.
(⁸) Joint Action 2002/962/CFSP (OJ L 334, 11.12.2002; Bull. 12-2002, point 1.6.122).
(⁹) Bull. 5-2002, point 1.6.125.
(¹⁰) Bull. 7/8-2002, point 1.6.143.
(¹¹) 1999 General Report, point 877
(¹²) Bull. 3-2002, point I.52.
(¹³) Bull. 4-2002, point 1.6.91.
(¹⁴) Bull. 5-2002, point 1.6.127.
(¹⁵) Common Position 2002/495/CFSP (OJ L 167, 26.6.2002; Bull. 6-2002, point 1.6.114)
(¹⁶) OJ L 146, 21.6.2000; 2000 General Report, point 1037.

national reconciliation; on 19 December (¹), it also repealed Common Positions 97/759/CFSP (²) and 98/425/CFSP (³). In a resolution of 4 July (⁴), Parliament recognised that priority had to go to Angola because of the dimension of the humanitarian problem and the political importance of peace. Under an action plan drawn up by the Commission, a financial package of EUR 125 million combining EU budget and EDF resources was allocated to a series of measures focused on emergency aid, food aid and food security, assistance for displaced persons and returnees to Angola and also mine clearance operations.

On 9 October, Mr Festus Mogae, President of Botswana, visited Brussels, where he was received by Mr Prodi.

Besides implementing the procedure suspending EU cooperation with Zimbabwe *(→ point 1004)*, the worsening human rights situation and the continuing political violence were condemned by the Council in its conclusions of 28 January (⁵) and 18 February (⁶). On 18 February (⁷), the Council also adopted restrictive measures against Zimbabwe prohibiting the supply of equipment capable of being used to repress the people of Zimbabwe and also freezing funds and financial assets. A regulation was adopted on 21 February (⁸) and then a decision on 13 September (⁹) in order to implement these measures at Community level. The situation in Zimbabwe was also discussed by the Barcelona European Council (¹⁰), which condemned the manner in which the elections were organised by the government. In a resolution of 16 May (¹¹), Parliament also described the elections as deeply flawed. The EU's concerns were reiterated by the Council on 15 April (¹²), 17 June (¹³) and 22 July (¹⁴), and by Parliament on 4 July (¹⁵), and 5 September (¹⁶).

1009.   Indian Ocean. In a resolution of 16 May (¹⁷), Parliament condemned all acts of political violence in Madagascar and called on the European Union to lend its support to an agreement between the parties to the internal conflict and to the holding of elections. It also called for the process of political dialogue

---

(¹) Common Position 2002/991/CFSP (OJ L 348, 21.12.2002; Bull. 12-2002, point 1.6.125).
(²) OJ L 309, 12.11.1997; 1997 General Report, point 1021.
(³) OJ L 190, 4.7.1998; 1998 General Report, point 951.
(⁴) Bull. 7/8-2002, point 1.6.144.
(⁵) Bull. 1/2-2002, point 1.6.154.
(⁶) Bull. 1/2-2002, point 1.6.155.
(⁷) Common Position 2002/145/CFSP (OJ L 50, 21.2.2002; Bull. 1/2-2001, point 1.6.157).
(⁸) Council Regulation (EC) No 310/2002 (OJ L 50, 21.2.2002; Bull. 1/2-2002, point 1.6.158).
(⁹) Council Decision 2002/754/CFSP (OJ L 247, 14.9.2002; Bull. 9-2002, point 1.6.92).
(¹⁰) Bull. 3-2002, point I.51.
(¹¹) Bull. 5-2002, point 1.6.135.
(¹²) Bull. 4-2002, point 1.6.98.
(¹³) Bull. 6-2002, point 1.6.124.
(¹⁴) Bull. 7/8-2002, point 1.6.157.
(¹⁵) Bull. 7/8-2002, point 1.6.156.
(¹⁶) Bull. 9-2002, point 1.6.91.
(¹⁷) Bull. 5-2002, point 1.6.132.

between the EU and Madagascar to be started in accordance with the provisions of the Cotonou Agreement.

1010.   *Caribbean.* Mr Nielson visited the Dominican Republic from 24 to 28 June.

1011.   *Pacific.* From 1 to 14 October, Mr Nielson went to the region where, in addition to Australia and New Zealand, he visited several ACP countries (Fiji, Micronesia, Papua New Guinea, Samoa and Tonga).

Relations with overseas countries and territories (OCTs)

1012.   *European Union-OCTs Forum.* On 19 and 20 September, Mr Nielson chaired this meeting, which was held in Bonaire (Dutch Antilles). There was a broad exchange of views on cooperation between the two sides, including regional cooperation, EDF allocations and procedures, ninth EDF programming and trade-related issues. On the eve of the forum, the OCTs ministerial conference set up the OCTs Association, comprising most of the countries and territories as full or associate members.

1013.   *Implementation of cooperation.* On 20 December, the Commission adopted Regulation (EC) No 2304/2002 ([1]), implementing Decision 2001/822/EC of 27 November 2001 on the association of the OCTs with the European Community ([2]). The aim of the regulation is to simplify the procedures for EDF financing by decentralising decision-making procedures and introducing the possibility of budget support alongside traditional funding for projects and programmes.

Financial and technical cooperation

1014.   In 2002, EUR 2 billion was granted for financial and technical cooperation under the European Development Fund. The breakdown by sector is shown in Table 20.

([1]) OJ L 348, 21.12.2002.
([2]) OJ L 314, 30.11.2001; 2001 General Report, point 1129.

TABLE 20

Annual breakdown of financing decisions for ACP countries

(EUR million)

Sector	Amount granted	
	2001 (¹)	2002 (²)
National and regional indicative programme	865	1 580
Structural adjustment	215	124
Sysmin	0	0
Stabex	0	0
Emergency aid	12	20
Aid for refugees	41	36
Risk capital	384	155
Interest rate subsidies	16	25
Debt relief initiative (HIPC)	0	60
Other and new initiatives	21	0
Total	1 554	2 000

(¹) Final figures.
(²) Provisional figures.

1015. *Financial regulation applicable to the ninth EDF.* On 18 July, the Commission presented a proposal for a financial regulation applying to the ninth EDF (Table II). On 17 December, Parliament, wishing to promote the idea of properly incorporating the EDF into the budget, refused to adopt an opinion on this proposal, stressing that its position should not have any negative implications for implementation of the various EDFs. On 28 November, the Commission presented its estimate of how much the Member States would have to contribute to cover spending for 2003 under the current EDFs, together with forecasts for commitments and payments for 2004–07 (¹).

(¹) COM(2002) 673; Bull. 11-2002, point 1.6.93.

Section 14

Diplomatic relations

1016. *Management of the external service.* On 2 July, the Commission approved a new communication on the management of its external service (¹), in which it undertook to pursue a personnel policy which made rotation of posts more flexible in order to cover even the most difficult posts more easily.

1017. *Delegations.* The Commission opened a delegation in Nepal and a representation office in Afghanistan. In continuing to implement the previous communication of 3 July 2001 on the development of its external service (²), the Commission regionalised its delegations in Costa Rica, Sri Lanka and Trinidad and Tobago.

1018. *Statistics.* At the end of the year, the Commission was accredited in 158 countries and international organisations and represented by 104 heads of delegation in a total of 131 external diplomatic missions.

(¹) SEC(2002) 745.
(²) COM(2001) 381; 2001 General Report, point 1130.

Chapter VII

Financing of Community activities, resource management

Section 1

Overview

1019.   *2002 was the first budget year covered by the cycle of strategic planning and programming under the objectives for 2000–05 which the Commission presented in February 2000 and which set out the key measures to be carried out during its term of office. The priorities laid down on this basis for the organisation of activities and the allocation of resources concerned the introduction of the euro, sustainable development, the new governance, enlargement, a consistent all-embracing policy of friendly relations with neighbouring third countries accompanied by a strengthening of the Euro-Mediterranean Partnership and global poverty reduction.*

In April Parliament granted discharge to the Commission in respect of the implementation of the 2000 budget.

In June the Council adopted the new financial regulation applicable to the Community budget which simplifies rules and procedures, provides a new structure for activity-based management and modernises financial management.

On 19 December Parliament adopted the 2003 budget which comes to EUR 99.686 billion in appropriations for commitments, virtually the same as in the previous budget, and to EUR 97.513 billion in appropriations for payments, 1.9 % higher than in 2002, although still no more than 1.02 % of the gross national income of the Member States.

As regards the protection of the financial interests of the Community, the Commission launched an information campaign and debate on the Green Paper published on this subject in 2001 and, in particular, on the establishment of a European prosecutor. The Convention on the Protection of the European Communities' Financial Interests signed in 1995 entered into force in October after being ratified by the final Member States.

Section 2

Budgets (¹)

General budget

Financial perspective

1020. *Adjustment for 2003.* On 19 February, in accordance with the interinstitutional agreement of 6 May 1999 on budgetary discipline and improvement of the budgetary procedure (²), the Commission sent the budgetary authority the results of the technical adjustment of the financial perspective for 2003 in line with movements in prices and gross national product (³), the latter because of the entry into force of the Council decision on the system of own resources (⁴) which defines gross national product (GNP) as gross national income (GNI) as determined by ESA 95 (⁵). The decision also adjusts the own resources ceiling expressed as a percentage of GNI to maintain unchanged the amount of financial resources placed at the disposal of the Communities. On 23 December, the Commission presented a communication on the result of the technical adjustment for 2004 (⁶).

Table 21 shows the financial perspective after the technical adjustment.

1021. *Establishment of the Solidarity Fund.* During the process for the adoption of the interinstitutional agreement providing the financial framework needed for the establishment of the European Union's Solidarity Fund (→ *point 362)*, a special trialogue meeting in Strasbourg on 23 September produced agreement between Parliament, the Council and the Commission on the text of the agreement and on the legal basis for the fund.

(¹) Further information is available on the Europa server (http://europa.eu.int/comm/budget/index_en.htm).
(²) OJ C 172, 18.6.1999; 1999 General Report, point 921.
(³) COM(2002) 86; Bull. 1/2-2002, point 1.7.5.
(⁴) Decision 2000/597/EC (OJ L 253, 7.10.2000; 2000 General Report, point 1052).
(⁵) Council Regulation (EC) No 2223/96 of 25 June 1996 on the European system of national and regional accounts in the Community (OJ L 310, 30.11.1996; 1996 General Report, point 95).
(⁶) COM(2002) 756; Bull. 12-2002, point 1.7.1.

TABLE 21

Financial perspective for 2000–06 after the technical adjustment for 2003

(EUR million)

Appropriations for commitments	Current prices				2003 prices		
	2000	2001	2002	2003	2004	2005	2006
1. Agriculture	41 738	44 530	46 587	47 378	46 285	45 386	45 094
— CAP (not including rural development)	37 352	40 035	41 992	42 680	41 576	40 667	40 364
— Rural development and accompanying measures	4 386	4 495	4 595	4 698	4 709	4 719	4 730
2. Structural operations	32 678	32 720	33 638	33 968	33 652	33 384	32 588
— Structural Funds	30 019	30 005	30 849	31 129	30 922	30 654	29 863
— Cohesion Fund	2 659	2 715	2 789	2 839	2 730	2 730	2 725
3. Internal policies ([1])	6 031	6 272	6 558	6 796	6 915	7 034	7 165
4. External action	4 627	4 735	4 873	4 972	4 983	4 994	5 004
5. Administration ([2])	4 638	4 776	5 012	5 211	5 319	5 428	5 536
6. Reserves	906	916	676	434	434	434	434
— Monetary reserve	500	500	250	0	0	0	0
— Emergency aid reserve	203	208	213	217	217	217	217
— Loan guarantee reserve	203	208	213	217	217	217	217
7. Pre-accession aid	3 174	3 240	3 328	3 386	3 386	3 386	3 386
— Agriculture	529	540	555	564	564	564	564
— Pre-accession structural instruments	1 058	1 080	1 109	1 129	1 129	1 129	1 129
— Phare (applicant countries)	1 587	1 620	1 664	1 693	1 693	1 693	1 693
Total commitment appropriations	93 792	97 189	100 672	102 145	100 974	100 046	99 207
Total payment appropriations	91 322	94 730	100 078	102 767	99 553	97 659	97 075
Payment appropriations as % of GNI (ESA 95)	1.07	1.08	1.10	1.08	1.02	0.98	0.95
Available for accession (payments)			4 397	7 266	9 626	12 387	15 396
— Agriculture			1 698	2 197	2 652	3 172	3 680
— Other expenditure			2 699	5 069	6 974	9 215	11 716
Ceiling on payment appropriations	91 322	94 730	104 475	110 033	109 179	110 046	112 471
Ceiling on payment appropriations (as % of GNI)	1.07	1.08	1.15	1.16	1.12	1.10	1.10
Margin for unforeseen expenditure (as % of GNI)	0.17	0.16	0.09	0.08	0.12	0.14	0.14
Own resources ceiling (as % of GNI)	1.24	1.24	1.24	1.24	1.24	1.24	1.24

([1]) In accordance with Article 2 of Decision No 182/1999/EC and Article 2 of Decision 1999/64/Euratom (OJ L 26, 1.2.1999), the amount of expenditure available during the period 2000–02 for research amounts to EUR 11.510 billion at current prices.

([2]) The expenditure on pensions included under the ceilings for this heading is calculated net of staff contributions to the pension scheme, within the limit of EUR 1.1 billion at 1999 prices for the period 2000–06.

Budgetary procedure for 2003

2003 budget

1022. *Guidelines.* In its conclusions of 5 March the Council emphasised the need for the same degree of budgetary restraint as exercised by Member States ([1]). It confirmed the importance it attached to the reform of the financial management undertaken within the Commission *(→ point 1150).* On 12 March, Parliament adopted a resolution setting out its priorities for the 2003 budget ([2]). It regarded enlargement and preparation of the administration for enlargement as 'absolute priorities'. The other political priorities included the reform of the Commission, external assistance to Afghanistan, and internal security in the European Union.

1023. *Preliminary draft budget (PDB).* The preliminary draft budget was approved by the Commission on 30 April ([3]). It totalled some EUR 100 billion in commitment appropriations (up by 1.4 % on 2002), leaving a margin of around EUR 2.3 billion in commitments and EUR 98.217 billion in payments (an increase of 2.7 % compared with 2002) beneath the 2003 ceiling set in the financial perspective for 2000–06 *(→ point 1020)*; the payments total, representing 1.03 % of Community gross national income (GNI), left a margin of EUR 4.720 billion, far below the ceiling in the financial perspective. For the third consecutive year, the preliminary draft was presented in accordance with both the traditional nomenclature and the activity-based budgeting approach.

The broad lines of the proposed preliminary draft by financial perspective heading were as follows:

- the budget for agriculture (EUR 45.118 billion, an increase of 1.9 % compared with 2002) left a margin of just under EUR 2.3 billion beneath the ceiling in the financial perspective. The situation on the agricultural markets seemed favourable for 2003, with domestic consumption and exports increasing and requirements for public storage falling significantly; the margin available within this heading could also cover any unforeseen events;

- the commitment appropriations proposed for structural operations (EUR 33.995 billion) slightly exceeded the ceiling because of the specific measure to promote the conversion of vessels and fishermen that were, up to 1999, dependent on the fisheries agreement with Morocco (EUR 27 million had to be entered in the budget for this purpose). It was therefore proposed to make

[1] Bull. 3-2002, point 1.7.1.
[2] Bull. 3-2002, point 1.7.2.
[3] SEC(2002) 464; Bull. 4-2002, point 1.7.1.

use of the flexibility instrument provided for in the interinstitutional agreement. Payment appropriations for the heading came to EUR 33.538 billion, an increase of 4.4 % compared with 2002;

- for internal policies, the Commission proposed EUR 6.714 billion in commitment appropriations and EUR 6.131 billion in payment appropriations (+ 2.4 % and − 0.4 % respectively compared with the 2002 budget). The proposal covered operations under the three policy priorities identified in the annual policy strategy for 2003: preparations for enlargement, stability and security, a sustainable and inclusive economy;

- on the external relations front, the commitment appropriations proposed came to EUR 4.912 billion, an increase of 2.3 % over the 2002 budget. The margin left beneath the ceiling was EUR 60 million. The total amount proposed for payment appropriations was virtually the same as in 2002 and would allow the Commission to continue its efforts to clear outstanding commitments. The stability and security objective received an additional EUR 93 million under heading 4. Most of it went to Asia following the Commission's pledge in respect of Afghanistan at the donors' conference in Tokyo in January 2002 (→ point 948). The priority given to a sustainable and inclusive economy was reflected in the increase in appropriations for the control of contagious diseases and the promotion of reproductive health;

- for pre-accession, the proposal contained measures under the three priorities set for 2003, in particular the strengthening of the administrative and judicial capacity of the future Member States under the Phare programme, the investment which the applicant countries need in order to play a full part in the trans-European networks, and measures to ensure the smooth operation of the internal market. The preliminary draft proposed a considerable increase in payment appropriations;

- the administrative budget came to EUR 5.447 billion (an increase of 5.2 % over 2002). The costs connected with the preparations for enlargement took expenditure above the ceiling. The priority was to take account of the administrative repercussions of enlargement. The well-established priorities were maintained, viz. the need to continue devolving management of external aid programmes to the delegations as initially planned and providing the resources for continuing the reform process. The creation of the European Communities Personnel Selection Office was also covered. The total scheduled for preparations for enlargement in 2003 was EUR 55.3 million, an increase of EUR 39.5 million compared with the budget provided for enlargement in 2002 (EUR 15.8 million). This increase was due, in particular, to the need to prepare for enlargement, which explains the request for appropriations for outside staff (including those from non-member countries) equivalent to 500 additional posts; as the whole body of Community law has to be published in the new languages, specific commitment appropriations of EUR 11 million were planned for the *Official Journal of the European Communities*. With the preliminary draft budget for 2003, the Commission proposed using the flexibility instrument to cover the additional administrative costs of enlargement preparations for all institutions.

In its resolution of 14 May Parliament discussed the estimates of its revenue and expenditure for 2003 ([1]).

1024. Draft budget. The draft 2003 budget established by the Council at first reading on 19 July ([2]) came to EUR 99.548 billion in appropriations for commitments and EUR 96.992 billion in appropriations for payments. Compared with the 2002 budget, these figures represented an overall increase of 0.9 % in appropriations for commitments and 1.4 % in appropriations for payments. The total amount of payment appropriations was thus equivalent to 1.02 % of Community GNP. The Council made a number of cuts to the preliminary draft, as shown in Table 22.

TABLE 22

Amendments made by the Council at first reading

(EUR million)

Heading of financial perspective	Appropriations for commitments	Appropriations for payments
1a	− 288	− 288
1b	0	0
2	− 27	− 525
3	− 41	− 19.6
4	− 20	− 11
5	− 71.8	− 71.8
7	0	− 300
Total	− 447.8	− 1 215.4

The main features of the draft budget were as follows:

- for agriculture, the Council adopted an across-the-board reduction of EUR 275 million in all budget chapters of subheading 1a (market expenditure) where the sum of appropriations was greater than EUR 1.5 billion. It was also decided to review the amounts in the light of the October letter of amendment *(→ point 1026)* and the Commission was called on to revise the figure for the eradication of animal diseases on this occasion. The Council

([1]) Bull. 5-2002, point 1.7.1.
([2]) Bull. 7/8-2002, point 1.7.1.

also accepted the Commission's preliminary draft as regards the appropriations for rural development (subheading 1b);

- for structural operations expenditure, the Council accepted the preliminary
  draft as regards commitment appropriations and made an across-the-board
  reduction of EUR 525 million for the Structural Funds because of the significant under-utilisation in recent years. With regard to surpluses from previous years, the Council underlined the need to establish the budget on the
  basis of realistic estimates and asked that any surplus in 2002 be carried over
  to the 2003 budget this autumn in a letter of an amendment;

- regarding expenditure on internal policies, the Council accepted the amounts
  proposed for multiannual programmes under the co-decision procedure. As
  regards the trans-European transport networks, the Council issued a statement to the effect that the reductions in appropriations for these networks
  would not affect projects relating to frontier regions bordering the candidate
  countries. It rejected two preparatory actions relating to non-Community
  areas (sport and cultural cooperation) for 2003 and increased the appropriations for special annual events relating to the world special Olympics 2003;

- as regards external operations, the Council increased appropriations in the
  preliminary draft for East Timor and the common foreign and security policy
  and agreed to retain the appropriations for the pre-accession strategy for
  Mediterranean countries under heading 4 of the financial perspective. The
  Council accepted the amounts proposed in the preliminary draft for international fisheries agreements. In a joint statement Parliament, the Council and
  the Commission accepted the possibility of using the emergency aid reserve
  for civilian crisis management; the Council and Parliament also decided to
  seek agreement on the amount for the CFSP in the light of the considerable
  new requirements and with the involvement of Parliament;

- the administrative expenditure of the institutions was reviewed on the basis
  of the Council conclusions of 5 March (→ point 1022) offering + 3.5% for
  each institution. The Council was categorically opposed to using the flexibility instrument for administrative expenditure as proposed by the Commission. Parliament was prepared to accept it only if it was accompanied by
  frontloading of expenditure in 2002 in order to ease the burden on the 2003
  budget. The Commission took the view that rejecting from the outset the use
  of the flexibility instrument compromised the administrative preparation of
  enlargement. Parliament and the Council agreed on the following: compliance with the ceiling of heading 5 and maintenance of a margin beneath the
  ceiling; agreement by the Council to extend the scope of the early retirement
  scheme to Parliament's temporary staff; increase in the Council's budget of
  11% (including publication of the *acquis communautaire*, 7% without it)

while Parliament would set its own budget; frontloading of expenditure in the 2002 budget with corresponding reductions in the 2003 budget: this operation, which applied to all institutions, would involve transfers within the institutions' budgets and between them at the end of the year; of the EUR 64 million cut planned by the Council, an initial EUR 11 million was returned to the Commission for enlargement in the form of a reserve, including the *acquis,* this being the exact amount needed for the *acquis*; the real cut in the Commission's preliminary draft was still EUR 53 million, but a reserve of EUR 18 million was created in the Council's budget and could be transferred to the Commission budget if the Council could frontload the corresponding amount in its own budget for the publication of the *acquis*;

- as regards expenditure on pre-accession instruments, the Council accepted the preliminary draft for commitment appropriations and decided on a reduction of EUR 300 million in the payment appropriations to take account of under-utilisation in past years.

1025. Use of the flexibility instrument. On 10 July, the Commission proposed that EUR 124.814 million be mobilised by the flexibility instrument to finance the specific action for the conversion of the Spanish and Portuguese fleets (EUR 27 million) *(→ point 359)*, the Community emergency measure for the scrapping of fishing vessels as part of the reform of the common fisheries policy (EUR 32 million) *(→ points 434 and 450)* and the amount in excess of the ceiling on administrative expenditure which the institutions need to prepare for enlargement (EUR 65.814 million) [1]. At the conciliation meeting of 25 November the budgetary authority decided to mobilise EUR 12.008 million under the flexibility instrument for the conversion of the Spanish and Portuguese fleets; [2] this was an exception to the principle that the flexibility instrument should not as a rule be used for the same needs two years in succession.

1026. Letters of amendment. On 17 July the Commission adopted letter of amendment No 1/2003 [3] to incorporate a line in the preliminary draft and EUR 32 million in reserve for the initial measures for scrapping vessels in support of the Commission's proposal to reform the common fisheries policy *(→ point 434)*. The budgetary authority deferred examination of this letter of amendment pending a legislative decision on the reform of the common fisheries policy.

Letter of amendment No 2/2003, adopted by the Commission on 18 September [4], proposed the budgetary structure needed to accommodate three new Commis-

---

[1] COM(2002) 399; Bull. 7/8-2002, point 1.7.2.
[2] Bull. 11-2002, point 1.7.1.
[3] Bull. 7/8-2002, point 1.7.1.
[4] Bull. 9-2002, point 1.7.1.

sion administrative offices *(→ point 1152)*; it was also intended to create lines in the 2003 budget to cover utilisation of the new European Solidarity Fund to provide Community disaster relief *(→ point 362)*; finally, it drew the budgetary authority's attention to the fact that the consequences of the new financial regulation had to be incorporated into the budget *(→ point 1048)*; however, the last point was not accepted by the budgetary authority, which called for a separate letter of amendment to be produced.

Letter of amendment No 3/2003 [1], adopted by the Commission on 30 October, covered the items provided for in the interinstitutional agreement of 6 May 1999: agriculture, international fisheries agreements and preliminary estimate of the 2002 budget out-turn. The letter of amendment cut agricultural spending by EUR 337.4 million, while the shift in the euro-dollar exchange rate produced some increases. The letter of amendment also proposed a line for genetic resources carrying EUR 1.5 million under heading 3; it also rebalanced amounts between the budget line and the reserve for fishery agreements, but the overall impact was neutral, and proposed entering in advance a surplus of EUR 500 million from the 2002 agricultural budget. The letter of amendment was approved in a single reading in the conciliation committee on 25 November but with amendments to reduce the reserve for fisheries agreements and the lines for food aid and humanitarian aid and increase the budget surplus for 2002 to EUR 1 billion for revenue that had been received.

On 28 November the Commission adopted letter of amendment No 4/2003 [2] dealing with the consequences of the new financial regulation and also proposed the harmonisation of the remarks for certain lines in order to clarify their application. In purely budgetary terms this letter of amendment was entirely neutral. It was subsequently approved by the Council and Parliament with some adjustments. The 2003 budget as finally adopted *(→ point 1029)* is therefore compliant with the financial regulation in force from 1 January 2003.

1027. Parliament's first reading. After Parliament's first reading on 24 October [3] the draft budget came to EUR 100.19 billion in appropriations for commitments and EUR 99.93 billion in appropriations for payments, 0.7 % and 4.5 % more than the appropriations in the 2002 budget. The appropriations for commitments, which Parliament increased by almost EUR 3 billion compared with the Council's draft, represents 1.04 % of Community GNI. Parliament's additions to the Council draft are set out in Table 23.

---

[1] Bull. 10-2002, point 1.7.2.
[2] Bull. 11-2002, point 1.7.1.
[3] Bull. 10-2002, point 1.7.2.

TABLE 23

Parliament's additions to the Council draft

(million EUR)

Heading of financial perspective	Appropriations for commitments	Appropriations for payments
1a	344.258	344.258
1b	0.000	0.000
2	27.000	1 508.349
3	119.354	121.324
4	155.350	270.864
5	– 2.201	– 2.201
7	0.000	699.000
Total	643.761	2 941.594

- Parliament made the following broad changes: for agriculture, Parliament overturned the Council's across-the-board cuts. It used part of the margin available for animal welfare, public health and genetic resources. On export subsidies for live animals Parliament requested transparency by splitting the lines for export refunds for meat from those for live animals;

- Parliament restored the payment appropriations cut by the Council for the Structural Funds, as well as the EUR 27 million for the restructuring of the fleets affected by the non-renewal of the Morocco fisheries agreement as proposed in the preliminary draft, thus exceeding the ceiling; it also decided to cut appropriations on the BA lines for administrative support and management expenditure for the programmes where implementation at 15 July is lower than 10 % and to increase the corresponding B lines by the same amount and to create global reserves where implementation is between 10 and 35 %;

- as regards internal policies, Parliament increased appropriations, leaving only a margin of EUR 2.7 million below the ceiling. It created several new pilot projects, for SMEs and enlargement, regions of knowledge, mobility of elderly people, and Kyoto clean development. It placed particular emphasis on the information policy and asked for a single interoperable database on EU legislation and the legislative procedure to be made accessible to the public;

- external policies were a particular problem to Parliament. In particular the appropriations for the Global Health Fund against HIV/AIDS, malaria and tuberculosis and for the reconstruction of Afghanistan were set at such a level the ceiling was exceeded. Parliament earmarked EUR 30 million for CFSP and EUR 10 million for the EU police mission in the Balkans on the CARDS line. It increased appropriations for mine-clearance and East Timor and proposed to put appropriations for KEDO (Korean peninsula energy programme) in the reserve;

- for administrative expenditure Parliament adopted the frontloading package, which brought forward to 2002, by way of an interinstitutional supplementary and amending budget (No 6/2002), expenditure initially planned for 2003 (→ point 1039). This should allow in 2003 preparation for enlargement and respect of the ceiling, as agreed with Council in July.

1028.   Council's second reading. This second reading was preceded by a conciliation meeting with Parliament on 25 November (¹). The negotiations centred on the use of the flexibility instrument for the programme to restructure the Spanish and Portuguese fishing fleets, the financing of heading 4, and in particular, the common foreign and security policy, as well as administrative expenditure and the overall increase in appropriations for payments. The amounts adopted by the Council came to EUR 99.454 billion in appropriations for commitments (0.02 % higher than in 2002) and to EUR 96.896 billion in appropriations for payments (1.3 % higher), equivalent to 1.01 % of Community GNI. The amounts adopted by the Council for each heading of the financial perspective are set out in Table 24.

TABLE 24

Council second reading

(EUR million)

Heading of financial perspective	Appropriations for commitments	Appropriations for payments
1a	40 082.45	40 082.45
1b	4 698.00	4 698.00
2	33 980.01	33 023.10
3	6 698.46	6 121.15
4	4 859.38	4 664.11
5	5 315.87	5 315.87
6	434.00	434.00
7	3 386.00	2 557.40
Total	99 454.18	96 896.08

- The Council made the following broad changes: as regards agriculture, the letter of amendment No 3/2003 was adopted as proposed by the Commission (→ point 1026), including the splitting of the line on export refunds for live bovine animals. Parliament and the Council recalled their joint declaration on recovery of beef and veal export refunds agreed on 21/22 November 2001 and invite the Commission to take the conclusions of the requested report into account when preparing the preliminary draft budget for 2004;

(¹) Bull. 11-2002, point 1.7.1.

- for structural measures, Parliament and the Council agreed to mobilise the flexibility instrument for an amount of EUR 12 million in order to finance the remaining part of the restructuring programme for the Spanish and Portuguese fleet. In November 2001 EUR 27 million for this programme had been left over for the next budget year; of this amount, transfer No 51/2002, approved at the conciliation meeting, provided EUR 14.9 million from unused appropriations inside the 2002 budget. Payment appropriations were lowered by EUR 1.5 billion in relation to Parliament's first reading;

- in the internal policies heading the Council and Parliament agreed a joint declaration on pilot projects. The Council restored a very large margin of EUR 97 million in this heading and accepted the genetic resources line as proposed in the letter of amendment (→ point 1026);

- for external policies, the Council and Parliament agreed to enter in the budget a total of EUR 47.5 million for common foreign and security policy (CFSP) to secure the financing of the EU police mission in Bosnia-Herzegovina. This amount had been negotiated against a joint declaration on the financing of the CFSP, which provides for more transparency and better information of Parliament. Agreement was also reached on entering EUR 42 million in the budget for the contribution to the Global Health Fund. At least the same amount should be added from the European Development Fund to secure a seat on the board of the Global Health Fund and thus an active role for the EU. Should the amount provided for so far not suffice, the Commission would make all necessary proposals. The assistance package of EUR 55 million to be financed from the emergency aid reserve for the famine in the Horn of Africa eased the pressure on the 2003 budget. Thus the budget lines for food aid and humanitarian aid were reduced by EUR 27.5 million each. The appropriations for KEDO were kept in the reserve. Pre-accession aid was not changed from the Council's first reading;

- on administrative expenditure the Council implemented the frontloading for the Commission only in so far as it related to savings and preparation for enlargement. The cuts on salaries in the first reading were confirmed, leading to a margin of around EUR 65 million beneath the ceiling of heading 5;

- finally, other joint declarations were agreed on potentially abnormal outstanding commitments, on the implementation profile, on the financial consequences of enlargement, on the evaluation before end-2003 of the implementation and the calculation methodology of aid granted by the EU Solidarity Fund.

1029. *Parliament's second reading.* The general budget for 2003 was adopted on 19 December after Parliament's second reading (¹). The budget as adopted

---

(¹) Bull. 12-2002, point 1.7.2.

totals EUR 99.686 billion for commitments and EUR 97.513 billion for payments. Compared with 2002, commitment appropriations remain at roughly the same level (an increase of 0.3 %). Appropriations for payments rise by a modest 1.9 %, which also reflects the consolidation efforts being made by Member States with their national budgets. This trend leaves a substantial margin of EUR 5.425 billion in payments and EUR 2.623 billion in commitments. The payment appropriations in the 2003 budget amount to 1.02 % of Member States' gross national income, the authorised limit being 1.24 %.

- Appropriations for agricultural expenditure are up by 1.2 % to EUR 44.780 billion, leaving a substantial margin of EUR 2.597 billion beneath the ceiling. The amount in the 2003 budget for rural development is the maximum possible.

- Expenditure for structural operations comes to EUR 33.980 billion, a figure which exceeds the ceiling by EUR 12 million financed by use of the flexibility instrument. The 2003 budget provides EUR 33.173 billion in payment appropriations for structural operations, an increase of 3.2 % over 2002. An amending budget may be presented should additional appropriations prove necessary in the course of the year. Within the overall allocation for structural operations the Cohesion Fund receives EUR 2.839 billion for commitments and EUR 2.650 billion for payments.

- The 2003 budget carries EUR 6.796 billion for internal policies, 5 % down on 2002 owing to the large increase in the 2002 budget as a result of supplementary and amending budget No 5/2002 which mobilised the European Solidarity Fund for the floods in Germany, Austria and France (→ point 1038). The research framework programme is awarded the same amount as in 2002, while there are large increases for transport, energy, the environment, the labour market and the social dimension employment. Payment appropriations are at much the same level as in 2002, with an increase of only 0.8 %. This heading also has a new line for genetic resources and for pilot projects launched by Parliament, including mobility for the elderly, preparation of SMEs for enlargement, regions of knowledge and Kyoto-Europe: clean development mechanism.

- The commitment appropriations for external action, up by 1.7 % on 2002, leave a margin of EUR 16.6 million. The food aid and humanitarian aid lines are down on 2002 as mobilisation of the emergency aid reserve late in the year for the famine in the Horn of Africa provided advance cover for some of the requirements. The European contribution to the Global Health Fund is set at EUR 42 million. A new line is entered, as a pilot project, for poverty-related diseases other than those covered by the Global Health Fund. The funds earmarked for CFSP total EUR 47.5 million. The transfer of the appropriations for Turkey from the Mediterranean chapter to the pre-accession chapter accounts for the marked changes in these chapters. The 2003 budget confirms the aid for the reconstruction of Afghanistan and the traditional priorities for external policies. In line with the objective of reducing outstanding commitments, the payment appropriations for this heading are 4 % up on 2002.

- For pre-accession aid, the commitment appropriations are, as always, at the ceiling. But this is nevertheless a reduction in relation to the 2002 budget, since the Czech Republic also received aid from the EU Solidarity Fund in 2002. Payment appropriations rise by 4.3 %, the biggest increase for all the headings, to cover the amounts committed since 2000 but not yet paid.

- A margin of EUR 20.9 million is left for administrative expenditure. Financing of the preparations for enlargement was arranged by bringing forward some interinstitutional spending in supplementary and amending budget No 6/2002 (→ point 1039). The increase over 2002 amounts to 3.5 %, with 0.7 % for the Commission, 6.7 % for the other institutions and 6.7 % for pensions. Administrative expenditure accounts for only 5.4 % of the total budget in terms of commitments.

1030.   Table 25 gives a breakdown, by heading of the financial perspective, of the amounts entered at the various stages of the 2003 budget procedure.

1031.   The *revenue* (see Table 28) required to finance the budget for 2003 represented 1 % of GNI. The uniform call-in rate for the VAT resource was 0.5366 % and the rate for the GNI resource was 0.6198 %. Traditional own resources (agricultural duties, sugar and isoglucose levies, and customs duties) represent 12.45 % of budget financing for 2003, the VAT resource 24.74 % and the fourth (GNI-based) resource 60.9 % (compared with 11.91, 24.05 and 48.61 % respectively for the 2002 budget). Miscellaneous revenue of EUR 837.4 million was also projected.

Own resources

1032.   On 12 February Parliament and the Council adopted Regulation (EC) No 359/2002 on the use of ESA 95 in the determination of Member States' payments to the VAT-based own resource (→ point 101). In its decision of 13 March [1] the Commission amended Decision 97/245/EC, Euratom laying down the arrangements for the transmission of information to the Commission by the Member States under the Communities' own resources system [2].

[1] Decision 2002/235/EC (OJ L 79, 22.3.2002).
[2] OJ L 97, 12.4.1997.

Implementation of the 2002 budget (^{1})

1033.   Implementation. On 2 July Parliament adopted a resolution on the
implementation profile of the 2002 budget (^{2}).

Supplementary and amending budgets 2002

1034.   Supplementary and amending budget No 1/2002. The Commission
adopted the preliminary draft on 22 February (^{3}) and the Council established the
draft on 26 February (^{3}); Parliament adopted it on 28 February (^{4}). Following the
interinstitutional agreement on the financing of the Convention on the Future
of the European Union *(→ point 7)*, it contained the new lines and transfers of
appropriations necessary for the three institutions (Commission, Council and
Parliament) to pay their contributions. On 28 February Parliament also adopted
supplementary estimates of its revenue and expenditure for 2002, taking this
contribution into account (^{5}).

1035.   Supplementary and amending budget No 2/2002. The Commission
adopted the preliminary draft on 27 February (^{6}) and the Council established the
draft on 12 March (^{7}). The purpose was to recalculate the revenue side of the
budget in accordance with the new own resources decision (^{8}) and enter as revenue an estimate of the positive balance resulting from implementation of the
2001 budget. This draft, which was amended by Parliament on 25 April to
reduce the balance entered (^{9}), was restored by the Council on 21 May (^{10}) and
the supplementary and amending budget was finally adopted by Parliament,
without amendment, on 30 May (^{11}). In a resolution adopted at the same time,
Parliament expressed its concern at the build-up of outstanding payments and
wished to achieve a more balanced relationship between commitments and
payments (^{12}).

(^{1}) http://europa.eu.int/comm/budget/execution/utilisation/details_fr.htm.
(^{2}) Bull. 7/8-2002, point 1.7.5.
(^{3}) Bull. 1/2-2002, point 1.7.6.
(^{4}) OJ L 81, 25.3.2002; Bull. 1/2-2002, point 1.7.6.
(^{5}) Bull. 1/2-2002, point 1.7.8.
(^{6}) Bull. 1/2-2002, point 1.7.7.
(^{7}) Bull. 3-2002, point 1.7.3.
(^{8}) Decision 2000/597/EC, Euratom (OJ L 253, 7.10.2000; 2000 General Report, point 1052).
(^{9}) Bull. 4-2002, point 1.7.2.
(^{10}) Bull. 5-2002, point 1.7.2.
(^{11}) OJ L 199, 29.7.2002; Bull. 5-2002, point 1.7.2.
(^{12}) Bull. 5-2002, point 1.7.1.

TABLE 25

2003 budget (appropriations for commitments) in euro

(EUR)

Heading	Appropriations entered in 2002 budget (¹)	Financial perspective 2003	Preliminary draft budget 2003 (²)	Difference (4)/(1)	Council (first reading) (³)	Difference (5)/(1)
	(1)	(2)	(3)	(4)	(5)	(6)
				%		%
Appropriations for commitments						
1. Agriculture	44 255 080 000	47 378 000 000	44 780 450 000	1.2	44 829 850 000	1.3
Margin	2 331 920 000		2 597 550 000		2 548 150 000	
Agricultural expenditure (excluding rural development)	39 660 080 000	42 680 000 000	40 082 450 000	1.1	40 131 850 000	1.2
Rural development and accompanying measures	4 595 000 000	4 698 000 000	4 698 000 000	2.2	4 698 000 000	2.2
2. Structural operations	33 838 000 000	33 968 000 000	34 027 000 000	0.6	33 968 000 000	0.4
Margin	– 200 000 000		– 59 000 000		0	
Structural Funds	31 049 000 000	31 129 000 000	31 188 000 000	0.4	31 129 000 000	0.3
Cohesion Fund	2 789 000 000	2 839 000 000	2 839 000 000	1.8	2 839 000 000	1.8
3. Internal policies	7 156 813 600	6 796 000 000	6 716 465 000	– 6.2	6 673 965 000	– 6.7
Margin	– 598 813 600		79 535 000		122 035 000	
4. External action	4 873 000 000	4 972 000 000	4 911 882 000	0.8	4 891 882 000	0.4
Margin	0		60 118 000		80 118 000	
5. Administration	5 178 461 138	5 381 000 000	5 436 332 143	5.0	5 364 526 883	3.6
Margin	538 862		– 55 332 143		16 473 117	
6. Reserves	676 000 000	434 000 000	434 000 000	– 35.8	434 000 000	– 35.8
Margin	0		0		0	
Monetary reserve	250 000 000			– 100.0		– 100.0
Guarantee reserve	213 000 000	217 000 000	217 000 000	1.9	217 000 000	1.9
Emergency aid reserve	213 000 000	217 000 000	217 000 000	1.9	217 000 000	1.9
7. Pre-accession aid	3 457 000 000	3 386 000 000	3 386 000 000	– 2.1	3 386 000 000	– 2.1
Margin	– 129 000 000		0		0	
Agriculture	555 000 000	564 000 000	564 000 000	1.6	564 000 000	1.6
ISPA	1 109 000 000	1 129 000 000	1 129 000 000	1.8	1 129 000 000	1.8
Phare (applicant countries)	1 664 000 000	1 693 000 000	1 693 000 000	1.7	1 693 000 000	1.7
European Union Solidarity Fund	129 000 000		p.m.	– 100.0	p.m.	– 100.0
Total appropriations for commitments	99 434 354 738	102 315 000 000	99 692 129 143	0.3	99 548 223 883	0.1
Margin	1 404 645 262		2 622 870 857		2 766 776 117	
Compulsory expenditure	41 294 401 100		41 538 154 321	0.6	41 587 554 321	0.7
Non-compulsory expenditure	58 139 953 638		58 153 974 822	0.0	57 960 669 562	– 0.3
Appropriations for payment						
Total appropriations for payment	95 656 387 238	102 938 000 000	97 880 144 143	2.3	96 991 638 883	1.4
Margin	4 588 612 762		5 057 855 857		5 946 361 117	
Compulsory expenditure	41 363 797 100		41 593 602 321	0.6	41 643 002 321	0.7
Non-compulsory expenditure	54 292 590 138		56 286 541 822	3.7	55 348 636 562	1.9
Appropriations for payments as percentage of GNI	1.05	1.07	1.02		1.01	

(¹) Including all supplementary and amending budgets.
(²) Including letters of amendment Nos 1/2003 to 4/2003.
(³) Including letter of amendment No 2/2003.
(⁴) Including letter of amendment No 2/2003.
(⁵) Including letters of amendment Nos 2/2003 to 4/2003.
(⁶) Including letters of amendment Nos 2/2003 to 4/2003.

(EUR)

Parliament (first reading) (³)	Difference (7)/(1)	Council (second reading) (⁴)	Difference (9)/(1)	Parliament (second reading) (⁴)	Difference (11)/(1)	Difference (11) – (3)	Difference (11) – (5)	Difference (11) – (7)	Difference (11) – (9)
(7)	(8)	(9)	(10)	(11)	(12)	(13)	(14)	(15)	(16)
	%		%		%				
45 174 108 000	2.1	44 780 450 000	1.2	44 780 450 000	1.2	0	– 49 400 000	– 393 658 000	0
2 203 892 000		2 597 550 000		2 597 550 000					
40 476 108 000	2.1	40 082 450 000	1.1	40 082 450 000	1.1	0	– 49 400 000	– 393 658 000	0
4 698 000 000	2.2	4 698 000 000	2.2	4 698 000 000	2.2	0	0	0	0
33 995 000 000	0.5	33 980 008 240	0.4	33 980 008 240	0.4	– 46 991 760	12 008 240	– 14 991 760	0
– 27 000 000		– 12 008 240		– 12 008 240					
31 156 000 000	0.3	31 141 008 240	0.3	31 141 008 240	0.3	– 46 991 760	12 008 240	– 14 991 760	0
2 839 000 000	1.8	2 839 000 000	1.8	2 839 000 000	1.8	0	0	0	0
6 793 319 000	– 5.1	6 698 465 000	– 6.4	6 795 801 000	– 5.0	79 336 000	121 836 000	2 482 000	97 336 000
2 681 000		97 535 000		199 000					
5 047 232 000	3.6	4 859 382 000	– 0.3	4 949 362 000	1.6	37 480 000	57 480 000	– 97 870 000	89 980 000
– 75 232 000		112 618 000		22 638 000					
5 362 325 098	3.6	5 315 870 128	2.7	5 360 071 098	3.5	– 76 261 045	– 4 455 785	– 2 254 000	44 200 970
18 674 902		65 129 872		20 928 902					
434 000 000	– 35.8	434 000 000	– 35.8	434 000 000	– 35.8	0	0	0	0
0		0		0					
	– 100.0		– 100.0		– 100.0	0	0	0	0
217 000 000	1.9	217 000 000	1.9	217 000 000	1.9	0	0	0	0
217 000 000	1.9	217 000 000	1.9	217 000 000	1.9	0	0	0	0
3 386 000 000	– 2.1	3 386 000 000	– 2.1	3 386 000 000	– 2.1	0	0	0	0
0		0		0					
564 000 000	1.6	564 000 000	1.6	564 000 000	1.6	0	0	0	0
1 129 000 000	1.8	1 129 000 000	1.8	1 129 000 000	1.8	0	0	0	0
1 693 000 000	1.7	1 693 000 000	1.7	1 693 000 000	1.7	0	0	0	0
p.m.	– 100.0	p.m.	– 100.0	p.m.	– 100.0	0	0	0	0
100 191 984 098	0.8	99 454 175 368	0.0	99 685 692 338	0.3	– 6 436 805	137 468 455	– 506 291 760	231 516 970
2 123 015 902		2 860 824 632		2 629 307 662					
41 927 832 321	1.5	41 504 890 321	0.5	41 504 890 321	0.5	– 33 264 000	– 82 664 000	– 422 942 000	0
58 264 151 777	0.2	57 949 285 047	– 0.3	58 180 802 017	0.1	26 827 195	220 132 455	– 83 349 760	231 516 970
99 933 233 398	4.5	96 896 082 128	1.3	97 502 937 098	1.9	– 377 207 045	511 298 215	– 2 430 296 300	606 854 970
3 004 766 602		6 041 917 872		5 435 062 902					
41 983 292 321	1.5	41 587 838 321	0.5	41 587 838 321	0.5	– 5 764 000	– 55 164 000	– 395 454 000	0
57 949 941 077	6.7	55 308 243 807	1.9	55 915 098 777	3.0	– 371 443 045	566 462 215	– 2 034 842 300	606 854 970
1.04		1.01		1.02					

1036. Supplementary and amending budget No 3/2002. The Commission adopted the preliminary draft on 5 June (^{1}) and the Council established the draft on 27 June (^{1}); the supplementary and amending budget was then adopted by Parliament on 3 July (^{2}). Its purpose was to update the estimate of own resources and the collection costs for the Member States and to enter the definitive amount of the balance of the 2001 budget. The supplementary and amending budget incorporated the Economic and Social Committee's request for the additional posts needed to take over the activities of the former ECSC Consultative Committee *(→ point 1125)* and the Court of Auditors' request for new budget remarks allowing it to cover the risk of industrial conflicts and terrorist attacks on its buildings. In its resolution accompanying adoption of the supplementary and amending budget Parliament noted that the final surplus for the 2002 financial year was EUR 15 billion and restated its concern at the build-up of outstanding payments (^{3}).

1037. Supplementary and amending budget No 4/2002. The Commission adopted the preliminary draft on 24 July (^{4}), which was then changed by letter of amendment No 1 that the Commission adopted on 18 September (^{5}); the Council established the draft on 20 September (^{5}); the supplementary and amending budget was then adopted by Parliament on 26 September (^{5}). The main purpose was to draw on the margin remaining under the ceiling of heading 4 (external action) of the financial perspective for reconstruction aid to Afghanistan. It also created two new lines to accommodate the appropriations for the European Union's Solidarity Fund to cover disaster relief in the Member States and the countries which have applied for accession *(→ point 362).*

1038. Supplementary and amending budget No 5/2002. The Commission adopted the preliminary draft on 13 November (^{6}) and the Council established the draft on 20 November (^{7}); the supplementary and amending budget was then adopted by Parliament on 21 November (^{8}). The purpose was to use the European Union's Solidarity Fund *(→ point 362)* for mobilising EUR 599 million for heading 3 (internal policies) and EUR 129 million for heading 7 (pre-accession aid) following the floods in Germany, Austria and the Czech Republic in August and in France in September.

1039. Supplementary and amending budget No 6/2002. The Commission adopted the preliminary draft on 13 November (^{9}) and the Council established

(^{1}) Bull. 6-2002, point 1.7.1.
(^{2}) OJ L 226, 22.8.2002; Bull. 7/8-2002, point 1.7.3.
(^{3}) Bull. 7/8-2002, point 1.7.5.
(^{4}) SEC(2002) 851, Bull. 7/8-2002, point 1.7.4.
(^{5}) Bull. 9-2002, point 1.7.2.
(^{6}) SEC(2002) 1221; Bull. 11-2002, point 1.7.3.
(^{7}) Bull. 11-2002, point 1.7.3.
(^{8}) OJ L 339, 16.12.2002; Bull. 11-2002, point 1.7.3.
(^{9}) SEC(2002) 1220; Bull. 11-2002, point 1.7.4.

the draft on 26 November (¹); the supplementary and amending budget was then adopted by Parliament on 5 December (²). The purpose was to bring forward to 2002 around EUR 77 million of administrative expenditure which would otherwise have been incurred in 2003, thus leaving a margin for manoeuvre to finance the expenditure needed in 2003 to prepare the institutions administratively for enlargement. This has been possible because of the savings made in 2002 in the various Community institutions covered by this supplementary and amending budget.

Out-turn of revenue and expenditure

Expenditure

1040.   The implementation rates for the 2002 budget are shown in Tables 26 and 27. Unused appropriations are estimated provisionally at EUR 4.080 billion in commitments and EUR 15.296 billion in payments.

Revenue

1041.   On the revenue side, total own resources for 2002 came to EUR 93 074.7 million, corresponding to 1.02 % of Community GNI. There was also EUR 1.257 billion in miscellaneous revenue. Revenue for 2002 is shown in Table 28 together with the revenue forecast for 2003.

Discharge procedure

1999

1042.   *Follow-up report.* In its resolution of 28 February (³) on the Commission report (⁴) on the measures taken in the light of the observations which it had made in its 1999 discharge resolution (⁵), Parliament welcomed the Commission's efforts to provide a quick reply and comment on the questions and observations made in the discharge decision. It also considered that, as the discharge authority, it must have the same access to Commission documents as the Court of Auditors. The Council also gave the follow-up report a favourable reception in its conclusions of 5 March (⁶).

(¹) Bull. 11-2002, point 1.7.4.
(²) Bull. 12-2002, point 1.7.4.
(³) OJ C 293 E, 28.11.2002; Bull. 1/2-2002, point 1.7.9.
(⁴) COM(2001) 696.
(⁵) OJ L 160, 15.6.2001; 2001 General Report, point 1159.
(⁶) Bull. 3-2002, point 1.7.9.

TABLE 26

Utilisation of appropriations for commitments (Commission)
at 31 December 2002 by financial perspective subdivision
(figures not final)

Heading	Appropriations entered in 2002 budget (including supplementary and amending budgets)	Appropriations entered in 2002 budget (including supplementary and amending budgets and transfers)	
1. Agriculture			
— Agricultural expenditure (excluding rural development) (Titles B1-1 to B1-3)	39 635.180	9 635.180	
— Rural development and ancillary measures B1-4 and B1-5)	4 595.000	4 595.000	
Total — Heading 1	44 230.180	44 230.180	
2. Structural operations			
— Objective 1 (Chapter B2-10)	21 329.628	21 329.628	
— Objective 2 (Chapter B2-11)	3 729.793	3 729.793	
— Objective 3 (Chapter B2-12)	3 646.007	3 646.007	
— Other structural measures (outside Objective 1 areas) (Chapter B2-13)	168.900	168.900	
— Community initiatives (Chapter B2-14)	1 860.322	1 803.408	
— Innovative measures and technical assistance (Chapter B2-16)	144.350	186.272	
— Other specific structural measures (Title B2-2)	170.000	184.992	
— Cohesion Fund (Title B2-3)	2 789.000	2 789.000	
Total — Heading 2	33 838.000	33 838.000	
3. Internal policies			
— Research and technological development (Subsection B6)	4 055.000	4 134.073	
— Other agricultural operations (Title B2-5)	55.320	54.983	
— Other regional policy operations (Title B2-6)	15.000	15.000	
— Transport (Title B2-7)	25.000	26.545	
— Other measures concerning fisheries and the sea (Title B2-9)	65.130	63.730	
— Education, vocational training and youth (Title B3-1)	523.350	534.067	
— Culture and audiovisual media (Title B3-2)	116.700	119.094	
— Information and communication (Title B3-3)	105.206	108.406	
— Social dimension and employment (Title B3-4)	148.855	156.095	
— Contributions to European political parties (Title B3-5)	7.000	7.000	
— Energy (Title B4-1)	33.000	33.611	
— Euratom nuclear safeguards (Title B4-2)	17.700	19.100	
— Environment (Title B4-3)	189.970	203.533	
— Consumer policy and health protection (Title B5-1)	22.500	21.958	
— Aid for reconstruction (Title B5-2)	0.898	0.898	
— Internal market (Title B5-3)	184.805	186.961	
— Industry (Title B5-4)	0.000	0.000	
— Labour market and technological innovation (Title B5-5)	99.600	106.698	
— Statistical information (Title B5-6)	34.000	34.543	
— Trans-European networks (Title B5-7)	677.000	676.998	
— Area of freedom, security and justice (Title B5-8)	103.460	125.671	
— Fraud prevention and expenditure in support of internal policies (Title B5-9)	6.100	6.100	
— European Union Solidarity Fund (Title B2-4)	0.000	599.000	
Total — Heading 3	6 485.594	7 234.061	

(million EUR)

Additional 2002 appropriations and carry-overs from 2001	Total appropriations available in 2002	Book commitments entered into in 2002	
		Amount	%
0.000	39 635.180	37 226.570	93.9
99.000	4 694.000	3 887.004	82.8
99.000	44 329.180	41 113.574	92.7
6.901	21 336.528	21 335.348	100.0
1.528	3 731.321	3 731.321	100.0
0.000	3 646.007	3 646.007	100.0
4.600	173.500	173.500	100.0
162.821	1 966.229	1 965.717	100.0
0.217	186.489	183.388	98.3
0.000	184.992	184.992	100.0
3.315	2 792.315	2 791.469	100.0
179.381	34 017.381	34 011.741	100.0
557.004	4 691.077	4 519.757	96.3
0.033	55.016	52.515	95.5
0.000	15.000	15.000	100.0
0.956	27.501	25.522	92.8
0.000	63.730	60.488	94.9
111.182	645.249	605.956	93.9
22.574	141.668	133.334	94.1
0.361	108.767	84.280	77.5
1.432	157.527	149.278	94.8
0.000	7.000	0.000	0.0
2.192	35.803	33.362	93.2
0.181	19.281	19.068	98.9
10.141	213.675	212.017	99.2
0.001	21.958	20.985	95.6
0.000	0.898	0.897	99.9
4.601	191.562	176.582	92.2
0.000	0.000	0.000	
2.965	109.663	103.934	94.8
5.169	39.711	35.113	88.4
1.768	678.765	641.229	94.5
1.041	126.712	121.553	95.9
0.000	6.100	5.854	96.0
0.000	599.000	599.000	100.0
721.603	7 955.664	7 615.722	95.7

TABLE 26 (continued)

4. External action		
— European Development Fund (Title B7-1)	—	—
— Food aid and support measures (Chapter B7-20)	455.000	510.000
— Humanitarian aid (Chapter B7-21)	441.845	521.845
— Cooperation with developing countries in Asia (Chapter B7-30)	488.000	558.000
— Cooperation with developing countries in Latin America (Chapter B7-31)	346.672	346.672
— Cooperation with southern Africa and South Africa (Chapter B7-32)	124.790	124.790
— Cooperation with third countries in the Mediterranean and the Middle East (Chapter B7-4)	861.320	783.320
— European Bank for Reconstruction and Development (Chapter B7-51)	0.000	0.000
— Cooperation with the new independent States and Mongolia (Chapter B7-52)	473.900	473.900
— Other Community operations for the CCEE, the NIS, Mongolia and the western Balkan countries (Chapter B7-53)	0.000	0.000
— Cooperation with the Balkan countries (Chapter B7-54)	765.000	758.000
— Other cooperation measures (Title B7-6)	419.579	419.579
— European initiative for democracy and human rights (Title B7-7)	104.000	104.000
— International fisheries agreements (Chapter B7-80)	149.369	191.738
— External aspects of certain Community policies (Chapters B7-81 to B7-87)	75.752	76.152
— Common foreign and security policy (Title B8-0)	24.700	30.000
— Pre-accession strategy for the Mediterranean countries (Chapters B7-04)	21.000	149.000
Total — Heading 4	4 750.926	5 046.995
5. Administration		
— Commission (excluding pensions)	2 689.237	2 743.966
— Pensions (all institutions)	688.099	682.579
Total — Heading 5	3 377.336	3 426.545
6. Reserves		
— Monetary reserve (Title B1-6)	250.000	250.000
— Guarantee reserve (Chapter B0-23 and B0-24)	213.000	213.000
— Emergency aid reserve (Chapter B7-91)	213.000	39.000
Total — Heading 6	676.000	502.000
7. Pre-accession aid		
— Agriculture (Chapter B7-01)	555.000	555.000
— Pre-accession structural instrument (Chapter B7-02)	1 109.000	1 109.000
— Phare (applicant countries) (Chapter B7-03)	1 664.000	1 664.000
— European Union Solidarity Fund (Chapter B7-09)	0.000	129.000
Total — Heading 7	3 328.000	3 457.000
Grand total	96 686.035	97 734.781

—	—	—	—
2.300	512.300	505.958	98.8
0.079	521.924	520.315	99.7
24.615	582.615	574.863	98.7
1.854	348.525	333.425	95.7
0.104	124.894	124.182	99.4
0.502	783.822	783.510	100.0
0.000	0.000	0.000	
5.320	479.220	444.494	92.8
0.000	0.000	0.000	
84.609	842.609	820.890	97.4
19.922	439.501	429.270	97.7
0.012	104.012	103.723	99.7
0.007	191.745	190.385	99.3
18.097	94.249	73.920	78.4
2.800	32.800	32.800	100.0
0.012	149.012	147.948	99.3
160.235	5 207.229	5 085.683	97.7
113.685	2 857.651	2 821.110	98.7
0.000	682.579	680.992	99.8
113.685	3 540.230	3 502.102	98.9
0.000	250.000	0.000	0.0
0.000	213.000	170.490	80.0
0.000	39.000	0.000	0.0
0.000	502.000	170.490	34.0
0.000	555.000	554.561	99.9
0.068	1 109.068	1 109.044	100.0
74.706	1 738.706	1 711.288	98.4
0.000	129.000	129.000	100.0
74.773	3 531.773	3 503.894	99.2
1 348.676	99 083.458	95 003.207	95.9

TABLE 27

**Utilisation of appropriations for payments (Commission)
at 31 December 2002 by financial perspective subdivision
(figures not final)**

Heading	Appropriations entered in 2002 budget (including supplementary and amending budgets)	Appropriations entered in 2002 budget (including supplementary and amending budgets and transfers)	
1. Agriculture			
— Agricultural expenditure (excluding rural development) (Titles B1-1 to B1-3)	39 635.180	39 635.180	
— Rural development and ancillary measures B1-4 and B1-5)	4 595.000	4 595.000	
Total — Heading 1	44 230.180	44 230.180	
2. Structural operations			
— Objective 1 (Chapter B2-10)	18 818.000	18 818.000	
— Objective 2 (Chapter B2-11)	4 360.000	3 405.000	
— Objective 3 (Chapter B2-12)	3 360.000	3 360.000	
— Other structural measures (outside Objective 1 areas) (Chapter B2-13)	380.000	380.000	
— Community initiatives (Chapter B2-14)	2 327.000	2 204.000	
— Innovative measures and technical assistance (Chapter B2-16)	245.000	245.000	
— Other specific structural Measures (Title B2-2)	39.000	39.000	
— Cohesion Fund (Title B2-3)	2 600.000	3 148.000	
Total — Heading 2	32 129.000	31 599.000	
3. Internal policies			
— Research and technological development (Subsection B6)	3 751.688	3 804.786	
— Other agricultural operations (Title B2-5)	61.220	61.018	
— Other regional policy operations (Title B2-6)	15.000	15.000	
— Transport (Title B2-7)	22.800	24.100	
— Other measures concerning fisheries and the sea (Title B2-9)	59.080	58.490	
— Education, vocational training and youth (Title B3-1)	523.075	533.732	
— Culture and audiovisual media (Title B3-2)	125.920	128.466	
— Information and communication (Title B3-3)	95.780	103.980	
— Social dimension and employment (Title B3-4)	132.145	144.961	
— Contributions to European political parties (Title B3)	6.300	6.300	
— Energy (Title B4-1)	34.550	35.183	
— Euratom nuclear safeguards (Title B4-2)	17.600	17.600	
— Environment (Title B4-3)	137.160	152.575	
— Consumer policy and health protection (Title B5-1)	20.000	20.407	
— Aid for reconstruction (Title B5-2)	0.898	0.898	
— Internal market (Title B5-3)	167.260	168.163	
— Industry (Title B5-4)	61.971	61.971	
— Labour market and technological innovation (Title B5-5)	125.093	129.908	
— Statistical information (Title B5-6)	31.500	32.003	
— Trans-European networks (Title B5-7)	600.930	603.134	
— Area of freedom, security and justice (Title B5-8)	111.570	119.751	
— Fraud prevention and expenditure in support of internal policies (Title B5-9)	5.000	5.000	
— European Union Solidarity Fund (Title B2-4)	0.000	599.000	
Total — Heading 3	6 106.540	6 826.426	

(million EUR)

Additional 2002 appropriations and carry-overs from 2001	Total appropriations available in 2002	Payments recorded in the accounts in 2002			
		Against commitments prior to 2002	Against 2002 commitments	Total	
		Amount	Amount	Amount	%
582.821	40 218.001	534.772	36 995.372	37 530.144	93.3
99.000	4 694.000	0.000	3 887.004	3 887.004	82.8
681.821	44 912.001	534.772	40 882.376	41 417.148	92.2
3.044	18 821.044	13 431.919	1 937.207	15 369.126	81.7
0.000	3 405.000	1 549.946	91.248	1 641.194	48.2
0.000	3 360.000	2 358.908	45.479	2 404.387	71.6
0.000	380.000	150.102	4.923	155.025	40.8
1.003	2 205.003	450.580	105.895	556.476	25.2
0.217	245.217	138.219	47.622	185.842	75.8
0.000	39.000	0.000	39.000	39.000	100.0
0.000	3 148.000	2 856.087	291.913	3 148.000	100.0
4.264	31 603.264	20 935.761	2 563.287	23 499.048	74.4
713.396	4 518.183	2 063.981	1 602.979	3 666.960	81.2
10.498	71.516	50.307	12.276	62.583	87.5
0.000	15.000	3.000	12.000	15.000	100.0
1.600	25.700	13.005	3.118	16.123	62.7
0.000	58.490	25.970	13.540	39.511	67.6
168.708	702.440	179.858	412.533	592.392	84.3
26.249	154.715	74.294	44.084	118.377	76.5
4.409	108.389	47.870	36.390	84.260	77.7
1.434	146.395	69.168	62.985	132.152	90.3
0.000	6.300	0.000	0.000	0.000	0.0
5.750	40.933	26.642	2.438	29.080	71.0
0.253	17.853	5.827	10.689	16.516	92.5
10.563	163.138	79.683	72.242	151.925	93.1
0.001	20.408	16.024	3.253	19.278	94.5
0.000	0.898	0.000	0.897	0.897	99.9
9.594	177.756	71.853	69.007	140.860	79.2
0.000	61.971	0.000	0.000	0.000	0.0
24.558	154.466	93.764	14.311	108.075	70.0
6.259	38.261	24.595	7.741	32.336	84.5
108.743	711.878	333.049	323.224	656.273	92.2
13.371	133.122	30.577	46.452	77.029	57.9
0.000	5.000	1.361	3.286	4.647	92.9
0.000	599.000	0.000	599.000	599.000	100.0
1 105.387	7 931.813	3 210.826	3 352.447	6 563.273	82.7

TABLE 27 (continued)

4. External action		
— European Development Fund (Title B7-1)	—	—
— Food aid and support measures (Chapter B7-20)	420.810	420.810
— Humanitarian aid (Chapter B7-21)	441.845	492.845
— Cooperation with developing countries in Asia (Chapter B7-30)	465.110	465.110
— Cooperation with developing countries in Latin America (Chapter B7-31)	318.366	233.366
— Cooperation with southern Africa and South Africa (Chapter B7-32)	148.470	136.115
— Cooperation with third countries in the Mediterranean and the Middle East (Chapter B7-4)	678.540	858.561
— European Bank for Reconstruction and Development (Chapter B7-51)	8.438	8.438
— Cooperation with the new independent States and Mongolia (Chapter B7-52)	542.720	468.261
— Other Community operations for the CCEE, the NIS, Mongolia and the western Balkan countries (Chapter B7-53)	0.000	0.058
— Cooperation with the Balkan countries (Chapter B7-54)	781.680	775.330
— Other cooperation measures (Title B7-6)	411.161	397.611
— European initiative for democracy and human rights (Title B7-7)	100.740	103.740
— International fisheries agreements (Chapter B7-80)	152.721	195.090
— External aspects of certain Community policies (Chapters B7-81 to B7-87)	87.962	79.952
— Common foreign and security policy (Title B8-0)	30.000	29.000
— Pre-accession strategy for the Mediterranean countries (Chapters B7-04)	20.432	28.967
Total — Heading 4	4 608.995	4 693.253
5. Administration		
— Commission (excluding pensions)	2 689.237	2 743.966
— Pensions (all institutions)	688.099	682.579
Total — Heading 5	3 377.336	3 426.545
6. Reserves		
— Monetary reserve (Title B1-6)	250.000	250.000
— Guarantee reserve (Chapter B0-23 and B0-24)	213.000	213.000
— Emergency aid reserve (Chapter B7-91)	213.000	180.000
Total — Heading 6	676.000	643.000
7. Pre-accession aid		
— Agriculture (Chapter B7-01)	370.000	370.000
— Pre-accession structural instrument (Chapter B7-02)	704.400	506.400
— Phare (applicant countries) (Chapter B7-03)	1 520.650	1 520.650
— European Union Solidarity Fund (Chapter B7-09)	0.000	129.000
Total — Heading 7	2 595.050	2 526.050
Grand total	93 723.100	93 944.455

—	—	—	—	—	—
0.000	420.810	205.811	210.605	416.416	99.0
50.079	542.924	165.565	308.689	474.253	87.4
2.457	467.567	300.776	147.981	448.758	96.0
0.104	233.470	162.771	15.265	178.036	76.3
0.000	136.115	90.291	28.139	118.431	87.0
4.721	863.282	462.023	376.764	838.787	97.2
0.000	8.438	8.438	0.000	8.438	100.0
3.820	472.081	328.522	58.875	387.398	82.1
0.000	0.058	0.058	0.000	0.058	99.3
118.624	893.954	337.914	408.651	746.565	83.5
66.143	463.753	232.717	154.161	386.879	83.4
0.012	103.752	58.929	34.829	93.758	90.4
0.007	195.097	4.060	182.115	186.174	95.4
18.340	98.292	37.775	26.787	64.562	65.7
7.035	36.035	14.140	16.792	30.933	85.8
0.012	28.979	12.493	6.376	18.870	65.1
271.355	4 964.608	2 422.284	1 976.031	4 398.314	88.6
368.723	3 112.690	220.070	2 473.598	2 693.668	86.5
0.007	682.586	0.000	679.346	679.346	99.5
368.730	3 795.275	220.070	3 152.944	3 373.014	88.9
0.000	250.000	0.000	0.000	0.000	0.0
0.000	213.000	0.000	170.490	170.490	80.0
0.000	180.000	0.000	0.000	0.000	0.0
0.000	643.000	0.000	170.490	170.490	26.5
0.000	370.000	123.810	0.061	123.871	33.5
0.010	506.410	329.531	67.048	396.578	78.3
74.706	1 595.356	693.803	390.502	1 084.305	68.0
0.000	129.000	0.000	129.000	129.000	100.0
74.715	2 600.765	1 147.144	586.611	1 733.754	66.7
2 506.273	96 450.728	28 470.857	52 684.186	81 155.043	84.1

TABLE 28

Budget revenue

(million EUR)

	2002	2003
Agricultural duties	1 180.2	1 173.1
Sugar and isoglucose levies	864.8	728.8
Customs duties	12 918.9	14 285.2
Own resources collection costs([1])	− 3 725.7	− 4 046.8
Regularisation of collection costs for 2001([2])	− 2 023.0	—
VAT own resources	22 687.4	24 121.2
GNI-based own resources	45 850.6	59 404.0
Balance of VAT and GNI own resources from previous years	− 53.5	p.m.
Surplus available from previous year	15 375.0	1 000.0
Other revenue	1 257.0	837.4
Total	94 331.7	97 502.9
	% of GNI	
Maximum own resources which may be assigned to the budget	1.24	1.24
Own resources actually assigned to the budget	1.02	1.00

([1]) The new financial regulation (→ *point 1048*) applicable from 1 January 2003 stipulates that the budget may not contain negative revenue. The collection costs shown in the column for 2003 are indicated only for the purposes of comparison with the previous year.

([2]) This figure corresponds to the amount repaid to the Member States to take account of the retroactive effects of the new own resources decision (→ *point 1032*) on the collection costs incurred by the Member States between March and December 2001.

1043.   Economic and Social Committee. On 25 April Parliament gave discharge to the Secretary-General of the Economic and Social Committee in respect of the implementation of its budget for the financial years from 1996 to 1999([1]).

2000

1044.   General budget. On 10 April, following the Council recommendation of 5 March ([2]), Parliament gave the Commission a discharge in respect of the implementation of the general budget of the European Union for the 2000 financial year and also closed the accounts for that year ([3]). The decision was accompanied by a resolution containing its comments. On 25 April Parliament also granted discharge to the Secretaries-General of the Council, the Court of Auditors, the Economic and Social Committee and the Committee of the Regions and to the Registrar of the Court of Justice and the Ombudsman in respect of the implementation of their budgets for the 2000 financial year ([4]).

([1]) Bull. 4-2002, point 1.7.9.
([2]) Bull. 3-2002, point 1.7.4.
([3]) OJ L 158, 17.6.2002; Bull. 4-2002, point 1.7.3.
([4]) OJ L 158, 17.6.2002; Bull. 4-2002, point 1.7.9.

1045.   Specific budgets. Following other recommendations adopted by the Council on 5 March (¹), Parliament on 10 April granted discharge to the Commission in respect of the financial management of the sixth, seventh and eighth European Development Funds (²) and discharge in respect of the implementation of the budget for Parliament (³); on the same date it granted discharge to the Management Board of the European Centre for the Development of Vocational Training (Cedefop) (⁴), to the Administrative Board of the European Foundation for the Improvement of Living and Working Conditions (Dublin Foundation) (⁵) and to the Director of the European Agency for Reconstruction (Kosovo) in respect of the implementation of their budget for the 2000 financial year (⁶).

ECSC operating budget

1046.   Discharge. On 10 April Parliament granted discharge to the Commission in respect of the implementation of the ECSC budget for the 2000 financial year (⁷).

1047.   Expiry of the ECSC Treaty. The consequences are set out in Section 11 ('Expiry of the ECSC Treaty') in Chapter I *(→ point 41)*.

Financial regulations

1048.   Recasting of the financial regulation applicable to the Community budget. On 25 June the Council adopted Regulation (EC, Euratom) No 1605/2002 as the new financial regulation applicable to the general budget of the European Communities (Table II). The regulation confines itself to stating the broad principles and basic rules governing the establishment and execution of the budget and financial control. The implementing rules have been moved to their own specific regulation *(→ point 1049)* in order to produce a better hierarchy of norms.

The new financial regulation, which is due to enter into force on 1 January 2003, has been changed as follows: simplification and legibility of the rules applicable to all stages of budget establishment and implementation; clarification of budgetary principles (unity, universality, specification, annuality, equi-

---

(¹) Bull. 3-2002, points 1.7.5 to 1.7.8.
(²) OJ L 158, 17.6.2002; Bull. 4-2002, point 1.7.4.
(³) OJ L 158, 17.6.2002; Bull. 4-2002, point 1.7.5.
(⁴) OJ L 158, 17.6.2002; Bull. 4-2002, point 1.7.6.
(⁵) OJ L 158, 17.6.2002; Bull. 4-2002, point 1.7.7.
(⁶) OJ L 158, 17.6.2002; Bull. 4-2002, point 1.7.8.
(⁷) OJ L 158, 17.6.2002; Bull. 4-2002, point 1.7.10.

librium, transparency, etc.); new structure, corresponding to the activity-based approach; more information for the budgetary authority; more flexibility, for example when making transfers from one budget line to another; rationalisation of management methods (centralised, decentralised or joint); modernisation of financial management geared to results and performance; fewer exceptions to the rules; modernisation of accounting rules; incorporation of provisions on public procurement procedures to improve transparency and prevention of fraud in this field.

1049. *Rules for the implementation of the financial regulation.* After presenting to the other institutions, for their opinion, a draft regulation transposing the principles and definitions of the new financial regulation into concrete rules (→ point 1048), the Commission adopted this regulation on 23 December (¹).

1050. *financial regulation applicable to the Community bodies.* On 17 July the Commission proposed a number of regulations (Table I) (Table II) so that the constituent acts of the Community bodies set up to carry out certain Community activities can be brought into line with the new financial regulation (→ point 1048) (²). On the same date it withdrew the amended proposals, which had been pending since 1998, to adjust the basic regulations of some of these bodies (Table II). On 23 December the Commission adopted a framework financial regulation governing the establishment, implementation and scrutiny of these bodies' budgets (³). The bodies will have to adopt their own financial rules on the basis of this framework regulation.

1051. *Statute of executive agencies for Community programmes.* On 19 December the Council adopted Regulation (EC) No 58/2003 on the statute of these agencies which will be involved in the implementation of Community programmes under the control and responsibility of the Commission (Table II).

1052. *Modernisation of the Community accounting system.* In a communication dated 17 December, the Commission presented the two strands of the planned guidelines for this reform: (⁴) a detailed proposal to allow the Commission to decide on the accounting framework, in particular on how generally accepted accrual accounting principles can be implemented; and options for the organisation of the project, resources and the timing of the work to develop an integrated computerised system.

(¹) Regulation (EC, Euratom) No 2342/2002 (OJ L 357, 31.12.2002; Bull. 12-2002, point 1.7.5).
(²) European Centre for the Development of Vocational Training, European Foundation for the Improvement of Living and Working Conditions, European Environment Agency, European Training Foundation, European Monitoring Centre for Drugs and Drug Addiction, European Agency for the Evaluation of Medicinal Products, European Agency for Health and Safety at Work, Translation Centre for the Bodies of the European Union, European Monitoring Centre on Racism and Xenophobia, European Agency for Reconstruction, European Food Safety Agency, European Aviation Safety Agency, European Maritime Safety Agency, Eurojust, Office for Harmonisation in the Internal Market and Community Plant Variety Office.
(³) Regulation (EC, Euratom) No 2343/2002 (OJ L 357, 31.12.2002; Bull. 12-2002, point 1.7.6).
(⁴) COM(2002) 755; Bull. 12-2002, point 1.7.10.

Section 3

Internal audit and financial control

1053.   Internal audit. In 2002, as well as completing the audits started in the previous year, the Commission's internal auditor carried out some new audits in the areas generally recognised as being high-risk. He also assessed the way in which the Commission's directorates-general fulfilled their obligation to produce annual activity reports and declarations of assurance, which were drawn up for the first time for the 2001 financial year *(→ point 1152)*. On 24 July the Commission took formal note of the Internal Auditor's report on that assessment and his annual audit report. In accordance with the White Paper on reforming the Commission ([1]), in-depth audits were launched in September, with the aim of covering all Commission departments by the end of 2003. As well as increasing the numbers of staff, efforts were made to support the development of the internal audit capacities and activities of the Commission's various departments.

1054.   Financial control. The process started following the White Paper on reforming the Commission, which proposed introducing a decentralised system of management and financial control in the long term, was continued in 2002. Accordingly, the Commission implemented the control concept defined in 2001 ([2]), which is basically aimed at maximising error detection, strengthening its departments' internal audit systems and improving the error notification and awareness of the directorates-general concerned. These basic functions consist mainly of the control and approval of financial transactions involving revenue and expenditure. They also cover consultation on draft Commission decisions with a financial impact and the general financial rules adopted by the Commission. For its part, the new financial regulation adopted on 25 June by the Council ([3]) *(→ point 1048)* abolishes from 1 January 2003 the obligation to obtain the prior approval of the financial comptroller before committing or authorising expenditure and decentralises the financial control system to each directorate-general. On 17 December the Commission assessed the readiness of its department for integrating the new financial regulation in their internal control systems ([4]) and also spelled out the organisation arrangements for the transfer of the work and staff of the Financial Control Directorate-General to the other departments on 31 March 2003 ([5]).

([1]) 2000 General Report, points 1079 and 1209.
([2]) 2001 General Report, point 1165.
([3]) http://europa.eu.int/eur-lex/en/archive/2002/l_24820020916en.html.
([4]) SEC(2002) 1362; Bull. 12-2002, point 1.7.11.
([5]) SEC(2002) 1366; Bull. 12-2002, point 1.7.12.

Section 4

Protection of the Communities' financial interests and the fight against fraud (¹)

1055. *Annual report from the Commission.* In its annual report under Article 280(5) of the EC Treaty, adopted on 2 July, the Commission gives an account of the main activities to protect the Community's financial interests and fight fraud in 2001 (²), covering all the action taken by national authorities in the Member States and by the Community. It reports that major progress was made in 2001 in adopting new measures at these various levels, with emphasis being placed on improving the legal and regulatory framework, on developing more effective mechanisms for cooperation with the Member States and between them, the applicant countries and other non-member countries and on continuing improvements to the internal organisation of the European Anti-Fraud Office (OLAF). The Commission also stresses the fall in the number of cases of irregularity notified by the Member States in 2001 across the various budget sectors, and the decrease in the total amounts involved. These findings are consistent with the trends observed in the figures for fraud and irregularities over the last few years. The Commission also notes that suspected cases of fraud and other irregularities that were the subject of OLAF investigations rose in 2001, with a total of 381 new cases, while 663 investigations were closed during the same period, representing a financial impact estimated at EUR 564.7 million. In its conclusions of 18 November, the Council took note of the Commission's report and of the considerable anti-fraud efforts being pursued both at Community level and in the Member States (³). It invited all those concerned to continue those efforts and stressed the importance of OLAF being able to continue to perform its tasks in an independent and efficient manner. It also underlined OLAF's importance in the incorporation of effective measures to prevent fraud and irregularities in legislative proposals and the need for improved cooperation with Europol and Eurojust. The Council considered that the new financial regulation of 25 June *(→ point 1048)* would help strengthen protection of the Communities' financial interests and step up the fight against fraud.

1056. *Activity reports of the European Anti-Fraud Office (OLAF).* In its conclusions of 7 May (⁴), the Council welcomed with interest the second activity

---

(¹) Further information is available on the Europa server (http://europa.eu.int/comm/anti_fraud/index_en.html).
(²) COM(2002) 348; Bull. 7/8-2002, point 1.7.15; Internet http://europa.eu.int/comm/anti_fraud/reports/index_en.html#ec.
(³) Bull. 11-2002, point 1.7.9.
(⁴) Bull. 5-2002, point 1.7.4.

reports of both OLAF and its Supervisory Committee (¹). It supported the objectives, methods and working principles set out in OLAF's activity report and noted that various measures had been taken to ensure OLAF's independence and the transparency of its operation and also to make the management and follow-up of its investigations more efficient. The Council also stressed the need to increase assistance to the applicant countries to enable them to adapt their national structures for combating fraud. Finally, it encouraged OLAF to pursue actively its operational work and submit an annual programme to the Supervisory Committee to ensure greater consistency in its operations at an early stage. On 17 October OLAF adopted its third activity report covering the period from 1 June 2001 to 30 June 2002 (²). The report bears witness to a steady increase in OLAF's investigative work, which has forced it to focus more on priority areas such as corruption within the Community institutions and cases involving applicant countries. The report also gives an account of OLAF's 'intelligence' activities, its support work, its follow-up to operational findings, its training and communication activities and cooperation with its partners in the fight against fraud.

1057.   Public consultation on the establishment of a European Public Prosecutor. The Commission has launched an information campaign and debate on the Green Paper on the criminal-law protection of financial interests and the establishment of a European public prosecutor (³). Over 11 000 copies of the Green Paper have been distributed and some 20 national seminars were held in the Member States and candidate countries, with Commission participation. Finally, on 16 and 17 September, the Commission held a public hearing to allow over 300 representatives from interested professional groups to air and exchange their views on the Green Paper. Discussions were spread over three sessions, which brought together in turn — from European, national and even regional level — those working in the institutional and legal framework, protagonists at the investigation, prosecution and trial stages and representatives of the interests to be protected and the rights of the defence. The hearing therefore provides a useful addition to the 70 written responses received since the adoption of the Green Paper, dealing with its main themes, i.e. the legal status and internal organisation of the European Prosecution Service, definitions of offences, procedure, judicial review of acts of the European public prosecutor, relations with other parties involved (⁴). The conclusions drawn by the Commission from the public consultation exercise as a whole will be used to produce a contribution to the Convention on the Future of the European Union *(→ point 12).* In a resolution adopted on 10 October (⁵) Parliament repeated its call for the introduction of a European public prosecutor for financial matters and welcomed the

---

(¹) Reports available on the Internet (http://europa.eu.int/comm/anti_fraud/reports/index_en.html).
(²) OJ C 328, 30.12.2002.
(³) COM(2001) 715; 2001 General Report, point 1173.
(⁴) The Green Paper, written comments on it and contributions to the public hearing are accessible on the Internet (http://europa.eu.int/comm/anti_fraud/green_paper/index_en.html).
(⁵) Bull. 10-2002, point 1.7.7.

Commission communication of November 2001 on the fraud-proofing of legislation and contract management ([1]).

1058.   Convention on the Protection of the Community's Financial Interests.
After being ratified by the last Member States ([2]), the Convention on the Protection of the European Communities' Financial Interests ([3]) came into force on 17 October ([4]), more than seven years after it was signed. Its first protocol ([5]), which defines active and passive corruption, also came into force, as did the protocol on the interpretation of the convention by the Court of Justice ([6]). However, the second protocol ([7]), which contains provisions on money laundering, the liability of legal persons, confiscation of the instruments and proceeds of offences, and cooperation with the Commission, is still awaiting ratification by five Member States. That is one of the reasons why the Commission has decided to maintain its proposal for a directive on the criminal-law protection of the Community's financial interests, while accepting some of the amendments made by Parliament at first reading. The purpose of the proposal is to incorporate the main elements of the 1995 convention and its protocols in a single Community instrument (Table I). In its conclusions of 18 November, the Council welcomed the ratifications that had taken place and called on those Member States which had not yet done so to ratify the remaining additional protocol ([8]).

1059.   Recovery of entitlements. In a communication dated 3 December on improving the recovery of Community entitlements arising from centralised and shared management of Community expenditure ([9]), the Commission assessed the progress made since the adoption of its first communication on the subject in December 2000 ([10]). On 17 December it revised and consolidated the internal procedure provisions ([11]) spelling out the distribution of roles resulting from the administrative reform (→ points 1150 et seq.) and the new regulatory framework (→ points 1048 and 1049).

([1]) SEC(2001) 2029; 2001 General Report, point 1172.
([2]) Belgium (12.3.2002), Ireland (3.6.2002) and Italy (19.7.2002).
([3]) OJ C 316, 27.11.1995; 1995 General Report, points 967 and 1008.
([4]) Bull. 10-2002, point 1.7.8.
([5]) OJ C 313, 23.10.1996;1996 General Report, points 958 and 1012.
([6]) OJ C 151, 20.5.1997; 1996 General Report, point 958.
([7]) OJ C 221, 19.7.1997; 1997 General Report, points 1038 and 1090.
([8]) Bull. 11-2002, point 1.7.9.
([9]) COM(2002)671; Bull. 12-2002, point 1.7.13.
([10]) SEC(2000) 204; Bull. 12-2000, point 1.10.14.
([11]) Bull. 12-2002, point 1.7.14.

Section 5

Borrowing and lending operations

1060.   On 3 December the Commission issued a report on the borrowing and lending activities of the Community in 2001 (¹). On 6 November, it proposed amending Decision 77/270/Euratom empowering it to issue Euratom loans for the purpose of contributing to the financing of nuclear power stations (Table II).

1061.   Table 29 shows the loans granted each year for 2000–02.

TABLE 29

Loans granted

(million EUR)

Instrument	2000	2001	2002
EC — Balance of payments	—	—	—
EC — Medium-term financial assistance to countries of central Europe and other non-member countries	160	305	12
EC — Food aid	—	—	—
ECSC	—	—	—
Euratom	—	40	40
EIB, of which:	36 031	36 776	39 618
— Community	30 642	31 184	33 442
— non-member countries, of which:	5 389	5 592	6 176
• ACP countries, OCTs and South Africa	541	670	348
• Mediterranean countries	1 214	1 401	1 588
• accession countries	2 948	2 659	3 641
• Latin America and Asia	532	543	174
• western Balkans	154	319	425
Total	36 191	37 121	39 670

(¹) COM(2002) 685.

Section 6

General budget guarantee for borrowing and lending operations

1062.   *General approach.* The guarantee by the Community budget covers lenders when the Community floats an issue under one of its financial instruments: balance-of-payments support facility, Euratom loans, medium-term financial assistance for certain non-member countries *(→ point 78)*. The budget guarantee is also given to the European Investment Bank (EIB) for loans it grants from its own resources to various non-member countries ([1]). At the end of 2002, the ceiling for authorised borrowing and lending operations guaranteed by the general budget was EUR 41.402 billion. At 31 December the guarantee was in operation for EUR 13.442 billion of Community borrowing and for EUR 13.756 billion granted by the EIB out of its own resources.

1063.   *The Guarantee Fund for external actions* ([2]). This fund, set up to reimburse the Community's creditors in the event of default by the recipient of a loan given or guaranteed by the Community in a non-member country ([3]), was not activated for payment defaults in 2002. In its communication of 21 January ([4]) the Commission considered that, given the strong pressures to increase lending through the Guarantee Fund instruments, it was now necessary to examine the means for finding further flexibility through the guarantee mechanism. Taking note of the existing situation, in particular the fact that the reserve for provisioning the Guarantee Fund was totally exhausted, it proposed increasing lending and guarantee capacity through some combination of decreasing the provisioning rate for the fund and reducing the extent of the guarantee granted for EIB loans. On 13 June the Commission presented a report on the Guarantee Fund and its management in 2001 ([5]).

---

[1] 1997 General Report, point 1092; 1999 General Report, point 967; 2000 General Report, point 1091; 2001 General Report, point 1175.
[2] http://europa.eu.int/scadplus/leg/en/lvb/l34006.htm.
[3] 1994 General Report, point 1133.
[4] COM(2002) 20; Bull. 1/2-2002, point 1.7.10.
[5] COM(2002) 305; Bull. 6-2002, point 1.7.3.

Chapter VIII

Community law

Section 1

Monitoring the application of Community law [1]

1064. In 2002 the Commission started 1 604 infringement proceedings (1 050 in 2001). Detailed information on the infringement proceedings instituted during the year and on the situation regarding transposal of Community directives into the national laws of the Member States will be given in the 20th annual report on monitoring the application of Community law, which will be published in 2003.

On 20 March the Commission adopted a communication on relations with the complainant in respect of infringements of Community law [2], which codifies all the administrative rules applicable to the handling of complaints. On 11 December it adopted a communication on the application of Community law [3], which takes up the 'better lawmaking' theme of the White Paper on European governance [4] (→ *points 23 and 24*).

---

[1] Further information is available on the Europa server (http://europa.eu.int/comm/secretariat_general/ sgb/droit_com/index_en.htm).
[2] COM(2002) 141 (OJ C 244, 10.10.2002).
[3] COM(2002) 725; Bull. 12-2002, point 1.9.1.
[4] COM(2001) 428; 2001 General Report, point 24; Internet http://europa.eu.int/comm/governance/white_ paper/index_en.htm.

Section 2

Decisions by the Court of Justice and the Court of First Instance (¹)

General principles of Community law

1065.   *Who is entitled to bring an action for annulment?* In its judgment in *Pequeños Agricultores*, delivered on 25 July (²), the Court of Justice had to consider an appeal filed by an association of small Spanish agricultural businesses against an order of the Court of First Instance dismissing as manifestly inadmissible the association's application for partial annulment of a regulation on the common organisation of the market in olive oil (³) on the ground that the members of the association were not individually concerned by the provisions of the regulation in question.

The same problem had earlier been considered in a case before the Court of First Instance, the *Jégo Quéré* case, in which that Court delivered judgment on 3 May (⁴); the Court of First Instance there took the view that the rule that such an applicant had to be 'individually concerned' needed to be interpreted more broadly if the applicant would otherwise be denied the right to an effective remedy, which was a right recognised by the constitutional traditions common to the Member States, by the European Convention of Human Rights and by the Charter of Fundamental Rights of the European Union. The Court of First Instance found that in order to be able to challenge a measure in such a case it was enough for the applicant to demonstrate that 'the measure in question affects his legal position, in a manner which is both definite and immediate, by restricting his rights or by imposing obligations on him'. Advocate General Jacobs, in his opinion on the *Pequeños Agricultores* appeal — which antedated the judgment of the Court of First Instance in *Jégo Quéré* — came to the same conclusion.

(¹) Statistics concerning the activities of the Court of Justice and the Court of First Instance in 2002 are published in the Court's annual report (2002 edition forthcoming) and on the Europa server (http://curia.eu.int/en/pei/rapan.htm).
(²) Case C-50/00 P *Unión de Pequeños Agricultores* v *Council* (2002) ECR p. I-06677; Bull. 9-2002, point 1.8.60.
(³) Regulation No 136/66/EEC (OJ 172, 30.9.1966), as last amended by Regulation (EC) No 1513/2001 (OJ L 201, 26.7.2001; 2001 General Report, point 455).
(⁴) Case T-177/01 *Jego Quéré & Cie* v *Commission* (2002) ECR, p. II-02365; Bull. 6-2002, point 1.8.114.

In its judgment in *Pequeños Agricultores*, the Court of Justice agreed that the European Community was a community based on the rule of law and that individuals were therefore entitled to effective judicial protection; but it considered that the EC Treaty had in fact established a complete system of legal remedies. Natural or legal persons who, by reason of the conditions for admissibility, could not directly challenge Community measures of general application were able to plead the invalidity of such measures in two ways: by challenging a Community measure implementing the disputed act, on the ground that the disputed act was unlawful (Article 241 of the EC Treaty); or by bringing an action before the national courts challenging the legality of a national measure taken under a Community regulation. The national courts, since they had no jurisdiction themselves to declare those measures invalid, would request the Court of Justice for a preliminary ruling (Article 234 of the EC Treaty). The Court concluded that any other interpretation of the notion of 'person individually concerned' would inevitably have the effect of setting aside the condition in question, which was expressly laid down in the EC Treaty. This would go beyond the jurisdiction conferred on the Community courts: only the Member States had the power to amend the Treaty and the system for judicial review of the legality of Community measures of general application. The Court of Justice, then, did not follow the line adopted either by its Advocate-General or by the Court of First Instance (*Jégo Quéré*), both of whom had sought to broaden the conditions of admissibility. The Court of First Instance has already acted on this ruling in an order delivered in another case, *VVG International*, on 8 August 2002, by strictly applying the settled case-law as upheld by the Court of Justice ([1]).

Fundamental rights

1066.   *Right to respect for family life.* On 17 September the Court of Justice delivered judgment in *Baumbast and R* ([2]), in which it had to consider whether persons admitted to the United Kingdom as members of the family of a migrant worker who was a Community national continued to enjoy the protection of Community law if they ceased to qualify as members of such a family and hence lost the status that had entitled them to residence. Mrs R. was a United States citizen, and was now divorced from her husband, who was a French national and a migrant worker in the United Kingdom; the children of the marriage continued to live with her. Mr Baumbast was a German national who had his centre of interests in the United Kingdom, although he was now employed in Germany, while his wife, who was of Colombian nationality, continued to live in the United Kingdom with their children.

([1]) Case T-155/02 *VVG International Handelsgesellschaft mbH*, OJ C 191, 10.8.2002.
([2]) Case C-413/99 *Baumbast and R v Secretary of State for the Home Department.*

The Court accepted, first of all, that the children were entitled to remain in the United Kingdom in order to attend courses of general education: the aim of Regulation (EEC) No 1612/68 (¹), namely freedom of movement for workers, required that the conditions for the integration of the migrant worker's family into the society of the host country be the best possible. That aim also required that the parent with custody of the child should have a right of residence; the Court here also cited the requirement of respect for family life laid down in Article 8 of the European Convention for the Protection of Human Rights and Fundamental Freedoms. Continuing the approach it had taken in the *Carpenter* case, where it emphasised the importance of the protection of family life (²), the Court accepted that the members of the family had a right of residence, even though on a restrictive interpretation of Community law they no longer qualified for any such entitlement.

The UK authorities had stated that Mr Baumbast no longer enjoyed right of residence as a worker, as a self-employed person, or as a person possessing 'sufficient resources'; the Court was asked whether he was entitled to residence by the mere fact of being a European Union citizen, in direct application of Article 18(1) of the EC Treaty, which concerns Union citizenship. In reply the Court for the first time expressly acknowledged that Article 18(1) had direct effect. But the relationship between the direct effect of Article 18(1) and the scope of the 'limitations and conditions' which it allows to be imposed on exercise of the entitlement has still to be clarified. The Court specified that these limitations and conditions, which were provided for in secondary legislation, had to be applied in compliance with the general principles of Community law, and in particular the principle of proportionality.

Competition

1067.   Professional bodies, the professions, competition. The case of *Wouters and Savelbergh*, in which the Court of Justice delivered judgment on 19 February (³), raised for the first time the important question of the conformity with Community law of a national decision prohibiting partnership between members of the bar and accountants. Mr Wouters and Mr Savelbergh, members of the Bar of the Netherlands, were refused permission by the Supervisory Board of the Bars of Amsterdam and Rotterdam to practise in partnership with the accountants Arthur Andersen and Price Waterhouse, both established in the

---

(¹) OJ L 257, 19.10.1968.
(²) Case C-60/00 *Mary Carpenter* v *Secretary of State for the Home Department* (2002) ECR, p. I-06279; Bull. 9-2002, point 1.8.61.
(³) Case C-309/99 *J. C. J. Wouters, J. W. Savelbergh and Price Waterhouse Belastingadviseurs BV* v *Algemene Raad van de Nederlandse Orde van Advocaten*, intervener Raad van de Balies van de Europese Gemeenschap (2002) ECR, p. I-2209; Bull. 3-2002, point 1.9.13.

Netherlands. This refusal was grounded by the General Council of the Bar of the Netherlands on the need to guarantee the independence of the legal profession. The Dutch supreme court, the *Raad van State*, to which the issue was referred as the court of final appeal, asked the Court of Justice for a preliminary ruling on the application to the professions of Community competition law. The Court of Justice found, first, that the General Council of the Bar of the Netherlands, as the body responsible for regulating the profession, had to be regarded as an association of undertakings for the purposes of Community competition law where it adopted a regulation binding on all its members. This professional body, which was composed exclusively of members of the profession and was not legally required to take its decisions in the general interest, constituted an association of undertakings where it adopted a regulation prohibiting professional partnerships. The Court found further that the prohibition of such multi-disciplinary partnerships did have the effect of restricting competition on the Dutch market for legal services. Moreover, it deprived clients from turning to a single structure offering a wide range of services (the 'one-stop-shop advantage'). The Dutch regulation also affected trade between Member States, because it applied equally to visiting lawyers who were registered members of the bar of another Member State, because economic and commercial law more and more frequently governed transnational transactions, and because firms of accountants looking for lawyers and partners were generally international groups present in several Member States. However, the Court acknowledged that there could be a degree of incompatibility between the 'advisory activities' carried out by a member of the Bar and the 'supervisory activities' carried out by an accountant. In the Netherlands accountants certifying accounts were not bound by a rule of professional secrecy comparable to that applicable to members of the Bar. Consequently, it was reasonable for the Dutch regulation to impose restrictions despite the adverse effects on competition, as they were necessary in order to ensure the proper practice of the legal profession. This reason was also invoked by the Court to validate the Dutch regulation in terms of the right of establishment and freedom to provide services.

1068.   Merger control. In judgments delivered on 22 and 25 October the Court of First Instance annulled two Commission decisions prohibiting mergers ([1]).

In *Schneider Electric*, following expedited proceedings lasting less than 10 months, the Court annulled a Commission decision prohibiting a merger between the French groups Schneider and Legrand, both of them manufacturers of low-voltage electrical equipment, and a second decision ordering a demerger. The Court found that the economic analysis the Commission had carried out in its prohibition decision was vitiated by errors and omissions which deprived it

---

([1]) Cases T-310/01 and T-77/02 *Schneider Electric SA* v *Commission,* Bull. 12-2002, point 1.9.78 and Cases T-5/02 and T-80/02 *Tetra Laval BV* v *Commission*; Bull. 12-2002, point 1.9.79.

of probative value save in relation to French sectoral markets. Except with respect to those markets, the Court found the Commission had overestimated the economic power of the merged group. With respect to the French markets the Court upheld the Commission's economic analysis in its entirety. But it found that there had been a 'substantial' change in the nature of the Commission's objections between the statement of objections it gave to the parties and the final decision, and that this infringed the rights of the defence. The annulment of the prohibition decision meant that the second decision, ordering the separation of Schneider and Legrand, was devoid of foundation, and automatically entailed its annulment too. Following the judgment the Commission decided to initiate the second stage of inquiry provided for in the merger regulation, Regulation (EEC) No 4064/89. The Schneider group subsequently sold its holding in Legrand to a consortium of investors, Wendel-KKR.

In its judgment in *Tetra Laval*, which likewise came at the end of expedited proceedings that lasted less than 10 months, the Court annulled a Commission decision prohibiting a merger between Tetra Laval, the world leader in carton packaging, and the French company Sidel, whose main business is the design and manufacture of packaging equipment and bottles in polyethylene terephthalate (PET). Here too the Court annulled a decision ordering the demerger of the companies. The Court found that the economic analysis of the conglomerate effects, based on the foreseeable conduct of the merged entity, was vitiated by certain errors of assessment. The Commission had to show that the anticipated conduct would follow 'in all likelihood'. The Commission should have taken account of incentives to avoid unlawful behaviour, and of the commitments offered by the company regarding its future conduct. The definition of the market in equipment for manufacturing PET bottles was too narrow, and the Commission's economic analysis relied on considerations which were not proved to the requisite standard, particularly in respect of the anticipated growth in demand for packaging for sensitive food products and PET bottles between now and 2005. The Court rejected a submission by Tetra Laval that its right of access to the file had been infringed. On 20 December the Commission decided to appeal against the judgment to the Court of Justice.

Free movement of capital

1069. Privatised undertakings. In judgments delivered on 4 June ([1]) the Court of Justice ruled on the compatibility with the fundamental freedoms of the legislation of Belgium, France and Portugal on special 'golden' shares, which restricts the acquisition of shares in newly privatised undertakings. In a 1997

([1]) Case C-367/98 *Commission* v *Portugal*, Case C-483/99 *Commission* v *France* and Case C-503/99 *Commission* v *Belgium* (2002) ECR pp. I-4731, 4781 and 4809; Bull. 6-2002, point 1.8.115.

communication (¹) the Commission expressed the view that the special powers reserved to Member States in the management of privatised undertakings, such as prior authorisations and rights of veto, could constitute an obstacle to the exercise of the fundamental freedoms enshrined in the Treaty, in particular the free movement of capital, although it accepted that they could be justified under exceptional circumstances and on strict conditions. Hence the three actions brought by the Commission against Portugal, France and Belgium for failure to fulfil their obligations. In its three rulings the Court fully upheld the 1997 communication, spelling out the following principles:

- the 'golden shares' and other special rights vested in public authorities constituted obstacles to the free movement of capital and to the right of establishment in as much as they might dissuade investors in other Member States from investing in the capital of the undertakings concerned;

- exceptions might be justified by overriding requirements of the general interest, such as, for example, the need to safeguard, for newly privatised public undertakings, security of supply of petroleum products in the event of a crisis.

However, these exceptions assumed that the following conditions were met: the State measures must be founded on overriding requirements of the general interest; they must not be discriminatory; and they must be proportional to the general interest objective being sought. The conditions were not met by measures which clearly discriminated against investors in other Member States or which were founded on a financial interest (Portugal) or measures which, although applying without distinction to all investors, stemmed from a wide discretionary power on the part of the State and not from specific objective criteria (France). By contrast, maintaining a minimum supply of gas in the event of a genuine and serious threat could constitute grounds for intervention by the public authorities in the management policy of a privatised undertaking provided it conformed to strict time-limits, was supported by a formal statement of reasons and was subject to effective review by the courts (Belgium).

Air transport

1070.   Open skies agreements. The Court of Justice had to consider infringement proceedings brought by the Commission against seven Member States which had concluded what are known as 'open skies' agreements with the United States, on the ground that the agreements infringed the Community's exclusive external competence. The Commission also accused those seven Member States

---

(¹) OJ C 220, 19.7.1997; 1997 General Report, point 210.

and the United Kingdom, which was a party to the bilateral Bermuda II agreement of 1977, of infringing the Treaty rules on freedom of establishment ([1]).

On the question of freedom of establishment, the Court found that according to the clause on the ownership and control of airlines the United States was, in principle, under an obligation to grant the rights provided for in the agreements to carriers controlled by the Member State with which it had concluded the agreement, and was entitled to refuse those rights to carriers controlled by other Member States which were established in that Member State ('Community airlines'). The Court agreed with the Commission that this was discrimination contrary to the freedom of establishment guaranteed by the Treaty, because it excluded Community airlines from the benefit of the treatment which the Member State concluding such an agreement thus reserved for its own airlines. On the question of the infringement of the Community's exclusive external competence, the Court said that Article 80(2) of the EC Treaty merely provided for a power for the Community to take action which was dependent on there being a prior decision of the Council. There was no express external Community competence in that regard. Nor was external competence implied by a need to exercise external competence at the same time as the Community's internal competence, since the Council had in fact been able to adopt the 'third package' without its being necessary to conclude an air transport agreement with the United States ([2]). Considering further the question of implied powers, the Court referred to the precedent in *AETR* ([3]): the rule established in that case applied where the Council had laid down common rules on the basis of Article 80(2) of the Treaty. In such circumstances Member States were no longer competent to enter into obligations towards non-member countries if those obligations affected the common rules. International commitments did affect the common rules where they fell within the scope of the common rules or, in any event, within an area which was already largely covered by such rules, or where the Community had included in its internal legislative acts provisions relating to nationals, in this case air carriers, of non-member countries. The Court then went on to examine the scope of the regulations cited, on a case-by-case basis. It concluded that some of the provisions on the establishment of fares and rates on intra-Community routes, and those relating to computerised reservation systems and the allocation of airport slots contained in the other regulations referred to, applied to air carriers of non-member countries. The Community therefore had exclusive competence for such matters. The Court granted the Commission's application on that point. But the bilateral agreements did not fall within an area already covered by the regulations relating to the granting by

---

([1]) Case C-466/98 *Commission* v *United Kingdom*, Case C-467/98 *Commission* v *Denmark*, Case C-468/98 *Commission* v *Sweden*, Case C-469/98 *Commission* v *Finland*, Case C-471/98 *Commission* v *Belgium*, Case C-472/98 *Commission* v *Luxembourg*, Case C-475/98 *Commission* v *Austria*, and Case 476/98 *Commission* v *Germany*; Bull. 12-2002, point 1.9.80.
([2]) Opinion 1/76 (1977) ECR 741; Eleventh General Report, point 569.
([3]) Case 22/70 *Commission* v *Council* (1971) ECR 263; Fifth General Report, point 604.

the Member States of operating licences in relation to air carriers established in the Community and the access of Community air carriers to intra-Community routes. Consequently, those regulations could not establish an external competence of the Community.

Under international law the sections of the agreements which have been held to be contrary to Community law are not automatically invalid. But the Member States must accept the consequences of these judgments: they can no longer negotiate on matters which are within the Community's exclusive external competence, and must in any event rectify any incompatibilities arising out of the agreements, even if this makes it necessary to denounce the agreements.

Food safety

1071. Precautionary principle. In two rulings handed down on 11 September ([1]) the Court of First Instance upheld Regulation (EC) No 2821/98 ([2]) banning the use of certain antibiotics as additives in feedingstuffs.

At the time the contested regulation was adopted, it had not been conclusively shown that there was a link between the use of these antibiotics in animal feedingstuffs and the development of resistance to them in humans via the food chain. This was the background against which the Council, when it adopted the regulation, invoked the precautionary principle. In these two judgments the Court spelled out the conditions for application of the precautionary principle. It confirmed the approach taken by the Commission in 2000 in its communication on the precautionary principle ([3]). The precautionary principle could be applied only where there was a risk, notably for human health, which had not yet been conclusively demonstrated, but it could not be based on unverified conjecture. Before any preventive measures were taken, the competent public authority had to conduct a risk assessment with two complementary components: a scientific component (as thorough a scientific risk assessment as possible taking account notably of the urgency of the situation) and a political component ('risk management'), with the public authority determining the desired level of protection and consequently deciding on an appropriate measure given the level of risk it had determined. 'Risk' thus constituted a function of the probability that use of a product or a procedure would adversely affect human health. 'Hazard' ('danger') was, in this context, commonly used in a broader sense and described any product or procedure capable of having an adverse

([1]) Case T-13/99 (ECR 1999, p. II-1961) *Pfizer Animal Health SA* v *Council* and Case T-70/99 *Alpharma Inc.* v *Council*; Bull. 9-2002, point 1.8.62.
([2]) OJ L 351, 29.12.1998; 1998 General Report, point 568.
([3]) COM(2000) 1; 2000 General Report, point 664.

effect on human health. The level of risk could not be placed at 'zero': the precautionary principle could not be applied where the risk was based on mere conjecture that had not been scientifically verified. The decision to ban a product had to be taken by the public authority that was politically responsible, and not by the scientific experts. Unless the legislation provided otherwise, the public authority was not bound by the scientific opinions. However, in order to be able to disregard them it must rely on a proper examination, carefully and impartially carried out, of all the relevant aspects of the individual case, which included the reasoning on which the scientific committee based its findings.

Section 3

Computerisation of Community law

1072.   Transparency. As in previous years, the Office for Official Publications of the European Communities (EUR-OP) continued its efforts to improve and update its techniques for collecting, processing and disseminating legal texts. Its objective is to make Community law more transparent and more accessible thanks to the online information services of CELEX (^{1}) and EUR-Lex (^{2}), which it manages. The Lex Interinstitutional Group (GIL) and the Council Working Party on Legal Data Processing (GIJC) coordinated this work. The coverage of the legal documentary bases managed by EUR-OP was extended, particularly thanks to the progress made in consolidating Community law and to the Commission's regular forwarding of preparatory acts. The forwarding of preparatory acts from the other institutions is being improved. The Office has also completed the collection of the texts of treaties available in EUR-Lex in accordance with Regulation (EC) N° 1049/2001 on public access to European Parliament, Council and Commission documents *(→ point 21).*

The year 2002 also saw the full opening of the EUR-Lex portal. The public now has access to the complete L and C Series of the *Official Journal of the European Communities* since it was placed on the Internet in January 1998 and to legislation in force, existing consolidated versions, preparatory acts and case-law. The fact that the EUR-Lex online service is free of charge has a major impact on income from the sale of subscriptions to the *Official Journal of the European Communities*. Sales of CELEX licences are holding up and go a long way towards financing the core of the CELEX system of information on Community legislation.

1073.   Statistics. The rate of use of EUR-Lex and CELEX is constantly increasing, as shown by the statistics on the number of documents consulted: for CELEX, 46 million (for the first eight months of 2002), compared with 30 million in 2001; for EUR-Lex, 145 million (for the first eight months of 2002), compared with 80 million in 2001.

(^{1}) http://europa.eu.int/celex/htm/celex_en.htm.
(^{2}) http://europa.eu.int/eur-lex/en/index.html.

Chapter IX

Institutions and other bodies

Section 1

Composition and functioning of the institutions and bodies

European Parliament (¹)

1074.   *Election of Members of the European Parliament.* On 25 June, the representatives of the Member States adopted the decision amending the act concerning the election of representatives of the European Parliament by direct universal suffrage (²), the purpose of which is to allow election in accordance with principles common to all the Member States from 2004. The common principles provide, in particular, for elections to be held by direct universal suffrage, freely and in secret, and for Members of the European Parliament to be elected on the basis of proportional representation using the list system or the single transferable vote. The office of Member of the European Parliament will be incompatible with that of member of a national parliament.

1075.   *Composition of Parliament.* At its part-session from 14 to 17 January, Parliament elected its officers for the second half of its legislature. Mr Pat Cox was elected President, and the 14 Vice-Presidents and five Quaestors were also elected, as were the members, chairs and vice-chairs of the various committees. In February, Mr Cox presented the outline of his work programme for the remainder of the parliamentary term. The distribution of the 626 seats among the political groups at 31 December was as follows:

- European People's Party and European Democrats (PPE-DE),
  chaired by Hans-Gert Pöttering (D)   232

(¹) http://www.europarl.eu.int/default.htm.
(²) OJ L 283, 21.10.2002; Bull. 6-2002, point 1.1.10.

- Party of European Socialists (PES),
  chaired by Enrique Barón Crespo (E)   175

- European Liberal Democrat and Reform Party (EDLR),
  chaired by Graham Watson (GB)   54

- Confederal Group of the European United Left —
  Nordic Green Left (GUE/NGL),
  chaired by Francis Wurtz (F)   50

- Greens/European Free Alliance (Verts/ALE),
  chaired by Daniel Cohn-Bendit (F)
  and Monica Frassoni (B)   45

- Europe of Nations Group (UEN),
  chaired by Charles Pasqua (F)   22

- Europe of Democracies and Diversities (EDD),
  chaired by Jens-Peter Bonde (DK),
  Johannes Blokland (NL) and Yves Butel (F)   17

- Non-affiliated (NI)   31

1076. Internal organisation. In January and February, Parliament adopted decisions on the numerical strength of committees and in February, it adopted a decision on the numerical strength of interparliamentary delegations. Also in January, it decided to set up a temporary committee on foot-and-mouth disease, whose report was adopted in December. At its part-session from 11 to 14 March ([1]), Parliament adopted a decision amending Rule 57 of its Rules of Procedure concerning the Commission's legislative and work programmes. In May, it adopted a decision annexing to its Rules of Procedure a list of documents directly accessible through its register of documents and a resolution on its revenue and expenditure estimates for 2003. In June, it adopted a decision amending its Rules of Procedure with regard to parliamentary immunity and three resolutions on the immunity of Italian members and the Italian authorities' practices in this respect and on social security for parliamentary assistants ([2]). It also adopted a decision on the general revision of its Rules of Procedure, a decision amending them to ensure balance between individual members and groups and a decision on the amendment of its provisions governing the justification of amendments. In October, it adopted decisions amending the regulation on Parliament's access to sensitive Council documents on security and defence and the discharge procedure. In December, it debated the statute of members. Parlia-

([1]) Bull. 3-2002, point 1.10.1.
([2]) Bull. 6-2002, point 1.9.1.

ment adopted the timetable for its part-sessions in 2003, and confirmed the abolition of Friday sittings in Strasbourg. Also, at the start of the sitting, the President of Parliament, Mr Cox, announced the opening of the official register of Parliament documents available to the public. Parliament also held special sessions on 20 March, to discuss the results of the Barcelona European Council ([1]) and on 11 September, in memory of the victims of the terrorist attacks on the United States on 11 September 2001.

1077.   *Relations with the other institutions*. In its relations with the other EU institutions and bodies, Parliament drafted resolutions on the decisions taken at the Barcelona ([2]), Seville ([3]), Brussels ([4]) and Copenhagen ([5]) European Councils. It also debated the work programmes and assessment of the Spanish and Danish Council Presidencies, the 2001 activity report presented by the European Ombudsman, Mr Jacob Söderman, the annual report of the European Central Bank (ECB) presented by Mr Wim Duisenberg *(→ point 68)*, and the 2000 and 2001 annual reports of the European Investment Bank (EIB) ([6]) in the presence of Mr Maystadt, and the 2001 annual report by the Court of Auditors *(→ point 1103)* presented by Mr Fabra Vallés. Parliament also adopted resolutions on the appointment of Mr Lucas Papademos to the office of Vice-President of the European Central Bank ([7]), reform of the Council and transparency *(→ point 1089)*, the proposal for a Council regulation amending the Staff Regulations of Officials of the European Communities, the termination of service of officials of the Commission, the General Secretariat of the Council and the European Parliament, the application of Regulation (EC) No 1049/2001 regarding public access to European Parliament, Council and Commission documents *(→ point 21)*, the Union's information and communication policy, the amendment of the protocol on the statute of the Court of Justice, and the Commission's evaluation activities. On 27 February, in the context of relations between Parliament and the Commission, Mr Prodi, President of the Commission, presented the Commission's annual policy strategy for 2003, which was discussed in greater detail by Ms de Palacio, Vice-President of the Commission, during a more in-depth debate on 20 March. On 20 November, Mr Prodi, President of the Commission, presented the Commission's legislative and work programme for 2003 *(→ point 1094)*.

1078.   *Institutional affairs and the future of the Union*. Parliament adopted resolutions on its relations with national parliaments in the field of European integration *(→ point 13)*, the legal personality of the European Union

([1]) Bull. 9-2002, point 1.10.2.
([2]) Bull. 1/2-2002, points 1.3.35 and 1.4.48.
([3]) Bull. 6-2002, point 1.1.11.
([4]) Bull. 11-2002, point 1.1.4.
([5]) Bull. 12-2002, point 1.1.2.
([6]) Bull. 1/2-2002, point 1.3.27; Bull. 11-2002, point 1.10.16.
([7]) Bull. 5-2002, point 1.3.1.

(→ *point 13*), the financing of the convention (→ *point 7*), the third Commission report on Union citizenship (→ *point 506*), the impact of the charter of fundamental rights of the European Union and its future status (→ *point 42*), the classification of acts and hierarchy of acts in the European Union (→ *point 13*), and the division of competences between the European Union and the Member States (→ *point 13*). On 5 December, Mr Prodi, President of the Commission, presented the Commission's second contribution to the work of the convention.

1079.   *Budget.* In May, Ms Schreyer, member of the Commission, presented the preliminary draft budget for 2003. Parliament completed both readings of the 2003 draft budget, which was signed by the President, Mr Cox, on 9 December. Parliament also adopted resolutions on the 1999 discharge (→ *point 1042*), the 2000 discharge (→ *point 1044*), the Financial Regulation applicable to the general budget of the European Communities (→ *point 1048*), the conciliation procedure on the 2003 budget (→ *point 1028*) and the 2002 supplementary and amending budgets (→ *points 1034 to 1039*).

1080.   *Economic and financial affairs.* Parliament approved resolutions on financial services (→ *point 162*), administrative cooperation in the field of indirect taxation (VAT) (→ *point 179*), the economic consequences of the attacks on 11 September 2001 (→ *point 653*), financial conglomerates (→ *point 167*), income tax ([1]), tax policy in the European Union (→ *point 175*), the 2002 broad guidelines of the economic policies of the Member States and the Community (→ *points 59 and 60*), international accounting standards (→ *point 187*), the risk capital action plan (→ *point 768*), the annual assessment of implementation of stability and convergence programmes (→ *point 63*), the Fiscalis 2007 programme (→ *point 177*) and the financial impact of enlargement (→ *point 711*). In addition, in January, the Commission made a statement on the introduction of the euro (→ *point 70*). In March, Mr Solbes, member of the Commission, gave a presentation on world governance in the wake of the world social forum in Porto Alegre and the world economic forum and New York. In May, he presented a communication on public finances in the euro zone. In September, Ms Diamantopoulou and Mr Solbes Mira, members of the Commission, gave statements on the coordination of economic and employment policy. In October, Mr Prodi and Mr Solbes Mira gave statements on the stability and growth pact.

1081.   *Internal policies.* The main internal policy topics which Parliament debated in 2002 were the environment, research, transport, energy, development cooperation, fisheries, agriculture, public health, food safety, regional policy, competition, education, culture, sport, tourism, the information society and telecommunications, equal opportunities and the Solidarity Fund. In November

---

([1]) Bull. 6-2002, point 1.3.41.

and December, Ms de Palacio, Vice-President of the Commission, made statements on the sinking of the oil tanker *Prestige* off the coast of Galicia.

In the field of justice and home affairs, Parliament gave its opinion on the progress made in 2001 in implementing the area of freedom, security and justice and the situation as regards fundamental rights in the European Union (→ *point 454*), drug-trafficking (→ *point 499*), combating racism and xenophobia (→ *point 481*), the fight against crime (→ *point 488*), combating terrorism (→ *point 492*), judicial cooperation in civil matters (→ *point 468*), police and judicial cooperation in criminal matters (→ *points 473 to 481*), asylum and immigration policy (→ *point 456*), checks at the common borders (→ *point 463*) and 'Echelon' (→ *point 200*). In May, Mr Patten, member of the Commission, addressed the House on progress and prospects in immigration and asylum policy.

1082.   External relations. Parliament focused mainly on enlargement (reports presented for the Commission by Mr Prodi and Mr Verheugen, in October, and a special debate with Members of Parliament from the candidate countries in November), the situation in the Middle East (→ *point 889*), Iraq (→ *point 54*), Afghanistan (→ *point 949*), Turkey (→ *point 54*), Hong Kong (→ *point 964*), Tibet (→ *point 54*), Chechnya (→ *point 917*), South Caucasus (→ *point 917*), Russia (→ *point 917*), Kaliningrad (→ *point 917*), Albania (→ *point 863*), Indonesia (→ *point 956*), India (→ *point 950*), Pakistan (→ *point 952*), Bangladesh (→ *point 54*), Nepal (→ *point 54*), Argentina (→ *point 54*), Zimbabwe (→ *point 1008*), Sudan (→ *point 54*), Egypt (→ *point 54*), Algeria and the Maghreb (→ *point 888*), Nigeria (→ *point 54*), Côte d'Ivoire (→ *point 1007*), Democratic Republic of Congo (→ *point 54*), the ACP countries (→ *point 990*) and international terrorism (→ *point 54*). Parliament also gave its opinion on the International Criminal Court (→ *point 53*), the Valencia Euro-Mediterranean Summit (→ *point 880*), the European Union–Latin America Summit (→ *point 969*), Mercosur (→ *point 970*), the American Servicemembers' Protection Act (→ *point 927*), transatlantic relations (→ *point 927*), the EU–United Nations partnership in the fields of development and humanitarian affairs (→ *point 831*), the Europe–Asia partnership (→ *point 945*) and antidumping activities. In April and November, Mr Solana, High Representative for the CFSP and Secretary-General of the Council, addressed the House in debates on the situation in the Middle East. In September and October, Mr Patten, member of the Commission, spoke on Iraq. As regards the common foreign and security policy (→ *points 748 to 761*), the House adopted resolutions on the current state of progress in the establishment of a common European security and defence policy and on relations between the European Union and NATO. On human rights issues (→ *point 54*), the House adopted a number of resolutions, in particular on the European Union's priorities for democratic rights with a view to the 58th session of the UN Commission on Human Rights, the European Union's policy on human rights, promoting human rights and democratisation in third countries and the situation in several countries. At the December part-session, the Sakharov Prize was awarded to Mr Payá Sardiñas. The President of Mexico, Vicente Fox, addressed the House in May, as did King Abdallah of Jordan in June, the President of Hungary, Ferenc Mádl, in October, and the President of Peru, Alejandro Toledo, in December.

1083.   *Questions to the Commission and the Council.* Parliament addressed 4 158 questions to the Commission: 3 517 written questions, 65 oral questions with debate and 576 during question time. Parliament addressed 788 questions to the Council: 411 written questions, 44 oral questions with debate and 333 during question time.

1084.   *Parliament's work.* A breakdown of Parliament's work in 2002 is shown in Table 30. At 31 December, the establishment plan of Parliament's Secretariat comprised 3 591 permanent posts and 103 temporary posts. The figures for legislative instruments adopted in co-decision with the Council are set out in Table 31 at the end of this section.

Council ([1])

1085.   *Barcelona European Council* ([2]). The European Council met on 15 and 16 March for its second annual spring meeting on the economic, social and environmental situation in the Union ([3]), and reviewed the progress made in implementing the Lisbon strategy ([4]). On economic affairs, the European Council pointed to the coordination of budgetary policies in the context of maintaining sound public finances sustainable in the long term with a view to consolidating the euro zone. It also approved the broad economic policy guidelines for 2002 *(→ point 60)*. On the environment, the European Council welcomed the ratification of the Kyoto Protocol, recognised the importance of the sixth action programme *(→ point 552)* and restated its commitment to sustainable development, in particular by expressing support for the Monterrey and Johannesburg Conferences. It also identified three areas worthy of particular attention: active policies towards full employment; connecting European economies; and encouraging a competitive economy based on knowledge. In the field of external relations, discussions centred on developing the Euro-Mediterranean partnership, Serbia and Montenegro, protectionist measures introduced by the United States, and Zimbabwe. The European Council also adopted a declaration on the situation in the Middle East.

([1]) http://ue.eu.int/en/summ.htm.
([2]) Bull. 3-2002, points I.2 to I.59 and Internet (http://www.europarl.eu.int/summits/index.htm).
([3]) Previous meeting: Stockholm, 23 and 24 March 2001 (2001 General Report, point 1204).
([4]) 2000 General Report, point 1145.

TABLE 30

Parliamentary proceedings from January to December — Resolutions and decisions adopted

Part-session	Consultations (single reading)	Co-decision procedure			Assent	Other opinions (¹)	Budget questions	Own-initiative reports and resolutions			Miscellaneous decisions, and resolutions (⁴)
		First reading	Second reading	Third reading				Report	Resolutions (²)	Urgent subjects (³)	
January	2	3	4	1	1	6		1		8	2
February I	13	6	1	2		7		6	6		2
February II		1	1			1	3	6	3	8	2
March	6	11	6			4	2	6	2	9	1
April I	15	5	6	1		6	8		5		
April II	3	1		2		5	2	1	1		
May I	8	8	6	1		10	1	4	5	4	1
May II	6	1	2	3		2	1	3	2		
June	14	7	6	1	1	8		3	1	9	
July	8	10	2	1	1	8	3	3	4	6	6
September I	2	12	1			5		6	2	3	1
September II	13	5	8	1	1	3	1	6	5		
October I	4	1	2			2		2	2		
October II	10	10	5			3	4	4	3	3	4
November I		2				2	1	1	4		1
November II	10	6	2			5	1	6	5	3	2
December I	9			2			2	2	3		1
December II	13	1	4	5		6	2	3	2	3	1
Total	136 (⁵)	90 (⁶)	56 (⁷)	20	4	83	31	63	55	56	24

(¹) Mainly opinions on Commission reports or communications.
(²) Resolutions in response to statements by other institutions or following oral questions.
(³) Resolutions on topical and urgent subjects of major importance.
(⁴) Decisions concerning waiver of immunity, amendments to the Rules of Procedure and interinstitutional agreements.
(⁵) Including 75 cases in which Parliament proposed amendments to the Commission proposal.
(⁶) Including 77 cases in which Parliament proposed amendments to the Commission proposal.
(⁷) Including 33 cases in which Parliament amended the Council's common position.

1086.   Seville European Council([1]). At its meeting on 21 and 22 June, the European Council gave its agreement to substantial reform of its working methods and those of the Council. It also expressed its determination to speed up the implementation of all aspects of the programme adopted in Tampere for the creation of an area of freedom, security and justice in the European Union. In this context it pointed to the need for further action in relation to immigration and asylum. Determined to reinforce the role of the European Union in the fight against terrorism, and recognising the important contribution of the common foreign and security policy, including the European security and defence policy, the European Council also adopted a declaration designed to take greater account of the capabilities required to combat terrorism. As regards enlargement, it confirmed that, subject to the present rate of progress in negotiations and reforms being maintained, the European Union was determined to conclude the negotiations with 10 countries by the end of 2002, if they are ready, and to sign the Treaty of Accession in spring 2003. The European Council also adopted a declaration on the problems caused by the ratification of the Treaty of Nice by Ireland. In the field of external relations it adopted declarations on the situation in India, the Middle East and Pakistan. It also supported the general approach followed by the Convention on the Future of the European Union and called for the conclusion of an interinstitutional agreement to improve the quality of Community legislation. On 12 July, the Council welcomed the results of this European Council, particularly as regards the structure, functioning and organisation of work within the Council ([2]).

1087.   Brussels European Council([3]). At its meeting on 24 and 25 October, the European Council confirmed that 10 candidate countries (Cyprus, the Czech Republic, Estonia, Hungary, Latvia, Lithuania, Malta, Poland, Slovakia and Slovenia) fulfilled the political criteria and would be able to fulfil the economic criteria from the beginning of 2004. It took decisions that would allow the European Union to present negotiating positions to these countries on all outstanding issues by early November 2002 at the latest, with a view to concluding the accession negotiations with them at the Copenhagen European Council in December, and signing the Accession Treaty in Athens in April 2003. Moreover, it endorsed the Commission proposals for providing in the Accession Treaty, besides a general economic safeguard clause, two specific safeguard clauses concerning the operation of the internal market and the area of justice and home affairs. The European Council also came to an agreement on the financing of enlargement and the conditions applicable to the new Member States in the agricultural sector. It also adopted guidelines for continuing the process with the countries which will not be included in the first enlargement (Bulgaria, Romania and Turkey). Finally, the European Council gave its opinion on the situation of

([1]) Bull. 6-2002, points I.1 to I.33 and Internet (http://www.europarl.eu.int/summits/index.htm).
([2]) Bull. 7/8-2002, point 1.3.2.
([3]) Bull. 10-2002, points I.1 to I.13 and Internet (http://www.europarl.eu.int/summits/index.htm).

the Russian enclave of Kaliningrad and relations between the European Union and NATO, including its readiness to take over the NATO military operation in the Former Yugoslav Republic of Macedonia, and issued a declaration on the hostage-taking in Moscow.

1088.   Copenhagen European Council (¹). At its meeting on 12 and 13 December, the European Council marked the conclusion of the accession negotiations with Cyprus, the Czech Republic, Estonia, Hungary, Latvia, Lithuania, Malta, Poland, Slovakia and Slovenia. The Union endorsed the result of the negotiations and the financial consequences of enlargement. The European Council stated that the Accession Treaty would be signed in Athens on 16 April 2003, and invited the current Member States and the acceding States to ratify the Treaty in time for it to enter into force on 1 May 2004. With regard to Cyprus, the European Council confirmed its preference for accession to the Union by a united Cyprus. It also set the objective of welcoming Bulgaria and Romania as members of the Union in 2007, depending on further progress in complying with the membership criteria. As for Turkey, the European Council stated that if, in December 2004, it fulfilled the Copenhagen political criteria, the Union would open accession negotiations without delay. The European Union and the acceding States also agreed on a joint declaration, 'One Europe', on the continuous, inclusive and irreversible nature of the enlargement process, which will be annexed to the final act of the Accession Treaty. Lastly, the European Council dealt with relations between the Union and NATO with a view to operations in Bosnia following SFOR, adopted declarations on Iraq and the Middle East, and expressed grave concern regarding the serious accident involving the oil tanker *Prestige*.

1089.   Reform of the Council. In a resolution of 16 May (²), the European Parliament stressed the need to rebalance the powers of the Union's institutions and to give precedence to the Community method in decision-making procedures. It also called for greater transparency in Council meetings. The Seville European Council in June, held a detailed discussion on the reform of the Council (³), and gave its agreement to a series of specific measures applicable, without amendment of the Treaties, to the organisation and functioning of the European Council (⁴) and of the Council (⁵).

1090.   Council Presidency. On 28 January, the Council adopted a decision to reverse the respective periods in which Germany and Finland will hold the office of President during the second six months of 2006 and the first six months of 2007 (⁶).

(¹) Bull. 12-2002, points I.1 to I. 17 and Internet (http://www.europarl.eu.int/summits/index.htm).
(²) Bull. 5-2002, point 1.1.4.
(³) Bull. 6-2002, point I.4.
(⁴) Bull. 6-2002, point I.27.
(⁵) Bull. 6-2002, point I.28.
(⁶) Council Decision 2002/105/EC, ECSC, Euratom (OJ L 39, 9.2.2002; Bull. 1/2-2002, point 1.9.4).

1091. *Council meetings and activities.* The Council held 77 meetings in 2002. Figures for the legislative instruments enacted this year are found in Table 31 at the end of this section.

1092. *Establishment plan.* At 31 December, the Council's establishment plan comprised 2 640 permanent posts and 61 temporary posts.

Commission ([1])

1093. *Annual policy strategy (APS) for 2003.* On 27 February, the Commission presented a communication to Parliament and the Council outlining its policy priorities for the year 2003: successful enlargement, the creation of a sustainable and inclusive economy, and the maintenance of stability and security for the citizens of the European Union ([2]). In its conclusions of 11 March ([3]) and 13 May ([4]), the Council welcomed the Commission's choice of priorities and its intention of conducting an in-depth dialogue on the strategic planning and programming of the activities for the adoption of its work programme for 2003. On 28 August, as part of the cycle of strategic planning and programming of its activities, the Commission presented a mid-term assessment of the annual policy strategy, taking into account its structured dialogue with Parliament and the Council ([5]).

1094. *Work programme for 2003* ([6]). On 30 October, the Commission adopted its legislative and work programme for 2003 ([7]). Based on a stocktaking document on the follow-up to its annual policy strategy for 2003, the Commission's programme reflects extensive preparatory consultation with Parliament and the Council on the policy priorities and key initiatives for the coming year. The programme contains a list of the legislative proposals and non-legislative acts that the Commission intends to adopt in 2003, in the three priority areas defined in the policy strategy as well as a second list of other proposals and acts which it may adopt in 2003. On the enlargement front, the Commission intends to support and monitor the acceding countries' preparations for accession, take steps to guarantee that it will be able to serve the enlarged Union effectively from the very first day of accession, and review Community policies so that they meet the needs of the enlarged Union. As regards stability and security, it will focus on helping the Council to adopt the legislation needed to create an area of freedom, security and justice, improving transport safety and security and civil

([1]) http://europa.eu.int/comm/index_en.htm.
([2]) Bull. 1/2-2002, point 1.9.15.
([3]) Bull. 3-2002, point 1.10.13.
([4]) Bull. 5-2002, point 1.9.11.
([5]) COM(2002) 427; Bull. 7/8-2002, point 1.10.9.
([6]) http://europa.eu.int/comm/off/work_programme/index_en.htm.
([7]) COM(2002) 590; Bull. 10-2002, point 1.9.11.

protection, safeguarding the frontiers of the enlarged Union, responding to crises across the world, and bringing people closer together. Lastly, focusing on the
objective of a sustainable and inclusive economy, the Commission aims to pursue the goal of making the European Union the most advanced knowledge-
based economy in the world, maintaining macroeconomic stability, promoting
sustainable development and working to ensure that the positive effects of globalisation are shared fairly. This year, however, the programme was adapted in
order to constitute a specific contribution to the Council's first annual operating
programme, due to be adopted in December 2003 ([1]). On the practical side, the
Commission will continue to provide the other institutions with a quarterly rolling programme, updated each month, and a report on the proposals adopted.
For the first time, too, this year's legislative and work programme contains a list
of proposals which will undergo an extended impact assessment in 2003. This
new mechanism will help to improve policy formulation and sustainable development by analysing the economic, social and environmental impact of proposals. In a resolution adopted on 5 December ([2]), Parliament welcomed the
work programme for its clarity and political focus, in keeping with the Commission's new political planning and programming strategy, but also wished for
further improvements to be made to the process through coordination of political programming at interinstitutional level in the coming years.

1095.   *Legislative activity.* The Commission met 46 times during the year. It
sent 516 proposals, recommendations and draft instruments with a view to
adoption by the Council or by Parliament and the Council together (54 directives, 193 regulations and 239 decisions). It also presented 265 communications
and reports, and 3 Green Papers. In addition to the new initiatives, programmes
and action plans adopted by the Commission, the debates launched and the
ongoing activities pursued under its work programme for 2003, these figures
include proposals for routine management instruments (for example in agriculture, fisheries, customs and commercial policy) and proposals for consolidating
existing legislation. The figures for legislative instruments adopted by the Commission are set out in Table 31 at the end of this section.

1096.   *Rules of procedure.* On 23 January, the Commission amended its Rules
of Procedure to annex new provisions covering document management ([3]).

1097.   *Establishment plan.* In 2002, the Commission's establishment plan
comprised 17 377 permanent posts (including 1 878 for the language service)
and 529 temporary posts (including 13 LA posts) for administrative duties;
3 556 permanent posts for research duties; 520 permanent posts for the Publications Office; 173 permanent posts and 127 temporary posts for the European

---

([1]) Bull. 6-2002, point I.28.
([2]) Bull. 12-2002, point 1.10.14.
([3]) Decision 2002/47/EC, ECSC, Euratom (OJ L 21, 24.1.2002; Bull. 1/2-2002, point 1.9.13).

Anti-Fraud Office; 36 permanent posts and 47 temporary posts for the European Centre for the Development of Vocational Training and 88 permanent posts for the European Foundation for the Improvement of Living and Working Conditions.

Under the secondment and exchange arrangements between the Commission and the Member States' government departments, 45 Commission officials (30.5 person-years) were seconded to national civil services and international organisations, and the number of national experts coming to work for the Commission was equivalent to 892 person-years.

Court of Justice and Court of First Instance [1]

1098. *Reform of the statute of the Court of Justice.* On 12 July, the Council amended Article 20 of the statute of the Court of Justice to adapt it to the international obligations arising from the agreement concluded by the Council with Iceland and Norway on the implementation of the Schengen *acquis* [2] and to anticipate the entry into force of any new agreements providing for the participation of non-member countries in preliminary-ruling proceedings [3].

1099. Composition of the Chambers of the Court of Justice for the 2002/03 court year:

- First Chamber: President: Mr Wathelet
  Judges: Mr Jann and Mr Rosas

- Second Chamber: President: Mr Schintgen
  Judges: Ms Colneric and Mr Skouris

- Third Chamber: President: Mr Puissochet
  Judges: Ms Macken, Mr Gulmann and Mr Cunha Rodrigues

- Fourth Chamber: President: Mr Timmermans
  Judges: Mr Edward, Mr La Pergola and Mr Von Bahr

- Fifth Chamber: President: Mr Wathelet
  Judges: Mr Timmermans, Mr Edward, Mr La Pergola,
  Mr Jann, Mr Von Bahr and Mr Rosas

[1] http://curia.eu.int/.
[2] OJ L 176, 10.7.1999; 1999 General Report, point 914.
[3] OJ L 218, 13.8.2002; Bull. 7/8-2002, point 1.10.12.

- Sixth Chamber: President: Mr Puissochet
  Judges: Ms Macken, Ms Colneric, Mr Schintgen,
  Mr Gulmann, Mr Skouris and Mr Cunha Rodrigues

1100.   Composition of the Chambers of the Court of First Instance for the 2002/03 court year:

- First Chamber: President: Mr Vesterdorf
  Judges: Mr Moura Ramos and Mr Legal

- Second Chamber: President: Mr Forwood
  Judges: Mr Pirrung and Mr Meij

- Third Chamber: President: Mr Lenaerts
  Judges: Mr Azizi and Mr Jaeger

- Fourth Chamber: President: Ms Tiili
  Judges: Mr Mengozzi and Mr Vilaras

- Fifth Chamber: President: Mr García-Valdecasas
  Judges: Ms Lindh and Mr Cooke

1101.   Establishment plan. At 31 December, the establishment plan of the Court of Justice and the Court of First Instance comprised 787 permanent posts and 290 temporary posts.

Court of Auditors [1]

1102.   Internal organisation. At its meeting on 16 January, the Court elected Mr Fabra Vallés President [2]. Information about the Court's composition is available on its web site [3]. At its 668th meeting, on 31 January, the Court of Auditors adopted new Rules of Procedure, defining its organisation and operation, and the procedures applicable [4].

1103.   Annual report for 2001 [5]. In July, the Court of Auditors agreed on the observations to feature in its annual report on the 2001 budget and sent them to the Commission and the other institutions concerned. The report was adopted by the Court on 10 October, and published in the *Official Journal of the European*

---

[1] http://www.eca.eu.int/.
[2] Bull. 1/2-2002, point 1.9.27.
[3] http://www.eca.eu.int/en/coa.htm.
[4] OJ L 210, 6.8.2002. Previous Rules of Procedure dated from 21 and 22 March 2001.
[5] http://www.eca.eu.int/en/reports_opinions.htm.

Communities in November, together with the replies by the other institutions (¹). It covers operations under the general budget and the activities of the sixth, seventh and eighth European Development Funds. The part devoted to the general budget is in nine chapters in which the Court analyses the accounts from the point of view of compliance with the principle of sound financial management. The first eight chapters cover the principal areas of revenue and expenditure (own resources, common agricultural policy, structural measures, internal policies, external action, pre-accession aid, administrative expenditure, financial instruments and banking activitites). The ninth chapter contains the statement of assurance on the reliability of the accounts and the legality and regularity of own resources, commitments and administrative expenditure. This year, this chapter also contains an assessment of the administrative reform of the Commission.

1104. Special reports. In 2002, the Court published seven special reports. These dealt with macro-financial assistance to third countries and structural adjustment facilities in the Mediterranean countries (²), the Socrates and Youth for Europe Community action programmes (³), the Community initiative 'Employment — Integra' (⁴), local actions for employment (⁵), the extensification premium and payment schemes in the common organisation of the market for beef and veal (⁶), the audit of the Commission's management of the EU oilseeds support scheme (⁷) and the sound financial management of the common organisation of markets in the banana sector (⁸).

1105. Specific annual reports. The Court produced 11 specific annual reports in 2002. These dealt with the audit of the operational efficiency of the management of the European Central Bank for the financial year 2001 (⁹), the financial statements for the financial year 2001 of the European Training Foundation (¹⁰), the Community Plant Variety Office (¹¹), the European Environment Agency (¹²), the European Agency for Safety and Health at Work (¹³), the European Agency for the Evaluation of Medicinal Products (¹⁴), the Translation Centre for the Bodies of the European Union (¹⁵), the European Foundation for the Improvement of Living and Working Conditions (¹⁶), the Euratom Supply

---

(¹) OJ C 295, 28.11.2002.
(²) Special Report No 1/2002 (OJ C 121, 23.5.2002; Bull. 3-2002, point 1.10.15).
(³) Special Report No 2/2002 (OJ C 136, 7.6.2002; Bull. 3-2002, point 1.10.16).
(⁴) Special Report No 3/2002 (OJ C 263, 29.10.2002; Bull. 7/8-2002, point 1.10.19).
(⁵) Special Report No 4/2002 (OJ C 263, 29.10.2002; Bull. 7/8-2002, point 1.10.20).
(⁶) Special Report No 5/2002 (OJ C 290, 25.11.2002; Bull. 7/8-2002, point 1.10.21).
(⁷) Special Report No 6/2002 (OJ C 254, 22.10.2002; Bull. 7/8-2002, point 1.10.22).
(⁸) Special Report No 7/2002 (OJ C 294, 28.11.2002; Bull. 7/8-2002, point 1.10.23).
(⁹) OJ C 259, 25.10.2002; Bull. 9-2002, point 1.9.11.
(¹⁰) OJ C 326, 27.12.2002; Bull. 9-2002, point 1.9.12.
(¹¹) OJ C 326, 27.12.2002; Bull. 9-2002, point 1.9.13.
(¹²) OJ C 326, 27.12.2002; Bull. 9-2002, point 1.9.14.
(¹³) OJ C 326, 27.12.2002; Bull. 9-2002, point 1.9.15.
(¹⁴) OJ C 326, 27.12.2002; Bull. 9-2002, point 1.9.16.
(¹⁵) OJ C 326, 27.12.2002; Bull. 9-2002, point 1.9.17.
(¹⁶) OJ C 326, 27.12.2002; Bull. 9-2002, point 1.9.18.

Agency (^{1}), the European Monitoring Centre for Drugs and Drug Addiction (^{2}) and the European Monitoring Centre on Racism and Xenophobia (^{3}).

1106. Opinions. The Court gave opinions on the Financial Regulation applicable to the general budget of the European Communities (^{4}), an amended proposal for a Council regulation amending Regulation (Euratom, ECSC, EEC) No 549/69 (^{5}), a proposal for a Council regulation introducing special measures to terminate the service of officials of the Commission of the European Communities as part of the reform of the Commission (^{6}), a proposal for a Council regulation introducing special measures to terminate the service of officials of the General Secretariat of the Council of the European Union (^{7}), a proposal for a Council regulation introducing special measures to terminate the service of European Parliament officials and temporary staff working in the political groups (^{8}), the financing of the common agricultural policy (^{9}), a proposal for amendment of the constituent acts of Community bodies following the adoption of the new Financial Regulation (^{10}), a Commission regulation on the framework financial regulation for the bodies referred to in Article 185 of the Financial Regulation applicable to the general budget (^{11}), the proposal for a regulation on the Financial Regulation applicable to the ninth European Development Fund in the framework of partnership with the ACP countries (^{12}) and a draft Commission regulation laying down detailed rules for the implementation of Regulation (EC, Euratom) No 1605/2002 (^{13}) on the Financial Regulation applicable to the general budget of the European Communities (^{14}).

European Central Bank (^{15})

1107. Composition of the ECB. By Decision 2002/386/EC (^{16}) of 23 May, taken on the recommendation of the Council (^{17}), Mr Lucas Papademos was appointed Vice-President of the ECB to replace Mr Christian Noyer.

(^{1}) Bull. 9-2002, point 1.9.19.
(^{2}) OJ C 326, 27.12.2002; Bull. 9-2002, point 1.9.20.
(^{3}) OJ C 326, 27.12.2002; Bull. 9-2002, point 1.9.21.
(^{4}) Opinion No 2/2002 (OJ C 92, 17.4.2002; Bull. 1/2-2002, point 1.9.29).
(^{5}) Opinion No 4/2002 (OJ C 225, 20.9.2002; Bull. 7/8-2002, point 1.10.14).
(^{6}) Opinion No 5/2002 (OJ C 236, 1.10.2002; Bull. 7/8-2002, point 1.10.15).
(^{7}) Opinion No 6/2002 (OJ C 236, 1.10.2002; Bull. 7/8-2002, point 1.10.16).
(^{8}) Opinion No 7/2002 (OJ C 236, 1.10.2002; Bull. 7/8-2002, point 1.10.17).
(^{9}) Opinion No 9/2002 (OJ C 285, 21.11.2002; Bull. 9-2002, point 1.9.22).
(^{10}) Opinion No 10/2002 (OJ C 285, 21.11.2002; Bull. 9-2002, point 1.9.23).
(^{11}) Opinion No 11/2002 (Bull. 9-2002, point 1.9.24).
(^{12}) Opinion No 12/2002.
(^{13}) OJ L 248, 16.9.2002; Bull. 6-2002, point 1.7.2.
(^{14}) Opinion No 13/2002.
(^{15}) http://www.ecb.int/.
(^{16}) OJ L 137, 25.5.2002; Bull. 5-2002, point 1.3.1.
(^{17}) OJ L 101, 17.4.2002; Bull. 4-2002, point 1.3.1.

1108.   *Activities of the ECB.* The activities of the European Central Bank and monetary policy are discussed in Section 1 ('Economic and monetary policy') of Chapter III *(→ point 68).*

European Economic and Social Committee (¹)

1109.   *Plenary sessions.* In the course of its nine plenary sessions in 2002, the European Economic and Social Committee (EESC) adopted 176 opinions and one information report. Of these opinions, 74 were on matters where consultation was mandatory, 56 were on matters where it was optional, and 46 were own-initiative opinions (including 5 exploratory opinions).

1110.   *New title.* On 17 July, the committee amended its Rules of Procedure, formally changing its name to European Economic and Social Committee (²).

1111.   *EESC priorities.* The committee played an active part in work on the major priorities on the European agenda. In March, it adopted a substantial opinion on governance *(→ point 15),* using its position as a bridge between the EU and civil society to make an effective and valuable contribution to the debate initiated by the White Paper on governance. The committee signalled its concern with economic and social cohesion by adopting opinions on the broad economic policy guidelines for the Member States *(→ point 59),* the economic policies of the euro-zone countries *(→ point 59)* and corporate social responsibility *(→ point 129).* The committee also had its say in the debate over the future of the CAP, issuing an own-initiative opinion *(→ point 394).* At its October plenary session, the committee elected Mr Roger Briesch, previously chairman of the Employee's Group and a member of the committee since 1990, as its new President. At the December session, the new President set out some of the priority lines of action for the EESC in its work programme for 2002–04. These included optimising the committee's role as a consultative body to Parliament, the Council and the Commission by stepping up cooperation, improving its representativeness and credibility as an institutional representative of civil society and reinforcing its presence in the debate on the future of Europe.

1112.   *Leading figures involved in EESC work.* The committee played host to a number of leading figures in 2002: Mr Dehaene, Vice-President of the convention, Mr Liikanen, member of the Commission, Ms de Palacio, Vice-President of the Commission, who reported on progress on the Lisbon strategy, Ms Diamantopoulou, member of the Commission, Mr Frederiksen, Danish Employment

---

(¹) http://www.ces.eu.int/index800.htm.
(²) OJ L 268, 4.10.2002.

Minister, who set out the Danish Presidency's priorities for employment, Mr Verheugen, member of the Commission, and Mr Cox, President of Parliament.

1113.   Cooperation between the Commission and the EESC. As in previous years, Ms de Palacio, Vice-President of the Commission responsible for relations with the EESC, sent the committee an indicative list of topics arising from the Commission's work programme for 2002 (¹) on which its opinion would be appreciated, as a way of helping the committee organise its work.

1114.   Consultations on Commission opinions. Of the committee's 176 opinions, 74 were on matters where consultation is mandatory. The most notable of these concerned: the Solidarity Fund *(→ point 362)*, giving unqualified approval to the Commission's proposal for the Solidarity Fund to be operational by the end of the year; working conditions for temporary workers *(→ point 130)*, supporting the Commission's proposal for a directive and emphasising the need to uphold the principle of non-discrimination; the single sky — air-traffic management action programme *(→ point 661)* and the sixth RTD framework programme *(→ point 299)*.

Of the 56 opinions on matters where consultation was optional, special mention should be made of those on the review of the single market strategy *(→ point 146)*, European transport policy for 2010 *(→ point 629)*, the social policy agenda *(→ point 111)*, and the open method of coordination for immigration and asylum policy *(→ point 466)*.

1115.   Right of initiative. The committee exercised its right of initiative on 41 occasions in 2002. The main opinions concerned the Lisbon strategy, the future of cohesion policy in the context of enlargement, direct company taxation, and European governance.

1116.   Exploratory opinions. In response to requests from members of the Commission the committee issued five exploratory opinions on transport security *(→ point 631)*, services of general interest *(→ point 171)*, the coordination of economic policies *(→ point 58)*, options for the reform of pension schemes *(→ point 118)* and simplifying and improving the regulatory environment *(→ point 25)*.

1117.   Establishment plan. At 31 December, the establishment plan of the committee comprised 501 permanent posts and 18 temporary posts, including 340 posts in the joint services with the Committee of the Regions.

(¹) 2001 General Report, point 1210.

Committee of the Regions (¹)

1118. *Plenary sessions.* At its six plenary sessions, the committee adopted 44 opinions and two resolutions. Of the opinions, 12 were on matters where consultation was mandatory and 32 where it was optional; 10 were own-initiative opinions.

1119. *Committee's priorities.* The committee began its work in 2002 by electing a new Bureau, which in turn elected its new President, Sir Albert Bore (PES/UK). The committee went on to adopt an opinion on European governance (→ *point 14*), in which it called for the regions to be involved in drawing up the European agenda. It subsequently adopted a resolution on sustainable development (→ *point 556*), welcoming the conclusions of the Gothenburg and Barcelona European Councils and urging the Community institutions to put them into practice. The committee played an active part in the work of the convention, in particular, by submitting its contribution (→ *point 14*), in which it reaffirmed its full support for the process of European integration and called for the European Union's current three-pillar legal structure to be simplified. It also set out its expectations of the convention, calling for recognition of its status as an institution and for its early involvement in the phase prior to the drawing-up of new policies likely to have an impact on the regional and local authorities.

1120. *Leading figures involved in its work.* The committee placed great importance on the debates with the members of the Commission and the representatives of the Council Presidency. In this connection, it welcomed the presence of Mr Lucas Jimenez on behalf of the Spanish Presidency, who presented his country's priorities for its six-month term, Mr Verheugen, for the Commission, who set out the strategy for enlarging the EU to include 10 new countries, Mr Haarder, Danish Minister for Foreign Affairs, who explained the priorities of the Danish Presidency, Mr Amato, Vice-Chairman of the convention, to whom it conveyed its aspirations for the outcome of the convention, and Mr Vitorino, member of the Commission, with whom it conducted an in-depth debate on the European Union's new information and communication strategy.

1121. *Cooperation with the Commission.* As has been the tradition since 1995, Ms de Palacio, for the Commission, sent the committee a list of items from its 2002 work programme (²) on which it was hoped the committee would make a contribution. She likewise kept the committee informed of the Commission's position in two reports about action taken to follow up its opinions.

1122. *Establishment plan.* At 31 December, the Committee of the Regions' establishment plan comprised 231 permanent posts and 19 temporary posts,

---

(¹) http://www.cor.eu.int/.
(²) 2001 General Report, point 1210.

including 131 posts in the joint services with the European Economic and Social Committee.

ECSC Consultative Committee [1]

1123.   Expiry of the ECSC Treaty [2]. Information about the expiry of the ECSC Treaty can be found in Section 11 ('Expiry of the ECSC Treaty') of Chapter I *(→ points 39 to 41).*

1124.   Committee sessions. In 2002, the Consultative Committee under the chairmanship of Mr Enrico Gibellieri — the Vice-Chairmen being Mr Wolfgang Reichel and Mr John O'Shea — held three ordinary sessions. On 27 June, a special session was held in Luxembourg to conclude the work of the Consultative Committee and mark the end of the Treaty establishing the European Coal and Steel Community.

1125.   Committee's activities. On being formally consulted by the Commission, the committee gave its view on the draft Commission decision on the position to be taken by the ECSC within the joint committee established by the agreement between the ECSC and Turkey on trade in products covered by the ECSC Treaty [3], the draft Commission decisions on the conclusion of agreements between the ECSC and Kazakhstan, Russia and Ukraine respectively on trade in certain steel products [4], and the draft Commission decisions on administering certain restrictions on imports of certain steel products from Kazakhstan, Russia and Ukraine [5]. The committee also gave its view on the position to be adopted by the Community within the Association Council established by the Europe Agreement with Poland with regard to an extension of the period foreseen in Article 8(4) of Protocol No 2 to the agreement, the conclusion of additional protocols to the Europe Agreements with the Czech Republic, Bulgaria and Romania respectively with regard to an extension of the period foreseen in Article 8(4) of Protocol No 2 to the Europe Agreement with the Czech Republic, Article 9(4) of Protocol No 2 to the Europe Agreement with Bulgaria and Article 9(4) of Protocol No 2 to the Europe Agreement with Romania [3], draft decisions on granting financial aid to technical steel [3] and coal [3] research projects, and the reports on the Community market for solid fuels in 2001 (final document) [3] and 2002 [3]. The committee also adopted an opinion on the Commission communication, 'European Union strategy for sustainable development' [3] and resolutions on the establishment of the Consultative Sub-

[1] http://europa.eu.int/comm/secretariat_general/sga/ceca/index_en.htm.
[2] http://europa.eu.int/ecsc/index_en.htm.
[3] Bull. 1/2-2002, point 1.9.41.
[4] Bull. 4-2002, point 1.9.16.
[5] Bull. 6-2002, point 1.9.22.

committee for Coal, Steel and Industrial Conversion (CSCSIC) within the European Economic and Social Committee and the criteria for appointing the 30 members from the ECSC industries [1], the decision by the President of the United States to introduce measures to protect the US steel industry [2] and, at the final session of the Consultative Committee, the legacy of the ECSC [3].

The Consultative Committee also held exchanges of views with the Commission on the application in 2001 of the Community rules for State aid to the coal industry [2], the Steel Aid Code [2], the multisectoral framework on regional aid for large investment projects and rescue and restructuring aid and closure aid for the steel sector [2], the Green Paper on the review of the merger regulation [2], the sectoral consequences of the expiry of the ECSC Treaty [3], certain aspects of the treatment of competition cases resulting from the expiry of the ECSC Treaty [3], and the regulation on State aid to the coal industry [3]. Exchanges of views were also held on the report on the Community market for solid fuels in 2001 and the outlook for 2002 [3], the monitoring of steel aid under Article 95 of the ECSC Treaty, the proposal for a Council regulation laying down transitional provisions concerning anti-dumping and compensatory measures adopted pursuant to Commission Decisions No 2277/96/ECSC and No 1889/98/ECSC as well as pending anti-dumping and anti-subsidy investigations, complaints and applications pursuant to those decisions [3] and Regulation (EC) No 560/2002 imposing provisional safeguard measures against imports of certain steel products [3].

TABLE 31

Legislative instruments enacted, repealed or expiring in 2002 [1]

Enacting institutions	Number of instruments	Regulations	Directives	Decisions	Recommendations
Parliament and Council	enacted in 2002	24	36	6	0
	repealed or expiring in 2002	5	3	4	4
Council alone	enacted in 2002	140	113	51	10
	repealed or expiring in 2002	144	48	21	1
Commission	enacted in 2002	602	44	610	17
	repealed or expiring in 2002	398	32	178	3

[1] Data received on 22 January 2003, from CELEX, the interinstitutional computerised documentation system on Community law (→ points 1072 and 1073), excluding instruments not published in the *Official Journal of the European Communities* and instruments listed in light type (routine management instruments valid for a limited period).

[1] Bull. 1/2-2002, point 1.9.41.
[2] Bull. 4-2002, point 1.9.16.
[3] Bull. 6-2002, point 1.9.22.

Section 2

Administration and management (¹)

Staff policy and Staff Regulations

Changes to the Staff Regulations

1126.   Auxiliary staff. By Regulation (EC, ECSC, Euratom) No 490/2002 of 18 March 2002, the Council extended the maximum duration of contracts of auxiliary staff to three years (Table II).

Equal opportunities and non-discrimination

1127.   Annual recruitment targets. To promote gender balance in category A, the targets for the recruitment and appointment of women in 2002 aimed for six women to be appointed to director-general and deputy director-general (grade A 1) or director (grade A 2) posts, including one paid from the 'Research' budget (one was appointed in grade A 1 and five in grade A 2), women to account for at least 20 % of appointments to middle management posts (heads of unit and advisors) (29 % were appointed), and as many women as possible to be recruited from the external reserve lists, with equal numbers of men and women recruited as far as the lists permit (56 women and 133 men were recruited in 2002).

1128.   Non-discrimination. As part of the reform *(→ points 1150 to 1153)*, new Staff Regulation provisions have been proposed on the definition of disability, moral and sexual harassment, and protection against discrimination in all its forms. To enable its staff to reconcile their professional and private lives better, the Commission also proposed improved family-related leave provisions and the introduction of more flexible working conditions. In addition, facilities with special computer equipment, allowing Internet access by the visually impaired, amongst others, were opened at the Albert Borschette Conference Centre in Brussels.

(¹) Additional information is available on the Europa server (http://europa.eu.int/comm/dgs/personnel_administration/index_en.htm).

Fixing and paying entitlements — Remuneration

1129.   In accordance with the method adopted in 1991 (¹) and extended to 30 June 2003 (²), the Council decided, on 16 December, to adjust remuneration (+ 2 %) with effect from 1 July 2002 (³) for all places of employment. Moreover, on 23 January, the Commission decided to adjust the daily subsistence allowances for missions outside the European Union. As part of the Commission reform, proposals were also made to simplify and modernise the system of staff allowances and to integrate the salary adjustment method into the Staff Regulations.

Career development

1130.   General implementing provisions were laid down for the new system of staff reports and promotion, and special reform-related training courses were organised. The first promotion exercise under the new system is to be carried out from 2003. The Commission also adopted guidelines on mobility and job descriptions in February. A job description exercise was carried out for all departments in the second half of 2002. Moreover, as part of its reform, the Commission proposed a new career structure based on two function groups rather than the existing four categories of officials. It also proposed the inclusion of 'contract agents' as a new type of employment in the conditions of employment of other servants of the European Communities.

Recruitment

1131.   *Open competitions.* In the course of 2002, the Commission launched a number of open competitions for categories A, B and C, with a view to drawing up reserve lists comprising over 1 500 successful candidates for potential recruitment between 2002 and 2003. These included open competitions to recruit administrators in the fields of finance and contracts, as well as environment, agriculture, fisheries and research. Internal competitions for transfer between categories and to upgrade staff were also published at the end of May, and should result in 343 successful candidates.

(¹) Twenty-fifth General Report, point 1198; Twenty-sixth General Report, point 1134.
(²) Council Regulation (EC, ECSC, Euratom) No 2805/2000 (OJ L 326, 22.12.2000; 2000 General Report, point 1185).
(³) Regulation (EC, Euratom) No 2265/2002 (OJ L 347, 20.12.2002).

Preparing for enlargement

1132.   Preparatory work involving the administrative aspects of enlargement continued and was intensified in 2002, both within the Commission and at interinstitutional level. An interim report on the measures undertaken and still pending, setting a timetable for those measures, was produced in July and transmitted to the European Parliament in September.

Joint sickness insurance scheme

1133.   The financial equilibrium of the scheme is still secure for at least the next 10 years, despite budgetary pressure as a result of the progressive ageing of the insured population. The aggregate surplus constitutes an adequate cushion to contend with this situation and with unforeseeable short-term situations.

Pensions

1134.   As part of the reform, the Commission proposed to the Council changes to the pension scheme, centred on achieving a better actuarial balance, neutrality in transfers of national pension rights to the Community scheme and a new approach to invalidity pensions and cost of living weightings.

Buildings policy and management; management of services and infrastructure

1135.   Within the framework of its communication of 16 December 1999 (¹), the Commission improved the terms of purchase of its new buildings by separating the process agreeing a price from the financing mechanism, and making use of a legal provision allowing it to benefit from the best interest rates available on the financial market. It also continued its purchase programme, increasing the number of buildings owned by the Commission from 49 to 51 %. The development of specific computer programs and deconcentration further improve the management of office space.

Interinstitutional cooperation

1136.   *Training.* Training in the languages of the applicant countries having been extended to all such languages (with the exception of Maltese), training

---

(¹) COM(1999) 713; 1999 General Report, point 1079.

opportunities in this area have been offered to the staff of all Community institutions.

1137.   Personnel Selection Office. On 25 July, the Secretaries-General of the European Parliament, the Council and the Commission, the Registrar of the Court of Justice, the Secretaries-General of the Court of Auditors, the European Economic and Social Committee, the Committee of the Regions, and the Representative of the European Ombudsman adopted Decision 2002/621/EC on the organisation and operation of the European Communities Personnel Selection Office ([1]).

Social policy and welfare at work

1138.   As part of the reform, the Commission modernised its social policy for staff in active employment and their families, and for retired staff. Under 'service agreements', the unit responsible will provide a client-oriented service facilitating integration, inclusion and the reconciliation of private and professional life, while consolidating a policy of prevention and organising accompanying activities, assistance and acknowledgement of work done.

Discipline

1139.   To improve the application of the obligations incumbent upon its officials under the Staff Regulations and of rules on professional ethics, the Commission adopted, on 19 February, a decision on the conduct of administrative inquiries and disciplinary proceedings. This decision sets up the Investigation and Disciplinary Office (IDOC). The publication of disciplinary decisions is an administrative practice that has not always been followed systematically, and will henceforth be incorporated into the IDOC activity report. The Commission also adopted, on 4 April, a decision on raising concerns about serious wrongdoings ('whistleblowing'): all officials must inform without delay the European Anti-Fraud Office (→ *points 1055 to 1059*) or their superior of any evidence which gives rise to a presumption of the existence of serious irregularities. The decision also provides protection for any official acting in accordance with this obligation, including where they further disclose this information, under certain conditions, in the absence of a response. In addition, as part of the reform, the Commission proposed amendments to the Staff Regulations to rationalise provisions on the opening and conduct of administrative or disciplinary proceedings, stabilise the composition of the disciplinary board and adapt the rules for suspending officials.

([1]) OJ L 197, 26.7.2002; Bull. 7/8-2002, point 1.10.7.

Information technology (¹)

1140.   Following the memorandum of June 2001 on the *e*Commission (²), general guidelines were laid down to support the implementation of reform initiatives and achieve this plan. The steering committee set up to this end produced a roadmap and work plan. It also identified the need to improve coordination of the existing administrative processes and further integrate the computer systems used in management.

1141.   In operational terms, 2002 saw the establishment of a contingency plan for 10 priority computer systems. The migration to a new reference configuration continued. A lot of work was put into developing 'corporate' computer systems for human resources management, budgetary management and setting up a central contracts database in collaboration with the horizontal departments concerned. Generalised access to the 'Europe by Satellite' broadcasts was opened up via the internal network. In addition, on 19 June, operational departments and the IT community met in a symposium to take stock of the progress made in implementing the *e*Commission project and to present the initial results achieved in fields such as the strategic planning of Commission actions, resource management, the introduction of a service culture, and electronic document management.

Translation (³)

1142.   *Strategic approach.* In 2002, the Translation Service stepped up the administrative preparations for enlargement so that it would be in a position to respond to this unprecedented challenge. In this context the Commission approved, in April, a communication on a strategy for the Translation Service (⁴), defining its mission as being to enable the Commission, in the most efficient and cost-effective way, to meet its legal and political obligations and needs with respect to the languages in which it has to conduct its written communications. In addition, as part of the new activity-based management introduced throughout the Commission, in June, the Translation Service set up an interdepartmental working group to examine ways of making better use of Commission translation resources and optimising control of demand for translations.

1143.   *Activities.* With particular regard to quality assurance within the context of the simplification of the language process, the Translation Service pro-

(¹) http://europa.eu.int/comm/di/index_en.htm.
(²) SEC(2001) 924; 2001 General Report, point 1253.
(³) http://europa.eu.int/comm/translation/en/index.html.
(⁴) SEC(2002) 382.

vided the following main services: translation, editing originals (4 317 pages), and summarising original documents (1 576 pages in writing and 855 pages orally). In 2002, it translated a total of 1 303 240 pages, including 3 456 pages out of and 5 600 pages into non-Community languages. Freelance translators accounted for 269 091 pages of translation and 9 400 pages of rapid post-editing of machine translations.

1144. Preparing for enlargement. The Translation Service continued language training for its translators with a view to meeting future needs, intensified contacts with the appropriate bodies in the applicant countries and started preparing for the establishment of local translation offices in those countries.

1145. Interinstitutional approach. The Translation Service continued its work in a number of areas, including within the Interinstitutional Committee for Translation and Interpreting (CITI), with a view to achieving synergy between the institutions in the language field. In 2002, the Translation Centre for Bodies of the European Union had a staff of 141 (including 66 LA officials) and translated 227 798 pages.

Interpreting and conferences [1]

1146. Preparing for enlargement. In 2002, the Joint Interpreting and Conference Service (SCIC) continued to focus on preparing for enlargement, an unprecedented challenge involving the addition of 10 new languages once the new Member States join the European Union. The strategy to this end, set out in the communication 'Conference interpreting and enlargement' [2], approved by the Commission on 9 April, recognises multilingualism as essential to ensuring the democratic legitimacy of the work of the European Union, while underlining the need to control costs by marrying requirements with the resources available. In pursuit of this objective, and in order to ensure the availability of sufficient high-quality interpreters, the SCIC has encouraged and promoted the training of interpreters in candidate countries and has made efforts to train its own staff in the use of language in these countries.

1147. Service agreements. In parallel with the objectives centred on enlargement, the SCIC has taken steps to improve the management of demand for its services by means of 'service agreements' with its main clients and the introduction of a new computer system for reserving interpreting and conference facilities.

[1] http://europa.eu.int/comm/scic/index_en.htm.
[2] SEC(2002) 349.

1148.   *Interinstitutional cooperation.* In June, in light of the conclusions of a working group specially mandated by the secretaries-general of the European institutions to examine any synergies and economies that might be gained from cooperation between the services concerned, the SCIC joined the extended Interinstitutional Committee for Translation and Interpreting (CITI). A new interpreting coordination unit, operational since September, is helping improve collaboration between the SCIC and the European Parliament and Court of Justice interpreting services. Agreements have also been reached for organising interinstitutional recruitment competitions for interpreters from the candidate countries and sharing their services.

1149.   *Activities.* In 2002, the activities of the SCIC concentrated on its central function of providing interpreting for the Commission, the Council and the other institutions and bodies for which it works. The overall tightening of budgetary discipline has produced a slight reduction in these services, with a total of 139 438 interpreter-days and 11 162 meeting days (146 249 and 11 767 respectively in 2001). The SCIC has also continued to organise conferences and provide consultancy services for the Commission departments. Concentrating on major events, it helped organise 36 conferences in 2002 (48 in 2001), with a total of around 23 000 participants (compared with 18 500 in 2001).

Section 3

Reform of the Commission (¹)

1150. *General approach.* The Commission continued and consolidated its implementation of the measures set out in the action plan reflecting the main points of the White Paper on reform adopted in March 2000 (²).

1151. *Development of a service-based culture.* As part of the modernisation and simplification of its working methods and progress towards an *e*Commission, on 23 January, the Commission amended (³) its Rules of Procedure (⁴) as regards the administration of its documents, principally in order to set up in due course an effective electronic system for administration and archiving.

1152. *Definition of priorities and efficient management of resources.* Now that the annual policy strategy (APS) exercise forms a well-established part of its practice, throughout the year the Commission held discussions with the other institutions on the priorities announced in the orientation debate in December 2001 *(→ point 1093)*. In connection with the activity-based management process, on 24 July, the Commission presented a synthesis of the annual activity reports for 2001 (⁵) which the directors-general are now required to produce as part of the new approach stemming from the reform.

In its communication of 28 May (⁶), the Commission set out guidelines on providing a legal framework within which the departments of the European institutions could set up office-type structures to carry out administrative and support duties. Unlike executive agencies, whose lifespan is closely linked to that of the programmes with which they are concerned and for which the Commission has proposed a framework regulation (⁷), the new offices will have permanent duties linked to a Commission department. On 6 November, the Commission set up three offices, a Paymaster's office responsible for determining, calculating and paying the individual entitlements of officials and two offices for infrastructure and logistics, one in Luxembourg and the other in Brussels, to deal with work on buildings policy and to manage the staff welfare infrastructure (⁸).

(¹) Further information is available on the Europa server (http://europa.eu.int/comm/reform/index_en.htm).
(²) COM(2000) 200; 2000 General Report, points 1205 to 1211.
(³) Decision 2002/47/EC, ECSC, Euratom (OJ L 21, 24.1.2002).
(⁴) OJ L 308, 8.12.2000.
(⁵) COM(2002) 426; Bull. 7/8-2002, point 1.10.8.
(⁶) COM(2002) 264; Bull. 5-2002, point 1.9.10.
(⁷) COM(2000) 788; 2000 General Report, point 1207.
(⁸) Bull. 11-2002, point 1.10.13.

As part of the reform begun by its communication of 16 May 2000 on the management of Community external assistance (¹), the Commission began the process of decentralising such management to its delegations, which is a key element of the reform. Since the aim is to extend the process of decentralisation to delegations located in 78 countries receiving assistance from the Community, it is taking place in three phases:

• an initial phase affecting 21 delegations, which are now working in a decentralised fashion;

• 24 of the 27 delegations affected by the second phase will enjoy decentralisation at the end of 2002;

• technical preparatory work on the third phase, affecting 30 delegations in the ACP States, has begun with a view to decentralisation at the end of 2003.

Besides the geographical programmes (EDF for the ACP States, CARDS for the western Balkans, Tacis for eastern Europe, MEDA for the Mediterranean, EPRD for South Africa, specific programmes for Asia and Latin America), once the simplification of budget structures and harmonisation of procedures has been achieved, decentralisation should also cover the implementation of the thematic or horizontal budget headings (food security, human rights and democracy, refugees, etc.).

1153.   *Human resources.* On 24 April, the Commission tabled a proposal for a regulation amending the Staff Regulations of Officials of the European Communities and the conditions of employment of other servants (Table II). This is the formal legislative proposal stemming from the reform package adopted by the Commission on 20 December 2001 (²), and includes some of the amendments adopted by the Staff Regulations Committee and the views expressed during the concertation process by the staff unions and professional associations. In its conclusions of 15 April (³), the Council expressed its support for the approach to staff policy on which the Commission had embarked.

On 5 June, the Commission adopted a communication setting out the impact of enlargement in terms of extra human resources (⁴). The aspects relating to conference interpreting were covered in its communication of 9 April (→ *point 1146).*

(¹) 2000 General Report, point 1207.
(²) SEC(2001) 2030; 2001 General Report, point 1264.
(³) Bull. 4-2002, point 1.9.7.
(⁴) COM(2002) 311; Bull. 6-2002, point 1.9.16.

On 25 July, a joint decision by the various Community bodies and institutions set up a Personnel Selection Office for European Community staff (→ *point 1137*). Specific provisions covering Commission management staff have been made or are planned (→ *point 1130*).

1154. Other information relating to the reform of the Commission may be found in Section 2 ('Administration and management') of this chapter (→ *points 1126 to 1149*).

Chapter X

Information and communication

Section 1

Information activities

1155. *General developments.* In 2002, the Commission continued to provide its various services, through a process of modernisation and innovation in line with the strategy adopted in 2001: decentralisation, integrated approach and partnerships with civil society, targeted information campaigns, sounding out citizens (opinion polls), Prince programme, greater collaboration between European Parliament offices and Commission representations in the Member States, new joint actions with the Member States. An evaluation methodology was also devised.

1156. *Representations in the Member States.* The 23 representations (15 in the capitals and eight in certain regions), were assigned a more prominent role as information relays for the media and citizens, providing a source of communication tailored to the specific national and local requirements of each Member State. As regards communication aimed at the general public, the Commission representations run, in cooperation with the European Parliament and the Member States, major information campaigns designed to raise public awareness of key European issues.

1157. *Networks and relays*(¹). On this front, the two objectives pursued in 2002 were geared to boosting collaboration and developing a new approach in line with the strategy introduced in 2001 (²). The network of documentation centres (EDCs) was upgraded by updating the directory, renewing contacts, the programming of meetings and rationalisation moves in the candidate countries. With the start-up of the Rome centre's activities, the major national and inter-regional centres were further consolidated and rationalised. The general assemblies of the Info-points Europe (IPE) and the rural information and promotion

---

(¹) http://europa.eu.int/comm/relays/index_en.htm.
(²) 2001 General Report, point 1278.

'carrefours', held in Trieste and Oldenburg respectively, paved the way for implementation of the new information and communication strategy. Representatives of the European Parliament, the Council, the Commission, the Committee of the Regions and the European Economic and Social Committee attended these general assemblies for the first time, and a dedicated Internet web site was opened. On the basis of priorities set by the Commission, a new approach was adopted for selecting projects for the European Movement and the Federation of Europe Houses. A procedure for analysing and evaluating all the relays and networks was launched with a view to establishing a single, second-generation multifunction network.

1158. *Europa* (¹). The Europa server on the Internet continued to host information from all the European Union institutions. It houses several million documents and more than 50 databases, which the public can access free of charge in most cases. Over the year, some 500 million documents were consulted or downloaded from the site. The main users were businesses, national authorities, universities, non-governmental organisations and the media. Mindful of the server's key strategic value, the Commission continued with setting up on-line information, interactive communication and transaction services under the 'Europa second generation (E2G)' project adopted in 2001 (²).

1159. *Publications.* In 2002, the Commission published, in the 11 official languages, 15 brochures and leaflets giving general information on the European Union's achievements and major topics of interest. A leaflet containing general information on the Union was also published in the languages of the candidate countries. As many as 17 million copies were distributed.

1160. *Audiovisual services.* The year 2002 saw the introduction of a 'TV and radio communication strategy' aimed at producing messages in key policy areas and establishing a closer partnership with the Member States. Initiatives were launched with television channels in some Member States to make programmes covering such issues as enlargement. Arrangements were also made to assist television journalists in the candidate countries, including the broadcasting on Europe by Satellite (EbS) of their material, and the schedule was revised to give more prominence to live transmission and more interinstitutional coverage, e.g. the work of the Convention on the Future of the Union (→ *points 8 to 10*) and the Council's public debates.

1161. *Public opinion.* This fundamental activity, gauging current public opinion, encompasses a wide range of products: a total of 63 surveys were carried out and some 370 000 citizens were interviewed. Particular emphasis was placed on Commission priorities, such as monitoring the introduction of the

---

(¹) http://europa.eu.int/.
(²) 2001 General Report, point 1279.

euro and enlargement. The exploitation of results also included summary notes on specific topics (the common foreign and security policy, sustainable development, young people and European integration, etc.). The Commission will henceforth discuss the Eurobarometer results twice a year. Within the Commission, closer cooperation was achieved with spokespersons and the offices and representations, as well as with the European Parliament and the Council, the Convention on the Future of the European Union and the Member States. The revamped public opinion[1] web site received more than 1 million hits for consultation or downloading over the year. Around 1 000 press articles were identified in the media.

1162. *Europe Direct*[2]. The Commission continued to operate this service, which was inaugurated in May 2000[3]. Access was made easier with the introduction, in July, of a single new freephone number[4] to replace the 16 numbers previously used. The visibility and use of 'Europe Direct' also grew.

---

[1] http://europa.eu.int/comm/public_opinion/index.htm.
[2] http://europa.eu.int/europedirect/.
[3] 2000 General Report, point 1212.
[4] 00 800 6 7 8 9 10 11.

Section 2

Press and communication activities (¹)

1163. The reforms launched in the press and communication field in 2000 and 2001 (²), were continued and consolidated in 2002 with intense activity on the media front reflected in a number of major campaigns including preparations for and launching of the campaign on enlargement and continuation of the campaign on the future of Europe.

1164. On 2 July, the Commission adopted a communication on information and communication (³) defining the content and methodology for implementation of the new strategy for which the institutional and operational framework was established in 2001 (⁴). The basic objectives of the approach proposed in the 2002 communication are:

- to provide the European Union with a genuine capacity to formulate and disseminate appropriate and targeted messages on various priority information topics drawing on a common reference framework;

- to establish a voluntary working partnership with the Member States based on a memorandum of understanding fostering genuine synergy between their structures and know-how and the activities of the European Union;

- to redefine and redesign an 'image' for the European Union and highlight its strengths.

Decentralisation is the key to the strategy and the focus will be on a small number of topics related to Europe: the area of freedom, security and justice, enlargement, the future of the European Union and Europe's role in the world.

The Committee of the Regions delivered an opinion on the Commission communication on 21 November (⁵) and the Council adopted conclusions on it on 10 December, in which it endorsed the four topics selected by the Commission, stressed that the information activities of the European Union institutions should be coordinated with those of the Member States and called on the Member States to take full advantage of the opportunities provided by the new strategy (⁶).

(¹) Further information is available on the Europa server (http://europa.eu.int/comm/dgs/press_communication/index_en.htm).
(²) 2000 General Report, point 1223; 2001 General Report, point 1277.
(³) COM(2002) 350; Bull. 7/8-2002, point 1.8.1.
(⁴) COM(2001) 354; 2001 General Report, point 1278.
(⁵) Bull. 11-2002, point 1.8.1.
(⁶) Bull. 12-2002, point 1.8.1.

Section 3

Activities of the Office for Official Publications of the European Communities (¹)

1165. New initiatives. In 2002, in addition to the work involved in projects already under way, the office launched other large-scale projects, including, in particular, the creation of a common Internet portal for the publications of the institutions and agencies and the setting up of a digital bookshop — known as the EU-Bookshop — coupled with an exhaustive electronic archive of publications and a mechanism for printing on request.

1166. Continuation of previous work. Among the projects already under way, mention should be made of the continuing work to consolidate Community legislation, which is due to be completed in 2003, and the development and marketing, since July, of a new version of the CD-ROM containing the *Official Journal of the European Communities*, L and C series. The office is also heavily involved in pre-enlargement work with a view to the publication of the Community *acquis* in the languages of the candidate countries (70 000 pages in each of the nine future official languages).

1167. EUR-Lex portal (²). After the whole body of Community legislation and case-law was made available to the public free of charge on line from 1 January, there was a very rapid increase in visits to the EUR-Lex portal. At the same time, the portal was improved by extending document coverage and adding new functions *(→ point 1072).*

(¹) Further information is available on the Internet (http://publications.eu.int/general/en/index_en.htm).
(²) http://europa.eu.int/eur-lex/en/index.html.

Section 4

Historical archives (^{1})

1168.   *Public release.* The Commission released for consultation, under the 30-year rule (^{2}), the historical archives of the ECSC High Authority, the EEC Commission, the Euratom Commission and the Commission of the European Communities for 1971 (^{3}), thereby adding 2 200 files to the 41 600 already made available to the public since 1952 in the case of the ECSC, since 1958 in the case of the EEC and Euratom and since 1967 in the case of the EC. Following the exceptional transfer of around 1.2 million files to a new archive depot in the Brussels region, the Archis database, set up in 1992 (^{4}), was adapted to the requirements of the new depot in order to facilitate and rationalise the management of transfers, research and file conservation. This measure falls in line with the Commission's initiative to encourage the transparency and accessibility of its documents *(→ point 21)*, given that they form part of Europe's archive heritage. On 19 August, the Commission proposed amendments to Regulation (EEC) No 354/83 concerning the opening to the public of the historical archives of the European Economic Community and the European Atomic Energy Community (^{5}) to bring it into line with Regulation (EC) No 1049/2001 regarding public access to European Parliament, Council and Commission documents (^{6}) (Table II). As part of its internal reform, the Commission launched a process aimed at modernising document administration *(→ point 1151)*.

1169.   *Publications.* The Commission published and distributed to interested parties the proceedings of the third DLM forum, *Access to and preservation of electronic information: best practices and solutions,* held in Barcelona from 6 to 8 May (^{7}). During the forum, the meaning of the acronym DLM was changed; it now stands for 'Document lifecycle management'. Keen to encourage measures to preserve archives in the short and long term, to ensure their transparency and to open up access to the public, the Commission welcomed the forum's conclusions on, among other things, the use of reference models for managing electronic documents in a number of European countries (^{8}), while also contributing to the strengthening of a European DLM network. It also continued publishing

---

(^{1}) Further information is available on the Europa server (http://europa.eu.int/historical_archives/intro_en.htm).
(^{2}) OJ L 43, 15.2.1983; Seventeenth General Report, point 54.
(^{3}) The historical archives files are kept at the European University Institute in Florence.
(^{4}) Twenty-sixth General Report, point 1162.
(^{5}) OJ L 43, 15.2.1983.
(^{6}) OJ L 145, 31.5.2001; 2001 General Report, point 21.
(^{7}) http://europa.eu.int/historical_archives/dlm_forum/.
(^{8}) 2001 General Report, point 1283.

the six-monthly newsletter *INSAR — Information summary on archives* ([1]), carried on updating the experts' report entitled *Archives in the European Union* ([2]) and published the third volume in the series of inventories of the ECSC High Authority files ([3]). It also contributed to various conferences on archives, in particular: the meetings between directors of national archives in the Member States and the applicant countries to discuss the coordination of archives in Europe (Valladolid, 11 and 12 March; Copenhagen, 10 and 11 October); the European conference on relations between the archives of the Member States and the archives of Hungary (Budapest, 6 June); the plenary session of archivists of foreign ministries (Madrid, 17 June); the European conference on the expiry of the ECSC Treaty (Luxembourg, 27 June); the congress of German archivists on the theme of 'Archives and research' (Trier, 17 and 18 September); and the seminar of European experts on methods of describing and opening up access to digitalised archives (Copenhagen, 21 and 22 November).

---

[1] 1996 General Report, point 654; Internet (http://europa.eu.int/historical_archives/insar_en.htm).
[2] 1994 General Report, point 710.
[3] Previous volume: 1999 General Report, point 1115.

The year in brief

January

1   The single currency is put into circulation and the dual-circulation period (euro and national currencies) begins *(→ point 70)*.

8   Instruments of ratification of the Nice Treaty are deposited by Austria *(→ point 1)*.

15   Pat Cox is elected President of the European Parliament *(→ point 1075)*.

18   Instruments of ratification of the Nice Treaty are deposited by Portugal *(→ point 1)*.

21   Parliament and Council sign a directive on undertakings for collective investment in transferable securities (UCITS) *(→ point 163)*.

21 *and* 22   Ministerial pledging conference for Afghanistan in Tokyo *(→ point 948)*.

23   Commission adopts a proposal for a directive on environmental liability *(→ point 595)*.

23 *and* 24   Commission adopts a package of proposals and a communication designed to develop the Community's railways *(→ point 640)*.

24   Commission adopts a communication entitled 'Life sciences and biotechnology: A strategy for Europe' *(→ point 290)*.

25   Instruments of ratification of the Nice Treaty are deposited by Sweden *(→ point 1)*.

28   Council adopts decisions on the accession partnerships *(→ point 712)*, a strategic document on terrorism in Europe *(→ point 492)* and a new regulation laying down the detailed rules and arrangements regarding Community structural assistance in the fisheries sector *(→ point 448)*.

       Parliament and Council sign a regulation concerning food law and food safety and establishing the European Food Safety Authority *(→ point 671)*, and a directive on the marketing of compound feedingstuffs *(→ point 682)*.

29   Instruments of ratification of the Nice Treaty are deposited by Finland *(→ point 1)*.

30   Commission adopts a communication on the common financial framework 2004–06 for the accession negotiations *(→ point 711)* and an issues paper on enlargement and agriculture *(→ point 708)*.

February

6   Sir Albert Bore is elected President of the Committee of the Regions (→ *point 1119*).

11   Instruments of ratification of the Nice Treaty are deposited by Germany (→ *point 1*).

12   Council adopts a directive on the structure and rates of excise duty applied to manufactured tobacco products (→ *point 178*).

Parliament and Council adopt a directive relating to ozone in ambient air (→ *point 581*).

18   Council adopts a recommendation on the implementation of the Member States' employment policies and a decision on guidelines for those policies in 2002 (→ *point 112*).

Parliament and Council adopt a regulation on the accelerated phasing-in of double-hull design requirements for single-hull oil tankers (→ *point 651*).

21   Commission adopts a report on implementation of the 2001 broad economic policy guidelines (→ *point 59*).

28   Inaugural session and opening of the Convention on the Future of the European Union (→ *point 9*).

Council adopts a series of decisions concerning relations with Switzerland (→ *point 855*) and a comprehensive plan to combat illegal immigration and trafficking in human beings in the European Union (→ *point 463*).

March

1   The euro is now the sole legal tender in the countries of the euro zone (→ *point 70*).

Commission approves a strategy document setting out the framework for cooperation between the EU and China over the period 2002–06 (→ *point 963*).

Parliament and Council adopt a decision establishing a Community action programme promoting non-governmental organisations primarily active in the field of environmental protection (→ *point 597*) and a regulation establishing a driver attestation for the transport of goods (→ *point 643*).

4   Commission adopts a proposal for a regulation on fighting poverty-related diseases (HIV/AIDS, malaria and tuberculosis) in developing countries (→ *point 827*).

6   Commission adopts a communication on education and training in the context of poverty reduction in developing countries (→ point 829).

7   Parliament and Council adopt a series of legislative instruments on the regulatory framework for communication networks and services (→ points 341 and 343).

11   Commission adopts a communication entitled 'Adapting to change in work and society: A new Community strategy on health and safety at work 2002–06' (→ point 131).

        Parliament and Council adopt a directive establishing a general framework for informing and consulting employees in the European Community (→ point 126) and a directive on the organisation of the working time of drivers in road transport (→ point 125).

15 and European Council meets at Barcelona to discuss, among other things, economic
16   matters (coordination of budget policies), social issues (guidelines for active policies geared to full employment) and the environment (ratification of the Kyoto Protocol). It also takes stock of progress made since the Lisbon European Council, discusses the development of the Euro-Mediterranean partnership and adopts a declaration on the situation in the Middle East (→ point 1085).

18 to 21 Fourth plenary ACP–EU Joint Parliamentary Assembly in Cape Town (South Africa) (→ point 988).

18 to 22 International Conference on Financing for Development in Monterrey (Mexico) (→ point 810).

22   Commission adopts a communication on health and poverty reduction in developing countries (→ point 827).

25   Commission adopts a communication on the enhanced safety of passenger ships in the Community and two proposals for directives in the same field (→ point 647).

        Council concludes Euro-Mediterranean association agreement with Jordan (→ point 892).

26   Parliament and Council adopt a directive introducing noise-related operating restrictions at Community airports (→ point 659).

April

9   Commission adopts a proposal for a recommendation adopting a multiannual programme for action in the field of energy (2003–06) (→ point 599).

10   Commission adopts a Green Paper on a Community return policy on illegal residents (→ point 464).

15   Parliament and Council adopt two regulations on the protection of the Community's forests against atmospheric pollution and against fire (→ point 572).

19   The Commission adopts a Green Paper on alternative dispute resolution in civil and commercial law (→ *point 470*).

22   Conference of Euro-Mediterranean foreign ministers opens in Valencia (→ *point 880*).

Euro-Mediterranean association agreements are signed with Algeria (→ *point 885*).

Parliament and Council adopt a regulation on the implementation of the '.eu' top-level domain (→ *point 338*).

25   Council approves the Kyoto Protocol to the United Nations Framework Convention on Climate Change (→ *point 587*) and adopts a regulation establishing a general Community framework of activities to facilitate the implementation of judicial cooperation in civil matters (→ *point 468*).

May

2   EU–US Summit in Washington (→ *point 926*).

3   Commission adopts a proposal for a regulation concerning jurisdiction and the recognition and enforcement of judgments in matrimonial matters and in matters of parental responsibility (→ *point 471*).

7   Commission adopts communications on integrated management of the external borders of the Member States of the European Union (→ *point 458*) and on consumer policy strategy 2002–06 (→ *point 693*).

Council designates Cork in Ireland as European Capital of Culture for 2005 (→ *point 535*).

Parliament and Council adopt a directive on undesirable substances in animal feed (→ *point 681*).

8   EU–Canada Summit in Toledo (→ *point 934*).

13   Parliament and Council adopt a regulation on air carrier liability in the event of accidents (→ *point 656*).

17 and   EU–Latin America/Caribbean Summit in Madrid (→ *point 969*).
18

21   Council adopts a regulation setting up the Galileo joint undertaking (→ *point 632*).

22   The Commission adopts a communication entitled 'A project for the European Union' for submission to the Convention on the Future of the European Union (→ *point 12*).

27   Parliament and Council adopt a regulation laying down common rules for the allocation of slots at Community airports (→ *point 657*).

28   Commission adopts communications on the reform of the common fisheries policy *(→ point 434)*, on a Community action plan to integrate environmental protection requirements into the common fisheries policy *(→ point 447)* and on 'eEurope 2005 — An information society for all' *(→ point 331)*.

Commission adopts a communication on a new type of office for managing support and administrative tasks in the Community institutions *(→ point 1152)*.

29   EU–Russia Summit in Moscow *(→ point 917)*.

30   Commission adopts a report on the application of Directive 94/80/EC laying down detailed arrangements for the exercise of the right to vote and to stand as a candidate in municipal elections *(→ point 508)*.

June

3   Instruments of ratification of the Nice Treaty are deposited by Greece *(→ point 1)*.

5   Commission adopts a series of communications dealing respectively with an action plan to simplify and improve the regulatory environment, assessment of the impact of Community legislation, European governance, minimum standards for consultations *(→ point 25)*, and the monitoring of commitments made by the negotiating countries in the accession negotiations *(→ point 710)*.

6   Parliament and Council adopt a directive on financial collateral arrangements *(→ point 164)*.

10   Parliament and Council adopt a decision on Community incentive measures in the field of employment *(→ point 112)*.

10 to 13   World Food Summit in Rome *(→ point 837)*.

12   Commission adopts a communication entitled 'Towards the full roll-out of third-generation mobile communications' *(→ point 346)*.

13   Council adopts a regulation establishing additional customs duties on imports of certain products originating in the United States *(→ point 801)*, a regulation laying down a uniform format for residence permits for third-country nationals *(→ point 459)* and an action programme concerning administrative cooperation in the fields of external borders, visas, asylum and immigration (ARGO) *(→ point 458)*. It also adopts framework decisions on combating terrorism *(→ point 492)*, on the European arrest warrant *(→ point 476)*, and on joint investigation teams in the field of police cooperation *(→ point 485)*.

17   Euro-Mediterranean association agreement signed with Lebanon *(→ point 893)*.

Council adopts a decision authorising the Commission to negotiate economic partnership agreements with ACP States and regions *(→ point 992)*.

21	Council adopts a recommendation on the broad economic policy guidelines of the Member States and the Community for 2002 (→ point 60).
21 and 22	European Council meets in Seville to discuss, among other things, the reform of its own working methods and those of the Council, the creation of an area of freedom, security and justice, the question of enlargement, and the fight against terrorism (→ point 1086).
24	Commission adopts a proposal for a directive concerning certain aspects of the organisation of working time (codified version) (→ point 125).
25	Council adopts a new Financial Regulation applicable to the general budget of the European Communities (→ point 1048) and a decision on the conclusion of the Cartagena Protocol on Biosafety (→ point 580).

Parliament and Council adopt a framework directive relating to the assessment and management of environmental noise (→ point 580).

26	Commission adopts a communication on the European social dialogue (→ point 133).
26 and 27	Annual G8 Summit at Kananaskis (→ point 924).
27	Council adopts a regulation on a temporary defence mechanism for the shipbuilding industry (→ point 805).

Parliament and Council adopt a directive establishing a Community monitoring system for maritime traffic (→ point 647) and a regulation establishing a European Maritime Safety Agency (→ point 647).

Parliament and Council adopt the sixth multiannual framework programme of the European Community for research, technological development and demonstration activities (2002–06) (→ point 299).

July

1	Parliament, Council and Commission adopt a decision on the regulations and general conditions for the performance of the duties of the European data protection supervisor (→ point 199).
2	Commission adopts communications dealing with corporate social responsibility (→ point 129) and an information and communication strategy for the European Union (→ point 1164), a proposal for a regulation concerning Community cooperation with Asian and Latin American countries (→ point 985) and the annual report for 2001 on the protection of the Communities' financial interests and the fight against fraud (→ point 1055).
8	Eleventh annual EU–Japan Summit in Tokyo (→ point 931).
9	Instruments of ratification of the Nice Treaty are deposited by Italy (→ point 1).

10   Commission adopts a communication on the mid-term review of the common agricultural policy *(→ point 393)*.

12   Council and Parliament adopt a directive on the processing of personal data and the protection of privacy in the electronic communications sector *(→ point 343)*.

15   Parliament and Council adopt a regulation laying down common rules in the field of civil aviation and establishing a European Aviation Safety Agency *(→ point 653)*.

19   Council adopts a framework decision to combat trafficking in human beings *(→ point 489)*.

22   Council adopts a framework programme on police and judicial cooperation in criminal matters (AGIS) *(→ point 457)*.

        Parliament and Council adopt a decision laying down the Community environment action programme 2001–10 *(→ point 552)*.

23   Expiry of the ECSC Treaty *(→ points 39 to 41)*.

        Council adopts a regulation on State aid to the coal industry *(→ point 240)*.

25   Instruments of ratification of the Nice Treaty are deposited by the United Kingdom *(→ point 1)*.

26   Commission adopts a proposal for a decision on a multiannual programme (2003–05) for the monitoring of eEurope, dissemination of good practices and the improvement of network and information security *(→ point 331)*.

31   Commission adopts a regulation on the application of Article 81(3) of the Treaty to categories of vertical agreements and concerted practices in the motor vehicle sector *(→ point 208)*.

August

26   Instruments of ratification of the Nice Treaty are deposited by Belgium *(→ point 1)*.

26 *Aug.*   World Summit on Sustainable Development in Johannesburg (South Africa), *to 4 Sept.* in the context of the United Nations Conference on Environment and Development *(→ points 556 to 558)*.

September

3   Commission adopts a communication on streamlining the annual economic and employment policy coordination cycles *(→ point 58)*.

10   Fifty-seventh session of the United Nations General Assembly opens in New York *(→ point 763)*.

Commission adopts a proposal for a regulation on drug precursors *(→ point 273)*.

11   Declaration by the Heads of State or Government of the European Union, the President of the European Parliament, the President of the Commission and the High Representative for the CFSP on the first anniversary of the attacks against the United States *(→ point 928)*.

16   Commission adopts a directive on competition in the markets for electronic communications networks and services *(→ point 229)*.

18   Commission adopts a communication on trade and sustainable development *(→ point 819)*.

22 to 24 Fourth Asia–Europe Summit (ASEM) in Copenhagen *(→ point 945)*.

23   Council adopts a regulation on additives in feedingstuffs *(→ point 683)*.

Parliament and Council sign directives on the protection of employees in the event of the insolvency of their employer *(→ point 128)*, on the principle of equal treatment for men and women as regards employment, vocational training and working conditions *(→ point 142)* and on the protection of consumers in respect of distance contracts *(→ point 697)*.

European Community and Chile sign agreement for scientific and technical cooperation *(→ point 312)*.

24   First EU–Korea Summit *(→ point 941)* and fifth EU–China Summit *(→ point 963)*.

October

2   Commission adopts a proposal for a directive on takeover bids *(→ point 189)*.

3   Council adopts decisions on the placing on the market of genetically modified organisms and their deliberate release into the environment *(→ point 580)*.

Parliament and Council sign a regulation laying down the health rules concerning animal by-products not intended for human consumption *(→ point 675)*.

7   Commission adopts a directive on the conditions of entry and residence of third-country nationals for the purpose of studies, vocational training or voluntary service *(→ point 466)*.

8   European Community signs protocol of accession to the European Organisation for the Safety of Air Navigation (Eurocontrol) *(→ point 661)*.

Council adopts decisions on mutual recognition agreements between the European Community and Japan, Canada, the United States, New Zealand and Australia *(→ point 791)*.

9	Commission adopts a strategy paper on enlargement and reports for 2002 on progress towards accession by the candidate countries (→ *point 705*).
10	Third European Union–India Summit in Copenhagen (→ *point 950*).
14	Commission adopts a communication on a Community return policy on illegal residents (→ *point 464*).
16	Commission adopts communications on structural indicators (→ *point 66*), a communication on the European research area (→ *point 292*) and a proposal for a directive on compensation to crime victims (→ *point 480*).
17	EU Troika visits Moscow (→ *point 917*).
23	Mr Briesch is elected President of the European Economic and Social Committee (→ *point 1111*).
23 Oct. to 1 Nov.	Conference on climate change in New Delhi (India) (→ *point 588*).
24	Commission adopts a proposal for a directive on the quality of bathing water (→ *point 566*).
24 and 25	European Council meets in Brussels. The main items discussed are enlargement, key aspects of the common agricultural policy and institutional affairs, including the work of the Convention on the Future of the European Union (→ *point 1087*).
28	Meeting in Copenhagen between the EU and the candidate countries (→ *point 707*).
30	Commission adopts a communication on its legislative programme and work programme for 2003 (→ *point 1094*).

November

3 to 15	Twelfth meeting of the Conference on International Trade in Endangered Species of Wild Fauna and Flora (CITES) in Santiago (Chile) (→ *point 571*).
5	Council adopts a decision on Portugal's excessive budget deficit and a recommendation on action to bring it to an end (→ *point 63*).
	Parliament and Council adopt a regulation and a directive on maritime safety and the prevention of pollution from ships (→ *point 651*) and a regulation on a common procurement vocabulary (→ *point 202*).
6	Commission adopts two communications, one on an action plan to counter the social, economic and regional consequences of the restructuring of the EU fishing industry (→ *point 449*) and nuclear safety (→ *point 627*).
7	Parliament, Council and Commission sign the interinstitutional agreement on the financing of the European Union Solidarity Fund (→ *point 362*).

11   Council adopts a regulation establishing the European Union Solidarity Fund (→ *point 362*).

         EU–Russia Summit in Brussels (→ *point 917*).

13   Commission adopts a communication on roadmaps for Bulgaria and Romania (→ *point 705*).

18   European Community and Chile sign association and free trade agreement in Brussels (→ *point 977*).

19   Commission adopts a proposal for a directive on investment services and regulated markets (→ *point 165*).

25   Council agreement on a common position on a proposal for a directive and a proposal for a regulation liberalising the markets in electricity and natural gas (→ *point 609*).

         Commission adopts a proposal for a directive on the energy performance of buildings (→ *point 617*).

26   Commission adopts a communication on an action plan to reduce discards of fish (→ *point 438*).

27   Commission adopts three communications on, respectively, euro-zone statistics and indicators (→ *point 100*), the need and the means to upgrade the quality of Community statistics (→ *point 58*) and strengthening the coordination of budgetary policies (→ *point 58*).

28   Social dialogue summit in Genval (Belgium) (→ *point 133*).

28 and
29   Council adopts a number of measures on illegal residents (→ *point 463*) and a decision setting up a European network for the protection of public figures (→ *point 485*).

December

2   Second ministerial pledging conference for Afghanistan in Bonn (→ *point 948*).

         Commission adopts proposals for decisions on trade in certain steel products and on the application of the double-checking system for Poland, the Czech Republic and Romania (→ *point 802*).

         Council adopts a recommendation on the prevention of smoking and on initiatives to improve tobacco control (→ *point 691*) and a resolution on the consumer policy strategy 2002–06 (→ *point 693*).

3   Commission adopts a communication on integrating migration issues in the EU's relations with third countries (→ *point 462*).

         Council adopts a directive to extend the facility allowing Member States to apply reduced rates of VAT to certain labour-intensive services (→ *point 179*).

Parliament and Council adopt a decision on the Fiscalis 2007 programme (→ *point 177*).

5 Commission adopts a communication on the institutional architecture of the European Union (→ *point 12*).

6 European Community and China sign agreement on maritime transport (→ *point 667*).

9 *and* 10 Ministerial accession conferences with Cyprus, the Czech Republic, Estonia, Hungary, Latvia, Lithuania, Malta, Poland, Slovakia and Slovenia (→ *point 706*).

9 *to* 13 Sixth meeting of the parties to the UN Framework Convention on the Control of Transboundary Movements of Hazardous Wastes (Basle Convention) (→ *point 562*).

10 Council adopts a decision on dock dues in the French overseas departments (→ *point 381*).

11 Commission adopts a communication on the review of the EU economy in 2002 (→ *point 61*).

Commission adopts a decision on merger control (→ *point 230*). It also tabled a report on European governance, together with four communications (→ *points 24 and 1064*), the report entitled 'Better lawmaking 2002' (→ *point 28*) and a proposal for a decision amending the arrangements for the exercise of its implementing powers (→ *point 37*).

12 Commission adopts a regulation on State aid for employment (→ *point 243*).

12 *and* 13 European Council meets in Copenhagen. This historic summit brought to an end the accession negotiations with 10 candidate countries, paving the way for a 25-member EU from 1 May 2004. It also confirmed the target date of 2007 for the accession of Bulgaria and Romania, and the opening of negotiations with Turkey by the end of 2004 if it can meet the Copenhagen criteria (→ *point 1088*).

13 Commission adopts proposal for a directive laying down Community measures to control foot-and-mouth disease (→ *point 676*) and a proposal for a regulation for the control of exports of dual-use items and technology (→ *point 790*).

16 Council adopts a new regulation recasting the rules for the application of the antitrust provisions in the EC Treaty (→ *point 207*) and a regulation laying down the animal-health rules governing products of animal origin intended for human consumption (→ *point 674*).

Parliament and Council adopt the Community statistical programme 2003–07 (→ *point 99*).

18 Instruments of ratification of the Nice Treaty are deposited by Ireland (→ *point 1*).

19 EU–Canada Summit in Ottawa *(→ point 934)*.

Parliament adopts the 2003 budget *(→ point 1029)*.

20 Commission adopts a Green Paper on a European order for payment procedure and on measures to simplify and speed up small claims litigation *(→ point 470)* and a proposal for a regulation on the accelerated phasing-in of double-hull design requirements for single-hull oil tankers *(→ point 648)*.

Council adopts three regulations dealing with the scrapping of fishing vessels *(→ point 450)*, Community structural assistance in the fisheries sector *(→ point 448)* and the conservation and sustainable exploitation of fisheries resources under the common fisheries policy *(→ point 438)*.

30 Commission adopts a proposal for a regulation concerning trade in certain equipment and products which could be used for capital punishment, torture or other cruel, inhuman or degrading treatment or punishment *(→ point 50)* and a proposal for a directive on minimum safety requirements for tunnels in the trans-European road network *(→ point 639)*.

Institutions and other bodies

European Parliament

Secretariat
Centre européen, Plateau du Kirchberg
L-2929 Luxembourg
Tel. (352) 43 00-1

Council of the European Union

General Secretariat
Rue de la Loi/Wetstraat 175
B-1048 Brussels
Tel. (32-2) 285 61 11

European Commission

Rue de la Loi/Wetstraat 200
B-1049 Brussels
Tel. (32-2) 299 11 11

Court of Justice

Boulevard Konrad Adenauer
L-2925 Luxembourg
Tel. (352) 43 03-1

European Court of Auditors

12, rue Alcide De Gasperi
L-1615 Luxembourg
Tel. (352) 43 98-1

European Economic and Social Committee

Rue Ravenstein 2
B-1000 Brussels
Tel. (32-2) 546 90 11

Committee of the Regions
Rue Belliard 79
B-1040 Brussels
Tel. (32-2) 282 22 11

European Investment Bank
100, boulevard Konrad Adenauer
L-2950 Luxembourg
Tel. (352) 43 79-1

European Central Bank
Kaiserstraße 29
D-60311 Frankfurt am Main
Tel. (49-69) 13 44-0

List of agencies

European Centre for the Development of Vocational Training (Cedefop)
BP 22427
GR-55102 Thessaloniki
Tel. (30) 23 10 49 01 11
Internet: http://www.cedefop.eu.int/

European Foundation for the Improvement of Living and Working Conditions
Wyattville Road
Loughlinstown
Dublin 18
Ireland
Tel. (353-1) 204 31 00
Internet: http://www.fr.eurofound.ie/

European Environment Agency (EEA)
Kongens Nytorv 6
DK-1050 Copenhagen K
Tel. (45) 33 36 71 00
Internet: http://www.eea.eu.int/

European Training Foundation (ETF)
Villa Gualino
Viale Settimio Severo 65
I-10133 Turin
Tel. (39) 01 16 30 22 22
Internet: http://www.etf.eu.int/

European Monitoring Centre for Drugs and Drug Addiction (EMCDDA)
Rua da Cruz de Santa Apolónia, 23-25
P-1149-045 Lisbon
Tel. (351) 218 11 30 00
Internet: http://www.emcdda.org/mlp/ms_fr-index.shtml

European Agency for the Evaluation of Medicinal Products (EMEA)
7 Westferry Circus
Canary Wharf
London E14 4HB
United Kingdom
Tel. (44-20) 74 18 84 00
Internet: http://www.emea.eu.int/

Office for Harmonisation in the Internal Market (OHMI)
Apartado de Correos 77
E-03080 Alicante
Tel. (34) 965 13 91 00
Internet: http://www.oami.eu.int/en/default.htm

European Agency for Safety and Health at Work
Gran Vía 33
E-48009 Bilbao
Tel. (34) 944 79 43 60
Internet: http://www.osha.eu.int/

Community Plant Variety Office (CPVO)
BP 2141
F-49021 Angers Cedex 02
Tel. (33) 241 25 64 00
Internet: http://www.cpvo.eu.int/

Translation Centre for the Bodies of the European Union
Bâtiment Nouvel Hémicycle
1, rue du Fort Thüngen
L-1499 Luxembourg
Tel. (352) 421 71 11
Internet: http://www.cdt.eu.int/

European Monitoring Centre on Racism and Xenophobia
Rahlgasse 3
A-1060 Vienna
Tel. (43-1) 58 03 00
Internet: http://www.eumc.eu.int/

European Agency for Reconstruction
BP 10177
GR-54110 Thessaloniki
Tel. (30) 23 10 50 51 00
Internet: http://www.ear.eu.int/

European Food Safety Authority (EFSA)
Internet: http://www.efsa.eu.int/index_en.html

European Maritime Safety Agency (AESM)
Internet: http://europa.eu.int/agencies/emsa/index_en.htm

European Aviation Safety Agency (AESA)
Internet: http://europa.eu.int/agencies/easa/index_en.htm

Publications cited

General Report on the Activities of the European Union
(abbr.: General Report), published annually by the Commission

Works published in conjunction with the General Report:

— *The Agricultural Situation in the European Union*
(abbr.: Agricultural Report), published annually

— *Report on Competition Policy*
(abbr.: Competition Report), published annually

— *Report on monitoring the application of Community law,* published annually

Bulletin of the European Union
(abbr.: Bull.), published monthly by the Commission

Official Journal of the European Communities
'Legislation' series (abbr.: OJ L)
'Information and notices' series (abbr.: OJ C)
'Supplement' series (abbr.: OJ S)

Reports of Cases before the Court
(abbr.: ECR), published by the Court of Justice in annual series, at irregular intervals
throughout the year

The above publications are printed and distributed through the Office for Official Publications of the European Communities, L-2985 Luxembourg.

Annexes

Table I — Co-decision procedure

	Commission proposal	ESC opinion/ COR opinion°	EP first reading a, b(^{1})	Amended Commission proposal	Common position Council*

The Community economic and social area
Statistical system
Policy aspects

	Commission proposal	ESC opinion/ COR opinion°	EP first reading a, b(^{1})	Amended Commission proposal	Common position Council*
99 Dec. No 2367/2002/EC: Community statistical programme 2003–07	OJ C 75 E/26.3.2002 COM(2001) 683 Bull. 11-2001/1.3.14	OJ C 125/27.5.2002 Bull. 3-2002/1.3.11	Bull. 4-2002/1.3.3 (b)		Bull. 9-2002/1.3.12
101 Reg. (EC) No 359/2002 amending Reg. (EC) No 2223/96: determination of Member States' payments to the VAT-based own resource	OJ C 29 E/30.1.2001 COM(2000) 583 Bull. 9-2000/1.3.6		OJ C 21 E/24.1.2002 Bull. 4-2001/1.3.5 (b)		OJ C 307/31.10.2001 Bull. 7/8-2001/1.3.9
101 Reg. (EC) No 1221/2002: quarterly non-financial accounts for general government	OJ C 154 E/29.5.2001 COM(2001) 100 Bull. 1/2-2001/1.3.33		OJ C 65 E/14.3.2002 Bull. 7/8-2001/1.3.8 (a)		
101 Prop. for a reg. amending Reg. (EC) No 2223/96: delays of transmission of the main aggregates of national accounts	OJ C 203 E/27.8.2002 COM(2002) 234 Bull. 5-2002/1.3.10		Bull. 9-2002/1.3.9 (a)		
101 Prop. for a reg.: nomenclature of territorial units for statistics (NUTS)	OJ C 180 E/26.6.2001 COM(2001) 83 Bull. 1/2-2001/1.3.31	OJ C 260/17.9.2001 Bull. 7/8-2001/1.3.5 OJ C 107/3.5.2002 Bull. 11-2001/1.3.11°	OJ C 112 E/9.5.2002 Bull. 10-2001/1.3.14 (b)		9.12.2002
102 Reg. (EC) No 1991/2002 amending Reg. (EC) No 577/98: organisation of a labour force sample survey in the Community	OJ C 270 E/25.9.2001 COM(2001) 319 Bull. 6-2001/1.3.8	OJ C 48/21.2.2002 Bull. 11-2001/1.3.12	OJ C 177 E/25.7.2002 Bull. 12-2001/1.3.17 (a)		Bull. 4-2002/1.3.5
102 Prop. for a reg.: Community statistics on income and living conditions (EU-SILC)	OJ C 103 E/30.4.2002 COM(2001) 754 Bull. 12-2001/1.3.20	OJ C 149/21.6.2002 Bull. 4-2002/1.3.6	Bull. 5-2002/1.3.9 (b)	COM(2002) 641 Bull. 11-2002/1.3.12	
102 Prop. for a reg.: labour cost index	OJ C 304 E/30.10.2001 COM(2001) 418 Bull. 7/8-2001/1.3.7	OJ C 48/21.2.2002 Bull. 11-2001/1.3.13	OJ C 293 E/28.11.2002 Bull. 1/2-2002/1.3.30 (a)		Bull. 9-2002/1.3.8
103 Reg. (EC) No 2150/2002: waste management statistics	OJ C 87/29.3.1999 COM(1999) 31 Bull. 1/2-1999/1.7.2	OJ C 329/17.11.1999 Bull. 9-1999/1.7.3	OJ C 72 E/21.3.2002 Bull. 9-2001/1.3.4 (b)	OJ C 180 E/26.6.2001 COM(2001) 137 Bull. 3-2001/1.3.15 COM(2001) 737 Bull. 12-2001/1.3.16	Bull. 4-2002/1.3.4
104 Reg. (EC) No 2056/2002 amending Reg. (EC, Euratom) No 58/97: structural business statistics	OJ C 154 E/29.5.2001 COM(2001) 38 Bull. 1/2-2001/1.3.29	OJ C 260/17.9.2001 Bull. 7/8-2001/1.3.6	OJ C 53 E/28.2.2002 Bull. 6-2001/1.3.9 (b)	OJ C 332 E/27.11.2001 COM(2001) 509 Bull. 9-2001/1.3.6	Bull. 6-2002/1.3.10
104 Prop. for a dec.: production and development of Community statistics on science and technology	OJ C 332 E/27.11.2001 COM(2001) 490 Bull. 7/8-2001/1.3.10		Bull. 7/8-2002/1.3.8 (b)	COM(2002) 554 Bull. 10-2002/1.3.6	
106 Prop. for a reg.: rail transport statistics	OJ C 180 E/26.6.2001 COM(2000) 798 Bull. 1/2-2001/1.3.30	OJ C 221/7.8.2001 Bull. 5-2001/1.3.7	OJ C 72 E/21.3.2002 Bull. 9-2001/1.3.5 (b) Bull. 10-2001/1.3.11 (a)		Bull. 6-2002/1.3.12
106 Prop. for a reg.: statistics on the carriage of passengers, freight and mail by air	OJ C 325/6.12.1995 COM(1995) 353 Bull. 9-1995/1.7.3	OJ C 39/12.2.1996 Bull. 11-1995/1.7.4	OJ C 54/25.2.2000 Bull. 9-1999/1.7.4 OJ C 78/18.3.1996 Bull. 1/2-1996/1.7.3		Bull. 6-2002/1.3.9* Bull. 9-2002/1.3.11

° Opinion of the Committee of the Regions.

* Council agreement.

(^{1}) a = adoption; b = amendments; c = rejection; d = EP failure to take a decision within three months; e = agreement on a common draft; f = failure to agree on a common draft.

TABLE I — CO-DECISION PROCEDURE   497

second reading a, b, c, d (¹)	Commission opinion	Conciliation Committee e, f (¹)	EP adoption of common draft	Adoption by Council*	EP and Council signature	Observations	
1-2002/1.3.9 (a)					OJ L 358/31.12.2002 Bull. 12-2002/1.3.10		99
177 E/25.7.2002 12-2001/1.3.19 (a)					OJ L 58/28.2.2002 Bull. 1/2-2002/1.3.28	Amended reg.: OJ L 310/30.11.1996	101
					OJ L 179/9.7.2002 Bull. 6-2002/1.3.7		101
						Reg. to be amended: OJ L 310/30.11.1996	101
							101
6-2002/1.3.8 (a)					OJ L 308/9.11.2002 Bull. 10-2002/1.3.7	Amended reg.: OJ L 77/14.3.1998	102
							102
.2002 12-2002/1.3.14							102
7/8-2002/1.3.9 (b)	COM(2002) 589 Bull. 10-2002/1.3.12				OJ L 332/9.12.2002 Bull. 11-2002/1.3.11		103
9-2002/1.3.10 (a)					OJ L 317/21.11.2002 Bull. 11-2002/1.3.10	Amended reg.: OJ L 14/17.1.1997	104
							104
					16.12.2002 Bull. 12-2002/1.3.12		106
.2002 12-2002/1.3.13							106

	Commission proposal	ESC opinion/ COR opinion°	EP first reading a, b (¹)	Amended Commission proposal	Common position Council*
107 Reg. (EC) No 1840/2002: prolongation of the ECSC steel statistics system after the expiry of the ECSC Treaty	OJ C 203 E/27.8.2002 COM(2002) 160 Bull. 3-2002/1.3.12		Bull. 5-2002/1.3.11 (a)		
107 Prop. for a reg.: production of annual Community statistics on steel for the reference years 2003–09	COM(2002) 584 Bull. 10-2002/1.3.10				
108 Dec. No 1919/2002/EC amending Dec. 96/411/EC: improving Community agricultural statistics	OJ C 126 E/28.5.2002 COM(2002) 80 Bull. 1/2-2002/1.3.29		Bull. 9-2002/1.3.6 (a)		

Employment and social policy
Employment

	Commission proposal	ESC opinion/ COR opinion°	EP first reading a, b (¹)	Amended Commission proposal	Common position Council*
112 Dec. No 1145/2002/EC: Community incentive measures in the field of employment	OJ C 337 E/28.11.2000 COM(2000) 459 Bull. 7/8-2000/1.3.10	OJ C 139/11.5.2001 Bull. 3-2001/1.3.19 OJ C 144/16.5.2001 Bull. 12-2000/1.3.9°	OJ C 276/1.10.2001 Bull. 1/2-2001/1.3.38 (b)	OJ C 180 E/26.6.2001 COM(2001) 124 Bull. 1/2-2001/1.3.38	OJ C 301/26.10.2001

Social protection and social security

	Commission proposal	ESC opinion/ COR opinion°	EP first reading a, b (¹)	Amended Commission proposal	Common position Council*
117 Prop. for a reg. amending, for the benefit of European parliamentary assistants, Reg. (EEC) No 1408/71: application of social security schemes to employed persons	OJ C 270 E/25.9.2001 COM(2001) 344 Bull. 6-2001/1.3.16		Bull. 6-2002/1.3.16 (b)	OJ C 331 E/31.12.2002 COM(2002) 405 Bull. 7/8-2002/1.3.16	

Labour law and industrial relations

	Commission proposal	ESC opinion/ COR opinion°	EP first reading a, b (¹)	Amended Commission proposal	Common position Council*
125 Prop. for a dir.: organisation of working time (consolidated version)	COM(2002) 336	Bull. 9-2002/1.3.19	17.12.2002 Bull. 12-2002/1.3.23		
125 Dir. 2002/15/EC: organisation of working time for mobile workers	OJ C 43/17.2.1999 COM(1998) 662 Bull. 11-1998/1.2.19	OJ C 138/18.5.1999 Bull. 3-1999/1.3.10	OJ C 219/30.7.1999 Bull. 4-1999/1.3.14 (b) OJ C 279/1.10.1999 Bull. 5-1999/1.2.12	OJ C 120 E/24.4.2001 COM(2000) 754 Bull. 11-2000/1.3.20	Bull. 12-2000/1.3.13* OJ C 142/15.5.2001
125 Prop. for a reg.: harmonisation of certain social legislation relating to road transport	OJ C 51 E/26.2.2002 COM(2001) 573 Bull. 10-2001/1.4.63	OJ C 221/17.9.2002 Bull. 5-2002/1.3.17			
126 Dir. 2002/14/EC: informing and consulting employees	OJ C 2/5.1.1999 OJ C 240 E/28.8.2001 COM(1998) 612 Bull. 11-1998/1.2.22	OJ C 258/10.9.1999 Bull. 7/8-1999/1.3.7 OJ C 144/16.5.2001 Bull. 12-2000/1.3.12°	OJ C 219/30.7.1999 Bull. 4-1999/1.3.16 (b) OJ C 54/25.2.2000 Bull. 9-1999/1.2.10	OJ C 240 E/28.8.2001 COM(2001) 296 Bull. 5-2001/1.3.16	Bull. 6-2001/1.3.19* OJ C 307/31.10.2001 Bull. 7/8-2001/1.3.16
128 Dir. 2002/74/EC amending Dir. 80/987/EEC on the approximation of the laws of the Member States relating to the protection of employees in the event of the insolvency of their employer	OJ C 154 E/29.5.2001 COM(2000) 832 Bull. 1/2-2001/1.3.46	OJ C 221/7.8.2001 Bull. 5-2001/1.3.15	15.11.2001 OJ C 153 E/27.6.2002 Bull. 11-2001/1.3.26 (b)		Bull. 12-2001/1.3.37* Bull. 1/2-2002/1.3.45
130 Prop. for a dir.: working conditions for temporary workers	OJ C 203 E/27.8.2002 COM(2002) 149 Bull. 3-2002/1.3.25	Bull. 9-2002/1.3.18	Bull. 11-2002/1.3.20 (b)	COM(2002) 701 Bull. 11-2002/1.3.20	

° Opinion of the Committee of the Regions.

* Council agreement.

(¹) a = adoption; b = amendments; c = rejection; d = EP failure to take a decision within three months; e = agreement on a common draft; f = failure to agree on a common draft.

TABLE I — CO-DECISION PROCEDURE **499**

P second reading a, b, c, d (¹)	Commission opinion	Conciliation Committee e, f (¹)	EP adoption of common draft	Adoption by Council*	EP and Council signature	Observations	
					OJ L 279/17.10.2002		107
							107
					OJ L 293/29.10.2002 Bull. 10-2002/1.3.9	Amended dec.: OJ L 162/1.7.1996	108
112 E/9.5.2002 10-2001/1.3.20 (b)	COM(2001) 730	26.2.2002	Bull. 4-2002/1.3.10	7.5.2002	OJ L 170/29.6.2002		112
						Reg. to be amended: OJ L 149/5.7.1971	117
							125
53 E/28.2.2002 6-2001/1.3.20 (b)	COM(2001) 415	Bull. 12-2001/1.3.38 (e)	OJ C 284E/21.11.2002 Bull. 1/2-2002/1.3.43	Bull. 1/2-2002/1.3.43	OJ L 80/23.3.2002 Bull. 3-2002/1.3.23		125
							125
112 E/9.5.2002 10-2001/1.3.24 (b)	COM(2001) 701	Bull. 12-2001/1.3.39 (e)	OJ C 284E/21.11.2002 Bull. 1/2-2002/1.3.46	Bull. 1/2-2002/1.3.46	OJ L 80/23.3.2002 Bull. 3-2002/1.3.22		126
5-2002/1.3.15 (b)	COM(2002) 265 Bull. 5-2002/1.3.15				OJ L 270/8.10.2002 Bull. 9-2002/1.3.20	Amended dir.: OJ L 283/28.10.1980	128
							130

	Commission proposal	ESC opinion/ COR opinion°	EP first reading a, b (¹)	Amended Commission proposal	Common position Council*

Health and safety at work

132 Dir. 2002/44/EC: protection of workers from physical agents (vibrations) Prop. for a dir.: protection of workers from agents	OJ C 77/18.3.1993 COM(1992) 560 Bull. 12-1992/1.3.158	OJ C 249/13.9.1993 Bull. 6-1993/1.2.149	OJ C 128/9.5.1994 Bull. 4-1994/1.2.160 (b) OJ C 54/**25.2.2000** **Bull. 9-1999/1.2.14**	OJ C 230/19.8.1994 COM(1994) 284 Bull. 7/8-1994/1.2.166	Bull. 11-2000/1.3.23* Bull. 6-2001/1.3.21* OJ C 301/26.10.2001 Bull. 6-2001/1.3.22 Bull. 10-2001/1.3.26
132 Prop. for a dir. amending Dir. 83/477/EEC: protection of workers from the risks related to exposure to asbestos at work	OJ C 304 E/30.10.2001 COM(2001) 417 Bull. 7/8-2001/1.3.18	OJ C 94/18.4.2002 Bull. 1/2-2002/1.3.47	**Bull. 4-2002**/1.3.15 (b)	OJ C 203 E/27.8.2002 COM(**2002**) 254 Bull. 5-**2002**/1.3.18	Bull. 6-2002/1.3.17* Bull. 9-2002/1.3.22

Equal opportunities

142 Dir. 2002/73/EC amending Dir. 76/207/EEC: implementation of the principle of equal treatment as regards access to employment	OJ C 337 E/28.11.2000 COM(2000) 334 Bull. 6-2000/1.3.27	OJ C 123/25.4.2001 Bull. 1/2-2001/1.3.49	OJ C 47 E/21.2.2002 Bull. 5-2001/1.3.17 (b)	OJ C 270 E/25.9.2001 COM(2001) 321 Bull. 6-2001/1.3.24	Bull. 6-2001/1.3.24* OJ C 307/31.10.2001 Bull. 7/8-2001/1.3.20

Internal market
Free movement of persons

159 Prop. for a dir.: recognition of professional qualifications	OJ C 181 E/30.7.2002 COM(2002) 119 Bull. 3-2002/1.3.32	Bull. 9-2002/1.3.33			

Freedom to provide services

163 Dir. 2001/108/EC amending Dir. 85/611/EEC: undertakings for collective investment in transferable securities	OJ C 280/9.9.1998 COM(1998) 449 Bull. 7/8-1998/1.3.27	OJ C 116/28.4.1999 Bull. 1/2-1999/1.3.55	OJ C 339/29.11.2000 Bull. 1/2-2000/1.3.48 (b)	OJ C 311/31.10.2000 COM(2000) 329 Bull. 5-2000/1.3.36	Bull. 10-2000/1.3.33* OJ C 297/23.10.2001 Bull. 6-2001/1.3.40
163 Dir. 2001/107/EC amending Dir. 85/611/EEC: management companies and simplified prospectuses	OJ C 272/1.9.1998 COM(1998) 451 Bull. 7/8-1998/1.3.27	OJ C 116/28.4.1999 Bull. 1/2-1999/1.3.56	OJ C 339/29.11.2000 Bull. 1/2-2000/1.3.48 (b)	OJ C 311/31.10.2000 COM(2000) 331 Bull. 5-2000/1.3.36	Bull. 3-2001/1.3.36* OJ C 297/23.10.2001 Bull. 6-2001/1.3.39
163 Prop. for a dir.: prospectus to be published when securities are offered to the public	OJ C 240 E/28.8.2001 COM(2001) 280 Bull. 5-2001/1.3.30	OJ C 80/3.4.2002 Bull. 1/2-2002/1.3.60	Bull. 3-2002/1.3.37 (b)	COM(2002) 460 Bull. 7/8-2002/1.3.30	Bull. 11-2002/1.3.27*
163 Prop. for a dir.: insider dealing and market manipulation (market abuse)	OJ C 240 E/28.8.2001 COM(2001) 281 Bull. 5-2001/1.3.29	OJ C 80/3.4.2002 Bull. 1/2-2002/1.3.61	Bull. 3-2002/1.3.38 (b)		Bull. 5-2002/1.3.28* Bull. 7/8-2002/1.3.29
164 Dir. 2002/47/EC: financial collateral arrangements	OJ C 180 E/26.6.2001 COM(2001) 168 Bull. 3-2001/1.3.41	OJ C 48/21.2.2002 Bull. 11-2001/1.3.45	OJ C 177 E/25.7.2002 Bull. 12-2001/1.3.49 (b)		Bull. 12-2001/1.3.49* Bull. 3-2002/1.3.34
165 Prop. for a dir.: investment services and regulated markets	COM(2002) 625 Bull. 11-2002/1.3.29				
166 Dir. 2002/12/EC amending Dir. 79/267/EEC: solvency margin requirements for life insurance undertakings	OJ C 96 E/27.3.2001 COM(2000) 617 Bull. 10-2000/1.3.34	OJ C 193/10.7.2001 Bull. 4-2001/1.3.28	OJ C 65 E/14.3.2002 Bull. 7/8-2001/1.3.28 (b)		

° Opinion of the Committee of the Regions.

* Council agreement.

(¹) a = adoption; b = amendments; c = rejection; d = EP failure to take a decision within three months; e = agreement on a common draft; f = failure to agree on a common draft.

TABLE I — CO-DECISION PROCEDURE **501**

EP second reading a, b, c, d (^{1})	Commission opinion	Conciliation Committee e, f (^{1})	EP adoption of common draft	Adoption by Council*	EP and Council signature	Observations	
112 E/9.5.2002 10-2001/1.3.25 (b) 3-2002/1.3.27 (b)	COM(2001) 717 COM(2002) 229 Bull. 5-2002/1.3.19	Bull. 4-2002/1.3.16 (e) Bull. 10-2002/1.3.18 (e)	Bull. 4-2002/1.3.16 (vibrations) Bull.12-2002/1.3.24 (noise)	Bull. 5-2002/1.3.19 (vibrations) Bull.12-2002/1.3.24 (noise)	OJ L 177/6.7.2002 (vibrations)		132
2.2002 12-2002/1.3.26						Dir. to be amended: OJ L 263/24.9.1983	132
112 E/9.5.2002 10-2001/1.3.27 (b)	COM(2001) 689	17.4.2002	Bull. 6-2002/1.3.20	Bull. 6-2002/1.3.20	OJ L 269/5.10.2002 Bull. 9-2002/1.3.23	Amended dir.: OJ L 39/14.2.1976	142
							159
112 E/9.5.2002 10-2001/1.3.39 (b)	COM(2001) 686				OJ L 41/13.2.2002 Bull. 1/2-2002/1.3.62	Amended dir.: OJ L 375/31.12.1985	163
112 E/9.5.2002 10-2001/1.3.39 (b)	COM(2001) 687				OJ L 41/13.2.2002 Bull. 1/2-2002/1.3.62	Amended dir.: OJ L 375/31.12.1985	163
							163
10-2002/1.3.24 (b)	COM(2002) 724						163
5-2002/1.3.30 (a)					OJ L 168/27.6.2002 Bull. 6-2002/1.3.32		164
							165
					OJ L 77/20.3.2002 Bull. 3-2002/1.3.33	Amended dir.: OJ L 63/13.3.1979	166

	Commission proposal	ESC opinion/ COR opinion°	EP first reading a, b (¹)	Amended Commission proposal	Common position Council*	
166 Dir. 2002/13/EC amending Dir. 73/239/EEC: solvency margin requirements for non-life insurance undertakings	OJ C 96 E/27.3.2001 COM(2000) 634 Bull. 10-2000/1.3.34	OJ C 193/10.7.2001 Bull. 4-2001/1.3.28	OJ C 65 E/14.3.2002 Bull. 7/8-2001/1.3.28 (b)			
166 Prop. for a dir. amending Dirs 72/166/EEC, 84/5/EEC, 88/357/EEC, 90/232/EEC and 2000/26/EC: insurance against civil liability in respect of the use of motor vehicles	OJ C 227 E/24.9.2002 COM(2002) 244 Bull. 6-2002/1.3.33					
166 Prop. for a dir.: insurance mediation	OJ C 29 E/30.1.2001 COM(2000) 511 Bull. 9-2000/1.3.26	OJ C 221/7.8.2001 Bull. 5-2001/1.3.32	OJ C 140 E/13.6.2002 Bull. 11-2001/1.3.42 (b)		Bull. 11-2001/1.3.42* Bull. 3-2002/1.3.39	
166 Dir. 2002/83/EC: life insurance (recast version)	OJ C 365 E/19.12.2000 COM(2000) 398 Bull. 6-2000/1.3.36	OJ C 123/25.4.2001 Bull. 1/2-2001/1.9.26	OJ C 343/5.12.2001 Bull. 3-2001/1.3.38 (a)		Bull. 5-2001/1.3.31* Bull. 5-2002/1.3.31	
166 Prop. for a dir.: activities of institutions for occupational retirement provision	OJ C 96 E/27.3.2001 COM(2000) 507 Bull. 10-2000/1.3.36	OJ C 155/29.5.2001 Bull. 3-2001/1.3.44	OJ C 65 E/14.3.2002 Bull. 7/8-2001/1.3.31 (b)		Bull. 6-2002/1.3.31* Bull. 11-2002/1.3.28	
167 Prop. for a dir. amending Dirs 73/239/EEC, 79/267/EEC, 92/49/EEC, 92/96/EEC, 93/6/EEC, 93/22/EEC, 98/78/EC and 2000/12/EC: supervision of credit institutions, insurance undertakings and investment firms in a financial conglomerate	OJ C 213 E/31.7.2001 COM(2001) 213 Bull. 4-2001/1.3.29	OJ C 36/8.2.2002 Bull. 10-2001/1.3.37	Bull. 3-2002/1.3.36 (b)		Bull. 5-2002/1.3.29* Bull. 9-2002/1.3.36	
170 Dir. 2002/39/EC amending Dir. 97/67/EC: opening to competition of Community postal services	OJ C 337 E/28.11.2000 COM(2000) 319 Bull. 5-2000/1.3.45	OJ C 116/20.4.2001 Bull. 11-2000/1.3.44 OJ C 144/16.5.2001 Bull. 12-2000/1.3.28°	OJ C 232/17.8.2001 Bull. 12-2000/1.3.28 (b)	OJ C 180 E/26.6.2001 COM(2001) 109 Bull. 3-2001/1.3.43	Bull. 10-2001/1.3.42* Bull. 12-2001/1.3.53	

Taxation

	Commission proposal	ESC opinion/ COR opinion°	EP first reading a, b (¹)	Amended Commission proposal	Common position Council*	
175 Prop. for a reg.: administrative cooperation in the field of VAT	OJ C 270 E/25.9.2001 COM(2001) 294 Bull. 6-2001/1.3.45	OJ C 80/3.4.2002 Bull. 1/2-2002/1.3.65	OJ C 284 E/21.11.2002 Bull. 1/2-2002/1.3.65 (b)			
175 Prop. for a dir. amending Dir. 77/799/EEC: mutual assistance by the competent authorities of the Member States in the field of direct and indirect taxation	OJ C 270 E/25.9.2001 COM(2001) 294 Bull. 6-2001/1.3.45	OJ C 80/3.4.2002 Bull. 1/2-2002/1.3.65	OJ C 284 E/21.11.2002 (a)			
175 Prop. for a dec.: computerising the movement and surveillance of excisable products	OJ C 51 E/26.2.2002 COM(2001) 466 Bull. 11-2001/1.3.53	OJ C 221/17.9.2002 Bull. 5-2002/1.3.36	Bull. 9-2002/1.3.41 (b)	COM(2002) 757 Bull. 12-2002/1.3.49		

° Opinion of the Committee of the Regions.

* Council agreement.

(¹) a = adoption; b = amendments; c = rejection; d = EP failure to take a decision within three months; e = agreement on a common draft; f = failure to agree on a common draft.

TABLE I — CO-DECISION PROCEDURE 503

EP second reading a, b, c, d (¹)	Commission opinion	Conciliation Committee e, f (¹)	EP adoption of common draft	Adoption by Council*	EP and Council signature	Observations	
					OJ L 77/20.3.2002 Bull. 3-2002/1.3.33	Amended dir.: OJ L 228/16.8.1973	166
						Dirs to be amended: 72/166/EC (OJ L 103/2.5.1972), 84/5/EEC (OJ L 8/11.1.1984), 90/232/EEC (OJ L 172/4.7.1988) and 2000/26/EC (OJ L 181/20.7.2000)	166
6-2002/1.3.34 (b)	COM(2002) 454			Bull. 9-2002/1.3.38	OJ L 9/15.1.2003 Bull. 12-2002/1.3.43		166
9-2002/1.3.37 (a)					OJ L 345/19.12.2002		166
							166
11-2002/1.3.30 (a)						Dirs to be amended: 73/239/EEC (OJ L 228/16.8.1973), 79/267/EEC (OJ L 63/13.3.1979), 93/6/EEC (OJ L 228/11.8.1992), 93/22/EEC (OJ L 360/9.12.1992), 98/78/EC (OJ L 330/5.12.1998) and 2000/12/EC (OJ L 126/26.5.2000)	167
3-2002/1.3.40 (b)	COM(2002) 217 Bull. 4-2002/1.3.27				OJ L 176/5.7.2002 Bull. 6-2002/1.3.35	Amended dir.: OJ L 15/21.1.1998	170
							175
						Dir. to be amended: OJ L 336/27.12.1977	175
							175

		Commission proposal	ESC opinion/ COR opinion°	EP first reading a, b(¹)	Amended Commission proposal	Common position Council*
177	Dec. No 2235/2002/EC: Community programme to improve the operation of taxation systems in the internal market (Fiscalis 2003–07 programme)	OJ C 103 E/30.4.2002 COM(2002) 10 Bull. 1/2-2002/1.3.66	OJ C 241/7.10.2002 Bull. 7/8-2002/1.3.35	Bull. 6-2002/1.3.40 (b)		Bull. 7/8-2002/1.3.35
181	Reg. (EC) No 792/2002 amending Reg. (EEC) No 218/92: administrative cooperation in the field of indirect taxation (measures regarding electronic commerce)	OJ C 337 E/28.11.2000 COM(2000) 349 Bull. 6-2000/1.3.40	OJ C 116/20.4.2001 Bull. 11-2000/1.3.48	OJ C 232/17.8.2001 Bull. 12-2000/1.3.33 (b) Bull. 4-2002/1.3.29 (a)		

Company law

		Commission proposal	ESC opinion/ COR opinion°	EP first reading a, b(¹)	Amended Commission proposal	Common position Council*
186	Prop. for a dir. amending Dir. 68/151/EEC: disclosure requirements in respect of certain types of companies	OJ C 227 E/24.9.2002 COM(2002) 279 Bull. 6-2002/1.3.41	11.12.2002 Bull. 12-2002/1.3.50			
187	Prop. for a dir. amending Dirs 78/660/EEC, 83/349/EEC and 91/674/EEC: annual and consolidated accounts of certain types of companies and insurance undertakings	OJ C 227 E/24.9.2002 COM(2002) 259 Bull. 5-2002/1.3.32				
187	Reg. (EC) No 1606/2002: application of international accounting standards	OJ C 154 E/29.5.2001 COM(2001) 80 Bull. 1/2-2001/1.3.71	OJ C 260/17.9.2001 Bull. 7/8-2001/1.3.29	Bull. 3-2002/1.3.35 (b)		
189	Prop. for a dir.: takeover bids	COM(2002) 534 Bull. 10-2002/1.3.28				

Intellectual property

		Commission proposal	ESC opinion/ COR opinion°	EP first reading a, b(¹)	Amended Commission proposal	Common position Council*
192	Prop. for a dir.: patentability of computer-implemented inventions	OJ C 151 E/25.6.2002 COM(2002) 92 Bull. 1/2-2002/1.3.71	Bull. 9-2002/1.3.45			

Public procurement

		Commission proposal	ESC opinion/ COR opinion°	EP first reading a, b(¹)	Amended Commission proposal	Common position Council*
202	Prop. for a dir.: coordination of procedures for the award of public supply contracts, public service contracts and public works contracts	OJ C 29 E/30.1.2001 COM(2000) 275 Bull. 5-2000/1.3.50	OJ C 193/10.7.2001 Bull. 4-2001/1.3.35 OJ C 144/16.5.2001 Bull. 12-2000/1.3.38°	OJ C 271 E/7.11.2002 Bull. 1/2-2002/1.3.72 (b)	OJ C 203 E/27.8.2002 COM(2002) 236 Bull. 5-2002/1.3.38	21.5.2002*
202	Prop. for a dir.: coordination of procurement procedures of entities operating in the water, energy and transport sectors	OJ C 29 E/30.1.2001 COM(2000) 276 Bull. 5-2000/1.3.50	OJ C 193/10.7.2001 Bull. 4-2001/1.3.36 OJ C 144/16.5.2001 Bull. 12-2000/1.3.38°	OJ C 271 E/7.11.2002 Bull. 1/2-2002/1.3.73 (b)	OJ C 203 E/27.8.2002 COM(2002) 235 Bull. 5-2002/1.3.39	Bull. 9-2002/1.3.48*
202	Reg. (EC) No 2195/2002: common procurement vocabulary (CPV)	OJ C 25 E/29.1.2002 COM(2001) 449 Bull. 7/8-2001/1.3.38	OJ C 48/21.2.2002 Bull. 11-2001/1.3.54 OJ C 192/12.8.2002 Bull. 3-2002/1.3.44°	Bull. 3-2002/1.3.44 (a)		Bull. 6-2002/1.3.45

° Opinion of the Committee of the Regions.

* Council agreement.

(¹) a = adoption; b = amendments; c = rejection; d = EP failure to take a decision within three months; e = agreement on a common draft; f = failure to agree on a common draft.

TABLE I — CO-DECISION PROCEDURE 505

EP second reading a, b, c, d (¹)	Commission opinion	Conciliation Committee e, f (¹)	EP adoption of common draft	Adoption by Council*	EP and Council signature	Observations	
10-2002/1.3.25 (a)					OJ L 341/17.12.2002 Bull. 12-2002/1.3.45		**177**
				Bull. 5-2002/1.3.35		Amended reg.: OJ L 24/1.2.1992	**181**
						Dir. to be amended: OJ L 65/14.3.1968	**186**
						Dirs to be amended: 78/660/EEC (OJ L 222/14.8.1978), 83/349/EEC (OJ L 193/18.7.1983) and 91/674/EEC (OJ L 374/31.12.1991)	**187**
					OJ L 243/11.9.2002		**187**
							189
							192
							202
							202
9-2002/1.3.47 (a)					OJ L 340/16.12.2002 Bull. 11-2002/1.3.42		**202**

	Commission proposal	ESC opinion/ COR opinion°	EP first reading a, b (¹)	Amended Commission proposal	Common position Council*

Enterprise policy

Industries and services

		Commission proposal	ESC opinion/ COR opinion°	EP first reading a, b (¹)	Amended Commission proposal	Common position Council*
273	Dir. 2002/45/EC amending Dir. 76/769/EEC: restrictions on the use of certain dangerous substances (chlorinated paraffins)	OJ C 337 E/28.11.2000 COM(2000) 260 Bull. 6-2000/1.3.32	OJ C 116/20.4.2001 Bull. 11-2000/1.3.35	OJ C 267/21.9.2001 Bull. 1/2-2001/1.3.58 (b)	OJ C 213 E/31.7.2001 COM(2001) 268 Bull. 5-2001/1.3.21	Bull. 5-2001/1.3.21* OJ C 301/26.10.2001 Bull. 6-2001/1.3.29
273	Dir. 2002/61/EC amending Dir. 76/769/EEC: restrictions on the marketing of certain dangerous substances and preparations (azocolourants)	OJ C 89 E/28.3.2000 COM(1999) 620 Bull. 12-1999/1.2.20	OJ C 204/18.7.2000 Bull. 5-2000/1.3.33	OJ C 135/7.5.2001 Bull. 9-2000/1.3.24 (b)	COM(2000) 785 Bull. 11-2000/1.3.34	Bull. 11-2001/1.3.38* Bull. 1/2-2002/1.3.55
273	Prop. for a dir.: 24th amendment of Dir. 76/769/EEC: restrictions on the marketing and use of dangerous substances (pentabromodiphenyl ether)	OJ C 154 E/29.5.2001 COM(2001) 12 Bull. 1/2-2001/1.3.58	OJ C 193/10.7.2001 Bull. 4-2001/1.3.16	OJ C 72 E/21.3.2002 Bull. 9-2001/1.3.25 (b)	OJ C 25 E/29.1.2002 COM(2001) 555 Bull. 9-2001/1.3.25	Bull. 9-2001/1.3.25* Bull. 12-2001/1.3.45
273	Prop. for a dir. amending Dir. 76/769/EEC: restrictions on the marketing and use of certain dangerous substances and preparations	OJ C 126 E/28.5.2002 COM(2002) 70 Bull. 1/2-2002/1.3.54	OJ C 221/17.9.2002 Bull. 5-2002/1.3.25	Bull. 6-2002/1.3.25 (b)		
273	Prop. for a dir.: restrictions on the marketing and use of nonylphenol, nonylphenol ethoxylate and cement	COM(2002) 459 Bull. 7/8-2002/1.3.26				
273	Prop. for a reg.: drug precursors	COM(2002) 494 Bull. 9-2002/1.4.9				
273	Prop. for a reg.: detergents	COM(2002) 485 Bull. 9-2002/1.3.27				
273	Prop. for a dir.: inspection and verification of good laboratory practice (GLP) (consolidated version)	COM(2002) 529 Bull. 9-2002/1.3.32				
273	Prop. for a dir.: application of the principles of good laboratory practice and the verification of their applications for tests on chemical substances	COM(2002) 530 Bull. 9-2002/1.3.32				
277	Prop. for a dir.: approximation of the laws of the Member States relating to electromagnetic compatibility	COM(2002) 759				
278	Prop. for a dir. amending Dir. 95/16/EC (machinery)	OJ C 154 E/29.5.2001 COM(2000) 899 Bull. 1/2-2001/1.3.56	OJ C 311/7.11.2001 Bull. 9-2001/1.3.21	Bull. 7/8-2002/1.3.25 (b)		
278	Prop. for a dir.: measuring instruments	OJ C 62 E/27.2.2001 COM(2000) 566 Bull. 9-2000/1.3.22	OJ C 139/11.5.2001 Bull. 3-2001/1.3.33	OJ C 65 E/14.3.2002 Bull. 7/8-2001/1.3.25 (b)	OJ C 126 E/28.5.2002 COM(2002) 37 Bull. 1/2-2002/1.3.50	
279	Prop. for a dir. amending Dir. 2001/83/EC: traditional herbal medicinal products	OJ C 126 E/28.5.2002 COM(2002) 1 Bull. 1/2-2002/1.3.52	Bull. 9-2002/1.3.31	Bull. 11-2002/1.3.24 (b)		
279	Prop. for a reg.: Community procedures for the authorisation and supervision of medicinal products for human and veterinary use and establishing a European Agency for the Evaluation of Medicinal Products	OJ C 75 E/26.3.2002 COM(2001) 404	Bull. 9-2002/1.3.30	Bull. 10-2002/1.3.20 (b)	COM(2002) 735	

° Opinion of the Committee of the Regions.

* Council agreement.

(¹) a = adoption; b = amendments; c = rejection; d = EP failure to take a decision within three months; e = agreement on a common draft; f = failure to agree on a common draft.

TABLE I — CO-DECISION PROCEDURE 507

EP second reading a, b, c, d (¹)	Commission opinion	Conciliation Committee e, f (¹)	EP adoption of common draft	Adoption by Council*	EP and Council signature	Observations	
C 153 E/27.6.2002 11-2001/1.3.39 (b)	COM(2002) 42	22.4.2002	Bull. 5-2002/1.3.24	Bull. 5-2002/1.3.24	OJ L 177/6.7.2002 Bull. 6-2002/1.3.27	Amended dir.: OJ L 262/27.9.1976	273
6-2002/1.3.26 (a)					OJ L 243/11.9.2002	Amended dir.: OJ L 262/27.9.1976	273
4-2002/1.3.22 (b)	COM(2002) 334	Bull. 11-2002/1.3.25 (e)	18.12.2002	9.12.2002 Bull. 12-2002/1.3.37		Dir. to be amended: OJ L 262/27.9.1976	273
						Dir. to be amended: OJ L 262/27.9.1976	273
							273
							273
							273
							273
							273
							277
						Dir. to be amended: OJ L 213/7.9.1995	278
							278
						Dir. to be amended: OJ L 311/28.11.2001	279
							279

		Commission proposal	ESC opinion/ COR opinion°	EP first reading a, b (¹)	Amended Commission proposal	Common position Council*	
279	Prop. for a dir. amending Dir. 2001/83/EC on the Community code relating to medicinal products for human use	OJ C 75 E/26.3.2002 COM(2001) 404	Bull. 9-2002/1.3.30	Bull. 10-2002/1.3.20 (b)			
279	Prop. for a dir. amending Dir. 2001/82/EC on the Community code relating to veterinary medicinal products	OJ C 75 E/26.3.2002 COM(2001) 404	Bull. 9-2002/1.3.30	Bull. 10-2002/1.3.20 (b)			
280	Draft dir.: seventh amendment of Dir. 76/768/EEC: approximation of the laws relating to cosmetic products	OJ C 311/31.10.2000 COM(2000) 189 Bull. 4-2000/1.3.15	OJ C 367/20.12.2000 Bull. 9-2000/1.3.21	OJ C 21 E/24.1.2002 Bull. 4-2001/1.3.15 (b)	OJ C 51 E/26.2.2002 COM(2001) 697 Bull. 11-2001/1.3.35	Bull. 11-2001/1.3.35* Bull. 1/2-2002/1.3.51	
281	Prop. for a dir. amending Dir. 94/25/EC: recreational craft	OJ C 62 E/27.2.2001 COM(2000) 639 Bull. 10-2000/1.3.24	OJ C 155/29.5.2001 Bull. 3-2001/1.3.31	OJ C 65 E/14.3.2002 Bull. 7/8-2001/1.3.21 (b)	OJ C 51 E/26.2.2002 COM(2001) 636	Bull. 10-2001/1.3.30* Bull. 4-2002/1.3.20	
285	Dec. No 2046/2002/EC amending Dec. No 1719/1999/EC: guidelines on trans-European networks for the electronic interchange of data (IDA) between institutions	OJ C 332 E/27.11.2001 COM(2001) 507 Bull. 9-2001/1.3.61	OJ C 80/3.4.2002 Bull. 1/2-2002/1.3.154	11.6.2002			
285	Dec. No 2045/2002/EC amending Dec. No 1720/1999/EC: interoperability of trans-European networks for the electronic interchange of data (IDA)	OJ C 332 E/27.11.2001 COM(2001) 507 Bull. 9-2001/1.3.61	OJ C 80/3.4.2002 Bull. 1/2-2002/1.3.154	Bull. 6-2002/1.3.108 (b)			

Research and technology
Community RTD policy

		Commission proposal	ESC opinion/ COR opinion°	EP first reading a, b (¹)	Amended Commission proposal	Common position Council*	
297	Prop. for a dec.: Community participation in a programme aimed at developing new clinical interventions to combat HIV/AIDS, malaria and tuberculosis	COM(2002) 474 Bull. 7/8-2002/1.3.86					
299	Dec. No 1513/2002/EC: multiannual framework programme 2002–06 (research)	OJ C 180 E/26.6.2001 COM(2001) 94 Bull. 1/2-2001/1.3.124	OJ C 260/17.9.2001 Bull. 7/8-2001/1.3.97 OJ C 107/3.5.2002 Bull. 11-2001/1.3.94°	OJ C 140 E/13.6.2002 Bull. 11-2001/1.3.94 (b)	OJ C 75 E/26.3.2002 COM(2001) 709 Bull. 11-2001/1.3.94	Bull. 12-2001/1.3.103* Bull. 1/2-2002/1.3.130	
301	Reg. (EC) No 2321/2002: rules for the participation and dissemination of research results for the implementation of the framework programme 2002–06	OJ C 332 E/27.11.2001 COM(2001) 500 Bull. 9-2001/1.3.45	OJ C 94/18.4.2002 Bull. 1/2-2002/1.3.129	Bull. 7/8-2002/1.3.84 (b)	OJ C 103 E/30.4.2002 COM(2001) 822 Bull. 1/2-2002/1.3.129 OJ C 262 E/29.10.2002 COM(2002) 413 Bull. 7/8-2002/1.3.84		

Information society
eEurope initiative

		Commission proposal	ESC opinion/ COR opinion°	EP first reading a, b (¹)	Amended Commission proposal	Common position Council*	
333	Prop. for a dir.: re-use and commercial exploitation of public sector documents	OJ C 227 E/24.9.2002 COM(2002) 207 Bull. 6-2002/1.3.95	11.12.2002 Bull. 11-2002/1.3.74°				
334	Prop. for a dec. amending Dec. No 276/1999/EC: action plan on promoting safer use of the Internet by combating illegal and harmful content on global networks	OJ C 203 E/27.8.2002 COM(2002) 152 Bull. 3-2002/1.3.67	Bull. 9-2002/1.3.73 Bull. 11-2002/1.3.73°				

° Opinion of the Committee of the Regions.

* Council agreement.

(¹) a = adoption; b = amendments; c = rejection; d = EP failure to take a decision within three months; e = agreement on a common draft; f = failure to agree on a common draft.

TABLE I — CO-DECISION PROCEDURE 509

P second reading a, b, c, d (¹)	Commission opinion	Conciliation Committee e, f (¹)	EP adoption of common draft	Adoption by Council*	EP and Council signature	Observations	
						Dir. to be amended: OJ L 311/28.11.2001	279
						Dir. to be amended: OJ L 311/28.11.2001	279
6-2002/1.3.23 (b)	COM(2002) 435					Amended dir: OJ L 262/27.9.1976	280
9-2002/1.3.26 (b)	COM(2002) 602 Bull. 11-2002/1.3.23					Dir. to be amended: OJ L 164/30.6.1994	281
				Bull. 6-2002/1.3.108*	OJ L 316/20.11.2002 Bull. 10-2002/1.3.67	Amended dec.: OJ L 203/3.8.1999	285
				Bull. 6-2002/1.3.108*	OJ L 316/20.11.2002 Bull. 10-2002/1.3.67	Amended dec.: OJ L 203/3.8.1999	285
							297
5-2002/1.3.71 (b)	COM(2002) 284 Bull. 5-2002/1.3.71				OJ L 232/29.8.2002		299
					OJ L 355/30.12.2002		301
							333
						Dec. to be amended: OJ L 33/6.2.1999	334

	Commission proposal	ESC opinion/ COR opinion°	EP first reading a, b (¹)	Amended Commission proposal	Common position Council*

Electronic communications

338	Reg. (EC) No 733/2002: implementation of the Internet .eu top level domain	OJ C 96 E/27.3.2001 COM(2000) 827 Bull. 12-2000/1.3.81	OJ C 155/29.5.2001 Bull. 3-2001/1.3.94	OJ C 65 E/14.3.2002 Bull. 7/8-2001/1.3.102 (b)	COM(2001) 535 Bull. 10-2001/1.3.102	Bull. 11-2001/1.3.103
341	Dir. 2002/21/EC: common regulatory framework for electronic communications networks and services	OJ C 365 E/19.12.2000 COM(2000) 393 Bull. 7/8-2000/1.3.94	OJ C 123/25.4.2001 Bull. 1/2-2001/1.3.128	OJ C 277/1.10.2001 Bull. 3-2001/1.3.88 (b)	OJ C 270 E/25.9.2001 COM(2001) 380	Bull. 4-2001/1.3.59* OJ C 337/30.11.2001 Bull. 9-2001/1.3.51
341	Dir. 2002/19/EC: access to, and interconnection of, electronic communications networks and associated facilities	OJ C 365 E/19.12.2000 COM(2000) 384 Bull. 7/8-2000/1.3.90	OJ C 123/25.4.2001 Bull. 1/2-2001/1.3.130	OJ C 277/1.10.2001 Bull. 3-2001/1.3.89 (b)	OJ C 270 E/25.9.2001 COM(2001) 369	Bull. 4-2001/1.3.60* OJ C 337/30.11.2001 Bull. 9-2001/1.3.52
341	Dir. 2002/20/EC replacing Dir. 97/13/EC: authorisation of electronic communications networks and services	OJ C 365 E/19.12.2000 COM(2000) 386 Bull. 7/8-2000/1.3.92	OJ C 123/25.4.2001 Bull. 1/2-2001/1.3.127	OJ C 277/1.10.2001 Bull. 3-2001/1.3.90 (b)	OJ C 270 E/25.9.2001 COM(2001) 372	Bull. 4-2001/1.3.61* OJ C 337/30.11.2001 Bull. 9-2001/1.3.53
341	Dir. 2002/22/EC: universal service and users' rights relating to electronic communications networks and services	OJ C 365 E/19.12.2000 COM(2000) 392 Bull. 7/8-2000/1.3.93	OJ C 139/11.5.2001 Bull. 3-2001/1.3.91 OJ C 144/16.5.2001 Bull. 12-2000/1.3.78°	OJ C 53 E/28.2.2002 Bull. 6-2001/1.3.88 (b)	OJ C 332 E/27.11.2001 COM(2001) 503 Bull. 9-2001/1.3.54	Bull. 6-2001/1.3.88* OJ C 337/30.11.2001 Bull. 9-2001/1.3.54
342	Dec. No 676/2002/EC: regulatory framework for radio spectrum policy in the EC	OJ C 365 E/19.12.2000 COM(2000) 407 Bull. 7/8-2000/1.3.96	OJ C 123/25.4.2001 Bull. 1/2-2001/1.3.129	OJ C 65 E/14.3.2002 Bull. 7/8-2001/1.3.103 (b)	OJ C 25 E/29.1.2002 COM(2001) 524 Bull. 9-2001/1.3.55	OJ C 9/11.1.2002 Bull. 10-2001/1.3.103
343	Dir. 2002/58/EC replacing Dir. 97/66/EC: processing of personal data and the protection of privacy in the electronic communications sector	OJ C 365 E/19.12.2000 COM(2000) 385 Bull. 7/8-2000/1.3.91	OJ C 123/25.4.2001 Bull. 1/2-2001/1.3.126	OJ C 140 E/13.6.2002 Bull. 11-2001/1.3.104 (b)		Bull. 12-2001/1.3.105* Bull. 1/2-2002/1.3.137

Trans-European networks
General approach

385	Prop. for a reg. amending reg. (EC) No 2236/95: granting of Community financial aid in the field of trans-European networks	OJ C 75 E/26.3.2002 COM(2001) 545 Bull. 10-2001/1.3.112	OJ C 125/27.5.2002 Bull. 3-2002/1.3.76	Bull. 7/8-2002/1.3.96 (b)	OJ C 151 E/25.6.2002 COM(2002) 134 Bull. 3-2002/1.3.76	

Transport

387	Prop. for a dec. amending Dec. No 1692/96/EC: Community guidelines for the development of the trans-European transport network	OJ C 362 E/18.12.2001 COM(2001) 544 Bull. 10-2001/1.3.113	OJ C 125/27.5.2002 Bull. 3-2002/1.3.77 OJ C 278/14.11.2002 Bull. 5-2002/1.3.85°	Bull. 5-2002/1.3.85 (b)	COM(2002) 542 Bull. 9-2002/1.3.78	

Telematics and telecommunications

388	Dec. No 1376/2002/EC: revision of Annex 1 to Dec. No 1336/97/EC on a series of guidelines for trans-European telecommunications networks	OJ C 103 E/30.4.2002 COM(2001) 742 Bull. 12-2001/1.3.121	OJ C 221/17.9.2002 Bull. 5-2002/1.3.80	Bull. 5-2002/1.3.80 (b)	OJ C 227 E/24.9.2002 COM(2002) 317 Bull. 6-2002/1.3.100	

° Opinion of the Committee of the Regions.

* Council agreement.

(¹) a = adoption; b = amendments; c = rejection; d = EP failure to take a decision within three months; e = agreement on a common draft; f = failure to agree on a common draft.

TABLE I — CO-DECISION PROCEDURE **511**

EP second reading a, b, c, d (^{1})	Commission opinion	Conciliation Committee e, f (^{1})	EP adoption of common draft	Adoption by Council*	EP and Council signature	Observations	
C 293 E/28.11.2002 . 1/2-2002/1.3.144 (b)	COM(2002) 165 Bull. 3-2002/1.3.69				OJ L 113/30.4.2002 Bull. 4-2002/1.3.81		338
C 177 E/25.7.2002 . 12-2001/1.3.107 (b)	COM(2002) 78 Bull. 1/2-2002/1.3.139				OJ L 108/24.4.2002		341
C 177 E/25.7.2002 . 12-2001/1.3.108 (b)	COM(2002) 75 Bull. 1/2-2002/1.3.140				OJ L 108/24.4.2002		341
C 177 E/25.7.2002 . 12-2001/1.3.109 (b)	COM(2002) 74 Bull. 1/2-2002/1.3.141				OJ L 108/24.4.2002	Replaced dir.: OJ L 117/7.5.1997	341
C 177 E/25.7.2002 . 12-2001/1.3.110 (b)	COM(2002) 77 Bull. 1/2-2002/1.3.142				OJ L 108/24.4.2002		341
C 177 E/25.7.2002 . 12-2001/1.3.111 (b)	COM(2002) 65 Bull. 1/2-2002/1.3.143				OJ L 108/24.4.2002		342
. 5-2002/1.3.79 (b)	COM(2002) 338 Bull. 6-2002/1.3.98				OJ L 201/31.7.2002 Bull. 7/8-2002/1.3.90	Replaced dir.: OJ L 24/30.1.1998	343
						Reg. to be amended: OJ L 228/23.9.1995	385
						Dec. to be amended: OJ L 228/9.9.1996	387
					OJ L 200/30.7.2002 Bull. 7/8-2002/1.3.91	Revised dec.: OJ L 183/11.7.1997	388

	Commission proposal	ESC opinion/ COR opinion°	EP first reading a, b (¹)	Amended Commission proposal	Common position Council*

Energy

390	Prop. for a dec. amending Dec. No 1254/96/EC: guidelines for trans- European energy networks	OJ C 151 E/25.6.2002 COM(2001) 775 Bull. 12-2001/1.3.122	OJ C 241/7.10.2002 Bull. 7/8-2002/1.3.99 OJ C 278/14.11.2002 Bull. 5-2002/1.3.87°	Bull. 10-2002/1.3.68 (b)		Bull. 11-2002/1.3.80*

Citizenship and quality of life

Union citizenship

Freedom of movement and right of residence

507	Prop. for a dir.: right of citizens to move around and reside freely	OJ C 270 E/25.9.2001 COM(2001) 257 Bull. 5-2001/1.4.3	OJ C 149/21.6.2002 Bull. 4-2002/1.4.11 OJ C 192/12.8.2002 Bull. 3-2002/1.4.3°			

Education and culture

Education and training

521	Prop. for a dec. amending Dec. No 253/2000/EC: second phase of the Community action programme 'Socrates'	OJ C 203 E/27.8.2002 COM(2002) 193 Bull. 4-2002/1.4.34	OJ C 241/7.10.2002 Bull. 7/8-2002/1.4.7	Bull. 9-2002/1.4.14 (a)		
524	Prop. for a dec.: programme for the enhancement of quality in higher education and the promotion of intercultural understanding through cooperation with third countries (Erasmus World) (2004–08)	OJ C 331 E/31.12.2002 COM(2002) 401 Bull. 7/8-2002/1.4.9				

Sport

546	Prop. for a dec.: European Year of Education through Sport 2004	OJ C 25 E/29.1.2002 COM(2001) 584 Bull. 10-2001/1.4.22	OJ C 149/21.6.2002 Bull. 4-2002/1.4.39 OJ C 278/14.11.2002 Bull. 5-2002/1.4.31°	Bull. 5-2002/1.4.31 (b)		Bull. 5-2002/1.4.31* Bull. 10-2002/1.4.25

Environment

Sixth action programme

552	Dec. No 1600/2002/EC: sixth environment action programme 2001–10	OJ C 154 E/29.5.2001 COM(2001) 31 Bull. 1/2-2001/1.4.28	OJ C 221/7.8.2001 Bull. 5-2001/1.4.30 OJ C 357/14.12.2001 Bull. 6-2001/1.4.24°	OJ C 47 E/21.2.2002 Bull. 5-2001/1.4.30 (b)		Bull. 6-2001/1.4.24* OJ C 4/7.1.2002 Bull. 9-2001/1.4.38

° Opinion of the Committee of the Regions.

* Council agreement.

(¹) a = adoption; b = amendments; c = rejection; d = EP failure to take a decision within three months; e = agreement on a common draft; f = failure to agree on a common draft.

TABLE I — CO-DECISION PROCEDURE   513

second reading a, b, c, d (^{1})	Commission opinion	Conciliation Committee e, f (^{1})	EP adoption of common draft	Adoption by Council*	EP and Council signature	Observations	
						Dec. to be amended: OJ L 161/29.6.1996	**390**
							507
						Dec. to be amended: OJ L 28/3.2.2000	**521**
							524
2.2002 12-2002/1.4.38							**546**
C 271 E/7.11.2002 1/2-2002/1.4.70 (b)	COM(2002) 84 Bull. 1/2-2002/1.4.70	Bull. 3-2002/1.4.14 (e)	Bull. 5-2002/1.4.32	Bull. 6-2002/1.4.31	OJ L 242/10.9.2002 Bull. 7/8-2002/1.4.12		**552**

	Commission proposal	ESC opinion/ COR opinion°	EP first reading a, b (¹)	Amended Commission proposal	Common position Council*

Sustainable development

562 Prop. for a dir.: waste electrical and electronic equipment	OJ C 365 E/19.12.2000 COM(2000) 347 Bull. 6-2000/1.4.30	OJ C 116/20.4.2001 Bull. 11-2000/1.4.34 OJ C 148/18.5.2001 Bull. 1/2-2001/1.4.33°	OJ C 34 E/7.2.2002 Bull. 5-2001/1.4.35 (b)	OJ C 240 E/28.8.2001 COM(2001) 315 Bull. 6-2001/1.4.28	Bull. 6-2001/1.4.28* Bull. 12-2001/1.4.36
562 Prop. for a dir.: restriction of the use of certain hazardous substances in electrical and electronic equipment	OJ C 365 E/19.12.2000 COM(2000) 347 Bull. 6-2000/1.4.30	OJ C 116/20.4.2001 Bull. 11-2000/1.4.34 OJ C 148/18.5.2001 Bull. 1/2-2001/1.4.33°	OJ C 34 E/7.2.2002 Bull. 5-2001/1.4.35 (b)	OJ C 240 E/28.8.2001 COM(2001) 316 Bull. 6-2001/1.4.28	Bull. 6-2001/1.4.28* Bull. 12-2001/1.4.36
562 Prop. for a dir. amending Dir. 94/62/EC on packaging and packaging waste	OJ C 103 E/30.4.2002 COM(2001) 729 Bull. 12-2001/1.4.37	OJ C 221/17.9.2002 Bull. 5-2002/1.4.40	Bull. 9-2002/1.4.25 (b)		Bull. 10-2002/1.4.29*
563 Recomm.: implementation of integrated coastal zone management in Europe	COM(2000) 545 Bull. 9-2000/1.4.34	OJ C 155/29.5.2001 Bull. 3-2001/1.4.23 OJ C 148/18.5.2001 Bull. 1/2-2001/1.4.34°	OJ C 65 E/14.3.2002 Bull. 7/8-2001/1.4.20 (b)	COM(2001) 533 Bull. 9-2001/1.4.33	Bull. 10-2001/1.4.24° Bull. 12-2001/1.4.38

Environmental quality and natural resources

566 Prop. for a dir.: quality of bathing water	COM(2002) 581 Bull. 10-2002/1.4.31				
572 Reg. (EC) No 804/2002 amending Reg. (EEC) No 3528/86: protection of the Community's forests against atmospheric pollution	OJ C 51 E/26.2.2002 COM(2001) 634 Bull. 11-2001/1.4.45	OJ C 80/3.4.2002 Bull. 1/2-2002/1.4.53	Bull. 3-2002/1.4.24 (b)		
572 Reg. (EC) No 805/2002 amending Reg. (EEC) No 2158/92: protection of the Community's forests against fire	OJ C 51 E/26.2.2002 COM(2001) 634 Bull. 11-2001/1.4.45	OJ C 80/3.4.2002 Bull. 1/2-2002/1.4.53	Bull. 3-2002/1.4.24 (b)		
572 Prop. for a reg.: monitoring of forests and environmental interactions in the Community (Forest Focus)	COM(2002) 404 Bull. 7/8-2002/1.4.16	12.12.2002			
574 Prop. for a dir. amending Dir. 96/82/EC: control of major accident hazards involving dangerous substances	OJ C 75 E/26.3.2002 COM(2001) 624 Bull. 12-2001/1.4.41	OJ C 149/21.6.2002 Bull. 4-2002/1.4.46	Bull. 7/8-2002/1.4.18 (b)	COM(2002) 540 Bull. 9-2002/1.4.32	Bull. 10-2002/1.4.34*

Environment and health

577 Prop. for a reg.: export and import of dangerous chemicals	OJ C 126 E/28.5.2002 COM(2001) 803 Bull. 1/2-2002/1.4.57	OJ C 241/7.10.2002 Bull. 7/8-2002/1.4.21	Bull. 10-2002/1.4.37		
580 Prop. for a reg.: transboundary movement of genetically modified organisms	OJ C 151 E/25.6.2002 COM(2002) 85 Bull. 1/2-2002/1.4.59	OJ C 241/7.10.2002 Bull. 7/8-2002/1.4.23 OJ C 278/14.11.2002°	Bull. 9-2002/1.4.35 (b)	COM(2002) 578 Bull. 10-2002/1.4.41	Bull. 10-2002/1.4.41*
581 Dir. 2002/3/EC: ozone in ambient air	OJ C 56 E/29.2.2000 COM(1999) 125 Bull. 6-1999/1.2.109	OJ C 317/6.11.2000 Bull. 6-2000/1.4.28°	OJ C 377/29.12.2000 Bull. 3-2000/1.4.22 (b)	OJ C 29 E/30.1.2001 COM(2000) 613 Bull. 10-2000/1.4.24	Bull. 10-2000/1.4.24* OJ C 126/26.4.2001 Bull. 3-2001/1.4.32
582 Dir. 2002/51/EC amending Dir. 97/24/EC: components and characteristics of two- or three-wheel motor vehicles	OJ C 337 E/28.11.2000 COM(2000) 314 Bull. 6-2000/1.4.32	OJ C 123/25.4.2001 Bull. 1/2-2001/1.4.43	OJ C 276/1.10.2001 Bull. 1/2-2001/1.4.43 (b)	OJ C 240 E/28.8.2001 COM(2001) 145 Bull. 5-2001/1.4.45	Bull. 3-2001/1.4.31* OJ C 301/26.10.2001 Bull. 7/8-2001/1.4.25

° Opinion of the Committee of the Regions.

* Council agreement.

(¹) a = adoption; b = amendments; c = rejection; d = EP failure to take a decision within three months; e = agreement on a common draft; f = failure to agree on a common draft.

TABLE I — CO-DECISION PROCEDURE 515

second reading a, b, c, d (¹)	Commission opinion	Conciliation Committee e, f (¹)	EP adoption of common draft	Adoption by Council*	EP and Council signature	Observations	
4-2002/1.4.40 (b)	COM(2002) 353 Bull. 6-2002/1.4.35	Bull. 10-2002/1.4.28 (e)	18.12.2002 Bull. 12-2002/1.4.44	16.12.2002 Bull. 12-2002/1.4.44	27.12.2002		562
4-2002/1.4.40 (b)	COM(2002) 354 Bull. 6-2002/1.4.35	Bull. 10-2002/1.4.28 (e)	18.12.2002 Bull. 12-2002/1.4.45	16.12.2002	27.12.2002 Bull. 12-2002/1.4.45		562
						Dir. to be amended: OJ L 365/31.12.1994	562
4-2002/1.4.41 (b)	COM(2002) 266 Bull. 5-2002/1.4.41				OJ L 148/6.6.2002 Bull. 5-2002/1.4.41		563
							566
					OJ L 132/17.5.2002 Bull. 4-2002/1.4.43	Amended reg.: OJ L 326/21.11.1986	572
					OJ L 132/17.5.2002 Bull. 4-2002/1.4.43	Amended reg.: OJ L 217/31.7.1992	572
							572
						Dir. to be amended: OJ L 10/14.1.1997	574
							577
							580
C 53 E/28.2.2002 , 6-2001/1.4.37 (b)	COM(2001) 476 Bull. 7/8-2001/1.4.26	Bull. 11-2001/1.4.58 (e)	OJ C 271 E/7.11.2002 Bull. 1/2-2002/1.4.60	Bull. 12-2001/1.4.46	OJ L 67/9.3.2002 Bull. 1/2-2002/1.4.60		581
C 177 E/25.7.2002 , 12-2001/1.4.45 (b)	COM(2002) 58 Bull. 1/2-2002/1.4.61	Bull. 3-2002/1.4.28 (e)	Bull. 5-2002/1.4.43	Bull. 6-2002/1.4.40	OJ L 252/20.9.2002 Bull. 7/8-2002/1.4.26	Amended dir.: OJ L 226/18.8.1997	582

	Commission proposal	ESC opinion/ COR opinion°	EP first reading a, b(¹)	Amended Commission proposal	Common position Council*
582 Prop. for a dir. amending Dir. 97/68/EC: measures against gas emissions from internal combustion engines to be installed in mobile machinery	OJ C 180 E/26.6.2001 COM(2000) 840 Bull. 12-2000/1.4.38	OJ C 260/17.9.2001 Bull. 7/8-2001/1.4.24	OJ C 87 E/11.4.2002 Bull. 10-2001/1.4.32 (b)	OJ C 51 E/26.2.2002 COM(2001) 626 Bull. 10-2001/1.4.32	Bull. 10-2001/1.4.32* Bull. 3-2002/1.4.30
582 Prop. for a dir. amending Dir. 1999/32/EC: sulphur content of marine fuels	COM(2002) 595 Bull. 11-2002/1.4.52				
582 Prop. for a dir.: limitation of emissions of volatile organic compounds and amending Dir. 1999/13/EC	COM(2002) 750				
582 Prop. for a dir. amending Dir. 97/68/EC: measures against the emission of gaseous and particulate pollutants from internal combustion engines to be installed in non-road mobile machinery	COM(2002) 765				
583 Prop. for a dir.: quality of petrol and diesel fuels and amending Dir. 98/70/EC	OJ C 213 E/31.7.2001 COM(2001) 241 Bull. 5-2001/1.4.43	OJ C 36/8.2.2002 Bull. 10-2001/1.4.33	OJ C 153 E/27.6.2002 Bull. 11-2001/1.4.55 (b)		Bull. 12-2001/1.4.44* Bull. 4-2002/1.4.47
584 Dir. 2002/49/EC: assessment and management of environmental noise	OJ C 337 E/28.11.2000 COM(2000) 468 Bull. 7/8-2000/1.4.37	OJ C 116/20.4.2001 Bull. 11-2000/1.4.36 OJ C 148/18.5.2001 Bull. 1/2-2001/1.4.44°	OJ C 232/17.8.2001 Bull. 12-2000/1.4.40 (b)		Bull. 12-2000/1.4.40* OJ C 297/23.10.2001 Bull. 6-2001/1.4.38

Climate change and international dimension

	Commission proposal	ESC opinion/ COR opinion°	EP first reading a, b(¹)	Amended Commission proposal	Common position Council*
587 Prop. for a dir. amending Dirs 70/156/EEC and 80/1268/EEC: measurement of carbon dioxide emissions and fuel consumption of N1 vehicles	OJ C 51 E/26.2.2002 COM(2001) 543 Bull. 10-2001/1.4.35	OJ C 125/27.5.2002 Bull. 3-2002/1.4.29	Bull. 9-2002/1.4.36 (b)		
587 Prop. for a dir. amending Dir. 96/61/EC establishing a scheme for greenhouse gas emission allowance trading within the Community	OJ C 75 E/26.3.2002 COM(2001) 581 Bull. 10-2001/1.4.44	OJ C 221/17.9.2002 Bull. 5-2002/1.4.45 OJ C 192/12.8.2002°	Bull. 10-2002/1.4.44 (b)	COM(2002) 680 Bull. 11-2002/1.4.55	9.12.2002*
589 Prop. for a reg. amending Reg. (EC) No 2037/2000: substances which deplete the ozone layer, as regards the critical uses and export of halons, the export of products and equipment	COM(2002) 642 Bull. 11-2002/1.4.53				

Governance, communication and civil society

	Commission proposal	ESC opinion/ COR opinion°	EP first reading a, b(¹)	Amended Commission proposal	Common position Council*
595 Prop. for a dir.: environmental liability with regard to the prevention and remedying of environmental damage	OJ C 151 E/25.6.2002 COM(2002) 17 Bull. 1/2-2002/1.4.67	OJ C 241/7.10.2002 Bull. 7/8-2002/1.4.29			
595 Prop. for a dir.: protection of the environment through criminal law	OJ C 180 E/26.6.2001 COM(2001) 139 Bull. 3-2001/1.4.39		Bull. 4-2002/1.4.53 (b)	COM(2002) 544 Bull. 9-2002/1.4.40	
596 Prop. for a dir.: public participation in the drawing up of plans and programmes relating to the environment and amendment of Dirs 85/337/EEC and 96/61/EC	OJ C 154 E/29.5.2002 COM(2000) 839 Bull. 1/2-2001/1.4.45	OJ C 221/7.8.2001 Bull. 5-2001/1.4.50 OJ C 357/14.12.2001 Bull. 6-2001/1.4.42°	OJ C 112 E/9.5.2002 Bull. 10-2001/1.4.48 (b)	OJ C 75 E/26.3.2002 COM(2001) 779 Bull. 12-2001/1.4.50	Bull. 12-2001/1.4.50* Bull. 4-2002/1.4.52

° Opinion of the Committee of the Regions.

* Council agreement.

(¹) a = adoption; b = amendments; c = rejection; d = EP failure to take a decision within three months; e = agreement on a common draft; f = failure to agree on a common draft.

TABLE I — CO-DECISION PROCEDURE 517

second reading a, b, c, d (¹)	Commission opinion	Conciliation Committee e, f (¹)	EP adoption of common draft	Adoption by Council*	EP and Council signature	Observations	
⁷/8-2002/1.4.25 (b)	COM(2002) 458 Bull. 7/8-2002/1.4.25				9.12.2002	Dir. to be amended: OJ L 59/27.2.1998	582
						Dir. to be amended : OJ L 121/11.5.1999	582
						Dir.to be amended: OJ L 85/29.3.1999	582
						Dir. to be amended: OJ L 59/27.2.1998	582
⁹-2002/1.4.37 (b)	COM(2002) 604 Bull. 10-2002/1.4.43	10.12.2002 Bull. 12-2002/1.4.57				Dir. to be amended: OJ L 350/28.12.1998	583
87 E/11.4.2002 10-2001/1.4.38 (b)	COM(2001) 621 Bull. 10-2001/1.4.38	Bull. 1/2-2002/1.4.62 (e)	Bull. 5-2002/1.4.44	Bull. 5-2002/1.4.44	OJ L 189/18.7.2002 Bull. 6-2002/1.4.41		584
						Dirs to be amended: 70/156/EEC (OJ L 42/23.2.1970) and 80/1268/EEC (OJ L 375/31.12.1980)	587
						Dir. to be amended: OJ L 257/10.10.1996	587
						Reg. to be amended: OJ L 244/29.9.2000	589
							595
							595
, 9-2002/1.4.39 (b)	COM(2002) 586 Bull. 10-2002/1.4.47	10.12.2002				Dirs to be amended: 85/337/EEC (OJ L 175/5.7.1985) 96/61/EC (OJ L 257/10.10.1996)	596

	Commission proposal	ESC opinion/ COR opinion°	EP first reading a, b (¹)	Amended Commission proposal	Common position Council*
596 Prop. for a dir.: public access to environmental information	OJ C 337 E/28.11.2000 COM(2000) 402 Bull. 6-2000/1.4.41	OJ C 116/20.4.2001 Bull. 11-2000/1.4.45 OJ C 148/18.5.2001 Bull. 1/2-2001/1.4.46°	OJ C 343/5.12.2001 Bull. 3-2001/1.4.38 (b)	OJ C 240 E/28.8.2001 COM(2001) 303 Bull. 6-2001/1.4.41	Bull. 6-2001/1.4.41* Bull. 1/2-2002/1.4.69
597 Dec. No 466/2002/EC: Community action programme promoting non-governmental organisations active in the field of environmental protection	OJ C 270 E/25.9.2001 COM(2001) 337 Bull. 6-2001/1.4.43	OJ C 36/8.2.2002 Bull. 10-2001/1.4.49	OJ C 112 E/9.5.2002 Bull. 10-2001/1.4.49 (b)		Bull. 10-2001/1.4.49* Bull. 12-2001/1.4.51

Energy

General strategy

	Commission proposal	ESC opinion/ COR opinion°	EP first reading a, b (¹)	Amended Commission proposal	Common position Council*
599 Prop. for a dec.: 'Intelligent energy for Europe programme' (2003–06)	OJ C 203 E/27.8.2002 COM(2002) 162 Bull. 4-2002/1.4.55	Bull. 9-2002/1.4.42 Bull. 11-2002/1.4.57°	Bull. 11-2002/1.4.57 (b)		Bull. 11-2002/1.4.57*

Internal energy market

	Commission proposal	ESC opinion/ COR opinion°	EP first reading a, b (¹)	Amended Commission proposal	Common position Council*
609 Prop. for a dir. amending Dir. 96/92/EC (internal market in electricity) and Dir. 98/30/EC (internal market in natural gas)	OJ C 240 E/28.8.2001 COM(2001) 125 Bull. 3-2001/1.4.43	OJ C 36/8.2.2002 Bull. 10-2001/1.4.52	Bull. 3-2002/1.4.38 (b)	OJ C 227 E/24.9.2002 COM(2002) 304 Bull. 6-2002/1.4.45	Bull. 11-2002/1.4.58*
609 Prop. for a reg.: conditions for access to the network for cross-border exchanges in electricity	OJ C 240 E/28.8.2001 COM(2001) 125 Bull. 3-2001/1.4.43	OJ C 36/8.2.2002 Bull. 10-2001/1.4.52	Bull. 3-2002/1.4.39 (b)	OJ C 227 E/24.9.2002 COM(2002) 304 Bull. 6-2002/1.4.45	Bull. 11-2002/1.4.58*
610 Prop. for a dir.: promotion of cogeneration based on a useful heat demand in the internal energy market	OJ C 291 E/26.11.2002 COM(2002) 415 Bull. 7/8-2002/1.4.32				
611 Prop. for a dir.: alignment of measures to safeguard the supply of petroleum products	OJ C 331 E/31.12.2002 COM(2002) 488 Bull. 9-2002/1.4.43				
611 Prop. for a dir.: measures to safeguard the supply of natural gas	OJ C 331 E/31.12.2002 COM(2002) 488 Bull. 9-2002/1.4.43				

New and renewable energy sources

	Commission proposal	ESC opinion/ COR opinion°	EP first reading a, b (¹)	Amended Commission proposal	Common position Council*
615 Prop. for a dir. promoting the use of biofuels for transport	OJ C 103 E/30.4.2002 COM(2001) 547 Bull. 11-2001/1.4.64	OJ C 149/21.6.2002 Bull. 4-2002/1.4.56 OJ C 278/14.11.2002 Bull. 5-2002/1.4.49°	Bull. 7/8-2002/1.4.34 (b)	OJ C 331 E/31.12.2002 COM(2002) 508 Bull. 9-2002/1.4.44	Bull. 11-2002/1.4.60

° Opinion of the Committee of the Regions.

* Council agreement.

(¹) a = adoption; b = amendments; c = rejection; d = EP failure to take a decision within three months; e = agreement on a common draft; f = failure to agree on a common draft.

TABLE I — CO-DECISION PROCEDURE **519**

second reading a, b, c, d (¹)	Commission opinion	Conciliation Committee e, f (¹)	EP adoption of common draft	Adoption by Council*	EP and Council signature	Observations	
5-2002/1.4.46 (b)	COM(2002) 498 Bull. 9-2002/1.4.41	Bull. 11-2002/1.4.56 (e)	18.12.2002 Bull. 12-2002/1.4.62	16.12.2002 Bull. 12-2002/1.4.62			596
271 E/7.11.2002 1/2-2002/1.4.68 (a)					OJ L 75/16.3.2002 Bull. 3-2002/1.4.36		597
							599
						Dirs to be amended: 96/92/EC (OJ L 27/30.1.1997) and 98/30/EC (OJ L 204/21.7.1998)	609
							609
							610
							611
							611
							615

	Commission proposal	ESC opinion/ COR opinion°	EP first reading a, b(¹)	Amended Commission proposal	Common position Council*

Energy efficiency and rational use of energy

		Commission proposal	ESC opinion/ COR opinion°	EP first reading a, b(¹)	Amended Commission proposal	Common position Council*
617	Dir. 2002/91/EC: energy performance of buildings	OJ C 213 E/31.7.2001 COM(2001) 226 Bull. 5-2001/1.4.56	OJ C 36/8.2.2002 Bull. 10-2001/1.4.55 OJ C 107/3.5.2002 Bull. 11-2001/1.4.66°	OJ C 284 E/21.11.2002 Bull. 1/2-2002/1.4.72 (b)	OJ C 203 E/27.8.2002 COM(2002) 192 Bull. 4-2002/1.4.57	Bull. 6-2002/1.4.46

Transport

Infrastructure

		Commission proposal	ESC opinion/ COR opinion°	EP first reading a, b(¹)	Amended Commission proposal	Common position Council*
639	Prop. for a dir.: minimum safety requirements for tunnels in the trans-European road network	COM(2002) 769 Bull. 12-2002				

Inland transport

		Commission proposal	ESC opinion/ COR opinion°	EP first reading a, b(¹)	Amended Commission proposal	Common position Council*
640	Prop. for a dir.: railway safety and amending Dir. 95/18/EC on the licensing of railway undertakings and Dir. 2001/14/EC on infrastructure capacity, levying of charges and certification	OJ C 126 E/28.5.2002 COM(2002) 21 Bull. 1/2-2002/1.4.81	Bull. 9-2002/1.4.50 Bull. 10-2002/1.4.52°			
640	Prop. for a dir. amending Council Dir. 96/48/EC and Dir. 2001/16/EC: interoperability of the trans-European rail system	OJ C 126 E/28.5.2002 COM(2002) 22 Bull. 1/2-2002/1.4.82	Bull. 9-2002/1.4.50 Bull. 10-2002/1.4.52°			
640	Prop. for a reg.: European Railway Agency	OJ C 126 E/28.5.2002 COM(2002) 23 Bull. 1/2-2002/1.4.83	Bull. 9-2002/1.4.50 Bull. 10-2002/1.4.52°			
640	Prop. for a dir. amending Dir. 91/440/EEC: development of the Community's railways	OJ C 291 E/26.11.2002 COM(2002) 25 Bull. 1/2-2002/1.4.85	Bull. 9-2002/1.4.50 Bull. 10-2002/1.4.52°			
642	Dir. 2002/7/EC amending Dir. 96/53/EC: maximum authorised dimensions for road vehicles in international traffic	COM(2000) 137 Bull. 3-2000/1.4.49	OJ C 123/25.4.2001 Bull. 1/2-2001/1.4.61 OJ C 144/16.5.2001 Bull. 12-2000/1.4.56°	OJ C 178/22.6.2001 Bull. 10-2000/1.4.37 (b)		Bull. 4-2001/1.4.26° OJ C 360/15.12.2001 Bull. 9-2001/1.4.48
642	Dir. 2002/85/EC amending Dir. 92/6/EEC: installation and use of speed limitation devices for certain categories of motor vehicles	OJ C 270 E/25.9.2001 COM(2001) 318 Bull. 6-2001/1.4.53	OJ C 48/21.2.2002 Bull. 11-2001/1.4.75	OJ C 284 E/21.11.2002 Bull. 1/2-2002/1.4.92 (b)	OJ C 227 E/24.9.2002 COM(2002) 351 Bull. 6-2002/1.4.50	Bull. 6-2002/1.4.50
642	Prop. for a dir.: EC type-approval of agricultural and forestry tractors, their trailers and interchangeable towed equipment, together with their systems, components and separate technical units	OJ C 151 E/25.6.2002 COM(2002) 6 Bull. 1/2-2002/1.3.57	OJ C 221/17.9.2002 Bull. 5-2002/1.3.87	Bull. 4-2002/1.3.25 (a)		Bull. 6-2002/1.3.28°
642	Prop. for a dir. amending Dir. 91/671/EEC: compulsory use of safety belts in vehicles of less than 3.5 tonnes	OJ C 96 E/27.3.2001 COM(2000) 815 Bull. 12-2000/1.4.55	OJ C 260/17.9.2001 Bull. 7/8-2001/1.4.35	OJ C 47 E/21.2.2002 Bull. 5-2001/1.4.61 (b)		Bull. 6-2002/1.4.49° Bull. 11-2002/1.4.67

° Opinion of the Committee of the Regions.

* Council agreement.

(¹) a = adoption; b = amendments; c = rejection; d = EP failure to take a decision within three months; e = agreement on a common draft; f = failure to agree on a common draft.

TABLE I — CO-DECISION PROCEDURE **521**

second reading a, b, c, d (¹)	Commission opinion	Conciliation Committee e, f(¹)	EP adoption of common draft	Adoption by Council*	EP and Council signature	Observations	
0-2002/1.4.50 (b)	COM(2002) 635 Bull. 11-2002/1.4.61				OJ L 1/4.1.2003		**617**
							639
						Dir. to be amended: 95/18/EC (OJ L 143/27.6.1995) and 2001/14/EC (OJ L 75/15.3.2001)	**640**
						Dir. to be amended: 96/48/EC (OJ L 235/17.9.1996) and 2001/16/EC (OJ L 4/9.1.2001)	**640**
							640
						Dir. to be amended: OJ L 237/24.8.1991	**640**
271 E/7.11.2002 1/2-2002/1.4.89 (a)				OJ L 67/9.3.2002 Bull. 1/2-2002/1.4.89		Amended dir.: OJ L 235/17.9.1996	**642**
9-2002/1.4.51 (a)				OJ L 327/4.12.2002 Bull. 11-2002/1.4.66		Amended dir.: OJ L 57/2.3.1992	**642**
							642
						Dir. to be amended: OJ L 373/31.12.1991	**642**

	Commission proposal	ESC opinion/ COR opinion°	EP first reading a, b(¹)	Amended Commission proposal	Common position Council*
643 Reg. (EC) No 484/2002: access to the market in the carriage of goods by road (driver attestation)	OJ C 96 E/27.3.2001 COM(2000) 751 Bull. 11-2000/1.4.52	OJ C 193/10.7.2001 Bull. 4-2001/1.4.28	OJ C 34 E/7.2.2002 Bull. 5-2001/1.4.60 (b)	OJ C 270 E/25.9.2001 COM(2001) 373 Bull. 7/8-2001/1.4.34	OJ C 9/11.1.2002 Bull. 10-2001/1.4.64
643 Prop. for a dir.: training of professional drivers for the carriage of goods	OJ C 154 E/29.5.2001 COM(2001) 56 Bull. 1/2-2001/1.4.62	OJ C 260/17.9.2001 Bull. 7/8-2001/1.4.36	OJ C 271 E/7.11.2002 Bull. 1/2-2002/1.4.87 (b)	COM(2002) 541 Bull. 9-2002/1.4.52	5.12.2002 Bull. 12-2002/1.4.70
644 Prop. for a reg.: ecopoints system for heavy goods vehicles (Austria)	OJ C 103 E/30.4.2002 COM(2001) 807 Bull. 12-2001/1.4.62	OJ C 221/17.9.2002 Bull. 5-2002/1.4.59			
644 Prop. for a dir.: transparent system of rules for restrictions on heavy goods vehicles	OJ C 198/24.6.1998 COM(1998) 115 Bull. 3-1998/1.2.115	OJ C 407/28.12.1998 Bull. 9-1998/1.2.95 OJ C 374/23.12.1999 Bull. 9-1999/1.2.84°	Bull. 7/8-2002/1.4.42 (b)	OJ C 120/24.4.2001 COM(2000) 759 Bull. 11-2000/1.4.53	

Maritime transport

	Commission proposal	ESC opinion/ COR opinion°	EP first reading a, b(¹)	Amended Commission proposal	Common position Council*
647 Reg. (EC) No 1406/2002: European Maritime Safety and Ship Pollution Prevention Agency	OJ C 120 E/24.4.2001 COM(2000) 802 Bull. 12-2000/1.4.60	OJ C 221/7.8.2001 Bull. 5-2001/1.4.63 OJ C 357/14.12.2001 Bull. 6-2001/1.4.55°	OJ C 53 E/28.2.2002 Bull. 6-2001/1.4.55 (b)	OJ C 103 E/30.4.2002 COM(2001) 676 Bull. 12-2001/1.4.63	Bull. 12-2001/1.4.63* Bull. 3-2002/1.4.47
647 Dir. 2002/59/EC: Community monitoring, control and information system for maritime traffic	OJ C 120 E/24.4.2001 COM(2000) 802 Bull. 12-2000/1.4.60	OJ C 221/7.8.2001 Bull. 5-2001/1.4.63 OJ C 357/14.12.2001 Bull. 6-2001/1.4.55°	OJ C 53 E/28.2.2002 Bull. 6-2001/1.4.55 (b)	OJ C 362 E/18.12.2001 COM(2001) 592 Bull. 10-2001/1.4.66	Bull. 12-2001/1.4.69
647 Prop. for a dir.: specific stability requirements for ro-ro passenger ships	COM(2002) 158 Bull. 3-2002/1.4.48	11.12.2002 Bull. 12-2002/1.4.76	Bull. 11-2002/1.4.72 (b)	COM(2002) 721	
647 Prop. for a dir. amending Dir. 98/18/EC: safety rules and standards for passenger ships	COM(2002) 158 Bull. 3-2002/1.4.48	11.12.2002 Bull. 12-2002/1.4.76	Bull. 11-2002/1.4.72 (b)	COM(2002) 720 Bull. 12-2002/1.4.76	
648 Prop. for a reg. amending Reg. (EC) No 417/2002: accelerated phasing-in of double-hull requirements and repealing Council Regulation (EC) No 2978/94	COM(2002) 780 Bull. 12-2002/1.4.78				
649 Dir. 2002/6/EC: reporting formalities for ships arriving in and departing from Community ports	OJ C 180 E/26.6.2001 COM(2001) 46 Bull. 1/2-2001/1.4.63	OJ C 221/7.8.2001 Bull. 5-2001/1.4.64 OJ C 19/22.1.2002 Bull. 9-2001/1.4.49°	OJ C 112 E/9.5.2002 Bull. 10-2001/1.4.67 (b)	OJ C 103 E/30.4.2002 COM(2001) 753 Bull. 12-2001/1.4.64	
649 Prop. for a dir.: market access to port services	OJ C 154 E/29.5.2001 COM(2001) 35 Bull. 1/2-2001/1.4.64	OJ C 48/21.2.2002 Bull. 11-2001/1.4.77 OJ C 19/22.1.2002°	OJ C 140 E/13.6.2002 Bull. 11-2001/1.4.77 (b)	OJ C 181 E/30.7.2002 COM(2002) 101 Bull. 1/2-2002/1.4.98	Bull. 6-2002/1.4.55* Bull. 11-2002/1.4.70
651 Reg. (EC) No 417/2002: accelerated phasing-in of double-hull requirements for oil tankers and repeal of Reg. (EC) No 2978/94	OJ C 212 E/25.7.2000 COM(2000) 142 Bull. 3-2000/1.4.51	OJ C 14/16.1.2001 Bull. 10-2000/1.4.41 OJ C 22/24.1.2001 Bull. 9-2000/1.4.64°	OJ C 228/13.8.2001 Bull. 11-2000/1.4.54 (b)	OJ C 154 E/29.5.2001 COM(2000) 848 Bull. 12-2000/1.4.61	Bull. 6-2001/1.4.57* OJ C 307/31.10.2001 Bull. 7/8-2001/1.4.37
651 Prop. for a reg.: fund for compensating oil pollution damage in European waters	OJ C 120 E/24.4.2001 COM(2000) 802 Bull. 12-2000/1.4.60	OJ C 221/7.8.2001 Bull. 5-2001/1.4.63 OJ C 357/14.12.2001 Bull. 6-2001/1.4.55°	OJ C 53 E/28.2.2002 Bull. 6-2001/1.4.55 (b)	OJ C 227 E/24.9.2002 COM(2002) 313 Bull. 6-2002/1.4.52	
651 Reg. (EC) No 2099/2002: Committee on Safe Seas and amendment of the regulations on maritime safety	OJ C 365 E/19.12.2000 COM(2000) 489 Bull. 9-2000/1.4.63	OJ C 139/11.5.2001 Bull. 3-2001/1.4.50 OJ C 253/12.9.2001 Bull. 4-2001/1.4.30°	OJ C 276/1.10.2001 Bull. 1/2-2001/1.4.66 (b)	OJ C 103 E/30.4.2002 COM(2001) 788 Bull. 12-2001/1.4.68	Bull. 3-2002/1.4.49* Bull. 5-2002/1.4.60

° Opinion of the Committee of the Regions.

* Council agreement.

(¹) a = adoption; b = amendments; c = rejection; d = EP failure to take a decision within three months; e = agreement on a common draft; f = failure to agree on a common draft.

TABLE I — CO-DECISION PROCEDURE 523

second reading a, b, c, d (^{1})	Commission opinion	Conciliation Committee e, f (^{1})	EP adoption of common draft	Adoption by Council*	EP and Council signature	Observations	
271 E/7.11.2002 /2-2002/1.4.88 (a)					OJ L 76/19.3.2002 Bull. 3-2002/1.4.46		643
							643
							644
							644
6-2002/1.4.53 (b)	COM(2002) 374 Bull. 7/8-2002/1.4.45				OJ L 208/5.8.2002 Bull. 6-2002/1.4.53		647
4-2002/1.4.61 (b)	COM(2002) 312 Bull. 6-2002/1.4.54				OJ L 208/5.8.2002 Bull. 6-2002/1.4.54		647
							647
						Dir. to be amended: OJ L 144/15.5.1998	647
						Reg. to be amended: OJ L 64/7.3.2002	648
					OJ L 67/9.3.2002		649
							649
177 E/25.7.2002 12-2001/1.4.67 (a)					OJ L 64/7.3.2002	Repealed reg.: OJ L 319/12.12.1994	651
							651
9-2002/1.4.54 (a)					OJ L 324/29.11.2002 Bull. 11-2002/1.4.69		651

	Commission proposal	ESC opinion/ COR opinion°	EP first reading a, b(¹)	Amended Commission proposal	Common position Council*
651 Dir. 2002/84/EC: maritime safety and the prevention of pollution by ships	OJ C 365 E/19.12.2000 COM(2000) 489 Bull. 9-2000/1.4.63	OJ C 139/11.5.2001 Bull. 3-2001/1.4.50 OJ C 253/12.9.2001 Bull. 4-2001/1.4.30°	OJ C 276/1.10.2001 Bull. 1/2-2001/1.4.66 (b)	OJ C 103 E/30.4.2002 COM(2001) 788 Bull. 12-2001/1.4.68	Bull. 3-2002/1.4.49* Bull. 5-2002/1.4.60
651 Prop. for a reg.: organotin compounds on ships	OJ C 262 E/29.10.2002 COM(2002) 396 Bull. 7/8-2002/1.4.46	11.12.2002	Bull. 11-2002/1.4.74 (b)		5.12.2002* Bull. 12-2002/1.4.77

Air transport

	Commission proposal	ESC opinion/ COR opinion°	EP first reading a, b(¹)	Amended Commission proposal	Common position Council*
653 Reg. (EC) No 1592/2002: common rules in the field of civil aviation and creation of a European Aviation Safety Agency	OJ C 154 E/29.5.2001 COM(2000) 595 Bull. 9-2000/1.4.67	OJ C 221/7.8.2001 Bull. 5-2001/1.4.66	OJ C 72 E/21.3.2002 Bull. 9-2001/1.4.51 (b)		Bull. 10-2001/1.4.76* Bull. 12-2001/1.4.73
653 Prop. for a dir.: safety of third countries' aircraft using Community airports	OJ C 103 E/30.4.2002 COM(2002) 8 Bull. 1/2-2002/1.4.100	OJ C 241/7.10.2002 Bull. 7/8-2002/1.4.51	Bull. 9-2002/1.4.56 (b)	COM(2002) 664 Bull. 11-2002/1.4.79	
654 Reg. (EC) No 2320/2002: common rules in the field of civil aviation security	OJ C 51 E/26.2.2002 COM(2001) 575 Bull. 10-2001/1.4.72	OJ C 48/21.2.2002 Bull. 11-2001/1.4.82	OJ C 153 E/27.6.2002 Bull. 11-2001/1.4.82 (b)		Bull. 12-2001/1.4.70* Bull. 1/2-2002/1.4.101
654 Prop. for a reg. amending Reg. (EEC) No 3922/91: harmonisation of technical requirements and administrative procedures in civil aviation	OJ C 311/31.10.2000 COM(2000) 121 Bull. 3-2000/1.4.52	OJ C 14/16.1.2001 Bull. 10-2000/1.4.45	OJ C 262/18.9.2001 Bull. 1/2-2001/1.4.71 (b) Bull. 9-2002/1.4.57 (b)	OJ C 227 E/24.9.2002 COM(2002) 30 Bull. 1/2-2002/1.4.102	
655 Prop. for a dir.: occurrence reporting in civil aviation	OJ C 120 E/24.4.2001 COM(2000) 847 Bull. 12-2000/1.4.65	OJ C 311/7.11.2001 Bull. 9-2001/1.4.52	OJ C 53 E/28.2.2002 Bull. 6-2001/1.4.60 (b)	OJ C 332 E/27.11.2001 COM(2001) 532	Bull. 6-2002/1.4.60
655 Prop. for a reg.: common rules on compensation and assistance to air passengers regarding flights	OJ C 103 E/30.4.2002 COM(2001) 784 Bull. 12-2001/1.4.72	OJ C 241/7.10.2002 Bull. 7/8-2002/1.4.50	Bull. 10-2002/1.4.56 (b)	COM(2002) 717	5.12.2002* Bull. 12-2002/1.4.79
656 Reg. (EC) No 889/2002 amending Reg. (EC) No 2027/97: air carrier liability in the event of accidents	OJ C 337 E/28.11.2000 COM(2000) 340 Bull. 6-2000/1.4.53	OJ C 123/25.4.2001 Bull. 1/2-2001/1.4.70	OJ C 21 E/24.1.2002 Bull. 4-2001/1.4.31 (b)	OJ C 213 E/31.7.2001 COM(2001) 273 Bull. 5-2001/1.4.65	Bull. 6-2001/1.4.61* Bull. 12-2001/1.4.74
657 Reg. (EC) No 894/2002 amending Reg. (EEC) No 95/93: common rules for the allocation of slots at Community airports	OJ C 103 E/30.4.2002 COM(2002) 7 Bull. 1/2-2002/1.4.99	OJ C 125/27.5.2002 Bull. 3-2002/1.4.50	OJ C 284 E/21.11.2002 Bull. 1/2-2002/1.4.99 (b)		Bull. 3-2002/1.4.50
657 Prop. for a reg. amending Reg. (EC) No 95/93: common rules for the allocation of slots at airports	OJ C 270 E/25.9.2001 COM(2001) 335 Bull. 6-2001/1.4.59	OJ C 125/27.5.2002 Bull. 3-2002/1.4.51	Bull. 6-2002/1.4.57 (b)	COM(2002) 623 Bull. 11-2002/1.4.76	
658 Prop. for a reg.: insurance requirements for air carriers and aircraft operators	COM(2002) 521 Bull. 9-2002/1.4.59				
659 Dir. 2002/30/EC: rules and procedures with regard to the introduction of noise-related operating restrictions at airports	OJ C 75 E/26.3.2002 COM(2001) 695 Bull. 11-2001/1.4.81	OJ C 125/27.5.2002 Bull. 3-2002/1.4.52 OJ C 192/12.8.2002 Bull. 3-2002/1.4.52°	Bull. 3-2002/1.4.52 (b)		
659 Prop. for a dir.: Community framework for noise classification of civil subsonic aircraft	OJ C 103 E/30.4.2002 COM(2001) 74 Bull. 12-2001/1.4.71	OJ C 221/17.9.2002 Bull. 5-2002/1.4.65	Bull. 9-2002/1.4.58 (b)	COM(2002) 683 Bull. 11-2002/1.4.81	
660 Prop. for a reg.: protection against subsidisation and unfair pricing practices in the supply of airline services from non-EC countries	OJ C 151 E/25.6.2002 COM(2002) 110 Bull. 3-2002/1.4.54	Bull. 9-2002/1.4.61			

° Opinion of the Committee of the Regions.

* Council agreement.

(¹) a = adoption; b = amendments; c = rejection; d = EP failure to take a decision within three months; e = agreement on a common draft; f = failure to agree on a common draft.

TABLE I — CO-DECISION PROCEDURE   525

second reading a, b, c, d (^{1})	Commission opinion	Conciliation Committee e, f (^{1})	EP adoption of common draft	Adoption by Council*	EP and Council signature	Observations	
9-2002/1.4.54 (a)					OJ L 324/29.11.2002 Bull. 11-2002/1.4.69		651
							651
4-2002/1.4.63 (b)	COM(2002) 241				OJ L 240/7.9.2002 Bull. 7/8-2002/1.4.47		653
							653
5-2002/1.4.62 (b)	COM(2002) 327 Bull. 6-2002/1.4.58	Bull. 10-2002/1.4.57 (e)	5.12.2002 Bull. 12-2002/1.4.80	9.12.2002 Bull. 12-2002/1.4.80	OJ L 355/30.12.2002 Bull. 12-2002/1.4.80		654
						Reg. to be amended: OJ L 373/31.12.1991	654
10-2002/1.4.55 (b)	COM(2002) 647 Bull. 11-2002/1.4.77						655
							655
3-2002/1.4.53 (a)					OJ L 140/30.5.2002 Bull. 5-2002/1.4.61	Amended reg.: OJ L 285/17.10.1997	656
5-2002/1.4.63 (a)					OJ L 142/31.5.2002 Bull. 5-2002/1.4.63	Amended reg.: OJ L 14/22.1.1993	657
						Reg. to be amended: OJ L 14/22.1.1993	657
							658
					OJ L 85/28.3.2002 Bull. 3-2002/1.4.52		659
							659
							660

	Commission proposal	ESC opinion/ COR opinion°	EP first reading a, b(^{1})	Amended Commission proposal	Common position Council*
661 Prop. for a reg.: framework for the creation of the single European sky	OJ C 362 E/18.12.2001 OJ C 103 E/30.4.2002 COM(2001) 123 Bull. 10-2001/1.4.70	OJ C 241/7.10.2002 Bull. 7/8-2002/1.4.48 OJ C 278/14.11.2002 Bull. 5-2002/1.4.64°	Bull. 9-2002/1.4.55 (b)	COM(2002) 658	5.12.2002* Bull. 12-2002/1.4.81
661 Prop. for a reg.: provision of air navigation services in the single European sky	OJ C 25 E/29.1.2002 OJ C 103 E/30.4.2002 COM(2001) 564 Bull. 10-2001/1.4.71	OJ C 241/7.10.2002 Bull. 7/8-2002/1.4.49 OJ C 278/14.11.2002°	Bull. 9-2002/1.4.55 (b)	COM(2002) 658 Bull. 11-2002/1.4.80	5.12.2002* Bull. 12-2002/1.4.81
661 Prop. for a reg.: organisation and use of the airspace in the single European sky	OJ C 25 E/29.1.2002 OJ C 103 E/30.4.2002 COM(2001) 564 Bull. 10-2001/1.4.71	OJ C 241/7.10.2002 Bull. 7/8-2002/1.4.49 OJ C 278/14.11.2002°	Bull. 9-2002/1.4.55 (b)	COM(2002) 658 Bull. 11-2002/1.4.80	5.12.2002* Bull. 12-2002/1.4.81
661 Prop. for a reg.: interoperability of the European air traffic management network	OJ C 25 E/29.1.2002 OJ C 103 E/30.4.2002 COM(2001) 564 Bull. 10-2001/1.4.71	OJ C 241/7.10.2002 Bull. 7/8-2002/1.4.49 OJ C 278/14.11.2002°	Bull. 9-2002/1.4.55 (b)	COM(2002) 658 Bull. 11-2002/1.4.80	5.12.2002* Bull. 12-2002/1.4.81

Intermodal transport

	Commission proposal	ESC opinion/ COR opinion°	EP first reading a, b(^{1})	Amended Commission proposal	Common position Council*
663 Prop. for a reg.: granting of Community financial assistance to improve the environmental performance of the freight transport system	OJ C 126 E/28.5.2002 COM(2002) 54 Bull. 1/2-2002/1.4.104	OJ C 241/7.10.2002 Bull. 7/8-2002/1.4.52 OJ C 278/14.11.2002 Bull. 5-2002/1.4.67°	Bull. 9-2002/1.4.60 (b)		5.12.2002*

International cooperation

	Commission proposal	ESC opinion/ COR opinion°	EP first reading a, b(^{1})	Amended Commission proposal	Common position Council*
668 Reg. (EC) No 893/2002 amending Reg. (EC) No 685/2001: distribution of authorisations received in connection with the EC–Romania Agreement — conditions for the carriage of goods by road	OJ C 270 E/25.9.2001 COM(2001) 334 Bull. 6-2001/1.4.64	OJ C 36/8.2.2002 Bull. 10-2001/1.5.8	OJ C 72 E/21.3.2002 Bull. 9-2001/1.5.18 (a)		

Health and consumer protection
Food safety

	Commission proposal	ESC opinion/ COR opinion°	EP first reading a, b(^{1})	Amended Commission proposal	Common position Council*
671 Reg. (EC) No 178/2002: establishment of the European Food Authority and procedures in matters of food safety	OJ C 96 E/27.3.2001 COM(2000) 716 Bull. 11-2000/1.4.57	OJ C 155/29.5.2001 Bull. 3-2001/1.4.59 OJ C 357/14.12.2001 Bull. 6-2001/1.4.67°	OJ C 53 E/28.2.2002 Bull. 6-2001/1.4.67 (b)	OJ C 304 E/30.10.2001 COM(2001) 475 Bull. 7/8-2001/1.4.41	28.6.2001* OJ C 4/7.1.2002 Bull. 9-2001/1.4.55
672 Dir. 2002/46/EC: food supplements	OJ C 311/31.10.2000 COM(2000) 222 Bull. 5-2000/1.4.51	OJ C 14/16.1.2001 Bull. 10-2000/1.4.51	OJ C 276/1.10.2001 Bull. 1/2-2001/1.4.77 (b)	OJ C 180 E/26.6.2001 COM(2001) 159 Bull. 3-2001/1.4.58	Bull. 9-2001/1.4.56* Bull. 12-2001/1.4.75
672 Prop. for a dir. amending Dir. 95/2/EC on food additives other than colours and sweeteners	COM(2002) 662 Bull. 11-2002/1.4.87				
673 Prop. for a dir. amending Dir. 94/35/EC: sweeteners for use in foodstuffs	OJ C 262 E/29.10.2002 COM(2002) 375 Bull. 7/8-2002/1.4.57	11.12.2002			

° Opinion of the Committee of the Regions.

* Council agreement.

(^{1}) a = adoption; b = amendments; c = rejection; d = EP failure to take a decision within three months; e = agreement on a common draft; f = failure to agree on a common draft.

TABLE I — CO-DECISION PROCEDURE 527

second reading a, b, c, d (^{1})	Commission opinion	Conciliation Committee e, f (^{1})	EP adoption of common draft	Adoption by Council*	EP and Council signature	Observations	
							661
							661
							661
							661
							663
					OJ L 142/31.5.2002 Bull. 5-2002/1.5.5	Amended reg.: OJ L 108/18.4.2001	668
177 E/25.7.2002 12-2001/1.4.77 (b)	COM(2001) 821 Bull. 1/2-2002/1.4.106				OJ L 31/1.2.2002 Bull. 1/2-2002/1.4.106		671
3-2002/1.4.56 (b)	COM(2002) 177 Bull. 4-2002/1.4.65				OJ L 183/12.7.2002 Bull. 6-2002/1.4.62		672
						Dir. to be amended: OJ L 61/18.3.1995	672
						Dir. to be amended: OJ L 237/10.9.1994	673

	Commission proposal	ESC opinion/ COR opinion°	EP first reading a, b(¹)	Amended Commission proposal	Common position Council*
673 Prop. for a reg.: smoke flavourings used or intended for use in or on foods	OJ C 262 E/29.10.2002 COM(2002) 400 Bull. 7/8-2002/1.4.58	11.12.2002			
673 Prop. for a dir. amending Dir. 95/2/EC: conditions of use for the food additive E 425 konjac	OJ C 331 E/31.12.2002 COM(2002) 451 Bull. 7/8-2002/1.4.59	11.12.2002			
673 Prop. for a dir. amending Dir. 2000/13/EC: indication of the ingredients present in foodstuffs	OJ C 332 E/27.11.2001 COM(2001) 433 Bull. 9-2001/1.4.61	OJ C 80/3.4.2002 Bull. 1/2-2002/1.4.120	Bull. 6-2002/1.4.80 (b)	OJ C 331 E/31.12.2002 COM(2002) 464 Bull. 9-2002/1.4.64	Bull. 11-2002/1.4.83*
673 Prop. for a reg.: hygiene of foodstuffs	OJ C 365 E/19.12.2000 COM(2000) 438 Bull. 7/8-2000/1.4.64	OJ C 155/29.5.2001 Bull. 3-2001/1.4.60	Bull. 5-2002/1.4.69 (b)		Bull. 6-2002/1.4.62*
673 Prop. for a reg.: specific hygiene rules for food of animal origin	OJ C 365 E/19.12.2000 COM(2000) 438 Bull. 7/8-2000/1.4.64	OJ C 155/29.5.2001	Bull. 5-2002/1.4.70 (b)		16.12.2002* Bull. 12-2002/1.4.88
673 Prop. for a reg.: traceability and labelling of genetically modified organisms and of food and feed products produced from GMOs and amending Dir. 2001/18/EC	OJ C 304 E/30.10.2001 COM(2001) 182 Bull. 7/8-2001/1.4.40	OJ C 125/27.5.2002 Bull. 3-2002/1.4.60 OJ C 278/14.11.2002 Bull. 5-2002/1.4.71°	Bull. 7/8-2002/1.4.55 (b)	OJ C 331 E/31.12.2002 COM(2002) 515 Bull. 9-2002/1.4.63	9.12.2002* Bull. 12-2002/1.4.84
673 Prop. for a reg.: genetically modified food and feed	OJ C 304 E/30.10.2001 COM(2001) 425 Bull. 7/8-2001/1.4.39	OJ C 221/17.9.2002 Bull. 5-2002/1.4.72 OJ C 278/14.11.2002 Bull. 5-2002/1.4.72°	Bull. 7/8-2002/1.4.56 (b)	COM(2002) 559 Bull. 10-2002/1.4.63	Bull. 11-2002/1.4.88*
673 Prop. for a dir.: monitoring of zoonoses, amending Dec. 90/424/EEC and repealing Dir. 92/117/EEC	OJ C 304 E/30.10.2001 COM(2001) 452 Bull. 7/8-2001/1.4.48	OJ C 94/18.4.2002 Bull. 1/2-2002/1.4.119	Bull. 5-2002/1.4.80 (b)	COM(2002) 684 Bull. 11-2002/1.4.84	Bull. 11-2002/1.4.84*
673 Prop. for a reg.: control of salmonella in the food chain and amending Dirs 64/432/EEC, 72/462/EEC and 90/539/EEC	OJ C 304 E/30.10.2001 COM(2001) 452 Bull. 7/8-2001/1.4.48	OJ C 94/18.4.2002 Bull. 1/2-2002/1.4.119	Bull. 5-2002/1.4.81 (b)	COM(2002) 684 Bull. 11-2002/1.4.85	Bull. 11-2002/1.4.85*
674 Prop. for a reg.: specific rules for the organisation of official controls on products of animal origin intended for human consumption	OJ C 262 E/29.10.2002 COM(2002) 377 Bull. 7/8-2002/1.4.63				
675 Reg. (EC) No 1774/2002: health rules concerning animal by-products not intended for human consumption	OJ C 96 E/27.3.2001 COM(2000) 574	OJ C 193/10.7.2001 Bull. 4-2001/1.4.38	OJ C 53 E/28.2.2002 Bull. 6-2001/1.4.70 (b)	OJ C 103 E/30.4.2002 COM(2001) 748 Bull. 12-2001/1.4.79	Bull. 6-2001/1.4.70* Bull. 11-2001/1.4.85
675 Dir. 2002/33/EC amending Dirs 90/425/EEC and 92/118/EEC: health requirements for animal by-products	OJ C 62 E/27.2.2001 COM(2000) 573 Bull. 10-2000/1.4.50	OJ C 193/10.7.2001 Bull. 4-2001/1.4.39	OJ C 53 E/28.2.2002 Bull. 6-2001/1.4.71 (b)	OJ C 103 E/30.4.2002 COM(2001) 747 Bull. 12-2001/1.4.80	Bull. 6-2001/1.4.71* Bull. 11-2001/1.4.86
676 Prop. for a dir. amending Dir. 96/22/EC: prohibition on the use of certain substances having a hormonal or thyrostatic action and of beta agonists	OJ C 337 E/28.11.2000 COM(2000) 320	OJ C 14/16.1.2001 Bull. 10-2000/1.10.34	OJ C 267/21.9.2001 Bull. 1/2-2001/1.4.79 (b)	OJ C 180 E/26.6.2001 COM(2001) 131 Bull. 3-2001/1.4.61	16.12.2002* Bull. 12-2002/1.4.97
681 Dir. 2002/32/EC: veterinary sector — undesirable substances and products in animal nutrition	OJ C 89 E/28.3.2000 COM(1999) 654 Bull. 12-1999/1.2.217	OJ C 140/18.5.2000 Bull. 3-2000/1.4.64	OJ C 178/22.6.2001 Bull. 10-2000/1.4.53 (b)	OJ C 96 E/27.3.2001 COM(2000) 861	19.6.2001* OJ C 4/7.1.2002 Bull. 9-2001/1.4.58

° Opinion of the Committee of the Regions.

* Council agreement.

(¹) a = adoption; b = amendments; c = rejection; d = EP failure to take a decision within three months; e = agreement on a common draft; f = failure to agree on a common draft.

TABLE I — CO-DECISION PROCEDURE   529

second reading a, b, c, d (¹)	Commission opinion	Conciliation Committee e, f (¹)	EP adoption of common draft	Adoption by Council*	EP and Council signature	Observations	
							673
						Dir. to de amended: OJ L 61/18.3.1995	673
						Dir. to be amended: OJ L 109/6.5.2000	673
							673
							673
						Dir. to be amended: OJ L 106/17.4.2001	673
							673
						Dec. to be amended: OJ L 224/18.8.1990 Dir. to be repealed: OJ L 62/15.3.1993	673
						Dirs to be amended: 64/432/EEC (OJ 121/29.7.1964) 72/462/EEC (OJ L 312/31.12.1972) 90/539/EEC (OJ L 303/31.10.1990)	673
							674
3-2002/1.4.59 (b)	COM(2002) 268	Bull. 9-2002/1.4.68 (e)	Bull. 9-2002/1.4.68	Bull. 9-2002/1.4.68	OJ L 273/10.10.2002 Bull. 10-2002/1.4.64		675
3-2002/1.4.58 (a)					OJ L 315/19.11.2002	Amended Dirs: 90/425/EEC (OJ L 224/18.8.1990) and 92/118/EEC (OJ L 62/15.3.1993)	675
						Dir. to be amended: OJ L 125/23.5.1996	676
177 E/25.7.2002 12-2001/1.4.84 (b)	COM(2002) 31 Bull. 1/2-2002/1.4.108	Bull. 3-2002/1.4.62 (e)	Bull. 4-2002/1.4.66	22.4.2002	OJ L 140/30.5.2002		681

	Commission proposal	ESC opinion/ COR opinion°	EP first reading a, b (¹)	Amended Commission proposal	Common position Council*
682 Dir. 2002/2/EC amending Dir. 79/373/EEC: marketing of compound feedingstuffs	COM(1999) 744 Bull. 1/2-2000/1.4.68	OJ C 140/18.5.2000 Bull. 3-2000/1.4.67	OJ C 178/22.6.2001 Bull. 10-2000/1.4.52 (b)	OJ C 120 E/24.4.2001 COM(2000) 780 Bull. 12-2000/1.4.80	OJ C 36/2.2.2001 Bull. 12-2000/1.4.80
683 Prop. for a reg.: additives for use in animal nutrition	OJ C 203 E/27.8.2002 COM(2002) 153 Bull. 3-2002/1.4.61	Bull. 9-2002/1.4.70	Bull. 11-2002/1.4.93 (b)	COM(2002) 771	16.12.2002* Bull. 12-2002/1.4.105
684 Prop. for a reg.: animal health requirements applicable to non-commercial movement of pet animals	OJ C 29 E/30.1.2001 COM(2000) 529 Bull. 9-2000/1.4.71	OJ C 116/20.4.2001 Bull. 11-2000/1.4.59	OJ C 27 E/31.1.2002 Bull. 5-2001/1.4.70 (b)	OJ C 270 E/25.9.2001 COM(2001) 349 Bull. 6-2001/1.4.74	Bull. 4-2002/1.4.67* Bull. 6-2002/1.4.65
684 Prop. for a dir. amending Council Dir. 86/609/EEC on the approximation of provisions regarding the protection of animals used for experimental and other scientific purposes	OJ C 25 E/29.1.2002 COM(2001) 703 Bull. 11-2001/1.4.88	OJ C 94/18.4.2002 Bull. 1/2-2002/1.4.114	Bull. 7/8-2002/1.4.60 (a)		

Public health

	Commission proposal	ESC opinion/ COR opinion°	EP first reading a, b (¹)	Amended Commission proposal	Common position Council*
685 Dec. No 1786/2002/EC: programme of action in the field of public health (2003–08)	OJ C 337 E/28.11.2000 COM(2000) 285 Bull. 5-2000/1.4.50	OJ C 116/20.4.2001 Bull. 11-2000/1.4.55 OJ C 144/16.5.2001 Bull. 12-2000/1.4.69°	OJ C 21 E/24.1.2002 Bull. 4-2001/1.4.64 (b)	OJ C 240 E/28.8.2001 COM(2001) 302 Bull. 6-2001/1.4.78	Bull. 6-2001/1.4.78* OJ C 307/31.10.2001
691 Prop. for a dir.: advertising and sponsorship of tobacco products	OJ C 270 E/25.9.2001 COM(2001) 283 Bull. 5-2001/1.4.79	OJ C 36/8.2.2002 Bull. 10-2001/1.4.88	Bull. 11-2002/1.4.96 (b)	COM(2002) 699 Bull. 11-2002/1.4.96	
692 Prop. for a dir.: standards of quality and safety for the donation, procurement, testing, processing, storage, and distribution of human tissues and cells	OJ C 227 E/24.9.2002 COM(2002) 319 Bull. 6-2002/1.4.74	11.12.2002 Bull. 12-2002/1.4.107			
692 Prop. for a dir.: standards of quality and safety relating to human blood and amending Dir. 89/381/EEC	OJ C 154 E/29.5.2001 COM(2000) 816 Bull. 12-2000/1.4.73	OJ C 221/7.8.2001 Bull. 5-2001/1.4.77 OJ C 19/22.1.2002 Bull. 9-2001/1.4.59°	OJ C 72 E/21.3.2002 Bull. 9-2001/1.4.59 (b)	OJ C 75 E/26.3.2002 COM(2001) 692 Bull. 11-2001/1.4.95	Bull. 11-2001/1.4.95* Bull. 1/2-2002/1.4.118

Consumer protection

	Commission proposal	ESC opinion/ COR opinion°	EP first reading a, b (¹)	Amended Commission proposal	Common position Council*
697 Dir. 2002/65/EC: distance contracts between suppliers and consumers for financial services and amending Dirs 90/619/EEC, 97/7/EC and 98/27/EC	OJ C 385/11.12.1998 COM(1998) 468 Bull. 10-1998/1.2.28	OJ C 169/16.6.1999 Bull. 4-1999/1.3.29	OJ C 279/1.10.1999 Bull. 5-1999/1.2.31 (b)	OJ C 177/27.6.2000 COM(1999) 385 Bull. 7/8-1999/1.3.22	Bull. 9-2001/1.4.63* Bull. 12-2001/1.4.88
700 Prop. for a dir.: harmonisation of the laws, regulations and administrative provisions concerning credit for consumers	OJ C 331 E/31.12.2002 COM(2002) 443 Bull. 9-2002/1.4.74				

° Opinion of the Committee of the Regions.
* Council agreement.
(¹) a = adoption; b = amendments; c = rejection; d = EP failure to take a decision within three months; e = agreement on a common draft; f = failure to agree on a common draft.

TABLE I — CO-DECISION PROCEDURE **531**

P second reading a, b, c, d(^{1})	Commission opinion	Conciliation Committee e, f(^{1})	EP adoption of common draft	Adoption by Council*	EP and Council signature	Observations	
21 E/24.1.2002 4-2001/1.4.37 (b)	COM(2001) 275 Bull. 5-2001/1.4.73	Bull. 10-2001/1.4.79 (e)	OJ C 177E/25.7.2002 Bull. 12-2001/1.4.76	Bull. 12-2001/1.4.76	OJ L 63/6.3.2002 Bull. 1/2-2002/1.4.109	Amended dir: OJ L 86/6.4.1979	682
							683
10-2002/1.4.65 (b)	COM(2002) 710 Bull. 12-2002/1.4.98						684
						Dir. to be amended: OJ L 358/18.12.1986	684
177 E/25.7.2002 12-2001/1.4.85 (b)	COM(2002) 29 Bull. 1/2-2002/1.4.117	8.5.2002	Bull. 7/8-2002/1.4.66	Bull. 6-2002/1.4.70	OJ L 271/9.10.2002 Bull. 9-2002/1.4.72		685
				2.12.2002*			691
							692
6-2002/1.4.73 (b)	COM(2002) 479 Bull. 7/8-2002/1.4.67		18.12.2002 Bull. 12-2002/1.4.109	16.12.2002 Bull. 12-2002/1.4.109	27.12.2002	Dir. to be amended: OJ L 181/28.6.1989	692
5-2002/1.4.83 (b)	COM(2002) 360 Bull. 6-2002/1.4.79				OJ L 271/9.10.2002 Bull. 9-2002/1.4.73	Amended Dirs: 90/619/EEC (OJ L 330/29.11.1990), 97/7/EC (OJ L 144/4.6.1997) and 98/27/EC (OJ L 166/11.6.1998)	697
							700

	Commission proposal	ESC opinion/ COR opinion°	EP first reading a, b (¹)	Amended Commission proposal	Common position Council*

Role of the Union in the world

Common commercial policy

Operation of the customs union, customs cooperation and mutual assistance

	Commission proposal	ESC opinion/ COR opinion°	EP first reading a, b (¹)	Amended Commission proposal	Common position Council*
782	Prop. for a dec. adopting an action programme for customs in the Community (Customs 2007)	OJ C 126 E/28.5.2002 COM(2002) 26 Bull. 1/2-2002/1.6.31	OJ C 241/7.10.2002 Bull. 7/8-2002/1.6.42	Bull. 9-2002/1.6.27 (b)	COM(2002) 575 Bull. 10-2002/1.6.35	
782	Prop. for a reg.: prevention of money laundering by means of customs cooperation	OJ C 227 E/24.9.2002 COM(2002) 328 Bull. 6-2002/1.3.37				

Development cooperation

North–south cooperation on health

	Commission proposal	ESC opinion/ COR opinion°	EP first reading a, b (¹)	Amended Commission proposal	Common position Council*
827	Prop. for a reg.: aid for poverty diseases in developing countries	OJ C 151 E/25.6.2002 COM(2002) 109 Bull. 3-2002/1.6.49				
828	Prop. for a reg.: aid for policies and actions on reproductive and sexual health and rights	OJ C 151 E/25.6.2002 COM(2002) 120 Bull. 3-2002/1.6.51				

Cooperation via non-governmental organisations and decentralised cooperation

	Commission proposal	ESC opinion/ COR opinion°	EP first reading a, b (¹)	Amended Commission proposal	Common position Council*
835	Reg. (EC) No 955/2002 extending and amending Reg. (EC) No 1659/98 on decentralised cooperation	OJ C 51 E/26.2.2002 COM(2001) 576 Bull. 10-2001/1.6.49		Bull. 3-2002/1.6.52 (b)		

Relations with Latin America

Cooperation measures

	Commission proposal	ESC opinion/ COR opinion°	EP first reading a, b (¹)	Amended Commission proposal	Common position Council*
985	Prop. for a reg.: Community cooperation with Asian and Latin American countries and amending Council Reg. (EC) No 2258/96	OJ C 331 E/31.12.2002 COM(2002) 340 Bull. 7/8-2002/1.6.134				

° Opinion of the Committee of the Regions.
* Council agreement.
(¹) a = adoption; b = amendments; c = rejection; d = EP failure to take a decision within three months; e = agreement on a common draft; f = failure to agree on a common draft.

TABLE I — CO-DECISION PROCEDURE 533

EP second reading a, b, c, d (¹)	Commission opinion	Conciliation Committee e, f(¹)	EP adoption of common draft	Adoption by Council*	EP and Council signature	Observations	
							782
							782
							827
							828
					OJ L 148/6.6.2002	Amended reg.: OJ L 213/30.7.1998	**835**
						Reg. to be amended: OJ L 306/28.11.1996	**985**

	Commission proposal	ESC opinion/ COR opinion°	EP first reading a, b (¹)	Amended Commission proposal	Common position Council*

Financing of Community activities, resource management

Budgets

Financial regulations

1050	Prop. for a reg. amending Reg. (EC) No 1210/90: budgetary and financial rules applicable to the European Environment Agency and access to the agency's documents	OJ C 331 E/31.12.2002 COM(2002) 406 Bull. 7/8-2002/1.7.8	11.12.2002	Bull. 10-2002/1.7.4 (b)	
1050	Prop. for a reg. amending Reg. (EC) No 178/2002: internal audit and control systems applicable to the European Food Safety Agency and access to the agency's documents	OJ C 331 E/31.12.2002 COM(2002) 406 Bull. 7/8-2002/1.7.8	11.12.2002	Bull. 10-2002/1.7.4 (b)	
1050	Prop. for a reg. amending Reg. (EC) No 1592/2002 concerning common rules in the field of civil aviation and creating a European Aviation Safety Agency	OJ C 331 E/31.12.2002 COM(2002) 406 Bull. 7/8-2002/1.7.8	11.12.2002	Bull. 10-2002/1.7.4 (b)	
1050	Prop. for a reg. amending Reg. (EC) No 1406/2002 concerning the setting up of a European Maritime Safety Agency	OJ C 331 E/31.12.2002 COM(2002) 406 Bull. 7/8-2002/1.7.8	11.12.2002	Bull. 10-2002/1.7.4 (b)	

Protection of the Communities' financial interests and the fight against fraud

1058	Prop. for a dir.: criminal law protection of the Community's financial interests	OJ C 240 E/28.8.2001 COM(2001) 272 Bull. 5-2001/1.7.10		OJ C 153 E/27.6.2002 Bull. 11-2001/1.7.12 (b)	COM(2002) 577 Bull. 10-2002/1.7.9	

° Opinion of the Committee of the Regions.

* Council agreement.

(¹) a = adoption; b = amendments; c = rejection; d = EP failure to take a decision within three months; e = agreement on a common draft; f = failure to agree on a common draft.

TABLE I — CO-DECISION PROCEDURE 535

P second reading a, b, c, d (¹)	Commission opinion	Conciliation Committee e, f (¹)	EP adoption of common draft	Adoption by Council*	EP and Council signature	Observations	
						Reg. to be amended: OJ L 120/11.5.1990	1050
						Reg. to be amended: OJ L 31/1.2.2002	1050
						Reg. to be amended: OJ L 240/7.9.2002	1050
						Reg. to be amended: OJ L 208/5.8.2002	1050
							1058

Table II — Consultation of the European Parliament

	Commission proposal	ESC opinion/ CoR opinion²	EP opinion	Amended Commission proposal	Adoption by Council*	Observations
Institutional questions and the future of the Union						
Implementing powers conferred on the Commission						
37 Prop. for a dec. amending Dec. 1999/468/EC: procedures for the exercise of implementing powers conferred on the Commission	COM(2002) 719					Dec. to be amended: OJ L 184/17.7.1999
The Community economic and social area						
Economic and monetary policy						
Monetary policy						
69 Reg. (EC) No 134/2002 amending Reg. (EC) No 2531/98: application of minimum reserves by the European Central Bank			OJ C 65 E/14.3.2002 Bull. 7/8-2001/1.3.3		OJ L 24/26.1.2002 Bull. 1/2-2002/1.3.21	Amended reg.: OJ L 318/27.11.1998
Financial operations						
77 Reg. (EC) No 332/2002: facility providing medium-term financial assistance for Member States' balances of payments	OJ C 180 E/26.6.2001 COM(2001) 113 Bull. 3-2001/1.3.10		OJ C 72 E/21.3.2002 Bull. 9-2001/1.3.2		OJ L 53/23.2.2002 Bull. 1/2-2002/1.3.24	
79 Dec. 2002/882/EC: provision of further macrofinancial assistance to the Federal Republic of Yugoslavia	OJ C 291 E/26.11.2002 COM(2002) 436 Bull. 7/8-2002/1.6.93		Bull. 10-2002/1.6.75		OJ L 308/9.11.2002 Bull. 11-2002/1.6.52	
79 Dec. 2002/883/EC: provision of further macrofinancial assistance to Bosnia and Herzegovina	OJ C 291 E/26.11.2002 COM(2002) 437 Bull. 7/8-2002/1.6.93		Bull. 10-2002/1.6.75		OJ L 308/9.11.2002 Bull. 11-2002/1.6.52	

TABLE II — CONSULTATION OF THE EUROPEAN PARLIAMENT 537

		Commission proposal	ESC opinion/ CoR opinion°	EP opinion	Amended Commission proposal	Adoption by Council*	Observations
80	Dec. 2002/1006/EC: provision of further financial assistance to Moldova	COM(2002) 538 Bull. 10-2002/1.6.89		5.12.2002 Bull.12-2002/1.6.95		OJ L 351/28.12.2002 Bull.12-2002/1.6.95	
81	Dec. 2002/639/EC providing supplementary macrofinancial assistance to Ukraine	OJ C 103 E/30.4.2002 COM(2002) 12 Bull. 1/2-2002/1.6.103		Bull. 5-2002/1.6.83		OJ L 209/6.8.2002 Bull. 7/8-2002/1.6.105	

Statistical system

Policy aspects

		Commission proposal	ESC opinion/ CoR opinion°	EP opinion	Amended Commission proposal	Adoption by Council*	Observations
101	Prop. for a reg.: harmonisation of gross national income at market prices (GNI regulation)	COM(2002) 558 Bull. 10-2002/1.3.8					

Employment and social policy

Employment

		Commission proposal	ESC opinion/ CoR opinion°	EP opinion	Amended Commission proposal	Adoption by Council*	Observations
112	Dec. 2 002/177/EC: guidelines for Member States' employment policies for 2002	OJ C 75 E/26.3.2002 COM(2001) 511 Bull. 9-2001/1.3.10	OJ C 36/8.2.2002 Bull. 10-2001/1.3.19 OJ C 107/3.5.2002 Bull. 11-2001/1.3.18°	OJ C 112 E/9.5.2002 Bull. 10-2001/1.3.19	OJ C 51 E/26.2.2002 COM(2001) 669 Bull. 11-2001/1.3.18	Bull. 12-2001/1.3.24* OJ L 60/1.3.2002 Bull. 1/2-2002/1.3.36	Council opinion: Bull.11-2001/1.3.20 and OJ C 47/21.2.2002 Council opinion: Bull. 11-2001/1.3.20 OJ C 47/21.2.2002

Social protection and social security

		Commission proposal	ESC opinion/ CoR opinion°	EP opinion	Amended Commission proposal	Adoption by Council*	Observations
117	Prop. for a reg.: extending the provisions of Regulation (EEC) No 1408/71 to nationals of third countries who are not already covered by these provisions solely on the ground of their nationality	OJ C 126 E/28.5.2002 COM(2002) 59 Bull. 1/2-2002/1.3.41		Bull. 11-2002/1.3.19		3.6.2002*	Extended reg.: OJ L 149/5.7.1971

° Opinion of the Committee of the Regions.
* Council agreement.

	Commission proposal	ESC opinion/CoR opinion³	EP opinion	Amended Commission proposal	Adoption by Council*	Observations

Health and safety at work

	Commission proposal	ESC opinion/CoR opinion³	EP opinion	Amended Commission proposal	Adoption by Council*	Observations
131	Recomm.: application of legislation governing health and safety at work to self-employed workers	COM(2002) 166 Bull. 4-2002/1.3.14	OJ C 241/7.10.2002 Bull. 7/8-2002/1.3.20 OJ C 287/22.11.2002 Bull. 7/8-2002/1.3.20*	Bull. 10-2002/1.3.16		3.12.2002* Bull.12-2002/1.3.25	

Social dialogue

	Commission proposal	ESC opinion/CoR opinion³	EP opinion	Amended Commission proposal	Adoption by Council*	Observations
133	Prop. for a dec.: establishing a tripartite social summit for growth and employment	OJ C 227 E/24.9.2002 COM(2002) 341 Bull. 6-2002/1.3.19	Bull. 11-2002/1.3.22*				

Internal market
Taxation

	Commission proposal	ESC opinion/CoR opinion³	EP opinion	Amended Commission proposal	Adoption by Council*	Observations
175	Prop. for a dir.: effective taxation of savings income in the Community	OJ C 270 E/25.9.2001 COM(2001) 400 Bull. 7/8-2001/1.3.32	OJ C 48/21.2.2002 Bull. 11-2001/1.3.48	Bull. 3-2002/1.3.41			
178	Dir. 2002/10/EC amending Dirs 92/79/EEC, 92/80/EEC and 95/59/EC: structure and rates of excise duty applied to manufactured tobacco	OJ C 180 E/26.6.2001 COM(2001) 133 Bull. 3-2001/1.3.46	OJ C 36/8.2.2002 Bull. 10-2001/1.3.44	OJ C 284 E/21.11.2002 Bull. 1/2-2002/1.3.67		6.11.2001* Bull. 1/2-2002/1.3.67	Amended dirs: 92/79/EEC and 92/80/EEC (OJ L 316/31.10.1992) and 95/59/EC (OJ L 291/6.12.1995)
179	Dir. 2002/92/EC amending Dir. 77/388/EEC: extension of the facility allowing Member States to apply reduced rates of VAT to certain labour-intensive services	COM(2002) 525 Bull. 9-2002/1.3.42	Bull. 10-2002/1.3.26	Bull. 11-2002/1.3.40		OJ L 331/7.12.2002 Bull.12-2002/1.3.43	Amended dir.: OJ L 145/13.6.1977
180	Prop. for a dir. amending Dir. 77/388/EEC: special scheme for travel agents	OJ C 126 E/28.5.2002 COM(2002) 64 Bull. 1/2-2002/1.3.68	OJ C 241/7.10.2002 Bull. 7/8-2002/1.3.36	Bull. 9-2002/1.3.40			Dir. to be amended: OJ L 145/13.6.1977
181	Dir. 2002/38/EC amending Dir. 77/388/EEC: VAT arrangements applicable to certain services supplied by electronic means	OJ C 337 E/28.11.2000 COM(2000) 349 Bull. 6-2000/1.3.40	OJ C 116/20.4.2001 Bull. 11-2000/1.3.48	OJ C 232/17.8.2001 Bull. 12-2000/1.3.33		Bull. 1/2-2002/1.3.69* OJ L 128/15.5.2002 Bull. 5-2002/1.3.35	Amended dir.: OJ L 145/13.6.1977
182	Prop. for a dir. amending Dir. 77/388/EEC as regards the rules on the place of supply of electricity and gas	COM(2002) 688					Dir. to be amended: OJ L 145/13.6.1977

TABLE II — CONSULTATION OF THE EUROPEAN PARLIAMENT 539

		Commission proposal	ESC opinion/ CoR opinion°	EP opinion	Amended Commission proposal	Adoption by Council*	Observations
183	Prop. for a dir. amending Dirs 92/81/EEC and 92/82/EEC introducing special tax arrangements for diesel fuel used for commercial purposes and aligning the excise duties on petrol and diesel fuel	OJ C 291 E/26.11.2002 COM(2002) 410 Bull. 7/8-2002/1.3.37					Dirs to be amended: 92/81/EEC and 92/82/EEC (OJ L 316/31.10.1992)
183	Prop. for a dir. amending Dir. 92/81/EEC; reduced rate of excise duty on certain mineral oils containing biofuels	OJ C 103 E/30.4.2002 COM(2001) 547 Bull. 11-2001/1.4.64	OJ C 149/21.6.2002 Bull. 4-2002/1.4.56 OJ C 278/14.11.2002 Bull. 5-2002/1.4.49°	Bull. 7/8-2002/1.3.34			Dir. to be amended: OJ L 316/31.10.1992

Intellectual property

		Commission proposal	ESC opinion/ CoR opinion°	EP opinion	Amended Commission proposal	Adoption by Council*	Observations
193	Prop. for a reg.: Community patent	OJ C 337 E/28.11.2000 COM(2000) 412 Bull. 7/8-2000/1.3.24	OJ C 155/29.5.2001 Bull. 3-2001/1.3.47	Bull. 4-2002/1.3.31			

Competition policy
Competition rules applying to businesses

		Commission proposal	ESC opinion/ CoR opinion°	EP opinion	Amended Commission proposal	Adoption by Council*	Observations
207	Reg. (EC) No 1/2003 amending Regs (EEC) No 1017/68, (EEC) No 2988/74, (EEC) No 4056/86 and (EEC) No 3975/87: implementation of the rules on competition laid down in Articles 81 and 82 of the EC Treaty	OJ C 365 E/19.12.2000 COM(2000) 582 Bull. 9-2000/1.3.29	OJ C 155/29.5.2001 Bull. 3-2001/1.3.50	OJ C 72 E/21.3.2002 Bull. 9-2001/1.3.28		Bull. 11-2002/1.3.46* OJ L 1/4.1.2003	Amended regs: (EEC) No 1017/68 (OJ L 175/23.7.1968), (EEC) No 2988/74 (OJ L 319/29.11.1974), (EEC) No 4056/86 (OJ L 378/31.12.1986) and (EEC) No 3975/87 (OJ L 374/31.12.1987)
230	Prop. for a reg.: control of concentrations between undertakings	COM(2002) 711					

State aid

		Commission proposal	ESC opinion/ CoR opinion°	EP opinion	Amended Commission proposal	Adoption by Council*	Observations
241	Reg. (EC) No 1407/2002: State aid to the coal industry	OJ C 304 E/30.10.2001 COM(2001) 423 Bull. 7/8-2001/1.4.33	OJ C 48/21.2.2002 Bull. 11-2001/1.4.69	Bull. 5-2002/1.3.55		Bull. 6-2002/1.3.59* OJ L 205/2.8.2002 Bull. 7/8-2002/1.3.69	ECSC Consultative Committee opinion: OJ C 321/16.11.2001

° Opinion of the Committee of the Regions.

* Council agreement.

Research and technology
Community RTD policy

	Commission proposal	ESC opinion / CoR opinion°	EP opinion	Amended Commission proposal	Adoption by Council*	Observations
299	Dec. 2002/668/Euratom: multiannual framework programme 2002–06 (Euratom)	OJ C 180 E/26.6.2001 COM(2001) 94 Bull. 1/2-2001/1.3.124	OJ C 260/17.9.2001 Bull. 7/8-2001/1.3.97	OJ C 140 E/13.6.2002 Bull. 11-2001/1.3.95	OJ C 75 E/26.3.2002 COM(2001) 709 Bull. 11-2001/1.3.95	Bull. 12-2001/1.3.103* OJ L 232/29.8.2002 Bull. 6-2002/1.3.84	
300	Dec. 2002/835/EC: specific programme 2002–06 for research, technological development and demonstration aimed at structuring the European research area	OJ C 240 E/28.8.2001 COM(2001) 279 Bull. 5-2001/1.3.55	OJ C 221/17.9.2002 Bull. 5-2002/1.3.72	Bull. 6-2002/1.3.85	OJ C 181 E/30.7.2002 COM(2002) 43 Bull. 1/2-2002/1.3.132	OJ L 294/29.10.2002 Bull. 9-2002/1.3.72	
300	Dec. 2002/834/EC: specific programme 2002–06 for research, technological development and demonstration aimed at integrating and strengthening the European research area	OJ C 240 E/28.8.2001 COM(2001) 279 Bull. 5-2001/1.3.55	OJ C 221/17.9.2002 Bull. 5-2002/1.3.72	Bull. 6-2002/1.3.87	OJ C 51 E/26.2.2002 COM(2001) 594 Bull. 10-2001/1.3.97 OJ C 181 E/30.7.2002 COM(2002) 43 Bull. 1/2-2002/1.3.132	OJ L 294/29.10.2002 Bull. 9-2002/1.3.72	
300	Dec. 2002/836/EC: specific programme 2002–06 for research, technological development and demonstration to be carried out by means of direct actions by the Joint Research Centre	OJ C 240 E/28.8.2001 COM(2001) 279 Bull. 5-2001/1.3.55	OJ C 221/17.9.2002 Bull. 5-2002/1.3.72	Bull. 6-2002/1.3.86	OJ C 181 E/30.7.2002 COM(2002) 43 Bull. 1/2-2002/1.3.132	OJ L 294/29.10.2002 Bull. 9-2002/1.3.72	
300	Dec. 2002/838/EC: specific programme 2002–06 for research and training	OJ C 240 E/28.8.2001 COM(2001) 279 Bull. 5-2001/1.3.55	OJ C 221/17.9.2002	Bull. 6-2002/1.3.89	OJ C 181 E/30.7.2002 COM(2002) 43 Bull. 1/2-2002/1.3.132	OJ L 294/29.10.2002 Bull. 9-2002/1.3.72	
300	Dec. 2002/837/Euratom: specific programme 2002–06 (Euratom) for research and training on nuclear energy	OJ C 240 E/28.8.2001 COM(2001) 279 Bull. 5-2001/1.3.55	OJ C 221/17.9.2002 Bull. 5-2002/1.3.72	Bull. 6-2002/1.3.88	OJ C 181 E/30.7.2002 COM(2002) 43 Bull. 1/2-2002/1.3.132	OJ L 294/29.10.2002 Bull. 9-2002/1.3.72	
301	Reg. (Euratom) No 2322/2002: rules for participation in the implementation of the Euratom framework programme 2002–06	OJ C 75 E/26.3.2002 COM(2001) 725 Bull. 12-2001/1.3.102	OJ C 241/7.10.2002 Bull. 7/8-2002/1.3.85	Bull. 7/8-2002/1.3.85	OJ C 103 E/30.4.2002 COM(2001) 823 Bull. 1/2-2002/1.3.131	OJ L 355/30.12.2002 Bull. 11-2002/1.3.68	

Information society
eEurope initiative

	Commission proposal	ESC opinion / CoR opinion°	EP opinion	Amended Commission proposal	Adoption by Council*	Observations
331	Prop. for a dec.: adoption of a multiannual programme (2003–05) for the monitoring of eEurope	OJ C 291 E/26.11.2002 COM(2002) 425 Bull. 7/8-2002/1.3.89	Bull. 10-2002/1.3.59				

TABLE II — CONSULTATION OF THE EUROPEAN PARLIAMENT 541

Economic and social cohesion

General outline

	Commission proposal	ESC opinion/ CoR opinion°	EP opinion	Amended Commission proposal	Adoption by Council*	Observations
361	Reg. (EC) No 2236/2002: financial contribution to the International Fund for Ireland (2003–04)		Bull. 11-2002/1.3.79		OJ L 341/17.12.2002	
362	Draft interinstitutional agreement: financing of the European Union Solidarity Fund and the conditions governing the resort to it 11.9.2002				Bull. 10-2002/1.4.35	
362	Reg. (EC) No 2012/2002 establishing a European Union Solidarity Fund	OJ C 331 E/31.12.2002 COM(2002) 514 Bull. 9-2002/1.4.30	Bull. 10-2002/1.4.36	Bull. 10-2002/1.4.36		OJ L 311/14.11.2002 Bull. 11-2002/1.4.44	

Innovative measures and other regional operations

	Commission proposal	ESC opinion/ CoR opinion°	EP opinion	Amended Commission proposal	Adoption by Council*	Observations
374	Reg. (EC) No 442/2002 amending Reg. (EEC) No 2019/93: specific measures for the smaller Aegean islands concerning certain agricultural products	OJ C 75 E/26.3.2002 COM(2001) 638 Bull. 11-2001/1.3.114	OJ C 80/3.4.2002 Bull. 1/2-2002/1.3.159	OJ C 284 E/21.11.2002 Bull. 1/2-2002/1.3.159		OJ L 68/12.3.2002 Bull. 1/2-2002/1.3.159	Amended reg.: OJ L 184/27.7.1993

Measures for the outermost regions

	Commission proposal	ESC opinion/ CoR opinion°	EP opinion	Amended Commission proposal	Adoption by Council*	Observations
380	Reg. (EC) No 579/2002 amending Reg. (EC) No 1587/98: scheme to compensate for the additional costs incurred in the marketing of certain fishery products from the Azores, Madeira, the Canary Islands, French Guiana and Réunion	OJ C 332 E/27.11.2001 COM(2001) 498 Bull. 9-2001/1.3.60		Bull. 3-2002/1.3.73		OJ L 89/5.4.2002 Bull. 3-2002/1.3.73	Amended reg.: OJ L 208/24.7.1998
381	Dec. 2002/166/EC authorising France to extend a reduced rate of excise duty on rum from its overseas departments	OJ C 270 E/25.9.2001 COM(2001) 347		OJ C 284 E/21.11.2002 Bull. 1/2-2002/1.3.152		OJ L 55/26.2.2002 Bull. 1/2-2002/1.3.152	

° Opinion of the Committee of the Regions.

* Council agreement.

	Commission proposal	ESC opinion/ CoR opinion°	EP opinion	Amended Commission proposal	Adoption by Council*	Observations
381 Dec. 2002/167/EC: Portugal — reduced rate of excise duty in Madeira (rum and liqueurs) and the Azores (liqueurs and eaux-de-vie)	OJ C 304 E/30.10.2001 COM(2001) 442		OJ C 284 E/21.11.2002 Bull. 1/2-2002/1.3.151		OJ L 55/26.2.2002 Bull. 1/2-2002/1.3.151	
381 Dec. 2002/546/EC: arrangements concerning the AIEM tax applicable in the Canary Islands	OJ C 75 E/26.3.2002 COM(2001) 732 Bull. 12-2001/1.3.118		Bull. 6-2002/1.3.107		OJ L 179/9.7.2002 Bull. 6-2002/1.3.107	
381 Dec. 2002/973/EC amending Dec. 89/688/EEC concerning the dock dues in the French overseas departments	COM(2002) 473 Bull. 7/8-2002/1.3.33		Bull. 11-2002/1.3.38		OJ L 337/13.12.2002 Bull. 12-2002/1.3.46	Amended dec.: OJ L 399/30.12.1989
382 Reg. (EC) No 704/2002: temporary suspension of autonomous Common Customs Tariff duties on imports of certain fishery products into the Canary Islands	OJ C 75 E/26.3.2002 COM(2001) 731 Bull. 12-2001/1.3.119		OJ C 284 E/21.11.2002 Bull. 1/2-2002/1.3.150		OJ L 111/26.4.2002 Bull. 3-2002/1.3.74	

Agriculture and rural development
Content of the common agricultural policy (CAP)

	Commission proposal	ESC opinion/ CoR opinion°	EP opinion	Amended Commission proposal	Adoption by Council*	Observations
397 Reg. (EC) No 1881/2002: amendment of Reg. (EC) No 2200/96 — starting date of the transitional period for the recognition of producer organisations	OJ C 227 E/24.9.2002 COM(2002) 252 Bull. 5-2002/1.3.89	Bull. 9-2002/1.3.81	Bull. 9-2002/1.3.81		OJ L 285/23.10.2002 Bull. 10-2002/1.3.69	Amended reg.: OJ L 297/21.11.1996

Agriculture and the environment, forests

	Commission proposal	ESC opinion/ CoR opinion°	EP opinion	Amended Commission proposal	Adoption by Council*	Observations
398 Prop. for a reg.: genetic resources in agriculture and amending Reg. (EC) No 1258/1999	OJ C 51 E/26.2.2002 COM(2001) 617 Bull. 10-2001/1.3.123	OJ C 149/21.6.2002 Bull. 4-2002/1.3.86				Reg. to be amended: OJ L 160/26.6.1999

Quality of agricultural products

	Commission proposal	ESC opinion/ CoR opinion°	EP opinion	Amended Commission proposal	Adoption by Council*	Observations
402 Prop. for a reg. amending Reg. (EEC) No 2081/92: protection of geographical indications and designations of origin for agricultural products and foodstuffs	OJ C 181 E/30.7.2002 COM(2002) 139 Bull. 3-2002/1.3.79	OJ C 241/7.10.2002 Bull. 7/8-2002/1.3.103 14.11.2001°	5.12.2002			Reg. to be amended: OJ L 208/24.7.1992

TABLE II — CONSULTATION OF THE EUROPEAN PARLIAMENT 543

Management of the common agricultural policy

	Commission proposal	ESC opinion/ CoR opinion°	EP opinion	Amended Commission proposal	Adoption by Council*	Observations
406	Prop. for a reg.: common organisation of the market in ethyl alcohol of agricultural origin	COM(2001) 101 Bull. 1/2-2001/1.3.170	OJ C 260/17.9.2001 Bull. 7/8-2001/1.3.127	Bull. 6-2002/1.3.115		
408	Prop. for a reg. amending Reg. (EEC) No 1766/92: calculation of import duties on certain cereals	COM(2002) 732				Reg. to be amended: OJ L 181/1.7.1992
409	Reg. (EC) No 962/2002 amending Reg. (EC) No 1868/94: production of potato starch	OJ C 51 E/26.2.2002 COM(2001) 677 Bull. 11-2001/1.3.125	OJ C 80/3.4.2002 Bull. 1/2-2002/1.3.162	Bull. 5-2002/1.3.92		OJ L 149/7.6.2002 Bull. 5-2002/1.3.92	Amended reg.: OJ L 197/30.7.1994
410	Reg. (EC) No 545/2002 extending the financing of quality and marketing improvement plans for certain nuts and locust beans and providing for a specific aid for hazelnuts	OJ C 51 E/26.2.2002 COM(2001) 667 Bull. 11-2001/1.3.127	OJ C 94/18.4.2002 Bull. 1/2-2002/1.3.164	Bull. 3-2002/1.3.82		OJ L 84/28.3.2002 Bull. 3-2002/1.3.82	
412	Reg. (EC) No 1873/2002: limits to the Community financing of work programmes drawn up by approved operators' organisations in the olive sector provided for in Reg. (EC) No 1638/98 and derogating from Reg. No 136/66/EEC	OJ C 262 E/29.10.2002 COM(2002) 343 Bull. 6-2002/1.3.116		Bull. 9-2002/1.3.84		OJ L 284/22.10.2002 Bull. 10-2002/1.3.71	Reg. (EC) No 1638/98 (OJ L 210/28.7.1998) and Reg. No 136/66/EEC (OJ 172/30.9.1996)
414	Reg. (EC) No 154/2002 amending Reg. (EEC) No 2358/71: common organisation of the market and fixing the aid granted in the seeds sector	OJ C 213 E/31.7.2001 COM(2001) 244 Bull. 5-2001/1.3.83	OJ C 311/7.11.2001 Bull. 9-2001/1.3.64	OJ C 177 E/25.7.2002 Bull. 12-2001/1.3.127		Bull. 12-2001/1.3.127* OJ L 25/29.1.2002 Bull. 1/2-2002/1.3.166	Amended reg.: OJ L 246/5.11.1971
415	Reg. (EC) No 546/2002 amending Reg. (EEC) No 2075/92: premiums and guarantee thresholds for leaf tobacco by variety group and Member State for the 2002, 2003 and 2004 harvests	OJ C 51 E/26.2.2002 COM(2001) 684 Bull. 11-2001/1.3.123	OJ C 94/18.4.2002 Bull. 1/2-2002/1.3.160	Bull. 3-2002/1.3.80		Bull. 3-2002/1.3.80* OJ L 84/28.3.2002 Bull. 3-2002/1.3.80	Amended reg.: OJ L 215/30.7.1992
416	Reg. (EC) No 2028/2002 amending Reg. (EEC) No 3950/92: additional levy in the milk and milk products sector	OJ C 227 E/24.9.2002 COM(2002) 307 Bull. 6-2002/1.3.117		Bull. 10-2002/1.3.73		OJ L 313/16.11.2002 Bull. 11-2002/1.3.85	Amended reg.: OJ L 405/31.12.1992

Financing the common agricultural policy: the EAGGF

	Commission proposal	ESC opinion/ CoR opinion°	EP opinion	Amended Commission proposal	Adoption by Council*	Observations
428	Prop. for a reg. amending Reg. (EC) No 1258/1999: financing of the common agricultural policy	COM(2002) 293 Bull. 6-2002/1.3.110	Bull. 9-2002/1.3.82	Bull. 9-2002/1.3.82			Reg. to be amended: OJ L 160/26.6.1999

° Opinion of the Committee of the Regions.
* Council agreement.

	Commission proposal	ESC opinion/ CoR opinion°	EP opinion	Amended Commission proposal	Adoption by Council*	Observations
428 Reg. (EC) No 2154/2002 amending Reg. (EEC) No 4045/89: scrutiny by Member States of transactions forming part of the system of financing by EAGGF	OJ C 51 E/26.2.2002 COM(2001) 663 Bull. 11-2001/1.3.129		Bull. 9-2002/1.3.85	COM(2002) 682 Bull. 11-2002/1.3.88	OJ L 328/5.12.2002	Amended reg.: OJ L 388/30.12.1989

Fisheries

Resource conservation and management

	Commission proposal	ESC opinion/ CoR opinion°	EP opinion	Amended Commission proposal	Adoption by Council*	Observations
437 Dec. 2002/70/EC amending Dec. 97/413/EC: restructuring the fisheries sector and achieving a balance on a sustainable basis	OJ C 270 E/25.9.2001 COM(2001) 322 Bull. 6-2001/1.3.120	OJ C 36/8.2.2002 Bull. 10-2001/1.3.129	OJ C 112 E/9.5.2002 Bull. 10-2001/1.3.129		Bull. 12-2001/1.3.143* OJ L 3/1.2.2002 Bull. 1/2-2002/1.3.177	Amended dec.: OJ L 175/3.7.1997
438 Prop. for a reg.: conservation and sustainable exploitation of fishery resources under the common fisheries policy	OJ C 203 E/27.8.2002 COM(2002) 185 Bull. 5-2002/1.3.97	12.12.2002°	5.12.2002		20.12.2002* OJ L 358/31.12.2002	
438 Reg. (EC) No 2347/2002: specific access requirements and associated conditions applicable to fishing for deep-sea stocks	OJ C 151 E/25.6.2002 COM(2002) 108 Bull. 3-2002/1.3.89		Bull. 10-2002/1.3.77		OJ L 351/28.12.2002 Bull.12-2002/1.3.11	
439 Reg. (EC) No 254/2002: measures to be applicable in 2002 for the recovery of the stock of cod in the Irish Sea (ICES Division VII a))	OJ C 75 E/26.3.2002 COM(2001) 699 Bull. 11-2001/1.3.132		OJ C 284 E/21.11.2002 Bull. 1/2-2002/1.3.179		OJ L 41/13.2.2002 Bull. 1/2-2002/1.3.179	
439 Prop. for a reg.: measures for the recovery of cod and hake stocks	OJ C 75 E/26.3.2002 COM(2001) 724 Bull. 12-2001/1.3.140		Bull. 6-2002/1.3.121	COM(2002) 773		
439 Prop. for a reg.: conservation of fishery resources through technical measures for the protection of juveniles of marine organisms	COM(2002) 672					
440 Prop. for a reg.: management of the fishing effort relating to certain Community fishing areas and resources and modifying Regulation (EEC) No 2847/93	COM(2002) 739 Bull.12-2002/1.3.120					
442 Prop. for a reg.: control measures applicable to fishing activities in the area covered by the Convention on the Conservation of Antarctic Marine Living Resources and repealing Regulations (EEC) No 3943/90, (EC) No 66/98 and (EC) No 1721/1999	OJ C 262 E/29.10.2002 COM(2002) 356 Bull. 7/8-2002/1.3.118					Regs to be repealed: (EEC) No 3943/90 (OJ L 379/31.12.1990), (EC) No 66/98 (OJ L 6/10.1.1998) and (EC) No 1721/1999 (OJ L 203/3.8.1999)
442 Prop. for a reg.: technical measures applicable to fishing activities in the area covered by the Convention on the Conservation of Antarctic Marine Living Resources	OJ C 262 E/29.10.2002 COM(2002) 355 Bull. 7/8-2002/1.3.119					

TABLE II — CONSULTATION OF THE EUROPEAN PARLIAMENT 545

	Commission proposal	ESC opinion/ CoR opinion°	EP opinion	Amended Commission proposal	Adoption by Council*	Observations
442	Prop. for a reg. amending Reg. (EC) No 1035/2001 establishing a catch documentation scheme for *Dissostichus spp.*	OJ C 291 E/26.11.2002 COM(2002) 424 Bull. 7/8-2002/1.3.120					Reg. to be amended: OJ L 145/31.5.2001
442	Prop. for a reg. amending Reg. (EC) No 973/2001: technical measures for the conservation of certain stocks of highly migratory species	OJ C 291 E/26.11.2002 COM(2002) 420 Bull. 7/8-2002/1.3.121					Reg. to be amended: OJ L 137/19.5.2001
442	Prop. for a reg. amending Reg. (EC) No 1936/2001: control measures applicable to fishing for certain stocks of highly migratory fish	OJ C 291 E/26.11.2002 COM(2002) 421 Bull. 7/8-2002/1.3.122					Reg. to be amended: OJ L 263/3.10.2001
442	Prop. for a reg.: system for the statistical monitoring of trade in bluefin tuna, swordfish and bigeye tuna	OJ C 331 E/31.12.2002 COM(2002) 453 Bull. 7/8-2002/1.3.123					

Fisheries and the environment

	Commission proposal	ESC opinion/ CoR opinion°	EP opinion	Amended Commission proposal	Adoption by Council*	Observations
447	Prop. for a reg.: removal of the fins of sharks on board vessels	OJ C 331 E/31.12.2002 COM(2002) 449 Bull. 7/8-2002/1.3.113					
447	Reg. (EC) No 2372/2002: specific measures to compensate the Spanish fisheries, shellfish industry and aquaculture affected by the oil spills from the *Prestige*	COM(2002) 776		19.12.2002		OJ L 358/31.12.2002 Bull.12-2002/1.3.131	

Structural action

	Commission proposal	ESC opinion/ CoR opinion°	EP opinion	Amended Commission proposal	Adoption by Council*	Observations
448	Reg. (EC) No 179/2002 amending Reg. (EC) No 2792/1999: fixing detailed rules and arrangements for structural assistance in the fisheries sector	OJ C 270 E/25.9.2001 COM(2001) 322 Bull. 6-2001/1.3.120	OJ C 36/8.2.2002 Bull. 10-2001/1.3.129	OJ C 112 E/9.5.2002 Bull. 10-2001/1.3.129		Bull. 12-2001/1.3.143* OJ L 31/1.2.2002 Bull. 1/2-2002/1.3.178	Amended reg.: OJ L 337/30.12.1999
448	Reg. (EC) No 2369/2002 amending Reg. (EC) No 2792/1999 laying down the detailed rules and arrangements regarding Community structural assistance in the fisheries sector	OJ C 203 E/27.8.2002 COM(2002) 187 Bull. 5-2002/1.3.101	12.12.2002°	5.12.2002		20.12.2002* OJ L 358/31.12.2002	Amended reg.: OJ L 337 du 30.12.1999
450	Reg. (EC) No 2370/2002 establishing an emergency Community measure for scrapping fishing vessels	OJ C 227 E/24.9.2002 COM(2002) 190 Bull. 5-2002/1.3.102	12.12.2002°	5.12.2002		20.12.2002* OJ L 358/31.12.2002 Bull.12-2002/1.3.130	

° Opinion of the Committee of the Regions.
* Council agreement.

Citizenship and quality of life

Area of freedom, security and justice

General

	Commission proposal	ESC opinion/ CoR opinion°	EP opinion	Amended Commission proposal	Adoption by Council*	Observations
455	Belgian, Spanish and French initiative for a dec. on the gradual abolition of border checks (amendment of Art. 40 of the Schengen Agreement)		Bull. 4-2002/1.4.21			Initiative of Belgium, Spain and France: OJ C 285/11.1.2001
457	Dec. 2002/630/JAI: framework programme on police and judicial cooperation in criminal matters (AGIS)		Bull. 4-2002/1.4.20		OJ L 203/1.8.2002 Bull. 7/8-2002/1.4.6	
457	French initiative for a dec. setting up a European judicial training network		24.9.2002			Initiative of France: OJ C 18/19.1.2001 and Bull. 1/2-2001/1.4.5

Internal borders, external borders and visa policy

	Commission proposal	ESC opinion/ CoR opinion°	EP opinion	Amended Commission proposal	Adoption by Council*	Observations
458	Dec. 2002/463/EC: action programme for administrative cooperation in the fields of external borders, visas, asylum and immigration (ARGO)	OJ C 278/14.11.2002 Bull. 5-2002/1.4.3°	Bull. 4-2002/1.4.8		Bull. 4-2002/1.4.8* OJ L 161/19.6.2002 Bull. 6-2002/1.4.6	
459	Prop. for a reg. amending Reg. (EC) No 1683/95: uniform format for visas	OJ C 180 E/26.6.2001 COM(2001) 157 Bull. 3-2001/1.4.4				Reg. to be amended: OJ L 164/14.7.1995
459	Reg. (EC) No 333/2002: uniform format for forms for affixing a visa	OJ C 180 E/26.6.2001 COM(2001) 157 Bull. 3-2001/1.4.4		OJ C 177 E/25.7.2002 Bull. 12-2001/1.4.14		Bull. 1/2-2002/1.4.7	
459	Reg. (EC) No 1030/2002: uniform format for residence permits for third-country nationals	OJ C 180 E/26.6.2001 COM(2001) 157 Bull. 3-2001/1.4.4		OJ C 177 E/25.7.2002 Bull. 12-2001/1.4.14		OJ L 157/15.6.2002 Bull. 6-2002/1.4.5	
459	Spanish initiative for a reg.: issue of visas at the border, including visas for seamen in transit						Initiative of Spain: OJ C 139/12.6.2002
459	Prop. for a reg. amending Reg. (EC) No 539/2001: list of third countries whose nationals must be in possession of visas when crossing the external borders of Member States	COM(2002) 679 Bull. 11-2002/1.4.13					Reg. to be amended: OJ L 81/21.3.2001

TABLE II — CONSULTATION OF THE EUROPEAN PARLIAMENT 547

	Commission proposal	ESC opinion/ CoR opinion°	EP opinion	Amended Commission proposal	Adoption by Council*	Observations
459 Prop. for a dir.: conditions in which third-country nationals shall have the freedom to travel in the territory of the Member States	OJ C 270 E/25.9.2001 COM(2001) 388 Bull. 7/8-2001/1.4.5	OJ C 192/12.8.2002 Bull. 3-2002/1.4.4°	OJ C 284 E/21.11.2002 Bull. 1/2-2002/1.4.3			

Asylum and immigration

	Commission proposal	ESC opinion/ CoR opinion°	EP opinion	Amended Commission proposal	Adoption by Council*	Observations
463 Framework dec. strengthening the penal framework to prevent the facilitation of unauthorised entry and residence			OJ C 276/1.10.2001 Bull. 1/2-2001/1.4.3		OJ L 328/5.12.2002	
463 Dir. 2002/90/EC defining the facilitation of unauthorised entry, movement and residence			OJ C 276/1.10.2001 Bull. 1/2-2001/1.4.3		OJ L 328/5.12.2002	Initiative of France: OJ C 253/4.9.2000 (Art. 67 EC)
465 Prop. for a dir.: short-term residence permit issued to victims of action to facilitate illegal immigration or trafficking in human beings who cooperate with the competent authorities	OJ C 126 E/28.5.2002 COM(2002) 71 Bull. 1/2-2002/1.4.4	OJ C 221/17.9.2002 Bull. 5-2002/1.4.5	5.12.2002			
466 Prop. for a dir.: right to family reunification	OJ C 116 E/26.4.2000 COM(1999) 638 Bull. 12-1999/1.5.4	OJ C 204/18.7.2000 Bull. 5-2000/1.4.5 OJ C 241/7.10.2002 Bull. 7/8-2002/1.4.1 Bull. 11-2002/1.4.3°	OJ C 135/7.5.2001 Bull. 9-2000/1.4.5	OJ C 62 E/27.2.2001 COM(2000) 624 Bull. 10-2000/1.4.2 OJ C 203 E/27.8.2002 COM(2002) 225 Bull. 5-2002/1.4.2		
466 Prop. for a dir.: status of third-country nationals who are long-term residents	OJ C 240 E/28.8.2001 COM(2001) 127 Bull. 3-2001/1.4.8	OJ C 36/8.2.2002 Bull. 10-2001/1.4.12 OJ C 19/22.1.2002 Bull. 5-2001/1.4.12°	OJ C 284 E/21.11.2002 Bull. 1/2-2002/1.4.2			
466 Prop. for a dir.: minimum standards for the qualification and status of third-country nationals and stateless persons as refugees	OJ C 51 E/26.2.2002 COM(2001) 510 Bull. 9-2001/1.4.9	OJ C 221/17.9.2002 Bull. 5-2002/1.4.4 OJ C 278/14.11.2002 Bull. 5-2002/1.4.3°	Bull. 10-2002/1.4.5			
466 Prop. for a dir.: minimum standards on procedures in Member States for granting and withdrawing refugee status	OJ C 62 E/27.2.2001 COM(2000) 578 Bull. 9-2000/1.4.6	OJ C 193/10.7.2001 Bull. 4-2001/1.9.5	OJ C 77 E/28.3.2002 Bull. 9-2001/1.4.10	OJ C 291 E/26.11.2002 COM(2002) 326 Bull. 6-2002/1.4.4		
466 Prop. for a reg.: criteria and mechanisms for the Member State responsible for examining an asylum application in one of the Member States	OJ C 304 E/30.10.2001 COM(2001) 447 Bull. 7/8-2001/1.4.6	OJ C 125/27.5.2002 Bull. 3-2002/1.4.1	Bull. 4-2002/1.4.2			

° Opinion of the Committee of the Regions.
* Council agreement.

		Commission proposal	ESC opinion/ CoR opinion°	EP opinion	Amended Commission proposal	Adoption by Council*	Observations
466	Prop. for a dir.: conditions of entry and residence of third-country nationals for the purposes of studies, vocational training or voluntary service	COM(2002) 548 Bull. 10-2002/1.4.1					
466	Prop. for a dir.: conditions of entry and residence of third-country nationals for the purpose of paid employment and self-employed economic activities	OJ C 332 E/27.11.2001 COM(2001) 386 Bull. 7/8-2001/1.4.3	OJ C 80/3.4.2002 Bull. 1/2-2002/1.4.6 OJ C 192/12.8.2002°				
466	Prop. for a dir.: minimum standards for the reception of applicants for asylum in Member States	OJ C 213 E/31.7.2001 COM(2001) 181 Bull. 4-2001/1.4.1	OJ C 48/21.2.2002 Bull. 11-2001/1.4.6 OJ C 107/3.5.2002 Bull. 11-2001/1.4.6°	Bull. 4-2002/1.4.7			

Judicial cooperation in civil and commercial matters

		Commission proposal	ESC opinion/ CoR opinion°	EP opinion	Amended Commission proposal	Adoption by Council*	Observations
468	Reg. (EC) No 743/2002: general framework for Community activities for the implementation of a European judicial area in civil matters	OJ C 213 E/31.7.2001 COM(2001) 221 Bull. 5-2001/1.4.7	OJ C 36/8.2.2002 Bull. 10-2001/1.4.13	OJ C 112 E/9.5.2002 Bull. 10-2001/1.4.13 Bull. 3-2002/1.4.6	OJ C 51 E/26.2.2002 COM(2001) 705 Bull. 11-2001/1.4.10	OJ L 115/1.5.2002 Bull. 4-2002/1.4.19	
469	Prop. for a dir.: minimum common rules relating to legal aid and other financial aspects of civil proceedings	OJ C 103 E/30.4.2002 COM(2002) 13 Bull. 1/2-2002/1.4.15	OJ C 221/17.9.2002 Bull. 5-2002/1.4.12	Bull. 9-2002/1.4.7		Bull. 10-2002/1.4.14*	
471	Prop. for a reg.: creating a European enforcement order for uncontested claims	OJ C 203 E/27.8.2002 COM(2002) 159 Bull. 4-2002/1.4.17	11.12.2002				
471	Prop. for a reg.: jurisdiction and the recognition and enforcement of judgments in matrimonial matters and in matters of parental responsibility repealing Reg. (EC) No 1347/2000 and amending Reg. (EC) No 44/2001 in matters relating to maintenance	OJ C 203 E/27.8.2002 COM(2002) 222 Bull. 5-2002/1.4.11	Bull. 9-2002/1.4.5	Bull. 11-2002/1.4.17		Bull. 11-2002/1.4.17*	Repealed reg.: (EC) No 1347/2000 (OJ L 160/30.6.2000) and amended reg.: (EC) No 44/2001 (OJ L 12/16.1.2001)

Judicial cooperation in criminal matters

		Commission proposal	ESC opinion/ CoR opinion°	EP opinion	Amended Commission proposal	Adoption by Council*	Observations
473	Dec. 2002/187/JAI setting up Eurojust to reinforce the fight against organised crime			OJ C 34 E/7.2.2002 Bull. 5-2001/1.4.11 OJ C 153 E/27.6.2002 Bull. 11-2001/1.4.20		OJ L 63/6.3.2002 Bull. 1/2-2002/1.4.13	Initiative of Belgium, France, Portugal and Sweden: OJ C 243/24.8.2000 (Art. 67 EC)

TABLE II — CONSULTATION OF THE EUROPEAN PARLIAMENT 549

	Commission proposal	ESC opinion/ CoR opinion°	EP opinion	Amended Commission proposal	Adoption by Council*	Observations
474 Prop. for a framework dec.: attacks against information systems	OJ C 203 E/27.8.2002 COM(2002) 173 Bull. 4-2002/1.4.12		Bull. 10-2002/1.3.61			
475 Belgian initiative for a dec. setting up a European network of national contact points for restorative justice						
475 French, Swedish and UK initiative for a framework dec. on the principle of mutual recognition of financial penalties						Initiative of France, Sweden and the United Kingdom: OJ C 278/2.10.2001
476 Framework dec. on the European arrest warrant and the surrender procedures between the Member States	OJ C 332 E/27.11.2001 COM(2001) 522 Bull. 9-2001/1.4.5		OJ C 153 E/27.6.2002 Bull. 11-2001/1.4.2 OJ C 284 E/21.11.2002 Bull. 1/2-2002/1.4.11		OJ L 190/18.7.2002 Bull. 6-2002/1.4.9	
477 Danish initiative for a framework dec.: confiscation of crime-related proceeds, instrumentalities and property			20.11.2002		19.12.2002*	Initiative of Denmark: OJ C 184/2.8.2002
477 Danish initiative for a framework dec.: execution in the EU of confiscation orders			20.11.2002			Initiative of Denmark: OJ C 184/2.8.2002
477 Belgian, French and Swedish initiative for a framework dec.: execution of orders freezing assets or evidence			OJ C 77 E/28.3.2002 Bull. 6-2002/1.4.15			Initiative of Belgium, France, and Sweden: OJ C 75/7.3.2001
478 Danish initiative for a dec.: increasing cooperation between Member States with regard to disqualifications			17.12.2002			Initiative of Denmark: OJ C 223/19.9.2002
479 Framework dec. on joint investigation teams			OJ C 140 E/13.6.2002 Bull. 11-2001/1.4.14		OJ L 162/20.6.2002 Bull. 6-2002/1.4.18	Initiative of Belgium, Spain, France and the United Kingdom: OJ C 295/20.10.2001
480 Prop. for a dir.: compensation to crime victims	COM(2002) 562 Bull. 10-2002/1.4.13					
481 Prop. for a dec. on combating racism and xenophobia	OJ C 75 E26.3.2002 COM(2001) 664 Bull. 11-2001/1.4.18		Bull. 7/8-2002/1.4.5			
482 German initiative for a framework dec.: criminal law protection against fraudulant anti-competitive conduct in relation to the award of public contracts			Bull. 6-2002/1.4.16			Initiative of Germany: OJ C 253/4.9.2000

° Opinion of the Committee of the Regions.

* Council agreement.

Police and customs cooperation

		Commission proposal	ESC opinion/ CoR opinion°	EP opinion	Amended Commission proposal	Adoption by Council*	Observations
483	Council Act drawing up a protocol amending the Europol convention			Bull. 5-2002/1.4.13		28.11.2002	Initiative of Belgium and Spain: OJ C 42/15.2.2002
483	Danish initiative amending the regs applicable to Europol staff						Initiative of Denmark: OJ C 286/22.11.2002
483	Danish initiative drawing up a protocol amending the Convention on the establishment of a European Police Office						Initiative of Denmark: OJ C 172/18.7.2002
483	Dec. adjusting the basic salaries of Europol staff (1 July 2001 to 1 July 2002)			Bull. 5-2002/1.4.15		13.6.2002	
484	Spanish initiative for a dec. setting up a European Institute of Police Studies			Bull. 5-2002/1.4.14			Initiative of Spain: OJ C 42/15.2.2002
485	Dec. setting up a European network for the protection of public figures			Bull. 5-2002/1.4.16			Initiative of Spain: OJ C 42/15.2.2002
485	Spanish initiative for a Council dec. setting up a network of contact points of national authorities responsible for private security			Bull. 5-2002/1.4.17		OJ L 333/10.12.2002	Initiative of Spain: JO C 42/15.2.2002
485	Dec. 2002/348/JAI: security in connection with football matches with an international dimension			Bull. 4-2002/1.4.24		OJ L 121/8.5.2002 Bull. 4-2002/1.4.24	
485	Danish initiative for a dec.: common use of liaison officers posted abroad by the law enforcement agencies of the Member States			20.11.2002			Initiative of Denmark: OJ C 176/24.7.2002
485	German, Belgian and French initiative for a Council Act: use of information technology for customs purposes (customs files identification database)			18.12.2002			

Prevention of and fight against crime

		Commission proposal	ESC opinion/ CoR opinion°	EP opinion	Amended Commission proposal	Adoption by Council*	Observations
488	Dec. 2002/494/JAI setting up a European network of contact points in respect of persons responsible for genocide, crimes against humanity and war crimes			Bull. 4-2002/1.4.16		OJ L 167/26.6.2002 Bull. 6-2002/1.4.12	Initiative of the Netherlands: OJ C 295/20.10.2001
488	Danish initiative for a dec.: investigation and prosecution of war crimes and crimes against humanity			17.12.2002			Initiative of Denmark: OJ C 223/19.9.2002
489	Framework dec. 2002/629/JAI on combating trafficking in human beings	OJ C 62 E/27.2.2001 COM(2000) 854 Bull. 12-2000/1.4.14	OJ C 357/14.12.2001 Bull. 6-2001/1.4.10°	OJ C 53 E/28.2.2002 Bull. 6-2001/1.4.10		Bull. 9-2001/1.4.21* OJ L 203/1.8.2002 Bull. 7/8-2002/1.4.4	
490	Danish initiative for a framework dec.: combating corruption in the private sector			20.11.2002			Initiative of Denmark: OJ C 184/2.8.2002

TABLE II — CONSULTATION OF THE EUROPEAN PARLIAMENT 551

Combating terrorism

	Commission proposal	ESC opinion/ CoR opinion°	EP opinion	Amended Commission proposal	Adoption by Council*	Observations
492	Framework dec. 2002/475/JAI on combating terrorism		OJ C 153 E/27.6.2002 Bull. 11-2001/1.4.1 OJ C 284 E/21.11.2002 Bull. 1/2-2002/1.4.10		Bull. 12-2001/1.4.6* OJ L 164/22.6.2002 Bull. 6-2002/1.4.8	
492	Prop. for a dec.: financing of certain activities carried out by Europol in connection with cooperation in the fight against terrorism	OJ C 331 E/31.12.2002 COM(2002) 439 Bull. 7/8-2002/1.4.3		5.12.2002 Bull.12-2002/1.4.7			
492	Dec. establishing a mechanism for evaluating national legal provisions relating to the fight against terrorism and their implementation			Bull. 9-2002/1.4.4		14.10.2002* OJ L 349/24.12.2002	Initiative of Spain: OJ C 151/25.6.2002
492	Dec.: police and judicial cooperation to combat terrorism (Article 4 of Common Position 2001/931/CFSP of the Council)			Bull. 9-2002/1.4.3		19.12.2002 Bull.12-2002/1.4.11	Initiative of Spain: OJ C 126/28.5.2002

Note: Row 492 first line Commission proposal: OJ C 332 E/27.11.2001 COM(2001) 521 Bull. 9-2001/1.4.4

Drugs

	Commission proposal	ESC opinion/ CoR opinion°	EP opinion	Amended Commission proposal	Adoption by Council*	Observations
499	Prop. for a framework dec.: constituent elements of criminal acts and penalties in the field of illicit drug trafficking	OJ C 270 E/25.9.2001 OJ C 304 E/30.10.2001 COM(2001) 259 Bull. 5-2001/1.4.19		Bull. 4-2002/1.4.29			

Education and culture
Education and training

	Commission proposal	ESC opinion/ CoR opinion°	EP opinion	Amended Commission proposal	Adoption by Council*	Observations
524	Dec. 2002/601/EC amending Dec. 1999/311/EC: adoption of the third phase of the trans-European cooperation scheme for higher education (Tempus III) (2000–06)	OJ C 151 E/25.6.2002 COM(2002) 47 Bull. 1/2-2002/1.4.38	OJ C 149/21.6.2002 Bull. 4-2002/1.4.37	Bull. 5-2002/1.4.26		30.5.2002* OJ L 195/24.7.2002 Bull. 6-2002/1.4.26	Amended dec.: OJ L 120/8.5.1999

° Opinion of the Committee of the Regions.
* Council agreement.

Environment

Environment and health

	Commission proposal	ESC opinion/ CoR opinion°	EP opinion	Amended Commission proposal	Adoption by Council*	Observations
577	Dec.: approval of the Rotterdam Convention on the Prior Informed Consent Procedure for Certain Hazardous Chemicals and Pesticides	OJ C 126 E/28.5.2002 COM(2001) 802 Bull. 1/2-2002/1.4.58		Bull. 10-2002/1.4.38			
585	Prop. for a dir.: control of high activity sealed radioactive sources	OJ C 151 E/25.6.2002 COM(2002) 130 Bull. 3-2002/1.4.31	OJ C 241/7.10.2002 Bull. 7/8-2002/1.4.27			19.12.2002 Bull.12-2002/1.4.53	

Climate change and international dimension

	Commission proposal	ESC opinion/ CoR opinion°	EP opinion	Amended Commission proposal	Adoption by Council*	Observations
587	Dec. 2002/358/EC: approval of the Kyoto Protocol to the United Nations Framework Convention on Climate Change	OJ C 75 E/26.3.2002 COM(2001) 579 Bull. 10-2001/1.4.42	OJ C 192/12.8.2002 Bull. 3-2002/1.4.32°	OJ C 284 E/21.11.2002 Bull. 1/2-2002/1.4.63		Bull. 3-2002/1.4.32* OJ L 130/15.5.2002 Bull. 4-2002/1.4.50	
589	Dec. 2002/215/EC: fourth amendment to the Montreal Protocol on Substances that deplete the Ozone Layer	OJ C 213 E/31.7.2001 COM(2001) 249 Bull. 5-2001/1.4.47		OJ C 87 E/11.4.2002 Bull. 10-2001/1.4.40		OJ L 72/14.3.2002 Bull. 3-2002/1.4.34	
593	Prop. for a dec.: accession to the 1979 Convention on Transboundary Air Pollution	OJ C 151 E/25.6.2002 COM(2002) 44 Bull. 1/2-2002/1.4.65		Bull. 7/8-2002/1.4.28			

Governance, communication and civil society

	Commission proposal	ESC opinion/ CoR opinion°	EP opinion	Amended Commission proposal	Adoption by Council*	Observations
595	Danish initiative for a framework decision: combating serious environmental crime			OJ C 121/24.4.2001 Bull. 7/8-2000/1.4.17 Bull. 4-2002/1.4.53		15.3.2001*	Initiative of Denmark: OJ C 39/11.2.2000

TABLE II — CONSULTATION OF THE EUROPEAN PARLIAMENT 553

Energy

Internal energy market

	Commission proposal	ESC opinion/ CoR opinion°	EP opinion	Amended Commission proposal	Adoption by Council*	Observations
611	Prop. for a dir. repealing Dirs 68/414/EEC and 98/93/EC (minimum stocks of cruce oil), and Dir. 73/238/EEC (measures to mitigate the effects of difficulties in the supply of crude oil)	OJ C 331 E/31.12.2002 COM(2002) 488 Bull. 9-2002/1.4.43				Dirs to be repealed: 68/414/EEC (OJ L 308/23.12.1968), 98/93/EC (OJ L 358/31.12.1998) and 73/238/EEC (OJ L 228/16.8.1973)

Transport

Galileo satellite radio-navigation programme

	Commission proposal	ESC opinion/ CoR opinion°	EP opinion	Amended Commission proposal	Adoption by Council*	Observations
632	Reg. (EC) No 876/2002: establishment of the Galileo joint undertaking	OJ C 270 E/25.9.2001 COM(2001) 336 Bull. 6-2001/1.4.51	OJ C 48/21.2.2002 Bull. 11-2001/1.4.71 OJ C 278/14.11.2002 Bull. 5-2002/1.4.56°	OJ C 284 E/21.11.2002 Bull. 1/2-2002/1.4.75		Bull. 3-2002/1.4.44* OJ L 138/28.5.2002 Bull. 5-2002/1.4.56	

Health and consumer protection

Food safety

	Commission proposal	ESC opinion/ CoR opinion°	EP opinion	Amended Commission proposal	Adoption by Council*	Observations
674	Prop. for a reg.: animal health rules governing the production, placing on the market and importation of products of animal origin intended for human consumption	OJ C 365 E/19.12.2000 COM(2000) 438 Bull. 7/8-2000/1.4.64	OJ C 155/29.5.2001	Bull. 5-2002/1.4.74		Bull. 11-2002/1.4.86*	
676	Prop. for a reg. amending Reg. (EC) No 1255/97: use of staging points	OJ C 291 E/26.11.2002 COM(2002) 414 Bull. 7/8-2002/1.4.64					Reg. to be amended: OJ L 174/2.7.1997

° Opinion of the Committee of the Regions.

* Council agreement.

	Commission proposal	ESC opinion°/CoR opinion°	EP opinion	Amended Commission proposal	Adoption by Council*	Observations
676 Prop. for a dir. amending Dir. 91/68/EEC: reinforcement of controls on movements of ovine and caprine animals	OJ C 331 E/31.12.2002 COM(2002) 504 Bull. 9-2002/1.4.66	11.12.2002 Bull. 12-2002/1.4.92	17.12.2002 Bull. 12-2002/1.4.92			Dir. to be amended: OJ L 46/19.2.1991
676 Prop. for a dir.: Community measures for the control of foot and mouth disease and amending Dir. 92/46/EEC	COM(2002) 736					Dir. to be amended: OJ L 268/14.9.1992
676 Prop. for a reg.: system for the identification and registration of ovine and caprine animals and amending Reg. (EEC) No 3508/92	COM(2002) 729					Reg. to be amended: OJ L 355/5.12.1992
676 Dir. 2002/60/EC amending Dir. 92/119/EEC: control of Teschen disease and African swine fever	OJ C 181 E/30.7.2002 COM(2002) 51 Bull. 1/2-2002/1.4.112				OJ L 192/20.7.2002 Bull. 6-2002/1.4.66	Amended dir.: OJ L 62/15.3.1993
676 Prop. for a dir. amending Dir. 88/407/EEC: animal health requirements applicable to intra-Community trade in and imports of semen of domestic animals of the bovine species	COM(2002) 527 Bull. 9-2002/1.4.67	11.12.2002 Bull.12-2002/1.4.96				Dir. to be amended: OJ L 194/22.7.1988
677 Dir. 2002/89/EC amending Dir. 2000/29/EC: protective measures against the introduction into the Community of organisms harmful to plants	OJ C 240 E/28.8.2001 COM(2001) 183 Bull. 4-2001/1.4.62	OJ C 36/8.2.2002 Bull. 10-2001/1.4.82	OJ C 53 E/28.2.2002 Bull. 6-2001/1.4.75		OJ L 355/30.12.2002 Bull. 11-2002/1.4.91	Amended dir.: OJ L 169/10.7.2000
678 Dir. 2002/53/EC consolidating Dir. 70/457/EEC: common catalogue of varieties of agricultural plant species	COM(95) 628 Bull. 12-1995/1.3.25	OJ C 153/28.5.1996 Bull. 1/2-1996/1.3.26	OJ C 320/28.10.1996 Bull. 9-1996/1.3.121 Bull. 4-2002/1.4.70	COM(1998) 470 Bull. 7/8-1998/1.3.219 COM(2001) 191	OJ L 193/20.7.2002 Bull. 6-2002/1.4.69	Consolidated dir.: OJ L 225/12.10.1970
678 Dir. 2002/54/EC consolidating Dir. 66/400/EEC: marketing of beet seed	COM(95) 622 Bull. 12-1995/1.3.24	OJ C 153/28.5.1996 Bull. 1/2-1996/1.3.25	OJ C 347/18.11.1996 Bull. 10-1996/1.3.134 Bull. 4-2002/1.4.68	COM(1998) 504 Bull. 9-1998/1.2.142 COM(2001) 177	OJ L 193/20.7.2002 Bull. 6-2002/1.4.68	Consolidated dir.: OJ L 125/11.7.1966
678 Dir. 2002/55/EC consolidating Dir. 70/458/EEC: marketing of vegetable seed	COM(95) 628 Bull. 12-1995/1.3.25	OJ C 153/28.5.1996 Bull. 1/2-1996/1.3.26	OJ C 26/19.9.1996 Bull. 7/8-1996/1.3.186 Bull. 4-2002/1.4.69	COM(1998) 505 Bull. 9-1998/1.2.143 COM(2001) 194	OJ L 193/20.7.2002 Bull. 6-2002/1.4.69	Consolidated dir.: OJ L 225/12.10.1970
678 Dir. 2002/56/EC consolidating Dir. 66/403/EEC: marketing of seed potatoes	COM(95) 622 Bull. 12-1995/1.3.24	OJ C 153/28.5.1996 Bull. 1/2-1996/1.3.25	OJ C 347/18.11.1996 Bull. 10-1996/1.3.134 Bull. 4-2002/1.4.68	COM(1998) 506 Bull. 9-1998/1.2.142 COM(2001) 192	OJ L 193/20.7.2002 Bull. 6-2002/1.4.68	Consolidated dir.: OJ L 125/11.7.1966
678 Dir. 2002/57/EC consolidating Dir. 69/208/EEC: marketing of seed of oil and fibre plants	COM(95) 622 Bull. 12-1995/1.3.24	OJ C 153/28.5.1996 Bull. 1/2-1996/1.3.25	OJ C 347/18.11.1996 Bull. 10-1996/1.3.134 Bull. 4-2002/1.4.68	COM(1998) 533 Bull. 9-1998/1.2.142 COM(2001) 195	OJ L 193/20.7.2002 Bull. 6-2002/1.4.68	Consolidated dir.: OJ L 169/10.7.1969
678 Dir. 2002/68/EC amending Dir. 2002/57/EC: marketing of seed of oil and fibre plants	OJ C 203 E/27.8.2002 COM(2002) 232 Bull. 5-2002/1.4.75	OJ C 241/7.10.2002 Bull. 7/8-2002/1.4.65	Bull. 7/8-2002/1.4.65		OJ L 195/24.7.2002 Bull. 7/8-2002/1.4.65	Amended dir.: OJ L 193/20.7.2002

TABLE II — CONSULTATION OF THE EUROPEAN PARLIAMENT 555

	Commission proposal	ESC opinion/ CoR opinion°	EP opinion	Amended Commission proposal	Adoption by Council*	Observations
678	Dir. 2002/11/EC amending Dir. 68/193/EEC: marketing of material for the vegetative propagation of the vine	OJ C 177 E/27.6.2000 COM(2000) 59 Bull. 1/2-2000/1.4.71	OJ C 268/19.9.2000 Bull. 7/8-2000/1.4.68	OJ C 197/12.7.2001 Bull. 10-2000/1.4.55		OJ L 53/23.2.2002 Bull. 1/2-2002/1.4.116	Amended dir.: OJ L 93/17.4.1968
678	Prop. for a dir. amending, as regards Community comparative tests and trials, Dirs 66/401/EEC, 66/402/EEC, 68/193/EEC, 92/33/EEC, 92/34/EEC, 98/56/EC, 2002/54/EEC, 2002/55/EC, 2002/56/EC and 2002/57/EC (marketing of seed)	COM(2002) 523 Bull. 9-2002/1.4.69	11.12.2002 Bull.12-2002/1.4.99				Dirs to be amended 66/401/EEC and 66/402/EEC (OJ 125/11.7.1966), 68/193/EEC (OJ L 93/17.4.1968), 92/33/EEC and 92/34/EEC (OJ L 157/10.6.1992), 98/56/EC (OJ L 226/13.8.1998) and 2002/54/EC, 2002/55/EC, 2002/56/EC and 2002/57/EC (OJ L 193/20.7.2002)
684	Draft dec.: conclusion of the protocol of amendment to the European Convention for the Protection of Vertebrate Animals used for Experimental and other Scientific Purposes	OJ C 25 E/29.1.2002 COM(2001) 704 Bull. 11-2001/1.4.51		Bull. 7/8-2002/1.4.61			

Public health

	Commission proposal	ESC opinion/ CoR opinion°	EP opinion	Amended Commission proposal	Adoption by Council*	Observations
690	Prop. for a recomm.: prevention and reduction of risks associated with drug dependence	COM(2002) 201 Bull. 5-2002/1.4.79	Bull. 10-2002/1.4.70 Bull. 11-2002/1.4.94°				
691	Prop. for a recomm.: prevention of smoking and initiatives to improve tobacco control	COM(2002) 303 Bull. 6-2002/1.4.76	Bull. 11-2002/1.4.97°				

Enlargement

Pre-accession strategy

Financial and technical assistance

	Commission proposal	ESC opinion/ CoR opinion°	EP opinion	Amended Commission proposal	Adoption by Council*	Observations
728	Prop. for a reg. amending Reg. (EC) No 1268/1999: Community support for pre-accession measures for agriculture and rural development in the countries of central and eastern Europe	OJ C 331 E/31.12.2002 COM(2002) 519 Bull. 9-2002/1.5.3	Bull. 10-2002/1.5.16				Reg. to be amended: OJ L 161/26.6.1999

° Opinion of the Committee of the Regions.

* Council agreement.

	Commission proposal	ESC opinion/CoR opinion°	EP opinion	Amended Commission proposal	Adoption by Council*	Observations

Role of the Union in the world

Development cooperation

North–south cooperation on health

	Commission proposal	ESC opinion/CoR opinion°	EP opinion	Amended Commission proposal	Adoption by Council*	Observations
827	Prop. for a reg.: trade diversion into the European Union of certain key medicines — COM(2002) 592 Bull. 10-2002/1.6.65					

Relations with Asia

Bilateral relations

	Commission proposal	ESC opinion/CoR opinion°	EP opinion	Amended Commission proposal	Adoption by Council*	Observations
949	Reg. (EC) No 881/2002: specific restrictive measures directed against certain persons and entities associated with Usama bin Laden, the Al-Qaida network and the Taliban, and repealing Reg. (EC) No 467/2001 — OJ C 151 E/25.6.2002 COM(2002) 117 Bull. 3-2002/1.6.85		Bull. 4-2002/1.6.70		OJ L 139/29.5.2002 Bull. 5-2002/1.6.105	Repealed reg.: OJ L 67/9.3.2001

ACP countries and OCTs

Financial and technical cooperation

	Commission proposal	ESC opinion/CoR opinion°	EP opinion	Amended Commission proposal	Adoption by Council*	Observations
1015	Prop. for a reg.: financial regulation applicable to the ninth European Development Fund — OJ C 262 E/29.10.2002 COM(2002) 290					

Financing of Community activities, resource management

Budgets

Financial regulations

	Commission proposal	ESC opinion/CoR opinion°	EP opinion	Amended Commission proposal	Adoption by Council*	Observations
1048	Reg. (EC, Euratom) No 1605/2002: financial regulation applicable to the budget of the European Communities — OJ C 96 E/27.3.2001 COM(2000) 461 Bull. 7/8-2000/1.7.9	OJ C 260/17.9.2001 Bull. 7/8-2001/1.7.6	OJ C 153 E/27.6.2002 Bull. 11-2001/1.7.4 Bull. 6-2002/1.7.2	OJ C 103 E/30.4.2002 COM(2001) 691 Bull. 12-2001/1.7.9	OJ L 248/16.9.2002 Bull. 6-2002/1.7.2	

TABLE II — CONSULTATION OF THE EUROPEAN PARLIAMENT 557

	Commission proposal	ESC opinion/ CoR opinion°	EP opinion	Amended Commission proposal	Adoption by Council*	Observations
1050	Prop. for a reg. amending Reg. (EC) No 2965/94: budgetary and financial rules applicable to the Translation Centre for the Bodies of the EU and access to the Centre's documents	OJ C 331 E/31.12.2002 COM(2002) 406 Bull. 7/8-2002/1.7.8				Reg. to be amended: OJ L 314/7.12.1994
1050	Prop. for a reg. amending Reg. (EC) No 2667/2000: budgetary and financial rules applicable to the European Agency for Reconstruction and access to the Agency's documents	OJ C 331 E/31.12.2002 COM(2002) 406 Bull. 7/8-2002/1.7.8				Reg. to be amended: OJ L 306/7.12.2000
1050	Prop. for a reg. amending Reg. (EEC) No 2309/93: budgetary and financial rules applicable to the European Agency for the Evaluation of Medicinal Products and access to the Agency's documents	OJ C 331 E/31.12.2002 COM(2002) 406 Bull. 7/8-2002/1.7.8				Reg. to be amended: OJ L 214/24.8.1993
1050	Prop. for a reg. amending Reg. (EEC) No 1360/90: budgetary and financial rules applicable to the European Training Foundation and access to the Foundation's documents	OJ C 331 E/31.12.2002 COM(2002) 406 Bull. 7/8-2002/1.7.8				Reg. to be amended: OJ L 131/23.5.1990
1050	Prop. for a reg. amending Reg. (EEC) No 1365/75: budgetary and financial rules applicable to the European Foundation for the Improvement of Living and Working Conditions and access to the Foundation's documents	OJ C 331 E/31.12.2002 COM(2002) 406 Bull. 7/8-2002/1.7.8				Reg. to be amended: OJ L 139/30.5.1975
1050	Prop. for a dec. amending Dec. 2002/187/JAI: setting up Eurojust with a view to reinforcing the fight against serious crime	OJ C 331 E/31.12.2002 COM(2002) 406 Bull. 7/8-2002/1.7.8				Dec. to be amended: OJ L 63/6.3.2002
1050	Prop. for a reg. amending Reg. (EC) No 2100/94: internal audit and control systems applicable to the Community Plant Variety Office and access to the Office's documents	OJ C 331 E/31.12.2002 COM(2002) 406 Bull. 7/8-2002/1.7.8				Reg. to be amended: OJ L 227/1.9.1994
1050	Prop. for a reg. amending Reg. (EEC) No 302/93: internal audit and control systems applicable to the European Monitoring Centre for Drugs and Drug Addiction and access to the Centre's documents	OJ C 331 E/31.12.2002 COM(2002) 406 Bull. 7/8-2002/1.7.8				Reg. to be amended: OJ L 36/12.2.1993
1050	Prop. for a reg. amending Reg. (EC) No 1035/97: internal audit and control systems applicable to the European Monitoring Centre on Racism and Xenophobia and access to the Centre's documents	OJ C 331 E/31.12.2002 COM(2002) 406 Bull. 7/8-2002/1.7.8				Reg. to be amended: OJ L 151/10.6.1997
1050	Prop. for a reg. amending Reg. (EC) No 40/94: internal audit and control systems applicable to the Office for Harmonisation in the Internal Market and access to the Office's documents	OJ C 331 E/31.12.2002 COM(2002) 406 Bull. 7/8-2002/1.7.8				Reg. to be amended: OJ L 11/14.1.1994
1050	Prop. for a reg. amending Reg. (EC) No 2062/94: internal audit and control systems applicable to the European Agency for Safety and Health at Work and access to the Agency's documents	OJ C 331 E/31.12.2002 COM(2002) 406 Bull. 7/8-2002/1.7.8				Reg. to be amended: OJ L 216/20.8.1994

° Opinion of the Committee of the Regions.
* Council agreement.

	Commission proposal	ESC opinion/ CoR opinion°	EP opinion	Amended Commission proposal	Adoption by Council*	Observations
1050	Prop. for a reg. amending Reg. (EEC) No 337/75: internal audit and control systems applicable to the European Centre for the Development of Vocational Training and access to the Centre's documents	OJ C 331 E/31.12.2002 COM(2002) 406 Bull. 7/8-2002/1.7.8					Reg. to be amended: OJ L 39/13.2.1975
1050	Prop. for a reg. amending Reg. (EC) No 40/94: Community trade mark	OJ C 335/6.11.1997 COM(97) 489 Bull. 10-1997/1.5.11		OJ C 104/6.4.1998 Bull. 3-1998/1.5.11	OJ C 194/20.6.1998 COM(1998) 289 Bull. 4-1998/1.5.16		Reg. to be amended: OJ L 11/14.1.1994, withdrawal by Commission: 17.7.2002
1050	Prop. for a reg. amending Reg. (EC) No 2100/94: plant variety rights	OJ C 335/6.11.1997 COM(97) 489 Bull. 10-1997/1.5.11		OJ C 104/6.4.1998 Bull. 3-1998/1.5.11	OJ C 194/20.6.1998 COM(1998) 289 Bull. 4-1998/1.5.16		Reg. to be amended: OJ L 277/1.9.1994, withdrawal by Commission: 17.7.2002
1050	Prop. for a reg. amending Reg. (EEC) No 2309/93: authorisation and supervision of medicinal products and the European Agency for the Evaluation of Medicinal Products	OJ C 335/6.11.1997 COM(97) 489 Bull. 10-1997/1.5.11		OJ C 104/6.4.1998 Bull. 3-1998/1.5.11	OJ C 194/20.6.1998 COM(1998) 289 Bull. 4-1998/1.5.16		Reg. to be amended: OJ L 214/24.8.1993, withdrawal by Commission: 17.7.2002
1050	Prop. for a reg. amending Reg. (EEC) No 1210/90 setting up a European Environment Agency and information network	OJ C 335/6.11.1997 COM(97) 489 Bull. 10-1997/1.5.11	OJ C 95/30.3.1998 Bull. 1/2-1998/1.6.9 OJ C 374/23.12.1999 Bull. 9-1999/1.6.4°	OJ C 104/6.4.1998 Bull. 3-1998/1.5.11	OJ C 194/20.6.1998 COM(1998) 289 Bull. 4-1998/1.5.16		Reg. to be amended: OJ L 120/11.5.1990, withdrawal by Commission: 17.7.2002
1050	Prop. for a reg. amending Reg. (EC) No 2062/94 setting up a European Agency for Safety and Health at Work	OJ C 335/6.11.1997 COM(97) 489 Bull. 10-1997/1.5.11		OJ C 104/6.4.1998 Bull. 3-1998/1.5.11	OJ C 194/20.6.1998 COM(1998) 289 Bull. 4-1998/1.5.16		Reg. to be amended: OJ L 216/20.8.1994, withdrawal by Commission: 17.7.2002
1050	Prop. for a reg. amending Reg. (EEC) No 302/93 setting up a European Monitoring Centre on Drugs and Drug Addiction	OJ C 335/6.11.1997 COM(97) 489 Bull. 10-1997/1.5.11		OJ C 104/6.4.1998 Bull. 3-1998/1.5.11	OJ C 194/20.6.1998 COM(1998) 289 Bull. 4-1998/1.5.16		Reg. to be amended: OJ L 36/12.2.1993, withdrawal by Commission: 17.7.2002
1050	Prop. for a reg. amending Reg. (EEC) No 1360/90 setting up a European Training Foundation	OJ C 335/6.11.1997 COM(97) 489 Bull. 10-1997/1.5.11		OJ C 104/6.4.1998 Bull. 3-1998/1.5.11	OJ C 194/20.6.1998 COM(1998) 289 Bull. 4-1998/1.5.16		Reg. to be amended: OJ L 131/23.5.1990, withdrawal by Commission: 17.7.2002
1050	Prop. for a reg. amending Reg. (EC) No 2965/94 setting up a Translation Centre for the bodies of the Union	OJ C 335/6.11.1997 COM(97) 489 Bull. 10-1997/1.5.11		OJ C 104/6.4.1998 Bull. 3-1998/1.5.11	OJ C 194/20.6.1998 COM(1998) 289 Bull. 4-1998/1.5.16		Reg. to be amended: OJ L 314/7.12.1994, withdrawal by Commission: 17.7.2002
1050	Prop. for a reg. amending Reg. (EC) No 1035/97 setting up a European Monitoring Centre on Racism and Xenophobia	OJ C 335/6.11.1997 COM(97) 489 Bull. 10-1997/1.5.11		OJ C 104/6.4.1998 Bull. 3-1998/1.5.11	OJ C 194/20.6.1998 COM(1998) 289 Bull. 4-1998/1.5.16		Reg. to be amended: OJ L 151/10.6.1997, withdrawal by Commission: 17.7.2002
1051	Reg.: statute for executive agencies to be entrusted with certain tasks in the management of Community programmes	OJ C 120 E/24.4.2001 COM(2000) 788 Bull. 12-2000/1.10.15		OJ C 65 E/14.3.2002 Bull. 7/8-2001/1.9.7	OJ C 103 E/30.4.2002 COM(2001) 808 Bull. 12-2001/1.9.18	19.12.2002 Bull.12-2002/1.10.13	

TABLE II — CONSULTATION OF THE EUROPEAN PARLIAMENT 559

	Commission proposal	ESC opinion/ CoR opinion°	EP opinion	Amended Commission proposal	Adoption by Council*	Observations

Borrowing and lending operations

| 1060 | Prop. for a déc. amending Dec. 77/270/Euratom empowering the Commission to issue Euratom loans for the purpose of contributing to the financing of nuclear power stations
COM(2002) 456
Bull. 11-2002/1.7.8 | | | | | Dec. to be amended: OJ L 88/6.4.1977 |

Institutions and other bodies

Administration and management

Staff policy and Staff Regulations

| 1126 | Reg. (EC, ECSC, Euratom) No 490/2002 amending Reg. (EEC, Euratom, ECSC) No 259/68: Staff Regulations of Officials and Conditions of Employment of Other Servants of the European Communities — contracts of auxiliary staff
OJ C 213 E/31.7.2001
COM(2001) 253 | | OJ C 284 E/21.11.2002
Bull. 1/2-2002/1.9.2 | | OJ L 77/20.3.2002 | Amended Reg.: OJ L 56/4.3.1968 |

Reform of the Commission

| 1153 | Prop. for a reg.: Staff Regulations of Officials and the Conditions of Employment of Other Servants of the European Communities
OJ C 291 E/26.11.2002
COM(2002) 213
Bull. 4-2002/1.9.7 | | | | | |

Information and communication

Historical archives

| 1168 | Prop. for a reg. amending Reg. (EEC, Euratom) No 354/83: opening to the public of the historical archives of the EEC and the European Atomic Energy Community
OJ C 331 E/31.12.2002
COM(2002) 462 | | | | | Reg. to be amended: OJ L 43/15.2.1983 |

*Opinion of the Committee of the Regions.

°Council agreement.

Table III — International agreements

	Commission recommendation	Council decision/ negotiating directives	Initials	Signature	Commission proposal/ conclusion	ESC opinion/ COR opinion°	EP opinion/ EP assent*	Council regulation (or decision)/ conclusion	Observations

The Community economic and social area
Competition policy
International cooperation

	Commission recommendation	Council decision/ negotiating directives	Initials	Signature	Commission proposal/ conclusion	ESC opinion/ COR opinion°	EP opinion/ EP assent*	Council regulation (or decision)/ conclusion	Observations
246 Draft EC–Japan agreement concerning cooperation on anti-competitive activities	8.6.2000				COM(2002) 230 Bull. 5-2002/1.3.64		Bull. 7/8-2002/1.3.79		

Research and technology
Community RTD policy

	Commission recommendation	Council decision/ negotiating directives	Initials	Signature	Commission proposal/ conclusion	ESC opinion/ COR opinion°	EP opinion/ EP assent*	Council regulation (or decision)/ conclusion	Observations
289 Draft framework agreement between the EC and the European Space Agency (ESA)	28.1.2002	Bull. 5-2002/1.3.70							

Implementation of the fifth framework programme 1998–2002

	Commission recommendation	Council decision/ negotiating directives	Initials	Signature	Commission proposal/ conclusion	ESC opinion/ COR opinion°	EP opinion/ EP assent*	Council regulation (or decision)/ conclusion	Observations
312 EC-Chile agreement on scientific and technical cooperation		Bull. 7/8-2001/1.3.98	26.10.2001	23.9.2002					Proposal signature: OJ C 181 E/30.7.2002 COM(2002) 151 Bull. 3-2002/1.3.66 Council decision concerning the signature: Bull. 5-2002/1.3.74

TABLE III — INTERNATIONAL AGREEMENTS 561

	Commission recommendation	Council decision/ negotiating directives	Initials	Signature	Commission proposal/ conclusion	ESC opinion/ COR opinion°	EP opinion/ EP assent*	Council regulation (or decision)/ conclusion	Observations
312 EC–India agreement on scientific and technical cooperation		12.2.2001	21.3.2001	Bull. 11-2001/1.3.97	OJ C 304 E/30.10.2001 COM(2001) 448 Bull. 7/8-2001/1.3.99		Bull. 5-2002/1.3.75	OJ L 213/9.8.2002 Bull. 6-2002/1.3.91	Entered into force: 14.10.2002 Proposal signature: OJ C 304 E/30.10.2001 COM(2001) 448 Bull. 7/8-2001/1.3.99 Council decision concerning the signature: Bull. 11-2001/1.3.97
312 Draft EC–Mexico agreement on scientific and technological cooperation		Bull. 7/8-2002/1.3.87							
312 Draft agreement on scientific and technical cooperation between the EC and Brazil			Bull. 12-2002/1.3.87						
312 Draft agreement on scientific and technical cooperation between the EC and Israel		Bull. 11-2002/1.3.69							
313 Additional protocol to the EC–Malta agreement on associating Malta with the implementation of the fifth framework programme of the EC for research, technological development and demonstration activities (1998–2002)		Bull. 4-2002/1.5.3		20.6.2001	OJ C 103 E/30.4.2002 COM(2001) 777 Bull. 12-2001/1.5.13		9.4.2002	OJ L 144/1.6.2002 Bull. 5-2002/1.5.4	
314 EC–Ukraine agreement on scientific and technological cooperation	24.7.2001	8.10.2001	13.11.2001	Bull. 7/8-2002/1.3.88	COM(2002) 550 Bull. 10-2002/1.3.57		Bull. 12-2002/1.3.88		Proposal signature: OJ C 203 E/27.8.2002 COM(2002) 178 Bull. 4-2002/1.3.79 Council decision concerning the signature: Bull. 6-2002/1.3.92

° Opinion of the Committee of the Regions.
* Agreement requiring Parliament's assent.

	Commission recommendation	Council decision/ negotiating directives	Initials	Signature	Commission proposal/ conclusion	ESC opinion/ COR opinion°	EP opinion/ EP assent*	Council regulation (or decision)/ conclusion	Observations

Agriculture and rural development

Management of the common agricultural policy

	Commission recommendation	Council decision/ negotiating directives	Initials	Signature	Commission proposal/ conclusion	ESC opinion/ COR opinion°	EP opinion/ EP assent*	Council regulation (or decision)/ conclusion	Observations
406 EC–South Africa agreements on trade in wines and spirituous beverages	Bull. 3-2002/1.4.97	Bull. 6-2002/1.4.118	30.11.2001	Bull. 1/2-2002/1.3.167	COM(2001) 757 Bull. 12-2001/1.3.131			OJ L 28/30.1.2002 Bull. 1/2-2002/1.3.167	Entry into force: 28.1.2002
406 EC–South Africa agreement in the form of an exchange of letters on trade in wines				28.1.2002	COM(2001) 759 Bull. 12-2001/1.3.132			OJ L 28/30.1.2002 Bull. 1/2-2001/1.3.168	Entry into force: 28.1.2002
408 Draft agreements between the EC and the United States and the EC and Canada relative to concession with cereals					COM(2002) 731 Bull. 12-2002/1.3.109			Bull. 12-2002/1.3.109	

Fisheries

Resource conservation and management

	Commission recommendation	Council decision/ negotiating directives	Initials	Signature	Commission proposal/ conclusion	ESC opinion/ COR opinion°	EP opinion/ EP assent*	Council regulation (or decision)/ conclusion	Observations
442 Convention on the conservation and management of fishery resources in the south-east Atlantic				20.4.2001	OJ C 75 E/26.3.2002 COM(2001) 679 Bull. 11-2001/1.3.138		Bull. 7/8-2002/1.3.124	OJ L 234/31.8.2002 Bull. 7/8-2002/1.3.124	Proposal signature: COM(2000) 807 Bull. 12-2000/1.3.128 Council decision concerning the signature: OJ L 111/20.4.2001 Bull. 1/2-2001/1.3.190
443 Draft EEC–Angola agreement on the extension of the protocol setting out the fishing opportunities and financial contribution (3.5.2002–2.8.2002)			26.4.2002		OJ C 262 E/29.10.2002 COM(2002) 368 Bull. 7/8-2002/1.3.114		Bull. 10-2002/1.3.79	OJ L 317/21.11.2002 Bull. 11-2002/1.3.93	Prop. for a reg. on the provisional application of the agreement: COM(2002)369 Bull. 7/8-2002/1.3.114 OJ C 262 E/29.10.2002. Council dec. on the provisional application of the agreement: OJ L 317/21.11.2002 and Bull.11-2002/1.3.93

TABLE III — INTERNATIONAL AGREEMENTS 563

	Commission recommendation	Council decision/ negotiating directives	Initials	Signature	Commission proposal/ conclusion	ESC opinion/ COR opinion°	EP opinion/ EP assent*	Council regulation (or decision)/ conclusion	Observations
443	Draft protocol setting out the fishing opportunities and financial contribution provided for in the EC–Cape Verde agreement (1.7.2001–30.6.2004)			7.7.2001		OJ C 332 E/27.11.2001 COM(2001) 470 Bull. 9-2001/1.3.68		OJ C 177 E/25.7.2002 Bull. 12-2001/1.3.146	OJ L 47/19.2.2002 Bull. 1/2-2002/1.3.182	
443	Draft protocol setting out the fishing opportunities and financial contribution provided for in the EC–Gabon agreement (3.12.2002–2.12.2005)			20.9.2001		OJ C 75 E/26.3.2002 COM(2001) 765 Bull. 12-2001/1.3.149		Bull. 3-2002/1.3.90	OJ L 89/5.4.2002 Bull. 3-2002/1.3.90	
443	Draft agreement in the form of an exchange of letters on the extension of the protocol setting out the fishing opportunities and the financial contribution provided for in the EC–Guinea agreement (1.1.2002–3.12.2002)			Bull. 5-2002/1.3.98		OJ C 126 E/28.5.2002 COM(2002) 41 Bull. 1/2-2002/1.3.183		14.5.2002	OJ L 144/1.6.2002 Bull. 5-2002/1.3.98	
443	Draft protocol setting out the fishing opportunities and financial contribution provided for in the EC–Guinea-Bissau agreement (16.6.2001–15.6.2006)			30.5.2001		OJ C 25 E/29.1.2002 COM(2001) 530 Bull. 10-2001/1.3.131		OJ C 177 E/25.7.2002 Bull. 12-2001/1.3.151	OJ L 40/12.2.2002 Bull. 1/2-2002/1.3.184	
443	Draft protocol setting out the fishing opportunities and financial contribution provided for in the EC–São Tomé and Príncipe agreement (1.6.2002–31.5.2005)			Bull. 1/2-2002/1.3.186						
443	Draft protocol setting out the fishing opportunities and financial contribution provided for in the EC–Senegal agreement (1.7.2002–30.6.2006)			Bull. 6-2002/1.3.122		COM(2002) 496 Bull. 10-2002/1.3.82			OJ L 349/24.12.2002 Bull. 12-2002/1.3.127	
443	Draft protocol setting out the fishing opportunities and financial contribution provided for in the EC–Seychelles agreement (18.1.2002–17.1.2005)			28.9.2001	19.6.2002	OJ C 126 E/28.5.2002 COM(2002) 55 Bull. 1/2-2002/1.3.187		Bull. 5-2002/1.3.99	OJ L 144/1.6.2002 Bull. 5-2002/1.3.99	
443	Draft EC-Kiribati agreement on fishing off the coast of Kiribati			Bull. 7/8-2002/1.3.116						Entry into force: 3.7.2002 Proposal signature: OJ C 126 E/28.5.2002 COM(2002) 56 Bull. 1/2-2002/1.3.187 Council decision concerning the signature: OJ L 134/22.5.2002 Bull. 4-2002/1.3.94

° Opinion of the Committee of the Regions.

* Agreement requiring Parliament's assent.

	Commission recommendation	Council decision/ negotiating directives	Initials	Signature	Commission proposal/ conclusion	ESC opinion/ COR opinion°	EP opinion/ EP assent*	Council regulation (or decision)/ conclusion	Observations
443 Draft EC–Mozambique agreement setting out the fishing opportunities and financial contribution	29.4.1996		Bull. 10-2002/1.3.80						
444 Draft additional protocol to the EC–Czech Republic association agreement laying down the conditions applicable to trade in certain fish and fishery products		COM(2001) 778 Bull. 12-2001/1.5.14			19.12.2001			OJ L 324/29.11.2002 Bull. 10-2002/1.5.13	
444 Draft EC–Bulgaria agreement on fishery products		29.5.2000		28.11.2002	OJ C 291 E/26.11.2002 COM(2002) 204 Bull. 4-2002/1.5.1			OJ L 335/12.12.2002 Bull. 11-2002/1.5.11	

Citizenship and quality of life

Area of freedom, security and justice

Judicial cooperation in civil and commercial matters

	Commission recommendation	Council decision/ negotiating directives	Initials	Signature	Commission proposal/ conclusion	ESC opinion/ COR opinion°	EP opinion/ EP assent*	Council regulation (or decision)/ conclusion	Observations
471 Council of Europe Convention on Contact Concerning Children									Proposal signature: COM(2002) 520 Bull. 10-2002/1.4.12
472 Draft convention between the EC and Denmark, Iceland, Norway and Poland on jurisdiction and the recognition and enforcement of judgments in civil and commercial matters		Bull. 10-2002/1.4.15							

Drugs

	Commission recommendation	Council decision/ negotiating directives	Initials	Signature	Commission proposal/ conclusion	ESC opinion/ COR opinion°	EP opinion/ EP assent*	Council regulation (or decision)/ conclusion	Observations
498 Draft EC–Turkey agreement on precursors and chemical substances frequently used in the illicit manufacture of narcotic drugs or psychotropic substances		5.4.2001			OJ C 331 E/31.12.2002 COM(2002) 500			Bull. 12-2002/1.4.27	Proposal signature: OJ C 331 E/31.12.2002 COM(2002) 500 Bull. 9-2002/1.4.10 Council decision concerning the signature: Bull. 12-2002/1.4.27

TABLE III — INTERNATIONAL AGREEMENTS 565

Environment

Environmental quality and natural resources

	Commission recommendation	Council decision/ negotiating directives	Initials	Signature	Commission proposal/ conclusion	ESC opinion/ COR opinion°	EP opinion/ EP assent*	Council regulation (or decision)/ conclusion	Observations
568 Draft protocol to the Barcelona Convention concerning cooperation in preventing pollution from ships and in combating pollution of the Mediterranean Sea by oil and noxious substances				25.1.2002					Proposal signature: COM(2002) 11 Bull. 1/2-2002/1.4.51 Council decision concerning the signature: Bull. 1/2-2002/1.4.51

Environment and health

	Commission recommendation	Council decision/ negotiating directives	Initials	Signature	Commission proposal/ conclusion	ESC opinion/ COR opinion°	EP opinion/ EP assent*	Council regulation (or decision)/ conclusion	Observations
580 Cartagena Protocol on Biosafety		Bull. 10-1995/1.3.160		Bull. 5-2000/1.4.32	OJ C 181 E/30.7.2002 COM(2002) 127 Bull. 3-2002/1.4.26		Bull. 6-2002/1.4.39	OJ L 201/31.7.2002 Bull. 6-2002/1.4.39	Proposal signature: COM(2000) 182 Bull. 3-2000/1.4.29 Council decision concerning the signature: Bull. 5-2000/1.4.32

Climate change and international dimension

	Commission recommendation	Council decision/ negotiating directives	Initials	Signature	Commission proposal/ conclusion	ESC opinion/ COR opinion°	EP opinion/ EP assent*	Council regulation (or decision)/ conclusion	Observations
594 Protocol on water and health to the 1992 convention on the protection and use of transboundary watercourses and international lakes					OJ C 332 E/27.11.2001 COM(2001) 483 Bull. 7/8-2001/1.4.29		OJ C 271 E/7.11.2002 Bull. 1/2-2002/1.4.64		

° Opinion of the Committee of the Regions.
* Agreement requiring Parliament's assent.

Transport
Inland transport

	Commission recommendation	Council decision/ negotiating directives	Initials	Signature	Commission proposal/ conclusion	ESC opinion/ COR opinion°	EP opinion/ EP assent*	Council regulation (or decision/ conclusion)	Observations
640					COM(2002) 24 Bull. 1/2-2002/1.4.84	Bull. 9-2002/1.4.50 10.10.2002°			
644				21.10.2002	COM(2002) 418 Bull. 7/8-2002/1.4.44		Bull. 10-2002/1.4.53		Proposal signature: COM(2002) 418 Bull. 7/8-2002/1.4.44 Council decision concerning the signature: 21.10.2002
645									Draft Commission decision concerning the memorandum of understanding: COM(2002)104 Bull.1/2-2002/1.4.94

Row 640: Convention concerning international carriage by rail (COTIF) of 9 May 1980, as amended by the Vilnius Protocol of 3 June 1999 (recommendation for a Council decision authorising the Commission to negotiate the conditions for accession)

Row 644: Draft agreement in the form of an exchange of letters between the EC and the former Yugoslav Republic of Macedonia concerning the system of ecopoints to be applied to transit traffic through Austria

Row 645: Protocol to the agreement concerning the development of the pan-European transport corridor No VII (the Danube)

Maritime transport

	Commission recommendation	Council decision/ negotiating directives	Initials	Signature	Commission proposal/ conclusion	ESC opinion/ COR opinion°	EP opinion/ EP assent*	Council regulation (or decision/ conclusion)	Observations
651					OJ C 51 E/26.2.2002 COM(2001) 675 Bull. 11-2001/1.4.79		Bull. 6-2002/1.4.51	OJ L 256/25.9.2002 Bull. 9-2002/1.4.53	
651							Bull. 6-2002/1.4.51		Proposal signature: OJ C 51 E/26.2.2002 COM(2001) 674 Bull. 11-2001/1.4.79 Council decision concerning the signature: OJ L 337/13.12.2002 Bull. 11-2002/1.4.73

Row 651: International Convention on Civil Liability for Bunker Oil Pollution Damage (ratification)

Row 651: International Convention on Liability and Compensation for Bunker Oil Pollution Damage (ratification)

TABLE III — INTERNATIONAL AGREEMENTS 567

Air transport

	Commission recommendation	Council decision/ negotiating directives	Initials	Signature	Commission proposal/ conclusion	ESC opinion/ COR opinion°	EP opinion/ EP assent*	Council regulation (or decision)/ conclusion	Observations
661 Protocol on the accession of the EC to the European Organisation for the Safety of Air Navigation (Eurocontrol)				Bull. 10-2002/1.4.54					Proposal signature: OJ C 262 E29.10.2002 COM(2002) 292 Bull. 6-2002/1.4.56 Council decision concerning the signature: 31.7.2002

International cooperation

	Commission recommendation	Council decision/ negotiating directives	Initials	Signature	Commission proposal/ conclusion	ESC opinion/ COR opinion°	EP opinion/ EP assent*	Council regulation (or decision)/ conclusion	Observations
667 EC–China agreement on maritime transport		Bull. 1/2-1998/1.3.192		6.12.2002	OJ C 181 E/30.7.2002 COM(2002) 97 Bull. 1/2-2002/1.4.105			Bull. 10-2002/1.4.59	Proposal signature: OJ C 181 E/30.7.2002 COM(2002) 97 Bull. 1/2-2002/1.4.105 Council decision concerning the signature: Bull. 10-2002/1.4.59
669 Interbus agreement between the EC and Bosnia and Herzegovina, Bulgaria, Croatia, Czech Republic, Estonia, Hungary, Latvia, Lithuania, Moldova, Romania, Slovakia, Slovenia and Turkey on international occasional transport	Bull. 12-1992/1.3.137	Bull. 12-1995/1.3.121		Bull. 6-2001/1.4.65	OJ C 51 E/26.2.2002 COM(2001) 540 Bull. 10-2001/1.4.59		Bull. 7/8-2002/1.4.53	OJ L 321/26.11.2002 Bull. 10-2002/1.4.58	Proposal signature: COM(2000) 799 Bull. 12-2000/1.4.67 Council decision concerning the signature: Bull. 6-2001/1.4.65

Health and consumer protection

Food safety

	Commission recommendation	Council decision/ negotiating directives	Initials	Signature	Commission proposal/ conclusion	ESC opinion/ COR opinion°	EP opinion/ EP assent*	Council regulation (or decision)/ conclusion	Observations
674 EC–New Zealand agreement on sanitary measures applicable to trade in live animals and animal products				28.11.2002	OJ C 331 E/31.12.2002 COM(2002) 503 Bull. 9-2002/1.4.65			OJ L 333/10.12.2002 Bull. 11-2002/1.4.89	

° Opinion of the Committee of the Regions.
* Agreement requiring Parliament's assent.

	Commission recommendation	Council decision/ negotiating directives	Initials	Signature	Commission proposal/ conclusion	ESC opinion/ COR opinion°	EP opinion/ EP assent*	Council regulation (or decision)/ conclusion	Observations
680									Proposal signature: COM(2002) 197 Bull. 4-2002/1.4.71 Council decision concerning the signature: Bull. 5-2002/1.4.77

International treaty on plant genetic resources for food and agriculture (row 680).

Enlargement

Pre-accession strategy

Europe agreements and other agreements

	Commission recommendation	Council decision/ negotiating directives	Initials	Signature	Commission proposal/ conclusion	ESC opinion/ COR opinion°	EP opinion/ EP assent*	Council regulation (or decision)/ conclusion	Observations
717		21.9.1992	10.7.2001	21.5.2002	OJ C 151 E/25.6.2002 COM(2002) 111 Bull. 3-2002/1.5.3			OJ L 202/31.7.2002 Bull. 6-2002/1.5.10	Entry into force: 1.9.02 Proposal signature: OJ C 151 E/25.6.2002 COM(2002) 111 Bull. 3-2002/1.5.3 Council decision concerning the signature: Bull. 5-2002/1.5.2
717		21.9.1992	10.7.2001	21.5.2002	OJ C 151 E/25.6.2002 COM(2002) 123 Bull. 6-2002/1.5.10			OJ L 202/31.7.2002 Bull. 6-2002/1.5.10	Entry into force: 1.9.02 Proposal signature: OJ C 151 E/25.6.2002 COM(2002) 123 Bull. 3-2002/1.5.3 Council decision concerning the signature: Bull. 5-2002/1.5.2
717		21.9.1992	10.9.2000	Bull. 11-2002/1.5.17	OJ C 291 E/26.11.2002 COM(2002) 432 Bull. 7/8-2002/1.5.8				Proposal signature: OJ C 291 E/26.11.2002 COM(2002) 432 Bull. 7/8-2002/1.5.8 Council decision concerning the signature: Bull. 11-2002/1.5.17

Row descriptions:
- First 717: Additional protocol to the EC–Latvia agreement on conformity assessment and the acceptance of industrial products
- Second 717: Additional protocol to the EC–Latvia agreement on conformity assessment and the acceptance of industrial products
- Third 717: Additional protocol to the EC–Slovenia agreement on conformity assessment and the acceptance of industrial products

TABLE III — INTERNATIONAL AGREEMENTS 569

	Commission recommendation	Council decision/ negotiating directives	Initials	Signature	Commission proposal/ conclusion	ESC opinion/ COR opinion°	EP opinion/ EP assent*	Council regulation (or decision)/ conclusion	Observations
717	Draft additional protocol to the Europe Agreement setting up an association between the EC and Slovakia on conformity assessment and the acceptance of industrial products				COM(2002) 588 Bull. 10-2002/1.5.12				Proposal signature: COM(2002) 588 Bull. 10-2002/1.5.12
717	Draft additional protocol to the EC–Estonia agreement on conformity assessment and acceptance of industrial products	21.9.1992	19.7.2002		COM(2002) 608 Bull. 11-2002/1.5.13				Proposal signature: COM(2002) 608 Bull. 11-2002/1.5.13
717	Draft agreements between the EC and candidate countries on conformity assessment for industrial products and on mutual recognition	Bull. 7/8-2002/1.5.4							
718	Draft protocol for the adaptation of the trade aspects of the EC–Estonia association agreement				COM(2002) 572 Bull. 10-2002/1.5.10				
718	Draft additional protocol for the adaptation of the trade aspects of the Europe Agreement establishing an EC–Poland association	30.3.1999			OJ C 262 E/29.10.2002 COM(2002) 363 Bull. 7/8-2002/1.5.3				
718	Draft additional protocol for the adaptation of the trade aspects of the EC–Slovenia European association agreement	30.3.1999			COM(2002) 607 Bull. 11-2002/1.5.16				
718	Draft additional protocol for the adaptation of the trade aspects of the EC–Latvia Europe Agreement	30.3.1999			COM(2002) 643 Bull. 11-2002/1.5.14				
718	Draft additional protocol for the adaptation of the trade aspects of the EC–Czech Republic Europe Agreement	30.3.1999			COM(2002) 657 Bull. 11-2002/1.5.15				
718	Draft additional protocol for the adaptation of the trade aspects of the EC–Lithuania European association agreement	30.3.1999			COM(2002) 690 Bull. 12-2002/1.5.11				

° Opinion of the Committee of the Regions.

* Agreement requiring Parliament's assent.

	Commission recommendation	Council decision/ negotiating directives	Initials	Signature	Commission proposal/ conclusion	ESC opinion/ COR opinion°	EP opinion/ EP assent*	Council regulation (or decision)/ conclusion	Observations
718 Draft additional protocol for the adaptation of the trade aspects of the EC–Hungary European association agreement		COM(2002) 707 Bull. 12-2002/1.5.10			10.12.2002				
718 Draft additional protocol for the adaptation of the trade aspects of the EC–Slovakia European association agreement		30.3.1999			COM(2002) 708 Bull. 12-2002/1.5.14				
718 Draft additional protocol for the adaptation of the trade aspects of the EC–Bulgaria European association agreement		30.3.1999			COM(2002) 749 Bull. 12-2002/1.5.9				
718 Draft additional protocol for the adaptation of the trade aspects of the EC–Romania European association agreement		30.3.1999			COM(2002) 553 Bull. 10-2002/1.5.14			Bull. 12-2002/1.5.9	
719 Draft EC–Cyprus and EC–Malta agreements on new mutual trading concessions relating to processed agricultural products		Bull. 11-2002/1.5.12							
721 Draft agreements between the EC and the countries of central and eastern Europe, Cyprus and Malta establishing an exchange of information on technical regulations and requirements applying to information society services		Bull. 10-2002/1.5.8							
723 Draft EC–Malta agreement in the form of an exchange of letters concluding an additional protocol to the EC–Malta agreement on mutual administrative assistance in the customs field					COM(2002) 509 Bull. 10-2002/1.5.11				
724 Memorandums of understanding setting up an association between the EC and the countries of central and eastern Europe, Cyprus, Malta and Turkey in connection with the sixth framework research programme (2003–06)				Bull. 10-2002/1.5.9					

TABLE III — INTERNATIONAL AGREEMENTS 571

	Commission recommendation	Council decision/ negotiating directives	Initials	Signature	Commission proposal/ conclusion	ESC opinion/ COR opinion°	EP opinion/ EP assent*	Council regulation (or decision)/ conclusion	Observations

Role of the Union in the world

Common commercial policy

Operation of the customs union, customs cooperation and mutual assistance

	Commission recommendation	Council decision/ negotiating directives	Initials	Signature	Commission proposal/ conclusion	ESC opinion/ COR opinion°	EP opinion/ EP assent*	Council regulation (or decision)/ conclusion	Observations
782	Protocol of amendment to the international convention on the simplification and harmonisation of customs procedures (Kyoto Convention)				COM(2002) 628 Bull. 11-2002/1.6.21				

Treaties, trade agreements and mutual recognition agreements

	Commission recommendation	Council decision/ negotiating directives	Initials	Signature	Commission proposal/ conclusion	ESC opinion/ COR opinion°	EP opinion/ EP assent*	Council regulation (or decision)/ conclusion	Observations
791	Mutual recognition agreement between the EC and Australia on conformity assessment, certificates and markings				OJ C 227 E/24.9.2002 COM(2002) 271 Bull. 6-2002/1.6.49			OJ L 27/8/16.10.2002 Bull. 10-2002/1.6.63	Dec. to be amended: 98/508/EC (OJ L 229/17.8.1998)
791	Mutual recognition agreement between the EC and Canada				OJ C 227 E/24.9.2002 COM(2002) 270 Bull. 6-2002/1.6.49			OJ L 27/8/16.10.2002 Bull. 10-2002/1.6.63	Dec. to be amended: 98/566/EC (OJ L 280/16.10.1998)
791	Mutual recognition agreement between the EC and Japan				OJ C 227 E/24.9.2002 COM(2002) 273 Bull. 6-2002/1.6.49			OJ L 27/8/16.10.2002 Bull. 10-2002/1.6.63	Dec. to be amended: 2001/747/EC (OJ L 284/29.10.2001)
791	Mutual recognition agreement between the EC and the United States				COM(2002) 250 Bull. 6-2002/1.6.49			OJ L 27/8/16.10.2002 Bull. 10-2002/1.6.63	Dec. to be amended: 1999/78/EC (OJ L 31/4.2.1999)
791	Mutual recognition agreement between the EC and New Zealand on conformity assessment				OJ C 227 E/24.9.2002 COM(2002) 272 Bull. 6-2002/1.6.49			OJ L 27/8/16.10.2002 Bull. 10-2002/1.6.63	Dec. to be amended: 98/509/EC (OJ L 229/17.8.1998)

° Opinion of the Committee of the Regions.

* Agreement requiring Parliament's assent.

	Commission recommendation	Council decision/ negotiating directives	Initials	Signature	Commission proposal/ conclusion	ESC opinion/ COR opinion°	EP opinion/ EP assent*	Council regulation (or decision/ conclusion)	Observations
793	EC–San Marino agreement on cooperation and customs union		Bull. 12-1990/1.4.26	Bull. 7/8-1991/1.3.28	Bull. 12-1991/1.3.23	OJ C 302/22.11.1991 COM(1991) 429 Bull. 11-1991/1.3.35		OJ C 241/21.9.1992 Bull. 7/8-1992/1.4.31	OJ L 84/28.3.2002 Bull. 1/2-2002/1.6.64	Recommendation for signature: Bull. 11-1990/1.4.20 Council decision concerning the signature: Bull. 12-1991/1.3.23 Entry into force: 1.4.2002

Individual sectors

	Commission recommendation	Council decision/ negotiating directives	Initials	Signature	Commission proposal/ conclusion	ESC opinion/ COR opinion°	EP opinion/ EP assent*	Council regulation (or decision/ conclusion)	Observations
803	ECSC–Russia agreement on trade in certain steel products		19.11.2001	7.3.2002	Bull. 7/8-2002/1.6.78	SEC(2002) 457				Proposal relating to the conclusion of the agreement at second reading: 8.7.2002 Bull.7/8-2002/1.6.78 Council assent: 17.6.2002
803	ECSC–Kazakhstan agreement on trade in certain steel products		19.11.2001	5.2.2002	Bull. 7/8-2002/1.6.78	SEC(2002) 453				Proposal relating to the conclusion of the agreement at second reading: 8.7.2002 Bull.7/8-2002/1.6.78 Council assent: 17.6.2002
804	Draft agreement in the form of a memorandum of understanding between the EC and Brazil on arrangements in the area of textile and clothing products		9.11.2000	8.8.2002						Proposal signature: COM(2002) 526 Bull. 9-2002/1.6.43 Council decision concerning the signature: OJ L 305/7.11.2002 Bull. 11-2002/1.6.38
804	Draft renewal of the EC–Nepal agreement on trade in textile products		Bull. 10-2002/1.6.64	Bull. 10-2002/1.6.64						Proposal signature: COM(2002) 653 Bull. 11-2002/1.6.39 Council decision concerning the signature: OJ L 348/21.12.2002 Bull. 12-2002/1.6.70

TABLE III — INTERNATIONAL AGREEMENTS 573

		Commission recommendation	Council decision/ negotiating directives	Initials	Signature	Commission proposal/ conclusion	ESC opinion/ COR opinion°	EP opinion/ EP assent*	Council regulation (or decision)/ conclusion	Observations
804	Draft renewal of the EC–Cambodia agreement on trade in textile products		Bull. 10-2002/1.6.64	18.10.2002						Proposal signature: COM(2002) 652 Bull. 11-2002/1.6.40 Council decision concerning the signature: OJ L 349/24.12.2002 Bull. 12-2002/1.6.69
804	Draft bilateral agreement with Vietnam on trade in textile products		Bull. 12-2002/1.6.69							
804	EC-Vietnam memorandum of understanding on the prevention of fraud in the trade in footwear		Bull. 11-2002/1.6.42							
806	Draft protocol amending the annex to the agreement on trade in civil aircraft					OJ C 151 E/25.6.2002 COM(2002) 112 Bull. 3-2002/1.6.42				

Development cooperation
Commodities and world agreements

		Commission recommendation	Council decision/ negotiating directives	Initials	Signature	Commission proposal/ conclusion	ESC opinion/ COR opinion°	EP opinion/ EP assent*	Council regulation (or decision)/ conclusion	Observations
823	Agreement establishing the terms of reference of the International Jute Study Group, 2001		8.3.2001			COM(2001) 738 Bull. 12-2001/1.6.55			OJ L 112/27.4.2002 Bull. 4-2002/1.6.39	Proposal signature: COM(2001) 738 Bull. 12-2001/1.6.55 Council decision concerning the signature: OJ L 112/27.4.2002
825	International cocoa agreement of 2001					OJ C 331 E/31.12.2002 COM(2002) 438 Bull. 7/8-2002/1.6.158			OJ L 342/17.12.2002 Bull. 11-2002/1.6.47	Proposal signature: COM(2002) 438 Bull. 7/8-2002/1.6.158 Council decision concerning the signature: OJ L 342/17.12.2002 Bull. 11-2002/1.6.47

° Opinion of the Committee of the Regions.
* Agreement requiring Parliament's assent.

European Economic Area, relations with EFTA countries

Relations with EFTA countries

	Commission recommendation	Council decision/ negotiating directives	Initials	Signature	Commission proposal/ conclusion	ESC opinion/ COR opinion°	EP opinion/ EP assent*	Council regulation (or decision)/ conclusion	Observations
855 EC–Switzerland agreement on the free movement of persons	Bull. 5-1995/1.3.102	Bull. 5-1995/1.3.102	Bull. 1/2-1999/1.4.70	Bull. 6-1999/1.3.61	COM(1999) 229 Bull. 5-1999/1.3.61			OJ L 114/30.4.2002 Bull. 1/2-2002/1.6.77	Proposal signature: COM(1999) 229 Bull. 5-1999/1.3.61 Council decision concerning the signature: Bull. 6-1999/1.3.61
855 EC–Switzerland agreement on air transport	Bull. 5-1995/1.3.102	Bull. 5-1995/1.3.102	Bull. 1/2-1999/1.4.70	Bull. 6-1999/1.3.61	COM(1999) 229 Bull. 5-1999/1.3.61			OJ L 114/30.4.2002 Bull. 1/2-2002/1.6.77	Proposal signature: COM(1999) 229 Bull. 5-1999/1.3.61 Council decision concerning the signature: Bull. 6-1999/1.3.61
855 EC–Switzerland agreement on rail and road transport	Bull. 5-1995/1.3.102	Bull. 5-1995/1.3.102	Bull. 1/2-1999/1.4.70	Bull. 6-1999/1.3.61	COM(1999) 229 Bull. 5-1999/1.3.61			OJ L 114/30.4.2002 Bull. 1/2-2002/1.6.77	Proposal signature: COM(1999) 229 Bull. 5-1999/1.3.61 Council decision concerning the signature: Bull. 6-1999/1.3.61
855 EC–Switzerland agreement on scientific and technological cooperation	Bull. 5-1995/1.3.102	Bull. 5-1995/1.3.102	Bull. 1/2-1999/1.4.70	Bull. 6-1999/1.3.61	COM(1999) 229 Bull. 5-1999/1.3.61			OJ L 114/30.4.2002 Bull. 1/2-2002/1.6.77	Proposal signature: COM(1999) 229 Bull. 5-1999/1.3.61 Council decision concerning the signature: Bull. 6-1999/1.3.61
855 EC–Switzerland agreement on government procurement	Bull. 5-1995/1.3.102	Bull. 5-1995/1.3.102	Bull. 1/2-1999/1.4.70	Bull. 6-1999/1.3.61	COM(1999) 229 Bull. 5-1999/1.3.61			OJ L 114/30.4.2002 Bull. 1/2-2002/1.6.77	Proposal signature: COM(1999) 229 Bull. 5-1999/1.3.61 Council decision concerning the signature: Bull. 6-1999/1.3.61
855 EC–Switzerland agreement on agricultural products	Bull. 5-1995/1.3.102	Bull. 5-1995/1.3.102	Bull. 1/2-1999/1.4.70	Bull. 6-1999/1.3.61	COM(1999) 229 Bull. 5-1999/1.3.61			OJ L 114/30.4.2002 Bull. 1/2-2002/1.6.77	Proposal signature: COM(1999) 229 Bull. 5-1999/1.3.61 Council decision concerning the signature: Bull. 6-1999/1.3.61

TABLE III — INTERNATIONAL AGREEMENTS 575

	Commission recommendation	Council decision/ negotiating directives	Initials	Signature	Commission proposal/ conclusion	ESC opinion/ COR opinion°	EP opinion/ EP assent*	Council regulation (or decision)/ conclusion	Observations
855	EC–Switzerland agreement on mutual recognition in relation to conformity assessment	Bull. 5-1995/1.3.102	Bull. 5-1995/1.3.102	Bull. 1/2-1999/1.4.70	Bull. 6-1999/1.3.61	COM(1999) 229 Bull. 5-1999/1.3.61			OJ L 114/30.4.2002 Bull. 1/2-2002/1.6.77	Proposal signature: COM(1999) 229 Bull. 5-1999/1.3.61 Council decision concerning the signature: Bull. 6-1999/1.3.61
855	Draft sectoral agreements between the EC and Switzerland (implementation of the Schengen *acquis*, the Dublin Convention, free trade in the service and audio-visual sector)	Bull. 4-2002/1.6.41	Bull. 6-2002/1.6.63							
857	EC–Norway agreement in the form of an exchange of letters concerning certain processed agricultural products covered by protocol No 2 of the Bilateral Free Trade Agreement between the EC and Norway			27.11.2002	OJ C 291 E/26.11.2002 COM(2002) 409			OJ L 341/17.12.2002 Bull. 11-2002	Entry into force: 27.11.2002

Relations with the western Balkans

Stabilisation and association agreements

	Commission recommendation	Council decision/ negotiating directives	Initials	Signature	Commission proposal/ conclusion	ESC opinion/ COR opinion°	EP opinion/ EP assent*	Council regulation (or decision)/ conclusion	Observations
863	Draft stabilisation and association agreement between the EC and Albania	28.11.2001	Bull. 10-2002/1.6.73							
865	EC–Croatia interim agreement on trade-related provisions			Bull. 10-2001/1.6.57	OJ C 362 E/18.12.2001 COM(2001) 429 Bull. 7/8-2001/1.6.80		OJ C 177 E/25.7.2002 Bull. 12-2001/1.6.67	OJ L 40/12.2.2002 Bull. 1/2-2002/1.6.80	Proposal signature: OJ C 362 E/18.12.2001 COM(2001) 429 Bull. 7/8-2001/1.6.80 Council decision concerning the signature: 28.1.2002 Entry into force: 1.3.2002

° Opinion of the Committee of the Regions.
* Agreement requiring Parliament's assent.

	Commission recommendation	Council decision/ negotiating directives	Initials	Signature	Commission proposal/ conclusion	ESC opinion/ COR opinion*	EP opinion/ EP assent*	Council regulation (or decision)/ conclusion	Observations
874	Draft EU-Albania agreement on the activities of the European Union monitoring mission in Albania	Bull. 5-2002/1.6.74							
875	Agreement between the EU and Bosnia-Herzegovina on the activities of the European Union Police Mission (EUPM) in Bosnia-Herzegovina	12.7.2002						Bull. 9-2002/1.6.55	Dec. 2002/845/PESC (OJ L 293/29.10.2002)

Relations with the southern Mediterranean and the Middle East

Maghreb

	Commission recommendation	Council decision/ negotiating directives	Initials	Signature	Commission proposal/ conclusion	ESC opinion/ COR opinion*	EP opinion/ EP assent*	Council regulation (or decision)/ conclusion	Observations
885	Euro-Mediterranean association agreement between the EC and Algeria	Bull. 4-1996/1.4.65	Bull. 6-1996/1.4.75	Bull. 12-2001/1.6.74	Bull. 4-2002/1.6.51	OJ C 262 E/29.10.2002 COM(2002) 157 Bull. 3-2002/1.6.68		Bull. 10-2002/1.6.82		Proposal signature: OJ C 262 E/29.10.2002 COM(2002) 157 Bull. 3-2002/1.6.68 Council decision concerning the signature: Bull. 4-2002/1.6.51

Mashreq, Palestinian territories, Israel

	Commission recommendation	Council decision/ negotiating directives	Initials	Signature	Commission proposal/ conclusion	ESC opinion/ COR opinion*	EP opinion/ EP assent*	Council regulation (or decision)/ conclusion	Observations
892	Euro-Mediterranean association agreement between the EC and Jordan	Bull. 6-1995/1.4.82	Bull. 4-1997/1.4.75	Bull. 4-1997/1.4.72	Bull. 11-1997/1.4.72	COM(1997) 554		OJ C 226/20.7.1998 Bull. 7/8-1998/1.4.99	OJ L 129/15.5.2002 Bull. 3-2002/1.6.71	Proposal signature: COM(1997) 554 Bull. 10-1997/1.3.73 Council decision concerning the signature: Bull. 11-1997/1.4.72 Entry into force: 1.5.2002

TABLE III — INTERNATIONAL AGREEMENTS 577

		Commission recommendation	Council decision/ negotiating directives	Initials	Signature	Commission proposal/ conclusion	ESC opinion/ COR opinion°	EP opinion/ EP assent*	Council regulation (or decision)/ conclusion	Observations
893	Euro-Mediterranean association agreement between the EC and Lebanon		Bull. 10-1995/1.4.82	Bull. 1/2-2002/1.6.95	Bull. 6-2002/1.6.75	COM(2002) 170 Bull. 4-2002/1.6.54				Proposal signature: COM(2002) 170 Bull. 4-2002/1.6.54 Council decision concerning the signature: Bull. 4-2002/1.6.54
893	Interim agreement between the EC and Lebanon				Bull. 6-2002/1.6.76	COM(2002) 210 Bull. 4-2002/1.6.55			OJ L 262/30.9.2002 Bull. 7/8-2002/1.6.100	Proposal signature: COM(2002) 210 Bull. 4-2002/1.6.55 Council decision concerning the signature: Bull. 4-2002/1.6.55
894	Draft Euro-Mediterranean association agreement between the EC and Syria		Bull. 1/2-2002/1.6.97 Bull. 12-1997/1.3.87							
895	Convention between the EC and the United Nations Relief and Works Agency for Palestine Refugees in the Near East (UNRWA) concerning the Community contribution to the 2002–05 UNRWA budget	Bull. 1/2-2002/1.6.100	Bull. 3-2002/1.6.70			OJ C 203 E/27.8.2002 COM(2002) 238 Bull. 5-2002/1.6.79		Bull. 9-2002/1.6.57	OJ L 281/19.10.2002 Bull. 9-2002/1.6.57	

Middle East

		Commission recommendation	Council decision/ negotiating directives	Initials	Signature	Commission proposal/ conclusion	ESC opinion/ COR opinion°	EP opinion/ EP assent*	Council regulation (or decision)/ conclusion	Observations
898	Draft EC-Iran agreement on trade and cooperation		Bull. 7/8-2002/1.6.102							

Relations with the independent States of the former Soviet Union and with Mongolia

Bilateral relations

		Commission recommendation	Council decision/ negotiating directives	Initials	Signature	Commission proposal/ conclusion	ESC opinion/ COR opinion°	EP opinion/ EP assent*	Council regulation (or decision)/ conclusion	Observations
918	Draft EC-Ukraine readmission agreement		Bull. 6-2002/1.4.3							

° Opinion of the Committee of the Regions.
* Agreement requiring Parliament's assent.

Relations with Asia

Bilateral relations

	Commission recommendation	Council decision/ negotiating directives	Initials	Signature	Commission proposal/ conclusion	ESC opinion/ COR opinion°	EP opinion/ EP assent°	Council regulation (or decision)/ conclusion	Observations
964	Draft agreement between the EC and the special administrative region of the People's Republic of China on the readmission of persons residing without authorisation	28.5.2001		Bull. 11-2002/1.4.4	SEC(2002) 412 Bull. 4-2002/1.6.76		Bull. 12-2002/1.4.5		Proposal signature: Bull. 4-2002/1.6.76

Relations with Latin America

Bilateral relations

	Commission recommendation	Council decision/ negotiating directives	Initials	Signature	Commission proposal/ conclusion	ESC opinion/ COR opinion°	EP opinion/ EP assent°	Council regulation (or decision)/ conclusion	Observations
976	Memorandum of understanding on cooperation between the EC and Brazil		28.5.2002	Bull. 11-2002/1.6.83					
977	EC–Chile association agreement	Bull. 11-1999/1.5.98	Bull. 6-2002/1.6.109	Bull. 11-2002/1.6.84	COM(2002) 536 Bull. 10-2002/1.6.112				Proposal signature: COM(2002) 536 Bull. 10-2002/1.6.112 Council decision concerning the signature: OJ L 352/30.12.2002 Bull. 11-2002/1.6.84

ACP countries and OCTs

Relations with ACP countries

	Commission recommendation	Council decision/ negotiating directives	Initials	Signature	Commission proposal/ conclusion	ESC opinion/ COR opinion°	EP opinion/ EP assent°	Council regulation (or decision)/ conclusion	Observations
990	EC–ACP Partnership Agreement	Bull. 1/2-1998/1.4.146	Bull. 6-1998/1.4.144		Bull. 6-2000/1.6.83	OJ C 240 E28.8.2001 COM(2000) 324 Bull. 5-2000/1.6.104		OJ C 271 E7.11.2002 Bull. 1/2-2002/1.6.138		Proposal signature: OJ C 240 E28.8.2001 COM(2000) 324 Bull. 5-2000/1.6.104 Council decision concerning the signature: Bull. 6-2000/1.6.83

TABLE III — INTERNATIONAL AGREEMENTS 579

		Commission recommendation	Council decision/ negotiating directives	Initials	Signature	Commission proposal/ conclusion	ESC opinion/ COR opinion°	EP opinion/ EP assent*	Council regulation (or decision)/ conclusion	Observations
992	Draft economic partnership agreements between the EC and the ACP countries and regions	Bull. 4-2002/1.6.87	17.6.2002							
999	Draft Agreement on guaranteed prices during the 2001/2002 to 2005/2006 delivery periods for cane sugar originating in the ACP countries set out in the Partnership Agreement and in the Republic of India		22.4.2002							

° Opinion of the Committee of the Regions.
* Agreement requiring Parliament's assent.

Index